CourseTutor
CoreEconomics

CourseTutor
CoreEconomics

Gerald W. Stone

Metropolitan State College of Denver

Worth Publishers

Senior Publisher: Craig Bleyer
Acquisitions Editor: Sarah Dorger
Development Editor: Bruce Kaplan
Development Editor, Media and Supplements: Marie McHale
Director of Market Development: Steven Rigolosi
Consulting Editor: Paul Shensa
Senior Marketing Manager: Scott Guile
Associate Managing Editor: Tracey Kuehn
Project Editors: Dana Kasowitz
           Jennifer Carey, Matrix Publishing Services
Art Director: Babs Reingold
Senior Designer: Kevin Kall
Cover and Interior Designer: Karen Quigley
Illustrations: Matrix Publishing Services
Photo Editor: Cecilia Varas
Production Manager: Barbara Anne Seixas
Composition: Matrix Publishing Services
Printing and Binding: RR Donnelley

Library of Congress Control Number: 2007938459

ISBN-13: 978-0-7167-9981-8
ISBN-10: 0-7167-9981-2

First printing 2007

Worth Publishers
41 Madison Avenue
New York, NY 10010
www.worthpublishers.com

*t*he study of economics is no easy task. You have to work carefully to follow the arguments presented in the text. Next, work through the tutorials and the questions and problems in this *CourseTutor,* checking your progress as you go along.

At the end of this course, if you do this work diligently, you will be able to analyze with more sophistication your everyday life. This will result in better decisions in areas ranging from career choice to studying, and from consumer purchases to marriage. You will be in a better position to analyze public policy issues such as taxation, education, antitrust, government spending, and foreign trade.

A good knowledge of economics means few public policymakers will be able to con you with talk of a free government lunch. You will always be on the lookout for unintended consequences of any public policy change. You will look at the incentives inherent in any transaction and from that review you will be able to generate expectations about the future.

Economics is an exciting subject to study. Less than 20 percent of Americans have ever taken a course in economics, so you will be in an elite crowd. Most of us know a lot about how the political system works and why we need to vote every couple of years. But not enough of us understand how our economy works.

Many people work and live in an economic environment 24/7, but often have little idea of how it works. Our ideas of how the economy sets prices and produces products vary from conspiracy theories involving multinational corporations to beliefs that government provides or regulates everything.

Because most of us end up working for corporations, we must be part of the conspiracy. But most of us wouldn't consider doing the things that corporations and businesses are often accused of doing. There is an inherent contradiction in what we see continually in the media. Furthermore, without corporations, much of what we enjoy today simply would not exist.

You will not find any conspiracy theories in this book. My goal is to give you the tools you need to do your own analysis of any economic situation.

Economists like everyone else are spread all across the political spectrum. The vast majority of economic analysis is agreed upon by the profession. But we all have different value systems, so it is not surprising that economists differ on which policy to use to solve a specific situation. Different policies have different side effects and it is often the nature of the side effects that lead economists to advocate different policy approaches to the same problem.

Because macroeconomic policies are generally of such a large magnitude (billions of dollars in spending, tax, or money supply changes), there is a lot of room for disagreement about the consequences of any policy and who or what groups will be affected. Further, forecasting the impacts of macroeconomic policy changes by Congress or the Federal Reserve is difficult at best. This, along with individual values about fighting inflation, reducing unemployment, or curbing rising deficits, leads economists to disagree about how to mitigate an economic downturn. When dealing with an economy as complex as ours, controversy is the norm.

I hope you find economics as exciting and as interesting as I did when I was a college sophomore. Economics pervades our lives and a good understanding of economic principles is essential. Enjoy the book and the course.

One more thing. This *CourseTutor* has been set up as your guide throughout the term. Each chapter of *CourseTutor* starts with a brief description of the chapter's contents, a list of key objectives, and a review of key terms. After studying these, move on to the tutorials. Start with the Frequently Asked Questions (FAQs). You will find that there is a FAQs section for each section of the chapter. Following each FAQs, there is a Quick Check of usually ten questions, designed to test your knowledge of the key concepts in each section. If you get all of these questions correct, go on to the next section. If you miss a few questions in a section, *CourseTutor* will give you further study suggestions, and often you will be given additional problems to work and solved problems to analyze. In this way, the tutorials are a buffet: Use what you need to obtain concept mastery, but move on to the next section if you know the material.

After you finish the tutorial portion of *CourseTutor,* you will find further hints and reminders to help you with chapter material, and Core Graphs and Core Equations will be presented for your review. Each chapter then contains 20 homework questions and problems. If your instructor requests, you can work these Homework Questions in the book and hand in individual answer sheets, or work the questions online. Then, examine the ExamPrep sheet for each chapter, which gives you a framework for thinking about the chapter. Fill out the ExamPrep sheet to help you study for exams.

After this material, every chapter contains the standard study guide material for your review, should you need additional help. There are matching questions, fill-in questions, true-false questions, multiple choice questions and problems, and essay questions. Answers to these questions and problems are provided to help you assess your progress through the text.

I personally cannot be with you every step of this journey. This *CourseTutor* is my attempt to be your guide.

Gerald W. Stone

CONTENTS

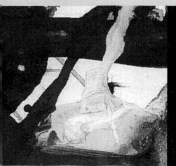

Exploring Economics

1

Economics Is a Rich Discipline of Wide Scope

In this first chapter, you are given a general introduction to economics. You will see the scope of economics as a way of thinking about the world, then you will look at how economists go about doing economics. Next, you will be presented with the key ideas in economics; you will meet these ideas throughout the course.

This is an introductory chapter. You are not expected to memorize all the ideas and issues covered in this first chapter. Rather, use this chapter as a way of familiarizing yourself with economics.

This Is What You Need to Know	STEP 1

After reading this chapter you should be able to

■ Explain the scope of economics and economic analysis.

■ Differentiate between microeconomics and macroeconomics.

■ Describe how economists use models.

■ Describe the *ceteris paribus* assumption.

■ Discuss the difference between efficiency and equity.

■ Describe the key ideas in economics.

Review the Key Terms	STEP 2

Microeconomics: The decision making by individuals, businesses, industries, and government.

Macroeconomics: The broader issues in the economy such as inflation, unemployment, and national output of goods and services.

Ceteris paribus: Assumption used in economics (and other disciplines as well), where other relevant factors or variables are held constant.

Efficiency: How well resources are used and allocated. The chief focus of efficiency: Do people get the goods and services they want at the lowest possible resource cost?

Equity: The fairness of various issues and policies.

Scarcity: Our unlimited wants clash with limited resources. Everyone faces scarcity. Economics focuses on the allocation of scarce resources to satisfy unlimited wants.

Opportunity costs: The next best alternative; what you give up to do something or purchase something.

Market failure: When markets fail to provide goods and services efficiently.

STEP 3 Work Through the Chapter Tutorials

What Is Economics About?

Frequently Asked Questions

Q: **What topics encompass economics?**

A: Economics is about almost everything. Economic analysis can be usefully applied to topics as diverse as how businesses make decisions to how college students allocate their time between studying and relaxing, from how individuals determine whether to "invest in themselves" by taking additional courses while on the job to how government deals with electric utilities that pollute nearby rivers.

Q: **How is economics divided as a subject?**

A: Economics is separated into two broad categories: microeconomics and macroeconomics.

Q: **What is the subject matter of microeconomics?**

A: Microeconomics deals with individual, firm, industry, and public decision making. For example, microeconomics deals with issues such as whether you should attend a concert or study, and if you study, how you allocate your study time among all your courses. Business firms consider issues such as how much output to produce and how many people to hire to produce the output.

Q: **What is the subject matter of macroeconomics?**

A: Macroeconomics focuses on the broader economic issues confronting the nation. Issues such as inflation (a general increase in prices economy-wide), employment and unemployment, and economic growth are the focus of macroeconomics.

Q: **How does model building characterize economics?**

A: Economics uses a stylized approach to a number of issues. Stylized models boil issues and facts down to their basic relevant elements. Then, using assumptions, stylized (simple) models are developed. Not all situations are covered by the models because economists seek to generalize about economic behavior and reach generally applicable results.

Q: What is the *ceteris paribus* assumption, and when is it used?

A: To build models means that we make use of the *ceteris paribus* assumption and hold some important variables constant. This useful device often provides surprising insights about economic behavior.

Q: How are efficiency and equity related?

A: Economists and policymakers often confront the tradeoff between efficiency and equity. Efficiency reflects how well resources are used and allocated; economic analysis often focuses on ensuring that efficient outcomes result from public policy. Sometimes the equity or fairness of the outcome is questioned. Because equity and fairness are subjective matters, there are differences of opinion about fairness, except at the extremes where people generally agree. For public policy issues, economics illuminates the tradeoffs between equity and efficiency. Economists have a lot to say about efficiency, but they tend to avoid the subjective issue of equity.

What Is Economics About? Quick Check

Circle the Correct Answer

1. (T/F) Microeconomics concentrates on such aggregates as economic growth and inflation.
2. (T/F) *Ceteris paribus* means that economists do economics by creating models.
3. Macroeconomics covers all *EXCEPT* which one of the following?
   a. the inflation rate
   b. the unemployment rate
   c. productivity rates
   d. sales of NIKE athletic shoes compared to Reeboks
4. Models are
   a. useless because they are too simple.
   b. stylized, simple representations of reality that can lead to important insights.
   c. exact, careful representations of reality.
   d. quite limited in their usefulness.

5. Concerning the efficiency versus equity tradeoff:
   a. Economists have much to say about both efficiency and equity.
   b. Economists have much more to say about equity than efficiency.
   c. Economists have much to say about efficiency but little to say about equity.
   d. Economists have much to say about equity but nothing to say about efficiency.

Score: ____

Answers: 1. F; 2. F; 3. d; 4. b; 5. c

If You Got All 5 Correct

You have a good sense of what economics is about. Go on to "Key Ideas of Economics" in the next section.

If You Didn't Get All of Them Correct

Spend a little time reviewing this material. It is not hard, but it provides a foundation for the remainder of this chapter. If you do not get this material straight, you might get lost later. Make a quick trip through the first section of the chapter again, looking at each heading and making sure you know what is covered under each topic. When you have a better sense of what economics is and how economists do what they do, go on to Key Ideas of Economics. ■

Key Ideas of Economics

Frequently Asked Questions

Q: **How is economics often defined?**

A: Our economy has limited resources. Our wants are limitless. This means that we face scarcity and must make tradeoffs in everything we do. Economics is often defined as the study of the allocation of scarce resources to competing wants.

Q: **What are opportunity costs?**

A: Everything we do involves opportunity costs. All activities require that we spend resources (e.g., time and money) that could be used in another activity. This other activity represents the opportunity cost of the current activity chosen. Opportunity costs apply to us as individuals and to societies as a whole.

Q: **What is thinking at the margin?**

A: Rational thinking requires that you think and make decisions at the margin. For example, making decisions at the margin for most businesses means deciding on the next employee to hire or the next advertising campaign, and for consumers, it means what will be the next product to purchase. Businesses use marginal analysis to determine how much output to produce and how many employees to hire. People use marginal analysis to determine which products to buy. Governments use marginal analysis to determine levels of regulation.

Q: **How do incentives affect people?**

A: People follow incentives. If society wants to discourage some behavior, society can tax it, punish it, or do a host of other things that increases its costs. Conversely, society can provide things such as tax benefits for behaviors it wishes to encourage.

Q: **What do markets do?**

A: Markets bring buyers and sellers together. Competition for the consumer's dollar forces firms to provide products at the lowest possible price, or some other firm will undercut their price. New products are introduced to the market and old products disappear. This dynamism is what makes markets efficient.

Q: **What is market failure, and how is it treated?**

A: Though markets are usually efficient, there are recognized times when they are not. Pollution is an example of this. Government action often provides a solution to problems of market failure.

Q: **What happens when people have information superiorities?**

A: Information is important. Superior information gives economic actors a decided advantage. Sometimes this is simply a facet of life. At other times, information advantages can result in dysfunctional markets.

Q: **What benefits do specialization and trade bring?**

A: Trading with other countries leads to better products for consumers at lower prices. Economies grow by producing those products where they have an advantage over other countries. This is why much of what we buy today comes from other countries. Specialization leads to tangible benefits.

Q: **Why is productivity important?**

A: Countries with the highest average per capita income are also the most productive. Their labor forces are highly skilled and firms employ huge amounts of capital with these workforces. This results in immense productivity and correspondingly high wages for the workers. High productivity growth results in high economic growth, which leads to high wages and high incomes, which stimulate large investments in education and research. All of this activity leads to higher standards of living.

Q: What can be done to deal with fluctuations in the overall economy?

A: The overall economy moves from growth spurts to recessions, then back to growth spurts. Economists have provided analyses that have helped governments smooth fluctuations in the overall economy.

Key Ideas of Economics Quick Check

Circle the Correct Answer

1. (T/F) Opportunity costs arise only when money is exchanged.
2. (T/F) Government can do things to make overall economic fluctuations less severe.
3. Which one of the following statements is *not* an underlying idea of economics?
   a. Markets are efficient.
   b. When markets fail, government can provide a solution.
   c. Individuals are always rational and always follow their incentives.
   d. Scarcity is the economic problem.
4. Which one of the following does *not* improve our standard of living?
   a. trade
   b. specialization
   c. productivity
   d. market failure.
5. When we have two soft drinks on a hot day and turn down the offer of a free third soft drink because we feel this might be too much and leave us waterlogged, we are
   a. thinking irrationally because it is free.
   b. helping alleviate scarcity by leaving something for someone else.
   c. thinking on the margin.
   d. using information to gain an advantage in the market.

Score: _____

Answers: 1. F; 2. T; 3. c; 4. d; 5. c

If You Got All 5 Correct

You have a good sense of the bedrock ideas in economics. Spend a few moments with "Hints, Tips, and Reminders."

If You Didn't Get All of Them Correct

Review the material. Then, go to the text and read through each heading in this section. Be sure you understand what concept is being discussed. If you are unclear about any of the ideas, reread the relevant passage in the text, then continue. ■

Consider These Hints, Tips, and Reminders   STEP 4

1. This chapter represents your *introduction* to the study of economics; treat it that way. No need to try and memorize all of the terms and topics—you will see them several times again throughout the course. Just read this chapter to get sense of the breadth of economics.

2. Reading and using graphs are a different story. The appendix to the chapter introduces you to the graphical methods you will encounter as you learn economics. Pick up any periodical such as the *New York Times, Wall Street Journal, Financial Times, Newsweek, Business Week,* and so on, and you will find them filled with graphs and figures that are part of the articles. Focus more of your study time on the Appendix and learn to interpret and read graphs—it will save you a lot of grief.

Do the Homework for Chapter 1
Exploring Economics

STEP 5

Instructor _____ Time _____ Student _____

Use the answer key below to record your answers to these homework questions.

1. (a) (b) (c) (d)   6. (a) (b) (c) (d)   11. (a) (b) (c) (d)   16. (a) (b) (c) (d)
2. (a) (b) (c) (d)   7. (a) (b) (c) (d)   12. (a) (b) (c) (d)   17. (a) (b) (c) (d)
3. (a) (b) (c) (d)   8. (a) (b) (c) (d)   13. (a) (b) (c) (d)   18. (a) (b) (c) (d)
4. (a) (b) (c) (d)   9. (a) (b) (c) (d)   14. (a) (b) (c) (d)   19. (a) (b) (c) (d)
5. (a) (b) (c) (d)   10. (a) (b) (c) (d)   15. (a) (b) (c) (d)   20. (a) (b) (c) (d)

1. Microeconomics focuses on
   a. what causes unemployment.
   b. what causes inflation around the world.
   c. decisions by firms.
   d. government deficits.

2. Macroeconomics is *not* generally concerned with
   a. what causes unemployment.
   b. what causes inflation around the world.
   c. pricing decisions by corporations.
   d. government deficits.

3. *Ceteris paribus* is
   a. an assumption used by economists to complicate models.
   b. the assumption that business maximizes profits.
   c. the assumption used by economists that all labor is equally productive.
   d. an assumption used by economists to hold all else constant.

4. Efficiency
   a. reflects how often economists make assumptions about important variables.
   b. reflects how well resources are allocated.
   c. reflects the fact that all labor is equally productive.
   d. is an assumption used by economists that holds important variables constant.

5. Equity refers to
   a. an assumption used by economists to complicate models.

   b. an individual's subjective judgment about fairness of policies.
   c. an assumption used by economists that all labor is equally productive.
   d. an assumption used by economists that holds important variables constant.

6. When you cannot go to a movie and play tennis at the same time, you are facing
   a. the fact that you cannot talk and chew gum at the same time.
   b. equity tradeoffs.
   c. efficiency versus equity tradeoff.
   d. opportunity costs.

7. Over a long period of time, our standard of living is determined by
   a. government regulation.
   b. productivity.
   c. opportunity costs.
   d. minimum wage laws.

8. We trade with other countries because
   a. the law requires us to.
   b. we can exploit developing nations, reducing their incomes.
   c. we are unable to produce most products ourselves.
   d. consumers get better products at lower prices.

Note to Student: There are 8 questions in this homework assignment.

Use the ExamPrep to Get Ready for Exams

This sheet (front and back) is designed to help you prepare for your exams. The chapter has been boiled down to its key concepts. You are asked to answer questions, define terms, draw graphs, and, if you wish, add summaries of class notes.

What Is Economics About?

Describe the following:

Microeconomics:

Macroeconomics:

Describe what *ceteris paribus* is and how it is used in economics:

Describe the tradeoff between efficiency and equity:

Key Ideas of Economics

List the 10 key ideas in economics and give an example of each:

Key Idea	Example

Additional Study Help Chapterwide Practice Questions

Matching

Match the description with the corresponding term.

____   1. Microeconomics
____   2. Macroeconomics
____   3. Models
____   4. *Ceteris paribus*
____   5. Efficiency
____   6. Equity
____   7. Scarcity
____   8. Opportunity Costs
____   9. Thinking at the margin
____   10. Productivity
____   11. Market failure
____   12. Business cycles
____   13. Specialization
____   14. Trade

a. Occurs when markets do not do what they are supposed to do.
b. Fairness.
c. When someone considers whether to eat an additional ice cream cone. Summed up in the phrase "the straw that broke the camel's back."
d. Simple, stylized descriptions of issues.
e. Considered the economic problem, resulting from our wants being greater than available resources.
f. Markets that provide the best quality products for the lowest possible cost.
g. How much output we produce over a specific time period; the greater the amount, the higher our standard of living will be.
h. Fluctuations in the overall economy, such as recessions.
i. The exchange of goods and services between countries or individuals.
j. When each of us concentrates on doing fewer things well rather than many things not as well.
k. All other relevant factors held constant.
l. The cost of what you have to give up.
m. A part of economics that looks at the decisions of individual consumers and businesses.
n. A part of economics that looks at the decisions of all consumers and all businesses.

Fill-In

Circle the word(s) in parentheses that complete the sentence.

1. (Macroeconomics, Microeconomics) _____ focuses on decision making by individuals, companies and governments while (macroeconomics, microeconomics) _____ addresses problems such as unemployment and inflation.

2. In creating models to determine how efficient and equitable policies are, economists use the concept of (efficiency, equity, *ceteris paribus*) _____ to focus attention on the important variables. How well resources are used and allocated are issues of (efficiency, equity, *ceteris paribus*) _____, while (efficiency, equity, *ceteris paribus*) _____ deals with the fairness of policies.

True-False

Circle the correct answer.

_T/F_   1. Analyzing whether you will buy more Vera Bradley handbags if the price drops would be considered part of microeconomics.

_T/F_   2. Analyzing whether everyone will buy more Vera Bradley handbags if the price drops would be considered part of macroeconomics.

_T/F_   3. *Ceteris paribus* means that models should be as simple as possible, but no simpler.

_T/F_   4. Because models are stylized versions of issues, they rarely have anything useful to say.

_T/F_   5. Economists generally have more to say about equity than efficiency.

_T/F_   6. Only people who are not rich are forced to make tradeoffs.

_T/F_   7. The opportunity cost of going to a concert is the price of the concert ticket.

_T/F_   8. Thinking "I am full, I cannot eat another mouthful" is an example of thinking at the margin.

_T/F_   9. Government policymakers find little use for economics when determining how to bring about desired changes.

_T/F_   10. Government is helpless in the face of recessions.

_T/F_   11. Markets are inefficient because someone is always better informed than someone else.

T/F   12. Trade is a one-way street: Rich nations benefit at the expense of poor nations.

T/F   13. Our standard of living is linked to productivity growth.

T/F   14. The opportunity cost of parking at school includes the amount of time I have to search for a parking space.

T/F   15. If I study for chemistry rather than history, I incur no opportunity cost because no monetary transaction takes place.

Multiple Choice

Circle the correct answer.

1. Which of the following is *not* a concern of microeconomics?
   a. The German firm BMW starts a new auto plant in North Carolina.
   b. You buy a music CD.
   c. Unemployment falls in the United States.
   d. Your sister finds a job after college.

2. Which of the following is *not* a concern of macroeconomics?
   a. Inflation climbs to 5% per year.
   b. Unemployment rates tumble.
   c. Coca-Cola expands overseas.
   d. Productivity rises in most businesses.

3. What does *ceteris paribus* mean?
   a. All people are considered equal.
   b. All relevant factors are held constant.
   c. Only important things are considered.
   d. The number of variables has to be kept under control.

4. What special insights can economics tell us about equity?
   a. Many things, because economics is a powerful way of looking at the world.
   b. Some things, because economics considers people to be rational.
   c. Not much, because each of us has to determine what is fair; economics has no special competence here.
   d. Only limited insights, in the special case when markets are completely competitive.

5. Which of the following is *not* an opportunity cost you incur if you see a Yankees baseball game?
   a. the parking fee, if you drive to the park
   b. the time spent in the after-game traffic jam

   c. the exorbitant price paid for hot dogs
   d. the $50 tickets that were given to you by a friend who could not go to the game

6. All *except* which one of the following is an example of thinking at the margin at an all-you-can-eat buffet?
   a. I am almost full, so I will have one dessert.
   b. If I eat five more egg rolls, I will be so full that I cannot eat a dessert.
   c. I have eaten seven egg rolls already.
   d. To eat another egg roll, I have to loosen my belt.

7. Pollution is an example of
   a. an inequitable outcome of markets.
   b. market failure.
   c. the problems that can arise with specialization.
   d. not thinking on the margin.

8. A company believing that offering airline frequent flyer miles with their product will lead to increased sales is following which key economic idea?
   a. People think at the margin.
   b. Information is important.
   c. People follow incentives.
   d. Government can deal with market failure.

9. A person who believes that hiring an automotive expert to help you negotiate with a car dealer about the purchase of a used car is following which key economic idea?
   a. Markets are efficient.
   b. Government can deal with market failure.
   c. People follow incentives.
   d. Information is important.

Essay-Problem

Answer in the space provided.

The questions below extend the material covered in this chapter. The answers you give may not correspond completely with ours; don't worry as long as they are fairly close.

1. Do you have a driver's license? If so, you probably had to wait for various lengths of time to take your initial driving test or get your license renewed. There are people who will wait in line for you if you pay them a fee. Why would you pay other people to do something that does not cost you in the first place?

2. Why should we *not* expect tax law to be as economically efficient in outcome as possible?

3. Is *ceteris paribus* unique to economics?

What's Next

You now have an introduction to economics. You have a sense of what economics is concerned with and how economists actually do economics. You also have been given an introduction to key ideas in economics. You are now ready to put this knowledge to work.

In the next chapter, we bring in several of the concepts from this chapter in looking at the crucial importance of economic growth. We present a stylized model of an economy and look at the major things that generate the economic growth that leads to higher living standards.

Answers to Chapterwide Practice Questions

Matching

1. m	5. f	9. c	13. j
2. n	6. b	10. g	14. i
3. d	7. e	11. a	
4. k	8. l	12. h	

Fill-In

1. Microeconomics, macroeconomics
2. *ceteris paribus*, efficiency, equity

True-False

1. T	5. F	9. F	13. T
2. F	6. F	10. F	14. T
3. F	7. F	11. F	15. F
4. F	8. T	12. F	

Multiple Choice

1. c	4. c	7. b
2. c	5. d	8. c
3. b	6. c	9. d

Essay-Problem

1. Time is an opportunity cost. You could be doing other things with your time. For especially lengthy waits incurred by busy business people, it is often worth it for them to pay someone to wait in line. High-paid individuals often have personal assistants to run their lives.

2. There is an efficiency versus equity tradeoff. Economists can propose the most economically efficient tax laws, but these have to go through a political process to become law. The political process ensures that equity considerations come into play. In other words, economists can propose various tax laws, but as soon as someone says that the proposed law is unfair to some person or some body, politicians will take notice and factor this in to the degree they think warranted.

3. No. It is common to the sciences. For example, physicists hold everything constant, then change one variable when they run various experiments. This is the logic behind taking one particle and seeing what happens under normal speeds, then taking the same particle and accelerating it to speeds near the speed of light.

Appendix: Working with Graphs and Formulas

Graphs, Charts, Tables, and Equations are the Language of Economics

Your study of economics will use a lot of graphs, some charts and tables, and a few simple equations. Knowing how to read, interpret, and use these methods of representing ideas and data will make your study of economics easier and make reading ordinary publications more enjoyable.

This Is What You Need to Know	STEP 1

After studying this appendix you should be able to

- Describe the four simple forms of data graphs.

- Make use of a straightforward approach to reading graphs.

- Read linear and nonlinear graphs and know how to compute their slopes.

- Use simple linear equations to describe a line and a shift in the line.

- Explain why correlation is not the same as causation.

Work Through the Appendix Tutorial	STEP 2

Frequently Asked Questions

Q: **What are the main types of graphs used to display economic data, and how do they differ?**

A: There are four main types of graphs used to display and analyze economic data: time series, scatter plots, pie charts, and bar charts. Time series graphs plot

15

data measures over time, whereas scatter plots plot two series (neither axis measures time) against each other. Pie charts split data into percentage parts of the whole and display them like pie slices. Bar charts present discrete data values as bars, which can be shown either vertically or horizontally.

Q: **Are there any rules for reading graphs?**
A: There are no formal rules, but a few simple suggestions might help. First, check the title to see what is being presented, then look to see what is measured on each axis, and look at the graph to see if it makes logical sense. Now look carefully at the graph to see if any interesting relationships shine through. Finally, read the caption associated with the graph to ensure you have not missed anything important.

Q: **What is a linear relationship, and how is its slope computed?**
A: A linear relationship is represented by a straight line. To compute the slope of a straight line, pick two points on the line and compute the ratio of the change in the variable on the vertical axis to the change in the variable on the horizontal axis (rise over run). In Figure APX-1, the slope of the line is computed by selecting two points such as a and b, then computing the ratio of changes in each variable:

$$(20 - 15) / (40 - 20) = 5 / 20 = .25$$

In this simple graph, when the number of cars on the road rises by 20, the commute time grows by 5 minutes, or 15 seconds for each additional car.

FIGURE APX-1

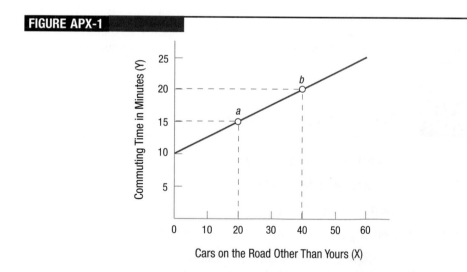

Q: **How is slope computed when the relationship is nonlinear?**
A: To find the slope of a nonlinear curve, pick a point and find the slope of a line tangent to that point. In Figure APX-2, the slope at point a is equal to

$$(16 - 13) / (30 - 20) = 3 / 10 = .3$$

Notice that in this case as more and more cars are on the road, congestion gets worse as an additional car enters the road (the slope gets steeper as more cars travel the road). This is a crucial difference from the linear curve where the slope was constant.

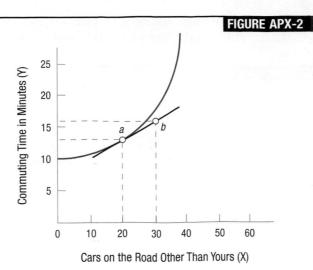

FIGURE APX-2

Q: **What simple equation represents a linear relationship?**

A: Straight lines can be represented by a simple equation of the form: $Y = a + bX$. In Figure APX-3 (Figure APX-1 reproduced), Y equals commuting time, a equals the vertical intercept of 10 minutes (the commute time when you are the only car on the road), b is equal to the slope of .25, and X is equal to the number of other cars on the road. Thus, the full equation is

$$Y = 10 + .25X$$

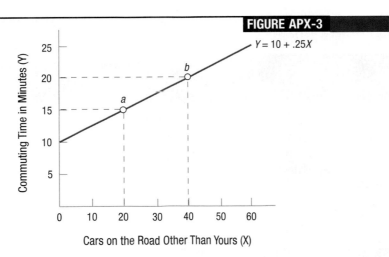

FIGURE APX-3

Q: **How can _ceteris paribus_ be represented in both graphs and equations?**

A: The term _ceteris paribus_ means to hold some additional important variables constant. So, for instance, in the commuting time model above, we might be assuming that the number of lanes available for travel is held constant. Assume that adding another lane reduces commuting time by 5 minutes, and removing a lane increases commute time by 5 minutes. We can add a variable L to our equation, representing lane additions or decreases so that our new equation now becomes

$$Y = 10 + .25X + L$$

where L is equal to -5 when a lane is added and $+5$ when a lane is reduced due to road work. Figure APX-4 on the next page shows the impact of this new variable on the commute time. Adding a new lane reduces commute time for all levels of traffic, while eliminating a lane increases commute time in all traffic conditions.

FIGURE APX-4

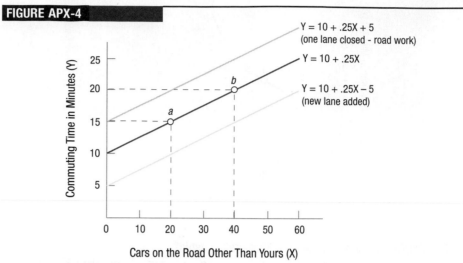

Q: Why does correlation not imply causality?

A: Just because two variables are related to each other does not mean one variable causes the other to change.

Key Point to Remember

Graphs, tables, charts, and equations are just other ways to view data and relationships between variables.

Working with Graphs and Formulas **Quick Check**

1. Figure APX-5 shows 2006 GDP per capita for selected countries, and the country's corresponding years of life expectancy at birth for both men and women. Russia's per capita GDP is roughly what percent of America's?

    a. 100%
    b. 1%
    c. 15%
    d. 50%

FIGURE APX-5

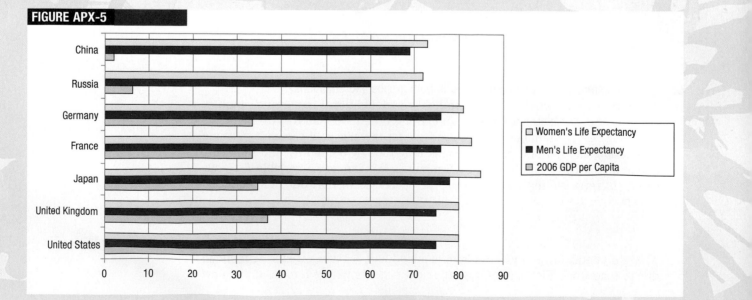

2. Using the same Figure APX-5, which country has the highest life expectancy for males/females?
   a. France/Germany
   b. United Kingdom/United States
   c. Japan/United Kingdom
   d. Japan/Japan
3. Figure APX-6 shows the median (middle person) duration of unemployment in weeks for each month for 2002–2004. Notice that there is a spike in how long people have been unemployed each June. Which of the following is probably the best explanation for these spikes in how long people have been unemployed?

   a. Employers do not like to hire people in June because they don't want to have to let new people go on vacation.
   b. The unemployed see the arrival of summer as a chance to surf and do not bother to look for a job.
   c. May and June represent graduation in both high school and college, so the job market becomes crowded and many unemployed individuals can't find work.
   d. Federal law restricts the number of people who can interview for federal jobs in the summer because of budget limitations.

FIGURE APX-6

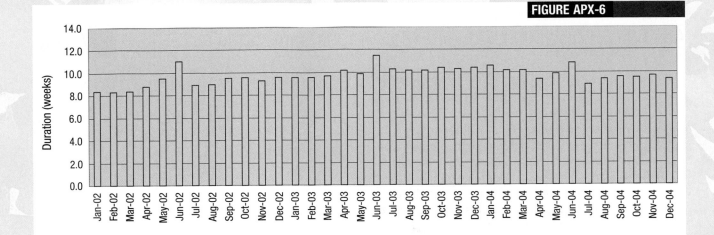

4. Figure APX-7 shows the relationship between the size of a video file in megabytes and the download time in minutes. What is the slope of the line?
   a. 0.4
   b. 0.3
   c. 0.2
   d. 0.1

5. Assume the line (relationship) in Figure APX-7 is for your medium-speed DSL line. Now assume you get a high-speed broadband network connection. How does that affect the line in Figure APX-7?
   a. No impact.
   b. The line will rotate downward with a smaller slope.
   c. The line will rotate upward with a larger slope.
   d. Broadband is so fast that the line will equal the horizontal axis.

Score: ____

FIGURE APX-7

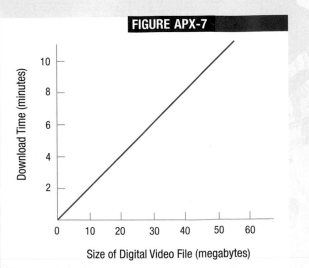

Size of Digital Video File (megabytes)

Answers: 1. c; 2. d; 3. c; 4. c; 5. b

If You Got All 5 Correct

You have a good working knowledge of how to read graphs, how to describe linear relationships, and how to calculate the slope of a line. Enjoy the rest of the course.

If You Didn't Get All of Them Correct

You should review this material again. You are going to see graphs throughout this course. Over the course of the semester you will be computing percentages, interpreting simple graphs, and on a rare occasion looking at simple equations such as that in this section. Don't worry about it at this point. You will get a lot of practice as the semester unfolds, and soon you won't give it a second thought. Good luck in the course.

Additional Study Help Working with Graphs and Formulas

1. Figure SH APX-1, from data in an article in *Business Week*, February 24, 2003, shows the source of America's imported oil in 2001. The United States consumed a total of 25 million barrels of oil a day or 9.125 billion barrels a year. Imported oil as a percent of total consumption was 70% in 2001. The pie chart below shows where that oil came from.
   a. With oil prices at $30 a barrel, approximately how much did the United States pay in 2001 for imported oil? _____
   b. What percentage of this went to OPEC?

   _____

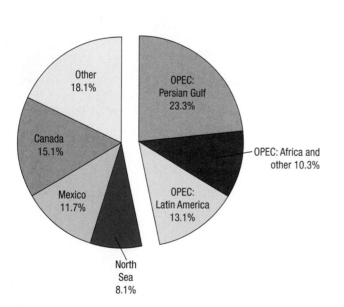

SH APX-1

2. Figure SH APX-2 is based on data in *The Wall Street Journal*, January 24, 2003. It shows the average number of children born to women during the early 1980s and the early 2000s in selected countries.

   a. How is the United States unique among these countries? _____
   b. What factors might account for the wide-ranging drop in fertility rates throughout most of the world?

   _____

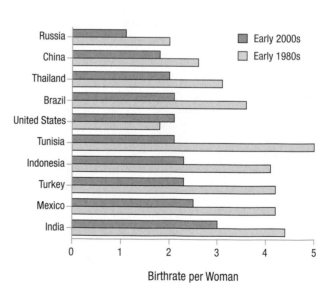

SH APX-2

3. Figure SH APX-3 shows educational attainment of Latinos in Los Angles, California in 2001. These data were included in a special survey in the *Economist*, November 2, 2002.
   a. What percent of foreign born have no college at all? _____
   b. By the third generation, what percent have not been to college? _____
   c. Between the second and third generations, what is the major change?

   _____

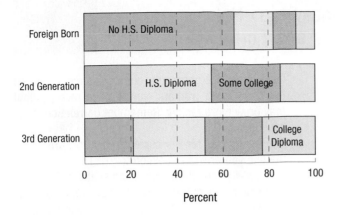

SH APX-3

5. Figure SH APX-5, using World Bank data, shows the population in the world living on under $1 a day.
   a. As a percent of the world's population, has poverty (as defined by living on $1 a day) declined? _____
   b. Where is poverty growing the fastest?

   _____

   c. Where has poverty declined the fastest?

   _____

4. Figure SH APX-4 graphs productivity change (output per hour worked) to changes in aggregate output (GDP) for the last several decades.
   a. Draw a smooth curve (or line) on the graph that shows the normal relationship between these two variables.
   b. Is this a positive or negative relationship that you graphed? _____
   c. State the relationship in words. Does it seem to make sense?

   _____

   d. Notice the two open circles. They represent years 2000 and 2001. Are these points above or below the line you drew on the graph?

   _____

   e. Could this help explain why job growth was slow in the years following the last two recessions? How?

   _____

   _____

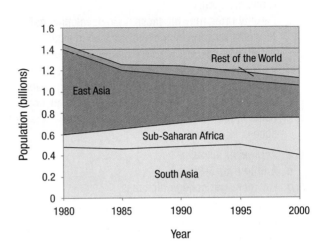

SH APX-5

6. Use the grid to answer the following questions.
   a. Plot the following equation: $Y = 2 + 0.5X$
   b. Plot the following equation: $Y = 10 - 1.5X$
   c. At what value of X is the value of Y equal for both equations? _____
   d. If $X = 2$, what would be the difference between the values for Y in equations a and b?

   _____

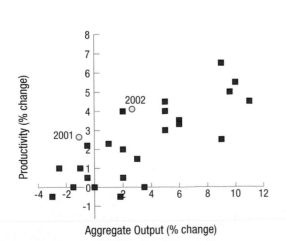

Aggregate Output (% change)

SH APX-4

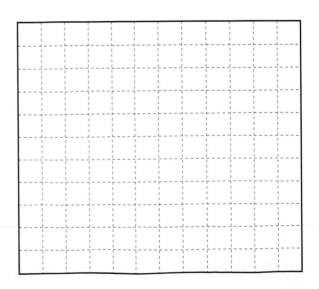

Answers to Additional Study Help
Working with Graphs and Formulas

1. a. (9.125   billion × .70) × $30 = 6.3875 × $30 = $191.625 billion.
   b. The percentage of imports from OPEC equals 23.3 + 10.3 + 13.1 = 46.7%.

2. a. Fertility rates have actually risen for the United States, unlike the remainder of the countries, where it has dropped.
   b. Fertility rates may be declining in developing nations for many reasons including increases in income, better access to birth control (better communications including telephones, satellite television, etc., have increased awareness about birth control in developing nations), increased urbanization (urban households have fewer children), and possibly greater access to education.

3. a. Approximately 82%
   b. A little over 50%
   c. Far more get college diplomas

4. a. A smooth line would be positively sloped and go roughly through the origin and up toward point $y = 5$; $x = 10$.
   b. Positive relationship
   c. This positive relationship suggests that when aggregate output is changing very rapidly, productivity is changing rapidly as well. Alternatively, rapidly growing aggregate output is associated with rapidly growing productivity. Yes, it makes sense that productiv-

ity change and aggregate output change would go together. When workers can produce more, output may grow more rapidly. Remember correlation is not causation.
   d. The two circles for the current recession are above the line you drew in question a.
   e. Productivity growth has been unusually high for the given change in output. This could be due to the possibility that the rapid technological buildup (computers, telecommunications, etc.) during the late 1990s is taking a while to be integrated into the economy. This could partly explain the rapid growth the economy experienced in 2004 and 2005. Productivity growth could hold back job growth in the sense that businesses can meet growing needs with their current number of workers—there is no need to hire more workers.

5. a. Yes. World population has grown in the last two decades, but world poverty has declined. One snag in these data is that they is are not adjusted for inflation. One dollar in 1980 probably translates into two dollars today.
   b. Sub-Saharan Africa
   c. East Asia

6. a and b: See Figure SHA APX-1.
   c. $x = 4$
   d. The difference is 4, as shown in the Figure SHA APX-1 (vertical arrow).

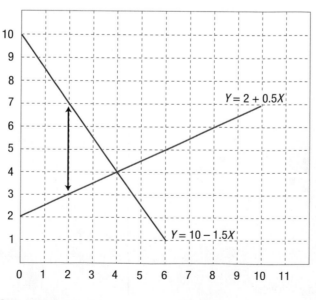

SHA APX-1

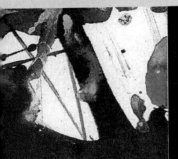

Production, Economic Growth, and Trade

2

Economic Growth and Trade Improve Our Standard of Living

Economic growth is crucial. It brings poor countries out of poverty and helps people in all countries better their conditions. We will return to the concept of growth again and again in this course. To understand how growth comes about, you will need to understand the determinants of growth. Also, you will need to know the benefits of trade.

This Is What You Need to Know	STEP 1

After studying this chapter you should be able to

- Describe the three basic questions that must be answered for any economy.

- Describe production and the factors that go into producing various goods and services.

- Describe the opportunity cost an economy incurs to increase the production of one product.

- Use a production possibilities frontier (PPF) or curve to analyze the limits of production.

- Describe economic growth and the impacts of expanding resources through increasing human resources, capital accumulation, and technological improvements.

- Describe the concepts of absolute and comparative advantage and explain what they tell us about the gains from trade when countries specialize in certain products.

- Describe the practical constraints on free trade and how some industries might be affected.

Review the Key Terms

Production: The process of converting resources (factors of production)—land, labor, capital, and entrepreneurial ability—into goods and services.

Resources: Productive resources include land (land and natural resources), labor (mental and physical talents of people), capital (manufactured products used to produce other products), and entrepreneurial ability (the combining of the other factors to produce products and assume the risk of the business).

Land: Includes natural resources such as mineral deposits, oil, natural gas, water, and land in the usual sense of the word. The payment to land as a resource is called rent.

Labor: Includes the mental and physical talents of individuals that are used to produce goods and services. Labor is paid wages.

Capital: Includes manufactured products such as welding machines, computers, and cellular phones that are used to produce other goods and services. The payment to capital is referred to as interest.

Entrepreneurs: Entrepreneurs combine land, labor and capital to produce goods and services. Entrepreneurs absorb the risk of being in business and receive profits in return.

Production efficiency: Goods and services are produced at their lowest resource (opportunity) cost.

Allocative efficiency: The mix of goods and services produced is just what people in society desire.

Production possibilities frontier (PPF): Shows the combinations of two goods that are possible for a society to produce at full employment. Points on or inside the PPF are feasible, and those outside of the frontier are unattainable.

Opportunity cost: The cost paid for one product in terms of the output (or consumption) of another product that must be foregone.

Absolute advantage: One country can produce more of a good than another country.

Comparative advantage: One country has a lower opportunity cost of producing a good than another country.

Work Through the Chapter Tutorials

Basic Economic Questions and Production

Frequently Asked Questions

Q: **What questions must every economy answer?**

A: *Every* economy must decide *what* to produce, *how* to produce it, and *who* will get the goods and services produced. The answers to these questions depend on how an economy is organized, whether capitalist, socialist, or communist.

Q: **What is the process by which goods and services are produced?**

A: Goods and services are produced by combining resources or the factors of production (land, labor, capital, and entrepreneurship) into products. Land includes all natural resources, labor includes the physical and mental talents of humans, capital represents all manufactured products used to produce other products, and the entrepreneur assumes the risk of production and combines the other three factors of production to produce goods and services.

Basic Economic Questions and Production Quick Check

Circle the Correct Answer

1. (T/F) In a capitalist economy, the distribution of most goods is determined by private markets.
2. (T/F) Land as a resource would include timber in a national forest, shale oil deposits in Colorado, and farm land in Iowa.
3. Which of the following is *not* a payment for a factor of production?
   a. interest
   b. wages
   c. rents
   d. capital gains on stock
4. Which of the following is *not* a form of capital as a factor of production?
   a. office computer
   b. stock certificates
   c. company car
   d. screwdriver for fastening parts on an assembly line
5. Producing the right mix of products for society is known as what?
   a. production efficiency
   b. factors of production
   c. basic economic questions
   d. allocative efficiency

Score: ____

Answers: 1. T; 2. T; 3. d; 4. b; 5. d

If You Got All 5 Correct

You have a good grasp of the concepts of production, the three basic economic questions, and efficiency. Go on to Production Possibilities and Economic Growth in the next section.

If You Didn't Get All of Them Correct

Take a moment and review the first part of the chapter in the book. This material is very simple, so when you have completed this review, go on to Production Possibilities and Economic Growth in the next section. But keep in mind that each new section builds on the previous ones. ■

Production Possibilities and Economic Growth

Frequently Asked Questions

Q: **What does a production possibilities frontier (PPF) show?**

A: The production possibilities frontier (PPF) or curve shows the different combinations of goods and services that a fully employed economy can produce, given available resources and current technology, with both factors assumed to be fixed in the short run. Production mixes inside and on the frontier are possible, but combinations that lie outside the curve are unattainable. In Figure 1, points a, b, and d are attainable, but point c is not.

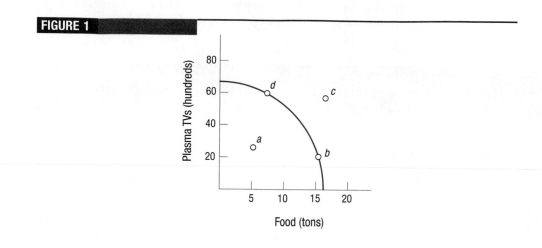

FIGURE 1

Q: What do points along the PPF represent?
A: Production on the frontier represents the maximum output attainable by the economy when all resources are fully employed.

Q: How is the concept of opportunity cost portrayed by the PPF?
A: Reallocating production from one product to another involves *opportunity costs*: The output of one product must be reduced to get the added output of the other. Producing more and more of one product eventually raises the opportunity costs for this product because of the unsuitability of some resources.

Q: What does the PPF model tell us about economic growth?
A: The production possibilities model suggests that economic growth comes from an expansion in resources or from improvements in technology. Expansions in resources expand the production possibilities frontier for all commodities. Technological advances in one industry directly expand production only in that industry, but nonetheless allow more of all types of goods to be produced. The new technology allows previous output to be produced using fewer resources, thus leaving some resources available for use in other industries.

Q: Can economic growth result from population growth?
A: Economic growth can be enhanced by increasing the quantity or quality of labor available for production. Population growth, caused by higher birthrates or immigration, will increase the quantity of labor available. Investments in human capital such as education will improve labor's quality.

Q: Does the type of products produced and consumed affect economic growth?
A: Greater capital accumulation will further improve labor's productivity and thus increase growth rates. This is shown in Figure 2 as a movement from point a outward, in contrast to a movement from point b outward—note how much greater is the growth when a society invests more rather than consumes more.

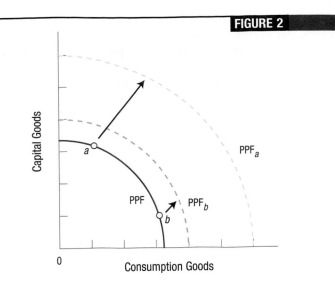

FIGURE 2

Production Possibilities and Economic Growth
Quick Check

Circle the Correct Answer

1. (T/F) A PPF curve will identify the best mix of products for a given society to produce.
2. (T/F) Production choices on, or to the left of, the PPF curve are attainable by the economy in question.
3. (T/F) If an economy can produce 10 more computerized drill presses only by producing 500 fewer jelly rolls, the opportunity cost of a drill press is 50 jelly rolls.
4. Opportunity cost is a measure of
   a. what it costs a firm to break into a new market.
   b. the increase in output that comes from adding inputs to the production process.
   c. the inputs a firm must purchase to be able to produce some good.
   d. the goods an individual or economy must forego to produce or consume more of some other good.
5. If an economy permits more immigration and invests in its school system, we would expect its PPF curve (PPF_0) in Figure 3 to
   a. shift in toward the origin to PPF_1.
   b. shift out away from the origin to PPF_2.
   c. remain in about the same place.
   d. react in any of the above ways—we cannot predict which.
6. Which economic policy is most likely to promote strong economic growth in the long run?
   a. more consumption goods and fewer capital goods
   b. producing more computerized drill presses and fewer jelly rolls

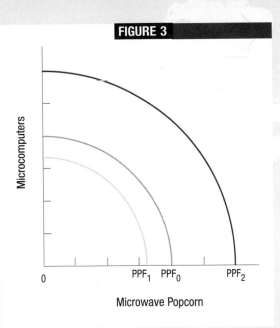

FIGURE 3

   c. high tax rates on capital investment by business
   d. more government retirement programs that encourage early retirement to make way for younger workers

7. If an economy is producing a mix of goods that lies directly on its production possibilities frontier, this indicates which of the following?
   a. Consumers are happy.
   b. The economy is operating at full employment.
   c. The economy is leaving some resources unused.
   d. The economy is growing.
8. The primary reasons underlying economic growth are
   a. falling consumer demand but improving technology.
   b. expanding resources and rising interest rates.
   c. rising exports and imports.
   d. expanding resources and improving technology.
9. If an economy produces computers and pizzas, and a technological innovation makes the production of computers cheaper, we would expect the economy's production of pizzas to
   a. decrease.
   b. not change.
   c. increase.
   d. decrease by an amount equal to the increase in computers.
10. Which production factors are easiest to influence through government policies?
   a. Land.
   b. Entrepreneurial talent.
   c. Capital and labor.
   d. None can be influenced.

Score: ____

Answers: 1. F; 2. T; 3. T; 4. d; 5. b; 6. b; 7. b; 8. d; 9. c; 10. c

If You Got 9 or 10 Correct

You have a good handle on the concepts of production possibilities frontiers and the determinants of economic growth. Go on to Specialization, Comparative Advantage, and Trade in the next section.

If You Didn't Get at Least 9 Correct

The next section on comparative advantage and trade builds on the concepts in this section. As you work through it, some of the concepts from these first two sections will begin to take hold. Take a moment to go back and review this section in the book. When you have completed this review, and before you move on, take a moment and work through the following solved problem.

Solved Problem: Production Possibilities

a. Using the grid on the previous page, plot a typical PPF for apples and office furniture, putting office furniture on the horizontal axis.

b. Draw a new PPF that reflects the economy a year after apple blight has killed nearly half of all apple trees.

c. Using the original PPF curve from part a, draw the new curve resulting from a technological breakthrough in apple production that greatly improves yields.

d. Explain why economies that produce more capital goods and fewer consumer goods have higher growth rates in the future. _____

Solution-Discussion: See Figure 4.

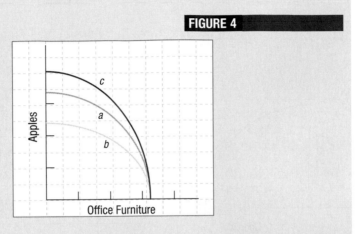

FIGURE 4

a. Your curve should be concave (bowed-out) from the origin with apples on the vertical axis and office furniture on the horizontal axis.

b. The new curve should be under the curve in part *a* but with the same end point on office furniture. The impact is on apple production only. Office furniture is unaffected.

c. The new curve should be outside curve in part *a* but with the same end point on office furniture. The impact is on apple production only. Office furniture is unaffected.

d. Producing more capital goods represents investment in future production that expands the PPF in the future because capital makes labor more productive.

Keep in Mind

This simple production possibilities model is based on the following simple assumptions:

■ Resources are fixed and limited.
■ Technology is given.
■ Production is efficient.
■ Two goods are assumed for simplicity.

From this simple set of assumptions, we get several important conclusions:

■ The economy faces a PPF curve and a tradeoff in the production of both goods.
■ Producing more of one good results in rising opportunity costs for that good.

■ Along the PPF, resources in the economy are fully employed.
■ Points inside the PPF represent unemployment.
■ Points outside the PPF are unattainable.

But most important, this simple, stylized model provides a guide to the kinds of policies that enhance economic growth:

■ Any policy that expands the quantity or improves the quality of resources will improve economic growth.
■ Any policy that improves technical progress will enhance growth.

Public policy can be viewed and analyzed through the lens of this simple PPF model. ■

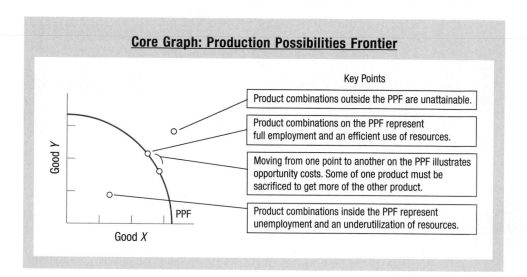

Core Graph: Production Possibilities Frontier

Key Points

Product combinations outside the PPF are unattainable.

Product combinations on the PPF represent full employment and an efficient use of resources.

Moving from one point to another on the PPF illustrates opportunity costs. Some of one product must be sacrificed to get more of the other product.

Product combinations inside the PPF represent unemployment and an underutilization of resources.

Specialization, Comparative Advantage, and Trade

Frequently Asked Questions

Q: **What is absolute advantage?**
A: An absolute advantage exists when one country can produce more of some good than another country.

Q: **What is comparative advantage?**
A: A country has a comparative advantage if its opportunity costs to produce a good are lower than the other country's.

Q: **What is the importance of comparative advantage for trade?**
A: Countries gain from voluntary trade if each specializes in producing those goods at which it enjoys a comparative advantage. Voluntary trade is thus a positive-sum game: Both countries stand to benefit from it.

Specialization, Comparative Advantage, and Trade
Quick Check

Circle the Correct Answer

1. (T/F) If two countries engage in voluntary trade, both can hope to gain from this trade, even though one country may have a much larger and more technologically advanced economy than the other.

2. (T/F) Countries that have an absolute advantage over other countries would not benefit from trade with them.

3. If one country has a comparative advantage over another, this means
   a. it can produce more of all products than the other country.
   b. it can produce one product at a lower opportunity cost than can the other country.
   c. its products are the best in the world.
   d. it has a bigger market share than the other country.

4. Two countries will benefit from trading with one another if
   a. each country concentrates on producing those goods at which it has an absolute advantage.
   b. the country with the greatest productive capacity does all of the production.
   c. each country concentrates on producing those goods at which it has the lowest opportunity cost.
   d. each country produces only goods that the other cannot.

5. In the table below, what is the opportunity cost for Japan of producing cameras rather than commercial airplanes?
   a. 27,500
   b. 5/6
   c. 50,000 to 1
   d. 1 to 500,000

	Aircraft	Cameras
United States	300	600,000
Japan	10	500,000

6. Which of the following does *not* typically limit international trade?
   a. transportation costs
   b. the risks of a falling standard of living as a result of trade
   c. the risks associated with overspecialization
   d. the prospect of short-term job losses in some sectors

7. In a zero-sum game involving two parties:
   a. Neither party can hope to make any gains.
   b. Both parties can be expected to make positive gains.
   c. One party can gain only if the other party also gains.
   d. One party can gain only if the other party loses.

Use the table below to answer Questions 8, 9, and 10.

	Athletic Shoes (pairs)	Music CDs
United States	10,000	20,000
Great Britain	5,000	15,000

8. What is the opportunity cost for Britain producing athletic shoes compared to music CDs?
   a. 2/3
   b. 3
   c. 2
   d. 1/2

9. If Britain produced music CDs only, then traded with the United States, which would occur?
   a. It would not benefit because the United States would still have an absolute advantage in producing athletic shoes.
   b. It would not benefit because its opportunity cost for producing music CDs is higher than that of the United States.
   c. It would not benefit because it does not have a comparative advantage.
   d. Both countries would benefit.

10. If Britain produced athletic shoes only, then traded with the United States, which would occur?
    a. It would not benefit because the United States would still have an absolute advantage in producing music CDs.
    b. It would not benefit because its opportunity cost for producing athletic shoes is higher than that of the United States.
    c. It would benefit because it has a comparative advantage.
    d. Neither country would benefit.

Score: _____

If You Got 9 or 10 Correct

You understand the concepts of specialization, comparative advantage, and voluntary trade. This chapter introduced the concepts of scarcity, production, tradeoffs, opportunity cost, and the benefits of specialization and voluntary trade. Most of this material is fairly straightforward, and you have probably mastered it. Just to be on the safe side, take a few moments and review the section on "Hints, Tips, and Reminders."

If You Didn't Get at Least 9 Correct

You should have scored 8 or better in this exercise even though questions 8–10 are difficult.

- Don't panic. Comparative advantage and voluntary trade are some of the more difficult concepts in the chapter and the book. It often takes students several attempts at this material to really master it.
- Take a moment and review this section in the book.
- Remember that people and nations voluntarily trade because each expects to benefit. Not many people would voluntarily trade (goods, hours worked, babysitting, or anything else) with someone else if they did not expect to benefit.
- Also, keep in mind that within countries there are winners and losers from trade. Typically consumers (a large group) benefit from trade and specific industries, and occupations (a smaller group) may lose. But overall, there are net gains from trade.

When you have completed this review, continue on, but you will probably want to review this chapter again. Maybe going through the "Hints, Tips, and Reminders" that follow will help. ■

STEP 4   Consider These Hints, Tips, and Reminders

1. Opportunity cost is an important concept that will resurface throughout the remainder of the course. Keep in mind that it is the value of your next-best alternative. The costs of going to a movie are your next best alternative—what you could have done with your money and time. The PPF makes this tradeoff clear—moving from one point to another involves opportunity costs.

2. The PPF is a really simple model of national economies but illustrates several important concepts:
   - **Scarcity**: Output possibilities beyond the boundary are impossible.
   - **Increasing opportunity cost**: As more of one good is produced, the opportunity cost of producing it rises because resources are not equally suitable for producing two different goods.
   - **Choice**: Societies must choose levels of output.
   - **Tradeoffs**: To pick one point on the PPF is to give up a different level of production.
   - **Opportunity cost**: Choices involve tradeoffs that involve opportunity costs—what society must give up to have more of another commodity or service.
   - **Full employment versus unemployment**: Along the PPF, resources are fully employed, while inside the PPF there is unemployment of resources.

■ **Economic growth**: Expanding the curve outward represents economic growth. Growth comes from improved technology and increases in resources

Keep in mind that this is a very simple model, but it provides insights into a lot of important issues.

3. The issues of specialization and trade are difficult to see at first, but keep in mind the following:
   ■ The basis for trade is comparative advantage and specialization. Whoever has the lowest opportunity costs to produce a given product or service has a comparative advantage.
   ■ This was Ricardo's main insight, so keep the principle of comparative advantage in mind as you work through problems.
   ■ Trade is controversial because there are winners and losers from trade. The winners are usually a large number of consumers, who each gain a little. The losers are typically a specific industry and its workers, who each lose a lot. There lies the controversy—many of us gain at the expense of a few.
   ■ Remember that comparative advantage applies to both people and resources. James Patterson and Stephen King have a comparative advantage over almost everyone when it comes to writing novels. Some land, for example, can produce crops more cheaply (in terms of resource cost) than other acreage.
   ■ It is important to remember that absolute advantage means nothing and is irrelevant for trade. Comparative advantages confer the benefits to trade between parties.
   ■ Comparative advantage and trade allow individuals and nations to consume levels of goods and services beyond their PPF. This is why people voluntarily trade! This principle holds true for individuals, communities, and nations. To make the point, look at an absurd set of examples: How would your life change if
      1. you could only buy American made goods?
      2. you could only buy goods made in your state?
      3. you could only buy goods made in the city where you live?
      4. you could only buy goods made by those living on your block?
      5. you couldn't buy goods from anyone, but you had to produce everything you consume yourself?

As you move down this list, most of us would agree that the quality of life as we know today would decline.

Do the Homework for Chapter 2	STEP 5
Production, Economic Growth, and Trade	

Instructor _____ Time _____ Student _____

_____

Use the answer key below to record your answers to these homework questions.

1. (a) (b) (c) (d)　　6. (a) (b) (c) (d)　　11. (a) (b) (c) (d)　　16. (a) (b) (c) (d)
2. (a) (b) (c) (d)　　7. (a) (b) (c) (d)　　12. (a) (b) (c) (d)　　17. (a) (b) (c) (d)
3. (a) (b) (c) (d)　　8. (a) (b) (c) (d)　　13. (a) (b) (c) (d)　　18. (a) (b) (c) (d)
4. (a) (b) (c) (d)　　9. (a) (b) (c) (d)　　14. (a) (b) (c) (d)　　19. (a) (b) (c) (d)
5. (a) (b) (c) (d)　　10. (a) (b) (c) (d)　　15. (a) (b) (c) (d)　　20. (a) (b) (c) (d)

1. Which of the following is *not* one of the basic questions all economies must answer?
   a. How are goods and services going to be produced?
   b. How will the level of technology be determined?
   c. Who will get the goods and services that the economy produces?
   d. What goods will be produced?

2. Land as a productive resource includes
   a. farm acreage.
   b. gold deposits.
   c. water and river systems.
   d. all of the above.

3. Profit is a return to
   a. land.
   b. labor.
   c. capital.
   d. entrepreneurship.

4. Productive efficiency means that
   a. General Motors must reduce its costs if it ever hopes to compete successfully with foreign automakers.
   b. companies must introduce new products continually to survive.
   c. products are produced at the lowest possible opportunity costs.
   d. capital costs are at their minimum, profits are low, and wages are high enough for a middle class lifestyle.

5. When an economy is producing the right mix of goods and services desired by society, we refer to that economy as
   a. entrepreneurial.
   b. productively efficient.
   c. capitalistic.
   d. allocatively efficient.

6. A point inside the PPF curve represents
   a. a situation of unemployed or underutilization of resources.
   b. negative returns.
   c. a growing economy.
   d. a fully employed economy.

Use Figure HW-1 to answer questions 7–9.

7. In the PPF curve shown in Figure HW-1, which points are attainable?
   a. *a* and *b*
   b. *b* and *c*
   c. *c*
   d. *b* only

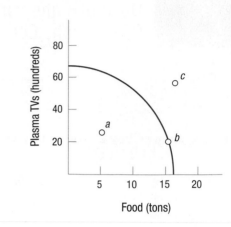

HW-1

8. Point *c* in the figure above represents
   a. how much more it costs to produce more food.
   b. negative returns to the production possibilities frontier.
   c. an impossible level of output for this economy to attain.
   d. unemployed or underutilization of resources.

9. Moving from point *a* to point *b* in the figure above would represent
   a. a more inefficient use of resources.
   b. diminishing returns.
   c. a losing situation because fewer plasma TVs are produced.
   d. a reduction in unemployment as the economy moves to full employment.

10. Using Figure HW-2, what might explain the shift in the PPF curve from *a* to *c*?
    a. More of the country's resources are devoted to soybean production.
    b. A technological improvement occurred in the production of PDAs.
    c. A technological improvement occurred in the production of soybeans.
    d. A reduction occurred in the number of idle resources.

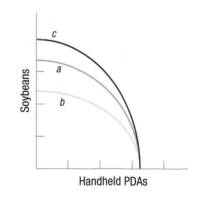

HW-2

11. In Figure HW-3, which of the points on PPF$_0$ represents the best choice for the economy?
    a. Point *a*.
    b. Point *b*.
    c. Point *c*.
    d. None of the above are necessarily correct.

12. In Figure HW-3, assume the economy is initially at point *b*. Which PPF curve will the economy most likely end up on in the future?
    a. PPF$_0$
    b. PPF$_1$
    c. PPF$_2$
    d. Point *c*

13. Using Figure HW-3, what might cause the production possibilities curve to shift from PPF$_1$ to PPF$_0$?
    a. Technology improves (lowers the cost) of producing consumer goods.
    b. Society decides it wants fewer consumer goods and more machinery.
    c. A large natural disaster occurs damaging the production base of the country.
    d. Society decides to reduce output today so they can produce more in the future.

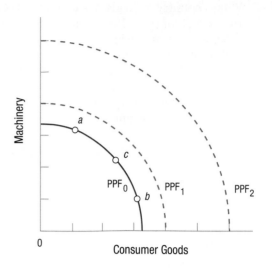

HW-3

Use the table at right to answer questions 14–15.

14. Using the table above, what is the opportunity cost of producing 800 tons of soybeans instead of 600 tons?
    a. There is no opportunity cost; this country can easily produce more tons of soybeans.
    b. 100 PDAs.
    c. Four PDAs for every ton of soybeans produced.
    d. 50 PDAs.

15. Using the table above, what is the opportunity cost of producing 175 PDAs instead of 150?
    a. Eight tons of soybeans for every additional PDA produced.
    b. 200 tons of soybeans.
    c. The amount of soybeans that must be given up for the additional PDAs.
    d. All of the above.

Production Possibilities

Combination	Soybeans (tons)	Handheld PDAs
A	1,000	0
B	800	100
C	600	150
D	400	175
E	200	190
F	0	200

---

16. The table at right depicts the production possibilities between Germany and the United States, assuming they produce only two products, movies and cameras. Assuming that free trade exists between the countries, how many movies should Germany produce so that both countries are better off after trading?
    a. 40
    b. 10
    c. 0
    d. 20

	Movies	Cameras
United States	30	600,000
Germany	10	500,000

17. When a country expands its trade with other countries, which of the following is likely to occur?
    a. Some job losses will occur in some industries.
    b. Most consumers in the country will complain and refuse to buy imported products.
    c. Incomes will drop in both countries.
    d. Unemployment will rise in both countries over a long period of time.

18. In a country with low standards of living and low levels of human capital, we would expect this country to focus on which of the following products?
    a. computers
    b. cellular phones
    c. clothing
    d. HDTV sets

19. Why would the United States want to trade with Spain, given that the United States is so much larger and more productive?

    a. The United States wants to acquire Spanish land.
    b. Spain leads the world in technical change and innovation.
    c. Absolute advantage.
    d. Comparative advantage.

20. If country A has an absolute advantage over country B in the production of a particular good, this means that
    a. country A has a technological advantage over country B.
    b. country A can produce more of a product than can country B.
    c. country A can produce a product at a lower opportunity cost than country B.
    d. country A is the market leader in producing the product.

| Use the ExamPrep to Get Ready for Exams | STEP 6 |

This sheet (front and back) is designed to help you prepare for your exams. The chapter has been boiled down to its key concepts. You are asked to answer questions, define terms, draw graphs, and, if you wish, add summaries of class notes.

Basic Economic Questions and Production

Describe the following:

A production function:

Increasing returns:

Diminishing returns:

Negative returns:

Constant returns:

Production Possibilities and Economic Growth

Use the grid below to diagram a typical production possibilities curve with increasing opportunity costs.

Add three points to the figure; full employment, underutilization of resources, and production that is not possible under the given constraints.

Describe how opportunity costs are shown on this diagram.

Describe the way economic growth can happen in the economy and show economic growth in the grid on the previous page.

Specialization, Comparative Advantage, and Trade

Define the following:

Absolute advantage:

Comparative advantage:

Describe the gains from trade associated with comparative advantage.

Describe some of the limits to trade and specialization.

Additional Study Help Chapterwide Practice Questions

Matching

Match the description with the corresponding term.

___ 1. Production
___ 2. Inputs
___ 3. Land
___ 4. Entrepreneurship
___ 5. Production possibilities frontier (PPF)
___ 6. Opportunity costs
___ 7. Economic growth
___ 8. Absolute advantage
___ 9. Comparative advantage

a. The price an economy or an individual must pay, measured in units of one product, to increase its production (or consumption) of another product.

b. That which goes into the production process to create finished products: land, labor, capital, and entrepreneurial ability.

c. Delineates the different possible mixes of goods an economy can produce when it is fully employing its resources.

d. When one country can produce a particular good at a lower opportunity cost than can the other county, trade will be beneficial.

e. A vacant, unimproved parking lot in the middle of Omaha, Nebraska.

f. The process of transforming inputs into outputs, or of turning factors of production—land, labor, capital, and entrepreneurial ability—into products and services.

g. When people and firms are continually increasing their production and consumption. Two primary explanations for this are expanding resources and improving technologies.

h. When one country can produce more of a particular good than another country.

i. Earns profits for its part in the production process.

Fill-In

Circle the word(s) in parentheses that complete the sentence.

1. No matter how the economy is structured, every economy must answer three basic questions including what goods and services to produce, who will get these goods and services, and (who will be in charge of the economy, how will the goods and services be produced, how will income will be distributed) _____.

2. Production involves turning (technology, resources) _____ into goods and services. Resources consist of land, entrepreneurship, labor and (energy, capital, profits) _____. Entrepreneurial ability is paid (profit, interest, rents) _____ for its efforts in assuming risk and combining the other factors of production to produce products and services for the market.

3. When the correct mix of goods and services are produced, the economy is said to be (capitalistic, allocatively efficient, productively efficient) _____. When goods and services are produced at their lowest opportunity cost, (allocative efficiency, productive efficiency) _____ prevails.

4. All points on the production possibilities frontier (PPF) represent output combinations that are (attainable, unattainable) _____; while points outside of the PPF are said to be (attainable, unattainable) _____. Points inside the PPF represent (unemployment, full employment) _____; while points on the PPF represent (unemployment, full employment) _____.

5. Moving from one point to another on the PPF results in (gains, opportunity costs) _____ as one product is traded for another. When the PPF is bowed out from the origin, opportunity costs are (increasing, decreasing, constant) _____.

6. When the PPF expands outward the economy has experienced (full employment, economic growth) _____, and this occurs because (government, costs, resources) _____ have expanded. Another source of economic growth according to the PPF model is (income redistribution, technology) _____.

7. An/A (absolute, comparative) _____ advantage occurs when one individual or nation can produce more of a good or service than another. An/A (absolute, comparative) _____ advantage occurs when one individual or nation can produce a good or service at a lower opportunity cost than another. An/A (absolute, comparative) _____ advantage is the reason why so many nations are trading with other nations.

True-False

Circle the correct answer.

__T/F__   1. Only socialist economies have to consider how goods and services will be produced.

__T/F__   2. Production involves turning land, labor, capital, and entrepreneurship into goods and services.

__T/F__   3. If an economy can produce 10,000 more gallons of peanut butter only by producing 5000 gallons less of jelly, the opportunity cost of 1 gallon of peanut butter is 2 gallons of jelly.

__T/F__   4. A PPF curve will identify the best mix of products for a given society to produce.

__T/F__   5. If an economy is operating at full employment, it can increase its production of one good only by decreasing its production of another.

__T/F__   6. If an economy initially produces a balanced mix of agricultural and manufactured goods, it could probably double its production of agricultural goods by devoting all of its productive resources to agriculture.

__T/F__   7. The two primary determinants of economic growth are expanding resources and improving technology.

__T/F__   8. In an economy that produces automobiles and video games, a technological advance in automobile manufacturing will likely have no effect on video game production levels.

__T/F__   9. The labor factor can be increased either by expanding the workforce or by making investments in human capital, such as offering on-the-job training.

__T/F__   10. The more an economy favors the production of consumption goods over capital goods, the stronger its economic growth is likely to be over time.

Multiple Choice

Circle the correct answer.

1. Which of the following is *not* one of the three basic questions any economy must answer?

a. How are goods and services to be produced?
b. Who will receive these goods and services?
c. How is the political leadership to be determined?
d. What goods and services are to be produced?

2. What are the primary factors of production for any industry?
a. political power, public relations, and advertising
b. land, labor, capital, and entrepreneurship
c. oil, coal, gas, and steel
d. business owners, workers, consumers, and government regulators

3. Production is about the relationship between
a. inputs and outputs.
b. workers and management.
c. firms and consumers.
d. the decisions of individual producers and the growth of the economy as a whole.

4. In production possibility frontier analysis, which mixes of goods are considered to be attainable by an economy?
a. only those mixes falling on the PPF curve
b. those mixes on, or to the left of, the PPF curve
c. those mixes on, or to the right of, the PPF curve
d. only those mixes falling to the left of the PPF curve

5. What does the PPF curve show?
a. the various levels of output producers are willing to supply at different price levels
b. the quantity of output an economy will produce at varying levels of labor or some other input
c. the best mix of goods for an economy to produce
d. the various mixes of goods an economy can produce at full employment of its resources

6. If an economy is producing a mix of goods that falls directly on its production possibilities frontier, this indicates that
a. consumers must be happy with the mix of good produced.
b. the economy is operating at full employment.
c. the economy is leaving some resources unused.
d. the economy is growing.

7. Opportunity cost is a measure of
a. what it costs a firm to break into a new market.
b. the increase in output that comes from adding inputs to the production process.
c. the inputs a firm must purchase to be able to produce some good.
d. the goods an individual or economy must forego to produce or consume more of some other good.

8. If an economy must forgo building 700 new homes to produce 3,500 new automobiles, what is the opportunity cost of one automobile?
   a. 0.2 home
   b. 1 home
   c. 5 homes
   d. 700 homes

9. An economy that devotes half of its resources to producing guns and half to producing butter turns out 1,000 guns and 1,000 pounds of butter every year. If this economy were to begin devoting all of its resources to producing guns, how many guns would we expect it to produce annually?
   a. Something less than 2,000 guns.
   b. Right around 2,000 guns.
   c. Something more than 2,000 guns.
   d. We have no grounds for making any predictions.

10. The primary reasons underlying economic growth are
    a. decreasing consumer demand and improving technology.
    b. expanding resources and rising interest rates.
    c. rising exports and declining imports.
    d. expanding resources and improving technology.

11. Which of the following would *not* be an investment in human capital?
    a. researching automated production techniques
    b. putting more money into the education system
    c. beginning a job-training program
    d. launching an employee physical fitness campaign

12. Which of the following would *not* be an expected outcome of investing in human capital?
    a. higher wages
    b. increased worker productivity
    c. an expanded PPF
    d. higher rates of workplace injuries

13. Which economic policy is most likely to promote strong economic growth in the long run? (Ignore the possibilities of international trade.)
    a. more consumption goods and fewer capital goods
    b. more capital goods and fewer consumption goods
    c. exclusively consumption goods
    d. more TIVO recorders

14. If an economy produces guns and butter, and a technological innovation makes the production of guns cheaper, we would expect the economy's production of butter to

a. decrease.
b. remain about the same.
c. increase.
d. be unpredictable.

15. Additional capital means that
    a. each unit of labor become less efficient.
    b. higher possible production throughout the economy.
    c. high production but only in a few parts of the economy.
    d. little difference in production or efficiency.

16. Which change would *not* be a way of stimulating economic growth?
    a. using more resources
    b. raising educational levels
    c. improving incentives for private firms to increase production
    d. restricting trade to protect the automobile industry

17. Which answer would *not* be an outcome of the ripple effect of technological change?
    a. new products
    b. improved goods and services
    c. increased efficiency
    d. improving efficiency in one industry, but not others

18. In Figure MC-1, assume that an economy starts with a PPF curve at PPF_0. Economic growth occurs when the economy
    a. moves on the PPF_0 curve from consumer goods to capital goods (point *b* to point *a*).
    b. moves from PPF_0 to PPF_1.

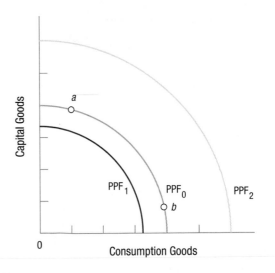

MC-1

   c. moves from PPF_0 to PPF_2.

   d. moves on the PPF_0 curve from capital goods to consumer goods (point a to point b).

19. In a positive-sum game involving two parties, which of the following is true?
   a. Both parties can and generally do make positive gains.
   b. For one party to gain, the other party must lose.
   c. Neither party can hope to make any gains.
   d. Both parties will invariably make equal gains.

20. If one country has a comparative advantage over another, which of the following can happen?
   a. It can produce more of some product than the other country.
   b. It can produce some product at a lower opportunity cost than can the other country.
   c. It produces higher quality products than the other country.
   d. It markets its products more quickly than the other country.

21. If one country has an absolute advantage over another, which of the following can happen?
   a. It can produce more of some product than the other country.
   b. It can produce some product at a lower opportunity cost than can the other country.
   c. It produces higher-quality products than the other country.
   d. It markets its products more quickly than the other country.

22. Two countries will benefit from trading with one another if
   a. each country concentrates on producing those goods at which it has an absolute advantage.
   b. the country with the greatest productive capacity does all of the production.
   c. each country concentrates on producing those goods at which it has a comparative advantage.
   d. each country produces only goods that the other cannot.

23. An economy with a highly educated workforce and large supply of capital, but relatively little land, would probably fare best in the global market by focusing on the production of which of these?
   a. wheat
   b. coal
   c. microcomputers
   d. timber

24. American standards of living have increased over the second half of the last century because of
   a. control of immigration.
   b. restrictions on trade.
   c. expansion of resources and technological progress.
   d. reductions in our trade deficit.

25. A likely outcome of signing the North American Free Trade Agreement (NAFTA) would be
   a. lower growth in the United States.
   b. job losses in some industries but increased potential for overall growth.
   c. job losses throughout the U.S. economy.
   d. no job losses in any part of the economy.

Essay-Problem

Answer in the space provided.

Some of the questions below are challenging. Don't get discouraged if your answers are not always the same as those we suggest. Use these as another way to assess your progress, but more important, to discover and learn some of the subtleties surrounding production, economic growth, and trade.

1. What is the essence of the three basic economic questions?

2. Describe the specific resources (factors of production) that a typical Apple computer store might use. Be specific in your description—do not just suggest "land, labor, capital, and entrepreneurial talent."

3. Is it likely that any country produces on its PPF?

4. If an economy that initially produces a balanced mix of corn and computers begins shifting more and more of its resources into the production of computers, why does the opportunity cost of computers eventually begin rising?

5. Has the Internet generated economic growth?

6. If expanding resources help an economy to grow, name some ways to expand resources.

7. How have computers spurred economic growth?

8. Name some of the short-term costs and long-term benefits of expanding international trade.

9. If international trade benefits both trading partners, why would countries erect trade barriers?

10. Explain how cell phones have helped countries around the world achieve quicker economic growth.

11. Using the information from the table below, draw a PPF curve for an economy that produces cars and boats. (Put cars on the horizontal axis.)

Possible Combinations

Cars	Boats
0	125
60	120
120	105
170	80
200	60
225	30
250	0

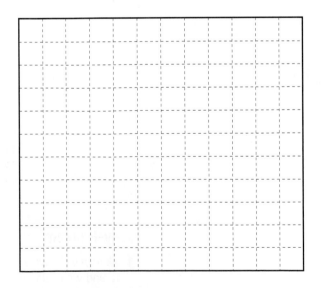

Which of the following mixes are attainable by the economy, and which are unattainable?
   a. 100 cars; 100 boats
   b. 200 cars; 75 boats
   c. 50 cars; 125 boats

What's Next

This chapter provided an introduction to how economic growth arises and how comparative advantage and international trade spur economic growth. We took individual and societal preferences for granted. In the next chapter, we look at demand and supply, the bedrock concept in economics. We will explore how individuals signal their demands for goods and services, and how firms respond to these signals.

Answers to Chapterwide Practice Questions

Matching

1. f	4. i	6. a	8. h
2. b	5. c	7. g	9. d
3. e			

Fill-In

1. how will the goods and services be produced
2. resources, capital, profit
3. allocatively efficient, productive efficiency
4. attainable, unattainable, unemployment, full employment
5. opportunity costs, increasing
6. economic growth, resources, technology
7. absolute, comparative, comparative

True-False

1. F	4. F	7. T	9. T
2. T	5. T	8. F	10. F
3. F	6. F		

Multiple Choice

1. c	8. a	14. c	20. b
2. b	9. a	15. b	21. a
3. a	10. d	16. d	22. c
4. b	11. a	17. d	23. c
5. d	12. d	18. c	24. c
6. b	13. b	19. a	25. b
7. d			

Essay-Problem

1. All economic systems have to answer the questions of what to produce, how to produce it, and who gets goods and services, but the answers can differ.
2. The typical Apple computer store hires labor (sales staff whom are very familiar with Apple products and computer technicians). Typically, they rent space in retail centers, the land component. Inside the stores are considerable fixtures, working products, inventory, and other capital including lights, registers, and phones. Some individual manages each store, and to this extent that person represents the entrepreneur.

3. Production possibilities analysis is very stylized and assumes that all inputs are used efficiently, a highly unlikely situation. Nevertheless, PPF analysis is still useful for thinking about production and growth.

4. In the initial situation, the economy likely uses those resources most suitable to corn production for producing corn, and those resources more suitable to computer production for producing computers. Most of the economy's low-skilled labor, for instance, will probably be working in the cornfields, whereas its high-skilled workers will be laboring efficiently in the computer industry. As ever more computers get produced, however, resources must be drawn from the corn industry, many of them suited more to corn production than to computer production. Low-skilled field hands, for instance, may suddenly find themselves in microchip factories, where they may be ill-suited to working efficiently. Such resource shifts significantly reduce the quantity of corn the economy can produce, while only marginally improving its output of computers. Thus, the more computers produced, the higher their opportunity cost will be, measured in terms of corn.

5. Among many specific answers, here is one. The Internet has enabled shoppers to compare prices of goods quickly. This has facilitated consumption, especially in less developed areas of the world. Increasing consumption has often been a motor to growth. The Internet has also significantly reduced transactions costs for many products. Auction firms like eBay have opened up huge markets for goods that were heretofore extremely difficult to obtain. Finding old books and obscure items previously involved incredible search costs.

6. One general way an economy can expand its labor factor is by increasing the number of people in the workforce. It might do this by increasing immigration, raising the national birthrate, or encouraging more potential workers to enter the workforce. By reducing discrimination in labor markets, the government was able to expand the labor force as more women and minorities entered. The second general way an economy can expand the labor factor is by raising the skill level of workers already employed, thereby increasing their productivity. This is known as investing in human capital. Some examples of investments in human capital are improving the educational system, providing on-the-job training, and improving employee health care.

7. Computers have spurred economic growth in many ways. Robotics, highly dependent on computers, have made production of products such as automobiles and snow blowers much more efficient and improved product quality. Computers have made planning much easier because making changes to numbers is not the cumbersome task it was before computerized spreadsheets. Computers have also become major communication devices, especially around the globe.

8. When a country expands its trade, it will generally increase its production of those goods at which it has a comparative advantage, shipping many of them abroad, while increasing its import of those goods at which it is at a comparative disadvantage. Domestic producers of the latter goods will see their profits fall when cheaper imports begin flooding the market; they may have to close down or lay off workers. The short-term pain for these firms and individuals is real. Nevertheless, if both entrepreneurs and workers begin moving into production sectors that are enjoying strong foreign sales, they stand to see their profits and wages rise in the long run. With global production and consumption rising as countries everywhere produce more of those goods at which they have comparative advantages, all of those who participate in expanded international trade should experience positive gains in the long run.

9. Trade, while beneficial to a country overall, may hurt specific industries that are now at a comparative disadvantage. These specific industries may seek political recourse. The political bark of a harmed industry often is much louder than the satisfaction of individuals benefiting from trade because the benefit may be small to each person, though great when summed together. Industries harmed by trade have an easier time focusing resources and lobbying efforts than can consumers.

10. Twenty years ago, telephone communication required huge expenditures in infrastructure: Telephone cable had to be laid or strung up on telephone poles. Today, cell-phone

towers are much, much cheaper to produce. Cell phones have spurred communication without massive expenditures in infrastructure.

11.

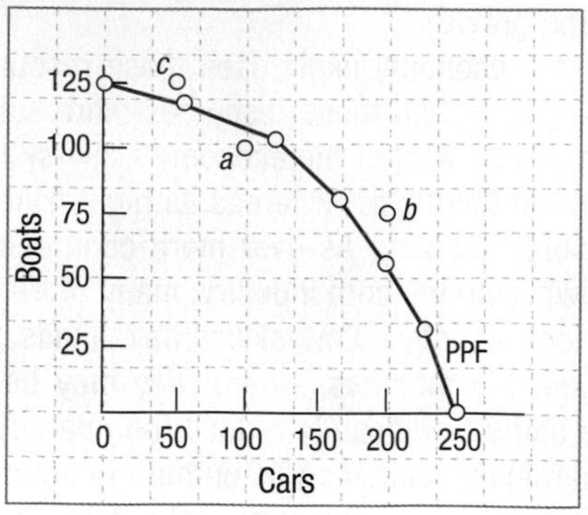

(a) attainable
(b) unattainable
(c) unattainable

Supply and Demand

3

Most Economic Issues Involve Supply and Demand in Some Way

Supply and demand form the foundation of economics. You will use these concepts throughout the remainder of the semester. To understand how market economies operate, you will need to have a firm grasp of supply and demand analysis. Nearly every economic problem you confront will be clarified in some way by this analysis.

This Is What You Need to Know	STEP 1

After studying this chapter you should be able to

- Describe the nature and purposes of markets.

- Describe the nature of demand, demand curves, and the law of demand.

- Describe the determinants of demand and be able to forecast how a change in one or more of these determinants will change demand.

- Describe the difference between a change in demand and a change in quantity demanded.

- Describe the nature of supply, supply curves, and the law of supply.

- Describe the determinants of supply and be able to forecast how a change in one or more of these determinants will change supply.

- Describe the difference between a change in supply and a change in quantity supplied.

- Determine market equilibrium price and output.

- Determine and predict how price and output will change given changes to supply and demand in the market.

Review the Key Terms

Markets: Institutions that bring buyers and sellers together so they can interact and transact with each other.

Price system: A name given to the market economy because prices provide considerable information to both buyers and sellers.

Demand: The maximum amount of a product that buyers are willing and able to purchase over some time period at various prices, holding all other relevant factors constant (the *ceteris paribus* condition).

Law of demand: Holding all other relevant factors constant, as price increases, quantity demanded falls, and as price decreases, quantity demanded rises.

Demand curve: Demand schedule information translated to a graph.

Horizontal summation: Market demand and supply curves are found by adding together how many units of the product will be purchased or supplied at each price.

Determinants of demand: Other nonprice factors that affect demand including tastes and preferences, income, prices of related goods, number of buyers, and expectations.

Normal good: A good where an increase in income results in rising demand.

Inferior good: A good where an increase in income results in declining demand.

Substitute goods: Goods consumers will substitute for one another depending on their relative prices.

Complementary goods: Goods that are typically consumed together.

Change in demand: Occurs when one or more of the determinants of demand changes, shown as a shift in the entire demand curve.

Change in quantity demanded: Occurs when the price of the product changes, and is shown as a movement along an existing demand curve.

Supply: The maximum amount of a product that sellers are willing and able to provide for sale over some time period at various prices, holding all other relevant factors constant (the *ceteris paribus* condition).

Law of supply: Holding all other relevant factors constant, as price increases, quantity supplied will rise, and as price declines, quantity supplied will fall.

Supply curve: Supply schedule information translated to a graph.

Determinants of supply: Other nonprice factors that affect supply including production technology, costs of resources (factor costs), prices of other commodities, expectations, number of sellers, and taxes and subsidies.

Change in supply: Occurs when one or more of the determinants of supply change, shown as a shift in the entire supply curve.

Change in quantity supplied: Occurs when the price of the product changes, and is shown as a movement along an existing supply curve.

Equilibrium: Market forces are in balance where the quantities demanded by consumers just equal quantities supplied by producers.

Equilibrium price: The price that results when quantity demanded is just equal to quantity supplied.

Equilibrium quantity: The output that results when quantity demanded is just equal to quantity supplied.

Surplus: Occurs when the price is above market equilibrium price, and quantity supplied exceeds quantity demanded.

Shortage: Occurs when the price is below market equilibrium price, and quantity demanded exceeds quantity supplied.

Work Through the Chapter Tutorials   STEP 3

Demand

Frequently Asked Questions

Q: What are markets, and why are they important?

A: Markets are institutions that enable buyers and sellers to interact and transact business with one another. Through their purchases, consumers signal their willingness to buy particular products at particular prices. These signals help businesses to decide what and how much to produce.

Q: What is demand, and how are price and quantity demanded related?

A: *Demand* refers to the quantity of products people are willing and able to purchase at various prices during some specific time period, all other relevant factors held constant. The *demand curve* shown in Figure 1 depicts the relationship between price and quantity demanded. Price and quantity demanded are negatively (inversely) related: As prices rise, consumers buy less, and vice versa. This inverse relation is known as the *law of demand*.

FIGURE 1

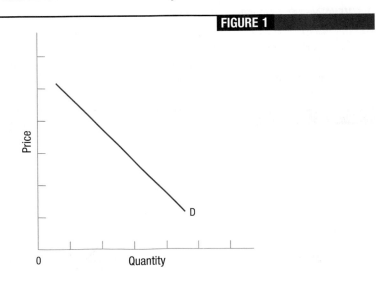

Q: What are the determinants of demand?

A: The *determinants of demand* include the following:
   ■ Consumer tastes and preferences
   ■ Income
   ■ Prices of substitutes and complements
   ■ The number of buyers in the market
   ■ Expectations regarding future prices, incomes, and product availability

Q: What causes the demand curve to shift?

A: *Demand changes (shifts)* when one or more of these determinants change. In Figure 2 a new popular ad campaign for Nalgene bottles would shift demand from D_0 to D_1. Alternatively, the ease of making digital copies could reduce the demand for music CDs, as shown by the demand curve declining from D_0 to D_2.

FIGURE 2

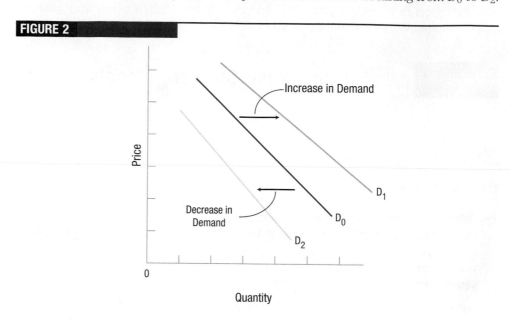

Q: How are market demand curves determined?

A: *Market demand curves* are found by horizontally summing individual demand curves. We simply add the total quantities demanded by all consumers for each possible price.

Q: What causes a change in demand?

A: *A change in demand* means a shift of the demand curve. As shown in Figure 3, a shift to the right (D_1) is an increase in demand, whereas a shift to the left (D_2) represents a decline in demand. These shifts in demand are caused by changes in one or more of the determinants of demand.

FIGURE 3

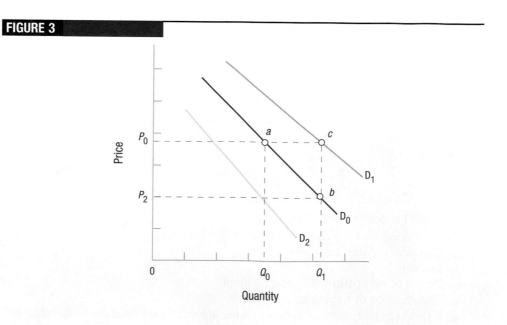

Q: How is a change in quantity demanded different from a change in demand?

A: A *change in quantity demanded* occurs only when the *price* of a product changes, leading consumers to adjust their purchases along an existing demand curve. This is shown in Figure 3 as a movement from point *a* to point *b*. Note in this case that a reduced price of P_2 was required to increase sales. Contrast this with the movement from point *a* to point *c* (an increase in demand), where much more is sold at the same price, P_0.

Demand Quick Check

Circle the Correct Answer

1. (T/F) The major benefit of markets is that they bring sellers and buyers together to transact business.
2. (T/F) The law of demand states that demand increases (demand curves shift to the right) when income increases.
3. (T/F) All markets have roughly the same number of buyers and sellers.
4. (T/F) Demand curves always have positive slopes reflecting the law of demand.
5. Which of the following is *not* a determinant of demand for orange juice?
   a. consumer after-tax income
   b. price of tomato juice
   c. medical research on the benefits of orange juice
   d. agricultural subsides (government payments) to farmers to grow more oranges
6. Which of the following will cause an increase in the demand for steel?
   a. Price of automobile tires increases because of a shortage of rubber from Malaysia.
   b. Concrete steel reinforcing rods are replaced by aluminum to reduce rust along the Atlantic seaboard.
   c. Gasoline prices are reduced by 50% because OPEC countries (the Middle East oil cartel) break into a quarrel and all countries expand production.
   d. McDonald's increases its production of hamburgers and fries to meet demand when a medical study concludes that fries are healthy alternatives to vegetables.
7. Which of the following is *not* a determinant of demand for MP3 players?
   a. the price of television sets
   b. consumer income
   c. the quality of music available in MP3 format
   d. the quantity of music available in MP3 format
8. An increase in demand means that
   a. the demand curve shifts upward and to the left.
   b. the demand curve shifts downward and to the right.
   c. more goods are purchased at the same price.
   d. fewer sellers are willing to sell the good.

9. The essence of a sale is (see Figure 4)
   a. reducing price to increase the quantity demanded.
   b. an attempt by sellers to increase consumer satisfaction.
   c. a movement from point *a* to point *c* in the figure.
   d. a shift in the demand curve from D_0 to D_1 in the figure.

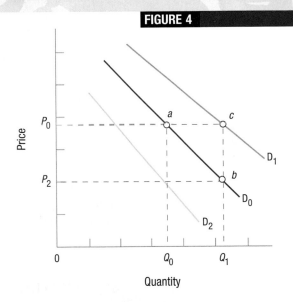

FIGURE 4

10. A decrease in quantity demanded in Figure 4 can be characterized by
    a. a shift in the demand curve from D_0 to D_1.
    b. a movement from point *a* to point *c*.
    c. a shift in the demand curve from D_0 to D_2.
    d. a movement from point *b* to point *a*.

Score: _____

Answers: 1. T; 2. F; 3. F; 4. F; 5. d; 6. c; 7. a; 8. c; 9. a; 10. d

If You Got 9 or 10 Correct

You have the concepts of demand, changes in demand, and changes in quantity demanded under control. Keep in mind that a change in one or more of the determinants of demand *shifts* the demand curve and is a *change in demand*, while a *change in quantity demanded* is caused by a change in the price of the product and is a movement *along* an existing demand curve. Go on to the next section, "Supply."

If You Didn't Get at Least 9 Correct

Keep in mind that it may take more than a cursory reading of the text to capture these concepts. To be able to use the analysis presented, it may take some time and effort. But given the importance of demand and supply analysis to the study of economics, give it a little more time than usual. Take a moment and go back and review the section on demand.

Keep in Mind

- Demand refers to
  - □ the amount of a product . . .
  - □ that people are willing and able to buy . . .
  - □ at various prices . . .
  - □ over some time period . . .
  - □ holding all other relevant factors constant.
- The other relevant factors are the determinants of demand:
  - □ tastes and preferences
  - □ income
  - □ prices of substitutes and complements
  - □ number of buyers in the market
  - □ expectations of future prices, income and product availability
- When a determinant changes, the demand curve shifts.
- A change in one or more of the determinants *shifts* the demand curve and is a *change in demand*, while a *change in quantity demanded* is caused by a change in the product's *price* and is a movement *along* an existing demand curve.

Now that you have reread the section, take a crack at the problem below. Once you have answered the questions yourself, follow along as the solution to the problem takes you through getting from individual demands to a market demand curve. ■

Solved Problem: Market Demands From Individual Demands

Use the table below, assuming the market consists only of the three people given. First, fill in the table by determining the market demand curve. Next, use the grid to construct the individual demand curves. Finally, construct the market

| | Quantity Demanded | | | | | |
Price	Lisa	Mildred	Nan	Market	50%	200%
100	0	1	1	___	___	___
80	1	2	3	___	___	___
60	2	3	5	___	___	___
40	3	4	7	___	___	___
20	4	5	9	___	___	___

demand curve. Now assume some event reduces the market demand by one half (50%). Complete the table and show the new demand curve on the graph. Next, assume that just the opposite occurs and the market doubles (200%). Again, complete the table and show the new market demand on the graph.

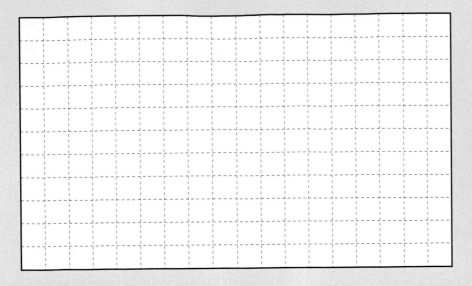

Solution-Discussion

The market demand curve is the horizontal summation of individual demands. When the price is $100, adding up the quantities demanded by each of the three individuals gives 2 (Mildred and Nan each are willing and able to buy one apiece, and Lisa wants none). When price is $60, Lisa buys 2 (point a); Mildred, 3 (point b); and Nan, 5 (point c). Adding all three quantities demanded equals 10 (point d) on the market demand curve. Doing the same for all five prices yields the market demand as shown. All four curves are plotted in Figure 5. Next, when demand drops by 50%, it equals half of the total of the original market demand, which in this instance is just equal to Nan's demand. When demand doubles (200%), all values double; demand shifts outward by twice the original demand curve and is shown as $D_{200\%}$.

FIGURE 5

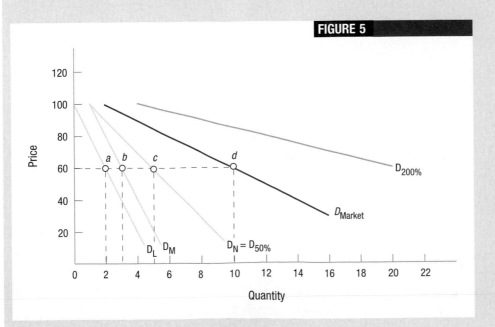

	Quantity Demanded					
Price	Lisa	Mildred	Nan	Market	50%	200%
100	0	1	1	2	1	4
80	1	2	3	6	3	12
60	2	3	5	10	5	20
40	3	4	7	14	7	28
20	4	5	9	18	9	36

Ideally, you now see the logic behind demand. If you are not comfortable with this section on demand, reread the "Frequently Asked Questions," then retake the quick quiz above. Because the supply section is quite similar in structure to demand, you will in all likelihood begin to see the pattern. Good luck with supply.

Supply

Frequently Asked Questions

Q: **What is supply, and how are price and quantity supplied related?**

A: *Supply* represents the quantity of a product producers are willing and able to put on the market at various prices, when all other relevant factors are held constant. The *law of supply* reflects the positive relationship between price and quantity supplied: As the supply curve in Figure 6 shows, the higher the market price, the more goods supplied, and vice versa. *Market supply*, as with market demand, is arrived at by horizontally summing the individual supplies of all firms.

FIGURE 6

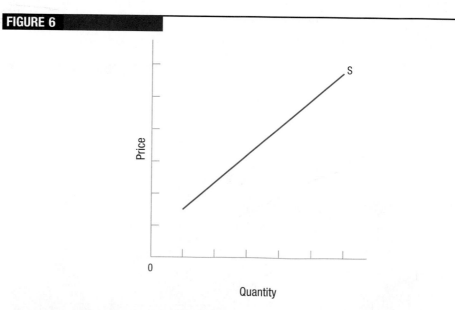

Q: **What are the determinants of supply?**

A: The *determinants of supply* are the following:
- production technology

■ the cost of resource inputs
■ prices of other commodities
■ expectations
■ number of sellers or producers in the market
■ taxes and subsidies

Q: How is a change in supply defined?

A: A *change in supply* results when one or more of the determinants of supply change. A shift to the right, as shown in Figure 7, reflects an increase in supply (from S_0 to S_1), whereas a shift to the left (from S_0 to S_2) represents a decrease in supply.

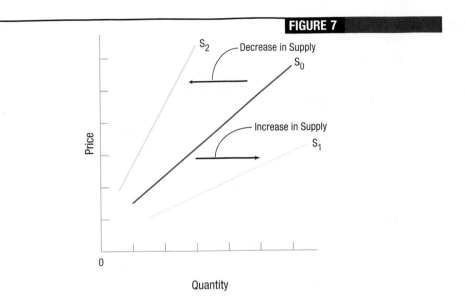

FIGURE 7

Q: How does a change in quantity supplied differ from a change in supply?

A: A *change in quantity supplied* is only caused by a change in the *price* of the product; it is a movement along an existing supply curve. A reduction in price results in a reduction of quantity supplied. This is shown in Figure 8 as a

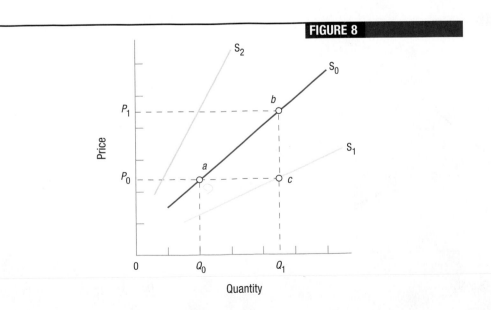

FIGURE 8

movement from point b to point a, on supply curve S_0. A price increase leads to an increase in quantity supplied. This is shown as the reverse movement from point a to point b.

Contrast this with the movement from point a to point c (an increase in supply) where much more is sold, even though the price is held to P_0.

Supply Quick Check

Circle the Correct Answer

1. (T/F) The law of supply states that higher prices will lead producers to offer less of their product for sale during a given period.
2. (T/F) A supply curve always slopes up and to the right to show that quantity supplied increases with price.
3. (T/F) If producers expect higher prices, that usually leads to an increase in supply.
4. Which of the following is *not* a determinant of supply?
   a. costs of resources
   b. consumer tastes and preferences
   c. production technology
   d. the number of sellers (producers) in the market
5. A decrease in supply will cause the supply curve to shift
   a. up and to the left.
   b. up and to the right.
   c. down and to the left.
   d. down and to the right.
6. When the price of a product increases from P_0 to P_1 in Figure 9,
   a. quantity supplied decreases from S_0 to S_2.
   b. quantity supplied increases from Q_0 to Q_1.
   c. supply decreases to S_2.
   d. supply increases to S_1.

7. The prices of other commodities affect supply because
   a. producers will switch to produce a more profitable commodity.
   b. consumers will buy more of a cheaper commodity.
   c. consumers will switch to complementary goods.
   d. producers will increase their price to keep pace with other commodities.
8. A change in supply of HDTV sets
   a. results from a change in consumer tastes and preferences.
   b. results from a price change.
   c. results in a change in the amount of HDTVs offered at every price.
   d. leads to a corresponding change in demand for HDTV sets.
   e. results from an improved picture aspect ratio.
9. Determinants of supply affect
   a. the entire supply curve.
   b. the quantity supplied only.
   c. the number of consumers who want the product.
   d. the quantity demanded.
10. Which of the following is correct concerning the market for baseball gloves shown in Figure 10?
   a. If glove manufacturers raise the price of their gloves from P_0 to P_1, quantity supplied decreases from S_0 to S_2.

FIGURE 9

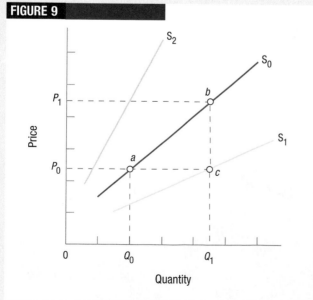

FIGURE 10

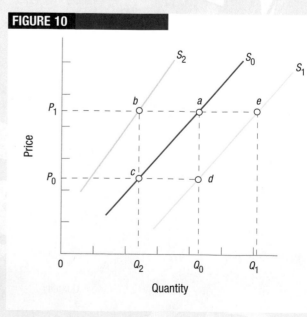

b. Excess livestock production leads to falling leather prices, so quantity supplied increases from Q_0 to Q_1.

c. Excess livestock production leads to falling leather prices, resulting in supply decreasing to S_2.

d. Excess livestock production leads to falling leather prices, so supply increases to S_1.

Score: ____

If You Got 9 or 10 Correct

You have mastered the concepts of supply, changes in supply, and changes in quantity supplied. You obviously noticed how closely the concepts of supply and demand structurally parallel each other. Keep in mind that a change in one or more of the determinants of supply *shifts* the supply curve and is a *change in supply*, while a *change in quantity supplied* is caused by a change in the product's price and is a movement *along* an existing supply curve. Go on to the next section, "Market Equilibrium."

If You Didn't Get at Least 9 Correct

You probably didn't do well on the previous section either. Both demand and supply follow the same general principles for different sides of the market. Demand focuses on consumers' decisions and what they wish and are able and willing to purchase, while supply looks at business decisions to supply goods, but in a quite similar way.

Keep in Mind

For both, changes in demand and changes in supply are defined in a similar fashion: They are caused by a change in one (or more) of the determinants. Similarly, a change in quantity demanded or a change in quantity supplied are both caused by just a change in the price of that product. A change in quantity demanded or supplied means a movement from one point on the curve to another. In contrast a change in demand or supply means that the market now faces an entirely new demand or supply curve.

Before you move on, work through the solved problem below. ■

Solved Problem: Supply

Use Figure 11 on the next page to answer the questions that follow.

a. Assume the market is initially at point a on S_0. A decline in quantity supplied would be represented by what point? _____

b. If the market was initially at point a, and production technology underwent substantial improvement, which curve would represent the resulting increase in supply? _____

c. Assume the market is initially at point d. An increase in quantity supplied would be represented by which point? _____

d. If supply is initially S_0, which curve represents a decline in supply? _____

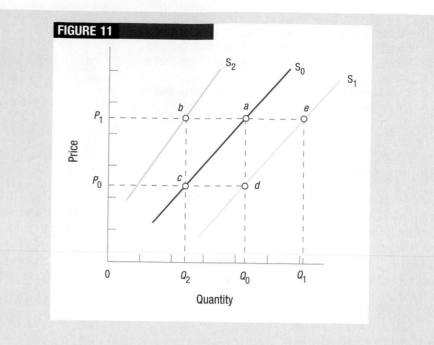

FIGURE 11

e. A move from point a to point c represents a _____ .

f. A movement from point c to point b represents a _____ .

Solution-Discussion

a. A decline in quantity supplied is a movement along an existing supply curve, so quantity supplied declines from point a to point c, and this is caused by a reduction in price from P_1 to P_0.

b. Supply curve S_1 would represent an improvement in technology increasing supplies to the market.

c. An increase in quantity supplied is caused by a change in price from point d to point e.

d. Supply curve S_2 represents a decrease in supply. Increases in input costs, for example, will shift the supply curve to the left.

e. A decrease in quantity supplied because it is a movement along an existing supply curve.

f. A decrease in supply, since the curve has shifted to the left. Note that on supply curve S_2, less is provided to the market at each price.

Now that you have worked through this solved problem, see if you can complete the following exercise before you go on to the next section on market equilibrium. This short exercise asks you to create both demand and supply curves and explain some of their features.

Exercise for You to Complete

1. Using the blank grid opposite, draw the axis lines and label the vertical axis "price" and the horizontal axis "quantity."

2. Draw a demand curve on this graph and label it D_0. Pick any point on the demand curve and label it point a. Pick another point on the demand curve with a lower price and label it point b.

3. Explain how points *a* and *b* illustrate the law of demand. _____

_____

_____

4. When price rises from point *b* to point *a* and quantity demanded drops, economists refer to this as a(n) _____

5. Recessions tend to put a damper on demand. Draw a new demand curve that represents a decrease in demand and label it D_1. How is this different from what you described in question 4?

_____

_____

6. Again, using the blank grid below, draw the axis lines and label the vertical axis "price" and the horizontal axis "quantity."

7. Draw a supply curve on this graph and label it S_0. Pick any point on the supply curve and label it point *c*. Pick another point on the supply curve with a higher price and label it point *d*.

8. Explain how points c and d illustrate the law of supply.

_____

_____

9. When price rises from point c to point d and quantity supplied grows, economists refer to this as a(n) _____.

10. When the cost of microcomputer chips falls, it increases supply. Draw a new supply curve in the graph reflecting this increase. How is this different from what you described in question 9?

_____

_____

Answers

(3) When the price of a product is reduced from point a to point b, quantity demanded increases. This is the law of demand. (4) Decrease in quantity demanded. (5) Shifting to a new curve is a decrease in demand: At all prices consumers want to buy less of the product. (8) When the price of a product is increased from point c to point d, quantity supplied increases. This is the law of supply. (9) Increase in quantity supplied. (10) Shifting to a new curve (the supply curve shifts rightward) is an increase in supply: At all prices firms are willing to provide more of the product to the market.

Keep in mind that supply and demand form the foundation of most of what you will study this semester. At this point, you may want to reread both of these sections in the text, then rework the previous two sections again. The next section on equilibrium brings the concepts of supply and demand together, and the level of complexity grows. Spend a little extra time here; it will pay dividends throughout the remainder of the course.

Market Equilibrium

Frequently Asked Questions

Q: What is market equilibrium?

A: Supply and demand together determine _market equilibrium_. Equilibrium occurs when quantity demanded and quantity supplied are equal. Equilibrium is shown in Figure 12 as point e. This means that producers offer for sale precisely that quantity that consumers are willing to purchase at that price. Equilibrium price, P_0, is that price where the market clears the equilibrium quantity of Q_0. If price temporarily gets above market equilibrium, inventories accumulate as consumers buy less than suppliers want to provide, so the market price drops to equilibrium. If price is temporarily below equilibrium, buyers want more than sellers are willing to sell, so prices begin rising toward equilibrium at point e.

Q: When supply or demand change, what can be predicted?

A: When supply and demand change (a shift in the curves), equilibrium price and output change. When only _one_ curve shifts, both resulting changes in equilibrium price and quantity can be predicted. For example, in Figure 13, if demand

FIGURE 12

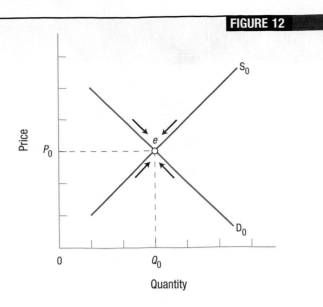

increases from D_0 to D_1, both equilibrium output and price will rise as equilibrium moves from point e to point c.

Q: When supply and demand both change, what can be predicted?

A: When *both* curves shift, the change in equilibrium price can be forecast in some instances, and the change in equilibrium output in others, but in no case can both be forecast without more information. For example, when demand rises and supply falls, equilibrium price will rise to P_2 (point b in Figure 13), but the change in equilibrium output is uncertain. Whether output will rise or fall depends on the relative size of the shifts between demand and supply. Alternatively, when demand rises and supply rises (people want more and more is available), equilibrium output will rise, but the change in equilibrium price is indeterminate without knowing about the relative size of the shifts between demand and supply.

FIGURE 13

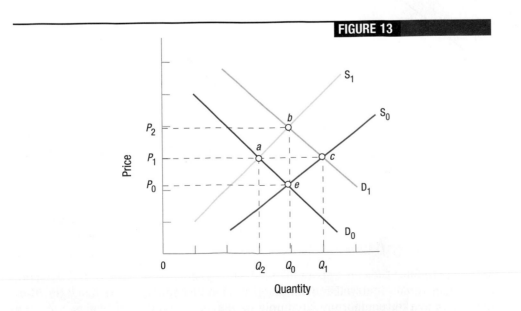

Market Equilibrium Quick Check

Circle the Correct Answer

1. (T/F) Markets clear at the equilibrium price.
2. (T/F) A product's equilibrium price is determined where the demand curve intersects the supply curve.
3. At equilibrium
   a. producers store surpluses for times of shortage.
   b. producers offer the exact amount of a product consumers want.
   c. producers switch to substitution products.
   d. consumers switch to complementary products.

Use Figure 14 to answer questions 4, 5, and 6. For questions 4 and 5, begin each question with market supply and demand equal to S_0 and D_0, respectively, with the market in equilibrium at point e. If demand or supply changes, assume it shifts to either D_1 or S_1.

4. If supply decreases and demand increases, the new equilibrium output is equal to?
5. The economic boom of the late 1990s caused incomes to rise dramatically in California. Assume the figure represents the housing market in San Jose, California. What is the new equilibrium price for housing?
6. (T/F) The movement from point a to point c in the figure is caused by an increase in both demand and supply.

7. Which of the following is *not* how markets adjust to shocks and disturbances?
   a. almost instantaneously
   b. after a period of adjustment
   c. only with government intervention
   d. differently

Use Figure 15 to answer questions 8, 9, and 10. For questions 8 and 9, begin each question with market supply and demand equal to S_0 and D_0, respectively, with the market in equilibrium at point e.

8. If supply increases and demand decreases, the new equilibrium price is equal to? _____
9. Nextel walkie-talkies are shown to increase worker productivity in auto glass delivery. This reduces costs to auto glass repair shops. Assume the figure represents the auto glass repair business. What is the impact on equilibrium price for auto glass repairs? _____
   _____
10. Describe what causes this market in the figure to move from point a to point c. _____
   _____

Score: _____

FIGURE 14

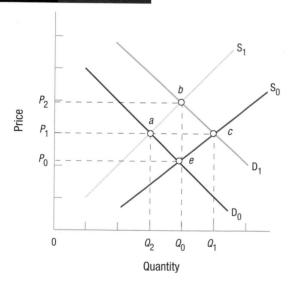

FIGURE 15

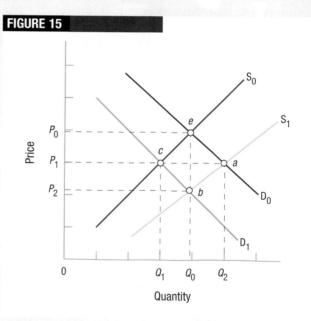

If You Got 9 or 10 Correct

You seem to have the concepts of demand, supply, changes in supply and demand, and market equilibrium well in hand. Keep in mind that supply and demand together determine market equilibrium. If supply *or* demand change, you can predict the change in *both* price and quantity sold. If both of the supply *and* demand curves shift, *either* price or quantity sold can be predicted, but not both; one will be indeterminate without information on the relative size of the shifts between demand and supply. This is a little tricky, but you seem to have mastered it. Take a moment to review the section on "Hints, Tips, and Reminders."

If You Didn't Get at Least 9 Correct

Don't panic. This is some of the most difficult material in the chapter and the book. It often takes students several attempts at this material to really master it. But keep in mind that it is probably the most important material in the book. Five years from now when you are moving up in your career, this is one of the three to four things you will remember from this course.

Keep in Mind

■ Equilibrium occurs where quantity supplied equals quantity demanded.
■ When supply or demand (one or the other curve) shifts, you can determine the change in *both* price and quantity sold. The table below summarizes the predicted changes from an initial equilibrium when either the supply or demand curve shifts.

Change in Demand or Supply	Change in Price	Change in Quantity Sold
Demand increases	Increase	Increase
Demand decreases	Decrease	Decrease
Supply increases	Decrease	Increase
Supply decreases	Increase	Decrease

■ When both curves shift, you can only predict the change in either price or quantity sold, but not both. The table below summarizes which variable (price or quantity sold) is predictable given that both curves have shifted.

Change in Demand	Change in Supply	Change in Price	Change in Quantity Sold
Increase	Increase	Indeterminate	Increase
Decrease	Decrease	Indeterminate	Decrease
Increase	Decrease	Increase	Indeterminate
Decrease	Increase	Decrease	Indeterminate

Before you move on, take some time and work through the solved problem below. Also, when you read the daily newspaper or the *Wall Street Journal*, look for articles where you can apply the concepts of supply and demand. You will find that there are several each week. This solved problem takes you through all that you have studied in this chapter. Pay particular attention to the description of the solution. ■

Solved Problem

The monthly supply and demand data for MP3 players is outlined in the table below.

Price	Quantity Demanded	Quantity Supplied	New Supply
130	600	1,200	_____
120	700	1,100	_____
110	800	1,000	_____
100	900	900	_____
90	1,000	800	_____
80	1,100	700	_____
70	1,200	600	_____

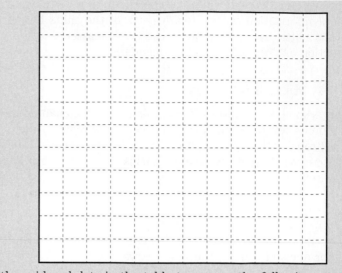

Use the grid and data in the table to answer the following questions.

a. Graph the curves in the grid above. Label the curves S_0 and D_0.

b. Equilibrium price is equal to _____.

c. Equilibrium output is equal to _____.

d. Assume initially that the price of MP3 players was set at $120.
Would there be a shortage or surplus in this market? _____
How large would the shortage or surplus be? _____

Describe the kind of pressures that would exist in this market to move the price toward equilibrium. _____

_____

e. Now, assume, as is so often the case in these types of markets, that technological improvements in electronics manufacturing mean that supply increases by 25%. List the new supply values for each price in the last column of the table. Plot the new supply curve and label it S_1.

f. What is the new equilibrium price? _____

g. What is the new equilibrium output? _____

Solution-Discussion

a.

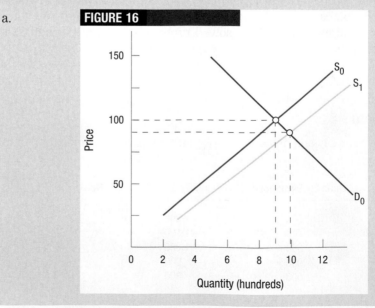

FIGURE 16

b. $100. At $100, quantity supplied (900) is equal to quantity demanded (900).

c. 900

d. Surplus, 400. Excess inventories lead to sales and other actions that would reduce prices.

e. See Figure 16. At every price, quantity supplied has increased by 25% (see table below).

Price	Quantity Demanded	Quantity Supplied	New Supply
130	600	1,200	1,500
120	700	1,100	1,375
110	800	1,000	1,250
100	900	900	1,125
90	1,000	800	1,000
80	1,100	700	875
70	1,200	600	750

f. $90

g. 1,000

As a final exercise, check and see what the new equilibrium price and output would be if demand now increased by 40%. This answer is that price rises to nearly $110, and output grows to around 1,200. Simple numerical problems like this provide the kind of insight you need when the questions gets complicated. Always draw the original supply and demand curves and then work out the shifts (always the hard part), and the answers will be clear.

Consider These Hints, Tips, and Reminders   STEP 4

1. Reminder: A change in one or more of the determinants of demand shifts the demand curve and is a change in demand, while a change in quantity demanded is caused by a change in the product's price and is a movement along an existing demand curve.

2. Reminder: A change in one or more of the determinants of supply shifts the supply curve and is a change in supply, while a change in quantity supplied is caused by a change in the product's price and is a movement along an existing supply curve.

3. Reminder: Supply and demand together determine market equilibrium. If supply or demand (one curve) changes (shifts), you can predict the change in both price and quantity sold. If both curves change (shift) either price or quantity sold can be predicted, not both; one variable will be indeterminate without more information on the relative size of the shifts between demand and supply.

4. The core graph below shows market equilibrium along with a surplus and shortage. Shortages (surpluses) result when price is temporarily below (above) equilibrium price.

5. One of the areas where students tend to falter is drawing graphs and working through changes in supply and demand in markets. One good approach to this

Core Graph: Market Equilibrium

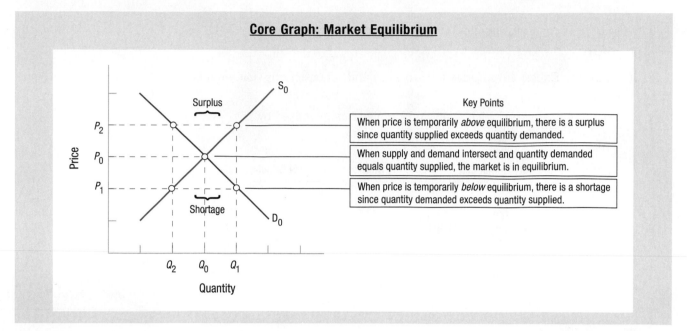

Key Points

When price is temporarily *above* equilibrium, there is a surplus since quantity supplied exceeds quantity demanded.

When supply and demand intersect and quantity demanded equals quantity supplied, the market is in equilibrium.

When price is temporarily *below* equilibrium, there is a shortage since quantity demanded exceeds quantity supplied.

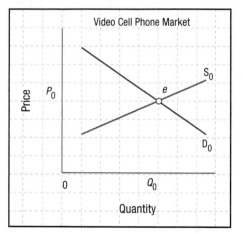

issue is to always draw a graph when you are confronted with a question or problem involving supply and demand. To begin your analysis, start with a graph like that for the video cell phone market shown here.

Use the subscript 0 for the original position. Begin with equilibrium labeled "e"; then ask "Is only price changing?" If so, you know that you are moving along an original supply or demand curve. If the answer is no, then ask "Do the facts of the question mean that a determinant is changing?" Note that the question could be such that nothing relevant is changing (this can be tricky). So, if a determinant is changing, is the impact on supply or demand? Figure out which, then shift the curve in the graph. Draw in the dot for the new equilibrium point, and make your conclusions. It may seem a little complex at first, but once you do it a few times, it will become commonplace.

6. To help you see the correct direction for shifts in supply and demand caused by changing determinants, exaggerate the change! For example, if you are looking at the demand for high-mileage hybrid cars, and gasoline prices rise, assume that gas prices jump by $5.00 a gallon. In this way it becomes obvious that demand for hybrid cars increases. By exaggerating the degree of change, the shift in the curve jumps out at you.

7. Here is another trap to avoid. When the price of a good rises (or falls), students (and commentators) often are heard to say that demand has fallen (risen) when they should be saying that quantity demanded has fallen (risen). The terminology is precise for a reason. Moving along an existing curve and selling more when price falls (a sale is in progress) is much different from selling more at the previous price because demand has risen (the entire demand curve shifts to the right). This also applies to supplies.

8. Here is one final trap to avoid. Supply and demand both increase when the curves shift to the right and decline when they shift to the left. Don't be tempted to think that an upward shift in the supply curve is an increase (as it is for demand) and that a shift downward in the supply curve is a decline (again this is true for demand). Thinking this way will lead to errors when you are faced with changes in the supply curve. Note that an upward shift in supply is a decrease in supply, and vice versa! Think of an increase as a shift to the right and a decrease as a shift to the left.

Do the Homework for Chapter 3	STEP 5

Do the Homework for Chapter 3
Supply and Demand

Instructor _____ Time _____ Student _____

Use the answer key below to record your answers to these homework questions.

1. (a) (b) (c) (d)	6. (a) (b) (c) (d)	11. (a) (b) (c) (d)	16. (a) (b) (c) (d)
2. (a) (b) (c) (d)	7. (a) (b) (c) (d)	12. (a) (b) (c) (d)	17. (a) (b) (c) (d)
3. (a) (b) (c) (d)	8. (a) (b) (c) (d)	13. (a) (b) (c) (d)	18. (a) (b) (c) (d)
4. (a) (b) (c) (d)	9. (a) (b) (c) (d)	14. (a) (b) (c) (d)	19. (a) (b) (c) (d)
5. (a) (b) (c) (d)	10. (a) (b) (c) (d)	15. (a) (b) (c) (d)	20. (a) (b) (c) (d)

1. Markets
   a. are institutions where sellers always have the advantage.
   b. are typically the same size.
   c. bring buyers and sellers together.
   d. are institutions where sellers offer only a physical product.

2. The law of demand states that
   a. prices of a product fall as demand rises.
   b. quantity demanded rises as price rises.
   c. demand rises as price falls.
   d. quantity demanded rises as price falls.

3. Which of the following is *not* a determinant of demand?
   a. profits of sellers
   b. prices of related products
   c. income
   d. tastes and preferences

Use Figure HW-1 to answer questions 4 and 5.

4. A shift in the demand curve for Apple iPods from D_0 to D_2 could be caused by which of the following?
   a. The economy grows faster than expected.
   b. Technology reduces the cost of production.
   c. Apple offers songs on its iTunes network for 10 cents each.
   d. An aging population turns to TV to satisfy its entertainment needs.

5. A shift in the demand curve for pizza from D_0 to D_2 could be caused by
   a. a recession that reduces peoples incomes.
   b. the Surgeon General reporting that fat from cheese and pepperoni is unhealthy.
   c. Subway cutting in half the prices of its sandwiches.
   d. all of the above.

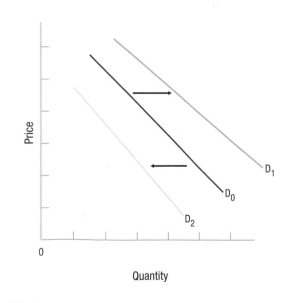

HW-1

6. Market demand curves are
   a. the average demand faced by business.
   b. the horizontal sum of individual demand curves.
   c. not a very useful concept; individual demands are most important.
   d. easily estimated for nearly all products and services.

Use Figure HW-2 to answer questions 7 and 8.

7. Assume the market is initially at point c with Q_1 sold at a price of P_0. An increase in quantity demanded would be represented by which of the following?
   a. a movement to point a
   b. a shift in the demand curve to D_1.
   c. a movement to point b.
   d. a shift in the demand curve to D_2.

8. Assume the market is initially at point c with Q_1 sold at a price of P_0. An increase in demand would be represented by which of the following?
   a. a movement from point a to point c.
   b. a shift in the demand curve to D_1
   c. a movement to point b
   d. a shift in the demand curve to D_2

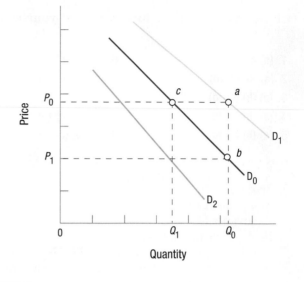

HW-2

---

9. The law of supply suggests that
   a. more will be demanded as the price falls.
   b. higher prices lead to greater quantity supplied.
   c. more advertising leads to consumers buying more.
   d. as prices rise, consumers find other (cheaper) products to buy.

Use Figure HW-3 to answer questions 10 and 11.

10. Assume the market is initially at point a. An increase in quantity supplied would be represented by a
    a. movement to point d.
    b. movement to point c.
    c. movement to point b.
    d. shift in the supply curve to S_2.

11. Assume the market is initially at point a. An increase in supply would be represented by a
    a. movement to point d.
    b. movement to point c.
    c. movement to point b.
    d. shift in the supply curve to S_2.

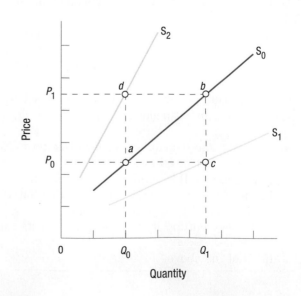

HW-3

12. Determinants of supply affect
    a. the quantity supplied.
    b. how much consumers demand.
    c. the entire supply curve.
    d. the quantity demanded.

13. A change in supply results from
    a. a change in one of the determinants of
       demand.
    b. a change in the price of the product.
    c. a shift in the demand curve.
    d. a change in one of the determinants of
       supply.

Use Figure HW-4 to answer questions 14–16.

14. Assume the market for cell phones is initially in
    equilibrium at point b with Q_0 units sold at a price
    of P_2. Now, assume that the Surgeon General
    releases a report that says that extensive use of
    cellular phones has a negative impact on hearing.
    The new equilibrium
    a. will be at point e.
    b. will be at point c.
    c. will be at point a.
    d. will not change.

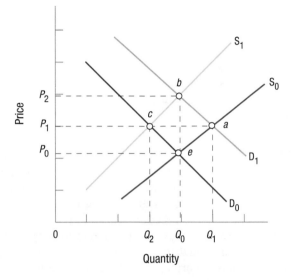

15. Assume the market for cell phones is initially in
    equilibrium at point c with Q_2 units sold at a price
    of P_1. Now assume that the industry develops a
    new method of producing phones that halves the
    cost. The new equilibrium
    a. will be at point e.
    b. will be at point b.
    c. will be at point a.
    d. will not change.

HW-4

16. Assume the market for tofu is initially in equilib-
    rium at point e with Q_0 units sold at a price of P_0.
    An Asian tsunami wipes out half of the Asian soy-
    bean crop. The new equilibrium
    a. will be at point a.
    b. will be at point b.
    c. will be at point c.
    d. will not change.

17. Assume the market for orange juice is shown in
    Figure HW-5 and the market is initially in equilib-
    rium at point e with Q_0 units sold at a price of P_0.
    Now, assume that the economy enters an extended
    recessionary period and incomes drop significantly.
    The new equilibrium for orange juice
    a. will be at point b.
    b. will be at point c.
    c. will be at point a.
    d. will not change.

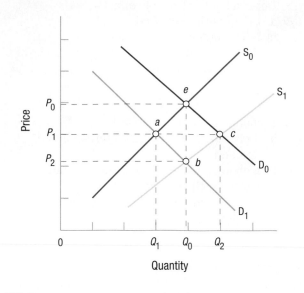

HW-5

Use the paragraph below to answer questions 18
through 20.

The *New York Times* reported on February 27, 2007,
that beekeepers across the nation are worried
because one third to two thirds of their bees have
gone missing. The bees are setting out each day in
search of nectar to make honey (and pollinate crops
along the way), but fail to return to the hive. Losses
of 20% from predators, chemicals, stress, and mites
are considered normal. The California almond crop
alone uses half of the nation's bee colonies to pollinate its trees in February.

18. What does this loss of bees suggest will happen to
    the rental fees farmers pay to have beehives placed
    near their fields to ensure crop pollination?
    a. Nothing, farmers will take up beekeeping.
    b. The fees will rise.

c. The fees will fall.
d. None of the above.

19. Given this situation confronting beekeepers and
    farmers, what will be the impact on walnut prices?
    a. No change.
    b. They will fall.
    c. They will rise.
    d. They will fall initially, then rise in a few years.

20. Three crops—almonds, apples, and blueberries—
    totaling nearly $6 billion in sales are almost
    entirely pollinated by honeybees. If something is
    not found to solve the "missing bees" problem,
    what will happen to the supply of these nuts and
    fruits to grocers?
    a. Supply will rise.
    b. No change in supply.
    c. Supply will fall.
    d. None of the above.

Use the ExamPrep to Get Ready for Exams	STEP 6

This sheet (front and back) is designed to help you prepare for your exams. The chapter has been boiled down to its key concepts. You are asked to answer questions, define terms, draw graphs, and, if you wish, add summaries of class notes.

Markets

Describe markets and their role:

Demand

Describe a demand curve:

Describe the law of demand:

Describe how we calculate market demand:

List the determinants of demand:

1. _____   2. _____

3. _____   4. _____

Define a change in quantity demanded:

Define a change in demand:

Now in Figure EP-1, draw a demand curve, show a change in quantity demanded, and show a change in demand.

EP-1

Supply

Describe a supply curve:

Describe the law of supply:

Describe how we calculate market supply:

List the determinants of supply:

1. _____   2. _____

3. _____   4. _____

Define a change in quantity supplied:

Define a change in supply:

Now in Figure EP-2, draw a supply curve, show a change in quantity supplied, and show a change in supply.

EP-2

Market Equilibrium

Define market equilibrium:

Show market equilibrium in Figure EP-3.

Now draw a shortage in the figure. What causes a shortage?

Now draw a surplus in the figure. What causes a surplus?

Predicting a New Market Equilibrium

When Only One Curve Shifts

Complete Figures EP-4 and EP-5 and the tables below (indicate whether equilibrium price and output increase or decrease). Start with an initial equilibrium where D_0 and S_0 cross at point e. In Figure EP-4 only shift demand, and in Figure EP-5 only shift supply.

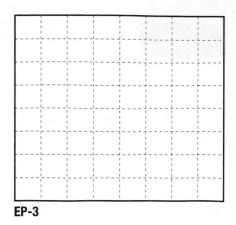

EP-3

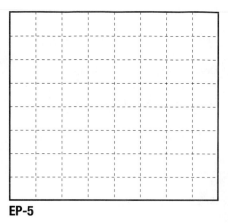

EP-4

EP-5

Only Demand Changes	Price	Quantity
Demand increases to D_1		
Demand decreases to D_2		

Only Supply Changes	Price	Quantity
Supply increases to S_1		
Supply decreases to S_2		

When Both Curves Shift

Complete Figures EP-6 and EP-7 and the tables below (indicate whether equilibrium price and output increase or decrease). Start with an initial equilibrium where D_0 and S_0 cross at point e. In Figure EP-6, show supply increasing, and have demand first increase and then decrease. In Figure EP-7, show supply decreasing, and have demand first increase and then decrease.

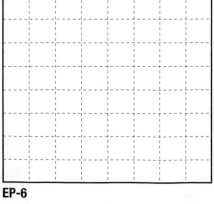

EP-6

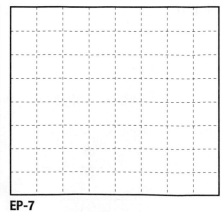

EP-7

Supply Increases	Price	Quantity
Demand increases to D_1		
Demand decreases to D_2		

Supply Decreases	Price	Quantity
Demand increases to D_1		
Demand decreases to D_2		

Additional Study Help Chapterwide Practice Questions

Matching

Match the description with the corresponding term.

___	1. Markets	___	5. Complements
___	2. Demand	___	6. Equilibrium
___	3. Supply	___	7. Shortage
___	4. Substitutes	___	8. Surplus

a. The amount of output that businesses are willing to produce and offer at various prices.

b. A balance between supply and demand where producers make exactly the amount of product that consumers want to buy.

c. An excess of a product caused by supply exceeding demand.

d. Institutions that bring buyers and sellers together to make transactions.

e. The amounts of a good or service that consumers are willing and able to buy at various prices.

f. Products that are used together.

g. Too little of a product is available in the market at current prices.

h. A competing product that consumers will switch to if the price of the original product rises.

Fill-In

Circle the word(s) in parentheses that complete the sentence.

1. Markets are institutions that permit (buyers and sellers, government and consumers) _____ to transact with each other and the market is often referred to as (capitalism, socialism, the price system) _____.

2. Demand refers to the goods and services that people (want, are willing and able) _____ to buy during some period of time. A negative relationship exists between price and (demand, quantity demanded) _____. This is known as the law of demand, which states that as price increases, (demand, quantity demanded) _____ falls, and vice versa.

3. Market demand curves are the (horizontal, vertical) _____ summation of individual demand curves. Market demands will change if one or more of the determinants change. These include tastes and preferences, income, (costs of resources, prices of related goods) _____, and expectations regarding future prices, income, the number of buyers and product availability.

4. When income rises and demand for a given product rises that product is a(n) (normal, inferior) _____ good. But if demand declines when income grows, the product is a(n) (normal, inferior) _____ good.

5. Movies and sporting events are (substitute, complementary) _____ goods, while coffee and cinnamon rolls are (substitute, complementary) _____ goods.

6. A change in price will result in a change in (demand, quantity demanded) _____, while a change in income will cause a change in (demand, quantity demanded) _____. When Taco Bell drops the price of its burritos to 50 cents, the demand for McDonald's hamburgers will (rise, fall) _____ because these two products are generally considered (substitutes, complements) _____. But when McDonald's raises the price of its hamburgers by 50 cents, its sales will fall because demand (falls, rises, remains constant) _____.

7. The law of supply states that there is a (direct, inverse) _____ relationship between price and quantity supplied. A change in price will result in a change in (supply, quantity supplied) _____, while a change in resource costs will cause a change in (supply, quantity supplied) _____. When General Motors finds that the price of steel has risen by 10%, its supply curve for Chevy Trucks will (shift to the right, shift to the left, not change) _____.

8. Market equilibrium results when quantity supplied equals quantity demanded. If price is set temporarily above equilibrium, a (surplus, shortage) _____ results, but if the price is set below equilibrium, a (surplus, shortage) _____ results.

9. When either the supply or demand curve shifts (one curve only), you are able to predict the new (price, quantity sold, both price and quantity sold) _____. If demand increases, equilibrium price will (rise, fall) _____, and equilibrium output will (rise, fall) _____. If supply increases, equilibrium price will (rise, fall) _____, and equilibrium output will (rise, fall) _____.

10. When both the supply and demand curves shift you are able to predict the new (price, quantity

sold, either price or quantity sold not both) _____. If demand increases and supply falls, equilibrium price will (rise, fall, be indeterminate) _____, and equilibrium output will (rise, fall, be indeterminate) _____. If both supply and demand increase, equilibrium price will (rise, fall, be indeterminate) _____, and equilibrium output will (rise, fall, be indeterminate) _____.

True-False

Circle the correct answer.

__T/F__   1. All markets offer a wide variety of products for sale.

__T/F__   2. You can only buy products in markets. Services are traded through a different mechanism.

__T/F__   3. The most basic component of markets is transactions.

__T/F__   4. According to the law of demand, quantity demanded is inversely related to price changes.

__T/F__   5. A demand curve always slopes up and to the right to show that quantity demanded increases with price.

__T/F__   6. When prices rise, demand decreases.

__T/F__   7. Demand refers to the goods and services people are willing and able to buy during a certain period of time.

__T/F__   8. According to the law of demand, all other factors held constant, as price increases, quantity demanded falls.

__T/F__   9. A supply curve shows the maximum amount of a good or service that businesses will offer at various prices.

__T/F__   10. If producers expect higher prices, that *usually* leads to an increase in supply.

__T/F__   11. A change in product price leads to a change in supply.

__T/F__   12. Signing a new union contract with substantial increases in wages and benefits typically will result in an increase in supply.

__T/F__   13. An improvement in technology only results in an increase in quantity supplied.

__T/F__   14. A product's equilibrium price is fully determined by the demand for that product.

__T/F__   15. A cleared market is a market in equilibrium.

__T/F__   16. The equilibrium price is also called the market clearing price.

__T/F__   17. All other relevant factors held constant, an increase in supply will lead to an increase in output and a decrease in price.

__T/F__   18. All other relevant factors held constant, if supply and demand both rise, price will necessarily rise.

__T/F__   19. If both the supply curve and the demand curve for a product change, you can't calculate either the new price or the new quantity produced.

__T/F__   20. When supply and demand move in opposite directions, it is easy to predict a change in output.

Multiple Choice

Circle the correct answer.

1. All markets
   a. offer the same basics products.
   b. bring buyers and sellers together to transact business.
   c. are the same size.
   d. offer either products or services, but not both.

2. How do markets best help buyers and sellers to communicate?
   a. by providing a place for buyers and sellers to interact online
   b. by providing information about the quality and quantity of government goods and services
   c. through price
   d. by providing technology for communication

3. Quantity demanded changes as a result of
   a. a change in demand.
   b. a change in supply.
   c. a change in product quality.
   d. a change in product price.

4. The law of demand states that
   a. quantity demanded rises as price falls.
   b. quantity demanded rises as price rises.
   c. demand rises as price rises.
   d. demand falls as price falls.

5. A demand curve always slopes
   a. up and to the right.
   b. down and to the right.
   c. consistent with the corresponding supply curve.
   d. parallel to the corresponding supply curve.

6. Which of the following is a determinant of demand?
   a. production technology
   b. resource input cost
   c. income
   d. number of sellers

7. Substitute goods are
   a. goods that are consumed together.
   b. goods whose quantity demanded does not fluctuate with price changes.
   c. related goods that consumers will turn to when prices rise.
   d. related goods that consumers will turn to when prices fall.

8. An increase in the number of buyers
   a. decreases demand.
   b. increases demand.
   c. decreases quantity demanded.
   d. increases quantity demanded.

9. Market demand curves are
   a. the horizontal sum of individual demand curves.
   b. the vertical sum of individual demand curves.
   c. the statistical average of individual demand curves.
   d. a graph of business demand for resources and employees.

10. An increase in demand means
    a. consumers will pay the same price for more output.
    b. consumers will buy more output at every price.
    c. consumers will only buy more output at the current price.
    d. consumers will only pay more for the current output.

11. Change in quantity demanded is caused by
    a. a change in consumer tastes.
    b. an increase in buyers.
    c. a change in income levels.
    d. a change in price.

12. Which statement best describes the law of demand?
    a. The higher the price of the product, the more of the product is likely to be produced.
    b. The lower a product's price, the more of that product consumers will purchase during a given time period.

c. The greater the need, the greater the demand.
d. Demand is related to many different factors.

13. Use Figure MC-1 to answer the questions that follow.

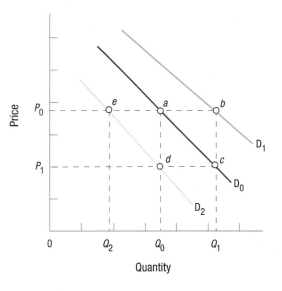

MC-1

a. Assume the market is initially at point a on D_0. An increase in quantity demanded would be represented by what point? _____
b. If the market was initially at point a and consumer income increased, an increase in demand would be represented by _____.
c. Assume the market is initially at point d. A decrease in quantity demanded would be represented by which point? _____
d. If demand is initially D_0, which curve represents a decline in demand? _____
e. A movement from point a to point d represents a(n) _____.
f. A movement from point c to point b represents a(n) _____.

14. Supply is
    a. dependent on consumer demand.
    b. the minimum amount of output producers will offer at a given price.
    c. the maximum amount of output producers will offer at various prices.
    d. an unimportant aspect of markets.

15. When the price of a product increases,
    a. quantity supplied decreases.
    b. quantity supplied increases.
    c. supply decreases.
    d. supply increases.

16. The idea that higher prices will lead to higher quantity supplied is part of
    a. the law of quantity supplied.
    b. the law of quantity demanded.
    c. the law of demand.
    d. the law of supply.

17. A supply curve shows
    a. the minimum amount of output businesses will make at various prices.
    b. the maximum amount of output businesses will offer for sale at various prices.
    c. the value consumers place on a good or service.
    d. the cost of the inputs required to sell a good or service.

18. Determinants of supply affect
    a. the entire supply curve.
    b. the quantity supplied.
    c. the number of consumers.
    d. the quantity demanded.

19. Improvements in production technology
    a. generally increase production cost.
    b. often allow for the creation of new products.
    c. have no effect on supply.
    d. generally decrease demand.

20. The prices of other commodities affect supply because
    a. when possible, producers will switch to produce a more profitable commodity.
    b. consumers will buy more of a cheaper commodity.
    c. consumers will switch to complementary goods.
    d. producers will increase their price to keep pace with other commodities.

21. An increase in the number of sellers of a product
    a. increases product price.
    b. has no long-term effect on supply.
    c. increases supply.
    d. decreases supply.

22. A change in supply
    a. results from a change of one of the determinants of demand.
    b. results in a price change.
    c. results in a change in the amount of product offered at every price level.
    d. leads to a corresponding change in demand.

23. A change in the price of a product causes a change in
    a. quantity supplied.
    b. supply.
    c. input cost.
    d. expectations.

24. When a market clears,
    a. producers bring more of a product to market that consumers are willing to purchase at the market price.
    b. producers bring less of a product to market than consumers would be willing to purchase at the market price.
    c. producers bring precisely the amount of a product to market that consumers wish to purchase at the market price.
    d. the price of a particular good is higher than the market will bear.

25. If there is a *surplus* of sports cars on the market, which of the following statements will *not* be true?
    a. Producer inventories of sports cars are rising.
    b. The market price of sports cars lies below their equilibrium price.
    c. Producers are bringing more sports cars to market than consumers are willing to purchase at the market price.
    d. The market price of sport cars exceeds their equilibrium price.

26. When the real estate market is in a "seller's market," which of the following can occur?
    a. Homebuyers can expect to find a wide selection of relatively inexpensive homes.
    b. There is a surplus of homes on the market.
    c. All real estate transactions take place in realtors' offices.
    d. There is a shortage of homes on the market.

27. All other relevant factors held constant, if there is a decrease in demand,
    a. price and output will drop.
    b. price will drop, but output will rise.
    c. price and output will rise.
    d. price will rise, but output will drop.

28. All other relevant factors held constant, if supply and demand both decrease,
    a. output will rise, but price will fall.
    b. output will fall, with the effect on price being indeterminate.
    c. output will rise, with the effect on price being indeterminate.
    d. price will rise, with the effect on output being indeterminate.

29. At equilibrium,
    a. producers store surpluses for times of shortage.
    b. producers offer the exact amount of a product consumers want.
    c. producers switch to substitution products.
    d. consumers switch to complementary products.

30. All markets respond to disturbances in equilibrium
    a. instantly.
    b. after a long period of adjustment.
    c. only when government intervenes.
    d. differently.

31. A cleared market is one that
    a. has a surplus.
    b. has a shortage.
    c. has an artificial price limit.
    d. is in equilibrium.

32. The market response to a surplus is
    a. increased demand.
    b. decreased demand.
    c. increased prices.
    d. decreased prices.

33. Equilibrium prices are
    a. *not* determined by the forces of supply and demand.
    b. easily determined by businesses.
    c. set by the government.
    d. the natural outcome of market forces.

34. If demand increases,
    a. equilibrium price and output increase.
    b. equilibrium price and output decrease.
    c. equilibrium price increases, and output decreases.
    d. equilibrium price decreases, and output increases.

Essay-Problem

Answer in the space provided.

Some of the questions below can be challenging. Don't get discouraged if your answers are not always the same as those we suggest. Use these sample answers as another way to assess your progress but, more important, to discover and learn some of the subtleties surrounding markets and supply and demand.

1. What is the essence of markets?

2. Explain how the laws of demand and supply differ.

3. Prices of related goods or other commodities are determinants for both demand and supply. How do they differ?

In the table below, use the spaces provided to answer whether in the market specified demand, supply, equilibrium quantity, and equilibrium price either increases ($\uparrow$), decreases ($\downarrow$), remains the same (NC), or is indeterminate (?). In the Comment-Discussion column briefly state the reasons for your answer.

Market Changes	Demand	Supply	Equilibrium Quantity	Equilibrium Price	Comment-Discussion
4. Assume there is a freeze in Florida that ruins its orange crop this year. What happens in the market for tomato juice?					
5. Again, assume there is a freeze in Florida that ruins its orange crop this year. Now what happens in the market for orange juice?					
6. Again, assume there is a freeze in Florida that ruins its orange crop this year. In addition, an extended drought in California significantly reduces the tomato crop. Now what happens in the market for tomato juice?					
7. Hard bargaining by southern California grocery unions results in higher wages and expanded health benefits for all workers in all stores. What will be the impact on the grocery market?					

(*continued*)

Market Changes	Demand	Supply	Equilibrium Quantity	Equilibrium Price	Comment-Discussion
8. Growth hormones are scientifically shown to increase vigor and quality of life without significant side effects. Advances in chip design make manufacturing these hormones nearly costless. What happens in the market for mountain bikes?					
9. Growth hormones are scientifically shown to increase vigor and quality of life without significant side effects. Advances in chip design make manufacturing these hormones nearly costless. What happens in the market for televisions?					
10. The Federal Reserve, becoming concerned with inflation, raises interest rates too high, accidentally driving the economy into a deep recession. At the same time, improved technology drives the costs of memory chips lower and lower. What happens in the MP3 player market?					

What's Next

You now have a good understanding of how markets work using supply and demand analysis. We have assumed throughout this chapter that markets have large numbers of buyers and sellers and are highly competitive. In addition, we assumed that both buyers and sellers had good information about prices and the products themselves.

In the next chapter, we look at some of the imperfections in markets and how our competitive market supply and demand analysis must be adjusted to account for these problems. For example, sometimes sellers have better information than buyers (used cars), and they use this knowledge to gain an edge on buyers. These issues do not, however, negate the usefulness of the analysis. Just be aware that the conclusions may have to be modified.

Answers to Chapterwide Practice Questions

Matching

1. d	3. a	5. f	7. g
2. e	4. h	6. b	8. c

Fill-In

1. buyers and sellers, the price system
2. are willing and able, quantity demanded, quantity demanded
3. horizontal, prices of related goods
4. normal, inferior
5. substitute, complementary

6. quantity demanded, demand, fall, substitutes, remains constant
7. direct, quantity supplied, supply, shift to the left
8. surplus, shortage
9. both price and quantity sold, rise, rise, fall, rise
10. either price or quantity sold not both, rise, be indeterminate, be indeterminate, rise

True-False

1. F	6. F	11. F	16. T
2. F	7. T	12. F	17. T
3. T	8. T	13. F	18. F
4. T	9. T	14. F	19. F
5. F	10. T	15. T	20. F

Multiple Choice

1. b	12. b	16. d	27. a
2. c	13. a. c	17. b	28. b
3. d	13. b. D$_1$	18. a	29. b
4. a	13. c. e	19. b	30. d
5. b	13. d. D$_2$	20. a	31. d
6. c	13. e. decrease in	21. c	32. d
7. c	demand	22. c	33. d
8. b	13. f. increase in	23. a	34. a
9. a	demand	24. c	
10. b	14. c	25. b	
11. d	15. b	26. d	

Essay-Problem

1. They bring buyers and sellers together.
2. Demand curves are negatively sloped while supply curves are positively sloped, and the two laws reflect these differences.
3. Price of related goods for demand refers to prices of substitutes or complements in consumption. The price of hamburger affects the demand for chicken. On the supply side, the prices of related commodities refer to substitutes in production. If firms can produce either of two commodities, and the market price of one rises, firms will produce more of that product and its supply will rise. This is an important distinction that you should analyze carefully when looking at changes to demand and supply caused by changes in determinants.

Market Changes	Demand	Supply	Equilibrium Quantity	Equilibrium Price	Comment-Discussion
4. Assume there is a freeze in Florida that ruins its orange crop this year. What happens in the market for tomato juice?	↑	NC	↑	↑	Demand for a substitute rises.
5. Again, assume there is a freeze in Florida that ruins its orange crop this year. Now what happens in the market for orange juice?	NC	↓	↓	↑	Supply of orange juice declines due to freeze.

(continued)

Market Changes	Demand	Supply	Equilibrium Quantity	Equilibrium Price	Comment-Discussion
6. Again, assume there is a freeze in Florida that ruins its orange crop this year. In addition, an extended drought in California significantly reduces the tomato crop. Now what happens in the market for tomato juice?	↑	↓	?	↑	Demand for substitute rises (tomato juice), drought reduces the supply of tomato juice. Price rises, but impact on output sold is indeterminate.
7. Hard bargaining by southern California grocery unions results in higher wages and expanded health benefits for all workers in all stores. What will be the impact on the grocery market?	NC	↓	↓	↑	Input costs (labor) rise, so supply declines.
8. Growth hormones are scientifically shown to increase vigor and quality of life without significant side effects. Advances in chip design make manufacturing these hormones nearly costless. What happens in the market for mountain bikes?	↑	NC	↑	↑	More healthy people will engage in mountain biking.
9. Growth hormones are scientifically shown to increase vigor and quality of life without significant side effects. Advances in chip design make manufacturing these hormones nearly costless. What happens in the market for televisions?	NC	NC	NC	NC	No impact. Television demand is unaffected by health issues.
10. The Federal Reserve, becoming concerned with inflation, raises interest rates too high, accidentally driving the economy into a deep recession. At the same time, improved technology drives the costs of memory chips lower and lower. What happens in the MP3 player market?	↓	↑	?	↓	The recession lowers income and demand, while technology reduces cost, increasing supply.

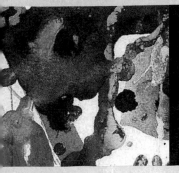

Market Efficiency, Market Failure, and Government Intervention

4

Buyers and Sellers Come Together in Markets

In the previous chapter, you learned the important tool of supply and demand analysis. In describing the workings of supply and demand, we used a stylized view of competitive markets, where buyers and sellers easily come together. Reality is not so clear cut. In this chapter, we explore the complexities inherent to most markets. This does not mean you have to toss out what you have just learned about supply and demand. Rather, market complexities will force you to adjust your supply and demand analysis: You still use it; you just have to adjust it.

This Is What You Need to Know

STEP 1

After studying this chapter you should be able to

- Understand how markets allocate resources.

- Define the conditions needed for markets to be efficient.

- Understand how markets impose discipline on producers and consumers.

- Understand and be able to use the concepts of consumer and producer surplus.

- Understand what market failure is, and when it occurs.

- Describe the different types of market failure.

- Recognize why government may control prices.

- Understand the effects of price ceilings and price floors.

- Recognize that taxes lead to deadweight losses.

Review the Key Terms

Property rights: The clear delineation of ownership of property backed by government enforcement.

Consumer surplus: The difference between market price and what consumers (as individuals or the market) would be willing to pay. It is equal to the area above market price and below the demand curve.

Producer surplus: The difference between market price and that price that firms would be willing to supply the product. It is equal to the area below market price and above the supply curve.

Asymmetric information: Occurs when one party to a transaction has significantly better information than another party.

Adverse selection: Asymmetric information problem such as found in health insurance that occurs when products of different qualities are sold at the same price.

Moral hazard: Asymmetric information problem that occurs when an insurance policy or some other arrangement changes the economic incentives and leads to a change in behavior.

Public goods: Goods that, once provided, no one person can be excluded from consuming (nonexclusion), and one person's consumption does not diminish the benefit to others from consuming the good (nonrivalry).

Free rider: When a public good is provided, consumers cannot be excluded from enjoying the product, so some consume the product without paying.

Common property resources: Resources that are owned by the community at large (parks, ocean fish, and the atmosphere) and therefore tend to be overexploited because individuals have little incentive to use them in a sustainable fashion.

External cost: Occurs when a transaction between two parties has an impact on a third party not involved with the transaction. With external costs such as pollution, the market provides too much of these products at too low a cost.

External benefits: Positive externalities (also called spillovers) such as education and vaccinations. Private markets provide too little at too high a price of goods with external benefits.

Price ceiling: A government-set maximum price that can be charged for a product or service. When the price ceiling is set below equilibrium, it leads to shortages. Rent control is an example.

Price floor: A government-set minimum price that can be charged for a product or service. If the price floor is set above equilibrium price it leads to surpluses. Minimum wage legislation is an example.

Deadweight loss: The loss in consumer and producer surplus due to inefficiency because some transactions cannot be made and therefore their value to society is lost.

Markets and Efficiency

Frequently Asked Questions

Q: What causes markets to be efficient?

A: Markets are efficient mechanisms for allocating resources. The prices and profits characteristic of market systems provide incentives and signals that are nonexistent or seriously flawed in other systems of resource allocation.

Q: What conditions must be met for markets to be efficient?

A: For markets to be efficient, they must have well-structured institutions. These include the requirements that (1) information is widely available; (2) property rights are protected; (3) private contracts are enforced; (4) spillovers are minimal; and (5) competition prevails.

Q: How do markets impose discipline on producers and consumers?

A: Producers would like to charge higher prices and earn greater profits. But their economic survival depends on turning out quality goods at reasonable prices. As consumers, we would all like to engage in frequent extravagant purchases. But given our limited resources, each of us must decide which products are most important to us. As a result, markets are also rationing devices.

Q: What are consumer and producer surplus?

A: Because many consumers are willing to pay more than equilibrium prices for goods, they receive a consumer surplus equal to what they would have been willing to pay and what the market sets as a price. In a similar way, producers receive a producer surplus. The difference between market price and what a firm would have been willing to provide products for (the area under market price but above the supply curve) is producer surplus.

Key Point to Remember

Competitive markets impose efficiency on both consumers and producers. Firms must produce what consumers want at reasonable prices in order to survive, or some other firm will, and consumers have limited resources, so they must allocate their income efficiently between competing products.

Markets and Efficiency Quick Check

Circle the Correct Answer

1. (T/F) Markets are only as efficient as the central government rules setting them up.
2. (T/F) Prices and profits are market signals to entrepreneurs in market systems.

3. (T/F) Efficient markets are markets where information is readily available to both buyers and sellers.
4. (T/F) Consumer surplus is the difference between what you would have been willing to pay to obtain a product and market price.

5. Which of the following describes producer surplus?
   a. The difference between what people are willing to pay and what firms are willing to supply the product for.
   b. The excess that producers earn from providing the product above market prices.
   c. The excess inventory that firms keep on hand to adjust to changing consumer tastes.
   d. The difference in price between what producers are willing to supply the product for and market price.
6. Which of the following is *not* a condition for markets to act efficiently?
   a. Contracts are enforced.
   b. Competitive markets prevail.
   c. Property rights are protected.
   d. Economic agents provide positive external benefits.
7. Which of the following describes the discipline imposed by markets?
   a. Producers would prefer to provide shoddy goods, but they are prevented by law from doing so.
   b. Consumers would prefer to purchase extravagant items, but the market system makes them too poor to spend profligately.
   c. If producers provide low-quality goods at high prices, they will go out of business.
   d. If consumers want something, they can buy it.
8. For markets to act efficiently, accurate information must be widely available because
   a. it is only fair.
   b. it reduces transactions costs.
   c. it is better to be open than secretive.
   d. all products have high informational requirements.
9. Which of the following is *not* correct?
   a. Property rights provide incentives for the optimal use of resources.
   b. Pollution is a negative externality and causes markets to work inefficiently.
   c. If a legal system is running well, informal rules are not needed to keep markets efficient.
   d. For markets to be efficient, they must be open to the entry of new participants and the exit of current participants.
10. The market is a rationing device for consumers because
    a. it forces each of us to decide which products are most important because our resources are limited.
    b. producers often provide shoddy goods.
    c. the rich take the good products, leaving us with a limited number of things from which to choose.
    d. producers are in business to make profits.

Score: ____

Answers: 1. F; 2. T; 3. T; 4. T; 5. d; 6. d; 7. c; 8. b; 9. c; 10. a

If You Got 9 or 10 Correct

You have a good handle on the way markets provide efficiency, and of the conditions needed for markets to work efficiently. Go on to "Market Failures" in the next section.

If You Didn't Get at Least 9 Correct

A simple review should be all that you need. And as you do so, jot down the conditions needed for markets to work efficiently. Take a moment and review why consumer and producer surplus exist and how they are measured.

Keep in Mind

The most difficult material in this section deals with consumer and producer surplus. Remember that consumer surplus is equal to the difference between what consumers would be willing to pay for the product (found on the demand curve) and what they actually have to pay (market price). Producer surplus in a similar fashion is the difference between market price and what producers would have been willing to provide the product for (found on the supply curve). Work through the problem that follows to make sure that you have these concepts down pat. ■

Solved Problem: Producer and Consumer Surplus

The table below contains supply and demand data.

Price	Quantity Demanded	Quantity Supplied
20	0	36
18	2	32
16	4	28
14	6	24
12	8	20
10	10	16
8	12	12
6	14	8
4	16	4
2	18	0

In the grid above, graph both supply and demand.

  a. What do equilibrium price and output equal?

  b. How large are consumer and producer surplus?

Now, assume that resource cost (labor and raw materials) used to produce this increased rapidly, adding $3 per unit to the cost of production.

  c. Plot the new supply curve and label it S_1.

  d. What is the new equilibrium price and output?

  e. How much has consumer surplus and producer surplus declined?

Solution-Discussion

The original supply and demand curves are plotted in Figure 1 on the next page (labeled S_0 and D_0 respectively).

  a. Original equilibrium price is $8, and equilibrium output is 12.

  b. Computing consumer surplus involves computing the area below the demand curve and above equilibrium price, and producer surplus is the area above the supply curve and below equilibrium price. We do this by computing

FIGURE 1

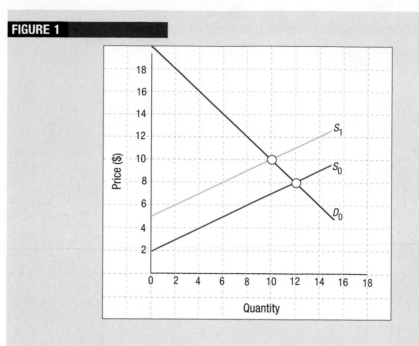

consumer surplus or producer surplus for each unit sold (price off the demand curve minus equilibrium price or price off the supply curve for producer surplus), or we can compute it by computing the area of the triangles. Remember that the area of a triangle is found by conputing one-half base times its height. It is this latter process we will use here:

Consumer surplus: $[(\$20 - \$8) \times 12] \div 2 = (\$12 \times 12) \div 2 = \$144 \div 2 = \$72$
Producer surplus: $[(\$8 - \$2) \times 12] \div 2 = (\$6 \times 12) \div 2 = \$72 \div 2 = \$36$

c. See the figure above.

d. Equilibrium price is $10, and equilibrium output is 10.

e. The new consumer and producer surplus values are:

Consumer surplus: $[(\$20 - \$10) \times 10] \div 2 = (\$10 \times 10) \div 2 = \$100 \div 2 = \$50$
Producer surplus: $[(\$10 - \$5) \times 10] \div 2 = (\$5 \times 10) \div 2 = \$50 \div 2 = \$25$

Thus, consumer surplus has fallen by $22, and producer surplus has fallen by $11.

Ideally, the solved problem has cemented in your mind how consumer and producer surplus are computed. If this is not the case, continue on, but be prepared to review this section again. Most of these are not difficult concepts (only consumer and producer surplus are a little difficult). The next section on market failures builds on this section and deals with the same issues. As you work through it, you will begin to see the pattern of what it takes to have an efficient market and how the absence of each of these elements leads to market failure. Keep this simple framework in mind as you read the next section.

Market Failures

Frequently Asked Questions

Q: What happens if markets do not meet one or more of the five requirements discussed in the previous section?

A: For markets to be efficient, they must meet the five institutional requirements identified above. When one or more of these conditions is not met, the market is said to fail.

Q: **Is market failure catastrophic?**

A: A: Market failure generally does not mean that a market totally collapses or fails to exist, but that it fails to provide the socially optimal goods and services. The exception to this is with pure public goods, where the market may totally fail to provide the goods.

Q: **What is asymmetric information?**

A: In some markets, one party to a transaction may have better information than the other. In this case, the market is said to fail because of asymmetric information. Asymmetric information can result in the inability of sellers to find buyers for the products, but it usually just involves adjustments in contracting methods.

Q: **What is adverse selection, and when does it occur?**

A: Adverse selection occurs when products of different qualities are sold at one price and involve asymmetric information. Individuals, for instance, know far more about their own health than do insurance companies. And because high-risk individuals are those who are most likely to purchase insurance, adverse selection skews the insurance pool, giving it a risk level higher than average.

Q: **What is moral hazard, and when does it occur?**

A: Moral hazard occurs when an insurance policy or some other arrangement changes the economic incentives people face, leading people to change their behavior, usually in a way detrimental to the market. The presence of lifeguards on the beach may cause people to take greater risks in the waves, and nets permit trapeze artists to perform more risky stunts.

Q: **What are private and public goods?**

A: Private goods are those goods that can be consumed only by the individuals who purchase them. Private goods are rival and exclusive. Public goods, in contrast, are nonrival and nonexclusive, meaning my consumption does not diminish your consumption and that once such a good has been provided for one person, others cannot be excluded from enjoying it.

Q: **What problem is caused by public goods, and how can it be overcome?**

A: Public goods give rise to the free rider problem. Once a public good has been provided, other consumers cannot be excluded from it, so many people will choose to enjoy the benefit without paying for it: They will free ride. And because of the possibility of free riding, the danger is that no one will pay for the public good, so it will no longer be provided by private markets, even though it is publicly desired. Pure public goods usually require public provision.

Q: **What happens to contracts when the legal system is inefficient?**

A: When an efficient legal system for the enforcement of contracts is lacking, contracts will be small because large contracts with complex financial provisions are difficult to enforce informally.

Q: **What happens to markets when external costs or benefits are present?**

A: Markets rarely produce the socially optimal output when external costs or benefits are present. The market overproduces goods with external costs, selling them at too low a price. Conversely, markets tend to provide too little of products that have external benefits.

Q: **How do monopolies make markets inefficient, and what can be done to overcome this problem?**

A: Some markets tend toward monopoly, and when a monopoly does control the market, prices go up. In the late 19th century, the monopolistic practices of the "robber barons" spurred passage of a series of antitrust laws that are still used today to promote competitive markets.

Core Graph: Externalities

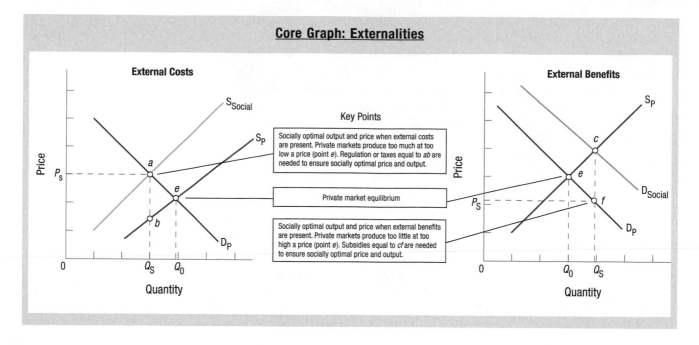

Key Points

Socially optimal output and price when external costs are present. Private markets produce too much at too low a price (point *e*). Regulation or taxes equal to *ab* are needed to ensure socially optimal price and output.

Private market equilibrium

Socially optimal output and price when external benefits are present. Private markets produce too little at too high a price (point *e*). Subsidies equal to *cf* are needed to ensure socially optimal price and output.

Key Point to Remember

Market failure occurs when information for buyers and sellers is not widely available, the market involves public goods, contracts are not enforced, externalities are present, or markets are not competitive. Market failure means that private markets will fail to provide the socially optimal output and price, so government intervention (typically rules or regulations) may be necessary. In the case of pure public goods, government often must provide them.

Market Failures Quick Check

Circle the Correct Answer

1. (T/F) When market failures occur, markets totally collapse and need government help.
2. (T/F) Asymmetric information causes markets to fail because sellers always have more information about products than buyers.
3. (T/F) Adverse selection occurs when insurance encourages high-risk individuals to obtain insurance but drives out low-risk individuals.
4. Which one of the following is an example of moral hazard?
   a. People prone to injuries obtain medical insurance, and the insurance company has no way of knowing about this tendency.
   b. People become less cautious about securing their property, saying: "Don't worry about it. It's insured."
   c. People think that all used cars are lemons.
   d. People prone to illness take out high-deductible health insurance policies.
5. Which one of the following is *not* an example of a public good?
   a. national defense
   b. local radio music broadcasts
   c. weather forecasts
   d. cell phone towers
6. Markets rarely produce the socially optimal output when negative externalities are present because
   a. externalities are nonrival and nonexclusive.
   b. producers and consumers do not pay all costs.
   c. consumers would balk at paying more.
   d. people cannot recognize a negative externality.
7. Public goods give rise to the free rider problem because
   a. not enough people pledge to give to public television.
   b. of the lemons problem.
   c. once a public good has been provided, other consumers cannot be excluded from it.
   d. when we consume them, we prevent other people from consuming them.
8. To overcome a problem of negative externalities, governments can use all *except* which one of the following?
   a. regulation
   b. taxation
   c. markets
   d. strict enforcement of contracts

9. Monopolies can hamper market efficiency because
    a. prices go up when monopolies control markets.
    b. the government is hampered by law from dealing with monopolies.
    c. antitrust polices have been ineffective against monopolies.
    d. of adverse selection and moral hazard.
10. Market failures are caused by all *except* which one of the following?
    a. Information is widely available, but not everyone makes use of it.

b. There are long delays in the legal system to enforce contracts.
c. Externalities are present.
d. Extensive monopoly power is present.

Score: ____

Answers: 1. F; 2. F; 3. T; 4. b; 5. d; 6. b; 7. c; 8. d; 9. a; 10. a

If You Got 9 or 10 Correct

Your understanding of why markets are efficient, why they sometimes fail, and how market failure might be remedied, is solid. Move on to the next section, "Government-Controlled Prices."

If You Didn't Get at Least 9 Correct

You should carefully review the material, keeping distinct the different types of market failure.

- Take a moment and jot down the different types of market failure.
- Contrast these with those conditions needed for markets to be efficient from the first section.
- Then, go back and check in the text, making sure your jotting did not leave out any type of market failure.
- Describe a remedy for each type of market failure.

Now might be a good time to spend some time reviewing the first two sections again. The heart of our economy is markets and their efficient operation. A lot of government intervention in the system stems from the types of institutional failures discussed in this chapter.

The next section, on government-controlled prices, shows what can happen when government steps in to regulate markets. In these instances, market failure may not be the reason for the intervention. Some people view market outcomes as unfair to many and encourage government to correct for this unfairness. The next section builds on concepts in the first two sections. If you have missed some of the concepts in the first two parts of this chapter, you will have to review them again. But first, work through the next section and see if it doesn't help you see some of what you missed in the earlier sections. ■

Government-Controlled Prices

Frequently Asked Questions

Q: **When does government use price ceilings and price floors?**
A: When competitive markets are left to determine equilibrium price and output, they clear; that is, businesses provide consumers with the quantity of goods

they want to purchase at the established prices. Nevertheless, the equilibrium price may not be what many people consider fair. The government may then use price ceilings or price floors to keep prices below or above the market equilibrium.

Q: **What are price ceilings, and what can happen with them?**

A: A price ceiling is the *maximum* legal price that can be charged for a product. Price ceilings set below market equilibrium result in shortages. In Figure 2, a price ceiling set at P_1 when the equilibrium price is P_e will result in shortage $Q_2 - Q_1$.

FIGURE 2

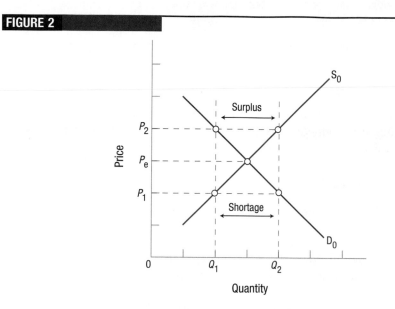

Q: **What are price floors, and what can happen with them?**

A: A price floor is the *minimum* legal price that can be charged for a product. Price floors set above market equilibrium result in surpluses. In Figure 2, a price floor set at P_2 when the equilibrium price is P_e will result in surplus $Q_2 - Q_1$.

Q: **Why do taxes cause a deadweight loss?**

A: Taxes drive a wedge between what consumers pay for a product and what business receives. They raise the price of products and reduce the quantity sold. The result is that some transactions that would have occurred in the absence of taxation do not, and this means that some consumer and producer surplus are lost to society.

Government-Controlled Prices Quick Check

Circle the Correct Answer

1. (T/F) Governments use price ceilings or price floors when markets do not clear.
2. (T/F) When price ceilings are set above the equilibrium price, shortages occur.
3. (T/F) Governments will use price ceilings when markets do not work.
4. If the government sets a price floor above an equilibrium price, this means

    a. shortages will occur.
    b. surpluses will occur.
    c. nothing will happen.
    d. the market will quickly return to equilibrium.

5. If the government sets a price ceiling below an equilibrium price, this means

    a. shortages will occur.
    b. surpluses will occur.
    c. nothing will happen.
    d. the market will quickly return to equilibrium.

6. If the government sets a price floor below an equilibrium price, this means
   a. shortages will occur.
   b. surpluses will occur.
   c. nothing will happen.
   d. the market will quickly return to equilibrium.

7. New York City politicians believe that private parking rates in Manhattan are too high, so they institute price ceilings below the current price. What happens to private parking spaces?
   a. Shortages occur.
   b. Surpluses occur.
   c. Nothing.
   d. The market adjusts quickly back to equilibrium.

8. Hospital orderlies convince the local government that they are being paid poorly for the work they do. The government decides to set a minimum wage that all hospitals must pay. After much discussion, the minimum wage is set $2.00 below the current wage. What happens to the number of hospital orderlies?
   a. There are fewer orderlies than wanted by hospitals.
   b. There are more orderlies than wanted by hospitals.
   c. Nothing.
   d. Dislocation happens at first, and then the market returns to equilibrium.

9. Now consider that the government sets the minimum wage at $2.00 above the current wage. What happens?
   a. There are fewer orderlies than wanted by hospitals.
   b. There are more orderlies than wanted by hospitals.
   c. Nothing.
   d. Dislocation happens at first, and then the market returns to equilibrium.

10. Some consumers convince state politicians that electricity is priced too high. They claim that families are being hurt by greedy utilities. The politicians then set a price ceiling at the current equilibrium price. Suddenly, the weather turns brutally hot in June, and people run their air conditioners much more. What happens?
   a. There is a surplus of electricity because the greedy utilities provide more in the hopes of making money from the situation.
   b. There is a shortage of electricity because utilities cannot meet the increased demand because of the price ceiling. There may be brownouts.
   c. Equilibrium is maintained because increased demand is a signal for utilities to increase supply.
   d. There are shortages at first because the utilities face an information problem of figuring out what demand is going to be, but this is solved quickly.

Score: ____

Answers: 1. F; 2. F; 3. F; 4. b; 5. a; 6. c; 7. a; 8. c; 9. b; 10. b

If You Got 9 or 10 Correct

You picked up the concepts of price ceilings, price floors, and the impact of taxes on consumer and producer surplus and the resulting deadweight loss. Even so, you might find it useful to take a quick look at the section titled "Hints, Tips, and Reminders."

If You Didn't Get at Least 9 Correct

You need to review this material slowly because the principles are straightforward:

▪ Start by looking again at Figure 2. Put your pencil above and then below the equilibrium price, and ask yourself what happens when the government institutes a price ceiling or a price floor. Remember that price ceilings are the highest price a firm can charge, and price floors are the lowest price a firm can charge or pay.

▪ Go back to the text and review the two Figures 5 and 6; they separate price ceilings from price floors. This may help you see why shortages and surpluses can result.

Key Point to Remember

Effective price ceilings and floors have an impact on markets. An effective price ceiling is the maximum price that can be charged, but if it is set below the equilibrium price, it will cause shortages. An effective price floor is the minimum price that can be charged or paid, but if it is set above equilibrium, it will cause surpluses.

Some of the questions in this section were a little difficult. Go back and reason out why you missed a question. Then take some time and work through the "Hints, Tips, and Reminders" section below. You will find some suggestions that will make your studying of this chapter easier. ■

Consider These Hints, Tips, and Reminders

1. Pay attention to the links between the first section, which describes the requirements for efficient markets, and the second section, which analyzes market failures. The list is the same!
   - Accurate information
   - Protected property rights
   - Private contracts are enforced
   - No externalities
   - Competitive markets

   When you look at this list, most government programs will fit into these five categories. When any of these elements are absent, the market does not provide the socially optimal level of output or pricing.

2. Keep in mind that market failure does not mean the market does nothing (with the exception of pure public goods); it simply provides a less than socially optimal result.

3. Profits drive markets (and individuals and corporations) to provide the products we take for granted. Higher profits act as signals that consumers want more of that commodity or service.

4. Markets are rationing devices. They separate us by how much we want a given product or service and ration out those who are unwilling (or unable) to pay the equilibrium market price.

5. Consumer surplus is just the difference between what you would have been willing to pay and market price. This is a benefit the market conveys to all of us. Anytime you "get a deal" on some product, you have received a consumer surplus.

6. Similarly, producer surplus is simply the difference between the price a firm would be willing to provide a product for and equilibrium market price. When gold-mining firms see the market price of gold rise (maybe because some event has created uncertainty in the world), they receive a producer surplus on each ounce of gold they sell.

7. A price ceiling places an upper limit (ceiling) on what you can sell a product for. Keep two points in mind:
   - If the price ceiling is equal to or above market price, *the ceiling has no effect.*
   - If the price ceiling is below equilibrium price, it is effective, but *it creates a shortage.*

   The first point is often used to create tricky exam questions—beware.

8. A price floor places a lower limit (floor) on what you can sell a product for. Again, keep two points in mind:
   - If the price floor is equal to or below market price, *the floor has no impact.*
   - If the price floor is above equilibrium price, it is effective, but *it generates a surplus.*

   Again, be alert for questions where the price floor has no effect.

Do the Homework for Chapter 4 Market Efficiency, Market Failure, and Government Intervention	STEP 5

Instructor _____ Time _____ Student _____

Use the answer key below to record your answers to these homework questions.

1. (a) (b) (c) (d)   6. (a) (b) (c) (d)   11. (a) (b) (c) (d)   16. (a) (b) (c) (d)
2. (a) (b) (c) (d)   7. (a) (b) (c) (d)   12. (a) (b) (c) (d)   17. (a) (b) (c) (d)
3. (a) (b) (c) (d)   8. (a) (b) (c) (d)   13. (a) (b) (c) (d)   18. (a) (b) (c) (d)
4. (a) (b) (c) (d)   9. (a) (b) (c) (d)   14. (a) (b) (c) (d)   19. (a) (b) (c) (d)
5. (a) (b) (c) (d)   10. (a) (b) (c) (d)   15. (a) (b) (c) (d)   20. (a) (b) (c) (d)

1. Which of the following conditions is *not* necessary for markets to be efficient?
   a. Good information must be widely available.
   b. Everyone must get their fair share of the fruits of the market.
   c. Externalities (spillovers) are minimal.
   d. Competition must prevail.

2. Businesses, corporations, and other producers all want to charge high prices for the products they produce and sell. Why is it that they seldom are able to do this?
   a. High prices scare away other firms.
   b. Market shortages push prices down.
   c. Competition from other firms drives down prices.
   d. Their patents expire.

3. Which of the following is *not* a characteristic of competitive markets?
   a. The market has many buyers and sellers.
   b. The market is open to entry and exit by firms.
   c. Products in these markets have close substitutes.
   d. Extensive government regulations ensure that firms act competitively.

4. Market failure occurs when
   a. one firm gets a competitive advantage over the others in the market.
   b. the market completely collapses.
   c. asymmetric information makes trading difficult.
   d. consumers fail to purchase a product from an industry.

5. Which of the following is an example of a public good?
   a. airline travel

   b. the light from a lighthouse
   c. ferry boat
   d. bicycle

6. If one firm is able to capture the entire market for a product or service, what will most likely happen in this market?
   a. Market efficiency is enhanced.
   b. This firm will increase spending on research and development to improve the quality of the product.
   c. Consumers will stop buying the product.
   d. The price of the product will rise.

7. A good that is nonrival in consumption means that
   a. everyone wants to buy and consume this product.
   b. no one is interested in this product.
   c. many people can consume the good simultaneously.
   d. two companies cooperate to produce and sell this product.

8. An example of an external cost or negative spillover is
   a. pollution caused by steel factories.
   b. a lighthouse.
   c. national defense and homeland security.
   d. immunization efforts in Africa.

9. A private market that creates negative spillovers or external costs will
   a. produce that output where all costs are built into the price.
   b. produce too much of the good at too low a price.
   c. voluntarily reduce output to the socially optimal level.
   d. collapse because no consumers will be willing to purchase the product.

10. Curbing monopoly or extensive monopoly power might require
    a. vigorous enforcement of antitrust laws.
    b. blocking mergers of large firms that control significant portions of a market.
    c. breaking up monopoly firms into smaller businesses.
    d. all of the above.

Use Figure HW-1 to answer questions 11–14. In each case assume that the market begins in equilibrium at point *e*.

11. How much will consumers purchase if the government placed a price floor of $8 on this market?
    a. 300
    b. 200
    c. 400
    d. none

12. What will be the impact if the government places a price floor of $4 on this market?
    a. a shortage equal to 200
    b. no impact at all
    c. equilibrium price would fall to $4
    d. a surplus equal to 200

13. How much will consumers purchase if the government places a price ceiling of $6 on this market?
    a. 300
    b. 400
    c. 200
    d. none

14. What would be the impact if the government placed a price ceiling of $4 on this market?
    a. a shortage equal to 200
    b. no impact at all
    c. a shortage equal to 300
    d. a surplus equal to 200

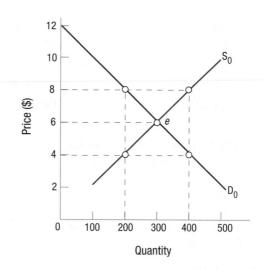

HW-1

Use Figure HW-2 to answer questions 15–17. In each case assume that the market begins in equilibrium at point *e*.

15. Consumer surplus is equal to
    a. $800
    b. $900
    c. $1,000
    d. $1,100

16. If the government places a price ceiling of $4 on this product, consumer surplus is equal to (This is tough, so crosshatch consumer surplus and then

compute the value. Remember consumers will not purchase at equilibrium price.)
a. $800
b. $1,000
c. $1,200
d. $1,400

17. If the government places a price ceiling of $4 on this product, combined producer and consumer surplus has dropped by? (Again, this is a tough question. Compute the triangle of consumer and producer surplus lost.)
a. $100
b. $200
c. $300
d. $400

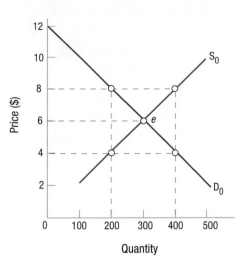

HW-2

18. Governments most often intervene in efficiently functioning markets to set prices because
a. too much of the product is being sold at quite low prices.
b. wages and benefits in the industry are excessive and are driving up prices.
c. prices or wages in the industry are not considered fair by some.
d. industry lobbyists push for, and politicians grant, price ceilings to prevent price gouging.

19. Which of the following is an example of a price floor?
a. rent controls
b. a discount on tile flooring
c. minimum wage laws
d. student discounts at the theater

20. Which of the following is an example of a price ceiling?
a. rent controls
b. a discount on tile flooring
c. minimum wage laws
d. student discounts at the theater

| | Use the ExamPrep to Get Ready for Exams | STEP 6 |

This sheet (front and back) is designed to help you prepare for your exams. The chapter has been boiled down to its key concepts. You are asked to answer questions, define terms, draw graphs, and, if you wish, add summaries of class notes.

Markets and Efficiency

Describe the following five institutional requirements for efficient markets and describe why they are important:

1. Widely available accurate information:

2. Well protected property rights:

3. Contracts enforced:

4. No externalities:

5. Competitive markets:

Describe the reasons for the overall efficiency of markets:

Market Failures

Define and describe the following reasons for market failure:

Asymmetric Information

Adverse selection:

Moral hazard:

Public Goods

Nonrivalry:

Nonexclusive:

Free rider:

Contract Enforcement

Explain why enforcing contracts is necessary:

Externalities

Use the grid at right to diagram external costs and benefits. Begin with the private market supply and demand curves labeled S_p and D_p.

External costs: Draw the new supply curve S_1 that includes negative spillovers. List the implications for efficient markets:

External benefits: Draw the new demand curve D_1 that includes positive externalities. List the implications for efficient markets.

Monopoly Power

Explain the harm from monopoly and the importance of competitive markets:

Government-Controlled Prices

Use the grid at right to describe price ceilings and floors. Begin with initial supply and demand curves labeled S_0 and D_0.

Price Ceilings

Draw a price ceiling below equilibrium price. What are the implications for the market?

List some examples of price ceilings:

Price Floors

Draw a price floor above the initial equilibrium price. What are the implications for the market?

List some examples of price floors:

Additional Study Help Chapterwide Practice Questions

Matching

Match the description with the corresponding term.

___   1. Property rights
___   2. Asymmetric information
___   3. Adverse selection
___   4. Moral hazard
___   5. Public goods
___   6. Externalities
___   7. Price ceilings
___   8. Price floors

a. Occurs when products of different qualities are sold at a single price due to asymmetric information.
b. Maximum legal prices that can be charged for products. If set below the equilibrium price, they result in shortages.
c. Both nonrival and nonexclusive goods. They give rise to the free rider problem.
d. A market failure caused when one party has better information than another.
e. Costs or benefits of economic activity that are not borne by the consumer or producer.
f. Occurs when insurance causes people to change their behavior in a detrimental way.
g. Minimum legal prices that can be charged for goods. If set above market equilibrium prices, they lead to surpluses.
h. Clear ownership of possessions. They foster an incentive not to waste.

Fill-In

Circle the word(s) in parentheses that complete the sentence.

1. The difference between what firms are willing to provide products for and market prices is (consumer, producer) _____ surplus, whereas the difference between what people would pay for a product and market price is (consumer, producer) _____ surplus.

2. Markets require (accurate, asymmetric, efficient) _____ information for efficient operation, but often (accurate, asymmetric, efficient) _____ information is a reality as one party has superior information over the other party.

3. When some contract or arrangement changes the economic incentives we face, economists refer to

this as (adverse selection, moral hazard) _____, and when products of different qualities are sold at the same price because of asymmetric information, we refer to this as (adverse selection, moral hazard) _____.

4. A product consumed by others without reducing the benefits to other consumers is referred to as a (public good, free rider) _____.

5. Pollution is an example of an external (benefit, cost) _____, while education represents an external (benefit, cost) _____. If everyone owns an asset, it is a (monopoly, common property resource, public good) _____, but when one firm controls the market for a resource, it is a (monopoly, common property resource, public good) _____.

6. The legally mandated highest price a firm can sell its products is a price (ceiling, floor) _____, but just the opposite, a legally mandated minimum price that can be charged for a product is a price (ceiling, floor) _____. An effective price (ceiling, floor) _____ will result in a surplus, while an effective price (ceiling, floor) _____ will cause shortages.

True-False

Circle the correct answer.

T/F   1. As messy as markets are, they are far more efficient at allocating resources than are systems of central planning.

T/F   2. An efficient market requires that accurate information be made available to both buyers and sellers.

T/F   3. Informal property rights tend to be more economically efficient than formal property rights because they involve less paperwork.

T/F   4. The larger the scale on which business operates, the more important it is that the legal system strictly enforces contract obligations.

T/F   5. Market failure implies that a market has completely collapsed, or ceased to exist as a market.

T/F   6. Market failure can result both from sellers knowing more about a product than the typical buyer and from buyers knowing more about a product than the typical seller.

T/F   7. The problem of moral hazard occurs when an insurance company provides incentives for behavior it is trying to discourage.

T/F   8. Public goods give rise to the free rider problem.

T/F   9. Informal contract enforcement tends to work best when contracts are small and the parties to them have long been acquainted with one another.

T/F   10. Markets tend to overproduce goods with external benefits and underproduce goods with external costs.

T/F   11. In theory, a "free market" should be one in which the government rarely intervenes, but in actual practice, the government often takes active steps to promote competition and guard against the rise of monopolies.

T/F   12. To be effective, a price floor must be set below the equilibrium price.

T/F   13. Price ceilings typically give rise to product shortages.

T/F   14. Price ceilings and floors are meant to achieve socially beneficial results, but they often have unintended detrimental consequences.

T/F   15. A raise in the minimum wage typically reduces unemployment among lower-skill workers.

Multiple Choice

Circle the correct answer.

1. Which of the following is *not* one of the requirements for an efficient market?
   a. The market is dominated by just one or two major firms.
   b. Private contracts are strictly enforced.
   c. Spillover effects from other economic actors are limited.
   d. Property rights are protected.

2. One of the requirements for an efficient market is that accurate information be made widely available. For which of the following products are informational requirements most difficult to satisfy?
   a. corn
   b. bricks
   c. prescription drugs
   d. paper towels

3. A villager is unable to use his family home as collateral for securing a small business loan because a legal title has never been issued for the house. Which requirement for an efficient market is not being met in this case?
   a. Accurate information is widely available.
   b. Private contracts are well enforced.
   c. Spillover effects from other economic factors are limited.
   d. Property rights are protected.

4. A small window-washing firm sues one of its clients for nonpayment. The court ultimately compels the client to pay, but only after legal process that lasts 3 years and costs the window-washing firms thousands of dollars in legal fees. Which requirement for an efficient market is not being met in this case?
   a. Competition prevails.
   b. Private contracts are well enforced.
   c. Spillover effects are limited.
   d. Property rights are protected.

5. A chemical company earns tremendous profits producing antifreeze, but the runoff from the production process begins killing off fish in the local river. Which requirement for an efficient market is not being met in this case?
   a. Competition prevails.
   b. Private contracts are well enforced.
   c. Spillover effects from other economic factors are limited.
   d. Property rights are protected.

6. When economists say the market rations goods to consumers, this means
   a. the government has issued ration coupons, which consumers can use to purchase the goods they most need.
   b. market discipline is forcing producers to offer high-quality goods for sale at relatively low prices.
   c. lawmakers have placed legal limits on the quantities of certain goods that individual consumers can purchase.

d. individual consumers have limited resources with which to purchase goods, so each consumer must decide which goods are most important to him or her.

7. Tobacco companies once promoted cigarettes as part of a healthy lifestyle, even after their own studies had shown that smoking causes lung cancer. What sort of market failure did this represent?
   a. asymmetric information
   b. adverse selection
   c. moral hazard
   d. the overproduction of negative externalities

8. An insurance company starts insuring businesses against the loss of data due to computer viruses, but this just leads firms to stop purchasing virus protection software. What sort of market failure does this represent?
   a. asymmetric information
   b. adverse selection
   c. moral hazard
   d. the free rider problem

9. A health insurance company begins offering free dental care as part of its basic insurance plan, but this just leads to a disproportionately large number of people with severe dental problems signing up for its plan. What sort of market failure does this represent?
   a. asymmetric information
   b. adverse selection
   c. moral hazard
   d. the overproduction of negative externalities

10. What sort of market failure did George Akerlof find to be most responsible for the low market price of used cars?
    a. asymmetric information
    b. adverse selection
    c. moral hazard
    d. the free rider problem

11. Normally, public goods are
    a. both exclusive and rival.
    b. exclusive, but nonrival.
    c. rival, but nonexclusive.
    d. both nonexclusive and nonrival.

12. Which of the following is an example of a public good?
    a. automobiles
    b. auto repair services
    c. highways
    d. bumper stickers

13. Which of the following is an example of a private good?
    a. Superbowl tickets
    b. National Public Radio
    c. the emergency broadcast system
    d. homeland security precautions

14. A musician releases a new CD in stores, but an Internet service allows users to download the CD for free. What sort of market failure problem does this represent?
    a. asymmetric information
    b. adverse selection
    c. moral hazard
    d. the free rider problem

15. What is the most likely effect of a single firm achieving monopoly status in its industry?
    a. Prices rise.
    b. Product quality goes up.
    c. Market efficiency increases.
    d. The firm's profit margin declines.

16. Which of the following is an example of a price ceiling?
    a. the minimum wage
    b. agricultural price supports
    c. rent controls
    d. unemployment insurance

17. Which of the following is an example of a price floor?
    a. rent controls
    b. caps on the Medicare payments made to doctors and hospitals
    c. a private company running a sale on its products
    d. agricultural price supports

18. A price ceiling set above a product's equilibrium price will generally result in
    a. a product shortage.
    b. a product surplus.
    c. the product being sold at its equilibrium price and clearing the market.
    d. none of the above.

19. A price floor set above a product's equilibrium price will generally result in
    a. a product shortage.
    b. a product surplus.
    c. the product being sold at its equilibrium price and clearing the market.
    d. none of the above.

20. A price ceiling set below a product's equilibrium price will generally result in
    a. a product shortage.
    b. a product surplus.
    c. the product being sold at its equilibrium price and clearing the market.
    d. none of the above.

Use Figure MC-1 to answer Questions 21–24. Equilibrium occurs at price P_e.

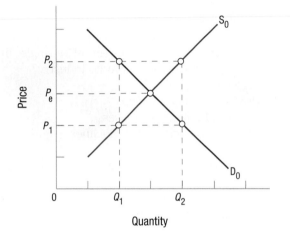

MC-1

21. What happens if the government sets a price ceiling at price P_2?
    a. Nothing.
    b. There will be a surplus of $Q_2 - Q_1$.
    c. There will be a shortage of $Q_2 - Q_1$.
    d. The market will settle back to equilibrium in a short period of time.

22. What happens if the government sets a price ceiling at price P_1?
    a. Nothing.
    b. There will be a surplus of $Q_2 - Q_1$.
    c. There will be a shortage of $Q_2 - Q_1$.
    d. The market will settle back to equilibrium in a short period of time.

23. What happens if the government sets a price floor at price P_2?
    a. Nothing.
    b. There will be a surplus of $Q_2 - Q_1$.
    c. There will be a shortage of $Q_2 - Q_1$.
    d. The market will settle back to equilibrium in a short period of time.

24. What happens if the government sets a price floor at price P_1?
    a. Nothing.
    b. There will be a surplus of $Q_2 - Q_1$.
    c. There will be a shortage of $Q_2 - Q_1$.
    d. The market will settle back to equilibrium in a short period of time.

Essay-Problem

Answer in the space provided.

The questions below can be challenging. Don't get upset if your answers are not always the same as those we suggest. Use our answers as a way to see if you are in the ballpark. More importantly use these questions and their answers to see the types of adjustments you must make when using supply and demand analysis to real markets.

1. What is the essence of markets?

2. Does market failure always require some government solution?

3. Sears has the motto "Satisfaction Guaranteed or Your Money Back." Is it in Sears' interest to accept returns with no questions asked? How does this motto overcome information problems?

4. Why do small businesses cultivate a "good name" (good reputation)?

5. An acquaintance said that the most important thing for him in buying an automobile was a warranty, such as "7 years–70,000 miles." How do warranties encourage you to buy? How might warranties cause problems for consumers?

6. Radio broadcasts are public goods. People with automobile radios, for example, cannot be prevented from listening to radio stations, and my listening to one station does not prevent you from listening to it. Yet, most radio stations are private, not public. What solves the public goods problem here, and can it be used to solve other public good problems? (Hint: break down the radio broadcast into its various segments. If it is a music station, do you hear music every moment? If it is a talk station, do you hear talk every moment?)

7. In some developing countries, land has been seized by the government from large landowners. This land is then parceled out to small farmers, but title to the land is kept by the government. Farmers are given low rents for set periods of time. Based on what you read in this chapter, what problems do you foresee with this arrangement?

8. If price ceilings such as rent control in Santa Monica, California, are economically inefficient, why not just get rid of them?

9. Agricultural price floors, initiated to give farmers a decent living, have led to agricultural surpluses in Europe and the United States. What happens to these surpluses?

10. If left on their own, why can we expect private companies to generate pollution?

What's Next

With this and the last chapter under your belt, you now have a good feel for how markets work. You have seen what is needed to make sure markets work efficiently, and what can be done to overcome market failure. Also, you have seen how the beneficial effects of markets can be overthrown if government steps in and institutes the wrong policies.

Answers to Chapterwide Practice Questions

Matching

1. h	3. a	5. c	7. b
2. d	4. f	6. e	8. g

Fill-In

1. producer, consumer
2. accurate, asymmetric
3. moral hazard, adverse selection
4. public good
5. cost, benefit, common property resource, monopoly
6. ceiling, floor, floor, ceiling

True False

1. T	5. F	9. T	13. T
2. T	6. T	10. F	14. T
3. F	7. T	11. T	15. F
4. T	8. T	12. F	

Multiple Choice

1. a	7. a	13. a	19. b
2. c	8. c	14. d	20. a
3. d	9. b	15. a	21. a
4. b	10. a	16. c	22. c
5. c	11. d	17. d	23. b
6. d	12. c	18. c	24. a

Essay-Problem

1. They bring buyers and sellers together.
2. No. Market failure may be quite mild, or can be overcome in other ways. Consider the lemons problem discussed in the chapter. A government solution is not necessary. The lemons problem will be overcome, for the most part, by used car dealers providing warranties or guarantees, buyers checking *Consumer Reports* or bringing mechanics to

inspect vehicles of interest, and private sellers going to great lengths to document the quality of their cars.

3. By using such a motto, Sears in effect says to its customers: Do not worry about the products; do not spend an inordinate amount of time researching products; buy what you want in the full knowledge that if things do not work out the way you expected, you will not have to pay for the product. This encourages buying, and it mitigates the information problem that all consumers face when purchasing any product. Of course, there is always the possibility of abuse on the part of customers. For example, Nordstrom's, which has a similar policy, was once approached by a man who wanted to return tires that dissatisfied him. Nordstrom's gave the man a credit. The problem was: Nordstrom's does not sell tires. So the man was abusing Nordstrom's. Such action occurs infrequently enough that stores such as Sears and Nordstrom's continue with their product guarantees.

4. A good name solves information problems and contracting problems. There are many small businesses. How do you choose which one to use? A good name keeps you from spending time hunting for information. For small tasks such as hiring a plumber for an emergency, a good reputation means you can proceed informally, rather than with some contract. Solving these information and contracting problems means lower transaction costs, which encourages you to engage in some transactions that you might otherwise avoid.

5. A warranty is a signal that a manufacturer stands behind its product. It assures you that if there are problems that fall within the warranty's terms, they will be taken care of at minimal cost. That is the good side of warranties. A problem may arise, for example, if an auto manufacturer knows its car does not come up to the standards of other cars but is willing to bear the possible costs of repairs as an inducement to get you to buy. The value of your time is also a cost of warranties: How many times do you want to take your car to the dealer for repairs? So a response to the acquaintance can be: Do you want a car that has a good warranty and you know is a good car, so you will not be spending so much time at the dealership, or do you want a great warranty with a car of unknown quality that may have you at the dealership again and again? This is one reason people look at the frequency of repair records in *Consumer Reports.*

6. Advertisements fund private radio stations, solving the public goods problem in this instance. Can advertising be used in other cases? Would advertisements in public parks work? How about letting a restaurant open in a small section of parkland and using the rent and tax revenue for park upkeep? The point is, the public good problem may be solvable in some cases by having private ventures bear the costs.

7. By keeping title in its hands, the government takes away the incentives small farm owners would have not to waste resources. If there was any doubt that the government would not renew leases, this would provide an incentive to waste the land, squeezing out of it whatever one could. Ownership brings about a long-term view.

8. Persistent rent control leads to winners and losers. The losers are people who would pay more for apartments but cannot find any. The winners are people who have lived in apartments for years and pay very low rents. Those who have benefited from rent control have benefited greatly and wield a large amount of political power. The point is this: Price ceilings create winners as well as losers, and winners will seek to defeat any change in the status quo.

9. Agricultural surpluses are exported or bought up by governments. In the United States, these surpluses also turn up as school breakfasts and lunches. To avoid the costs of dealing with surpluses, governments have turned to payments not to farm specific acreage.

10. Pollution is a negative externality, caused by private firms not bearing the true cost of business. It costs money to clean up pollution, and if one private firm incurs these costs, its price may not be competitive in the market. People buying the product in Arizona may not care that the firm has a clean production process in Maine. Once a private firm is

forced to bear this cost, say, by a government regulatory agency, the private firm will either produce less, thereby decreasing pollution, or produce the same amount but clean up the pollution. The private company will seek to minimize the additional cost it now has to bear. But all firms must now meet the same pollution control standards, so being competitive is not an issue.

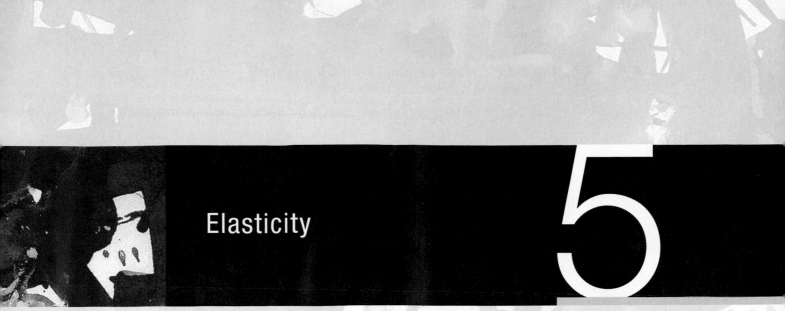

Elasticity

Elasticity Is an Important Summary Measure of Demand and Supply

Elasticity is an important extension of supply and demand concepts. In the previous chapters, we saw that when price changes, quantity demanded and quantity supplied change as well. But by how much? The answer to this is given in a simple number that economists call "elasticity." Elasticity is the change in one variable caused by the change in another variable. You will see that this simple concept of elasticity provides a tremendous amount of information.

This Is What You Need to Know

STEP 1

After studying this chapter you should be able to

- Understand the concept of elasticity and why percentages are used to measure it.

- Describe the difference between elastic and inelastic demand.

- Compute price elasticities of supply and demand.

- Use income elasticity of demand to define normal, inferior, and luxury goods.

- Describe cross elasticity of demand and use this concept to define substitutes and complements.

- Describe the relationship between total revenue and price elasticity of demand.

- Describe the determinants of elasticity of demand and supply.

- Use the concept of price elasticity of supply to measure the relationship between quantity supplied and changes in product price.

- Describe the time periods economists use to study elasticity, and describe the variables that companies can change during these periods.
- Describe the relationship between elasticity and the burden and incidence of taxes.

STEP 2   Review the Key Terms

Price elasticity of demand: A measure of the responsiveness of quantity demanded to a change in price, equal to the percentage change in quantity demanded divided by the percentage change in price.

Elastic demand: The absolute value of the price elasticity of demand that is greater than 1. Elastic demands are very responsive to changes in price. The percentage change in quantity demanded is greater than the percentage change in price.

Inelastic demand: The absolute value of the price elasticity of demand that is less than 1. Elastic demands are not very responsive to changes in price. The percentage change in quantity demanded is less than the percentage change in price.

Unitary elasticity of demand: The absolute value of the price elasticity of demand equal to 1. The percentage change in quantity demanded is just equal to the percentage change in price.

Total revenue: Price times quantity demanded (sold). If demand is elastic and price rises, quantity demanded falls off significantly and total revenue declines, and vice versa. If demand is inelastic and price rises, quantity demanded does not decline much and total revenue rises, and vice versa.

Income elasticity of demand: Measures how responsive quantity demanded is to changes in consumer income.

Normal goods: Goods that have positive income elasticities but less than 1. When consumer income grows, quantity demanded rises for normal goods, but less than the rise in income.

Luxury goods: Goods that have income elasticities greater than 1. When consumer income grows, quantity demanded rises more than the rise in income for luxury goods.

Inferior goods: Goods that have income elasticities that are negative. When consumer income grows, quantity demanded falls for inferior goods.

Cross elasticity of demand: Measures how responsive the quantity demanded of one good is to changes in the price of another good. Substitute goods have positive cross elasticities; complementary goods have negative cross elasticities.

Substitutes: Goods consumers will substitute for one another depending on their relative prices such as chicken and beef, cable TV and satellite service, and coffee and tea. Substitutes have a positive cross elasticity of demand.

Complements: Goods that are typically consumed together such as coffee and sugar, automobiles and tires, and iPods and iTunes. Complements have a negative cross elasticity of demand.

Price elasticity of supply: Measures the responsiveness of quantity supplied to changes in price. An elastic supply curve has elasticity greater than 1, whereas inelastic supplies have elasticities less than 1. Time is the most important determinant of the elasticity of supply.

Elastic supply: Price elasticity of supply is greater than 1. The percentage change in quantity supplied is greater than the percentage change in price.

Inelastic supply: Price elasticity of supply is less than 1. The percentage change in quantity supplied is less than the percentage change in price.

Unitary elastic supply: Price elasticity of supply is equal to 1. The percentage change in quantity supplied is equal to the percentage change in price.

Market period: Time period so short that the output and the number of firms are fixed.

Short run: A period of time when plant capacity and the number of firms in the industry cannot change. Firms can employ more people, use overtime with existing employees, or hire part-time employees to produce more, but this is done in an existing plant.

Long run: A period of time long enough for firms to alter their plant capacities and for the number of firms in the industry to change. Existing firms can expand or build new plants, or firms can enter or exit the industry.

Incidence of taxation: Refers to who bears the economic burden of a tax. The economic entity bearing the burden of a particular tax will depend on the price elasticities of demand and supply.

Work Through the Chapter Tutorials

STEP 3

Elasticity of Demand

Frequently Asked Questions

Q: **What is price elasticity of demand?**

A: Price elasticity of demand measures how sensitive the quantity demanded of a product is to price changes. Price elasticity of demand typically is expressed in absolute value terms. It is determined by dividing the percentage change in quantity demanded by the percentage change in price. Elasticity measures permit comparisons among products.

Q: **What is the difference between elastic and inelastic demand curves?**

A: When the absolute value of the price elasticity of demand is greater than 1, that product is said to have an elastic demand. Elastically demanded products have many substitutes, and their demand is quite sensitive to price changes. Foreign vacations and furniture have relatively elastic demand curves. When elasticity is less than 1, demand is inelastic. Quantity demanded is not very sensitive to price. Necessities like gasoline, prescription drugs, and tobacco have relatively inelastic demand curves. A value of elasticity equal to 1 is a unitary elastic curve, where the percentage change in quantity demanded is equal to the percentage

FIGURE 1

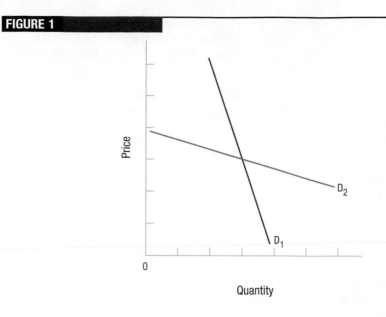

change in price. Figure 1 has two demand curves: D_1 is relatively inelastic, and D_2 is relatively elastic.

Q: What are the determinants of elasticity?

A: There are four major determinants of elasticity. Elasticity is influenced by the availability of substitute products, the percentage of income spent on the product, whether the product is a necessity or a luxury good, and the length of time consumers have to adjust to price changes.

Q: How is elasticity computed?

A: To avoid the problem of getting two different elasticity calculations for the same price change whether price is rising or falling, we use the midpoint formula to compute elasticity:

$$E_d = \frac{Q_1 - Q_0}{(Q_1 + Q_0)/2} \div \frac{P_1 - P_0}{(P_1 + P_0)/2}$$

For example, in Figure 2, the elasticity between points a and b (price drops from \$25 to \$20) is

$$
\begin{aligned}
&= [(400 - 200)/300] \div [(20 - 25)/22.5] \\
&= 200/300 \div -5/22.5 \\
&= .67 \div -.22 \\
&= -3.05 \\
&= |3.05|
\end{aligned}
$$

Q: Why does elasticity vary along a linear demand curve?

A: Along a linear (straight line) demand curve, elasticity varies from elastic at higher prices to inelastic at lower prices. When price is high, a 1-unit change in price is a small percentage change, but a big change in quantity demanded, and thus the demand is elastic. The opposite is true when price is low. In Figure 2, for example, between point a and point b demand is elastic, and it is inelastic between point d and point e. At point c, price elasticity of demand is unitary (1).

FIGURE 2

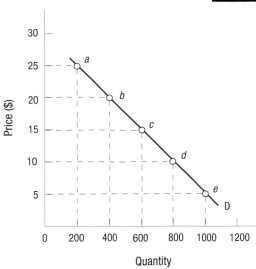

Q: How is total revenue affected by changing prices when demand is *inelastic?*

A: An inelastically demanded product may, for example, have more brand loyalty. Consequently, quantity demanded is less sensitive to price changes. So, when prices rise, total revenue rises, since quantity demanded falls off less than price increases. When price declines, total revenue falls since quantity sold grows at only a fraction of the price decline.

Q: How are total revenue and price related when demand is elastic?

A: An elastic demand means a price change can lead to large shifts in quantity demanded. Thus, when prices fall for an elastically demanded good, sales surge and total revenue rises. However, when price is raised, consumers find substitutes easily and sales plunge, resulting in lower total revenues.

Q: How are elasticity and total revenue related along a linear demand curve?

A: Figure 3 on the next page shows the relationship between price elasticity and total revenue along a straight line demand curve. Note how total revenue keeps rising as one moves down the demand curve (price falling) in the elastic range, and how total revenue falls as one moves down the demand curve in the inelastic range. Total revenue is maximized at the point of unitary elasticity.

Q: What is income elasticity of demand?

A: Income elasticity of demand measures how quantity demanded varies with consumer income. Normal goods have a positive income elasticity of demand but less than 1. *Luxury* goods have income elasticities greater than 1. *Inferior* goods have negative income elasticities. As income rises, spending on luxury goods grows faster than income, while spending on inferior goods falls. When income rises, spending on *normal* goods rises, but at a pace that is less than the increase in income.

Q: What is cross elasticity of demand?

A: Cross elasticity of demand measures how responsive quantity demanded of one good is to changes in the price of another good. If cross elasticity of demand is positive, the two goods are *substitutes*. If negative, the two goods are *complements*.

FIGURE 3

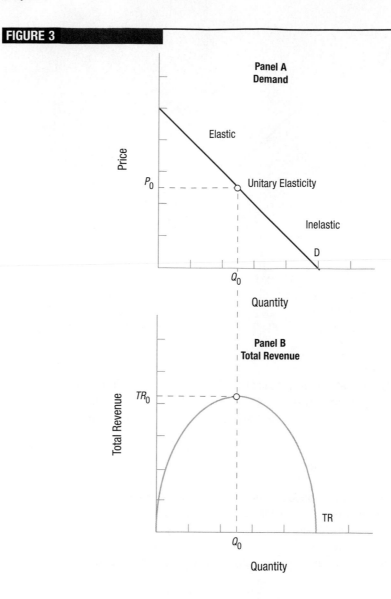

Panel A
Demand

Elastic

Unitary Elasticity

Inelastic

Panel B
Total Revenue

Key Point to Remember

When demand is inelastic ($E_d < 1$), a change in price leads to a *smaller percentage change* in quantity demanded. So when price *rises* total revenue *rises*, and vice versa. Alternatively, when demand is elastic ($E_d > 1$), a change in price leads to a *larger percentage change* in quantity demanded, and so when price *rises* total revenue *falls*, and vice versa.

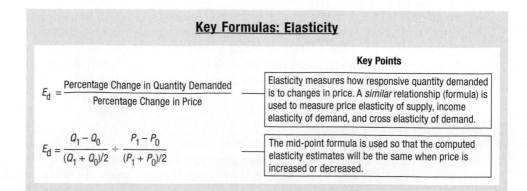

Key Formulas: Elasticity

	Key Points
$E_d = \dfrac{\text{Percentage Change in Quantity Demanded}}{\text{Percentage Change in Price}}$	Elasticity measures how responsive quantity demanded is to changes in price. A *similar* relationship (formula) is used to measure price elasticity of supply, income elasticity of demand, and cross elasticity of demand.
$E_d = \dfrac{Q_1 - Q_0}{(Q_1 + Q_0)/2} \div \dfrac{P_1 - P_0}{(P_1 + P_0)/2}$	The mid-point formula is used so that the computed elasticity estimates will be the same when price is increased or decreased.

Elasticity of Demand Quick Check

Circle the Correct Answer

1. (T/F) If price elasticity of demand is low (inelastic), a small change in price will result in a relatively large change in quantity demanded.
2. (T/F) If demand is inelastic and the price of the product falls, total revenue will rise.
3. (T/F) If price elasticity of demand (expressed as an absolute value) is less than 1, demand is inelastic.
4. (T/F) If the demand is elastic and the price of the good rises, total revenue will rise because the change in quantity demanded is less than the change in price.
5. Which of the following is *not* a determinant of the elasticity of demand?
   a. the time period under consideration
   b. whether the good is a luxury or a necessity
   c. how easy it is to substitute other products
   d. the price of the product
6. If price drops from $8 to $4, and sales rise from 20 units to 40 units, what is the absolute value of the price elasticity of demand?
   a. 0.5
   b. 0.66
   c. 1
   d. 2
7. In Figure 4, the price elasticity of demand, expressed as an absolute value
   a. must be less than 1 at point *a*.
   b. must be less than 1 at point *b*.
   c. increases from point *b* to point *c*.
   d. must be greater than 1 at point *e*.
8. An income superior good is one for which income elasticity of demand E_Y is
   a. $E_Y < 0$.
   b. $E_Y = 0$.
   c. $E_Y < 1$.
   d. $E_Y > 1$.
9. If price rises from $2.00 to $2.80 and quantity demanded falls from 160 to 80 units, what is the absolute value of the price elasticity of demand?
   a. 0.5
   b. 0.66
   c. 1
   d. 2
10. Using Figure 5, what is the elasticity of demand between points *a* and *b* (remember to express the answer in absolute value terms)?
   a. 0.85
   b. 1.0
   c. 1.75
   d. 2.2

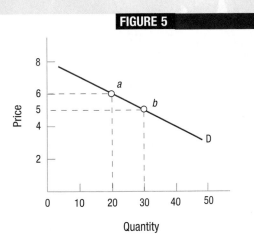

FIGURE 5

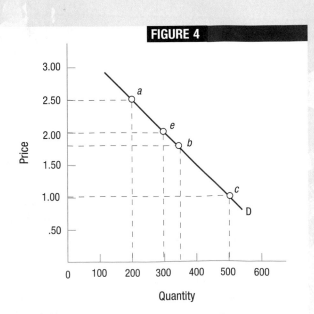

FIGURE 4

Score: _____

If You Got 9 or 10 Correct

You have a good grasp of the concept of elasticity of demand, how it is calculated, the relationship between elasticity and total revenue, and the concepts of cross elasticity of demand and income elasticity of demand. These were not simple questions and that is a lot of material to absorb in one lesson. Congratulations. Go on to the next section, "Elasticity of Supply."

If You Didn't Get at Least 9 Correct

- First note that the concept of elasticity and its computation are difficult and tedious. You need to keep a focus to get through this material.
- Also, keep in mind that there is a lot of material in this section.
- Go back and review the first part of the chapter in the text.
- When you have completed this review, work through the solved problem below, then go to the next section, "Elasticity of Supply."

Solved Problem: Elasticity of Demand

The following data (see table) for gasoline sales and prices in the United States are from the United States Department of Energy. Prices are in dollars, and sales are in millions of gallons per day.

Price	Sales (gal/day millions)
3.50	330
3.25	340
3.00	350
2.75	360
2.50	370
2.25	380
2.00	390
1.75	400
1.50	410
1.25	420
1.00	430

a. Compute the elasticity of demand when the price increases from $3.00 to $3.25.

b. Compute the elasticity of demand when the price increases from $1.25 to $1.50.

c. Why would the values be different?

d. When average gas prices are $1.50 a gallon, what does total revenue per day equal? What is total revenue when price is $3.00 a gallon? Is this consistent with your elasticity estimates in questions a and b?

e. A prominent economist, N. Gregory Mankiw (*Wall Street Journal*, October 20, 2006, p. A12), suggested that the government increase gasoline taxes by $1.00 a gallon. He suggested this tax increase would be good for the environment, reduce road congestion, help the federal budget, and improve national security, among other reasons. Assume that the current price of gasoline is $2.00 a gallon and the government followed Professor Mankiw's advice, slapping on a $1.00 tax per gallon of gasoline. Further assume that this raised the price to $3.00 a gallon (the last section of the chapter looks at the impact of taxes and elasticity estimates). Using the data in the table, how much revenue would the government collect in a *year?*

f. Why might such a tax be good for the environment, reduce road congestion, help the federal budget, and improve national security?

Solution-Discussion

a. The elasticity of demand when price rises from $3.00 to $3.25 is equal to the percentage change in quantity demanded divided by the percentage change in price. Using the midpoint formula:

$$E_d = [(350 - 340)/((350 + 340)/2)] \div [(3.00 - 3.25)/((3.00 + 3.25)/2)]$$
$$= (10/345) \div (-.25/3.125) = .02899 \div .08 = |-.36| = .36.$$

b. In a similar fashion to question a, the elasticity of demand when price rises from $1.25 to $1.50 is

$$E_d = [(420 - 410)/((420 + 410)/2)] \div [(1.25 - 1.50)/((1.25 + 1.50)/2)]$$
$$= (10/415) \div (-.25/1.375) = .02410 \div .1818 = |-.13| = .13.$$

c. First, the demand relationship shown in the table is a linear relationship (if you plot the line, you will see it is a straight line). And we know that elasticity varies over a linear demand curve. Second, when prices rise, we would expect to see the elasticity become more elastic and this is the case in the table. As prices rise, consumers buy less as they find other substitutes for gasoline. In the short run, quantity demanded drops off maybe at 2% for every rise in price of 10%. People take fewer trips and consolidate those trips to accomplish more. Some people may even move to public transportation, leaving their cars home. In the long run, people will purchase cars with higher gas mileage or substitute smaller cars for their existing SUVs.

d. At $1.50 a gallon, 410 million gallons a day are sold, so total revenue is equal to $1.50 × 410 = $615 million a day. At $3.00 a gallon, total revenue is $3.00 × 350 = $1,050 million a day. Yes, it is consistent. When demand is inelastic and price increases, total revenue will rise, since the percentage increase in price is greater than the percentage decrease in sales.

e. If the government put a $1.00 tax per gallon on gasoline, and we assume that the price would rise to $3.00, tax revenue per day would be $1 × 350 = $350 million. Annual revenue would equal $350 million × 365 = $127.750 billion.

f. Burning gasoline is harmful to the environment, increasing pollution and potentially adding to global warming. Increasing the gasoline tax will reduce automobile travel, thereby reducing both environmental harm and road congestion. We saw in question e that substantial tax revenue can be collected. The national security argument is a little more nuanced in that since the United States is a substantial part of world oil consumption, our demand may be what keeps oil prices high, resulting in large flows of cash to the Middle East. Also, our dependence on oil leads to concern with sometimes incendiary Middle East politics.

Now that you have reviewed this section, the "Elasticity of Supply" section will be easier since you now have a better understanding of elasticity of demand. As you read the material in the next section you will see that supply closely parallels demand. ■

Elasticity of Supply

Frequently Asked Questions

Q: **What is the price elasticity of supply, and how is it measured?**
A: The price elasticity of supply measures how sensitive the quantity of a product supplied is to changes in price for that product. Economists find the price elasticity of supply by taking the percentage change in the quantity supplied and dividing it by the percentage change in price (essentially the same formula as that for the price elasticity of demand). The slope of the supply curve is positive, so the price elasticity of supply is always positive.

Q: **How are elastic and inelastic supply curves defined?**
A: An elastic supply curve has a price elasticity of supply greater than 1. Elasticity for inelastic supplies is less than 1, and unitary if equal to 1. Figure 6 shows three supply curves: S_1 is inelastic, S_2 is unitary elastic, and S_3 is elastic.

FIGURE 6

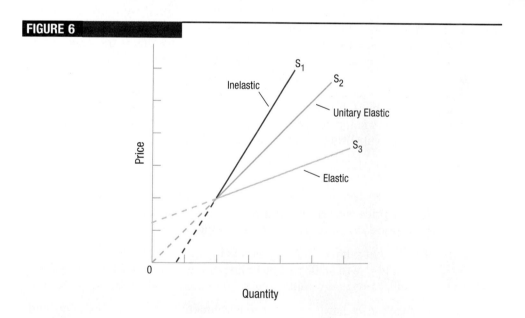

Q: **Why is time important in determining elasticity of supply?**
A: The market period, short run, and long run are the time periods economists use to study elasticity. The market period, shown in Figure 7 as S_{MP}, is so short that the output of firms is fixed (perfectly inelastic). The short-run supply curve is shown as S_{SR}. In the short run, companies can change the amount of labor and other variable factors to alter output, but physical plant is usually assumed to be fixed. In the long run (S_{LR}), companies have time to build new production facilities and to enter or to exit the industry.

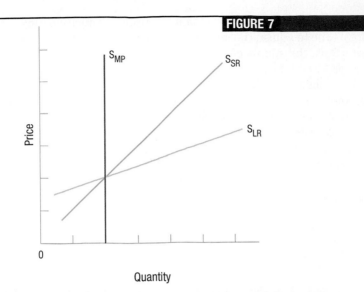

FIGURE 7

Elasticity of Supply Quick Check

Circle the Correct Answer

1. (T/F) In the market period, the elasticity of supply is perfectly elastic.
2. (T/F) If a supply curve is linear and it intersects the quantity axis, the curve is inelastic.
3. (T/F) During the short run, plant capacity and the number of firms in an industry are fixed, but firms can adjust their output in response to market changes by adjusting the amount of inputs they employ.
4. The supply curve for the long run, S_{LR}, is
   a. relatively elastic.
   b. relatively inelastic.
   c. unitarily elastic.
   d. indeterminate.

5. If demand for Talking Elmo dolls suddenly increases because Sesame Street features Elmo more in its programs, what can suppliers do in the short run?
   a. Nothing.
   b. Increase supply to a small degree by using more labor and other variable inputs.
   c. Flood the market with additional dolls by building a new doll manufacturing plant.
   d. Increase supply greatly by converting a bicycle manufacturing plant into a doll plant.

Score: ____

Answers: 1. F; 2. T; 3. T; 4. a; 5. b

If You Got All 5 Correct

Your knowledge of supply elasticity is solid. Go on to the next section that focuses on taxes and elasticity.

If You Didn't Get All of Them Correct

These were relatively simple questions, so if you had trouble here, you probably haven't done well up to this point. Elasticity is not an easy concept to keep straight. It typically requires a little extra time and effort to get it down.

Keep in Mind

- Elasticity of supply roughly follows the same structure as elasticity of demand.
- Computing elasticity of supply is done the same way as elasticity of demand, but since the supply curve is positively sloped, the resulting number will be positive.

■ The most important determinant of supply elasticity is time. When firms have a long time to adjust, the supply curve will be more *elastic*. As the adjustment time shortens, the supply curve becomes less elastic.

You might consider a quick review of the first two sections of the chapter at this point. The next section, on "Taxes and Elasticity," puts together both elasticity of demand and supply and assumes that you have a good feel for both concepts. After this review, continue on to the next section. ■

Taxes and Elasticity

Frequently Asked Questions

Q: How does the elasticity of demand affect who actually pays a tax?

A: Elasticity affects the burden and incidence of taxes. The more elastic the demand, the less a company can shift part of a tax to consumers in the form of price increases. Consumers can readily substitute for an elastically demanded product when its price has increased due to taxes.

Q: Why do consumers pay more of a tax when demand is inelastic?

A: An inelastically demanded product can absorb the increase in pcrice due to taxes without much impact on quantity demanded. In Figure 8, point *a* represents a tax levied on a product with relatively inelastic demand. Note the larger increase in price compared to the smaller decrease in quantity demanded, and the ability suppliers have to shift most of this tax on to consumers because demand, D_0, is relatively inelastic.

FIGURE 8

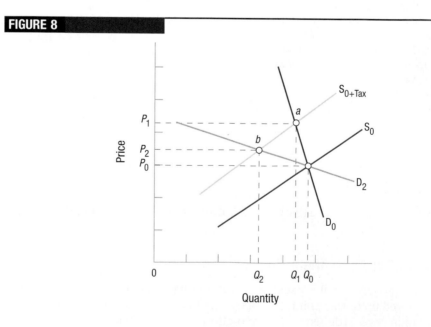

Q: Why do sellers bear most of the tax burden when demand is relatively elastic?

A: When demand is relatively elastic, consumers have a lot of alternatives to the taxed product so quantity demanded is highly sensitive to changes in price. Demand curve D_2 in Figure 8 is relatively elastic, and point *b* shows the impact of the tax. Price rises very little, but quantity sold falls considerably to Q_2. In this case, firms (and their employees) bear the greater burden of this tax.

Q: How does the elasticity of supply affect tax burdens?

A: The more inelastic the supply, the less consumers bear the burden of a tax. In Figure 9, the tax shifts the curve upward from S_0 to S_{0+tax}. Price rises from P_0 to P_1 and the consumer's burden is relatively small. Firms bear some of the price increase, but the reduction in output is small. Contrast this with a perfectly elastic supply S_2 (the dashed supply curve) and its corresponding supply curve S_{2+tax} when the tax is applied. Consumers bear the full burden of the tax as price increases from P_0 to P_2. Notice that output falls to Q_2, so the firm bears the burden of lower output.

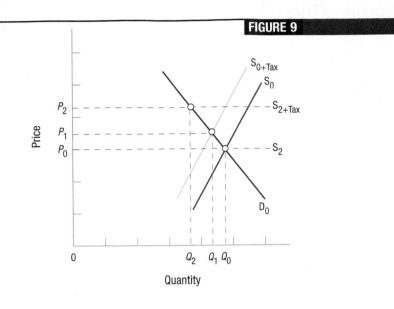

FIGURE 9

Q: What is deadweight loss of taxes, and why is it important?

A: The deadweight loss of a tax is the loss of consumer and producer surplus over and above the tax revenue collected. We want to minimize deadweight losses because they represent inefficiencies associated with collecting taxes.

Taxes and Elasticity Quick Check

Circle the Correct Answer

1. (T/F) The more elastic the demand, the more the burden of an excise tax falls on producers.
2. (T/F) Where the supply is perfectly elastic, producers bear the greatest burden of an excise tax.
3. When an excise tax is placed on a product with relatively inelastic demand, which of the following occurs?
   a. Less revenue is collected than if the demand were elastic.
   b. Most of the tax is avoided through product substitution by consumers.
   c. Most of the tax is borne by the purchaser.
   d. Most of the tax is borne by the supplier.
4. If the excise tax on a product with relatively elastic demand is raised, sales of the product will
   a. rise.
   b. fall.
   c. remain constant.
   d. do any of the above; tax rates do not affect sales.
5. Excise taxes are usually placed on goods such as gasoline, cigarettes, and liquor because
   a. collection costs are lowest for these taxes.
   b. revenues collected are so small, ensuring that constituents will not be upset.
   c. government only taxes those products that are detrimental to public health.
   d. the demand for these products is relatively inelastic.

Score: ____

You should have correctly answered all of these questions. If you didn't, continue on, but you will undoubtedly have to review this chapter again. As you read through the "Hints, Tips, and Reminders" that follow, if you are unable to understand the suggestions you will want to go back and review the entire chapter again. This is difficult (and sometimes tedious) stuff, but it will show up again in several more chapters. ■

STEP 4   Consider These Hints, Tips, and Reminders

1. The basic idea of elasticity is how *responsive* quantity changes are to price changes; hence the general formula for elasticity is the percentage change in quantity (demanded, supplied, etc.) *divided by* percentage change in (price, income, etc.).

2. Keep in mind that as the table below shows, quantity is always the numerator of each elasticity equation.

Elasticity	Equation
Price elasticity of demand	$\dfrac{\text{Percentage Change in } \textit{Quantity} \text{ Demanded}}{\text{Percentage Change in Price}}$
Price elasticity of supply	$\dfrac{\text{Percentage Change in } \textit{Quantity} \text{ Supplied}}{\text{Percentage Change in Price}}$
Income elasticity of demand	$\dfrac{\text{Percentage Change in } \textit{Quantity} \text{ Demanded}}{\text{Percentage Change in Income}}$
Cross elasticity of demand	$\dfrac{\text{Percentage Change in } \textit{Quantity} \text{ Demanded of product a}}{\text{Percentage Change in Price of product b}}$

You should *always* be dividing something into quantity to determine the value of elasticity.

3. We use midpoints to keep elasticity estimates consistent whether price rises or falls. But keep in mind that if you are given the percentage changes for both quantity and price, you can compute elasticity directly from those values (percentage change in quantity demanded divided by percentage change in price). For example, a recent article in the *New York Times* cited a study by economist Christopher Knittel, who showed that between November 1975 and November 1980 when gasoline prices rose by 20%, consumers cut gas consumption by 6%.[1] But comparing a recent 5-year period (March 2001 to March 2006), when gas prices rose by 20%, consumers only reduced their purchases of gasoline by 1%. In the earlier case, elasticity averaged 0.3 (6% ÷ 20%), while for 2006, the elasticity is much more inelastic at 0.05 (1% ÷ 20%). Why would this be the case? The author suggested that it might be due to longer commutes as a consequence of suburban sprawl, slower growth of mass transit over this period, and the fact that more two-earner households exist where earnings are high enough that gasoline prices have become a smaller portion of the household budget.

    The important point here is that you will often be given these numbers (percentage changes) in newspaper and magazine articles, and they can quickly be converted to elasticities without resorting to midpoint calculations.

---

[1]Clifford Krauss, "Drivers Offer a Collective Ho-Hum as Gsoline Prices Soar," *New York Times*, March 20, 2007, p. C1.

Do the Homework for Chapter 5
Elasticity

Instructor _____ Time _____ Student _____

Use the answer key below to record your answers to these homework questions.

1. (a) (b) (c) (d)   6. (a) (b) (c) (d)   11. (a) (b) (c) (d)   16. (a) (b) (c) (d)
2. (a) (b) (c) (d)   7. (a) (b) (c) (d)   12. (a) (b) (c) (d)   17. (a) (b) (c) (d)
3. (a) (b) (c) (d)   8. (a) (b) (c) (d)   13. (a) (b) (c) (d)   18. (a) (b) (c) (d)
4. (a) (b) (c) (d)   9. (a) (b) (c) (d)   14. (a) (b) (c) (d)   19. (a) (b) (c) (d)
5. (a) (b) (c) (d)   10. (a) (b) (c) (d)   15. (a) (b) (c) (d)   20. (a) (b) (c) (d)

1. Price elasticity of demand measures
   a. how much demand falls when prices rise.
   b. the percentage change in demand caused by price increases.
   c. the percentage change in quantity demanded caused by changes in price.
   d. how sensitive consumer tastes and preferences are to advertising.

2. An elastic demand means that
   a. quantity demanded will decline rapidly when price falls.
   b. demand will rise dramatically in response to new product introductions.
   c. quantity demanded will drop dramatically in response to a rise in price.
   d. quantity demanded will hardly change when price rises.

3. An inelastic demand means that
   a. quantity demanded will decline rapidly when price falls.
   b. demand will rise dramatically in response to a good advertisement.
   c. quantity demanded will drop dramatically in response to a rise in price.
   d. quantity demanded will hardly change when price rises.

4. Which of the following is *not* a determinant of elasticity of demand?
   a. the more substitutes available for the product
   b. how much of the household budget is spent on the product
   c. the time period under consideration
   d. how hard it is to find the good in stores

Use Figure HW-1 to answer questions 5–7.

5. What is the absolute value of the elasticity of demand between points *b* and *c* in the figure?
   a. 1.0
   b. .75
   c. .50
   d. .25

6. What is the absolute value of the elasticity of demand between points *a* and *b* in the figure?
   a. 1.5
   b. 1.6
   c. 1.7
   d. 1.8

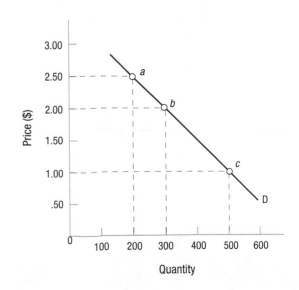

HW-1

7. When price falls from $2.50 to $2.00 in the figure, total revenue will
   a. rise.
   b. fall.
   c. remain the same.
   d. no way to tell.

8. When the demand is inelastic and price increases,
   a. quantity demanded will decline substantially.
   b. total revenue will rise for the firm.
   c. total revenue will decline.
   d. consumers will find many new substitutes for the product.

9. When price increases from P_0 to P_1 in Figure HW-2, total revenue
   a. does not change.
   b. rises.
   c. falls.
   d. not enough information to answer the question.

10. The demand curve D between prices P_0 and P_1 shown in Figure HW-2 is
    a. relatively elastic.
    b. unitarily elastic.
    c. representative of a good where there are lots of substitutes.
    d. relatively inelastic.

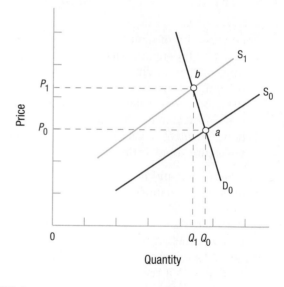

HW-2

11. The price elasticity of supply measures
    a. the responsiveness of quantity supplied to changes in price.
    b. how flexible households are to changes in product supplies.
    c. how rapidly changes in technology are reflected in lower prices.
    d. the percentage change in supply to a fixed percentage change in product price.

Use Figure HW-3 to answer questions 12 and 13.

12. Which of the curves in the figure represents an elastic supply curve?
    a. S_1
    b. S_2
    c. S_3
    d. none of the above

13. Which of the curves in the figure represents an inelastic supply curve?
    a. S_1
    b. S_2
    c. S_3
    d. none of the above

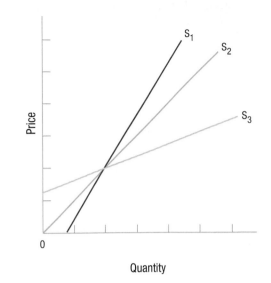

HW-3

14. The supply curve for the market period is
    a. highly elastic.
    b. relatively elastic.
    c. unitary elastic.
    d. highly inelastic.

15. The supply curve for the long run is
    a. relatively elastic.
    b. relatively inelastic.
    c. unitary elastic.
    d. highly inelastic.

16. Chips and salsa
    a. are clearly inferior goods.
    b. have a positive cross elasticity of demand.
    c. sales are not affected by changes in price.
    d. have a negative cross elasticity of demand.

17. Lima beans and rice are examples of
    a. luxury goods.
    b. normal goods.
    c. inferior goods.
    d. complementary goods.

18. It has been noted that when the price of coffee rises by 20%, sales of tea rise by 8%. These two products
    a. are complements.
    b. have a cross elasticity of demand of 2.5.
    c. are normal inferior goods.
    d. have a cross elasticity of demand of .4.

19. In Figure HW-4, assume a tax is levied equal to
    $a - b$ or $P_2 - P_1$, and equilibrium moves from
    point e to point a. In this instance, the largest bur-
    den of the tax falls on which of the following?
    a. businesses
    b. workers
    c. consumers
    d. government because tax revenues are small

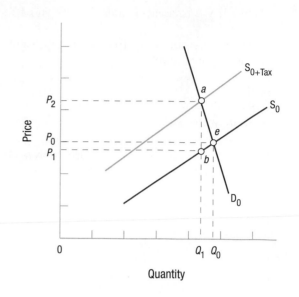

HW-4

20. In Figure HW-5 assume a tax is levied equal to $b -$
    a or $P_2 - P_1$, and equilibrium moves from point e
    to point b. In this instance the largest burden of
    the tax falls on which of the following?
    a. businesses and workers
    b. nonprofit groups as their donations to impor-
       tant causes fall
    c. consumers
    d. government because tax revenues are unex-
       pectedly large

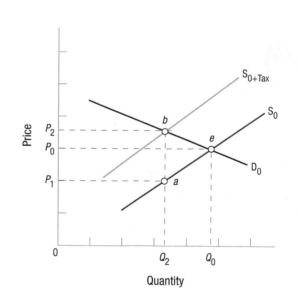

HW-5

| | Use the ExamPrep to Get Ready for Exams | STEP 6 |

This sheet (front and back) is designed to help you prepare for your exams. The chapter has been boiled down to its key concepts. You are asked to answer questions, define terms, draw graphs, and, if you wish, add summaries of class notes.

Elasticity of Demand

Define the general concept of elasticity of demand:

General formula for elasticity:

Describe the following:
Perfectly elastic demand curve:

Perfectly inelastic demand curve:

Unitary elastic demand curve:

In the grid below, draw the following:

- A perfectly elastic demand curve
- A perfectly inelastic demand curve
- A relatively elastic demand curve
- A relatively inelastic demand curve

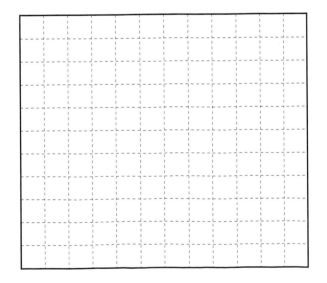

List the determinants of elasticity of demand:

Give the midpoint formula for computing elasticity:

Elasticity and Total Revenue

Complete the table below, describing the relationship among total revenue, price changes, and elasticity by indicating what happens to total revenue.

Elasticity	Change in Total Revenue	
	Price Increases	Price Decreases
Elastic		
Inelastic		
Unitary		

Other Elasticities of Demand

Income elasticity of demand:
List the formula:

Define normal goods:

Define luxury goods:

Define inferior goods:

Cross elasticity of demand:
List the formula:

Define substitute goods:

Define complements:

Elasticity of Supply

List the formula for price elasticity of supply:

Define the following:
Elastic:

Inelastic:

Unitary elastic:

List the three time periods for supply and their relative elasticity.

Taxes and Elasticity

Fill in the following table with an approximation of who bears the highest excise tax burden (sellers or buyers):

	Demand Inelastic	Demand Elastic
Supply inelastic		
Supply elastic		

Additional Study Help Chapterwide Practice Questions

Matching

Match the description with the corresponding term.

___ 1. Price elasticity of demand
___ 2. Elastic demand
___ 3. Inelastic demand
___ 4. Unitary elasticity of demand
___ 5. Normal goods
___ 6. Inferior goods
___ 7. Cross elasticity of demand
___ 8. Substitutes
___ 9. Complements
___ 10. Price elasticity of supply
___ 11. Market period
___ 12. Short run
___ 13. Long run

a. A measure of how responsive the quantity demanded of one good is to the change in the price of another. It is defined as the percentage change in the quantity demanded of product a over the percentage change in the price of product b.

b. A length of time so short that firms have no ability to change their production levels in response to changes in markets. Output is fixed during this period, as are input levels, plant sizes, and the number of firms.

c. Quantity demanded is unresponsive to price changes. A large change in price will cause only a small change in quantity sold.

d. A measure of how responsive quantity demanded is to changes in price defined as the percentage change in quantity demanded over the percentage change in price.

e. Goods and services that are consumed as a replacement for another if price increases. They have a positive cross elasticity of demand.

f. If the percentage change in quantity demanded is precisely equal to the percentage change in price.

g. Goods that are usually consumed together. Their cross elasticity of demand is less than 0.

h. A period of time long enough for firms to adjust their production levels in response to market changes by adjusting labor and other inputs, but not long enough for changes in plant capacity or the number of firms in an industry.

i. The quantity demanded is responsive to price changes. The absolute value of price elasticity of demand is greater than 1.

j. Goods that have positive income elasticities but less than 1.

k. A measure of how responsive quantity supplied is to price changes for a given product. It is defined as the percentage change in quantity supplied over the percentage change in price.

l. Goods that have income elasticities that are negative.

m. Firms can change their plant capacity and enter or exit the industry during this time period. The supply curve is relatively elastic.

Fill-In

Circle the word(s) in parentheses that complete the sentence.

1. Price elasticity of demand is a measure of how responsive (price, quantity demanded) _____ is to changes in (price, quantity demanded) _____. If the absolute value of elasticity is greater than one, demand is (inelastic, elastic, unitarily elastic) _____, when it is equal to one, demand is (inelastic, elastic, unitarily elastic) _____, and when it is less than one, demand is (inelastic, elastic, unitarily elastic) _____.

2. The more substitutes available the more (inelastic, elastic) _____ is demand, and the smaller the fraction of household income spent on a product the more (inelastic, elastic) _____ is demand. The longer the time period consumers have to consider the purchase of a product, the more (inelastic, elastic) _____ is demand.

3. When elasticity is inelastic and price increases, total revenue will (rise, fall, remain the same) _____, and (rise, fall, remain the same) _____ when price falls. When elasticity is elastic and price increases, total revenue will (rise, fall, remain the same) _____, and (rise, fall, remain the same) _____ when price falls.

4. When a product has an income elasticity coefficient greater than 1 it is a (normal, inferior, luxury) _____ good, and when its income elasticity is less than 1 but greater than 0, it is a (normal, inferior, luxury) _____ good, but if its income elasticity is less than 0 it is a (normal, inferior, luxury) _____ good.

5. When cross elasticity is greater than 0, the two goods are (substitutes, complements) _____. When cross elasticity is negative, the two goods are (substitutes, complements) _____.

6. When the price elasticity of supply is greater than 1, supply is (elastic, inelastic) _____, and when the price elasticity of supply is less than 1, supply is (elastic, inelastic) _____. The primary determinate of elasticity of supply is (price, quantity, time) _____. The (market period, short run, long run) _____ is long enough for firms to change all variables, while the (market period, short run, long run) _____ period restricts output and the number of firms in the industry, while the (market period, short run, long run) _____ allows firms to change the amount of labor and raw materials to adjust their output to changing market conditions.

7. When demand is (elastic, inelastic) _____, consumers bear much of the burden of excise taxation, and when supply is (elastic, inelastic) _____, consumers still tend to bear a higher burden of the excise taxes.

True-False

Circle the correct answer.

T/F   1. If price elasticity of demand is high (elastic), a small change in price will result in a relatively large change in quantity demanded.

T/F   2. If price elasticity of demand (expressed as an absolute value) is less than 1, demand is inelastic.

T/F   3. A perfectly elastic demand curve will be vertical.

T/F   4. If the price of computer desks rises by 9% and sales fall by 6%, price elasticity of demand is -1.5.

T/F   5. Income elasticity of demand is greater than 1 for a normal good.

T/F   6. Products are complements if their cross elasticity of demand is greater than 0.

T/F   7. If price elasticity of demand is unitary, a 10% rise in price will result in a 10% rise in total revenue.

T/F   8. If the demand for a product is elastic, a decline in its price will result in an increase in total revenue.

T/F   9. The more substitutes a product has, the more elastic demand for it will be.

T/F   10. Firms with elastically demanded products experience dramatic changes in sales in response to price changes.

T/F   11. Restaurants might offer a "buy one, get one free" offer because of the relatively high elasticity of demand in their industry.

T/F   12. All linear demand curves have an upper portion that is inelastic and a lower part that is elastic.

T/F   13. Changing brands is more likely to occur when a product's price is high, and when a product has fewer substitutes, its elasticity of demand will be higher.

T/F   14. In general, the smaller the proportion of consumers' income spent on a product, the higher the elasticity of demand.

T/F   15. If a supply curve is linear and it intersects the quantity axis, the curve is inelastic.

T/F   16. During the market period, plant capacity and the number of firms in an industry are fixed, but firms can adjust their output in response to market changes by adjusting the amount of inputs they employ.

T/F   17. The main determinant of the price elasticity of supply is time.

T/F   18. Most excise taxes are levied on goods with relatively inelastic demand curves.

T/F   19. If an excise tax is placed on a good with perfectly inelastic demand, the full burden of the tax will fall on consumers in the form of higher prices.

Multiple Choice

Circle the correct answer.

1. In general, elasticity is a measure of
   a. consumer tastes and preferences.
   b. the responsiveness of one variable to changes in another.

c. input price levels in different industries.

d. worker productivity.

2. If a small rise in price causes a relatively large decrease in the quantity demanded of a product, the product's demand is
   a. relatively elastic.
   b. unitary elastic.
   c. relatively inelastic.
   d. perfectly inelastic.

3. Price elasticity of demand is defined as
   a. percentage change in quantity demanded over percentage change in price.
   b. percentage change in quantity supplied over percentage change in quantity demanded.
   c. absolute change in quantity demanded (number of units) over absolute change in price (dollars).
   d. percentage change in quantity demanded over the percentage change in income.

4. 1f the price of laptop computers drops by 4% and sales go up 2%, what is the price elasticity of demand for laptops expressed as an absolute value?
   a. 0.5
   b. 1
   c. 2
   d. 4

5. If the price of bananas rises from $0.84/lb to $1.05/lb, what is the percentage change in the price of bananas?
   a. −21%
   b. 21%
   c. 25%
   d. 84%

6. If the price of a certain sports car rises from $20,000 to $22,000 and the quantity demanded consequently drops from 7,500 to 6,000, what is the sports car's price elasticity of demand, expressed as an absolute value?
   a. 1.0
   b. 1.5
   c. 2.0
   d. 2.3

7. If a demand curve is perfectly elastic, it will be
   a. horizontal.
   b. linear and falling.
   c. falling, bowed in toward the origin.
   d. vertical.

8. If price rises from $1.00 to $1.40 and quantity demanded falls from 80 to 40 units, what is the price elasticity of demand, expressed as an absolute value?
   a. 1.0
   b. 1.5
   c. 2.0
   d. 2.5

9. If price drops from $400 to $200 and sales rise from 400 units to 800 units, what is the price elasticity of demand, expressed as an absolute value?
   a. 0.5
   b. 0.66
   c. 1
   d. 2

10. If quantity demanded changes by 25% and price changes by −20%, what is the elasticity of demand, expressed as an absolute value?
    a. 0.8
    b. 1.0
    c. 1.25
    d. 2

11. A normal good is one for which
    a. quantity demanded rises as income rises, but not as fast as the increase in income.
    b. quantity demanded rises as income increases, rising faster than the increase in income.
    c. quantity demanded falls as income rises.
    d. quantity demanded is unaffected by changes in incomes.

12. An luxury good is one for which income elasticity of demand E_Y is
    a. $E_Y < 0$.
    b. $E_Y = 0$.
    c. $0 < E_Y < 1$.
    d. $E_Y > 1$.

13. If the cross elasticity of demand for two products is less than 0, the two products are
    a. substitutes.
    b. complements.
    c. unrelated.
    d. identical.

14. If the price of an inelastically demanded good goes up, total revenue will
    a. rise.
    b. remain constant.
    C. fall.
    d. be indeterminate without further information.

15. If the price of a good demanded with unitary elasticity falls, total revenue will
    a. rise.
    b. remain constant.
    c. fall.
    d. any of the above—indeterminate without further information.

16. On a linear demand curve, the portion of the curve where P is low and Q is high has an elasticity of demand that is
    a. high, or elastic.
    b. unitary.
    c. low, or inelastic.
    d. the same as when P is high and Q is low.

17. When consumers have time to adjust their consumption patterns, what can happen to the elasticity of demand?
    a. It becomes less elastic.
    b. It tends to be more elastic.
    c. Anything can happen to elasticity of demand.
    d. There will be no change.

18. In response to incremental increases in gasoline prices, production of smaller, more fuel-efficient cars might increase. This would be an example of
    a. the impact of arc elasticity on suppliers.
    b. proportion of income spent on a product.
    c. the impact of time period and substitutability on elasticity of demand.
    d. perfect elasticity.

19. Which statement is *not* true of the long run?
    a. Firms may decide to leave the industry if they perceive the market as unfavorable.
    b. New firms can enter the business.
    c. Existing firms can alter their production capacity.
    d. The supply curve in the long run is inelastic.

20. If price elasticity of supply is greater than 1, supply is
    a. elastic.
    b. inelastic.
    c. unitary.
    d. inexhaustible.

21. If a supply curve is elastic, it will intersect
    a. the price axis.
    b. the quantity axis.
    c. the origin.
    d. none of the above.

22. Plant capacity, the number of firms in an industry, and quantity of variable inputs employed are all fixed during the
    a. purchasing period.
    b. market period.
    c. short run.
    d. long run.

23. If an excise tax is levied on a product for which there is relatively inelastic demand, most of the tax burden will be shifted onto
    a. consumers.
    b. sellers.
    c. the government.
    d. workers.

24. Most excise taxes are levied on goods for which demand is
    a. perfectly elastic.
    b. relatively elastic.
    c. unitarily elastic.
    d. relatively inelastic.

25. For products with excise taxes levied on them, as elasticity of supply declines, the portion of the tax burden borne by sellers
    a. increases.
    b. decreases.
    c. falls to zero.
    d. remains constant.

Essay-Problem

Answer in the space provided.

The questions below are challenging. Don't get discouraged if your answers are not always the same as those we suggest. Use these as another way to assess your progress but more importantly to discover some of the subtleties surrounding the concept of elasticity.

1. We saw in the text that the price elasticity of demand for newspapers is 0.1. With such an inelastic demand, should the *Wall Street Journal*, the premier U.S. business newspaper, make it a policy to raise its prices by at least 25 cents every year? Why or why not?

2. Consider two products—laptop computers and mainframe computers—and explain why elasticity is computed in percentage terms.

3. Consider three products: a cup of coffee, a cup of cappuccino, and a cup of cappuccino at Starbucks. Which one is relatively most price inelastic? Which one is relatively most price elastic?

4. Consider a sweater purchased at three different stores: Banana Republic, The Gap, and Old Navy. At which store would you expect the sweater to be most price elastic?

5. Is it always a good idea for firms to lower prices in an attempt to increase total revenue?

6. Name three inferior goods.

7. Name two superior goods.

8. Why are economists so vague in defining the short run and the long run? Why not use a fixed amount of time, such as one year?

9. Why do governments consistently tax gasoline and cigarettes?

10. Why does the actual payer of an excise tax not always bear the tax burden?

What's Next

Having completed this chapter, you now have a good understanding of the concept of elasticity. Often elasticity is intuitively grasped by simply keeping in mind which is changing the most (in percentage terms)—quantity or price. Elasticity estimates provide useful information that consumers, decision makers, and governments can use. Elasticity helps to explain why some people flee some products at the merest hint of a price increase, and yet stay with other products when a price increase is large.

This is a tough, dense, and challenging chapter. But understanding these concepts will be necessary in later chapters on market structures: competition, monopoly, and oligopoly. In the next chapter, we look at how people determine whether prices of products are too high or just right. We focus on what underlies the demand curve.

Answers to Chapterwide Practice Questions

Matching

1. d	5. j	8. e	11. b
2. i	6. l	9. g	12. h
3. c	7. a	10. k	13. m
4. f			

Fill-In

1. quantity demanded, price, elastic, unitary elastic, inelastic
2. elastic, inelastic, elastic
3. rise, fall, fall, rise
4. luxury, normal, inferior
5. substitutes, complements
6. elastic, inelastic, time, long run, market period, short run
7. inelastic, elastic

True-False

1. T	6. F	11. T	16. F
2. T	7. F	12. F	17. T
3. F	8. T	13. F	18. T
4. F	9. T	14. F	19. T
5. F	10. T	15. T	

Multiple Choice

1. b	8. c	14. a	20. a
2. a	9. c	15. b	21. a
3. a	10. c	16. c	22. b
4. a	11. a	17. b	23. a
5. c	12. d	18. c	24. d
6. d	13. b	19. d	25. a
7. a			

Essay-Problem

1. Although price elasticity of demand for newspapers in general is highly inelastic, we have to look at the possibility of substitutes for a specialized newspaper like the *Wall Street Journal*. Eventually, readers of the *Wall Street Journal* will question whether the premium price is worth it, and they will look at substitutes such as the *New York Times*, which has a large business section, though not as extensive as the *Wall Street Journal*. Furthermore, as the *New York Times* senses discontent, it will increase its business coverage. A price increase would increase total revenue in the short run, but might backfire in the long run. And continual price increases would exacerbate the problem. Additionally, newspapers in general—like gasoline—have an inelastic demand, but specific brands have more elastic demands.

2. Laptops sell for $1,000, and mainframes can sell for hundreds of thousands of dollars. A small change in the price of mainframes may be more than the total cost of a laptop. If we are going to compare the relative changes, we need a number that allows for this huge difference in price. Elasticity, measured in percentage terms, lets us directly compare changes in differently priced products.

3. The cup of coffee is the most price inelastic—we are more likely to do without cappuccino than coffee altogether, since cappuccino is more expensive. As to whether cappuccino or Starbucks cappuccino is more price elastic, that depends on the relative prices of the two: Starbucks cappuccino is likely to be more expensive than grocery store cappuccino, but it might be less expensive than a fancy restaurant's cappuccino.

4. We would expect the sweater would be most expensive at Banana Republic since the stores—all part of The Gap empire—can be placed on the price spectrum from (most expensive to least expensive) Banana Republic to The GAP to Old Navy. Therefore, we would expect the sweater at Banana Republic to be most price elastic. But we could be wrong: It is possible that the demand curve for all three stores is similar, and more substitutes are available on the low end rather than the high end, so it may be that the Old Navy sweater is most price elastic of the three.

5. No. Take a look at Figure 4 in the text again. In the elastic range, lowering price will increase total revenue. But if the price is in the inelastic range and the firm lowers the price, total revenue actually will fall. This is why it is important for firms to estimate the elasticity for their products.

6. Beans, ramen noodles, hot dogs. The key thing here is to consider goods you buy when budgets are very tight, but that you would avoid if you had more money.

7. Coach handbags and Burberry scarves.

8. Economists use, for example, the ability to change plant capacity to determine the long run, but industries differ in the amount of time needed to change plant capacity. A computer chip plant may take years to build, so a one-year short-run–long-run limitation would be incorrect for this industry. In other industries, actual building may not take long, but, say, obtaining the necessary environmental clearance may take years. Therefore, the definition must fit the particular situation and so must remain adjustable.

9. Governments might put forward the "sin tax" argument for taxing something such as cigarettes ("they are bad for you") as a way of obtaining popular support for such a tax, but it is a little harder to make that argument for gasoline. The answer is that gasoline and cigarettes have relatively inelastic demands, so increases in the tax have little effect on quantity demanded, which means that in the short run at least, tax revenues will be substantial and reasonably predictable.

10. Here is where elasticity's usefulness as a concept can be seen. Even though a tax might be levied on a producer of a good and so paid by the producer, if price elasticity of demand is relatively inelastic, this tax can be shifted to the consumer in the form of higher prices. So the producer might pay the tax to the government, then recoup almost all of the payment by obtaining higher prices from consumers.

Consumer Choice and Demand

6

The Important Logic of Consumer Choice

Supply and demand analysis is based on the premise that consumers and producers make rational decisions about what they want and what they will produce. This chapter looks at the choices that we as consumers make, and the next chapter focuses on producers. You will see how the two major theories for understanding how consumers make choices will give you a better sense of what demand really is and how you go about making product selections every day.

This Is What You Need to Know

STEP 1

After studying this chapter you should be able to

- Use a budget line to determine the constraints on consumer choices.
- Describe the difference between total and marginal utility.
- Describe the law of diminishing marginal utility.
- Understand consumer surplus.
- Use marginal utility analysis to derive demand curves.

Review the Key Terms

STEP 2

Marginal utility analysis: A theoretical framework underlying consumer decision making. This approach assumes that satisfaction can be measured and that consumers maximize satisfaction when the marginal utilities per dollar are equal for all products and services.

Budget line: Graphically illustrates the possible combinations of two goods that can be purchased with a given income, given the prices of both products.

Utility: A hypothetical measure of consumer satisfaction.

Total utility: The total satisfaction that a person receives from consuming a given amount of goods and services.

Marginal utility: The satisfaction received from consuming an additional unit of a given product or service.

Law of diminishing marginal utility: As we consume more of a given product, the added satisfaction we get from consuming an additional unit declines.

Utility maximizing rule: Utility is maximized where the marginal utility per dollar is equal for all products, or $MU_a/P_a = MU_b/P_b = \ldots = MU_n/P_n$.

Consumer surplus: The difference between what consumers would be willing to pay and what they actually pay for a product in the market.

STEP 3   Work Through the Chapter Tutorials

Marginal Utility Analysis

Frequently Asked Questions

Q: **What is the budget line, and why is it important for consumer decisions?**

A: Because consumer budgets are limited, consumption decisions often require making tradeoffs. More of one good can be purchased only if less of another is bought. The budget line shown in Figure 1 graphically represents both this outer limit on consumption decisions and the various combinations of goods that can be purchased with this given level of income, in this case two goods (pizza and wall climbing).

FIGURE 1

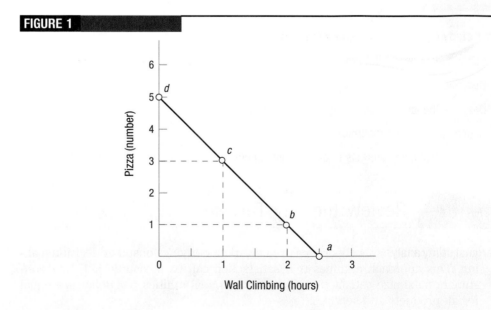

Wall Climbing (hours)

Q: What is utility?

A: The *utility* of a product is a hypothetical measure of how much satisfaction a consumer derives from the product. Though it can't be measured directly like weight or length, economists estimate the utility of various products at different levels of consumption to understand consumer preference and predict consumer behavior. The standard unit of utility is the *util*.

Q: How are total utility and marginal utility defined?

A: *Total utility* is the entire amount of satisfaction a consumer derives from consuming some product; it is equal to the sum of the utility derived from the consumption of each individual unit of this product. *Marginal utility* is the amount of utility derived from consuming one more unit of a given product. As a person consumes more units of a product, marginal utility will change. Consuming the fifth unit of a product may lead to a different increase in total utility than did consuming the third unit. Figure 2 graphs total utility and marginal utility for two particular goods. Note how total utility keeps rising but marginal utility falls.

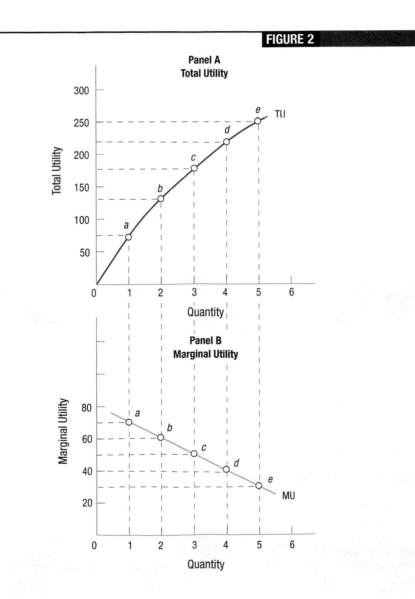

FIGURE 2

Q: What is the law of diminishing marginal utility?

A: The *law of diminishing marginal utility* states that as more units of any product are consumed, marginal utility will decline. Panel B of Figure 2 shows this law of diminishing marginal utility.

Q: How does marginal utility help us understand consumer decision making?

A: Marginal utility analysis provides a theoretical framework that economists use to understand how consumers make their consumption decisions among different products at varying price levels.

Q: How do consumers maximize their satisfaction with their limited income?

A: Marginal utility analysis reasons that consumers try to maximize utility within limited budgets by adjusting their spending to the point where the marginal utility derived from the last dollar spent on any product is equal to the marginal utility from the last dollar spent on other products. So for products a, b, c, through n, the consumer utility maximizing condition is

$$\frac{MU_a}{P_a} = \frac{MU_b}{P_b} = \frac{MU_c}{P_c} = \cdots = \frac{MU_n}{P_n}$$

In reality, the applicability of marginal utility theory is restricted. It assumes consumers can measure utility accurately and perform complex calculations of utility in their heads. Despite this drawback, marginal utility theory provides economists with a reasonable approach to how consumers make decisions about consumption choices with limited budgets.

Marginal Utility Analysis Quick Check

Circle the Correct Answer

1. (T/F) A consumer's budget line with two products graphs the consumer's budget and the market supply of the two products.
2. (T/F) The law of diminishing marginal utility states that marginal utility will fall as more units of a product are consumed.
3. (T/F) Economists believe that utility is readily observable and measurable.
4. (T/F) Marginal utility is the satisfaction a consumer derives from an additional unit of some product consumed.
5. If the utility derived from consuming the first unit is 12; from the second unit, 10; from the third unit, 8; from the fourth unit, 6; and from the fifth unit, 4; then the total utility derived from consuming four units is
   a. 6
   b. 4
   c. 36
   d. 40
6. Using marginal utility analysis, consumers maximize their satisfaction when they
   a. are able to get much more of one product than another.
   b. are able to get credit and spend more than their current income.
   c. are completely satiated.
   d. spend their income in such a way that the marginal utilities per dollar are equal for all products.

Complete the table below and use it to answer questions 7 and 8.

7. Assume a $20 food budget, spent in $4 increments. Bread costs $4 a loaf, and cereal costs $4 a box. Utility will be maximized by consuming which of the following?
   a. 1 loaf of bread and 2 boxes of cereal
   b. 2 loaves of bread and 3 boxes of cereal
   c. 3 loaves of bread and 2 boxes of cereal
   d. 4 loaves of bread and 1 boxes of cereal
8. The marginal utility per dollar for 3 boxes of cereal is
   a. 2.5
   b. 5.0
   c. 7.5
   d. 10.0
9. Marginal utility analysis assumes
   a. consumers make similar choices.
   b. consumers will consume products only when marginal utility rises; they will shun products when marginal utility falls.
   c. consumers try to maximize utility within limited budgets by adjusting their spending to the point where the utility derived from the last dollar spent on any product is equal to the utility from the last dollar spent on other products.
   d. marginal utility is generally the same for each unit consumed.
10. Total utility is which of the following?
   a. the utility a consumer receives from consuming a given number of units of the product
   b. the sum of the marginal utilities for a given number of units of the product
   c. generally grows at a diminishing rate as more of a given product is consumed
   d. all of the above

Score: _____

Total and Marginal Utility for Bread and Cereal

Bread				Cereal			
(1)	(2)	(3)	(4)	(5)	(6)	(7)	(8)
Quantity (loaves of bread)	Total Utility	Marginal Utility	Marginal Utility per Dollar (price = $4)	Quantity (boxes of cereal)	Total Utility	Marginal Utility	Marginal utility per Dollar (price = $4)
0	0	___	___	0	0	___	___
1	70	___	___	1	50	___	___
2	125	___	___	2	90	___	___
3	165	___	___	3	120	___	___
4	190	___	___	4	140	___	___
5	200	___	___	5	150	___	___

If You Got 9 or 10 Correct

You have a good grasp of the basics of marginal utility analysis. This is an important step in using the logic of utility analysis that follows in the next section.

If You Didn't Get at Least 9 Correct

▪ Go back and reread the first part of the chapter on the basics of marginal utility analysis.

▪ Take a few moments and look back at the questions you missed in the quiz. Some of these are difficult questions. They really test your knowledge of marginal utility analysis. Be sure you can answer them correctly before you go on.

Keep in Mind

One of the most important conclusions from marginal utility analysis is that utility (or consumer satisfaction) is maximized when the marginal utilities per dollar are equal for all products. Thus, if the price of one product rises, that product's ratio of marginal utility to price (MU/P) is now smaller, and consumers will now purchase less of that product. This makes marginal utility analysis consistent with the law of demand (quantity demanded is inversely related to prices). And further, this is how we derive demand curves with marginal utility analysis, discussed in the next section. ■

Core Equation: Utility Maximizing Equation

$$\frac{MU_a}{P_a} = \frac{MU_b}{P_b} = \frac{MU_c}{P_c} = \dots = \frac{MU_n}{P_n}$$

Solved Problem: Utility Maximization

Here we solve question 7 in the Quick Check on the previous pages. You were asked to complete the table and solve where utility was maximized given a $20 food budget, spent in $4 increments where both a loaf of bread and a box of cereal cost $4 each. The table is completed below:

Bread				Cereal			
(1) Quantity (loaves of bread)	(2) Total Utility	(3) Marginal Utility	(4) Marginal Utility per Dollar (price = $4)	(5) Quantity (boxes of cereal)	(6) Total Utility	(7) Marginal Utility	(8) Marginal Utility per Dollar (price = $4)
0	0	—	—	0	0	—	—
1	70	70	17.5	1	50	50	12.5
2	125	55	13.8	2	90	40	10
3	165	40	10	3	120	30	7.5
4	190	25	6.25	4	140	20	5
5	200	10	2.5	5	150	10	2.5

Solution-Discussion

Columns 4 and 8 ($MU/\$$ for each good) are where the decisions are made. Consumers make decisions at the margin! Your first $4 will be spent on bread (17.5 > 12.5). The second $4 will again be spent on bread (again, 13.8 > 12.5), but the third $4 will go to cereal, because the marginal utility per dollar has dropped to 10 for bread. The last two $4 expenditures will be for both bread and cereal since both the third loaf of bread and the second box of cereal have a $MU/\$$ ratio of 10.

So, the solution is 3 loaves of bread and 2 boxes of cereal.

Now, how does the utility maximizing combination change when the price of cereal drops to $2 a box?

Discussion

The marginal utility per dollar figures in column 8 now double since the cost of cereal has been cut in half. Write these new figures out to the side of column 8. The first $4 will be spent on cereal, then 1 loaf of bread, then another loaf of bread, then 2 boxes of cereal, and finally another loaf of bread and another box of cereal. The new expenditure combination will be 3 loaves of bread and 4 boxes of cereal. Note that as the price of cereal fell, this consumer purchased more cereal, consistent with the law of demand.

It is time to move on, but know that you will have to go over this section again. As you progress through the next section, "Using Marginal Utility Analysis," which builds on this section, you may see how everything comes together. If not, review the marginal utility section carefully, and ask yourself if this is how you make choices between goods and services. Just how do you make the decision about whether to go to a movie or spend the time studying economics?

Using Marginal Utility Analysis

Frequently Asked Questions

Q: **What is consumer surplus, and how is it computed?**

A: *Consumer surplus* is the difference between what consumers would be willing to pay for a product and what they must actually pay for the product in the market. Figure 3 depicts this, where the equilibrium price is $20 per hour, and consumer surplus is the area in the shaded triangle *fdb.*

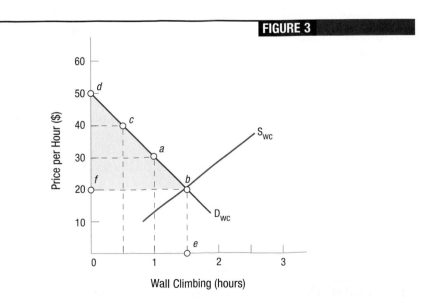

FIGURE 3

Using Marginal Utility Analysis Quick Check

1. (T/F) Demand curves derived from marginal utility analysis are *not* consistent with the law of demand.
2. (T/F) To derive a demand curve using marginal utility analysis, you have to be concerned with the total utility derived from each product per dollar.
3. Consumer surplus is
   a. the extra utility from consuming one more unit of the product.
   b. the difference between total and marginal utility.
   c. the difference between the price consumers would be willing to buy a good for and the price in the market.
   d. the difference between the price consumers would be willing to buy a good for and the good's marginal utility to the consumer.
4. If the price of one good falls, marginal utility analysis concludes that
   a. consumers will continue to make the same choices as before the price change.
   b. consumers will consume more of the products where prices are the same because they are more valuable now.

c. consumers try to maximize utility within limited budgets by buying more of the product that has fallen in price.
   d. consumers will ignore the price change because all that matters is the size of marginal utility from consuming a particular product.
5. What is a serious critique of marginal utility theory?
   a. It has limited ability to explain how consumers make choices.
   b. It has been refuted by the behavioral economists.
   c. Consumer demand curves cannot be derived using marginal utility analysis.
   d. A basic assumption is that consumers can measure the utility of all products they consume.

Score: ____

Answers: 1. F; 2. F; 3. c; 4. c; 5. d

You should have scored 4 or 5 correct in this exercise. If you didn't, you will probably have to review this chapter again. Take a few moments and look at the "Hints, Tips, and Reminders" that follow. ■

STEP 4 — Consider These Hints, Tips, and Reminders

1. Treat the budget line as similar to the linear production possibilities frontier (PPF) we looked at in Chapter 2. Along (and on) the budget line you are spending all of your income on some mix of the two goods. You can't spend beyond the budget constraint, and at points inside you are spending less than your total income (saving some). Keep in mind that your total income divided by the price of a product represents the most of one product you can buy, and these are the end points of the budget line.

2. This chapter really brings home the "thinking at the margin" concept discussed in Chapter 1. How do you decide to eat or buy *one more* piece of pizza? The answer is that you weigh the benefits to the costs, or *MU/P*. Marginal utility is the benefit and price is the cost. And most important, you do this kind of calculation for each additional piece you eat or buy.

3. So, each step in the consumer maximizing equation,

$$MU_a/P_a = MU_b/P_b = \ldots = MU_n/P_n$$

is really a series of incremental steps. The simple story is that you purchase that product first where *MU/P* is the highest, and then proceed to purchase that product with the highest ratio next, and so on until your budget is exhausted. Don't let the equation throw you; it is a simple "getting the *most* for your money" process.

4. Computing consumer surplus can often appear daunting, but it is really very easy. First, let's remind ourselves that consumer surplus is the amount above market price we would be willing to pay for a product and is equal to the area under the demand curve but above market price (the shaded area in Figure 4). The actual calculation of consumer surplus is straightforward if we remember one simple trick shown in the figure. If market price is $10 (point *e*) and 8 units are purchased, consumer surplus can be computed as follows: The shaded triangle (consumer surplus) is equal to *one half* of the dashed rectangle, and that rectangle is equal to ($30 − $10) × 8 = $20 × 8 = $160. Thus, consumer surplus is equal to one half of $160 or $80.

FIGURE 4

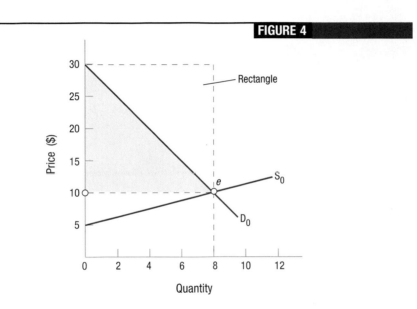

Do the Homework for Chapter 6 Consumer Choice and Demand	STEP 5

Instructor _____ Time _____ Student _____

Use the answer key below to record your answers to these homework questions.

1. (a) (b) (c) (d)	6. (a) (b) (c) (d)	11. (a) (b) (c) (d)	16. (a) (b) (c) (d)
2. (a) (b) (c) (d)	7. (a) (b) (c) (d)	12. (a) (b) (c) (d)	17. (a) (b) (c) (d)
3. (a) (b) (c) (d)	8. (a) (b) (c) (d)	13. (a) (b) (c) (d)	18. (a) (b) (c) (d)
4. (a) (b) (c) (d)	9. (a) (b) (c) (d)	14. (a) (b) (c) (d)	19. (a) (b) (c) (d)
5. (a) (b) (c) (d)	10. (a) (b) (c) (d)	15. (a) (b) (c) (d)	20. (a) (b) (c) (d)

1. Utility theory or utilitarianism developed by Jeremy Bentham
   a. looks at which products people purchase and then uses this information to determine how prices are determined.
   b. argues that utility or satisfaction cannot be measured accurately enough to be useful in analyzing consumer decisions.
   c. uses indifference curves to explain how consumers would maximize their satisfaction.
   d. developed a theory of consumer choice based on allocating limited resources to maximize happiness (utility).

2. The budget line or constraint shows
   a. the amount of money you have to spend if that raise is forthcoming.
   b. the amount of money you have to spend after retirement savings are deducted.
   c. a couple of combinations of goods and services that can be purchased given prices and expected future income after you graduate.
   d. the possible purchasing combinations of two goods given your limited income.

3. Assume the budget line or constraint shown in Figure HW-1 represents your weekly budget. If pizzas go for $5 each, your weekly budget is which of the following?
   a. $75
   b. $100
   c. $125
   d. $150

4. Assume the budget line or constraint shown in Figure HW-1 represents your weekly budget. If pizzas go for $5 each, how much do music CDs cost?
   a. $7.50
   b. $10.00
   c. $12.50
   d. $15.00

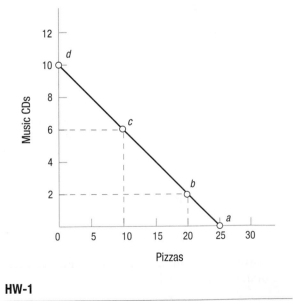

HW-1

5. The law of diminishing marginal utility states that
   a. satisfaction for consuming more of a good is often low and then rises as more and more units of that good are consumed.
   b. total utility will drop as soon as you consume the second unit of a product.
   c. utility can be measured.
   d. the gains to total utility from consuming additional units of a product declines.

6. To maximize their total utility, consumers should
   a. allocate their budget between goods so that the marginal utilities per dollar are equal for the last units purchased.
   b. spend their money so that each product has the same total utility as all others.
   c. buy amount of each good up to the point where diminishing marginal utility sets in.
   d. allocate their budget between goods so that the total utilities per dollar are just equal for the last units purchased.

7. Consumer surplus is
   a. the maximum amount of a product you will buy for a particular price, all other relevant factors held constant.
   b. that level of consumption where the next unit consumed adds less utility to total utility than the last unit consumed.
   c. the situation where you are indifferent to two different levels of consumption of two goods.
   d. the difference between what you would be willing to pay for a product and what you must actually pay.

8. Marginal utility will
   a. equal total utility for the last unit consumed.
   b. rise with every unit of the product consumed.
   c. remain unchanged with every unit of the product consumed.
   d. diminish with every unit of the product consumed.

Use the table below to answer questions 9–12.

Trail Mix		Oranges	
Quantity (pounds)	Total Utility	Quantity (pounds)	Total Utility
0	0	0	0
1	140	1	100
2	250	2	180
3	330	3	240
4	380	4	280
5	400	5	300

9. The marginal utility of the fourth pound of oranges is which of the following?
   a. 280
   b. 50
   c. 40
   d. 10

10. Assume that you have $8 to spend, trail mix and oranges each cost $4 per pound, and you can only buy these commodities in 1-pound increments. What mix of these goods would you purchase to maximize utility?
    a. 1 pound of trail mix and 1 pound of oranges
    b. 1 pound of oranges
    c. 2 pounds of trail mix
    d. 1 pound of trail mix

11. Assume that you have $20 to spend, trail mix and oranges each cost $4 per pound, and you can only buy these commodities in 1-pound increments. What mix of these goods would you purchase to maximize utility?
    a. 1 pound of trail mix and 4 pounds of oranges
    b. 2 pounds of oranges and 3 pounds of trail mix
    c. 2 pounds of trail mix and 3 pounds of oranges
    d. 4 pounds of trail mix and 1 pound of oranges

12. Assume that you have $20 to spend, trail mix and oranges each cost $4 per pound, and you can only buy these commodities in 1-pound increments. What will be the maximum total utility possible given these limitations?
    a. 420 utils
    b. 510 utils
    c. 570 utils
    d. 160 utils

Use Figure HW-2 to answer questions 13 and 14.

13. When market supply is equal to S_0, consumer surplus is equal to
    a. $1,050
    b. $1,075
    c. $1,100
    d. $1,125

14. Increasing resource cost results in supply declining from S_0 to S_1. Consumer surplus has been *reduced* by how much?
    a. $600
    b. $625
    c. $650
    d. $675

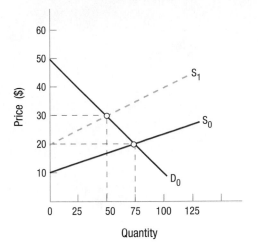

HW-2

15. Marginal utility helps explain how consumers select goods and services to purchase, but it faces some criticisms, including the following:
    a. Consumers usually buy more than two goods.
    b. Marginal utility analysis is judged to be too elegant and logical.
    c. It assumes that consumers are able to measure the utility they get from the products they consume.
    d. It doesn't help explain consumer surplus.

Note to Student: There are 15 questions in this homework assignment.

Use the ExamPrep to Get Ready for Exams	STEP 6

This sheet (front and back) is designed to help you prepare for your exams. The chapter has been boiled down to its key concepts. You are asked to answer questions, define terms, draw graphs, and, if you wish, add summaries of class notes.

Marginal Utility Analysis

Define the following terms:

Utility:

Marginal Utility:

Describe the law of diminishing marginal utility:

Describe the process of maximizing utility and the simple equation used to describe the utility maximization process:

Consumer Surplus

Use the grid below to illustrate consumer surplus:

Describe the concept of consumer surplus:

Describe some of the problems and limitations of marginal utility analysis:

Additional Study Help Chapterwide Practice Questions

Matching

Match the description with the corresponding term.

___ 1. Budget line
___ 2. Utility
___ 3. Total utility
___ 4. Marginal utility
___ 5. Law of diminishing marginal utility
___ 6. Marginal utility analysis

a. The amount of utility derived from consuming one more unit of a product.
b. Shows the different combinations of goods that can be purchased at a given level of income.
c. As more of any product is consumed, marginal utility declines.
d. A hypothetical measure of consumer satisfaction.
e. The entire satisfaction a consumer derives from consuming some product.
f. This framework for understanding consumer choices assumes consumers try to maximize the utility they receive on their limited budgets, by adjusting their spending to the point where the utility derived from the last dollar spent on any product is equal to the utility from the last dollar spent on other products.

Fill-In

Circle the word(s) in parentheses that complete the sentence.

1. The total satisfaction people receive from products and services is called (total, marginal, average) _____ utility, and the satisfaction received from consuming one more unit of the product is called (total, marginal, average) _____. The law of diminishing marginal utility implies that (total, marginal, average) _____ utility will decline.

2. Consumers maximize utility by purchasing goods up to the point were the marginal utility per dollar is (highest, equal, lowest) _____ for all goods.

3. Consumer surplus grows as prices (rise, fall, remain the same) _____, and it will (rise, fall, remain the same) _____ when prices rise.

True-False

Circle the correct answer.

T/F 1. A budget line graphically represents the various combinations of two goods a consumer can afford on a particular budget.

T/F 2. A rise in income will push a consumer's budget line out and to the right.

T/F 3. Utility is something that is easily measured, like weight or length.

T/F 4. If a consumer purchases 5 units of a product, her marginal utility is the utility she derives from consuming all 5 units.

T/F 5. If a consumer prefers peaches to bananas, he can be sure to maximize his total utility by devoting his entire fruit budget to peaches, and none to bananas.

T/F 6. The law of diminishing marginal utility suggests that the consumer surplus from each additional purchase will eventually disappear as ever more units of some good are consumed.

T/F 7. Consumers can be expected to maximize their utility by spending each dollar of their limited budgets on the goods that provide them with the highest marginal utility per dollar.

Multiple Choice

Circle the correct answer.

1. To economists, utility is
a. a readily observable and measurable property of consumer goods.
b. equivalent to a product's equilibrium price.
c. a hypothetical measure of consumer satisfaction.
d. a measure of the energy costs going into the production of a particular good.

2. Total utility is:
a. the satisfaction a consumer derives from the last unit of some product consumed.
b. the satisfaction a consumer derives from all of the units of some product consumed.

c. the satisfaction a consumer derives from receiving a consumer surplus.

d. something that doesn't change for each successive unit consumed.

3. Marginal utility is

a. the satisfaction a consumer derives from an additional unit of some product consumed.

b. the satisfaction a consumer derives from all of the units of some product consumed.

c. equivalent to consumer surplus.

d. something that is constant for each unit consumed.

4. Marginal utility will

a. diminish with every additional unit consumed.

b. rise indefinitely with every unit consumed.

c. remain constant for each unit consumed.

d. be of little use to economists in understanding consumer behavior, since it cannot be precisely measured.

Questions 5–9 refer to the table below. Complete the table. Assume that you have a $10 budget, and music downloads and poor boy sandwiches cost $2 each.

5. How will you spend your $10 budget to maximize utility?

a. 4 music downloads and 1 poor boy sandwich

b. 3 music downloads and 2 poor boy sandwiches

c. 2 music downloads and 3 poor boy sandwiches

d. 1 music download and 4 poor boy sandwiches

6. What is the marginal utility for the third music download?

a. 10

b. 20

c. 30

d. 40

7. What is the marginal utility per dollar for the fourth poor boy sandwich?

a. 5

b. 10

c. 15

d. 20

8. If the price of poor boy sandwiches doubles to $4, how many will you purchase to maximize utility?

a. 1

b. 2

c. 3

d. none

9. If the price of music downloads drops to $1 (poor boy sandwiches are still $2), how many music downloads will you purchase?

a. 1

b. 2

c. 3

d. 4

10. The difference between what consumers would be willing to pay for a product and what they must actually pay for the product in the market is known as which of the following?

a. the indifference curve

b. marginal utility

c. consumer surplus

d. optimal consumer choice

11. If you would be willing to spend $20 to purchase your first CD, but CDs cost only $15 each, your consumer surplus on that first CD would be

a. $5

b. $15

c. $20

d. unknowable without further information

Total and Marginal Utility for Music Downloads and Poor Boy Sandwiches

Music Downloads				Poor Boy Sandwiches			
(1) Quantity (downloads)	(2) Total Utility	(3) Marginal Utility	(4) Marginal Utility per Dollar (price = $2)	(5) Quantity (poor boy sandwiches)	(6) Total Utility	(7) Marginal Utility	(8) Marginal Utility per Dollar (price = $2)
0	0	___	___	0	0	___	___
1	80	___	___	1	50	___	___
2	140	___	___	2	90	___	___
3	180	___	___	3	120	___	___
4	200	___	___	4	140	___	___
5	210	___	___	5	150	___	___

12. Assume that you would be willing to spend $25 to purchase your first CD, $20 to purchase the second, and $15 for the third. The market price for CDs is $15 each. Thus, your consumer surplus on your purchase of three CDs would be
    a. $5
    b. $10
    c. $15
    d. $20

13. Which of the following assumptions does marginal utility analysis *not* make?
    a. Consumers will seek to maximize their utility in making their purchasing decisions.
    b. All consumers have similar tastes and preferences.
    c. Consumers are able to accurately measure utility.
    d. Consumers are able to perform complex computations regarding utility in their heads.

14. Why is marginal utility theory not entirely satisfactory?
    a. It doesn't seem to fit actual consumer behavior.
    b. It assumes that consumers can measure the utility of consumption.
    c. It isn't helpful in understanding consumer choices.
    d. Its conclusions are contradicted by the law of demand.

Essay-Problem

Answer in the space provided.

The questions below can be challenging but are designed to improve your understanding of consumer choice. Don't get discouraged if your answers are not always the same as those we suggest. Use these as another way to assess your progress, but more important, to discover and learn some of the subtleties surrounding consumer choice and demand.

1. What is the essence of consumer choice theory?

2. Do young children follow the law of diminishing marginal utility?

3. Can marginal utility ever be negative?

4. The Cabbage Patch Kids were a hot toy and some parents reportedly flew to London to obtain the doll. Considering this doll fad, do you think there ever could be consumer surplus more than twice the price of a product?

5. Why are dollars a good proxy for utils?

6. To use marginal utility theory, do we have to assume that people act rationally all of the time?

7. Is the thought of people with internal utility calculators so silly that we should abandon marginal utility analysis?

What's Next

This chapter gives you a good understanding of what lies behind demand: consumers making rational decisions about how particular products add to their satisfaction. In the next chapter, we look at what lies behind supply, with how producers decide how much of any product to provide to the market. We saw that the assumptions behind marginal utility analysis are a little far-fetched. This does not, however, negate the usefulness of the analysis. Just be aware of what demand analysis rests on.

Answers to Chapterwide Practice Questions

Matching

1. b
2. d
3. e
4. a
5. c
6. f

Fill-In

1. total, marginal, marginal
2. equal
3. fall, fall

True-False

1. T	3. F	5. F	7. T
2. T	4. F	6. T	

Multiple Choice

1. c	3. a	4. a	5. b
2. b			

Total and Marginal Utility for Music Downloads and Poor Boy Sandwiches

Music Downloads				Poor Boy Sandwiches			
(1)	(2)	(3)	(4)	(5)	(6)	(7)	(8)
Quantity (downloads)	Total Utility	Marginal Utility	Marginal Utility per Dollar (price = $2)	Quantity (poor boy sandwiches)	Total Utility	Marginal Utility	Marginal Utility per Dollar (price = $2)
0	0	—	—	0	0	—	—
1	80	80	40	1	50	50	25
2	140	60	30	2	90	40	20
3	180	40	20	3	120	30	15
4	200	20	10	4	140	20	10
5	210	10	5	5	150	10	5

6. d	9. d	11. a	13. b
7. b	10. c	12. c	14. b
8. a			

Essay-Problem

1. Consumers make product choices in some rational way.
2. Even children follow the law of diminishing marginal utility, though the number of times they may say "more" leads one to think that marginal utility falls slower than it would with an adult. Just how many times can one watch the *Bambi* movie without getting bored?
3. Yes. Consider eating ice cream on a hot day. The first ice cream may be wonderful. So may the second. Eventually (possibly after the 15th cone), if ice cream makes you violently sick, total utility will have gone down at that point, so marginal utility for that unit will be negative.
4. Yes. To calculate consumer surplus in this case, the cost of the airfare has to be added in to the actual price paid for a Cabbage Patch Kid doll; this puts consumer surplus many times greater than the doll. There is no defined limit to how high consumer surplus may be.
5. We normally think of utility in terms of goods purchased. Since the purchase price is given in dollars, we can think of a dollar as equal to one util (we could also think of $1 = 100 utils rather than 1 util, but this is just a case of scale).
6. No. People act irrationally every day. But they do not act irrationally a large part of the time, so marginal utility analysis is useful as a conceptual device.
7. No. As silly as this aspect of marginal utility analysis may appear, the general usefulness of the analysis remains. The theory has strong predictive power as to how consumers make choices. We may be bothered by the thought of people as calculators; this should spur economists to come up with better theories, not abandon theories that are useful.

Appendix: Indifference Curve Analysis

The Important Logic of Consumer Choice

Marginal utility analysis requires that utility be measured and that marginal utility per dollar be computed for each product. Indifference curve analysis only assumes that consumers can distinguish between bundles of goods and services and select those they prefer. With this analysis, satisfaction (or utility) does not have to be explicitly measured.

This Is What You Need to Know

After studying this appendix you should be able to

- Understand the properties of indifference curves and preference maps.

- Use indifference curves to derive demand curves and measure income and substitution effects.

Review the Key Terms

Indifference curve: Shows all combinations of two goods where the consumer is indifferent (gets the same level of satisfaction).

Indifference map: An infinite set of indifference curves where each curve represents a different level of utility or satisfaction.

Income effect: When higher prices essentially reduce consumer income, the quantity demanded for normal goods falls.

157

Substitution effect: When the price of one good rises, consumers will substitute other goods for that good, so the quantity demanded for the higher-priced good falls.

STEP 3   Work Through the Appendix Tutorial

Frequently Asked Questions

Q: **What are indifference curves?**

A: *Indifference curve analysis* seeks to avoid the problems with measurement faced by marginal utility analysis. The *indifference curve* graphically represents all the combinations of two products that provide the same level of satisfaction to consumers. The indifference curve identifies a set of possible consumption combinations that leaves the consumer indifferent (equally satisfied).

Q: **How are indifference curves used to determine consumer purchases?**

A: Indifference curve analysis helps economists understand how consumers allocate their limited budgets among diverse goods. Figure APX-1 has three indifference curves superimposed over a budget line, with two products considered. Note that the optimum point is where the budget line is just tangent at one point to an indifference curve.

FIGURE APX-1

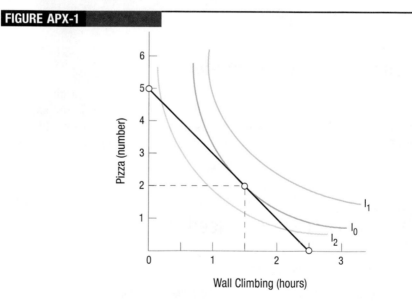

Q: **Why use indifference curve analysis?**

A: Indifference curve analysis leads to the same theoretical conclusions as marginal utility analysis but is subject to fewer restrictive assumptions. It does not require that consumers measure utility or calculate marginal utility per dollar, but only that consumers be able to decide which bundles of goods they would prefer to consume under varying circumstances.

Q: **What is the income effect of a price change?**

A: The *income effect* is a change in quantity demanded that comes as a result of a change in income due to a change in price. When the price of some regularly purchased good rises, this leaves consumers with less money to spend buying goods of all sorts. The rise in price therefore effectively reduces consumer income, resulting in a drop in quantity demanded for most normal goods.

Q: **What is the substitution effect?**

A: When the price of some good rises, quantity demanded for the good will typically fall as consumers begin purchasing cheaper substitute products; this is the
substitution effect. Note that when the price of a product rises, quantity
demanded for it will typically fall, partially due to the income effect and partially due to the substitution effect; indifference curve analysis helps us determine how much of this drop in demand is due to each effect.

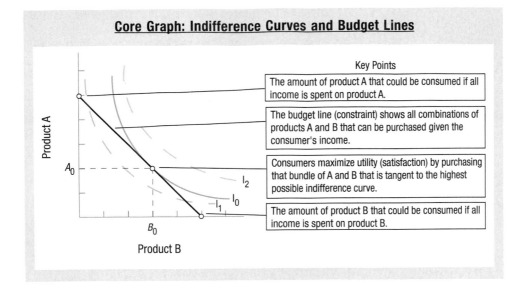

Core Graph: Indifference Curves and Budget Lines

Key Points

The amount of product A that could be consumed if all income is spent on product A.

The budget line (constraint) shows all combinations of products A and B that can be purchased given the consumer's income.

Consumers maximize utility (satisfaction) by purchasing that bundle of A and B that is tangent to the highest possible indifference curve.

The amount of product B that could be consumed if all income is spent on product B.

Indifference Curve Analysis Quick Check

Circle the Correct Answer

1. (T/F) Indifference curve analysis assumes that people can choose between different bundles of goods without calculating the total utility of each bundle.
2. (T/F) Because of the law of diminishing marginal utility, indifference curves are *not* straight lines.
3. (T/F) Consumer satisfaction is maximized where two indifference curves intersect.
4. To maximize satisfaction on a limited budget, consumers must make choices
   a. at the point where two indifference curves intersect.
   b. on the indifference curve that cuts the budget line twice.
   c. on the indifference curve that is tangent to the budget line.
   d. anywhere on indifference curves that are above the budget line.

5. If the price of heating oil rises during the winter, con-sumers will purchase less of other goods because of
   a. the substitution effect.
   b. the income effect.
   c. the law of diminishing marginal utility.
   d. changes in tastes and preferences.
6. If the price of J. Crew sweaters goes up, and consumers purchase fewer J. Crew sweaters and more Gap sweaters, this is an example of
   a. the substitution effect.
   b. the income effect.
   c. the law of diminishing marginal utility.
   d. changes in tastes and preferences.
7. An indifference curve is
   a. concave (bowed out) to the origin because of the law of diminishing marginal utility.
   b. concave to the origin because of the law of indiffer-ence curves.

c. convex (bowed in) to the origin because of the law of diminishing marginal utility.

d. convex to the origin because of the law of substitution.

Use Figure APX-2 to answer question 8.

FIGURE APX-2

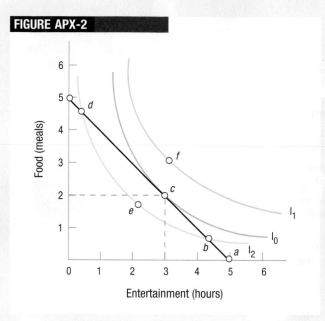

8. Satisfaction for this consumer would be maximized
   a. anywhere on indifference curve l_1.
   b. at either point b or point d on l_2.
   c. at point c on l_0.
   d. anywhere on the budget line.

9. If the price of gasoline goes up and you take an airplane to Disney World rather than drive, this would be an example of
   a. the income effect.
   b. the substitution effect.
   c. the law of diminishing marginal utility.
   d. the law of supply.

10. Indifference curve analysis is preferred to marginal utility analysis because
    a. it is easier to draw indifference curves than to fill in marginal utility tables.
    b. it deals with bundles of goods while marginal utility analysis can only deal with two goods.
    c. it is more scientific.
    d. it does not require that consumers measure utility for innumerable possible consumption choices.

Score: _____

Answers: 1. T; 2. T; 3. F; 4. c; 5. b; 6. a; 7. c; 8. c; 9. b; 10. d

If You Got 9 or 10 Correct

You have mastered a tough concept. Indifference curve analysis is the modern method of determining consumer preferences, deriving demand curves, and analyzing many different issues involving decision making.

If You Didn't Get at Least 9 Correct

Take a moment and go back and review the Appendix at the end of this chapter. Pay particular attention to the uniqueness of indifference curves and how, combined with the budget line, consumer choice is determined. Finally, spend a few moments and review those questions you missed to make sure you know why you missed them. Missing questions can be helpful—you won't make that same mistake again! ■

STEP 4   ## Consider These Hints, Tips, and Reminders

1. Keep in mind that indifference curve analysis essentially leads us to the same conclusions as marginal utility analysis without the restrictive assumptions that consumers can actually measure utility.

2. The other advantage of indifference curves is that the concept is easily applied to many other areas as the terrorist example suggests. The indifference concept is more widely applicable than marginal utility.

Do the Homework for Chapter 6 Appendix
Indifference Curve Analysis

Instructor _____ Time _____ Student _____

Use the answer key below to record your answers to these homework questions.

1. (a) (b) (c) (d)   6. (a) (b) (c) (d)   11. (a) (b) (c) (d)   16. (a) (b) (c) (d)

2. (a) (b) (c) (d)   7. (a) (b) (c) (d)   12. (a) (b) (c) (d)   17. (a) (b) (c) (d)

3. (a) (b) (c) (d)   8. (a) (b) (c) (d)   13. (a) (b) (c) (d)   18. (a) (b) (c) (d)

4. (a) (b) (c) (d)   9. (a) (b) (c) (d)   14. (a) (b) (c) (d)   19. (a) (b) (c) (d)

5. (a) (b) (c) (d)   10. (a) (b) (c) (d)   15. (a) (b) (c) (d)   20. (a) (b) (c) (d)

1. Which of the following is *not* a property of indifference curves?
   a. They slope upward and to the right.
   b. They are subject to the law of diminishing marginal utility.
   c. They have a negative slope.
   d. They are convex (bowed in) to the origin.

Use Figure HW APX-1 to answer questions 2–4.

2. Looking at indifference curve I_0, what can we say about points a and d?
   a. Neither is very desirable to the consumer.
   b. The consumer would rather be at point b than at points d or a.
   c. The consumer is indifferent between the two bundles of commodities.
   d. The consumer would prefer to be at point e rather than at point a or d.

3. What can we say about point e?
   a. It is preferred to points a and d.
   b. All points on I_0 are preferred to point e.
   c. It is preferred to all other points noted in the figure.
   d. The consumer will select point e over point f.

4. What can we say about point f?
   a. It is preferred to points a and d.
   b. All points on I_0 are preferred to point f.
   c. It is not preferred to all other points on I_0.
   d. The consumer will select point e over point f.

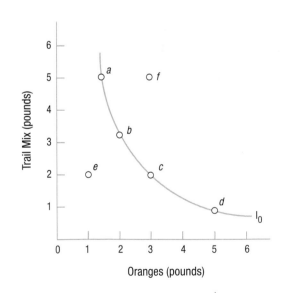

HW APX-1

5. Indifference curves are used to
   a. measure total utility of two bundles of goods.
   b. derive demand curves.
   c. determine why consumers prefer luxury goods to necessities.
   d. evaluate marketing campaigns for expensive products and services.

6. Maximizing satisfaction using indifference curves requires that consumers
   a. measure utility and purchase where the marginal utility per dollar is maximized.
   b. focus their consumption on that one good that provides the highest level of satisfaction.
   c. find that point where two indifference curves intersect.
   d. select that combination of goods that is on the highest possible indifference curve given the consumer's budget constraint.

7. If the price of oil jumps from $50 a barrel to $100, and consumers reduce their purchases of many other goods, this would be an example of
   a. the substitution effect.
   b. the income effect.
   c. the budget effect.
   d. the indifference curve effect.

Note to Student: There are 10 questions in this homework assignment.

8. If the price of oil jumps from $50 a barrel to $100 and consumers take fewer long distance vacations, this would be an example of
   a. the substitution effect.
   b. the income effect.
   c. the budget effect.
   d. the indifference curve effect.

9. Indifference curve analysis is generally preferred to marginal utility analysis because
   a. consumers measure utility and purchase where the marginal utility per dollar is maximized.
   b. it does not require that consumers actually measure utility.
   c. it is easier to understand intuitively.
   d. it is newer analysis than marginal utility analysis.

10. Indifference curves do not cross because
   a. at the point where they cross, consumer income could not be determined.
   b. each point on any indifference curve represents different levels of income.
   c. marginal utility cannot be measured at this point.
   d. each indifference curve represents different levels of satisfaction, and the point where they cross would be inconsistent with this assumption.

| Use the ExamPrep to Get Ready for Exams | STEP 6 |

This sheet (front and back) is designed to help you prepare for your exams. The chapter has been boiled down to its key concepts. You are asked to answer questions, define terms, draw graphs, and, if you wish, add summaries of class notes.

Indifference Curve Analysis

Describe an indifference curve:

Describe the properties of indifference curves:

Deriving a Demand Curve

Use the blank grids to illustrate the following:

■ Draw a budget line in Panel A for two products.
■ In Panel A, draw an indifference map of three indifference curves.
■ Show the optimal consumer choice between these two goods.
■ Set up Panel B with output of the good on the horizontal axis and its price on the vertical axis of Panel B. (Hint: This should be the good on the horizontal axis of Panel A.)
■ Transfer the optimal consumer choice (both price and output) to Panel B.
■ Now change the price of the product shown in Panel B and shift the budget line in Panel A.
■ Show the new consumer equilibrium.
■ Show that new point in Panel B. Connect the points. You now have the demand curve.

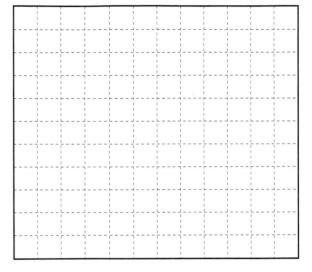

Panel A

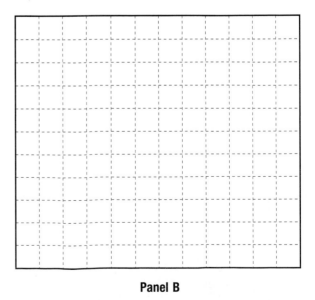

Panel B

Income and Substitution Effects

Describe the substitution effect:

Describe the income effect:

Additional Study Help Appendix Practice Questions

True-False

Circle the correct answer.

T/F   1. Two indifference curves for the same set of products will never intersect.

T/F   2. To say that a consumer is at a point of indifference between two bundles of goods means that she does not really want to purchase either bundle.

T/F   3. Indifference curves are bowed-in, or convex toward the origin, due to the law of diminishing marginal utility.

T/F   4. Maximizing satisfaction on limited income requires purchasing some bundle of goods on the highest possible indifference curve given your limited income.

T/F   5. A rise in the price of an essential consumer good such as food effectively reduces consumer incomes.

Multiple Choice

Circle the correct answer.

1. An indifference curve shows
   a. the quantity of a product a consumer would demand at various price levels.
   b. all combinations of two products that provide consumers with the same level of satisfaction.
   c. the level of supply at which producers are indifferent to whether or not they supply any additional units of a product.
   d. the level of spending at which consumers are indifferent to whether or not they purchase any more products.

2. An indifference curve has
   a. a positive slope and is convex to the origin.
   b. a positive slope and is concave to the origin.
   c. a negative slope and is convex to the origin.
   d. a negative slope and is concave to the origin.

3. Indifference curves can be used to derive
   a. measurements of total utility.
   b. demand curves.
   c. predictions regarding consumer incomes.
   d. supply curves.

4. A preference map contains
   a. a set of demand curves reflecting different levels of consumer income.

b. a set of indifference curves that intersect at strategic points.
   c. a set of indifference curves representing different levels of satisfaction.
   d. a set of supply curves representing the producer preference for supplying various goods at different price levels.

5. Maximizing satisfaction on a limited budget requires
   a. selecting a point on the highest possible indifference curve given a limited budget.
   b. selecting a point where two indifference curves cross.
   c. selecting one of two goods.
   d. selecting more of one good in exchange for more of another.

6. If consumers cut back on their purchases of many different goods because the price of heating oil has gone up, this behavior would be an example of
   a. the substitution effect.
   b. the energy effect.
   c. the environmental effect.
   d. the income effect.

7. If consumers purchase fewer cucumbers and more tomatoes because the price of cucumbers has gone up, this would be an example of
   a. the substitution effect.
   b. consumer preference for red vegetables.
   c. the income effect.
   d. the complementary goods effect.

Use Figure MC APX-1 to answer questions 8 and 9.

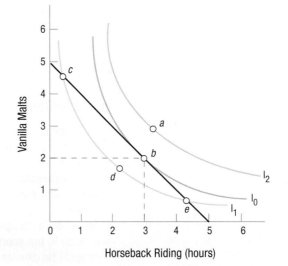

MC APX-1

8. What level of satisfaction *cannot* be achieved with this budget line and these indifference curves?
   a. point *d*
   b. point *c*
   c. point *e*
   d. point *a*

9. With a limited budget, satisfaction will be maximized at
   a. point *e*.
   b. point *a*.
   c. point *b*.
   d. point *d*.

Essay-Problem

Answer in the space provided.

The questions below apply the indifference curve analysis of consumer choice. Your answers may not always be the same as those we suggest, but they should be in the same ballpark.

1. In comparing vacation A to vacation B, why would indifference curve analysis be preferred to marginal utility analysis?

2. When might the income effect predominate over the substitution effect?

3. Is the substitution effect the same for all products?

Answers to Appendix Practice Questions

True-False

1. T	3. T	5. T
2. F	4. T	

Multiple Choice

1. b	4. c	7. a
2. c	5. a	8. d
3. b	6. d	9. c

Essay-Problem

1. Indifference curve analysis would be easier because people would simply have to decide if bundle A (vacation A) would give more satisfaction than bundle B (vacation B). With marginal utility analysis, some attempt would have to be made to calculate utility for the various aspects of each vacation.
2. The income effect might dominate when the item in question is a large portion of one's budget.
3. As we saw in the previous chapter, products with inelastic demand have few substitutes, at least in the short run. Health care is one of these. We would expect the substitution effect to be weaker with inelastically demanded products than with elastically demanded products.

Production and Cost

Production and Cost are Behind Decisions About Supply

Having looked in the last chapter at what lies behind demand curves by examining how consumers make choices, in this chapter we turn to what lies behind supply curves by examining how producers decide what to produce. It is important to understand why firms exist and how they determine their costs, in both the short run and the long run.

After studying this chapter you should be able to

- Describe the nature of firms and markets.

- Describe the nature of economic costs and profits.

- Differentiate between the short run and long run.

- Describe the nature of short-run production, total product, marginal product, and average product.

- Differentiate between increasing, constant, and decreasing returns.

- Describe the nature of short-run costs, fixed costs, variable costs, average costs, and marginal costs.

- Use graphs to show the relationship between short-run average fixed cost, average variable cost, average total cost, and marginal cost curves.

- Describe long-run costs.

- Describe the reasons for economies and diseconomies of scale.

Review the Key Terms

Firm: An economic institution that transforms resources (factors of production) into outputs for consumers.

Sole proprietor: A type of business structure comprised of a single owner who supervises and manages the business and is subject to unlimited liability.

Partnership: Similar to a sole proprietorship, but involves more than one owner who shares the managing of the business. Partnerships are also subject to unlimited liability.

Corporation: A business structure that has most of the legal rights of individuals, and in addition, the corporation can issue stock to raise capital. Stockholders' liability is limited to the value of their stock.

Profit: Equal to the difference between total revenue and total cost.

Revenue: Equal to price per unit times quantity sold.

Economic costs: The sum of explicit and implicit costs.

Explicit costs: Those expenses paid directly to another economic entity including wages, lease payments, taxes, and utilities.

Implicit costs: The opportunity costs of using resources that belong to the firm including depreciation, depletion of business assets, and the opportunity cost of the firm's capital employed in the business.

Sunk costs: Those costs that have been incurred and cannot be recovered including, for example, funds spent on existing technology that have become obsolete and past advertising that has run in the media.

Economic profits: Profits in excess of normal profits. These are profits in excess of both explicit and implicit costs.

Normal profits: The return on capital necessary to keep investors satisfied and keep capital in the business over the long run.

Short run: A period of time over which at least one factor of production (resource) is fixed, or cannot be changed.

Long run: A period of time sufficient for firms to adjust all factors of production including plant capacity.

Production: The process of turning inputs into outputs.

Marginal product: The change in output that results from a change in labor ($\Delta Q/\Delta L$).

Average product: Output per worker, found by dividing total output by the number of workers employed to produce that output (Q/L).

Increasing marginal returns: A new worker hired adds more to total output than the previous worker hired so that both average and marginal products are rising.

Diminishing marginal returns: An additional worker adds to total output, but at a diminishing rate.

Fixed costs: Costs that do not change as a firm's output expands or contracts, often called overhead. These include items such as lease payments, administrative expenses, property taxes, and insurance.

Variable costs: Costs that vary with output fluctuations, including expenses such as labor and material costs.

Average fixed cost: Total fixed cost divided by output (TFC/Q).

Average variable cost: Total variable cost divided by output (TVC/Q).

Average total cost: Total cost divided by output (TC/Q). Average total cost is also equal to AFC + AVC.

Marginal cost: The change in total costs arising from the production of additional units of output (ΔTC/ΔQ). Since fixed costs do not change with output, marginal costs are the change in variable costs associated with additional production (ΔTVC/ΔQ).

Long-run average total cost (LRATC): In the long run, firms can adjust their plant sizes so LRATC is the lowest unit cost at which any particular output can be produced in the long run.

Economies of scale: As a firm's output increases, its LRATC tends to decline. This results from specialization of labor and management, and potentially a better use of capital and complementary production techniques.

Constant returns to scale: A range of output where average total costs are relatively constant. Fast-food restaurants and movie theatres are examples.

Diseconomies of scale: A range of output where average total costs tend to increase. Firms often become so big that management becomes bureaucratic and unable to efficiently control its operations.

Economies of scope: By producing a number of products that are interdependent, firms are able to produce and market these goods at lower costs.

Work Through the Chapter Tutorials   STEP 3

Firms, Profits, and Economic Costs

Frequently Asked Questions

Q: **What are firms and what do they do?**

A: Firms produce the goods and services we consume. Firms are economic institutions that transform inputs (factors of production) into outputs (products and services).

Q: **How are entrepreneurs grouped?**

A: Entrepreneurs are organized into three basic business structures: sole proprietorships, partnerships, and corporations.

Q: **What is a sole proprietorship?**

A: A sole proprietorship is composed of one owner who usually supervises the business's operation. Sole proprietorships are easily established and managed, but proprietors are limited in their ability to raise capital and their personal assets are subject to unlimited liability.

Q: **What is a partnership, and how does it differ from a sole proprietorship?**

A: A partnership is similar to a sole proprietorship, except that it has more than one owner. Partnerships can raise capital more easily and spread around the management responsibilities, but as with sole proprietors, partners are subject to unlimited liability for the entire partnership.

Q: What is a corporation, and how does it differ from sole proprietorships and partnerships?

A: Corporations are the premier form of business organization in most of the world. Corporations possess most of the legal rights of individuals, and they are able to issue stock to raise capital. Most significantly, the liability of individual owners (stockholders) is limited to the amount they have invested in the stock.

Q: How are profits defined, and how do they relate to the goals of firms?

A: Profits are the difference between total revenue and total cost. Firms are assumed to seek to maximize their profits. Although other assumptions about the goals of firms are possible, profit maximization is the typical assumption economists use.

Q: How are economic costs defined?

A: Economic costs are separated into explicit (out-of-pocket) and implicit (opportunity) costs. Explicit costs are paid to some other entity. They include wages, lease expenses, taxes, and so on. Implicit costs are not directly paid to others. These costs include the depreciation and depletion of company assets, as well as the cost of the capital the firm employs.

Q: What are normal profits?

A: Economists define a normal return as the return on capital that keeps investors willing to invest their capital in an industry over the long run. Firms earning just this level of profit are said to be earning normal profits. Firms earning more than this are earning economic profits, and firms earning less are suffering economic losses.

Q: How are the short and long run defined?

A: The short run is a period of time during which at least one factor of production is fixed, usually plant capacity. Firms can vary output in the short run by hiring more labor or changing other variable factors. In the long run, firms are able to vary all factors, including plant size. Moreover, existing firms can leave the industry, and new firms can enter.

Firms, Profits, and Economic Costs Quick Check

Circle the Correct Answer

1. (T/F) Firms transform inputs and outputs into goods and services for consumers.
2. (T/F) Total revenue is the difference between the amount of money a firm receives from the sale of its products and its total costs.
3. (T/F) Total revenue equals number of units sold times price per unit.
4. (T/F) Depreciation is an explicit cost.
5. Which of the following is *not* an explicit cost in your new business?
   a. rent
   b. insurance
   c. the amount of wages you pay yourself
   d. the amount of wages you give up if you quit your old job to start your new business.

6. A normal rate of return on capital is
   a. a return that generates economic profits in excess of zero.
   b. the same for every business and industry.
   c. a profit just sufficient to keep investors satisfied and thus to keep capital in a business over the long run.
   d. okay in the short run but not okay in the long run.

7. Which of the following factors of production is usually assumed to be fixed in the short run?
   a. Quantity of raw materials purchased.

b. Number of workers employed.
c. Number of shifts a factory operates.
d. Plant size.

8. Economic profits are equal to
   a. total revenue minus explicit costs.
   b. total revenue minus explicit and implicit costs.
   c. total revenue minus implicit costs.
   d. total revenue minus capital costs.

9. Opportunity costs
   a. do not have to be considered in figuring profit.
   b. are explicit costs.
   c. are implicit costs.
   d. are zero when economic profits are normal.

10. The long run is usually the longest, in terms of actual months and years, for
    a. small, family-run businesses.
    b. firms that use labor-intensive production methods.
    c. large corporations that operate massive factories.
    d. industries capable of making quick adjustments to changes in market demand.

Score: ____

Answers: 1. F; 2. F; 3. T; 4. F; 5. d; 6. c; 7. d; 8. b; 9. c; 10. c

If You Got 9 or 10 Correct

You have a good understanding of the nature of firms, entrepreneurs, profits, implicit and explicit costs, and the short run versus the long run. These are the basic concepts underlying production and cost. These are also the easiest ideas presented in the chapter. Go on to the next section, "Production in the Short Run," and get ready for a little more of a challenge.

If You Didn't Get at Least 9 Correct

You need to do a few things. These are relatively intuitive concepts, so first take a moment and reread the list of terms you need to know. That may be enough to cement these concepts in your mind. If not, reread the first section of the chapter, and go back and make sure you know why you missed the questions you did. As you work through the next section, "Production in the Short Run" (a little harder section), this material should become clearer.

But before you move on, take a piece of paper, define explicit and implicit costs, and list three examples of each. Now define normal profits, think of an example of some small business earning economic profits, then have costs increase sufficiently to cause the firm to earn only normal profits. Keeping these four concepts straight will make the remaining material in the chapter a lot easier. ■

Production in the Short Run

Frequently Asked Questions

Q: How are average and marginal products defined?

A: In the short run, firms can vary the output they produce by varying their labor inputs. The total product curve relates labor inputs to outputs. Marginal product is the change in output resulting from a change in labor input ($\Delta Q/\Delta L$). Marginal product is thus the change in output associated with hiring one additional worker. Average product or output per worker is equal to total output divided by labor input (Q/L).

Q: **What do typical marginal and average product curves look like?**

A: Figure 1 graphs total, average, and marginal product for a hypothetical firm. Note that the marginal product curve cuts the average product curve at its maximum point (point *b*); once marginal product (the output from one additional worker) is less than average product, it pulls the average down (see the movement from point *b* to *c*). Marginal returns diminish between points *a* and *c* and negative returns occur after 12 workers are hired (point *c*).

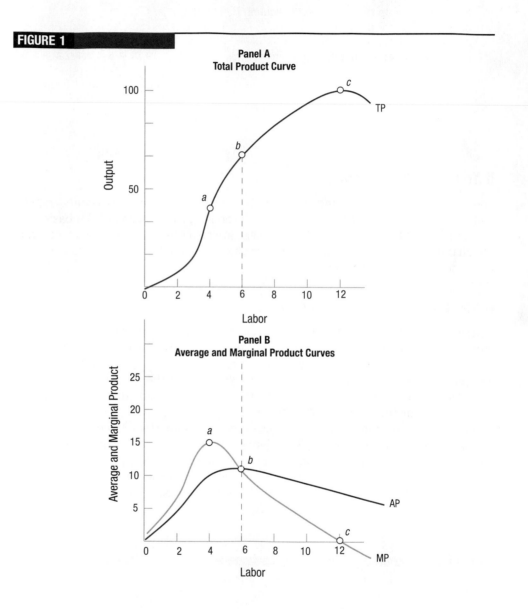

FIGURE 1

Panel A
Total Product Curve

Panel B
Average and Marginal Product Curves

Q: **What are increasing and decreasing returns?**

A: Typical production functions exhibit both increasing and decreasing returns. When increasing returns are present, each additional worker adds more to total output than previous workers. This can occur because of specialization. All production is eventually subject to the law of diminishing returns, whereby additional workers add less and less to total output.

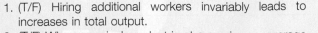

Production in the Short Run Quick Check

Circle the Correct Answer

1. (T/F) Hiring additional workers invariably leads to increases in total output.
2. (T/F) When marginal product is at a maximum, average product will always be at a maximum.
3. If hiring an additional worker yields a negative marginal return, this means that
   a. hiring the additional worker will still raise total output, but at a diminishing rate.
   b. hiring the additional worker will actually reduce total output.
   c. hiring the additional worker will increase average product.
   d. the additional worker will be paid a lower wage than other employees.

Use Figure 2 to answer questions 4 and 5.
4. Going from 8 workers to 9 workers illustrates
   a. decreasing average returns.
   b. diminishing marginal returns.
   c. negative returns.
   d. increasing returns.
5. Rational firms would never hire more than how many workers?
   a. 8   c. 22
   b. 12   d. indeterminate

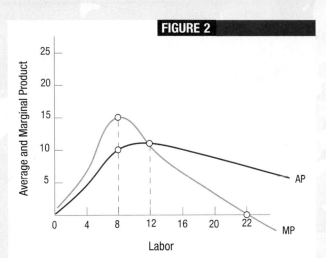

FIGURE 2

Score: ____

Answers: 1. F; 2. F; 3. b; 4. b; 5. c

If You Got All 5 Correct

Short-run production is not a problem for you. This is relatively difficult material with its average and marginal product curves and the law of diminishing returns. Move on to "Costs of Production" the next section, which builds on this section.

If You Didn't Get All of Them Correct

You should review this section. First, reread the text. Then keep the following in mind and work through the solved problem on the next page.

Key Point to Remember

Remember that in the short run at least one factor of production is fixed (usually capital or plant size). Therefore, output varies directly with labor input. *Average product* is average output per worker or Q/L. If 10 workers can produce 200 units of output, then average product is 20. *Marginal product* is the extra output the firm produces when one more worker is hired. So, if 10 workers can produce 200 units, the firm hires a new worker (the 11th), and total output rises to 225, then marginal product is 25 ($\Delta Q = 25$, $\Delta L = 1$, so $\Delta Q/\Delta L = 25/1 = 25$).

Don't make this material harder than it is. It is really quite straightforward. Take some time and review the solved problem below. It will help you a lot when you get to the next section, "Costs of Production."

Solved Problem: Production in the Short Run

Complete the following table, and graph average product and marginal product in the grid provided. Try to complete this before looking at the solution. After you have completed this review, move on to "A Final Check."

L	Q	MP	AP
0	0		
1	14		
2	30		
3	50		
4	80		
5	108		
6	130		
7	150		
8	168		
9	180		

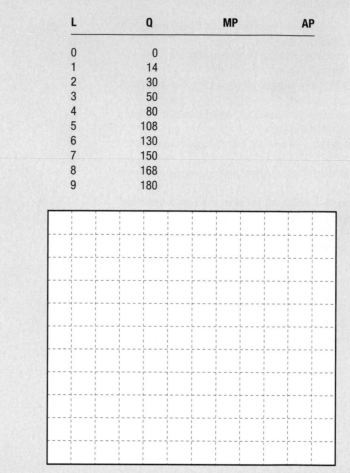

Solution-Discussion

Values for marginal and average product are shown in the table below. Notice that both marginal and average product initially increase then marginal product declines until both are roughly equal when 6 units of output are produced, and then both continue to decline.

L	Q	MP	AP
0	0	—	—
1	14	14	14.00
2	30	16	15.00
3	50	20	16.66
4	80	30	20.00
5	108	28	21.60
6	130	22	21.66
7	150	20	21.42
8	168	18	21.00
9	180	12	20.00

Both marginal and average product are shown in Figure 3.

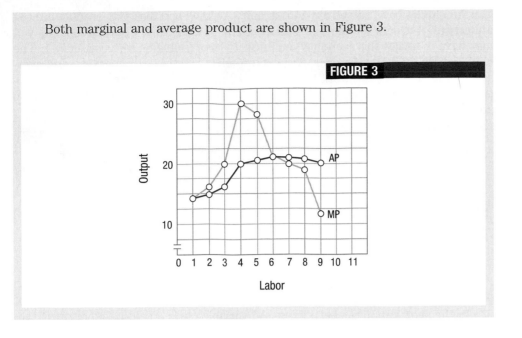

FIGURE 3

Production in the Short Run A Final Check

1. (T/F) Marginal product is the change in output that results from hiring one additional worker.
2. (T/F) Total product equals average product plus marginal product.

   Use Figure 4 to answer questions 3 and 4.

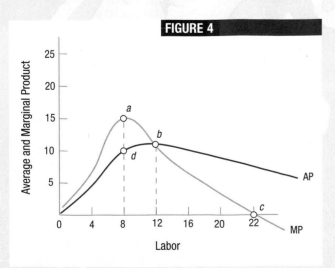

FIGURE 4

3. Should the firm hire more than 8 workers?
   a. No, because that is where production is maximized.
   b. No, because after that the firm will face diminishing returns.
   c. No, because after that the firm faces negative returns.
   d. Yes, because average and marginal product are still positive.
4. After which point will there be negative returns?
   a. a
   b. b
   c. c
   d. d
5. Which of the following is true?
   a. Average product will be at its maximum when marginal product is at its maximum.
   b. Average product will be at its maximum when marginal product is zero.
   c. Average product will be at its maximum when marginal product equals average product.
   d. Average product never reaches a maximum.

Score: ____

You should not have missed any in this quiz. Average and marginal product are the underlying concepts for the cost curves in the next section. Continue on, but you may have to review this section if you begin to have problems with cost curves. The next section on costs, however, gives you further practice with marginal and average calculations. As you work through these problems, the concepts from production may take hold. This is fundamental material that may take a little time to absorb. ■

Costs of Production

Frequently Asked Questions

Q: What are fixed and variable costs?

A: In the short run, firms have fixed and variable costs. Fixed costs, or overhead, are those costs the firm incurs whether it produces anything or not. These costs include administrative overhead, lease payments, and insurance. Variable costs are those costs that vary with output, such as wages, utilities, and raw materials costs. Total costs are equal to total fixed costs plus total variable costs (TC = TFC + TVC).

Q: How are average total costs, average fixed costs, and average variable costs computed?

A: *Average total cost* (ATC) represents total cost per unit of production, or TC/Q. *Average fixed cost* (AFC) is equal to TFC/Q, and *average variable cost* (AVC) is equal to TVC/Q. Consequently, ATC = AFC + AVC.

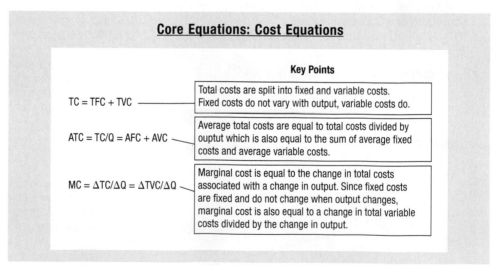

Core Equations: Cost Equations

Key Points

TC = TFC + TVC ——— Total costs are split into fixed and variable costs. Fixed costs do not vary with output, variable costs do.

ATC = TC/Q = AFC + AVC —— Average total costs are equal to total costs divided by ouptut which is also equal to the sum of average fixed costs and average variable costs.

MC = ΔTC/ΔQ = ΔTVC/ΔQ —— Marginal cost is equal to the change in total costs associated with a change in output. Since fixed costs are fixed and do not change when output changes, marginal cost is also equal to a change in total variable costs divided by the change in output.

Q: What do typical ATC, AFC, and AVC curves look like when graphed?

A: Figure 5 graphs average total cost, average fixed cost, and average variable cost. Note that average fixed cost declines continuously as output increases, because this fixed amount of cost is being spread over larger quantities of output. In contrast, average variable cost and average total cost first decrease, then increase because of diminishing returns.

FIGURE 5

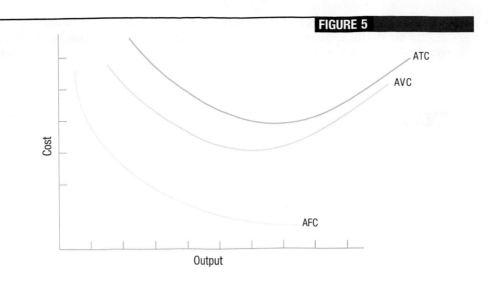

Q: How are marginal costs defined and graphed?

A: Marginal cost (MC) is the change in total costs associated with producing one additional unit. Since fixed costs do not change in the short run (ΔTFC = 0), marginal cost is equal to the change in variable costs when one additional unit is produced; hence, MC = ΔTVC/ΔQ. Figure 6 graphs marginal cost along with average variable cost and average total cost. Note that marginal costs cut the average variable cost curve and the average total cost curve at their minimum points.

FIGURE 6

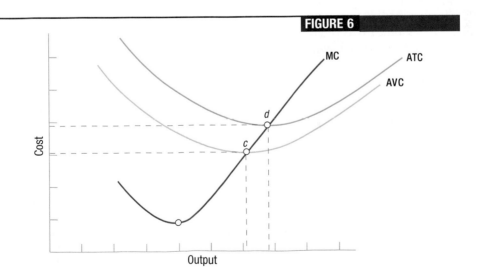

Q: How is the long-run average total cost curve (LRATC) determined?

A: In the long run, all factors of production are variable, and firms can enter or leave the industry. The long-run average total cost curve (LRATC) represents the lowest unit costs (ATC) for any specific output level in the long run.

Figure 7 graphs the long-run average total cost curve as the minimum parts of several short-run average cost curves, using the assumption that in the long run, firms will build plants of the size best fitting the levels of output desired.

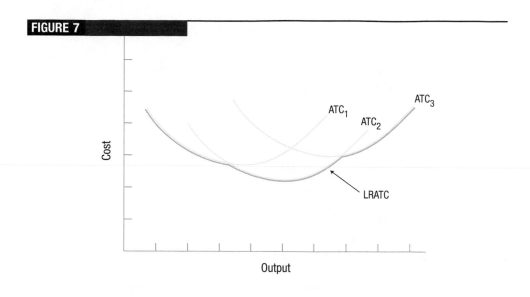

FIGURE 7

Q: Why do firms face economies and diseconomies of scale?

A: Economies of scale associated with larger firm size result from such factors as specialization in labor and management. As a firm grows, the average cost of production falls. Eventually, however, a firm will encounter diseconomies of scale when its size becomes so large that efficient management becomes impossible. At this point, average costs begin to rise. Today, advanced computer and communications technologies have radically increased the size of firms that can be efficiently managed.

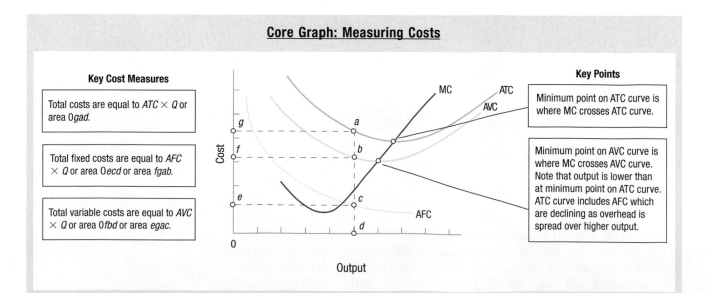

Core Graph: Measuring Costs

Key Cost Measures

Total costs are equal to $ATC \times Q$ or area $0gad$.

Total fixed costs are equal to $AFC \times Q$ or area $0ecd$ or area $fgab$.

Total variable costs are equal to $AVC \times Q$ or area $0fbd$ or area $egac$.

Key Points

Minimum point on ATC curve is where MC crosses ATC curve.

Minimum point on AVC curve is where MC crosses AVC curve. Note that output is lower than at minimum point on ATC curve. ATC curve includes AFC which are declining as overhead is spread over higher output.

Costs of Production Quick Check

Circle the Correct Answer

1. (T/F) Fixed costs include insurance and rent.
2. (T/F) Average variable costs equal average total costs minus average fixed costs.
3. In Figure 8, at what point will average variable cost exactly equal the cost of hiring one additional worker?
   a. *c*
   b. *d*
   c. cannot tell because average fixed costs are not included
   d. at the minimum point of the marginal cost curve
4. A firm's long-run average total costs (LRATC) curve is formed by combining a number of curves that represent:
   a. the firm's average total costs at various times, plant size being held constant.
   b. the firm's average variable cost, average fixed cost, and marginal cost.
   c. the firm's total product, average product, and marginal product.
   d. the firm's short-run average total costs for a variety of different plant sizes.
5. Diseconomies of scale result when
   a. fixed costs are large.
   b. a firm shrinks so much that individual workers must perform multiple tasks.
   c. a firm grows so large that it becomes difficult to manage in an efficient manner.
   d. a firm grows large enough that it can purchase advanced machinery.

Score: ____

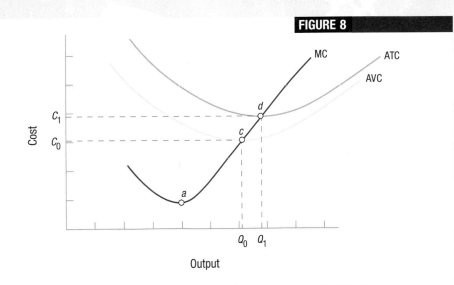

FIGURE 8

If You Got All 5 Correct

Short-run and long-run costs are not a problem for you. You might find the "Hints, Tips, and Reminders" in the next section useful.

If You Didn't Get All of Them Correct

You will need to review this section again. Even though this is difficult material, it is essential that you understand costs of production and cost curves to be able to master the concepts of profit maximization and market structure analysis that follow in the next few chapters. Review this section in the text and be sure to work the material in the "Chapterwide Practice Questions" section. When you have completed this work, study carefully the solved problem below. First, work the problem on your own, then read through the answer and the description of how each cost was determined. When you are done, take the short "Final Quiz" after this solved problem.

Solved Problem: Costs of Production

Complete the table below assuming that fixed costs are $1,500 and wages are $100 per worker.

L	Q	MP	AP	TVC	TC	ATC	AVC	MC
0	—	—	—	—	—	—	—	—
1	5	—	—	—	—	—	—	—
2	12	—	—	—	—	—	—	—
3	18	—	—	—	—	—	—	—
4	22	—	—	—	—	—	—	—
5	25	—	—	—	—	—	—	—

Solution-Discussion

The table below shows the answers. Keep in mind the following:

■ Average product is equal to Q/L, so when 3 workers are hired, output is 18, so average product is 6(18/3 = 6).

■ Marginal product is equal to the change in output associated with an increase in labor, or $\Delta Q/\Delta L$. Thus, when the fourth worker is hired, output grows from 18 to 22 units, and marginal product is 4.

■ Total variable cost in this case is just equal to labor cost, and each worker costs 100, so when 5 workers are hired, TVC = 500.

■ Total cost is equal to total fixed cost plus total variable cost (TC = TFC + TVC). Fixed cost is 1,500, so adding 1,500 to TVC will give us total cost.

■ Average total cost is total costs divided by output (TC/Q), so when output is equal to 12, total cost is 1,700, so AVC = 1,700/12 = 141.7.

■ Average variable cost is equal to total variable cost divided by output. Thus, when output is equal to 22, total variable cost is 400, so AVC = 400/22 = 18.2.

■ Marginal cost is just the change in total cost (but since fixed cost is fixed, we can use total variable cost) divided by the change in output. When labor goes from 3 to 4 units, output increases from 18 to 22 units, so marginal cost is $\Delta TVC/\Delta Q = 100/4 = 25$.

L	Q	MP	AP	TVC	TC	ATC	AVC	MC
0	—	—	—	—	1500	—	—	—
1	5	5	5	100	1600	320.0	20.0	20.0
2	12	7	6	200	1700	141.7	16.7	14.3
3	18	6	6	300	1800	100.0	16.7	16.7
4	22	4	5.4	400	1900	86.4	18.2	25.0
5	25	3	5	500	2000	80.0	20.0	33.3

If the firm has 3 workers, total cost is $1,800.00. If the firm can sell the 18 units of output it produces for $100.00 each, revenue to the firm is also $1,800.00, so the firm breaks even (earns a normal profit—remember that the cost curves include opportunity costs).

Now complete the Final Check section on the following page.

Costs of Production Final Check

1. (T/F) Fixed cost is considered fixed in the short run but not in the long run.
2. Average cost, or cost per unit of output (TC/Q), is equal to
   a. TFC + TVC
   b. TFC/Q + TVC/Q
   c. TC – TFC/Q
   d. PVC + PDQ
3. Which curve is *not* typically bowl-shaped?
   a. the average total cost curve
   b. the average fixed cost curve
   c. the short-run average cost curve
   d. the average variable cost curve
4. In Figure 9, output in the range from Q_0 to Q_1 is considered
   a. economies of scale.
   b. constant returns to scale.
   c. diseconomies of scale.
   d. an example of the law of diminishing returns.
5. Marginal cost
   a. crosses through the minimum point of the total cost curve.
   b. crosses through the minimum point of the ATC curve before crossing through the minimum point of the AVC curve.
   c. doesn't cross through the minimum point of the AFC curve.
   d. is equal to the change in average fixed costs divided by the change in output.

Score: ____

Answers: 1. T; 2. b; 3. b; 4. b; 5. c

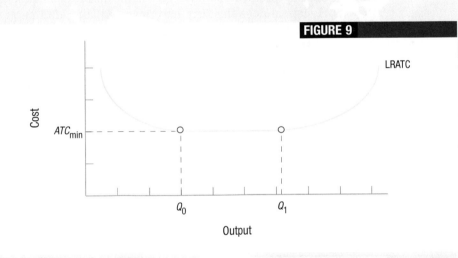

FIGURE 9

You shouldn't miss any in this exercise. If you did, this is a sign that you are still having trouble with the material in this chapter. If you have consistently had problems with this chapter, start at the beginning, reread the text, and work through the material again to this point. Since cost and production are so fundamental to much of the rest of the book, you will want to make sure you have these concepts down pat. ■

Consider These Hints, Tips, and Reminders   STEP 4

1. Sunk costs can often be a difficult concept to grasp. Because you have already spent money on some activity and the money cannot be recovered, this spending is sunk and should have no impact on future decisions. This takes a little getting used to. Money spent on a cell phone last year should not affect your decision to buy a new phone that is many times better for less money.

2. Don't let the distinction between economic and accounting costs fool you. Accounting costs focus on those costs that are essentially out of pocket; costs for which you pay cash or for which you write checks. Economic costs include accounting costs plus opportunity costs.

   When you start a business, two opportunity costs are nearly always present. First, you quit a job (you were working, weren't you?), so you have given up that salary and benefits. Second, you put some of your savings (capital) into the business that could have earned interest in the bank. Adding these two opportunity costs to the explicit costs of running your business represents your economic costs. You will not earn an economic profit until all economic costs are covered. Note that your firm will earn a normal profit if the business *just* covers your economic costs.

3. The cost curves that economists draw include opportunity costs in the curves and therefore represent economic costs. Thus, when economists assume that total costs are equal to X, this X includes a reasonable return on the firm's capital invested in the business.

   So, when you see some report that says Company ABC earned an obscene accounting profit of so many billions of dollars, you should ask yourself, How much capital does this firm have invested, and after subtracting a reasonable return to their capital, how big is the resulting profit? Keep in mind that any profit that remains is "economic profit."

4. The most important cost curves you learned about in this chapter are ATC, AVC, and MC. You will see and use these curves in the next three chapters. You will need to be able to draw the curves fairly precisely, so remember: Both ATC and AVC are bowl shaped, and MC passes through the minimum points on both curves.

5. The best way to draw the ATC, AVC, and MC curves is to draw a positively sloped MC curve first, then draw the ATC and AVC curves. Figure 10 shows step by step how to construct the curves.

FIGURE 10

Step 1: Draw a positively sloped MC curve.
Step 2: Plot two points *a* and *b* that will represent the minimum points on the two average cost curves.
Step 3: Note that point *a* will be the minimum point on the ATC; and point *b*, the minimum point of the AVC curve. Note that point *b* will always occur at a lower output than point *a*, because ATC = AVC + AFC. As long as there are some fixed costs, point *b* on AVC will always be at a lower output than point *a* on ATC.
Step 4: Draw two bowl-shaped curves through these two points. Note that the right tail on the AVC curve gets closer to the ATC curve, but never touches it because of the spreading of fixed costs. Label the curves and axes.

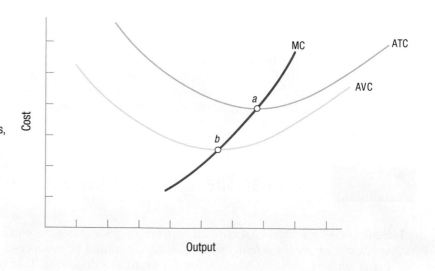

6. You will need to become proficient with computing TVC from AVC and TC from ATC. Since AVC = TVC/Q, the relationship is straightforward: TVC = AVC × Q. Similarly, ATC = TC/Q, so TC = ATC × Q.

  This is shown graphically in Figure 11. For three different points a, b, and c on the AVC curve, TVC is just equal to AVC × Q. For point a, this is $C_2 \times Q_2$ which is equal to the shaded area. For point b, TVC would be $C_1 \times Q_1$, and for point c it would be $C_3 \times Q_3$. Note these areas are not shaded. The exact same process applies for ATC and TC.

FIGURE 11

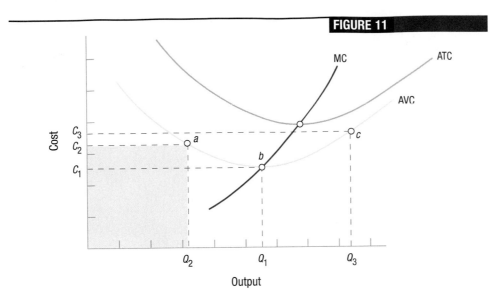

Do the Homework for Chapter 7
Production and Cost

Instructor _____ Time _____ Student _____

Use the answer key below to record your answers to these homework questions.

1. (a) (b) (c) (d)	6. (a) (b) (c) (d)	11. (a) (b) (c) (d)	16. (a) (b) (c) (d)
2. (a) (b) (c) (d)	7. (a) (b) (c) (d)	12. (a) (b) (c) (d)	17. (a) (b) (c) (d)
3. (a) (b) (c) (d)	8. (a) (b) (c) (d)	13. (a) (b) (c) (d)	18. (a) (b) (c) (d)
4. (a) (b) (c) (d)	9. (a) (b) (c) (d)	14. (a) (b) (c) (d)	19. (a) (b) (c) (d)
5. (a) (b) (c) (d)	10. (a) (b) (c) (d)	15. (a) (b) (c) (d)	20. (a) (b) (c) (d)

1. Economic costs for the entrepreneur include which of the following?
   a. rent on buildings
   b. utility and communications bills
   c. interest income foregone on the capital in the business
   d. all of the above

2. Which of the following costs are usually assumed to be fixed?
   a. leases on buildings
   b. utility bills
   c. wages and salaries
   d. all of the above

3. Which of the following differentiates the short run from the long run?
   a. the time it takes the firm to hire another CEO
   b. one factor of production is variable
   c. the rate at which firms can vary labor
   d. one factor of production is fixed

4. Total profits are defined as
   a. the difference between total costs and variable costs.
   b. what is left over after variable costs are subtracted from total revenues.
   c. the difference between total revenues and total costs.
   d. fixed costs plus variable costs plus implicit costs.

5. Normal profits are
   a. explicit costs plus implicit costs.
   b. necessary to keep investors willing to put capital into a firm.
   c. a rate of return on capital just equal to the average for the industry.
   d. zero as reported to the Internal Revenue Service.

6. The long run is defined by the fact that
   a. firms inevitably earn losses.
   b. firms continue to change production techniques to earn economic profits.
   c. firms are able to vary all of the factors of production.
   d. the plant capacity of firms is fixed.

7. Subtracting total costs from total revenues yields
   a. fixed costs.
   b. variable costs.
   c. the rate of return to the firm.
   d. profit.

Use Figure HW-1 to answer questions 8–11.

8. At which point will a new unit of labor hired add the most to total output of the firm?
   a. point *a*
   b. point *b*
   c. point *c*
   d. point *d*

9. At which point will each worker produce the most output?
   a. point *a*
   b. point *b*
   c. point *c*
   d. point *d*

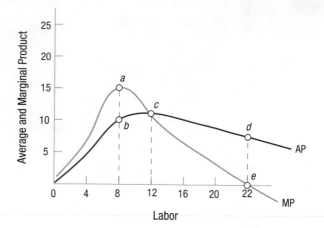

HW-1

10. Point *a* to point *e* on the marginal product (MP) curve illustrates
    a. the law of increasing returns.
    b. constant returns to scale.
    c. the law of diminishing returns.
    d. falling average product.

11. When 12 units of labor are hired, which of the following is *not* true?
    a. Marginal product is higher than average product.
    b. Marginal product is declining.
    c. Average product is equal to marginal product.
    d. Average product is at its maximum.

12. Marginal cost equals
    a. the change in average total costs divided by the change in output.
    b. the change in total variable costs divided by the change in output.
    c. the change in total fixed costs divided by the change in output.
    d. the change in total costs minus the change in fixed costs.

Use Figure HW-2 to answer questions 13–16.

13. Total fixed costs are equal to which of the following?
    a. $1,200
    b. $2,400
    c. $3,600
    d. $4,800

14. Total variable costs are equal to which of the following?
    a. $1,200
    b. $2,400
    c. $3,600
    d. $4,800

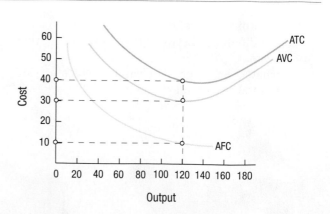

HW-2

15. Total costs are equal to which of the following?
    a. $1,200
    b. $2,400
    c. $3,600
    d. $4,800

16. Marginal cost at output equal to 120 units is equal to which of the following?
    a. $10
    b. $20
    c. $30
    d. $40

17. When the average total cost curve is rising, the marginal cost curve
    a. will be falling.
    b. will be above the average total cost curve.
    c. will be rising slower than the average variable cost curve.
    d. will be rising slower than the average total cost curve.

18. Which of the following helps generate economies of scale as firms grow larger?
    a. a growing rift between management and workers
    b. the inability of large firms to efficiently use their natural resources
    c. larger firms are able to purchase and implement more advanced equipment
    d. the labor force becomes too large to efficiently manage

19. When firms become so large that they are difficult to manage in an efficient manner, this is an example of
    a. increasing marginal costs.
    b. increasing average costs.
    c. economies of scale.
    d. diseconomies of scale.

20. The firm's long-run average total cost curve is derived from
    a. the short-run marginal cost curves of the firm.
    b. the summation of the firm's average variable and average fixed cost curves.
    c. the firm's short-run average cost curves for different plant sizes.
    d. a combination of the firm's short-run average variable cost and average total cost curves.

Use the ExamPrep to Get Ready for Exams   STEP 6

This sheet (front and back) is designed to help you prepare for your exams. The chapter has been boiled down to its key concepts. You are asked to answer questions, define terms, draw graphs, and, if you wish, add summaries of class notes.

Firms

Define each of the following terms:

Firm:

Sole proprietor:

Partnership:

Corporation:

Profit:

Explicit costs:

Normal profit:

Economic profit:

Short run:

Long run:

Production in the Short Run

Use the grids at right to illustrate the following:

■ Draw a total product curve in Panel A.
■ In Panel B, draw marginal and average product curves.
■ Label the areas of increasing returns, diminishing returns, and negative returns.

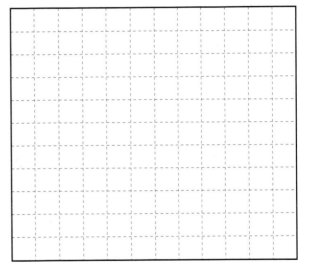

Panel A

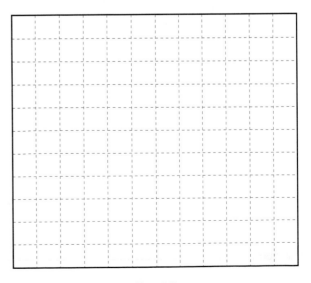

Panel B

Costs of Production

Short-Run Costs

Define the following (use formulas where appropriate):

Fixed costs:

Variable costs:

Average fixed costs:

Average variable costs:

Average total costs:

Marginal costs:

Use the grid below to illustrate the following short-run curves:

Average fixed costs
Average variable costs
Average total costs
Marginal costs

(Hint: Keep in mind that the minimum point on the AVC curve comes at a lower output than the minimum point on the ATC curve. Also, the marginal cost curve goes through both minimum points)

Long-Run Costs

Describe the long-run average total cost curve:

Describe economies and diseconomies of scale:

Describe the role technology plays in reducing long-run average cost:

Additional Study Help Chapterwide Practice Questions

Matching

Match the description with the corresponding term.

___ 1. Firms
___ 2. Revenue
___ 3. Economic costs
___ 4. Explicit costs
___ 5. Implicit costs
___ 6. Economic profits
___ 7. Normal profits
___ 8. Short run
___ 9. Long run
___ 10. Production
___ 11. Average product
___ 12. Marginal product
___ 13. Fixed costs
___ 14. Variable costs
___ 15. Marginal costs
___ 16. Economies of scale
___ 17. Diseconomies of scale
___ 18. Constant returns to scale

a. Costs a firm pays in the course of doing business, including both explicit and implicit costs.
b. The time period over which one production factor, usually plant capacity, is fixed.
c. A firm's output per unit of labor input.
d. Costs that change with the level of production.
e. The profit level where revenue exceeds both implicit and explicit costs.
f. Costs that do not change with the level of production in the short run.
g. A range of production output where long-run average total costs remain the same.
h. The range of production output where long-run average total cost goes up as output goes up.
i. The minimum level of profits necessary to keep investors willing to put capital in a firm.
j. A time period over which all production variables can change, including plant capacity and number of firms in the market.
k. Institutions or organizations that produce goods and services by transforming inputs into outputs.
l. The money a firm actually pays out while doing business.
m. A firm's output.
n. The amount of additional output created by adding one additional worker.
o. The opportunity costs of doing business.
p. The cost to a firm to produce one more unit of output.
q. The money a firm brings in from selling its goods or services.
r. The range of production output where long-run average total cost goes down as output goes up.

Fill-In

Circle the word(s) in parentheses that complete the sentence.

1. The risks associated with production are assumed by (labor, capital, entrepreneurs) _____.

2. Price times units sold is equal to (explicit costs, total revenue, implicit costs, sunk costs, normal profits, economic profits) _____. Out-of-pocket expenses are (explicit costs, total revenue, implicit costs, sunk costs, normal profits, economic profits) _____, but opportunity costs are (explicit costs, total revenue, implicit costs, sunk costs, normal profits, economic profits) _____. Profits that just equal a normal rate of return are equal to (explicit costs, total revenue, implicit costs, sunk costs, normal profits, economic profits) _____, while profits in excess of a normal return are called (explicit costs, total revenue, implicit costs, sunk costs, normal profits, economic profits) _____.

3. Total output divided by number of workers is equal to (marginal, average, total) _____ product, while the change in total output divided by the change in the number of employees is equal to (marginal, average, total) _____ product.

4. Costs that do not change in the short run are called (fixed, variable, average, marginal) _____ costs. Labor and wages are an example of (fixed, variable, average, marginal) _____ costs. When additional labor is hired and costs change, this change in costs represents (fixed, variable, average, marginal) _____ costs whereas cost per unit represents (fixed, variable, average, marginal) _____ costs.

5. As output increases, marginal cost first passes through the minimum point on the (average total, average variable) _____ cost curve, then passes through the minimum point on the (average total, average variable) _____ cost curve.

6. When long-run average total costs are rising, firms are encountering (economies, diseconomies) _____ of scale and when long-run average total costs are falling, firms are facing (economies, diseconomies) _____ of scale.

True-False

Circle the correct answer.

__T/F__   1. Firms located in areas with high labor costs will tend to use labor-intensive production methods.

__T/F__   2. A firm's primary goal is to maximize its profits.

__T/F__   3. Explicit costs include all out-of-pocket expenses.

__T/F__   4. Total revenue is the amount of money a firm receives from the sale of its products or services.

__T/F__   5. Investors will remove capital from a firm earning zero economic profit.

__T/F__   6. In the short run, plant capacity is generally assumed to be fixed.

__T/F__   7. In the long run, all factors of production may vary, but the number of firms remains fixed.

__T/F__   8. Marginal product remains the same no matter what the level of output.

__T/F__   9. Marginal product is the change in profit that results from adding one additional worker.

__T/F__   10. The law of diminishing returns states that at some point additional workers will no longer improve output.

__T/F__   11. In the long run, all costs are fixed.

__T/F__   12. Variable costs include wages and expenditures for raw materials.

__T/F__   13. Average total cost is equal to average fixed cost minus average variable cost.

__T/F__   14. Marginal cost equals change in total fixed costs over change in output plus change in total variable costs over change in output.

__T/F__   15. The marginal cost curve will always intersect the maximum points of both the average variable cost curve and the average total cost curve.

__T/F__   16. Firms will encounter constant returns to scale indefinitely as they grow in size.

__T/F__   17. Diseconomies of scale is caused by inefficiency once a firm grows past a certain point.

Multiple Choice

Circle the correct answer.

1. Firms
   a. operate in only one market.
   b. produce goods and services.
   c. try to achieve zero profits.
   d. transform products into inputs.

2. Firms use low-technology, labor-intensive production methods in areas where
   a. labor is scarce and expensive.
   b. technology is advanced and inexpensive.
   c. labor is plentiful and cheap.
   d. product inputs are expensive.

3. The difference between a firm's total revenue and its total cost is
   a. profit.
   b. operating margin.
   c. marginal income.
   d. marginal return.

4. As a rule, firms try to maximize
   a. sales.
   b. market share.
   c. customer satisfaction.
   d. profits.

5. Number of units sold times price per unit equals
   a. marginal revenue.
   b. net profit.
   c. total revenue.
   d. gross profit.

6. A firm's out-of-pocket expenses are
   a. explicit costs.
   b. implicit costs.
   c. marginal costs.
   d. fixed costs.

7. Which of the following is an explicit cost?
   a. opportunity costs
   b. the cost of capital
   c. depreciation
   d. wages

8. An implicit cost
   a. is a direct out-of-pocket expense.
   b. is an opportunity cost of doing business.
   c. is a onetime expense.
   d. is offset by explicit costs.

9. To keep investors willing to put capital into a firm, that firm must
   a. earn more than zero economic profit.
   b. earn more than normal economic profit.
   c. earn zero economic profit.
   d. have a positive marginal profit.

10. Zero economic profit is considered
    a. a normal profit.
    b. a sign of a failing firm.
    c. an excess profit.
    d. insufficient profit.

11. Total revenue minus explicit and implicit costs equals
    a. economic profit or loss.
    b. zero profit.
    c. normal economic profit.
    d. marginal profit.

12. The number of firms in an industry can change
    a. only in the long run.
    b. in the short run if there is a market shortage.
    c. in the short run if there is a market surplus.
    d. only in the short run.

13. The change in output from adding one additional worker is
    a. marginal product.
    b. total product.
    c. marginal profit.
    d. total income.

14. Total output divided by the number of workers employed equals
    a. marginal product.
    b. marginal return.
    c. total product.
    d. average product.

15. When hiring one more worker increases output by an amount less than the average output of existing workers, hiring this additional worker will
    a. decrease average productivity.
    b. decrease total productivity.
    c. increase average productivity.
    d. have no effect on productivity.

16. If hiring an additional worker will actually reduce total output, this is an example of
    a. increasing returns.

b. positive marginal return.
   c. negative marginal return.
   d. diseconomies of scale.

Use Figure MC-1 to answer questions 17 and 18.

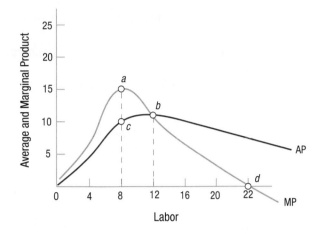

MC-1

17. Going from 15 workers to 16 workers illustrates
    a. constant return.
    b. decreasing returns.
    c. increasing returns.
    d. economy of scale.

18. At which point are workers, on average, producing the most output?
    a. *a*
    b. *b*
    c. *c*
    d. *d*

19. In the short run, total cost equals
    a. total fixed cost.
    b. total variable cost.
    c. total variable cost minus total fixed cost.
    d. total variable cost plus total fixed cost.

20. Which of the following is typically regarded as a fixed cost?
    a. shipping costs
    b. insurance payments
    c. raw material costs
    d. wages

21. Change in output does *not* cause changes in
    a. variable cost.
    b. average fixed cost.
    c. marginal cost.
    d. total fixed cost.

22. TFC/Q + TVC/Q is the formula for
    a. average total cost.

b. marginal cost.

c. total cost.

d. variable cost.

23. Marginal cost equals
   a. change in total variable cost divided by change in total fixed cost.
   b. change in total variable cost divided by change in quantity.
   c. change in total fixed cost divided by change in quantity.
   d. change in total variable cost minus change in total fixed cost.

24. If a firm can produce 100 DVDs for $100 and 200 DVDs for $150, what is the marginal cost per DVD of the additional 100 DVDs?
   a. $1.00
   b. $.75
   c. $.50
   d. $.25

25. The long-run average total cost (LRATC) curve is able to portray the lowest unit cost at which any specific output can be produced in the long run because
   a. fixed costs are stable in the long run.
   b. it takes into account changes in plant size.
   c. it ignores changes in plant size.
   d. it ignores changes in variable costs.

26. A firm's long-run average total cost (LRATC) curve shows
   a. the lowest unit cost for any level of output.
   b. the highest unit cost for any level of output.
   c. the marginal cost for any level of output.
   d. the variable cost for any level of output.

27. When a firm grows so large that it becomes difficult to manage in an efficient manner, this is an example of
   a. economies of scale.
   b. constant returns to scale.
   c. diseconomies of scale.
   d. increasing returns to scale.

Use Figure MC-2 to answer questions 28 and 29.

28. In the figure, ATC_1, ATC_2, and ATC_3 represent
   a. different levels of output in relation to worker productivity.
   b. different levels of output in relation to demand.
   c. different levels of output in relation to cost.
   d. different levels of output in relation to plant size.

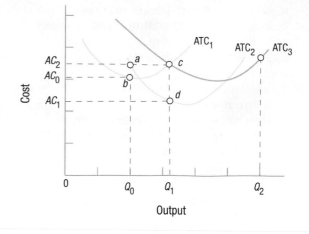

MC-2

29. If you wanted to produce output Q_1, you would operate which plant size?
   a. Plant 1 associated with ATC_1
   b. Plant 2 associated with ATC_2
   c. Plant 3 associated with ATC_3
   d. Plant 1 associated with ATC_1, but add more capital

Essay-Problem

Answer in the space provided.

Learning and applying cost and production concepts can be challenging. Don't get discouraged if your answers below are not always the same as those we suggest. Use these as guidelines, but more importantly to help you learn some of the difficult issues surrounding firms, production, and costs.

1. Why are entrepreneurs important for any economy?

2. Was profit maximization the goal of Enron?

3. To get a porch built on your house, you have to apply for a permit, go before the local zoning board and explain your request, and hire a contractor to do the work. Why is appearing before the zoning board an implicit cost in this case?

4. If interest rates go up, will existing normal profits be sufficient to keep investors in the firm happy?

5. Why is it important for small businesses to have an accurate estimate of fixed costs?

6. In the short run, why is marginal cost so much more important for average variable cost than for average fixed cost?

7. Will the LRATC curve for an oil refinery be bumpy or smooth?

8. Hotrod Skateboards manufactures skateboards. It has the following costs:

   wages
   rent
   wheels
   boards
   paint
   insurance

   Which of these are fixed costs, and which are variable costs?

9. Would you categorize the personal computer industry as operating under economies of scale, constant returns to scale, or diseconomies of scale?

10. Fill in the following table.

Number of Workers	Total Product	Marginal Product	Average Product
50	100	_____	_____
55	120	_____	_____
60	150	_____	_____
65	200	_____	_____
70	225	_____	_____
75	235	_____	_____
80	240	_____	_____

11. Complete the following production and cost table. Plot the ATC, AVC, and MC curves in Figure EP-1.

L	Q	MP	AP	TFC	TVC	TC	AFC	ATC	AVC	MC
0	0	_	_	_	_	_	_	_	_	_
1	7	_	_	_	_	_	_	_	_	_
2	15	_	_	_	_	_	_	_	_	_
3	25	_	_	_	_	_	_	_	_	_
4	40	_	_	_	_	_	_	_	_	_
5	54	_	_	_	_	_	_	_	_	_
6	65	_	_	_	_	_	_	_	_	_
7	75	_	_	_	_	_	_	_	_	_
8	84	_	_	_	_	_	_	_	_	_
9	90	_	_	_	_	_	_	_	_	_
10	95	_	_	2000	20000	_	_	_	_	_

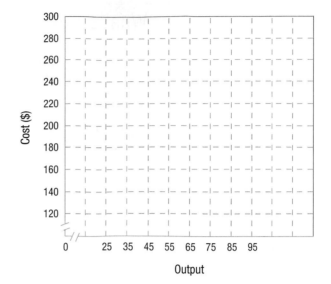

EP-1

12. Use Figure EP-2 to answer the following questions.

   a. What output level has the lowest average variable cost?

   b. At what point is marginal cost equal to average variable cost?

   c. Minimum average total cost is equal to _____.
   d. Why is the minimum point on ATC at 35 units greater than the minimum point on the AVC curve at 30 units?

   e. Why does the marginal cost curve cross through the minimum points on the ATC and AVC curves?

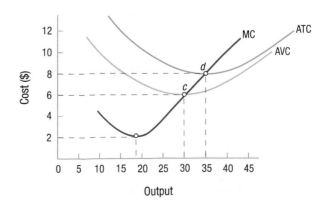

EP-2

What's Next

You now should have a good understanding of what lies behind supply curves. Firms seek out profitable business opportunities. Once they gauge a business need, they have to determine how they are going to produce the good or service, then determine the cost. With this information in hand, they can determine if there is a profit to be made.

In the next chapter, we look at competitive markets and see the forces that shape supply and demand in these markets. In that chapter, we give the assumption of profit maximization a much clearer analytical base.

Answers to Chapterwide Practice Questions

Matching

1. k	6. e	11. c	15. p
2. q	7. i	12. n	16. r
3. a	8. b	13. f	17. h
4. l	9. j	14. d	18. g
5. o	10. m		

Fill-In

1. entrepreneurs
2. total revenue, explicit costs, implicit costs, normal profits, economic profits
3. average, marginal
4. fixed, variable, marginal, average
5. average variable, average total
6. diseconomies, economies

True-False

1. F	6. T	10. T	14. T
2. T	7. F	11. F	15. F
3. T	8. F	12. T	16. F
4. T	9. F	13. F	17. T
5. F			

Multiple Choice

1. b	9. c	16. c	23. b
2. c	10. a	17. b	24. c
3. a	11. a	18. b	25. b
4. d	12. a	19. d	26. a
5. c	13. a	20. b	27. c
6. a	14. d	21. d	28. d
7. d	15. a	22. a	29. b
8. b			

Essay-Problem

1. Entrepreneurs see new business opportunities by finding unmet market needs. Meeting these needs helps economies to grow.

2. Yes. The problem was that this goal conflicted with the goals of some of the officers of the corporation, who sought to profit at Enron's expense. This sorry episode shows that profit maximization may indeed be the goal of the firm, but it may not be the goal of all of the members of that firm: This is the point at which trouble begins. The profit maximization assumption does not mean companies do *anything* to make higher profits. Economists limit this assumption to lawful behavior. Keep in mind that long-run profit concerns mean not doing things in the short run (illegal or unethical behavior) that threaten the long-run viability of the firm.

3. It is not an explicit cost because you do not pay yourself anything to go before the board. It is an opportunity cost and so should be included in the total costing for the project because you could have done other things with your time. Now, if your alternative was to play golf, then the opportunity cost may be low. But if you had to take time off from work, the cost is the wages foregone, or the personal day taken.

4. No. Economists link normal profits to the cost of capital. If interest rates go up, the cost of capital will go up. Therefore, what previously was considered normal profits will have to increase to meet the new cost of capital rate. Think of it this way: If you could get 5% interest from the bank, the cost of capital would have to be at least this rate to get you to invest your money in something else; when the interest rate the bank pays you goes up, you will need a higher rate from an investment to even consider taking the money out of the bank and investing it in an enterprise.

5. In the short run, fixed costs—rent, insurance—are fixed. Small businesses often have widely fluctuating sales and, therefore, fluctuating income. Fixed costs are the minimum a small business has to pay each month (often called "the nut"). Without accurate estimates of what these fixed costs are, small businesses owners may be surprised to find that they do not have the cash to pay these costs at various times of the year.

6. In the short run, fixed costs are fixed. Marginal costs have no bearing on fixed costs.

7. The LRATC is constructed by combining the ATC curves for a firm for different plant sizes, with the lowest possible production costs at every possible level of production. An oil-refining firm may have only a few different options for the size of its refineries, with the building of new refineries requiring investments of hundreds of millions of dollars. With only a few options for plant size being realistically available, any change in plant size can be expected to have a major impact on average costs, thus resulting in a bumpy LRATC curve for this firm.

8. Fixed: rent, insurance. Variable: wages, wheels, boards, paint.

9. Because the price of personal computers has fallen consistently over the years and is still falling, we would expect the industry as a whole to be operating under economies of scale. Individual companies, however, could be operating at any one of the three places on the LRATC.

10.

Number of Workers	Total Product	Marginal Product	Average Product
50	100	—	2.00
55	120	4	2.18
60	150	6	2.50
65	200	10	3.08
70	225	5	3.21
75	235	2	3.13
80	240	1	3.00

11. See the following table and Figure EPA-1.

L	Q	MP	AP	TFC	TVC	TC	AFC	ATC	AVC	MC
0	0	0	—	2000	0	2000	—	—	—	—
1	7	7	7	2000	2000	4000	285.71	571.43	285.71	285.71
2	15	8	7.50	2000	4000	6000	133.33	400.00	266.67	250.00
3	25	10	8.33	2000	6000	8000	80.00	320.00	240.00	200.00
4	40	15	10.00	2000	8000	10000	50.00	250.00	200.00	133.33
5	54	14	10.80	2000	10000	12000	37.04	222.22	185.19	142.86
6	65	11	10.83	2000	12000	14000	30.77	215.38	184.62	181.82
7	75	10	10.71	2000	14000	16000	26.67	213.33	186.67	200.00
8	84	9	10.50	2000	16000	18000	23.81	214.29	190.48	222.22
9	90	6	10.00	2000	18000	20000	22.22	222.22	200.00	333.33
10	95	5	9.50	2000	20000	22000	21.05	231.58	210.53	400.00

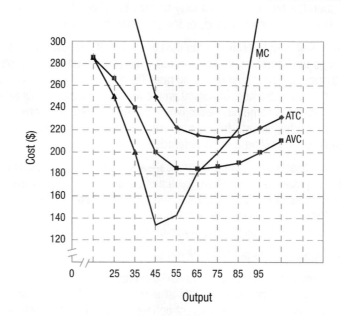

EPA-1

12. a. 30
    b. *c*
    c. $8
    d. Because fixed costs are included in ATC. This spreading of overhead means that ATC reaches a minimum after AVC.
    e. Marginal cost is the cost to produce one more unit of output. If MC is less than ATC, then ATC must fall (adding a smaller number to the average will bring the average down). Similarly, if MC is higher than ATC, ATC must be rising (again, adding a larger number to the average will increase the average). Only when MC = ATC is ATC at its minimum. The same analysis applies to AVC.

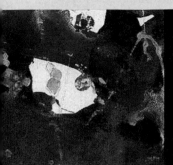

Competition

8

The Competitive Market Model Is a Cornerstone of Microeconomics

If supply and demand is the foundation of economics, the analysis of market structure is a close second. It is here where you will see how firms put together the profit equation of revenues minus costs. You looked at production and costs in the last chapter. Here, we start putting some of these ideas to work when we bring in revenues and show how costs help determine what a firm will produce. Pay special attention to the market model discussed in this chapter—competition—because what you learn here will make it much easier to understand other market structures in the following chapters.

After studying this chapter you should be able to

- Name the primary market structures and describe their characteristics.

- Define a competitive market and the assumptions that underlie it.

- Distinguish the differences between competitive markets in the short run and the long run.

- Analyze the conditions for profit maximization, loss minimization, and plant shutdown for a firm.

- Derive the firm's short-run supply curve.

- Use the short-run competitive model to determine long-run equilibrium.

- Describe why competition is in the public interest.

Review the Key Terms

Market structure analysis: By observing a few industry characteristics such as number of firms in the industry or the level of barriers to entry, economists can use this information to predict pricing and output behavior of the firm in the industry.

Competition: Exists when there are many relatively small buyers and sellers, a standardized product, with good information to both buyers and sellers, and no barriers to entry or exit.

Price taker: Individual firms in competitive markets get their prices from the market since they are so small they cannot influence market price. For this reason, competitive firms are price takers and can produce and sell all the output they produce at market determined prices.

Marginal revenue: The change in total revenue from selling an additional unit of output. Since competitive firms are price takers, P = MR for competitive firms.

Profit maximizing rule: Firms maximize profit by producing output where MR = MC. No other level of output produces higher profits.

Normal profits: Equal to zero economic profits; where P = ATC.

Shutdown point: When price in the short run falls below the minimum point on the AVC curve, the firm will minimize losses by closing its doors and stopping production. Since P < AVC, the firm's variable costs are not covered, so by shutting the plant, losses are reduced to fixed costs.

Short-run supply curve: The marginal cost curve above the minimum point on the average variable cost curve.

Productive efficiency: Goods and services are produced and sold to consumers at their lowest resource (opportunity) cost.

Allocative efficiency: The mix of goods and services produced are just what society desires. The price that consumers pay is equal to marginal cost and is also equal to the least average total cost.

Increasing cost industry: An industry that in the long run faces higher prices and costs as industry output expands. Industry expansion puts upward pressure on resources (inputs), causing higher costs in the long run.

Decreasing cost industry: An industry that in the long run faces lower prices and costs as industry output expands. Typically the result of technological advances.

Constant cost industry: An industry that in the long run faces roughly the same prices and costs as industry output expands. Some industries can virtually clone their operations in other areas without putting undue pressure on resource prices, resulting in constant operating costs as they expand in the long run.

Work Through the Chapter Tutorials

Market Structure Analysis

Frequently Asked Questions

Q: What is market structure analysis, and why is it useful?

A: Market structure analysis is used by economists to categorize industries by looking at a few key characteristics. Once categorized, an industry's behavior in pricing and output can be predicted.

Q: **What are the basic market structures, and how are they defined?**

A: Economists have identified four basic market structures: competition, monopolistic competition, oligopoly, and monopoly. They are defined by the following factors: the number of firms in the industry, the nature of the product produced, the extent of barriers to entry and exit, and the degree to which individual firms can control prices.

Q: **What are the main characteristics of the competitive market structure?**

A: The competitive market structure assumes, first, a market with many buyers and sellers, none large enough to influence product prices. Second, it assumes that a homogeneous or standardized product is produced. Third, it assumes all buyers and sellers have all relevant information about prices and product quality. Fourth, barriers to entry and exit are insignificant.

Q: **What does it mean to say that competitive firms are price takers?**

A: Competitive firms are price takers because they cannot significantly alter the sales price of their products. Product prices are determined in broad markets. Figure 1 depicts a competitive market, and the firm faces a horizontal demand curve—the firm cannot affect the price; it can only accept it.

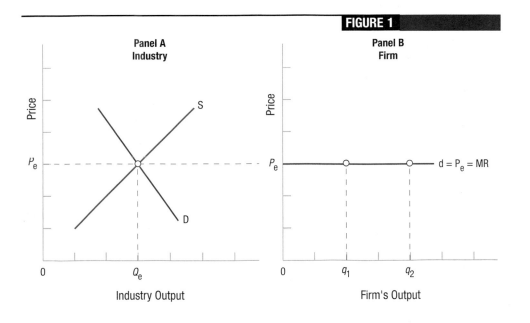

FIGURE 1

Panel A
Industry

Panel B
Firm

Q: **How is the short run defined?**

A: In the short run at least one factor of production (usually plant capacity) is fixed. Also in the short run, firms cannot enter or exit the industry.

Q: **How is the long run defined?**

A: In the long run, all factors of production are variable, with short-run profit levels inducing entry or exit.

Keep in Mind

Market structure analysis is a way to look at definable characteristics of an industry. Based on this assessment, one can predict industry pricing and output behavior. Competitive firms are price takers and have to accept market prices as given.

Market Structure Analysis Quick Check

Circle the Correct Answer

1. (T/F) Monopolies have substantial control over price.
2. (T/F) Competitive markets have homogeneous products.
3. (T/F) All markets have roughly the same number of buyers and sellers.
4. (T/F) In the short run, plant size and the number of firms in the industry are regarded as fixed.
5. Airlines represent what market structure?
   a. competition
   b. monopolistic competition
   c. oligopoly
   d. monopoly
6. Competitive markets
   a. are usually dominated by one or two large firms.
   b. have many sellers but often have few buyers.
   c. set up effective barriers to entry.
   d. put individual sellers in the position of price takers.
7. In a competitive market, a firm
   a. will sell its product for less than the market price in the hope of increasing sales.
   b. will try to influence government in the hope of getting the price raised.
   c. will try to maximize its profit by setting its sales price above the market price.
   d. will accept the market price as a given.

8. Competitive markets are characterized by
   a. many buyers and sellers, of varying sizes ranging from small to large.
   b. easy entry and exit from the industry in the short run.
   c. little opportunity to make profits in the short run.
   d. buyers and sellers having all the information they need about prices and product quality to make informed decisions.
9. Individual firms in competitive markets face horizontal demand curves. This means that any individual firm
   a. is a price maker.
   b. is a price taker.
   c. is not concerned with price.
   d. has a bowl-shaped marginal revenue curve.
10. Corn farming is an example of
    a. competitive markets.
    b. monopolistically competitive markets.
    c. oligopolistic markets.
    d. monopoly markets.

Score: ____

Answers: 1. T; 2. T; 3. F; 4. T; 5. c; 6. d; 7. d; 8. d; 9. b; 10. a

If You Got 9 or 10 Correct

You have a good grasp of the general concept of market structure, and more particularly of the characteristics of the competitive model. Go on to the next section, "Short-Run Decisions.".

If You Didn't Get at Least 9 Correct

Do a careful review of this introductory material because it is the foundation for this chapter and the next two chapters. First, be sure you can list the four major market structures. Second, jot down the main characteristics of the competitive market model. Finally, list the difference between the short run and the long run—this difference becomes important at the end of the chapter. Continue on, but be prepared to review this section again. Working through the next section, "Short-Run Decisions," will probably help you see why it is important to understand the assumptions of competitive markets. ■

Competition: Short-Run Decisions

Frequently Asked Questions

Q: How is marginal revenue defined, and how is it related to market price for a competitive firm?

A: Total revenue equals price per unit times quantity sold (TR = $p \times q$). Marginal revenue is equal to the change in total revenue that comes from producing an added unit of the product (MR = ΔTR/Δq). In a competitive market, a firm can sell all it wants at the market price, so marginal revenue is equal to market price for the competitive firm.

Q: **How will a competitive firm maximize its profits?**

A: Firms will maximize their profits by selling a level of output at which marginal revenue is just equal to marginal cost (MR = MC). For the competitive firm this translates into MR = MC = P. In the short run, a firm can earn economic profits, normal profits, or economic losses, depending on a product's market price.

Q: **How do average total costs determine profits for the competitive firm in the short run?**

A: If price is above the minimum point on the ATC curve, a firm will earn economic profits in the short run. If price is just equal to the minimum point on the ATC curve, the firm will earn normal profits. If price should fall below the minimum ATC, the firm will earn economic losses.

Q: **Why is the minimum point on the AVC curve known as the shutdown point?**

A: If price falls below the minimum point on the AVC curve, the firm will shut down and incur a loss equal to its fixed costs, since firms will not operate if they cannot cover their variable costs.

Q: **What is the short-run supply curve for the competitive firm?**

A: The short-run supply curve for the competitive firm is the marginal cost curve above the minimum point on the AVC curve.

Q: **At what price will a competitive firm in the short run earn economic profits? Normal profits? Losses?**

A: Figure 2 shows the short-run supply curve for a competitive firm. It also shows the profit possibilities discussed above. The competitive firm will earn economic profits with a price above P_1 (above point b), normal profits at a price of P_1 (at point b), and it will lose money at a price below P_1. The firm will remain in business in the short run at prices between P_0 and P_1 even though losses are incurred because variable costs will be covered and some revenue will be available to pay fixed costs. Below a price of P_0, the firm will shut down because it will not be able to cover all of its variable costs, much less any of its fixed costs.

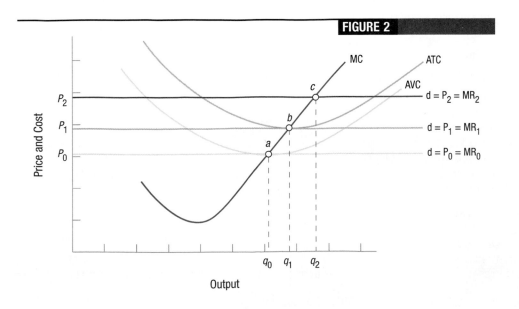

FIGURE 2

Key Point to Remember

Competitive firms are price takers so MR = P. Competitive firms (and firms in all of the market structures you will study) maximize profits by producing output where MR = MC. Thus, competitive firms maximize profits where P = MR = MC.

Core Equation: Profit Maximization

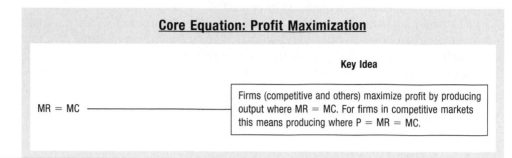

Key Idea

MR = MC ———————————— Firms (competitive and others) maximize profit by producing output where MR = MC. For firms in competitive markets this means producing where P = MR = MC.

Competition: Short-Run Decisions Quick Check

Circle the Correct Answer

1. (T/F) If a company earns an additional $1,500 in revenue by selling 10 additional units, its marginal revenue is $1,500.

2. (T/F) A firm in a competitive market will maximize its profits by producing a level of output where marginal revenue equals marginal cost.

3. (T/F) If a company earns $3,000 in revenue, hires an additional worker for $100 in wages and then earns a total of $3,500 in revenue, its marginal revenue is $400.

4. (T/F) A firm in a competitive market will always want to produce as much output as it can because it will maximize its profits.

5. If a competitive firm produces at the point where the marginal cost curve intersects the average total cost curve at its minimum point, the firm will earn
   a. economic profits.
   b. normal profits.
   c. no profits.
   d. a short-run loss.

6. Should the competitive firm keep producing even if it faces short-run losses if it is producing at a point on the marginal cost curve that is above the minimum point of its average variable cost curve?
   a. Yes, because it is producing normal profits at this point.
   b. Yes, because it is still producing more than zero economic profits at this point.
   c. Yes, because it still covers its variable costs and has some revenue to pay for fixed costs.
   d. No, it should never incur losses.

7. For a competitive firm, the portion of the marginal cost (MC) curve that exists above the minimum point on the average variable cost (AVC) curve is actually
   a. the firm's short-run demand curve.
   b. the firm's long-run demand curve.
   c. the firm's average total costs curve.
   d. the firm's short-run supply curve.

8. If a competitive firm produces at the point where the marginal cost curve intersects the average variable cost curve at its minimum point, the firm will
   a. earn economic profits.
   b. earn normal profits.
   c. have a short-run loss, but it will just cover its variable costs.
   d. have a short-run loss, but it will not cover its variable costs.

9. A competitive firm seeking to minimize its losses in the short run should shut down its plant as soon as
   a. it suffers economic losses.
   b. profits drop to zero.
   c. losses exceed normal profits.
   d. losses exceed total fixed costs.

10. The short-run supply curve for the competitive firm is a portion of
    a. the average total cost (ATC) curve.
    b. the average variable cost (AVC) curve.
    c. the average fixed cost (AFC) curve.
    d. the marginal cost (MC) curve.

Score: _____

If You Got 9 or 10 Correct

You have been able to pick up some relatively difficult material including an understanding of the profit possibilities for the competitive firm in the short run and the derivation of the competitive firm's short-run supply curve. You can move on to "Competition: Long-Run Adjustments," the last section in this chapter. However, because of the importance of the competitive model, we suggest you do a quick review of the solved problem below. This review should be worth it.

If You Didn't Get at Least 9 Correct

Don't get upset—this is tough material. A patient review will be worth it. Reflect on the role played by profit maximizing and when and why the firm would shut the plant.

Next, put this reflection to work by looking again at the figures in this section. Be sure you know the relationship between price, the average total costs curve, and profits. Read the caption to each figure and make sure you see why each figure is different and what ideas are conveyed. This approach to marginal decision making (profits are maximized by equating MR and MC) will show up continually in upcoming chapters. Take a moment to study the Solved Problem below.

Solved Problem: Short-Run Competitive Decisions

Figure 3 represents a firm in a competitive industry. Answer the following questions:

 a. At what price will this firm shut down and produce no output at all?

 b. If the market sets a price of $10 a unit, how much output will this firm produce? Will it make an economic profit? If so, roughly how much?

 c. If market price falls to $8 a unit, how much output will the firm produce? Will it make a profit? If so, roughly how much?

 d. If market price is $7 a unit, how much will the firm produce? Again, will it make a profit? How much?

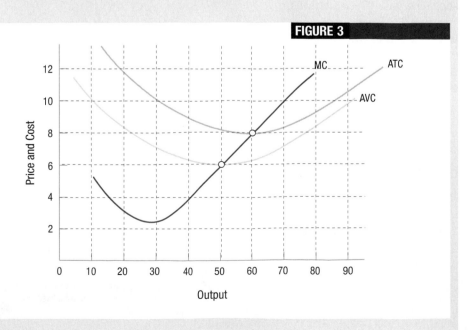

FIGURE 3

Solution-Discussion

a. The minimum point on the AVC curve is at $6 a unit. At a price below $6, the firm is unable to cover its variable costs and losses exceed fixed costs, so the firm is better off closing its doors.

b. At $10 a unit, the firm will produce 70 units of output. Because price is above ATC, the firm will earn an economic profit. Profit per unit is roughly $1.50 a unit (P − ATC at an output of 70), so total economic profit is roughly $105 ($1.50 × 70 = $105).

c. At a price of $8, the firm will produce 60 units. This is the minimum point on the ATC curve, so the firm's TR = TC, and therefore it earns a normal profit.

d. At $7 a unit, the firm equates MR and MC at roughly 55 units of output. This price is below ATC, but above AVC so the firm is earning a loss. Because P > AVC, the firm is able to pay its variable costs and contribute to overhead (fixed costs), so by producing 55 units, it is minimizing losses (losses are smaller than fixed costs and are roughly $55).

Hint: To see the answers for each of these questions, draw a horizontal line at the price and see where it intersects the MC curve.

Keep in Mind

The approach contained in short-run competitive decision making is too important for future chapters to have only partial knowledge. You owe it to yourself to make sure you understand this material thoroughly. The approach is used over and over again throughout economics.

Examine the figures again, and be sure you know how profit is determined in the short run for the competitive firm. Take a little time and draw your own graph for ATC, AVC, and MC. Draw a horizontal line for price and outline the profit maximizing output and shade in profit (or loss). Do not continue on until you are confident you understand how to determine profits and costs and can show and describe a situation when the firm is just earning normal profits. As the Core Graph below shows, you only need *two* points on the standard cost curve graph to be able to show the following situations:

■ Economic profits.
■ Normal profits.
■ Economic losses, but the firm keeps operating.
■ Economic losses exceeding fixed costs, so the firm shuts down.

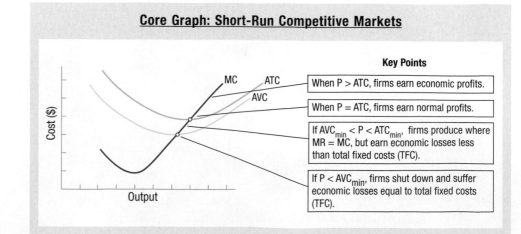

Core Graph: Short-Run Competitive Markets

Key Points

When P > ATC, firms earn economic profits.

When P = ATC, firms earn normal profits.

If $AVC_{min} < P < ATC_{min}$, firms produce where MR = MC, but earn economic losses less than total fixed costs (TFC).

If $P < AVC_{min}$, firms shut down and suffer economic losses equal to total fixed costs (TFC).

Once you have these concepts down, continue on. The next section on long-run adjustments in competitive markets provides perspective on these short-run competitive decisions. ■

Competition: Long-Run Adjustments

Frequently Asked Questions

Q: How is the long run defined?

A: In the long run, all factors of production are variable, including the ability to exit or enter an industry.

Q: How are profits and losses long run signals to other firms?

A: When the firms in an industry earn economic profits in the short run, this attracts new firms to the industry, reducing product price until firms are just earning normal profits. A corresponding adjustment occurs when the firms in an industry suffer short-term economic losses: Some firms leave the industry, thus raising prices until the remaining firms are again earning normal returns.

Q: How do competitive markets serve the public interest?

A: Competitive markets serve the public interest by ensuring that firms price their products at their marginal cost, which also equals $LRATC_{min}$. Therefore, the quantity of products consumers want is provided at the lowest possible opportunity cost ($LRATC_{min}$). This is shown in Figure 4.

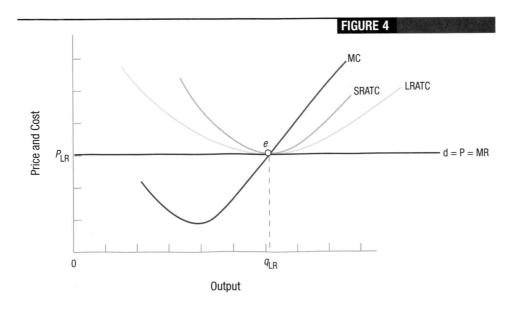

FIGURE 4

Q: What are increasing cost, decreasing cost, and constant cost industries?

A: An industry may be an increasing cost industry (average total costs increase in the long run as more output is produced), a decreasing cost industry (average total costs decrease in the long run as more output is produced), or a constant cost industry (average total costs remain constant in the long run even as output is increased) depending on the industry's precise structure, the current state of technology, and the degree of economies and diseconomies of scale.

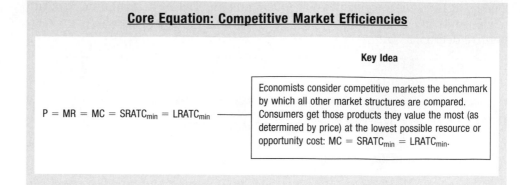

Core Equation: Competitive Market Efficiencies

Key Idea

$$P = MR = MC = SRATC_{min} = LRATC_{min}$$

Economists consider competitive markets the benchmark by which all other market structures are compared. Consumers get those products they value the most (as determined by price) at the lowest possible resource or opportunity cost: $MC = SRATC_{min} = LRATC_{min}$.

Key Point to Remember

Entry and exit are unrestricted in competitive markets. As a result, short-run profits and losses act as signals to existing firms and potential entrants. In the long run, economic profits encourage entry and economic losses encourage exit by existing firms. These dynamic movements ensure that firms in competitive markets only earn normal (zero economic) profits in the long run. Economists find the long-run dynamics of competitive markets a thing of beauty. The analysis (story) shows why competitive markets are the standard by which other market structures are compared.

Competition: Long-Run Adjustments Quick Check

Circle the Correct Answer

1. (T/F) In the long run, competitive markets are both productively and allocatively efficient.
2. (T/F) In an increasing cost industry, expansion leads to upward pressure on inputs such as raw materials, leading to higher prices and costs.

3. What will happen in the long run in Figure 5?
   a. Short-run profits will encourage more firms to enter the market, and they will earn economic profits.
   b. Short-run profits will encourage more firms to enter the market, and they will earn normal profits.

FIGURE 5

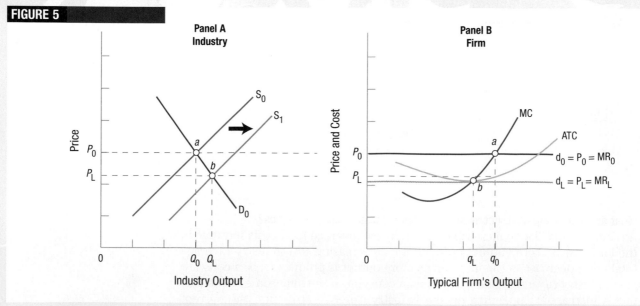

c. Short-run losses will encourage some firms to leave the market, and the remaining firms will earn economic profits.

d. Short-run losses will encourage some firms to leave the market, and the remaining firms will earn normal profits.

4. In the long run, the individual competitive firm in Figure 5 will earn
   a. economic profits equal to $(MC \times P_0) - (ATC \times P_L)$.
   b. economic profits equal to OP_0aq_0.
   c. economic losses.

d. zero economic profits.

5. When a competitive market is in long-run equilibrium, price (P) is *not* equal to which of the following terms?
   a. MC
   b. $LRATC_{min}$
   c. MR
   d. $SRATC_{min}$

Score: _____

Answers: 1. T; 2. T; 3. b; 4. d; 5. d

If You Got All 5 Questions Correct

You seem to have the story down pat. Just in case you got lucky with this quick quiz, take a few moments and work through the next section, "Outlining the Transition From Short Run to Long Run in Competitive Markets."

If You Didn't Get All of Them Correct

Keep in mind that long-run adjustments in competitive markets can be some of the more difficult material to absorb in the book. It may take you several attempts to really master this material. For both short-run economic profits and losses, the transition to the long run is really a stylistic story. In the following we break the story down into its parts. Work through this material and it should help you get the process straight.

Outlining the Transition from Short Run to Long Run in Competitive Markets

The transition of competitive markets from short-run to long-run equilibrium can be thought of as a stylized story with a series of steps. We will do this for both short-run economic profits and short-run economic losses. As you work through this section, make sure you understand the reasons for each step before you move on.

Short-Run Economic Profits to Long-Run Normal Profits

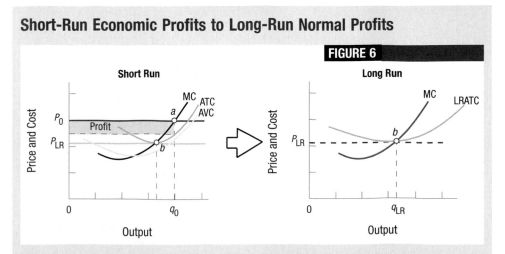

FIGURE 6

1. In the short run, firms earn *economic profits* and profit maximizing output is found at point a in Figure 6 where $P = MR = MC$.

2. Notice that at point *a*, the firm is producing beyond the *minimum* point on the ATC curve (point *b*). Also note that the AVC curve (grayed out) is there for reference in the short run, but it is not crucial when the firm is earning economic profits.

3. The shaded area in the short run is equal to economic profits.

4. The economic profits attract *new* firms seeking these above normal returns.

5. As new firms enter the industry, supply *expands* and price *falls*.

6. As price declines, individual firm output *falls* and economic profits *decline*.

7. Once entry is sufficient to reduce price to P_{LR} (point *b*), only *normal profits* are earned and the incentive for new firms to enter no longer exists.

8. In long-run equilibrium (point *b*), P = MC = SRATC$_{min}$ = LRATC$_{min}$. Consumers get the product at the lowest possible opportunity (resource) cost.

Short-Run Economic Losses to Long-Run Normal Profits

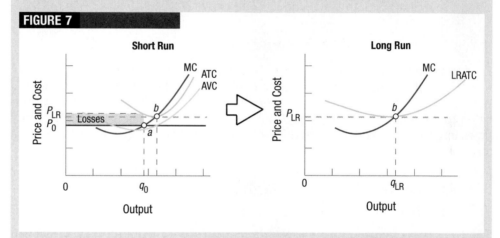

FIGURE 7

1. In the short run, firms earn *economic losses*, and loss-minimizing output is found at point *a* in Figure 7 where P = MR = MC. Losses are smaller than fixed costs because price is above the AVC curve. So, the firm continues to produce.

2. Notice that at point *a*, the firm is producing *less* output than that associated with the *minimum* point on the ATC curve (point *b*).

3. The shaded area in the short run is equal to economic losses.

4. These economic losses lead some existing firms to *leave* the industry.

5. As these firms exit the industry, supply *falls* and price *rises*.

6. As price increases, individual firm output *grows* and economic losses *decline*.

7. Once exit is sufficient to raise price to P_{LR} (point *b*), *normal profits* are earned and the incentive for firms to leave the industry no longer exists.

8. In long-run equilibrium (point *b*), P = MC = SRATC$_{min}$ = LRATC$_{min}$. Consumers get the product at the lowest possible opportunity (resource) cost.

At this point you should understand how profits and losses work as signals and why competitive markets are so efficient. Now see how you do on the questions that follow.

Competition: Long-Run Adjustments Final Check

1. (T/F) In the long run, the price of finished goods will drop in constant cost industries.
2. Competitive markets are efficient because
   a. $P = MC = LRAVC_{min}$
   b. $P = MC = LRAFC_{min}$
   c. $P = MC = LRATC_{min}$
   d. $P = MC = LRTR_{min}$
3. What will happen in the long run in Figure 8?
   a. Short-run profits will encourage more firms to enter the market, and they will earn economic profits.
   b. Short-run profits will encourage more firms to enter the market, and they will earn normal profits.
   c. Short-run losses will encourage some firms to leave the market, and the remaining firms will earn economic profits.
   d. Short-run losses will encourage some firms to leave the market, and the remaining firms will earn normal profits.

4. In the long run, the individual competitive firm in Figure 6 will
   a. earn economic profits.
   b. earn normal profits.
   c. earn zero profits.
   d. incur economic losses.
5. When a competitive market is in long-run equilibrium, price (P) is equal to which of the following terms?
   a. MR
   b. $LRATC_{min}$
   c. MC
   d. all of the above

Score: ____

Answers: 1. F; 2. c; 3. d; 4. b; 5. d.

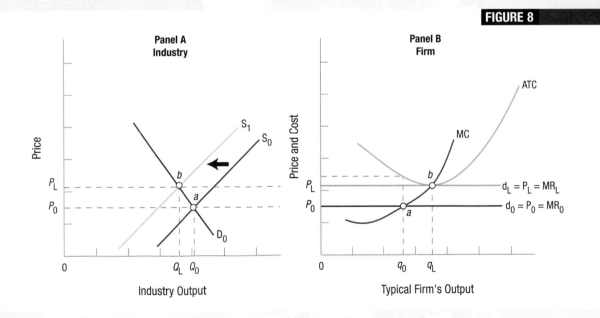

FIGURE 8

You should have got all of these correct. If not, you should review this material one more time. ■

___

Consider These Hints, Tips, and Reminders   STEP 4

1. What you must take away from this chapter:
   ■ Profits are maximized by producing output where MR = MC.

- In the short run,
  - ☐ If P > ATC, the firm makes an economic profit.
  - ☐ If P < ATC, the firm makes losses.
  - ☐ If AVC < P < ATC, the firm produces output but makes losses.
  - ☐ If P < AVC, the firm shuts down and minimizes losses (losses equal fixed costs).
- In the long run,
  - ☐ Short-run economic profits encourage entry, and short-run losses result in exit by some existing firms.
  - ☐ Entry and exit drive profits to normal levels.
- Competitive markets are the benchmark to which all other market structures are compared. Competitive markets serve the public interest because consumers get what they want at the lowest price; $P = MC = SRATC_{min} = LRATC_{min}$.

2. Market structure analysis is a very powerful analytic approach. You look at the industry's characteristics and forecast how its firms will determine price and output. This may seem straightforward when markets are competitive, but it gets a little more complex when other market structures are considered. Keep in mind that profits are maximized when MR = MC. This will be how you analyze all other market structures as well.

Do the Homework for Chapter 8
Competition

Instructor _____ Time _____ Student _____

Use the answer key below to record your answers to these homework questions.

1. (a) (b) (c) (d)	6. (a) (b) (c) (d)	11. (a) (b) (c) (d)	16. (a) (b) (c) (d)
2. (a) (b) (c) (d)	7. (a) (b) (c) (d)	12. (a) (b) (c) (d)	17. (a) (b) (c) (d)
3. (a) (b) (c) (d)	8. (a) (b) (c) (d)	13. (a) (b) (c) (d)	18. (a) (b) (c) (d)
4. (a) (b) (c) (d)	9. (a) (b) (c) (d)	14. (a) (b) (c) (d)	19. (a) (b) (c) (d)
5. (a) (b) (c) (d)	10. (a) (b) (c) (d)	15. (a) (b) (c) (d)	20. (a) (b) (c) (d)

1. Which of the following is *not* an assumption of competitive markets?
   a. homogeneous products in this market
   b. a large number of buyers and sellers
   c. barriers to entry or exit
   d. good knowledge by both buyers and sellers

2. Which of the following markets is likely to be the most competitive?
   a. cable television
   b. automobiles and trucks
   c. oil refining
   d. farm commodities

3. In a competitive market, firms will
   a. reduce their prices to increase their market share.
   b. advertise the uniqueness of their products.
   c. produce at the lowest possible cost to maximize per unit profits.
   d. generally accept the market price as a given.

4. The demand curve facing a competitive firm is
   a. upward sloping.
   b. highly inelastic.
   c. horizontal.
   d. downward sloping.

5. If the demand curve facing the competitive firm in Figure HW-1 is d_2, the competitive price will be which of the following?
   a. $10
   b. $15
   c. $20
   d. $25

6. If the demand curve facing the competitive firm in Figure HW-1 is d_2, profits earned by this firm will be roughly equal to which of the following?
   a. 0
   b. $2,240
   c. $2,800
   d. $560

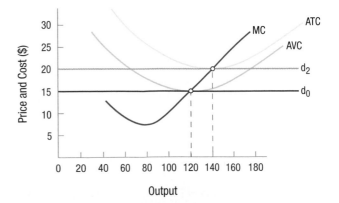

HW-1

7. If the demand curve facing the competitive firm in Figure HW-1 is d_2, total variable costs for this

firm will be roughly equal to which of the following?
a. $2,800
b. $1,800
c. $2,000
d. $2,240

8. If the demand curve facing the competitive firm in Figure HW-1 is d_2, total costs for this firm will be roughly equal to which of the following?
a. $2,400
b. $2,600
c. $2,800
d. $3,000

9. If the demand curve facing the competitive firm in Figure HW-1 is d_0, total profits for this firm will be roughly equal to:
a. a loss equal to $720
b. just a normal profit
c. losses equal to total variable costs
d. a loss equal to $1,800

10. In Figure HW-1, if the price falls below _____, the firm will shut down.
a. $30
b. $25
c. $20
d. $15

11. If the firm in Figure HW-1 represents the typical firm in the industry, long-run equilibrium price will be which of the following?
a. $30
b. $25
c. $20
d. $15

12. If the firm in Figure HW-1 is producing 140 units of output, average fixed cost will roughly equal
a. $6
b. $5
c. $4
d. $3

13. If in Figure HW-1 the short-run equilibrium price for the industry is $17, what will happen in this industry in the long run?
a. Short-run profits will encourage more firms to enter the market, and industry output will expand.
b. Short-run profits will discourage new firms from entering since the competitive pressures are so intense.
c. Short-run losses will encourage some firms to leave the industry, and industry and individual firm output will decline.
d. Short-run losses will encourage some firms to leave the industry, and industry output will decline, but the remaining firms will earn normal profits.

14. If in Figure HW-1 the short-run equilibrium price for the industry is $25, what will happen in this industry in the long run?
a. Short-run profits will encourage more firms to enter the market, and industry output will expand, but individual firm output and profit will decline.
b. Short-run profits will discourage new firms from entering since the competitive pressures are so intense.
c. Short-run profits will encourage new firms to enter the industry, but the intense competition will cause industry and individual firm output to decline.
d. Short-run losses will encourage some firms to leave the industry, and industry output will decline, but the remaining firms will earn normal profits.

15. In Figure HW-1 the short-run supply curve for this firm will be:
a. There is no supply curve for this firm.
b. The marginal cost curve above a price of $10.
c. The marginal cost curve above a price of $15.
d. The marginal cost curve above a price of $20.

16. For a competitive firm in the short run, if marginal revenue is greater than marginal costs, then the firm should
a. shut the plant and move the capital into a more profitable industry.
b. decrease production until MR = MC.
c. not do anything because if MR > MC profits must be maximized.
d. increase production until MR = MC.

17. For a competitive firm in the short run, if marginal revenue is less than marginal costs, then the firm should
a. shut the plant and move the capital into a more profitable industry.
b. decrease production until MR = MC.
c. not do anything because if MR > MC profits must be maximized.
d. increase production until MR = MC.

18. For a competitive firm, if marginal revenue equals marginal cost, which equals average total cost, and this is just equal to average revenue or price, then the firm is
    a. making economic profits.
    b. making such large losses that it needs to close the firm.
    c. making normal profits.
    d. not producing enough output to make a profit.

19. The most important reason that competitive firms only earn normal profits in the long run is because
    a. supply cannot exceed demand.
    b. of easy entry and exit into and out of the industry.
    c. corporate income taxes reduce profits to zero.
    d. fixed costs are extremely low for most industries.

20. To maximize profits, a competitive firm
    a. produces where average total costs are minimized.
    b. sets a price that maximizes total revenue.
    c. produces an output where marginal revenue is just equal to total costs.
    d. produces an output where marginal revenue is just equal to marginal costs.

		STEP 6
Use the ExamPrep to Get Ready for Exams		

This sheet (front and back) is designed to help you prepare for your exams. The chapter has been boiled down to its key concepts. You are asked to answer questions, define terms, draw graphs, and if you wish, add summaries of class notes.

Market Structure Analysis

List the characteristics of each market structure in the following table.

Competition	Monopolistic Competition	Oligopoly	Monopoly

Competition: Short-Run Decisions

Define marginal revenue:

Why is marginal revenue a straight line at the market price for the competitive firm?

Profit Maximizing Output

Use the grid below to draw the following short-run cost curves:

- Average variable costs
- Average total costs
- Marginal costs

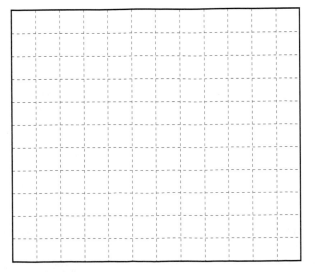

(Hint: Keep in mind that the minimum point on the AVC curve comes at a lower output than the minimum point on the ATC curve. Also, the marginal cost curve goes through both minimum points.)

Draw in a demand curve for this firm that is above the minimum point on the ATC curve and label it d$_{profits}$. Now cross-hatch in total profits and label the area "profits."

Draw in a demand curve for this firm that is just equal to the minimum point on the ATC curve and label it d$_{normal\ profits}$. Economic profits equal _____? Does this firm earn a profit at all? Explain:

Loss Minimizing Output

Use the grid below to draw the following short-run cost curves:

- Average variable costs
- Average total costs
- Marginal costs

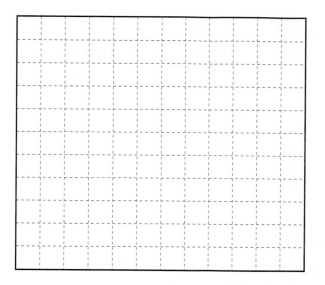

(Hint: Keep in mind that the minimum point on the AVC curve comes at a lower output than the minimum point on the ATC curve. Also, the marginal cost curve goes through both minimum points.)

Draw in a demand curve for this firm that is below the minimum point on the ATC curve and label it d$_{losses}$. Now cross-hatch in total losses and label the area "losses." Why does the firm continue to operate if it incurs losses?

Use the two figures you have drawn to explain why the marginal cost curve above the minimum point on the AVC curve is the firm's supply curve.

Competition: Long-Run Adjustments

Explain what happens in a competitive industry in the long run when firms are earning economic profits in the short run.

Explain what happens in a competitive industry in the long run when firms are earning economic losses in the short run.

Why in both instances do firms only earn normal profits in the long run?

Explain why the competitive market is the ideal market structure.

Additional Study Help Chapterwide Practice Questions

Matching

Match the description with the corresponding term.

___ 1. Market structure
___ 2. Competitive markets
___ 3. Profit maximization
___ 4. Shutdown point
___ 5. Increasing cost industry
___ 6. Decreasing cost industry
___ 7. Constant cost industry

a. Losses exceed total fixed costs and revenues are not even enough to cover variable costs.

b. An industry that expands in the long run without enjoying economies or suffering diseconomies.

c. According to this principle, firms will continue to produce and sell output until marginal revenue, the change in total revenue that results from the sale of one more unit of the product, equals marginal cost.

d. When the firms in an industry expand or new firms enter it, added demands push up the price of raw materials and labor. These diseconomies cause costs to increase.

e. Economists categorize industries as competitive, monopolistically competitive, oligopolistic, or monopolistic.

f. An industry that enjoys economies as it expands, thus reducing average production costs.

g. Many buyers and sellers but none large enough to influence product prices, homogeneous products, complete information for buyers and sellers, no barriers to entry or exit, and thus no long term economic profits.

Fill-In

Circle the word(s) in parentheses that complete the sentence.

1. When just a few firms that are mutually interdependent control an industry, the industry is representative of (competition, monopolistic competition, oligopoly, monopoly) _____ market structure. When many firms exist in an industry with standardized products, the industry represents (competition, monopolistic competition, oligopoly, monopoly) _____ market structure. A one firm industry is a (oligopoly, monopoly) _____.

2. An important assumption of competitive markets is (differentiated products, no barriers to entry or exit) _____, while for monopolistically competitive markets, an important assumption is (differentiated products, no barriers to entry or exit) _____.

3. For the competitive firm marginal revenue is equal to (profit, price, output) _____, and profit maximizing output is found where marginal revenue equals (price, marginal cost) _____.

4. When market price is greater than the minimum of average total costs, the firm earns (normal profits, economic profits, economic losses) _____. If market price falls below the minimum of average total costs, but average variable costs are covered, the firm earns (normal profits, economic profits, economic losses) _____; but when average variable costs cannot be covered, the firm (closes its doors, minimizes losses by producing and selling some output where MR = MC) _____. When market price is just equal to the minimum of average total costs, the firm can expect to earn (normal profits, economic profits, economic losses) _____.

5. Short-term (normal profits, economic profits, economic losses) _____ attract firms into the industry, resulting in (normal profits, economic profits, economic losses) _____ over the long run. Short-term (normal profits, economic profits, economic losses) _____ cause the industry to contract, causing market price to (rise, fall, remain the same) _____, and ultimately lead to (normal profits, economic profits, economic losses) _____ over the long run.

6. Competitive industries exhibit (allocative, productive) _____ efficiency because products are produced at the lowest opportunity cost and also achieve (allocative, productive) _____ efficiency because consumers get the products they want at marginal cost.

True-False

Circle the correct answer.

T/F 1. Competitive markets have virtually no barriers to entry or exit.

T/F 2. The individual firms in an oligopoly have little control over the price of their products.

T/F   3. In a competitive market, an individual firm's demand curve will be vertical.

T/F   4. If a company earns an additional $700 in revenue by selling 5 additional units, it marginal revenue is $140.

T/F   5. If a bicycle company in a competitive market finds it can sell as many mountain bikes as it produces at $400 each, it will definitely want to produce and sell as many mountain bikes as it can.

T/F   6. A firm in a competitive market will maximize its profits by producing a level of output where marginal revenue equals marginal cost.

T/F   7. A firm that is earning zero economic profits is not earning any profits at all.

T/F   8. As soon as a firm begins to suffer economic losses, it can be expected to shut down its production facilities.

T/F   9. To minimize losses, a competitive firm will shut down its plant once prices fall below the minimum point on the average variable costs curve.

T/F   10. A competitive firm's short-run supply curve is the marginal cost curve above the minimum point on the average variable costs curve.

T/F   11. In a competitive market, individual firms may earn economic profits in the short run, but they will earn zero economic profits in the long run.

T/F   12. If the individual firms in a competitive market are earning normal profits, this will draw new firms into the market in the long run.

T/F   13. Competitive markets are both productively and allocatively efficient.

T/F   14. Easy entry and exit ensure that only normal profits are earned by competitive firms in the long run.

T/F   15. A decreasing cost industry enjoys certain economies as it expands its output, thereby reducing the price of finished products.

Multiple Choice

Circle the correct answer.

1. In what way do competitive markets, as described by Adam Smith, resemble the realm of biological life, as described by Charles Darwin?
   a. Money is essential for determining the courses of both.
   b. In both, minor adjustments take thousands of years to complete.
   c. The best place to observe both is the Galapagos Islands.
   d. In both, only the most efficient survive.

2. What does market structure analysis allow economists to do?
   a. Predict the long-range viability of various products.
   b. Predict the pricing and production behavior of firms in various industries.
   c. Understand the physical layout of stores and other marketplaces.
   d. Predict consumer behavior in various markets.

3. Which of the following factors are *not* relevant to determining the market structure of a particular industry?
   a. the size of the industry in terms of total revenues
   b. the extent of barriers to market exit and entry
   c. the extent to which individual sellers can control prices
   d. the number of firms in the industry

4. The benchmark for comparing other market structures is which of the following
   a. competition
   b. monopolistic competition
   c. oligopoly
   d. monopoly

5. Which market structure features many buyers and sellers, differentiated products, no barriers to entry or exit, no long-run economic profits, and some control over price on the part of individual sellers?
   a. competition
   b. monopolistic competition
   c. oligopoly
   d. monopoly

6. Which market structure features few firms, mutually dependent decision making, substantial barriers to entry, the potential for long-run economic profits, and shared market power, with consider-

able control over price on the part of individual sellers?
a. competition
b. monopolistic competition
c. oligopoly
d. monopoly

7. Which of the following is *not* assumed of competitive markets?
a. The market contains many buyers and sellers.
b. Firms have no potential for long-term economic profits.
c. Individual sellers have some control over market prices.
d. Homogeneous products are offered for sale.

8. Which of the following is *not* assumed of monopolies?
a. Firms have no potential for long-run economic profits.
b. The industry contains only one firm.
c. There are major and effective barriers to market entry.
d. The individual firm has substantial control over the price of its products.

9. An individual firm is a price taker if
a. it has some control over the sales price of its product.
b. it has complete control over the sales price of its product.
c. market prices are irrelevant to its production decisions.
d. it has little choice but to sell its product at the established market price.

10. The individual firms in a competitive market produce goods that are
a. highly differentiated.
b. moderately differentiated.
c. homogeneous, or standardized.
d. typically of low quality.

11. In a competitive market, a firm
a. can be expected to sell its product for less than the market price.
b. could conceivably sell its product for less than the market price, but would normally have no reason to do so.
c. can maximize its profit by setting its sales price above the market price.
d. will rarely pay attention to the market price in setting the price of its own product.

12. Why are the individual firms in a competitive market price takers?
a. The industry has so many firms, and each is so small, that none have much control over the price of their products.
b. The managers in such firms rarely have time to figure out their own prices, so they just go with the prices the market sets.
c. The industry has so few firms, and each is so large, that none of them has much control over the price of their products.
d. High barriers to entering or exiting the market force individual firms to accept the market price.

13. Which of the following industries is least likely to be in a competitive market structure?
a. soybeans
b. semiconductors
c. military aircraft
d. sheet metal

14. Why do firms in competitive markets have little control over the price of their products?
a. The government regulates the prices of such firms.
b. Competitive markets are dominated by one or two giant corporations, which largely determine product price.
c. There are so many small firms in competitive markets that none can have much influence over product price.
d. High exit barriers prevent such firms from leaving the market.

15. In the short run, which factors are usually regarded as fixed?
a. number of workers employed and the quantity of raw materials purchased
b. plant size and the number of firms in the industry
c. number of workers employed and the number of shifts the plant operates
d. total costs and total revenues

16. Marginal revenue is equal to
a. change in revenue over change in quantity sold.
b. price per unit times quantity sold.
c. change in revenue over change in price.
d. total revenue over quantity sold.

17. For firms in competitive industries, marginal revenue is equivalent to
a. total revenue.
b. change in quantity sold.
c. profit per unit.
d. price per unit.

18. If price is above the minimum point on a firm's ATC curve in the short run, the firm will
    a. incur economic losses.
    b. earn normal profits.
    c. earn economic profits.
    d. be producing at a level of output in which MC exceeds MR.

19. In Figure MC-1, if the firm were to expand its production from 84 to 87 units of output, it would be
    a. operating at a level of optimal productive efficiency.
    b. reducing its profits by producing where marginal cost exceeds price.
    c. increasing its profits by producing and selling more units.
    d. realizing economies of scale by increasing its output.

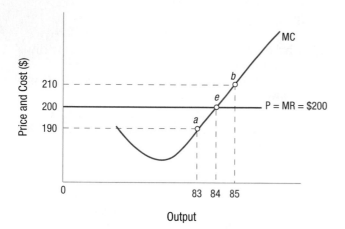

MC-1

20. In a competitive industry, a profit-maximizing firm will continue producing and selling output until
    a. marginal revenue equals average cost.
    b. total revenue equals marginal cost.
    c. marginal revenue equals marginal cost.
    d. average cost exceeds marginal revenue.

21. When a competitive firm is earning normal economic profits
    a. it is earning zero economic profits.
    b. other firms can be expected to enter the industry.
    c. existing firms can be expected to leave the industry.
    d. it is earning economic profits greater than zero.

22. A competitive firm seeking to minimize its losses in the short run should shut down its plant as soon as
    a. it begins suffering economic losses.
    b. total losses exceed total variable costs.

    c. total losses exceed total fixed costs.
    d. profit per unit falls below zero.

23. For a competitive firm, what does the marginal cost (MC) curve above the minimum point on the average variable costs (AVC) curve represent?
    a. the firm's short-run supply curve
    b. the firm's long-run demand curve
    c. the firm's average variable costs curve
    d. the firm's short-run demand curve

Use Figure MC-2 to answer questions 24–28. Figure MC-2 portrays the cost curves for a competitive firm in the short run.

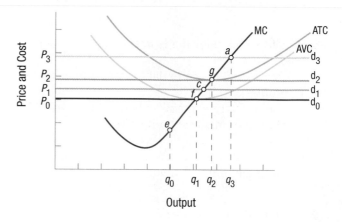

MC-2

24. If the market price is P_3, and the firm produces q_3 units of output, the firm will
    a. earn economic profits.
    b. earn normal profits.
    c. incur a loss, though not enough to shut down.
    d. incur a loss greater than fixed costs, so it will shut down.

25. If the market price is P_2 and the firm produces q_2 units, the firm will
    a. earn economic profits.
    b. earn normal profits.
    c. incur a loss.
    d. incur a loss equal to fixed costs.

26. If the market price is P_0, and the firm produces q_1 units, the firm will be at the point of
    a. economic profits.
    b. normal profits.
    c. zero economic profits.
    d. shutdown.

27. Competitive firms will never produce at point
    a. g
    b. a
    c. f
    d. e

28. At point *c,* firms will
    a. reap a normal profit.
    b. face a loss but continue producing because some fixed costs are covered.
    c. face a loss and shut down because variable costs are not covered.
    d. face a loss and shut down because competitive firms should never incur a loss.

29. If the firms in an industry are earning economic profits, what happens in the long run?
    a. Some existing firms will exit the industry.
    b. New firms can be expected to enter the industry.
    c. There will be no pressure for firms to either enter or exit the industry.
    d. Total revenues in the industry can be expected to fall.

30. If the firms in an industry are earning economic losses, what happens in the long run?
    a. Some existing firms can be expected to exit the industry.
    b. New firms can be expected to enter the industry.
    c. There will be no pressure for firms either to enter or to exit the industry.
    d. Total revenues in the industry can be expected to rise.

31. In the long run, the firms in a competitive industry can be expected to
    a. suffer economic losses.
    b. earn economic profits.
    c. set their prices above market prices.
    d. earn normal profits.

32. If a large number of firms, having suffered economic losses, exit a competitive market, which of the following would we *not* expect to take place?
    a. a shift to the left of the industry supply curve
    b. the establishment of a new equilibrium at a higher level of output
    c. a reduction of the losses suffered by firms remaining in the market
    d. the establishment of a new equilibrium at a higher price level

33. What does productive efficiency mean?
    a. The market allocates the production of various goods in accord with consumer wants.
    b. A market contains the minimum number of producers feasible.
    c. Goods are produced and sold to consumers at their lowest possible opportunity cost.
    d. The market allocates the production of various goods in accord with government directives.

34. What does allocative efficiency mean?
    a. A market allocates the production of various goods in accord with consumer wants.
    b. The market contains the minimum number of producers feasible.
    c. Goods are produced and sold to consumers at their lowest possible opportunity cost.
    d. The market allocates the production of various goods in accord with government directives.

35. When a competitive market is in long-run equilibrium, price (P) is *not* equal to which of the following terms?
    a. MC
    b. LRATC$_{min}$
    c. MR
    d. TC

36. In a competitive market, the most efficient level of production occurs when
    a. P = MR
    b. MR = AVC
    c. MC = LRATC$_{min}$
    d. all of the above

37. In an increasing cost industry,
    a. as the industry expands, the price of necessary inputs falls.
    b. as the industry expands, the price of necessary inputs rises.
    c. as the industry expands, the price of its finished goods falls.
    d. industry size does not affect the price of inputs or of its finished goods.

38. In a constant cost industry,
    a. as the industry expands, the price of necessary inputs falls.
    b. as the industry expands, the price of necessary inputs rises.
    c. as the industry expands, the price of its finished goods falls.
    d. industry size does not affect the price of inputs or of its finished goods.

39. Which of the following factors does *not* affect whether an industry is an increasing cost, constant cost, or decreasing cost industry?
    a. consumer demand for the industry's products
    b. the nature of economies of scale
    c. the extent of diseconomies of scale
    d. the current state of technology

Essay-Problem

Answer in the space provided.

The questions below are challenging. Don't get discouraged if your answers are not always the same as those we suggest. Use these as another way to assess your progress, but more importantly, to learn more about the competitive model.

1. Why do economists put industries into market structure categories?

2. Why does the competitive model require that there are many buyers and many sellers?

3. Why is the demand curve horizontal for a firm in a competitive market?

4. Why are costs so important for a competitive firm?

5. The profit maximizing rule for a competitive firm is to produce until marginal revenue equals marginal cost. What would happen if the competitive firm produced where marginal cost was lower than marginal revenue? Marginal cost was higher than marginal revenue?

6. In the long run, why are economic profits signals?

7. Why are competitive markets in the public interest?

8. Give an example of an increasing cost industry and a decreasing cost industry, and explain why they are so.

9. Do firms like to be in competitive markets?

10. In the long run, competitive markets squeeze out economic profits. Can any competitive firm hope to generate economic profits in the long run, or is it just dreaming?

What's Next

This chapter gave you an introduction to market structure, how competitive markets determine output in the short and long runs, and why economists use the competitive model as a measuring stick for all other market structures. Now you can go on to these other market structures and see why they do not achieve the production and allocative efficiencies of competitive markets.

Answers to Chapterwide Practice Questions

Matching

1. e	3. c	5. d	7. b
2. g	4. a	6. f	

Fill-In

1. oligopoly, competition, monopoly
2. no barriers to entry or exit, differentiated products
3. price, marginal cost
4. economic profits, economic losses, closes its doors, normal profits
5. economic profits, normal profits, economic losses, rise, normal profits
6. productive, allocative

True-False

1. T	5. F	9. T	13. T
2. F	6. T	10. T	14. T
3. F	7. F	11. T	15. T
4. T	8. F	12. F	

Multiple Choice

1. d	11. b	21. a	31. d
2. b	12. a	22. c	32. b
3. a	13. c	23. a	33. c
4. a	14. c	24. a	34. a
5. b	15. b	25. b	35. d
6. c	16. a	26. d	36. c
7. c	17. d	27. d	37. b
8. a	18. c	28. b	38. d
9. d	19. b	29. b	39. a
10. c	20. c	30. a	

Essay-Problem

1. Grouping industries into a few categories allows economists to predict the pricing and production behavior of firms in that industry.
2. The competitive model requires that buyers and sellers be price takers: No one consumer or firm has any power to influence the price. This requirement of the model is best met when there are many buyers and many sellers. We will see in later chapters what happens when a buyer or seller has some pricing power.

3. A horizontal demand curve means that the firm is a price taker. It must simply accept the established market price, at which price it is assumed the firm can sell as much of its product as it wants. If the individual firm were to try setting its price above the market price, consumers would not buy anything from it, since other firms are offering the same product at the lower market price. Conceivably, the firm could set its price below the market price, but it would have no reason to do so, since it can sell all the product its wants at the higher market price.

4. The profit equation is: profit = total revenues minus total costs. In competitive markets, firms have no power to set the prices that determine revenues. All they can do is adjust output to maximize profits.

5. If marginal cost was lower than marginal revenue, the firm could continue to hire more workers (variable inputs) and still come out ahead. The amount paid out to the additional worker is less than the amount added to revenues, so profit will rise. If marginal cost was higher than marginal revenue, the cost of each additional worker would be greater than the additional revenue brought in, so profits would fall; the firm would be worse off than if it did nothing more.

6. Economic profits tell firms outside the industry that there are profit possibilities greater than the opportunity cost of capital. Economic profits attract new market entrants the way honey attracts bees.

7. The competitive market is productively efficient. Products are produced and sold to consumers at their lowest possible opportunity cost. Competitive markets are also allocatively efficient. If output falls below equilibrium, marginal cost is less than price. Consumers place a higher value on that product than it costs to produce. Therefore, society will be better off if more of it is in the market. If output is above equilibrium, marginal cost exceeds price, and we will be better off if those resources are used to produce another product more highly valued by society. But competitive markets ensure that equilibrium is at the most efficient point.

8. In an increasing cost industry, as total industry output rises, the average total costs of production similarly rise, thereby raising the price of the finished products. Industries depending on very specialized forms of labor, known only to a few people—many sorts of indigenous artwork, for instance—fit into this category. This sort of specialized labor is in such short supply that its price will rise dramatically if the demand for some form of indigenous art should rise, thus driving up the average costs of production.

  In a decreasing costs industry, as total industry output rises, average total costs of production will fall. This is because the industry begins to realize economies of scale as it increases its total output. The semiconductor industry is a good example of a decreasing cost industry: As the demand for semiconductors has soared, new methods for producing them inexpensively come into play, thus decreasing the average total costs of semiconductors. Most manufacturing processes exhibit economies of scale.

9. In general, no. Firms in competitive markets have no power over price; to be profitable, all they can do is produce the profit maximizing output and only earn normal returns in the long run. Firms would prefer to have some pricing power and be under less cost pressure and have the opportunity to earn economic profits longer.

10. In reality, firms might generate long-run economic profits if they continually are the low-cost producer. Prospects are not great for a firm to be able to do this over the long run, but it can happen. Our competitive model has such restrictive assumptions that economic profits are not possible in the long run.

Monopoly

If Competition Serves the Public Interest, Why Do Firms Want to Be Monopolies?

Monopoly is the other extreme on the market structure spectrum, opposite from the competitive market ideal. You will put to work what you have learned in the previous chapter on competitive markets to analyze monopoly markets. Unlike competitive firms, which are price takers, monopolists are *price makers*. Their monopoly power allows monopolists to adjust their output in ways that give them significant control over product price. You will see that while competitive markets are in the public interest, monopolies definitely are not. The chapter will show you what can be done to alleviate this situation.

This Is What You Need to Know

STEP 1

After studying this chapter you should be able to

- Describe the characteristics of a monopoly and monopoly power.

- Describe the ways in which monopoly power is maintained.

- Use monopoly market analysis to determine the equilibrium level of output and price for a monopoly.

- Describe the differences between monopoly and competition.

- Describe the different forms of price discrimination.

- Describe the different approaches to regulating a natural monopoly.

- Relate the history and purpose of antitrust legislation to monopoly analysis.

■ Apply concentration ratios and Herfindahl-Hirshman Indexes to analyze the likelihood of regulation in a given market.

■ Describe the conditions of a contestable market and its significance.

Review the Key Terms

Monopoly: A one-firm industry with no close product substitutes and with substantial barriers to entry.

Economies of scale: As the firm expands in size, average total costs decline.

Rent seeking: Resources expended to protect a monopoly position, such as lobbying, extending patents, and restricting the number of licenses permitted.

X-inefficiency: The inefficiency that arises when monopolies are protected from competitive pressures. Spending on corporate jets, travel, and other perks of business represent x-inefficiency.

Price discrimination: Charging different consumer groups different prices for the same product. The conditions necessary for successful price discrimination include some monopoly power (the firm needs some control over price), different consumer groups with different elasticities of demand, and the ability of the firm to prevent arbitrage (keeping low-price buyers from reselling to high-price buyers).

Natural monopoly: Large economies of scale mean that the minimum efficient scale of operations is roughly equal to market demand.

Marginal cost pricing rule: Regulators would prefer to have natural monopolists price where $P = MC$, but this would result in losses (long term) because $ATC > MC$. Thus, regulators often must use an average cost pricing rule.

Average cost pricing rule: Requires a regulated monopolist to produce and sell output where price equals average total costs. This permits the regulated monopolist to earn a normal return on investment over the long term and so remain in business.

Rate of return regulation: Permits product pricing that allows the firm to earn a normal return on capital invested in the firm.

Price caps: Maximum price at which a regulated firm can sell its product. They are often flexible enough to allow for changing cost conditions.

Antitrust law: Laws designed to maintain competition and prevent monopolies from developing.

Concentration ratios: The share of industry shipments or sales accounted for by the top four or eight firms.

Herfindahl-Hirshman index (HHI): A way of measuring industry concentration, equal to the sum of the squares of market shares for all firms in the industry.

Contestable markets: Markets that look monopolistic but have entry costs so low that the sheer threat of entry keeps prices low.

Network externalities: Markets in which as more people use the network, the network becomes more valuable.

Monopoly Markets

Frequently Asked Questions

Q: **How are monopolies defined?**

A: For economists, a monopoly is defined by three key characteristics. First, the market has just one seller; the monopolistic firm *is* the industry. Second, no close substitutes exist for the monopolist's product, so consumers cannot easily substitute other products for the product sold by the monopolist. Third, significant barriers to entry keep other firms from entering the industry. This means the monopolist faces no competition, even in the long run.

Q: **For the monopolist, how are price and output linked?**

A: Monopoly power is the degree to which a firm can control the price of its product by adjusting output. Competitive firms are price takers, meaning that they have no monopoly power; the prices for their products are determined by competitive markets. Monopolists, in contrast, are price makers. They enjoy considerable monopoly power and much freedom in deciding what to charge for their products.

Q: **Where does monopoly power come from?**

A: Monopoly power is caused by significant barriers to entry.

Q: **Why are economies of scale a barrier to entry?**

A: The economies of scale in an industry can be so large that demand will support only one firm in what economists would refer to as a "natural monopoly." Utilities have traditionally been considered natural monopolists because of the high fixed costs associated with power plants.

Q: **Can control over an important production input be a barrier to entry?**

A: If a firm owns or has control over an important input into the production process, that firm can keep potential rivals out of the market.

Q: **Can government provide barriers to entry?**

A: Government provides some barriers to market entry. For instance, it may grant a franchise to a firm, giving permission to provide specific goods or services, while prohibiting others from doing so. Patents protect firms and individuals that invent new products and processes. Copyrights give firms or individuals the exclusive right to produce intellectual products for a long period of time.

Q: **How is product price determined in a monopolistic market?**

A: Because the monopolist constitutes the entire industry, it faces a downward sloping demand curve. Product price is determined in a monopoly by how much the monopolist wishes to produce. This contrasts with the competitive firm, which can sell all it wishes, but only at the market determined price.

Q: **How does a monopolist maximize profit?**

A: Like the competitive firm, the monopolist maximizes its profit at output where $MR = MC$. This is shown in Figure 1 on the next page. Because of the monopolist's downward sloping demand curve, marginal revenue is less than price. To determine the monopolist's profit maximizing price, extend a vertical line through the point where $MR = MC$ (point e) to the demand curve (point a). This intersection determines the price (P_M) to be found on the vertical axis. The monopolist's profit equals the difference between this price and average total costs ($a - b$), multiplied by the number of units sold (Q_M).

FIGURE 1

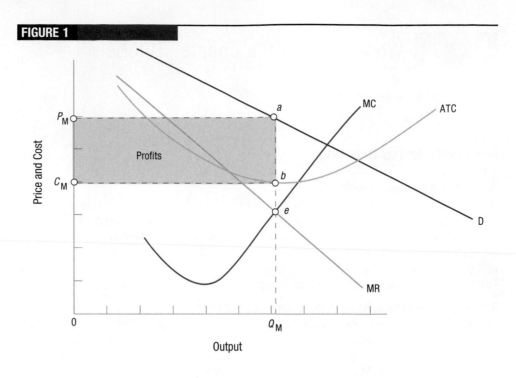

Q: Do monopolists always make economic profits?

A: Monopolies are not guaranteed economic profits. If a monopolist's profit maximizing price is lower than its average total costs, it will suffer a loss. Just like competitive firms, as long as price exceeds average variable costs, the monopolist will minimize its losses in the short run by continuing to produce. But if price should fall below average variable costs, the monopolist will shut down. If these losses persist, the monopolist will exit the industry in the long run.

Q: How does monopoly output and price compare to competitive markets?

A: Monopoly output is lower and monopoly price is higher. Monopolies earn economic profits by reducing consumer surplus.

Q: What is the deadweight loss from monopoly?

A: The loss to society from monopoly output and pricing is known as deadweight loss, or welfare loss. This is shown as area *cab* in Figure 2.

FIGURE 2

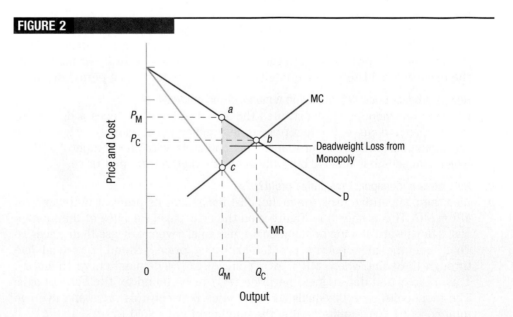

Q: What is rent-seeking behavior?

A: To maintain their advantageous position, monopolists engage in rent-seeking behavior. They undertake a variety of activities to avoid competition, such as hiring lawyers and lobbyists to obtain favorable treatment, for example, tariff protection from Congress. All these activities are inefficient, in that they shift resources from one group to another without producing a useful good or service, and so rent seeking represents an added loss to society from monopoly.

Q: What is x-inefficiency?

A: Some economists argue that monopolies do not operate efficiently because they are protected from competitive pressures; this is known as x-inefficiency. Management can offer itself perks, for instance, without worrying about whether costs are kept at efficient levels.

Key Points to Remember

- A monopolist *is* the industry, there are no good substitutes for the monopolist's product, and substantial barriers to entry exist.
- Because monopoly demand is downward sloping, MR < P.
- Monopolies are price makers and maximize profits by producing where MR = MC, but set price off the demand curve.
- Monopolies sell less output at higher prices than competitive markets.

Monopoly Markets Quick Check

Circle the Correct Answer

1. (T/F) Monopolists are price makers, not price takers.
2. (T/F) A natural monopoly can arise in an industry when economies of scale are so large that demand will support only a single firm.
3. (T/F) For a firm to have monopoly power, it must have nearly complete control over the price at which it sells its product.
4. (T/F) For the monopolist, MR = P.
5. Which of the following will be true for a monopoly?
   a. D = MR
   b. P = MR
   c. P < MR
   d. P > MR
6. What determines the price at which a monopolist can sell its product?
   a. Rules imposed by government regulatory agencies.
   b. The price set by competitors.
   c. The level of output at which the monopolist decides it wants to produce.
   d. The monopolist can earn a profit by selling at any price.
7. In Figure 3, area P_CP_Mac represents
   a. x-inefficiency.
   b. the maximum amount of rent-seeking behavior we might expect from this monopoly.
   c. the deadweight loss from monopoly.
   d. normal profits for the monopolist.

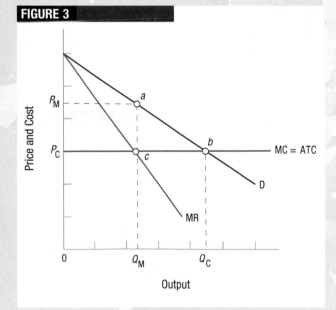

FIGURE 3

8. The profit maximizing output for the monopolist is found where
   a. MR = MC.
   b. MR = ATC.
   c. MR = P.
   d. ATC = P.

9. Which of the following is *not* an example of rent-seeking behavior?
   a. increasing management salaries and perks
   b. lobbying Congress for laws limiting imports
   c. hiring lawyers to extend patent protection
   d. securing a government franchise
10. Which one of the following is *not* correct?
   a. Monopolists are price makers; competitive firms are price takers.
   b. Monopolists produce less at higher prices than competitive firms.
   c. Monopolists tend to be inefficient because they do not face the same market pressures as competitive firms.
   d. Monopolists never lose money, while competitive firms may do so.

Score: ____

Answers: 1. T; 2. T; 3. F; 4. F; 5. d; 6. c; 7. b; 8. a; 9. a; 10. d

If You Got 9 or 10 Correct

You have a good start on monopoly. The important concepts are monopoly pricing and output decisions and the differences between monopoly and competition. Make sure you get this and then go on to the next section. There is a lot to learn in this first section, so an extra review might be helpful.

If You Didn't Get at Least 9 Correct

Don't worry. This is tough material. Take it slowly through this section again. List the differences between the monopoly and the competitive models. Review each figure again. Pay particular attention to how monopolies set price and output for their market. Work through the solved problem below to make sure you understand these concepts. Once you finish this review, go to the next section, "Monopoly Market Issues."

Solved Problem: Monopoly Price, Output, and Profits

The market in Figure 4 is controlled by one firm with the demand and cost curves shown.

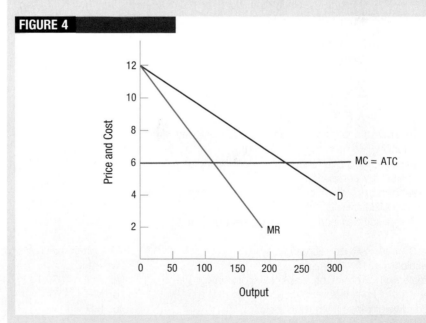

FIGURE 4

a. What would be the profit maximizing output and price?

b. How large are economic profits?

Solution-Discussion

a. Profits are maximized by producing output where MR = MC. In this case, output is equal to 115 (point *c* in Figure 5), and the price is found on the demand curve at $9 (point *a*).

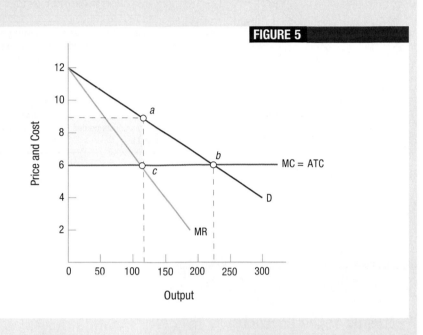

FIGURE 5

b. Profit is equal to the shaded area in Figure 5, and is equal to (P − ATC) times output. Price is $9, average total cost (ATC) is $6, and output is equal to 115 units, so profit = ($9 − $6) × 115 = $3 × 115 = $345.

Keep in Mind

1. Monopolies (and all firms) maximize profit by producing where MR = MC (point *c* in Figure 5). Monopoly output is equal to roughly 115.

2. Monopoly price is found on the demand curve, roughly $9 in this case.

3. Monopoly profit is equal to the shaded area in Figure 5 and is equal to (P − ATC) × Q = ($9 − $6) × 115 = $3 × 115 = $345.

4. Competitive price and output will be at point *b* where P = ATC and economic profits will equal zero (normal profits). Competitive price is $6 and output is 225.

5. Monopolists sell less output at higher price than competitive markets.

6. The deadweight loss (consumer and producer surplus lost from lower output at higher prices from monopoly) is equal to triangle *abc*. ▪

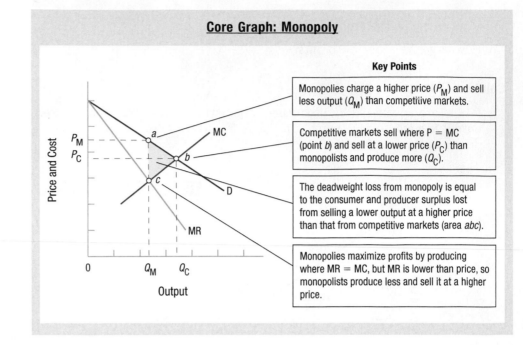

Core Graph: Monopoly

Key Points

Monopolies charge a higher price (P_M) and sell less output (Q_M) than competitive markets.

Competitive markets sell where P = MC (point *b*) and sell at a lower price (P_C) than monopolists and produce more (Q_C).

The deadweight loss from monopoly is equal to the consumer and producer surplus lost from selling a lower output at a higher price than that from competitive markets (area *abc*).

Monopolies maximize profits by producing where MR = MC, but MR is lower than price, so monopolists produce less and sell it at a higher price.

Monopoly Market Issues

Frequently Asked Questions

Q: **What is price discrimination?**

A: When firms with monopoly power price discriminate, they charge different consumers different prices for the same product. The goal is to maximize profits by charging each customer (or group) as much as each is willing to pay.

Q: **What is needed for successful price discrimination?**

A: Several conditions are required for successful price discrimination. First, sellers must have some monopoly power, or some control over price. Second, sellers must be able to separate the market into different consumer groups based on their elasticities of demand. Third, sellers must be able to prevent arbitrage; that is, it must be impossible or prohibitively expensive for low price buyers to resell to higher price buyers.

Q: **What is first-degree price discrimination?**

A: First-degree (or perfect) price discrimination involves charging each customer the maximum price each is willing to pay. This is exemplified by the flea market, where sellers and buyers haggle and barter for each product.

Q: **What is second-degree price discrimination?**

A: Second-degree price discrimination involves charging different customers different prices based on the quantities of the product they purchase. Many firms charge a high price for the first units of a product sold to a customer, but then offer a bulk discount on the sale of added units.

Q: **What is third-degree price discrimination?**

A: The most common form of price discrimination is third-degree price discrimination. This involves charging different groups of people different prices, as when airlines set different ticket prices for business travelers and vacationers.

Q: **What causes a natural monopoly, and what can be done about this?**

A: A natural monopoly exists when economies of scale are so large that the min-
      imum efficient scale of operation is roughly equal to market demand. In such
      cases, policymakers employ a variety of measures to prevent natural monopo-
      lists from abusing their positions of market dominance.

Q: **What is a marginal cost regulatory pricing rule?**

A: A marginal cost pricing rule requires the monopolist to set its price where P =
      MC, the profit maximizing rule in competitive markets. But, because this price
      is often below the monopolist's average total costs, losses result, equal to dis-
      tance dc per unit in Figure 6. For the monopoly to remain in business, it must
      be heavily subsidized by the government. For this reason, this approach is sel-
      dom used.

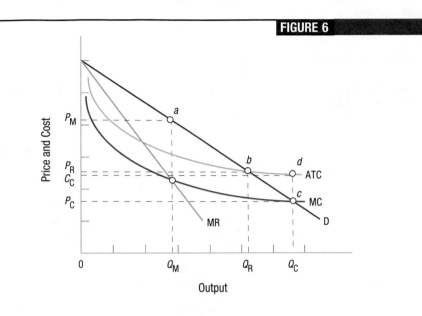

FIGURE 6

Q: **What is an average cost regulatory pricing rule?**

A: An average cost pricing rule requires the monopolist to produce and sell at the
      level where demand equals average total costs (point b in Figure 6). The result
      is that the firm earns a normal return. Consumers do lose something, in that
      they must pay a higher price for a lower output than they would under com-
      petitive conditions. Still, the normal profits keep the firm in business, and the
      losses to consumers are significantly less than if the firm were left unregulated.

Q: **Why do regulators use rate of return or price caps to regulate natural monopolies, and
      what are they?**

A: In practice, estimating demand and cost curves is extremely difficult, so regu-
      lators often abandon the theoretical regulatory strategies noted above and turn
      to rate of return or price cap regulation. Rate of return regulation allows the
      monopolist to price its product in such a way that it can earn a normal return
      on capital invested. Price caps place maximum limits on the prices firms can
      charge for products.

Key Point to Remember

Price discrimination occurs when firms with monopoly power can group its customers with different elasticities of demand and charge different prices for the same
product. Firms do this because it increases profits. Note that firms do not have to
be monopolists, but they must have some control over price. We see price discrimination everyday in airline tickets, hotel prices, and movie tickets.

Monopoly Market Issues Quick Check

Circle the Correct Answer

1. (T/F) For price discrimination to be successful, it must be very difficult for low-price buyers to resell to higher-price buyers.
2. (T/F) Regulators have trouble determining actual demand and cost curves.
3. (T/F) To price discriminate successfully, sellers must be able to separate the market into different consumer groups based on their elasticities of demand.
4. Which of the following is an example of first-degree price discrimination?
   a. early-bird discounts given to people who have dinner before 6 P.M.
   b. half-price discounts for children going to movies
   c. a bulk discount for electricity after the purchase of a certain fixed amount
   d. an owner of a rare Pez dispenser who offers it for sale on eBay

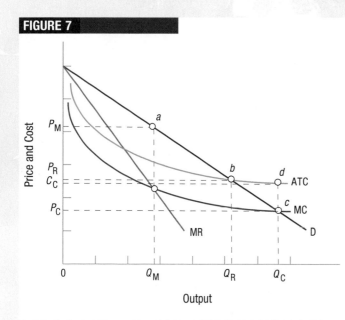

FIGURE 7

5. In Figure 7, the MC and ATC curves decline continually because
   a. MC and ATC curves for a monopoly, unlike competitive firms, are never bowl-shaped.
   b. natural monopolies enjoy economies of scale.
   c. natural monopolies can price discriminate.
   d. natural monopolies are not as efficient as competitive firms, and so always face declining cost curves rather than bowl-shaped ones.

6. In Figure 7, if the government mandates a marginal cost pricing rule,
   a. the monopolist would produce at point *b*.
   b. the monopolist would face a loss of *dc* per unit and ultimately would shut down.
   c. the monopolist would earn a normal profit.
   d. the monopolist would *not* produce at the socially optimal point.
7. What type of price discrimination occurs when a hotel in Key West, Florida, increases its prices between January 1 and April 1?
   a. First-degree price discrimination.
   b. Second-degree price discrimination.
   c. Third-degree price discrimination.
   d. None of the above; this is not an example of price discrimination.
8. What type of price discrimination occurs when customers are charged one rate for the first 100 kilowatt hours of energy used in one month and another rate for the next 100 kilowatt hours?
   a. First-degree price discrimination.
   b. Second-degree price discrimination.
   c. Third-degree price discrimination.
   d. None of the above; this is not an example of price discrimination.
9. What happens when the government imposes rate of return regulation on a natural monopolist?
   a. The monopolist will see its economies of scale evaporate.
   b. The monopolist will suffer economic losses unless it is publicly subsidized.
   c. The monopolist is prohibited from selling its product above a stipulated maximum price.
   d. The monopolist will be able to earn a normal rate of return on capital invested.
10. When government uses rate of return to regulate a natural monopoly, which one of the following does *not* occur?
   a. Monopolists try to include as many expenses as possible under the category "legitimate business expenses."
   b. Regulatory commissions wind up having large staffs to consider the monopolist's attempts to include every expense as a business expense.
   c. Monopolists take regulatory commissions to court.
   d. Monopolists appear before the regulatory commission every few months to have price increases approved.

Score: _____

These are relatively easy questions. You should have answered them all correctly. The issues of price discrimination and regulating natural monopolies all show how important and broad the analysis of monopoly can be applied. You can use this analysis to answer subtle questions about firms and industries with monopoly power even if they are not pure monopolists.

Concerns about monopoly power and monopoly were behind the European Union's half-billion-dollar fine of Microsoft in 2004 and the requirements that it split the Windows operating system into several different versions (bare bones and expanded) and not add additional functions without EU permission. Microsoft appealed both the fine and the new regulations. A similar situation again plagued Microsoft in Europe with its introduction of Windows Vista in early 2007. European regulators again required multiple versions to exclude specific functions.

If You Got 9 or 10 Correct

Go on to the "Antitrust" section, which focuses on the policies designed to eliminate monopolies and prevent attempts to monopolize.

If You Didn't Get at Least 9 Correct

We suggest you review this section once more. The material is tough, but the review will be useful. Do the normal stuff like rereading the section and reworking the quiz to be sure you know why you missed the questions you did.

Keep in Mind

- Firms price discriminate (sell the same product to different customers at different prices) because it is *profitable* to do so. Ask yourself why few new-car dealerships have a meaningful posted price on their cars. Most retailers post their prices and sell at those posted prices. Car dealers (and their sales staff) operate in a way to get you to pay the highest price you are willing to pay rather than do without the car. You are negotiating against both the salesperson and the manager in back. Your job as a buyer is to find the dealer's lowest price at which it is willing to sell the car. Auto purchases are a classic example of first-degree or perfect price discrimination.
- Price discrimination requires that arbitrage not be possible. If low-cost buyers can sell to high-cost buyers, price discrimination will fail (everyone will pay a low price). Along the borders of Mexico and Canada, people with large prescription drug bills routinely cross the border to purchase low-cost medicines. American pharmaceutical manufacturers sell the same drugs more cheaply in both countries. Since most people do not live on the border, the few who buy drugs are not a serious problem for drug companies. However, with Internet pharmacies from both countries now selling low-priced prescriptions, big pharma's multiprice model is in jeopardy. Ask yourself who stands to lose and who will benefit if pharmaceutical firms cannot price discriminate.
- The answer to the question just posed is complex, but as a beginning, since price discrimination leads to higher revenue and profits for drug companies, eliminating multiple prices will lead to lower prices in the United States and to higher prices elsewhere, but reduced profits and revenues for the companies. This could ultimately lead to reduced research and development and fewer drug breakthroughs in the future.
- Regulation is tricky and complex and, where possible, should be avoided. Both airlines and trucking are more robust industries since deregulation. In both, output has expanded and real prices have fallen. The only calls for re-regulation

come from the industry itself, for reasons George Stigler outlined several decades ago.

Continue on, but be prepared to review this section and the section on monopoly again. The next section, "Antitrust," discusses the major policies and laws used by the federal government to eliminate monopolies and, more importantly, to keep them from forming in the first place. ■

Antitrust Policy

Frequently Asked Questions

Q: **What are the major antitrust laws?**

A: Since 1890, the United States Congress has passed a series of major statutes that form the core of the country's antitrust laws. These include the Sherman Act (1890), the Clayton Act (1914), the Federal Trade Commission Act (1914), the Robinson-Patman Act (1936), and the Celler-Kefauver Antimerger Act (1950).

Q: **What was the purpose of the early antitrust laws?**

A: The early antitrust acts were passed with the intention of promoting the equitable distribution of wealth and protecting small businesses against predatory monopolies. The intensity of antitrust enforcement has varied with presidential administrations and courts over the past century.

Q: **What is the purpose of antitrust policy today?**

A: There is general agreement among economists and judges that some antitrust regulation is needed, and that its basic purpose is to prevent the inefficiencies associated with significant monopoly power.

Q: **How is market concentration measured?**

A: Economists have developed several means of measuring market concentration. The most widely used of these, the n-firm concentration ratio, reports the share of industry sales accounted for by the n largest firms. Typically, the 4- and 8-firm concentration ratios are reported.

Q: **What is the Herfindahl-Hirshman index, and how is it defined?**

A: The Herfindahl-Hirshman index (HHI) is the principal measure of concentration used by the U.S. Justice Department to evaluate mergers and judge monopoly power. The HHI is defined by the equation: HHI = $(S_1)^2 + (S_2)^2 + (S_3)^2 + \ldots + (S_n)^2$ where $S_1, S_2, \ldots S_n$ are the percentage market shares of each firm in the industry. By squaring market shares, the HHI gives greater weight to those firms with large market shares.

Q: **What are contestable markets?**

A: Contestable markets are those with entry costs so low that firms can enter or leave the industry rapidly. If a firm is earning economic profits, new firms will enter the market until returns have been driven back down to normal levels. The sheer threat of entry therefore keeps prices in contestable markets low, even if the market is now a monopoly. Monopoly firms in potentially contestable markets must, moreover, avoid x-inefficiency, since they always need to be ready for the possibility of facing competition.

Antitrust Policy Quick Check

Circle the Correct Answer

1. (T/F) Antitrust legislation began, among other reasons, as a way to protect the country against "robber barons."
2. (T/F) Contestable markets have low entry costs.
3. (T/F) The Sherman Act, the first major piece of antitrust legislation, was passed in 1914.
4. (T/F) Lawmakers who passed the early antitrust legislation were mainly concerned with improving the allocative efficiency of the marketplace.
5. Antitrust cases can be filed by all of the following *except*
   a. the Antitrust Division of the Department of Justice.
   b. the Federal Trade Commission.
   c. lawyers for private plaintiffs.
   d. the monopolist itself.
6. If an industry contains 4 firms with market shares of 40, 25, 20, and 15%, respectively, its Herfindahl-Hirshman index is which of the following?
   a. 100
   b. 10,000
   c. 2,850
   d. 7,150
7. Which one of these features does *not* tend to make monopolies in the "new economy" transitory?
   a. Much of what the new economy produces is intellectual property, which tends to be easy to clone.
   b. Easy entry and exit.
   c. Modest capital requirements.
   d. Low rates of innovation.
8. Which one of the following has *not* been a rationale for antitrust legislation?
   a. protecting small businesses from the predatory practices of monopolies
   b. protecting consumers from market concentration, with the expectation that market concentration will lead to more monopoly pricing power
   c. prohibiting price discrimination
   d. forcing monopolists to follow the $P = MC$ rule
9. If an industry contains 4 firms with market shares of 35, 25, 25, and 15, respectively, its Herfindahl-Hirshman index would classify it as being
   a. unconcentrated.
   b. moderately concentrated.
   c. highly concentrated.
   d. monopolistic.
10. If the price charged by a monopolist is close to what would be charged by a competitive firm, it is likely that
    a. the monopolist cannot price discriminate.
    b. the market is contestable.
    c. the monopolist is public spirited.
    d. the monopolist is a price taker in this particular market.

Score: _____

Answers: 1. T; 2. T; 3. F; 4. F; 5. d; 6. c; 7. d; 8. d; 9. c; 10. b.

If You Got 9 or 10 Correct

Move on to Step 4 and study the "Hints, Tips, and Reminders."

If You Didn't Get at Least 9 Correct

This is not difficult material. If you didn't get nine or more correct, this is not good! You are clearly focused on something other than economics. Work through the "Hints, Tips, and Reminders" in the next section. Maybe something there will get you on the right track. If you still are having problems, you may want to start again from the beginning of this chapter, proceeding slowly. Some of the early material in the chapter can be tough. ∎

Consider These Hints, Tips, and Reminders   STEP 4

1. Keep in mind that a monopoly is a one-firm industry, so the downward sloping industry demand is the monopoly firm's demand, not horizontal like the competitive firm. This means that marginal revenue (MR) lies below price on the demand curve.

2. When drawing graphs for a monopoly, use this simple trick to draw the MR curve. First draw a straight-line demand curve beginning somewhere on the vertical or price axis (point *a* in Figure 8) with a negative slope (remember the law of demand?). To put in the marginal revenue curve, split the distance from a point on the demand curve (point *c*) at a relatively low price (P_0). This results in point *b*. Remember that distance $P_0 b$ = distance *bc*. Now connect a straight line from the beginning of the demand curve (point *a*) through this new point *b*. This is the MR curve that bisects the linear demand curve. This simple technique of bisecting the linear demand curve to get an accurate MR curve will make drawing monopoly graphs easier.

FIGURE 8

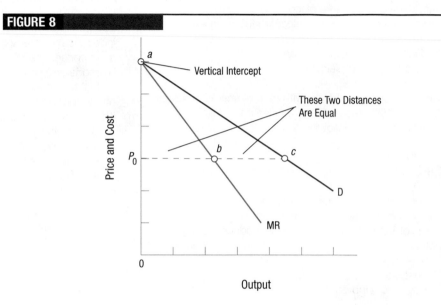

3. This chapter focuses on monopoly—a one-firm industry. Pure monopolies are rare and represent what we would prefer to avoid. Every firm, however, strives for a monopoly position but most only obtain some *monopoly power*. This may come from location, superior product, and so on. The issue eventually comes down to how much monopoly power is too much and that is the focus of antitrust laws.

4. Why do firms price discriminate? Because they make more profit! Therefore, firms that can separate customers into different groups with different elasticities of demand will price discriminate. Firms are not being *nice* to seniors, students, or flyers who book 14 days in advance and stay over a weekend. Firms do this to make money.

5. Another technique to simplify your graphs is to use a horizontal ATC curve so that the curve represents MC as well. In the same way that P = MR for a horizontal demand curve (competitive model), MC = ATC when the ATC curve is horizontal. This simplifies your graph by reducing the number of distinct points you have to consider.

Do the Homework for Chapter 9
Monopoly

Instructor _____ Time _____ Student _____

Use the answer key below to record your answers to these homework questions.

1. (a) (b) (c) (d)	6. (a) (b) (c) (d)	11. (a) (b) (c) (d)	16. (a) (b) (c) (d)
2. (a) (b) (c) (d)	7. (a) (b) (c) (d)	12. (a) (b) (c) (d)	17. (a) (b) (c) (d)
3. (a) (b) (c) (d)	8. (a) (b) (c) (d)	13. (a) (b) (c) (d)	18. (a) (b) (c) (d)
4. (a) (b) (c) (d)	9. (a) (b) (c) (d)	14. (a) (b) (c) (d)	19. (a) (b) (c) (d)
5. (a) (b) (c) (d)	10. (a) (b) (c) (d)	15. (a) (b) (c) (d)	20. (a) (b) (c) (d)

---

1. Which of the following is *not* an assumption of monopoly markets?
   a. homogeneous products in this market
   b. no close substitutes for the seller's product
   c. barriers to entry or exit
   d. one seller in the market

2. The monopolist's demand curve will be
   a. upward sloping.
   b. smaller than the market itself.
   c. downward sloping.
   d. horizontal at the market set price.

3. A monopolist maximizes profit by producing an output where
   a. marginal revenue is equal to price.
   b. average total costs are equal to average revenue.
   c. marginal revenue is equal to price.
   d. marginal revenue is equal to marginal cost.

---

4. The monopolist in Figure HW-1 maximizes profit
   a. by producing output where marginal revenue is equal to price.
   b. by producing 12,000 units where average total costs are equal to average revenue.
   c. by producing 12,000 units where marginal revenue is equal to price.
   d. by producing 12,000 units where marginal revenue is equal to marginal cost.

5. The monopolist in Figure HW-1
   a. produces 12,000 units where marginal revenue is equal to price.
   b. maximizes profit by selling 12,000 units at a price of $20.
   c. maximizes profit by producing 12,000 units where marginal revenue is equal to total cost.
   d. maximizes profit by producing 12,000 units and selling this output at a price of $30.

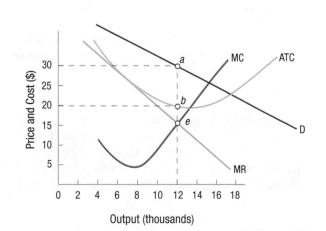

HW-1

6. The monopolist in Figure HW-1
   a. produces 12,000 units where marginal revenue is equal to price.
   b. maximizes profit equal to $120,000.
   c. maximizes profit by producing 12,000 units where marginal revenue is equal to total cost.
   d. maximizes profit by producing 12,000 units and selling this output at a price of $20.

7. The monopolist in Figure HW-1
   a. produces 12,000 units where marginal revenue is equal to price.
   b. maximizes profit by producing and selling 12,000 units at a price of $20.
   c. sells 12,000 units with total costs equal to $240,000.
   d. sells 12,000 units with total costs equal to $360,000.

---

8. Profits for the profit maximizing monopolist will equal
   a. marginal costs times output.
   b. price minus average total costs, times output.
   c. zero economic profits most of the time.
   d. price minus marginal costs, times output.

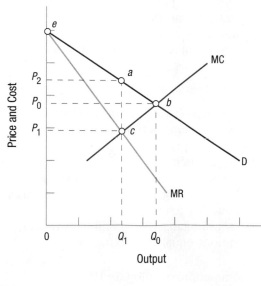

9. Area cab in Figure HW-2 is called
   a. monopoly profit.
   b. profit margin.
   c. normal profits.
   d. deadweight loss of monopoly.

10. In Figure HW-2,
    a. a monopoly would produce output Q_1 and sell it for P_1.
    b. a competitive firm would produce at point b.
    c. even a competitive firm would earn economic profits in the long run.
    d. monopoly profits would equal area cab.

11. In Figure HW-2, the monopoly
    a. will earn monopoly profits equal to area cab.
    b. will produce and sell Q_0 units at price P_0.
    c. will produce and sell Q_1 units at price P_2.
    d. will earn monopoly profits equal to area P_2P_1ac.

HW-2

---

12. In Figure HW-3, the monopoly
    a. will earn monopoly profits equal to area cab.
    b. will produce and sell Q_0 units at price P_0.
    c. will produce and sell Q_1 units at price P_1.
    d. will earn monopoly profits equal to area P_0P_1ab.

13. In Figure HW-3, the monopoly
    a. will earn monopoly profits equal to area P_0P_1ac.
    b. will produce and sell Q_0 units at price P_0.
    c. will produce and sell Q_1 units at price P_0.
    d. will earn monopoly profits equal to area P_0P_1ab.

14. In Figure HW-3, a competitive firm will
    a. earn economic profits equal to area P_0P_1ac.
    b. produce and sell Q_0 units at price P_0.
    c. produce and sell Q_1 units at price P_0.
    d. earn economic profits equal to area P_0P_1ab.

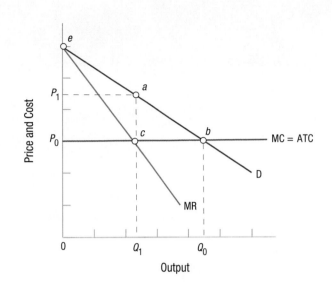

HW-3

---

15. Which of the following is an example of rent-seeking behavior?
    a. fees paid to lawyers for copyright and trademark services
    b. fees paid to public relations firms and advertising agencies to market a brand
    c. fees paid to lobbyists for extensions on tariffs
    d. fees paid to lawyers for drafting contracts

16. When a firm is able to perfectly price discriminate,
    a. it can separate its customers into a few groups and charge different prices to each of these groups.
    b. it is able to provide quantity discounts to some customers.
    c. it can vary the product just slightly enough to convince customers that the higher price is worth it.
    d. it can charge each customer just what they are willing to pay for the product.

17. When a firm is able to use second-degree price discrimination,
    a. it can separate its customers into a few groups and charge different prices to each of these groups.
    b. it is able to provide quantity discounts to some customers.
    c. it can vary the product just slightly enough to convince customers that the higher price is worth it.
    d. it can charge each customer just what they are willing to pay for the product.

18. When a firm is able to use third-degree price discrimination,
    a. it can separate its customers into a few groups and charge different prices to each of these groups.
    b. it is able to provide quantity discounts to some customers.
    c. it can vary the product just slightly enough to convince customers that the higher price is worth it.
    d. it can charge each customer just what they are willing to pay for the product.

19. Concentration ratios measure
    a. the degree to which an industry is concentrated in one regional location such as Silicon Valley.
    b. the percent of an industry's sales controlled by the largest firm.
    c. the share of industry sales accounted for by the industry's largest few firms.
    d. how concentrated patents are in the industry.

20. The Herfindahl-Hirshman index
    a. measures the degree to which an industry is concentrated in one regional location such as Silicon Valley.
    b. is the percent of an industry's sales controlled by the largest firm.
    c. is the share of industry sales accounted for by the industry's largest few firms.
    d. is the measure used by the Justice Department to approve or disapprove mergers.

Use the ExamPrep to Get Ready for Exams   STEP 6

This sheet (front and back) is designed to help you prepare for your exams. The chapter has been boiled down to its key concepts. You are asked to answer questions, define terms, draw graphs, and if you wish, add summaries of class notes.

Monopoly Markets

List the key characteristics of a monopoly market:

List the main sources of monopoly power:

Monopoly Pricing and Output Decisions

Describe why marginal revenue is less than price for a monopolist:

Use the grid below to draw the following

- Average total costs
- Marginal costs

(Hint: keep in mind that the marginal cost curve goes through the minimum point of the ATC curve.)

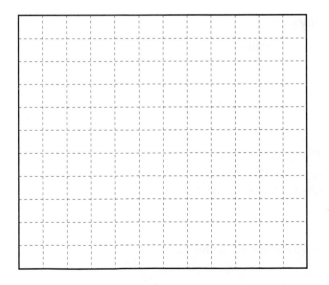

Now draw in a demand and marginal revenue curve for a monopolist. (Hint: remember that the marginal revenue curve bisects [splits] a linear demand curve.)

Show the profit maximizing output and price, and shade in and label profit.

Show the price and output that a competitive industry would produce.

Discuss why monopolies are less efficient than competition.

Monopoly Market Issues

Price Discrimination

Discuss the three forms of price discrimination:

Why do firms price discriminate?

Regulating the Natural Monopolist

Define a natural monopoly:

Describe the marginal cost pricing rule and why it is seldom used:

Describe the average cost pricing rule:

Discuss the complications of implementing regulations:

Antitrust Policy

Describe the major antitrust laws:

Describe the following tools that economists use to define the relevant market:

Concentration ratios:

Herfindahl-Hirshman index (HHI):

List the merger guidelines from the Justice Department using the HHI:

Discuss the concept of contestable markets and its usefulness:

Additional Study Help Chapterwide Practice Questions

Matching

Match the description with the corresponding term.

___ 1. Economies of scale
___ 2. Monopoly
___ 3. Rent seeking
___ 4. Price discrimination
___ 5. Contestable markets
___ 6. Marginal cost pricing rule
___ 7. Average cost pricing rule
___ 8. Concentration ratios
___ 9. Herfindahl-Hirshman index (HHI)

a. A measure of industry concentration defined by adding the percentage market shares squared of each firm in the industry.
b. When monopolists devote resources to protecting their monopoly position.
c. The result when increases in output reduce the average costs of production.
d. Markets with entry costs so low that firms can enter or leave the industry rapidly.
e. Charging different customers different prices for the same product.
f. A regulatory mandate compelling a monopolist to produce and sell at levels of output and price where price equals average total costs.
g. A regulatory mandate compelling a monopolist to sell its product at levels of output and price where price equals the marginal cost of production.
h. A measure of the degree to which an industry's production and sales are primarily in the hands of a few firms.
i. A market with just one seller, no close substitutes for the firm's product, and significant barriers to entry.

Fill-In

Circle the word(s) in parentheses that complete the sentence.

1. A monopolist is (the industry, a factor of production) _____. Monopolies often have (the best technology, high quality products, a patent) _____.

2. For the monopolist, price is (below, greater than, equal to) _____ marginal revenue, and profits are maximized when marginal cost is (below, greater than, equal to) _____ marginal revenue.

3. When comparing monopoly price and output with competitive prices and output, monopoly price is (higher than, lower than, about the same as) _____ those in competitive markets, and monopoly output is (higher, lower, about the same) _____.

4. Monopoly behavior designed to reduce competitive pressures through lobbying for special circumstances is called (x-inefficiency, rent seeking) _____, and when monopolists aren't as attentive to levels of costs, economists refer to this as (x-inefficiency, rent seeking) _____.

5. When firms can charge customers the maximum amount they would be willing to pay, economists refer to this as (perfect, second-degree, third-degree) _____ price discrimination. When customers are split into groups and are charged different prices, that is an example of (perfect, second-degree, third-degree) _____ price discrimination; and finally when customers are charged different prices for different blocks of consumption, (perfect, second-degree, third-degree) _____ price discrimination is present.

6. The share of an industry's sales accounted for the four largest firms is a (contestable market, concentration ratio, Herfindahl-Hirshman index) _____ while the sum of the market shares squared is the (contestable market, concentration ratio, Herfindahl-Hirshman index) _____. When prices in an industry approach competitive levels because entry is easy, economists refer to this as a (contestable market, concentration ratio, Herfindahl-Hirshman index) _____.

True-False

Circle the correct answer.

_T/F_ 1. Monopolists are price takers.

_T/F_ 2. Monopoly power implies that a firm has some control over the price at which its product sells.

_T/F_ 3. A natural monopoly is an industry with economies of scale so large that demand will support only a single firm.

T/F   4. For the monopolist, marginal revenue is greater than price.

T/F   5. For the monopolist, profit maximizing output is at that level where marginal revenue equals average total costs.

T/F   6. Deadweight loss is the loss to society that comes about as a result of a monopoly market.

T/F   7. Because monopolists do not get bogged down in competition, they tend to operate more efficiently than competitive firms.

T/F   8. First-degree price discrimination involves charging different groups of consumers different prices.

T/F   9. Pricing movie tickets differently for children, adults, and seniors is an example of third-degree price discrimination.

T/F   10. If everything else is equal, prices will be lower in a contestable market than in a noncontestable market.

T/F   11. Contestable markets often require more regulatory oversight than other markets.

T/F   12. If regulators require a natural monopolist to sell its output for a price equal to the firm's average total costs, the firm will suffer economic losses and require government subsidies to stay in business.

T/F   13. Rate of return regulation allows monopolists to price their products such that they can earn a normal rate of return on the capital they invest.

T/F   14. In the early 1900s, most policymakers who supported antitrust legislation did so because they wanted to ensure the allocative efficiency of the marketplace.

T/F   15. Antitrust cases can be filed by the Antitrust Division of the Department of Justice, the Federal Trade Commission (FTC), state attorneys general, and lawyers for private plaintiffs.

T/F   16. The Herfindahl-Hirshman index measures market concentration by adding together the squares of the market shares of all the firms in a particular industry.

T/F   17. The HHI is inconsistent with our intuitive notions about market power.

T/F   18. Monopolies are often transitory in the "new economy."

Multiple Choice

Circle the correct answer.

1. Which of the following is *not* a defining characteristic of monopolies?
   a. No close substitutes for the seller's product.
   b. Significant barriers to market entry.
   c. Sellers are price makers.
   d. Many sellers in the market.

2. Monopoly power is
   a. a market containing just one seller.
   b. the power a firm has to control price by adjusting output.
   c. a market containing numerous sellers.
   d. the power the government has to regulate monopolies.

3. Which of the following statements concerning monopoly power is most accurate?
   a. Most firms have some monopoly power, though true monopolists enjoy the most such power.
   b. Only firms that are true monopolies enjoy any monopoly power.
   c. Monopoly power is a market structure that contains a single seller, has no close substitutes, and has high entry barriers.
   d. Most firms have some monopoly power, though competitive firms enjoy the most such power.

4. Which of the following is *not* a typical source of monopoly power?
   a. patents
   b. economies of scale
   c. control over a significant factor of production
   d. product homogeneity

5. Which of the following industries would *not* traditionally be a natural monopoly?
   a. electric power
   b. waste treatment
   c. baked goods
   d. local telephone service

6. A natural monopoly is an industry
   a. with economies of scale so large that a single firm encompasses the market.
   b. that could support multiple firms, but is limited to a single firm by government mandate.

c. that contains only a single firm at the moment, but is highly contestable.

d. that is rarely regulated in this country.

7. What does a government franchise do?
   a. It provides the inventor of a new product or process with protection against competition for a limited period of time.
   b. It grants a particular firm permission to provide a specific good or service, while prohibiting other firms from doing so.
   c. It grants the author of a piece of intellectual property the exclusive right to reproduce that product for a certain period of time.
   d. It gives government regulators the power to appropriate specified products for public consumption.

8. What is the typical length of a patent in the United States?
   a. 6 months
   b. 5 years
   c. 20 years
   d. 50 years

9. Which of the following will be true for an unregulated monopoly?
   a. $P < MR$
   b. $P = MR$
   c. $P > MR$
   d. $D - MR$

10. A monopolist's demand curve will be
    a. relatively more inelastic than for competition.
    b. the industry's demand curve.
    c. downward sloping.
    d. all of the above.

11. What determines the price at which a monopolist can sell its product?
    a. The price at which other firms in the industry are selling their products.
    b. The level of output at which the monopolist decides it wants to produce.
    c. Rules imposed by government regulatory agencies.
    d. Nothing—the monopolist can earn a profit by selling at any price.

12. The profit maximizing output for the monopolist is found where?
    a. $MR = P$
    b. $ATC = P$
    c. $MR = MC$
    d. $MR = ATC$

13. The profit maximizing monopolist will earn profits equal to which of the following?
    a. $(P - ATC) \times Q$
    b. $(P - MC) \times Q$
    c. $(ATC - MR) \times Q$
    d. $(ATC - MC) \times Q$

14. When will the profit maximizing monopolist shut down its plant?
    a. Never—monopolists can always earn economic profits, so they never have reason to shut down.
    b. When marginal revenue drops below price.
    c. When price drops below average total costs.
    d. When price drops below average variable costs.

15. The profit maximizing monopolist will produce Q_M units, as shown in Figure MC-1. Profit will be
    a. distance ae times Q_M.
    b. distance ab times Q_M.
    c. distance be times Q_M.
    d. none of the above.

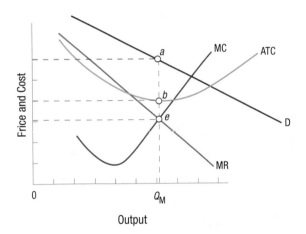

MC-1

16. Monopolists generally offer consumers _____ and _____ than competitive firms.
    a. lower output; lower prices
    b. lower output; higher prices
    c. higher output; lower prices
    d. higher output; higher prices

17. Which of the following is *not* an example of rent-seeking behavior?
    a. securing a patent extension
    b. lobbying Congress for a protective tariff
    c. running an advertisement touting the firm's product
    d. securing a government franchise

18. Rent seeking involves any behavior on the part of a monopolist that is intended to
    a. protect its monopoly position.
    b. generate a normal return.
    c. increase its customer base.
    d. improve efficiency so as to discourage potential competitors from entering the industry.

19. Monopolists tend to be x-inefficient because
    a. they often hold numerous patents.
    b. they produce at higher levels of output than competitive firms.
    c. they face such large economies of scale.
    d. they are not subjected to the pressures of the market.

20. In Figure MC-2, the deadweight loss from this monopolist is which of the following?
    a. $200
    b. $225
    c. $250
    d. $300

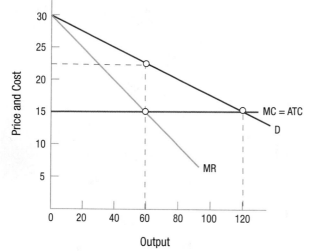

MC-2

21. In Figure MC-2, the monopoly profit earned by this monopolist is which of the following?
    a. $350
    b. $400
    c. $450
    d. $500

22. Which of the following is an example of first-degree price discrimination?
    a. movie tickets for children, adults, and seniors
    b. a garage sale

c. a bulk discount for buying laundry detergent in large quantities
d. airline rates that vary for all sorts of reasons

23. Which of the following is *not* among the conditions required for firms to be able to price discriminate successfully?
    a. Sellers must be able to separate the market into different consumer groups based on their elasticities of demand.
    b. Sellers must be able to prevent arbitrage.
    c. Sellers must have a patent to maintain their monopoly power.
    d. Sellers must have some monopoly power, or some control over price.

24. When a delivery company will ship packages at $2 per pound for the first 10 pounds, then at $1.50 per pound for every pound after that, which sort of price discrimination is this an example of?
    a. First-degree price discrimination.
    b. Second-degree price discrimination.
    c. Third-degree price discrimination.
    d. None of the above; this is not an example of price discrimination.

25. What type of price discrimination occurs when a restaurant offers seniors a 10% discount?
    a. First-degree price discrimination.
    b. Second-degree price discrimination.
    c. Third-degree price discrimination.
    d. None of the above; this is not an example of price discrimination.

Figure MC-3 shows the demand and marginal revenue curves for a restaurant engaging in price discrimination. Use this figure to answer questions 26–28.

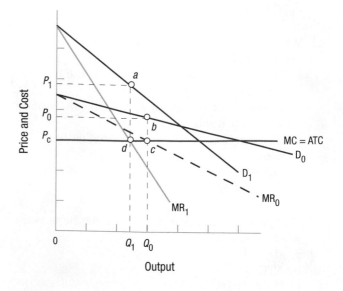

MC-3

26. Which point represents the price and quantity that the monopolist will supply for regular customers (those with the least elastic demand curve)?
    a. *a*
    b. *b*
    c. *c*
    d. *d*

27. Which point represents the price and quantity that the monopolist will supply for potential customers who need a discount as an inducement to buy from the restaurant?
    a. *a*
    b. *b*
    c. *c*
    d. *d*

28. Had the monopolist not price discriminated, it would have priced at P_1. What is the profit gained by offering a discount to nonregular customers (price discriminating)?
    a. $0P_0bQ_0$
    b. P_CP_0bc
    c. $P_CP_1ad - P_CP_0bc$
    d. $aQ_10P_1 - bQ_00P_0$

29. Contestable markets are those
    a. with low entry costs, such that new firms can enter the market rapidly.
    b. with a large number of firms selling homogeneous products.
    c. that tend to be among the most inefficient in the economy.
    d. that cannot support more than one firm in the industry.

30. What holds price to something close to a competitive level in a contestable market, even if that market should be a monopoly?
    a. the fact that the market contains numerous firms selling a homogeneous product
    b. the potential for other firms to enter the market and offer the monopolist some competition
    c. government-imposed price caps
    d. the weakness of consumer demand, which defines contestable markets

31. Which of the following are *not* among the questions a firm considering hit-and-run entry into a contestable market must ask itself?
    a. Can the firm earn a profit at the industry price after the firm has entered the market?
    b. Are the entry costs low enough to make market entry worthwhile?

c. Can the firm make some sales quickly, before the established firm in the market has had a chance to respond?
    d. Can the firm earn a profit over the long run at the current industry price?

32. Which of the following is *not* among the traditional approaches to regulating a natural monopoly?
    a. Firms desiring a monopoly right must compete for it; the winner is offered a franchise stipulating certain price and output conditions that were contained in the original competitive bid.
    b. Monopolistic firms are publicly owned and thus ultimately subject to political control.
    c. The firm that can first establish market dominance is allowed to set price and output levels as it sees fit.
    d. Monopolistic firms are privately owned, but subject to government regulations, especially regarding pricing and output.

33. If the monopolist in Figure MC-4 were a private, unregulated firm, it would produce at what point?
    a. *a*
    b. *b*
    c. *c*
    d. *d*

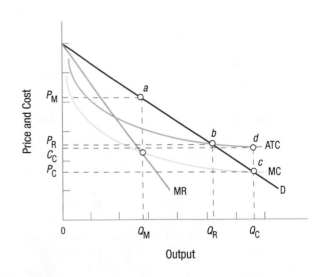

MC-4

34. What would happen if regulators invoked a $P = MC$ rule (the competitive market ideal) and forced the monopolist in Figure MC-4 to produce Q_C units at price P_C?
    a. This is the best of all worlds for everyone because it is precisely the quantity demanded by the market at that price.

b. The monopolist would earn normal profits at this point, just as a competitive firm would with a P = MC rule.

c. The monopolist would earn zero economic profits at this point, just as a competitive firm would with a P = MC rule.

d. The monopolist would face a loss of *cd* per unit because price is lower than average total costs.

35. If regulators invoked an average cost pricing rule on the monopolist in Figure MC-4, which of the following would *not* happen?

a. The monopolist would produce at point *b* and earn a normal return.

b. The monopolist would produce at point *d*.

c. The monopolist would produce more than if left on its own, but less than the socially optimal amount.

d. The monopolist would produce at a price less than if left on its own, but higher than the socially optimal price.

36. In what year did the Congress pass the Sherman Act, the first major piece of American antitrust legislation?

a. 1866

b. 1890

c. 1914

d. 1950

37. What was the purpose of the Robinson-Patman Act?

a. It outlawed any combination or conspiracy in restraint of trade or commerce.

b. It amended the Clayton Act in 1936 to prohibit price discrimination and to protect mom and pop stores.

c. It closed a merger loophole in the Clayton Act.

d. It established the Federal Trade Commission.

38. If an industry contains eight firms with market shares of 25, 18, 15, 12, 10, 10, 6, and 4, respectively, its 4-firm concentration ratio is which of the following?

a. 30

b. 70

c. 100

d. 1,318

39. The Justice Department would classify an industry with an HHI of 1,345 as

a. unconcentrated.

b. moderately concentrated.

c. highly concentrated.

d. monopolistic.

40. These days, roughly what percent of all mergers are rapidly approved by the government?

a. less than 2%

b. 70%

c. 50%

d. 99%

Essay-Problem

Answer in the space provided.

The questions in this section often ask you to apply what you have learned and can be challenging. Use our answers as guides and as another way to assess your progress.

1. What is the difference between being a monopoly and having monopoly power?

2. What are the three primary sources of monopoly power? Describe each one.

3. Why is rent-seeking behavior such as lobbying inefficient from a public interest perspective?

4. Construct an argument in favor of monopoly.

5. What is a major benefit of price discrimination to the monopolist, and a major loss to consumers?

6. Why are price-discriminating monopolists more likely to offer senior discounts and child discounts than general discount coupons mailed to a prospective consumer group that has a high elasticity of demand for the product?

7. Why does the federal government continue to subsidize Amtrak?

8. George Stigler showed that regulators can be "captured" by the monopolies they are supposed to regulate and wind up helping them rather than promoting the public interest. How does this happen?

9. How can regulated monopolies possibly justify country club memberships for their managers as legitimate business expenses?

10. If the initial push for antitrust legislation over 100 years ago did not have allocative efficiency as its goal, how can it be said to have an economic rationale behind it?

11. The table below shows sales and market shares for the top 10 firms in the semiconductor industry.

Company	Revenue ($billion)	Market Share (%)
Intel	27.1	15.3
Samsung Electronics	10.5	5.9
Renesas Technology	7.9	4.5
Texas Instruments	7.4	4.2
Toshiba	7.4	4.1
STMicroelectronics	7.2	4.0
Infineon Technologies	6.9	3.9
NEC Electronics	6.3	3.6
Motorola	4.6	2.6
Phillips Semiconductor	4.5	2.5

a. What is the 4-firm concentration ratio?
b. What is the 8-firm concentration ratio?
c. Assume these firms represent the entire industry, and these market shares represent the market shares for the entire industry (don't recalculate market shares so they total 100%). What is the HHI for this industry?
d. Is this industry rather competitive or tending toward monopoly?
e. If Intel and Samsung wanted to merge, would they be permitted under the HHI guidelines?

What's Next

By completing this chapter, you now have a good understanding of the two market structures at the extreme: the competitive model and monopoly. You have seen the public benefits from the competitive model and the problems that arise with monopolies. In the next chapter, we look at the two market structures between these two poles.

Answers to Chapterwide Practice Questions

Matching

1. c	4. e	7. f
2. i	5. d	8. h
3. b	6. g	9. a

Fill-In

1. the industry, a patent
2. greater than, equal to
3. higher than, lower
4. rent seeking, x-inefficiency
5. perfect, third-degree, second-degree
6. concentration ratio, Herfindahl-Hirshman index, contestable market

True-False

1. F	6. T	11. F	16. T
2. T	7. F	12. F	17. F
3. T	8. F	13. T	18. T
4. F	9. T	14. F	
5. F	10. T	15. T	

Multiple Choice

1. d	11. b	21. c	31. d
2. b	12. c	22. b	32. c
3. a	13. a	23. c	33. a
4. d	14. d	24. b	34. d
5. c	15. b	25. c	35. b
6. a	16. b	26. a	36. b
7. b	17. c	27. b	37. b
8. c	18. a	28. b	38. b
9. c	19. d	29. a	39. b
10. d	20. b	30. b	40. b

Essay-Problem

1. A monopoly is defined as a market containing a single seller where there are no close substitutes for the monopolist's product, and market entry is nearly impossible. Monopoly power, on the other hand, is the power a monopolist (or any firm) has to control the price of its product in virtue of its market strength. Nearly every firm has some monop-

oly power, in the sense that it often has some control over price. As markets approach competitive conditions, this control over price becomes minor; as markets approach the monopoly structure, control over price becomes more important.

2. The three primary sources of monopoly power are economies of scale, control over a significant factor of production, and legal mandates. Some industries have economies of scale so large that demand can support only a single firm in the industry. The investment necessary for other firms to enter the market would be so large that the entry of competitors into the industry is virtually impossible. When one firm has exclusive control over some key ingredient in a product's production, it can monopolize production of that product. For many years, Alcoa Aluminum monopolized the production of aluminum by controlling most of the world's supply of bauxite. In a similar way, De Beers controlled the supply of the world's diamonds for over half a century. Government patents, franchises, and copyrights all grant specific individuals or firms the exclusive right to produce certain products for an extended period of time.

3. Hiring lobbyists costs the firm resources that could be devoted to things that would better serve the rest of society, such as increased production or research and development of new products. The most a lobbyist does is maintain or increase a monopolist's position.

4. "My firm operates in an industry with extremely large economies of scale; thus it requires extremely large investments just to enter the industry. Given these high capital costs, demand in my industry will support only a single firm. If the industry were broken into multiple, smaller firms, none of them would survive. Furthermore, by investing in enormous—and enormously expensive—factories and machines, my firm is able to offer consumers more output at a lower price than multiple firms could manage, each of them producing on a smaller, less efficient scale. Finally, with my firm's massive budget, I am able to make large investments in research and development, thus paving the way for even better, less expensive products down the road. If the industry were broken into smaller competitive firms, all of them having tight budgets, none of them would make these R&D investments, and thus new products would never be developed."

5. Monopolists (or firms with pricing power) benefit from price discrimination because they can charge different prices to different people, and so better capture what each person or group Is wIlllng to pay, leading to much greater profit possibilities than if only one price were charged. While consumers pay what they are willing to pay under price discrimination, and so, in this sense, they are not hurt, but they do not get the consumer surplus that arises when only one price is available.

6. Seniors and children are easily identifiable groups. General discount coupons mailed to a prospective group may find their way into the hands of people with inelastic demand, either by accident or because acquaintances with highly elastic demand give them to people with inelastic demand. For price discrimination to work, the seller must clearly identify groups and prevent arbitrage between groups with elastic and inelastic demand.

7. The simplest answer is that it believes it is in the public interest to subsidize this money-losing monopoly. Amtrak does face competition from the airlines for many locations on its routes, but it also goes to places not served by the airlines. Furthermore, its prices usually are lower than airline prices. And people in areas served by Amtrak can be very vocal politically about the need for its train service, while the general populace is affected by its subsidies only to a minor degree, and so it does not get worked up about the subsidy. These reasons explain why Amtrak is subsidized; they do not explain whether the subsidy makes good economic sense.

8. In a straightforward sense, regulators hear a monopolist's arguments over and over. Over time, regulators can tune these arguments out or become sympathetic to the problems faced by monopolists. The arguments can become sophisticated and clever. When the usual topics of conversation are a monopolist's problems, and where public input is lacking, it is not surprising that regulators become more conciliatory to monopolists. In a less favorable sense, regulators sometimes wind up in the private sector with higher-paying jobs, working for the very monopolist that they had regulated. Did expectations of a future job lead to more sympathetic behavior?

9. Two arguments are usually given. First, the firm claims that business is transacted at the country club: Just as a business meal eases business activities, so does playing golf at an exclusive country club. Second, the firm claims that this is simply a cost of hiring people, that the top people would not be attracted by low salaries or must have what their colleagues in the unregulated sectors have. Because regulators are open to public scrutiny, it is harder for firms to make these claims to regulators than to shareholders of a private firm.

10. There was a general sense that large firms wielded monopoly power, especially against small businesses. There was—and is—a general inclination to think that big firms have muscle that they are not shy about exercising. Bigness may not always be bad, but as we have seen in this chapter, big firms with monopoly power can be expected to use that power to some degree to increase profits. Consumers and society lose when this happens. Preventing these losses is a good rationale for antitrust policy.

11. a. 29.9
    b. 45.5
    c. 380.78
    d. competitive
    e. New HHI = 561.32. Yes, the merger would be allowed.

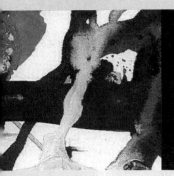

Monopolistic Competition, Oligopoly, and Game Theory

10

Competition, Monopoly: Now What Is in the Middle?

We have already analyzed competition and monopoly, which are market structure extremes. We now want to look at the two structures in the middle: monopolistic competition and oligopoly. This will round out our discussion of market structures. Furthermore, in looking at oligopoly, we look at game theory, an area of much fer ment in economics because it is useful in exploring oligopolistic behavior.

This Is What You Need to Know   STEP 1

After studying this chapter you should be able to

■ Describe product differentiation and its impact on the firm's demand curve.

■ Describe short-run pricing and output decisions for monopolistically competitive firms.

■ Describe the reasons why in the long run monopolistically competitive firms only earn normal profits.

■ Compare the efficiency of monopolistic competition to competition.

■ Describe and recognize oligopolistic industries.

■ Describe cartels and the reasons for their instability.

■ Describe the kinked demand curve model and why some economists feel prices are relatively stable in oligopoly industries.

■ Describe the Prisoner's Dilemma and determine the outcome of other games using the approach of minimizing your maximum loss.

■ Understand the nature of Nash equilibria and their importance to economists.

Review the Key Terms

Monopolistic competition: Involves a large number of small firms and is similar to competition, with easy entry and exit, but unlike the competitive model, the firms have differentiated their products, whether real or imagined.

Product differentiation: One firm's product is distinct from another's through such things as advertising, innovation, and location.

Oligopoly: A market with just a few firms dominating the industry where (1) each firm recognizes that it must consider its competitors' reactions when making its own decisions (mutual interdependence), and (2) there are significant barriers to entry into the market.

Mutual interdependence: When only a few firms constitute an industry, each firm must consider the reactions of its competitors to its decisions.

Cartel: An agreement between firms in an industry (or countries) to formally collude on price and output, then agree on the distribution of production.

Kinked demand curve: An oligopoly model that assumes that if a firm raises its price, competitors will not raise theirs; but if the firm lowers its price, all of its competitors will lower their price to match the reduction. This leads to a kink in the demand curve and relatively stable market prices.

Game theory: An approach to analyzing oligopoly behavior using mathematics and simulation by using different assumptions about the players, time involved, level of information, strategies, and other aspects of the game.

Prisoner's Dilemma: A noncooperative game where players cannot communicate or collaborate in making their decisions about whether to confess or not and thus results in inferior outcomes for both players. Many oligopoly decisions can be framed as a Prisoner's Dilemma.

Nash equilibrium: An important proof that an n-person game where each player chooses his optimal strategy, given that all other players have done the same, has a solution. This was an important proof because economists now knew that even complex models (or games) had an equilibrium or solution.

Static games: One-off games (not repeated) where decisions by the players are made simultaneously and are irreversible.

Dynamic games: Sequential or repeated games where the players can adjust their actions based on the decisions of other players in the past.

Predatory pricing: Selling below cost to consumers in the short run hoping to eliminate competitors so that prices can be raised in the longer run to earn economic profits.

Trigger strategies: Action is taken contingent on your opponent's past decisions. For example, a grim trigger strategy is defined as any unfavorable decision by your opponent that is met by a permanent retaliatory decision forever.

Tit-for-tat strategies: Simple strategies that repeat the prior move of competitors. If your opponent lowers price, you do the same. This approach has the efficient quality that it rewards cooperation and punishes unfavorable strategies (defections).

Work Through the Chapter Tutorials	STEP 3

Monopolistic Competition

Frequently Asked Questions

Q: **What are the key characteristics of monopolistic competition?**

A: Monopolistic competition assumes nearly the same characteristics as the competitive model, including a large number of small firms with insignificant market share and an absence of barriers to entry and exit, but the products sold by these firms are differentiated. Product differentiation is the key to this market structure. Products are similar, but consumers view them as different because of brand preference, physical location, inherent product differences, or many other factors.

Q: **How does product differentiation affect the demand curve?**

A: Product differences are often modest. Because of these differences, each firm nonetheless faces a downward sloping demand curve with an associated marginal revenue curve. Note, however, that this demand curve is highly elastic.

Q: **What is the short-run pricing and output for a monopolistically competitive firm?**

A: Monopolistically competitive pricing and output behavior in the short run looks a lot like that for a weak monopolist. Profit is maximized by selling an output where MR = MC. This is shown in Figure 1. Profits are maximized by selling q_0 units at P_0, and profits are equal to the shaded area.

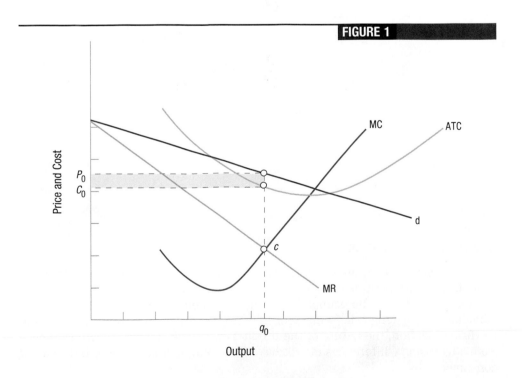

FIGURE 1

Q: **What happens in the long run to the profits of the monopolistically competitive firm?**

A: In the long run, easy entry and exit of other firms eliminates short-run profits or losses. If short-run profits exist, entry will reduce individual demand curves until the demand curve is just tangent to the long-run average total cost curve. If short-run losses are the rule, exit will expand the demand curve of remaining firms until, again, the demand curve is just tangent to the long-run ATC curve.

Q: **What is the cost to consumers of product differentiation?**

A: At long-run equilibrium, P = LRATC, and the firm earns normal profits. Note that this output level is not equal to the minimum point on the LRATC curve. This can be seen in Figure 2. Because the demand curve has a negative slope, the tangent occurs at point a an output level that is lower than that needed to minimize costs (minimum point on the LRATC curve). This represents the cost to consumers for product differentiation. The immense selection of goods available does not come without costs. Costs of advertising, rapid innovation, and "me too" copying are all included in the price of the products we purchase. Figure 2 compares long-run equilibrium of monopolistic competition (point a) with the competitive model (point b), and it shows that output is less and price higher under monopolistic competition.

FIGURE 2

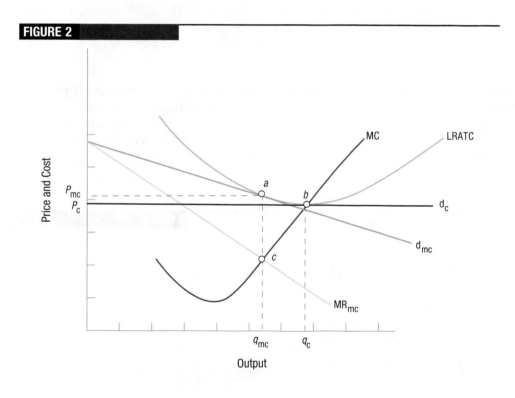

Key Point to Remember

The key characteristic about monopolistic competition is *product differentiation*. This gives the firms some control over price (monopoly power). But, entry and exit are easy, so the economic profits from their limited monopoly power is eliminated in the long run. Remember that product differentiation can come from the firm's location, the nature of the product or service, or perceived differences from advertising (differences do not have to be real, just considered different by consumers).

Monopolistic Competition Quick Check

Circle the Correct Answer

1. (T/F) Monopolistically competitive firms sell differentiated products.
2. (T/F) Because of product differentiation, the demand curve facing a monopolistically competitive firm will be relatively inelastic.
3. (T/F) In the short run, the monopolistically competitive firm will produce at the point where MR = MC.
4. In the short run, profit maximization for the monopolistically competitive firm will be similar to that for
   a. a monopolist, but will tend to be more.
   b. a monopolist, but will tend to be less.
   c. a competitive firm, but will tend to be more.
   d. a competitive firm, but will tend to be less.
5. In the long run, a monopolistically competitive firm will earn
   a. economic profits because of product differentiation.
   b. economic profits because of entry restrictions.
   c. normal profits because economic profits will attract new firms and there are no entry restrictions.
   d. normal profits because costs are high for monopolistically competitive firms.
6. In Figure 3, in the long run, the monopolistically competitive firm will
   a. produce at point *b* because it will earn normal profits only, just as the competitive firm does.
   b. produce at point *b* because it is at the minimum of the long-run ATC curve.

c. produce at point *a* because it faces a demand curve that is somewhat elastic due to its product differentiation.
   d. produce at point *a* because its profit will be distance *ac* times q_{mc} units.
7. In the run long, the monopolistically competitive firm
   a. will produce more than the monopolist, but at a higher price because of product differentiation.
   b. will produce less than the competitive firm, but at a higher price.
   c. will produce less than the competitive firm, but at a lower price because it faces relatively elastic demand.
   d. will produce more than the competitive firm because it offers a differentiated product, rather than a standardized one.
8. In the long run, which one of the following will *not* happen for the monopolistically competitive firm?
   a. Economic profits will tend to evaporate because they will attract new entrants to the market because entry is easy.
   b. Quantity of output produced will be less than with competitive firms, and at a higher price.
   c. Short-run profits will be less than with a monopoly.
   d. Long-run output will be produced at the minimum of the long-run average total cost curve.
9. Which one of the following is *not* an example of a monopolistically competitive product?
   a. Coach handbags
   b. Armani suits

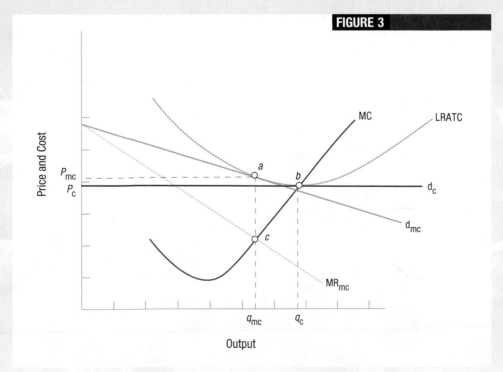

FIGURE 3

c. Burberry raincoats
d. Safeway brand salt
10. Monopolistic competition is similar to competition *except* for which one of the following?
    a. Both have a large number of small firms.
    b. Both face easy entry and exit to the market.

c. Both are price takers.
d. Both do not earn long-run economic profits.

Score: ____

Answers: 1. T; 2. F; 3. T; 4. b; 5. c; 6. c; 7. b; 8. d; 9. d; 10. c

If You Got 9 or 10 Correct

You're solid on monopolistic competition. Go on to the next section, "Oligopoly."

If You Didn't Get at Least 9 Correct

Spend some time reviewing this material. If you understood competition and monopoly, you should have little trouble understanding monopolistic competition. Keep in mind that a monopolistically competitive firm prices like a monopolist (with little monopoly power) in the short run, but easy entry and exit reduces profits to zero (normal) in the long run.

Remember, monopolistic competition is essentially the same as the competitive model with product differentiation instead of homogeneous products. This means that consumers will have some brand loyalty that is absent in competitive markets with standardized products. The costs of differentiating products are the inefficiency associated with this market structure. These costs are relatively small and are considered the price we pay for innovation, advertising, and brand preference.

Monopolistic competition is quite close in market structure to the competitive model. In the next section, "Oligopoly," you will look at a model that is significantly different from the three models you have studied so far. ∎

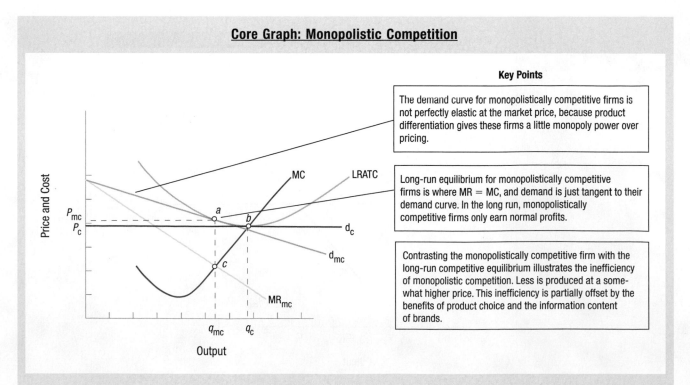

Core Graph: Monopolistic Competition

Key Points

The demand curve for monopolistically competitive firms is not perfectly elastic at the market price, because product differentiation gives these firms a little monopoly power over pricing.

Long-run equilibrium for monopolistically competitive firms is where MR = MC, and demand is just tangent to their demand curve. In the long run, monopolistically competitive firms only earn normal profits.

Contrasting the monopolistically competitive firm with the long-run competitive equilibrium illustrates the inefficiency of monopolistic competition. Less is produced at a somewhat higher price. This inefficiency is partially offset by the benefits of product choice and the information content of brands.

Oligopoly

Frequently Asked Questions

Q: What is an oligopoly?

A: Oligopoly industries are those in which the market is controlled by just a few firms. What constitutes a few firms is not precisely defined. Oligopoly products can be the same or differentiated and barriers to entry are usually substantial. Because there are only a few firms, decisions by one firm are dependent on the decisions of other firms in the industry. Economists refer to this as mutual inter-dependence.

Q: What are cartels?

A: Cartels are illegal in the United States and the European Union, but are per-mitted in other parts of the world. Firms in a cartel collude and agree to set monopoly prices and share the market according to some formula. Cartels are inherently unstable because cheating is immensely profitable.

Q: What is the kinked demand curve model of oligopoly?

A: The kinked demand curve model of oligopoly answers the question of why oli-gopoly prices often appear stable. The model assumes that if the firm raises its price, competitors will not react and raise their prices, but if the firm lowers prices, other firms will lower theirs in response. These *reactions* by competitors create a "kink" in the firm's demand curve and a discontinuity in the MR curve. This discontinuity permits marginal costs to vary considerably (between points *a* and *b* in Figure 4) before the firm will change its price. Study the kinked demand curve model of oligopoly in Figure 4 before going on to work the problems.

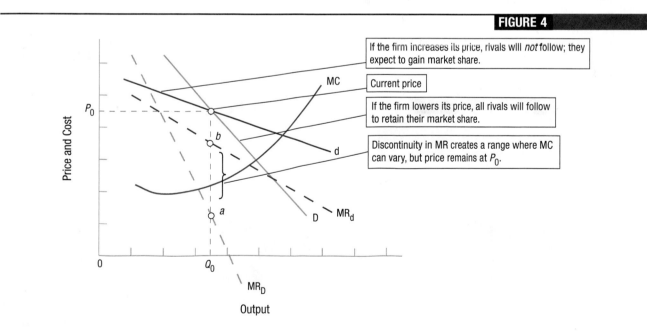

FIGURE 4

If the firm increases its price, rivals will *not* follow; they expect to gain market share.

Current price

If the firm lowers its price, all rivals will follow to retain their market share.

Discontinuity in MR creates a range where MC can vary, but price remains at P_0.

Key Point to Remember

Oligopolies are industries with a *few* firms with fairly substantial barriers to entry. Because there are only a few firms, their decisions are *mutually interdependent*. When only a few firms compete, if one firm makes a decision that enhances its com-petitive advantage, the other firms will react to mitigate this competitive advantage.

Oligopoly Quick Check

Circle the Correct Answer

1. (T/F) Oligopoly firms can set prices without considering competitors because each firm is so large.
2. (T/F) There are only two oligopoly models: cartels and kinked-demand curves.
3. (T/F) Oligopolies represent an industry having few firms and significant barriers to entry.
4. (T/F) Mutual interdependence in decision making between firms is the key characteristic of oligopolies.
5. Cartels are *not* found in the United States because
   a. they require many member firms, making them too large to police.
   b. there are too many incentives to cheat in our competitive economy.
   c. they require collusion, which is difficult to accomplish with a prying press corps.
   d. they are prohibited by law.
6. In Figure 5, if an oligopoly firm raises prices at any point to the left of point *a* demand curve d, rival firms will
   a. have the same price increase because oligopolies are mutually interdependent.
   b. have the same price increase because they want to obtain the same economic profits.
   c. ignore the price increase because the first-moving firm will find that its price increase leads to reduced market share, with the other firms picking up new customers.
   d. ignore the price increase because rival firms' costs will be in between points *b* and *c*, not at either point.

7. The oligopolist in Figure 5 will price its product
   a. somewhere between P_1 and P_2 because it faces kinked demand.
   b. at P_2.
   c. at P_1.
   d. at P_0.
8. Cartels are inherently unstable because
   a. they are prevented by law.
   b. they require secrecy, which is very hard to achieve.
   c. the demand curve for their product is highly elastic.
   d. cheating is highly profitable.
9. In the kinked demand curve model, a lowering of price by one oligopoly firm will cause rivals to
   a. ignore the price decrease so as not to decrease profits.
   b. ignore the price decrease because demand is kinked.
   c. match the price decrease so as not to lose market share.
   d. match the price increase because demand is relatively inelastic.
10. In the kinked demand curve model, the profit maximizing point is which of the following?
    a. MR = MC = P
    b. MR > MC = P
    c. MR = MC < P
    d. MR = MC > P

Score: ____

FIGURE 5

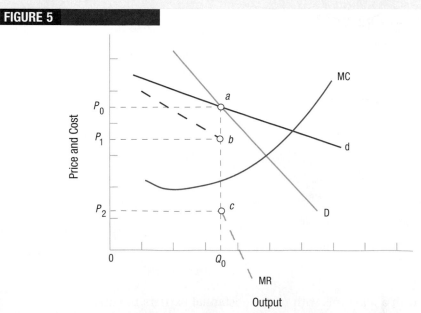

If You Got 9 or 10 Correct

Oligopoly and the two models covered in the text (cartels and the kinked demand curve) are no problem for you. Go on to "Game Theory," the last section in the chapter. You will find this section a little more challenging.

If You Didn't Get at Least 9 Correct

Review the material carefully. Cartels probably will be easier to understand than the kinked demand curve. Do all the standard stuff: Reread the text and spend some time rereading the captions for the figures.

If you had trouble with monopolistic competition, sit down and, using the table below, list the attributes of both monopolistic competition and oligopoly and list some industries that fit those characteristics.

Monopolistic Competition		Oligopoly	
Characteristics	Examples	Characteristics	Examples
_____	_____	_____	_____
_____	_____	_____	_____
_____	_____	_____	_____

Ask yourself how you would expect firms in these two market structures to differ. Keep in mind that monopolistic competition is closer to the competitive ideal and oligopoly is closer to monopoly.

Now take a few moments and work through the solved problem on the kinked demand curve model below.

Solved Problem: Kinked Demand Curve

The data in the table below are for two different demand curves facing an oligopolist, where demand curve D_0 represents the firm's demand curve when their competitors will match their changes in price, and demand curve D_1 reflects demand when competitors do not follow the firm's price changes. Using these data, answer the questions below:

P	D_0	D_1	MR_1	MR_0
20	0	0	0	0
18	20	0	0	10
16	40	0	0	20
14	60	40	20	30
12	80	80	40	40
10	100	120	60	50
8	120	160	80	60
6	140	200	100	70
4	160	240	120	80
2	180	280	140	90
0	200	320	160	100

a. Use the grid that follows to plot the demand and marginal revenue curves. (Hint: The marginal revenue curves bisect each demand curve.)

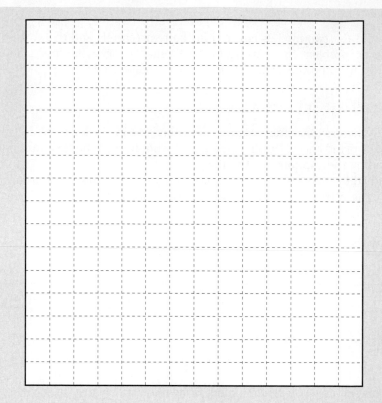

b. At what price do the two demand curves cross? Assume this is the current price charged by the firm.

c. Now describe what happens if the firm raises or lowers its price. Darken the relevant portions of the demand curve facing the firm. Now darken the relevant portions of the marginal revenue curves.

d. Given the discontinuity in the marginal revenue curve, what is the range for marginal cost before the firm will change its price?

e. What behavioral implications does this model provide about oligopoly pricing behavior?

f. What is one criticism of this kinked demand curve model?

Solution-Discussion

a. See Figure 6 on the following page.

b. $12. The curves cross at point e.

c. If the firm raises its price, competitors do not match the price increase, so the upper portion of D_1 above point e has been darkened. If the firm lowers price all competitors lower their prices as well, thus, the lower portion of D_0 below point e has been darkened. The darkened portion of the two demand curves represents the demand curve facing our oligopolist.

d. Output for this firm will remain at 80 units as long as marginal cost is between roughly $4.50 and $8.00 ($MC_0$ and MC_1).

e. Prices tend to be relatively stable in oligopolistic industries where competitors react in the way formulated by this model. Another implication of this model is that there is a wide range of possible oligopoly models depending on the behavioral reaction of competitors. It does illustrate that the most important aspect of oligopolies is their mutual interdependence and the importance of how they react to their competitor's decisions.

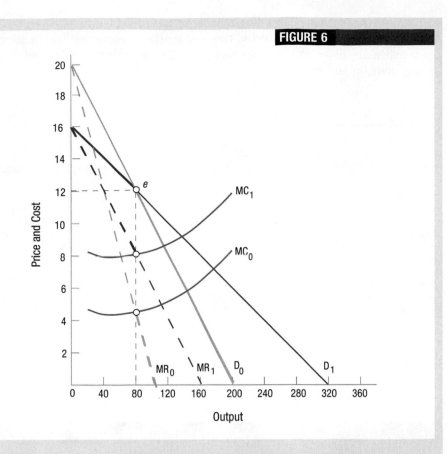

FIGURE 6

f. A major shortcoming of the kinked demand curve model is that we really don't know how the $12 price was established in the first place. Why has the industry set that price as the initial equilibrium price and not some other price?

The kinked demand curve model usually requires a second viewing. After this, go on to the next section on game theory. ▪

Game Theory

Frequently Asked Questions

Q: What is the Prisoner's Dilemma?

A: The Prisoner's Dilemma is a noncooperative game where each player must anticipate whether the other is going to confess or not. Both would be better off by not confessing, but each will confess in the end. Both players end up minimizing their worst outcome, prison time. The Prisoner's Dilemma is applicable to many other areas including business pricing, advertising, war, and research and development decisions.

Q: What important point did John Nash make about game theory?

A: John Nash, in a very short paper, showed that in an n-person game, if each player chooses his optimal strategy given that all other players have done the same, that game has a solution. This was an important result that allowed economists to develop realistic but complex games of market interactions, because they knew a solution existed.

Q: How can the four key market structures be summarized?

A: At this point, you have covered the four market structures. The major characteristics are listed in the table below. Study the summary table before checking your understanding.

	Competition	Monopolistic Competition	Oligopoly	Monopoly
Number of firms	Many	Many	Few	One
Product	Homogeneous	Differentiated	Homogeneous or differentiated	Unique
Barriers to entry or exit?	No	No	Yes	Yes
Strategic interdependence?	No	No	Yes	Not Applicable
Long-run price decision?	P = ATC	P = ATC	P > ATC	P > ATC
Long-run profits?	Zero	Zero	Usually economic	Economic
Key summary characteristic	Price taker	Product differentiation	Mutual interdependence	One firm industry

Game Theory Quick Check

Circle the Correct Answer

1. (T/F) In the Prisoner's Dilemma, each participant chooses a strategy that leads to the highest possible outcome.
2. (T/F) John Nash proved that some complex games could have a solution, now known as a Nash Equilibrium.
3. (T/F) In a Prisoner's Dilemma, prisoners communicate with each other to determine the best strategy to take.
4. (T/F) Game theory helps explain both market structures in the middle: oligopolies and monopolistically competitive firms.

Use the payoff matrix below to answer question 5. Assume that oligopolists A and B both charge $15 for the product and face roughly the same costs.

	Firm B's Price	
Firm A's Price	$15	$10
$15	$200,000,$200,000	$100,000,$500,000
$10	$500,000,$100,000	$150,000,$150,000

5. If Firm A lowers its price to $10,
   a. it will gain $300,000 in profit.
   b. Firm B will gain $300,000 in profit.

c. Firm B will match Firm A's price, leading to lower profits for both.
   d. Firm B will match Firm A's price, and both will gain $150,000 in profit.
6. Which one of the following is *not* correct?
   a. Competitive firms are price takers.
   b. Monopolies are price makers.
   c. Oligopolies have some pricing power.
   d. Monopolistically competitive firms are price takers.
7. Which one of the following is *not* correct?
   a. Oligopolies are mutually interdependent.
   b. Monopolies enjoy significant barriers to entry.
   c. Monopolistically competitive firms have differentiated products.
   d. Competitive firms achieve long-run economic profits if they price at P > ATC.
8. If one airline lowers its price, game theory suggests that
   a. the other airlines will do nothing.
   b. the other airlines will do nothing because they are at a Nash equilibrium.
   c. the other airlines will immediately do the same to minimize profits.
   d. the other airlines will immediately do the same to minimize the effect of the first-moving airline on their profits.
9. Which one of the following is *not* correct?
   a. Competitive firms produce only homogeneous products.

b. Oligopolies produce only homogeneous products.
c. Monopolies price at P > ATC in the long run.
d. Monopolistically competitive firms face no significant barriers to entry.

10. Which one of the following is *not* correct?
a. Monopolistically competitive firms are mutually inter-dependent.
b. Monopolies earn economic profits in the long run.

c. Oligopolies price at P > ATC in the long run.
d. Competitive firms maximize profit where MR = MC.

Score: _____

If You Got 9 or 10 Correct

You have a good grasp of the basics of game theory and the essence of market structures. Spend a few moments with the "Hints, Tips, and Reminders," the next step.

If You Didn't Get at Least 9 Correct

Look back and make sure that you know why your answers were incorrect. Market structure analysis forces you to pull together this and the previous two chapters. If often takes a little time for the material to sink in, and students often need several attempts to really master this material.

If you had trouble with this chapter, now is the time to solve this problem.

Keep in Mind

- Product differentiation distinguishes monopolistic competition from competition. This leads to slight monopoly power and a highly elastic demand curve.
- Short-run equilibrium for a monopolistically competitive firm looks like a weak monopolist.
- In the long run, entry and exit eliminate economic profits for a monopolistically competitive firm, and price and output are determined where the demand curve is tangent to the average total cost curve.
- Oligopolies involve few firms that are mutually interdependent; their decisions are based on expected reactions by rivals. This makes oligopoly models numerous and complex.
- The kinked demand curve model assumes that rivals will not follow price increases, but match price reductions. This leads to a gap in the marginal revenue curve that permits a range of cost conditions before the firm will change its price. This model predicts price stability in oligopolistic markets.
- Game theory is another way of modeling oligopoly mutual interdependence.

If you get a handle on these items, you have the essence of the chapter down pat. Read through the "Hints, Tips, and Reminders" that follow. ■

Consider These Hints, Tips, and Reminders   STEP 4

1. Here is something to keep in mind as you work through all of the market structure analysis and try to graph each market: The firm's cost curves are drawn the same for all market structures, only the demand curves change.
- Competition—horizontal at market price due to standardized product.

- Monopolistic competition—modestly downward sloping due to product differentiation.
- Oligopoly—more of a downward slope because of firm's size (maybe with a kink) and more reflective of the industry if a cartel.
- Monopoly—the industry's demand curve.

2. Also keep in mind that monopolistic competition is closer to the competitive model, and oligopoly is closer to monopoly (see the continuum below).

```
         |--------|----------------------------------|-----------|
      Competition Monopolistic                    Oligopoly   Monopoly
                  Competition
```

Do the Homework for Chapter 10
Monopolistic Competition, Oligopoly,
and Game Theory

Instructor _____ Time _____ Student _____

Use the answer key below to record your answers to these homework questions.

1. (a) (b) (c) (d)	6. (a) (b) (c) (d)	11. (a) (b) (c) (d)	16. (a) (b) (c) (d)
2. (a) (b) (c) (d)	7. (a) (b) (c) (d)	12. (a) (b) (c) (d)	17. (a) (b) (c) (d)
3. (a) (b) (c) (d)	8. (a) (b) (c) (d)	13. (a) (b) (c) (d)	18. (a) (b) (c) (d)
4. (a) (b) (c) (d)	9. (a) (b) (c) (d)	14. (a) (b) (c) (d)	19. (a) (b) (c) (d)
5. (a) (b) (c) (d)	10. (a) (b) (c) (d)	15. (a) (b) (c) (d)	20. (a) (b) (c) (d)

1. Which of the following is *not* an assumption of monopolistically competitive markets?
   a. There are just a few firms.
   b. Each of the firms produce slightly differentiated products.
   c. Firms have some control over the price of their products.
   d. There are no significant barriers to entry into this market.

2. Monopolistic competitive markets are similar to competitive markets in that
   a. there are just a few firms.
   b. differentiated products are produced.
   c. the socially optimal level of output is produced in the long run.
   d. both earn normal profits in the long run.

3. A monopolistically competitive market is one in which
   a. only one firm produces a differentiated product.
   b. all firms sell the exact same product.
   c. many firms sell a slightly differentiated product.
   d. most firms sell the same products, and just a few are able to differentiate their products.

4. In the short run for monopolistically competitive firms,
   a. price is equal to marginal cost.
   b. the firm only earns normal profits.
   c. the firm's demand curve is horizontal.
   d. price is greater than marginal cost.

5. In Figure HW-1, in the long run, the profit maximizing price for this monopolistically competitive firm is which of the following?
   a. P_0
   b. P_1
   c. point c
   d. point b

6. In Figure HW-1, in the long run, the profit maximizing output for this monopolistically competitive firm is which of the following?
   a. P_0
   b. P_1
   c. q_1
   d. q_0

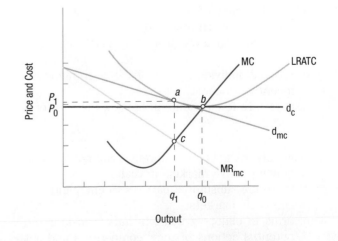

HW-1

7. In Figure HW-1, in the long run, total economic profit for this monopolistically competitive firm is
   a. a positive economic profit.
   b. a negative economic loss.
   c. equal to area P_0P_1ab.
   d. equal to zero.

8. In Figure HW-1, if this industry were a competitive industry, profit maximizing output
   a. is not shown in this figure.
   b. would be nothing, because the industry would be shut down since losses are inevitable.
   c. would be q_1.
   d. would be q_0.

9. A major difference between a monopoly and an oligopoly is that
   a. oligopolies produce where price is greater than marginal cost.
   b. oligopolies are able to earn long-run economic profits.
   c. unlike monopolies, oligopolies produce the socially optimal level of output in the long run.
   d. oligopolies must consider the reactions of competitors to their policies.

10. Which of the following is *not* an assumption of oligopoly markets?
    a. There are substantial barriers to entry into oligopolistic markets.
    b. The products sold in oligopolistic markets are differentiated.
    c. There are only a few firms in an oligopolistic industry.
    d. Oligopolies must consider the reactions of competitors to their policies.

11. One reason that cartels are inherently unstable is that
    a. keeping track of who cheats in a cartel is simple with modern technology.
    b. there are no laws protecting cartel arrangements.
    c. rational individual firms have a tremendous incentive to cheat.
    d. there are few benefits in being a member of a cartel.

12. Oligopoly markets are different from monopolistically competitive markets in that
    a. there are substantial barriers to entry into oligopolistic markets.
    b. firms in oligopoly markets must consider the potential actions of their competitors and act strategically.

c. there are only a few firms in an oligopolistic industry.
d. all of the above.

13. Which of the following is an assumption of monopolistically competitive markets and *not* an assumption of oligopoly markets?
    a. There are substantial barriers to entry.
    b. The products sold are differentiated.
    c. There are only a few firms in the industry.
    d. Firms in the industry must consider the reactions of competitors to their policies.

14. Which of the following is the best example of an oligopolistic industry?
    a. California apple growers
    b. fitness club industry
    c. cigarettes
    d. Los Angles restaurant market

15. When oligopolists are able to collude,
    a. both price and output usually rise.
    b. both price and output usually fall.
    c. price falls and output rises.
    d. price rises and output falls.

16. In which of the following industries is there a cartel?
    a. computer memory chips
    b. oil
    c. movies
    d. wheat

17. A cartel fixes price in order to
    a. increase the market share of the cartel itself.
    b. restrict entry into the cartel.
    c. eliminate competition.
    d. increase profits.

18. Modern game theory owes its origins to
    a. John Maynard Keynes.
    b. Adam Smith.
    c. John von Neumann.
    d. Milton Friedman.

Use the payoff matrix below to answer questions 19 and 20.

Firm A's Price	Firm B's Price	
	$50.00	$30.00
$50.00	$300,000, $300.000	$150,000, $450,000
$30.00	$450,000, $150,000	$200,000, $200,000

19. In the payoff matrix, two possible pricing policies for Firms A and B are shown, and the profit payoff to each firm (A, B) is shown in the table. If Firm B sets its price at $30, what will Firm A do?
    a. Nothing, because what Firm B does has no impact on Firm A.
    b. Set its price at $50 to keep profits at a maximum.
    c. Exit the business, since losses are inevitable.
    d. Set its price at $30.

20. In the payoff matrix, two possible pricing policies for Firms A and B are shown and the profit payoff to each firm (A, B) is shown in the table. If the two firms are able to successfully collude, which of the following will happen?
    a. Both will set their prices at $30.
    b. Firm A will charge $50, and Firm B will charge $30.
    c. Firm A will charge $30, and Firm B will charge $50.
    d. Both will set their prices at $50.

Use the ExamPrep to Get Ready for Exams STEP 6

This sheet (front and back) is designed to help you prepare for your exams. The chapter has been boiled down to its key concepts. You are asked to answer questions, define terms, draw graphs, and, if you wish, add summaries of class notes.

Monopolistic Competition

List the characteristics of monopolistic competition:

Short-Run Price and Output under Monopolistic Competition

Use the grid below for the following:

Draw the following curves: Average total cost and marginal cost. (Hint: Keep in mind that the marginal cost curve goes through the minimum point of the ATC curve.)

Now draw in a demand and marginal revenue curve for a monopolistically competitive firm. (Hint: Remember that the marginal revenue curve bisects [splits] a linear demand curve and that the demand is highly elastic.)

In the figure show the profit maximizing output and price, and shade in and label profit. (Hint: This is essentially the same as for a monopolist, but demand is more elastic and economic profits are considerably smaller.)

Long-Run Price and Output under Monopolistic Competition

Use the grid on the next page for the following:

Again, draw the following curves: Average total cost and marginal cost.

Now draw in a demand and marginal revenue curve for a monopolistically competitive firm.

Show the profit maximizing output and price in the long run. What kind of profits do these firms earn? Why?

Contrast the price and output that a monopolistically competitive industry would produce with that for a competitive firm.

Discuss why monopolistically competitive firms are less efficient than competitive firms.

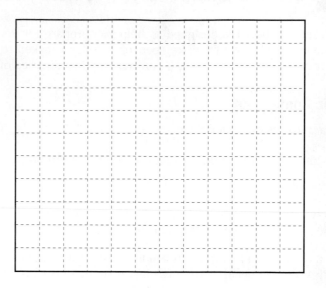

Oligopoly

List the characteristics of an oligopoly:

Cartels

Describe cartels and their chances for long-run success:

The Kinked Demand Curve Model

List the assumptions of the kinked demand curve model:

What happens when an oligopolistic firm raises its price?

Lowers its price?

Describe why prices are inherently stable in the kinked demand curve model.

Game Theory

In the Prisoner's Dilemma (a noncooperative game), why will each prisoner confess?

Complete the Summary of Market Structures shown in the table below.

Summary of Market Structures

	Competition	Monopolistic Competition	Oligopoly	Monopoly
Number of firms				
Product				
Barriers to entry or exit?				
Strategic Interdependence?				
Long-run price decision?				
Long-run profits?				
Key summary characteristic				

Additional Study Help Chapterwide Practice Questions

Matching

Match the description with the corresponding term.

___   1. Monopolistic competition
___   2. Product differentiation
___   3. Oligopoly
___   4. Mutual interdependence
___   5. Cartel
___   6. Kinked demand curve
___   7. Game theory
___   8. Prisoner's Dilemma
___   9. Nash equilibrium

a. Caused by the reactions of competing firms to match price decreases but not follow price increases.
b. An industry containing a few firms.
c. A Nobel Prize was won for this analysis.
d. Something that makes consumers desire one product versus another.
e. Why decisions made independently are often different from those made collectively or collusively.
f. Many firms vying for the consumer's dollar through innovation and product differentiation.
g. Any rule-governed situation with a well-defined outcome, characterized by strategic interdependence.
h. The most important aspect of oligopolistic decision making.
i. An industry where the firms get together and agree to set price and output quotas and share the market.

Fill-In

Circle the word(s) in parentheses that complete the sentence.

1. The most important characteristic of monopolistic competition that causes it to differ from competitive markets is (homogeneous, differentiated) _____ products. In the short run, both firms in monopolistic competition and competitive markets can earn (normal, economic) _____ profits, but in the long run both will end up earning (normal, economic) _____ profits.

2. Compared to competitive firms, monopolistically competitive firms produce (more, less, the same) _____ and charge a (higher, lower, the same) price. Both maximize profit where (P < MC, P = MC, MR = MC) _____.

3. Oligopoly industries involve (many, few, one) _____ firm(s), that have (few, many, no) _____ barriers to entry and are mutually (independent, interdependent) _____.

4. The kinked demand curve model assumes that if the firm increases its product price, the other firms in the industry (will, will not) _____ follow, but if the firm lowers its price other firms in the industry (will, will not) _____ follow. This model leads to (highly variable, stable) _____ prices.

5. The Prisoner's Dilemma is a (cooperative, noncooperative) _____ game where ultimately, both will (confess, go free) _____. In static games decisions are made (sequentially, simultaneously) _____, but with dynamic games players decisions occur (sequentially, simultaneously) _____.

True-False

Circle the correct answer.

T/F   1. The source of market power for monopolistically competitive firms is their differentiated products.

T/F   2. The demand curve facing the firm in a monopolistically competitive environment is flat at the market price due to product differentiation.

T/F   3. Monopolistic competition is defined by a small number of firms selling differentiated products.

T/F   4. In the short run, the monopolistically competitive firm sets prices and output in a manner similar to a monopolist.

T/F   5. In the long run, the monopolistically competitive firm can earn economic profits, but not as large as a monopoly firm.

T/F   6. Oligopoly represents an industry with few firms with insignificant market power.

T/F   7. The key aspect of oligopolies is the mutual interdependence in decision making between firms.

<u>T/F</u>   8. Oligopolies typically earn normal profits.

<u>T/F</u>   9. In oligopoly markets, there are no significant barriers to entry.

<u>T/F</u>   10. Pricing models of oligopoly are easy to devise because there are so few firms to be concerned with in the construction of the model.

<u>T/F</u>   11. Game theory is used to analyze highly competitive markets.

<u>T/F</u>   12. The Prisoner's Dilemma is an unrealistic game.

<u>T/F</u>   13. Participants in Prisoner's Dilemma situations try to select a strategy that guarantees the highest possible outcome.

<u>T/F</u>   14. All game theory models result in stable and predictable outcomes.

<u>T/F</u>   15. John Nash's proof of a game theory equilibrium under certain circumstances set game theory back for decades.

Multiple Choice

Circle the correct answer.

1. Monopolistic competition is *not* characterized by which of the following?
   a. a large number of sellers
   b. product differentiation
   c. downward sloping demand curve
   d. stable prices for the product

2. The demand for the monopolistically competitive firm's product is downward sloping because
   a. quantity demanded rises as price falls.
   b. these firms have immense market power and can charge whatever price they desire.
   c. of product differentiation.
   d. many firms competing for business increases the demand.

Use Figure MC-1 depicting a monopolistically competitive firm to answer questions 3–5.

3. What will be equilibrium output in the short run?
   a. 340 units
   b. 320 units
   c. 300 units
   d. no output

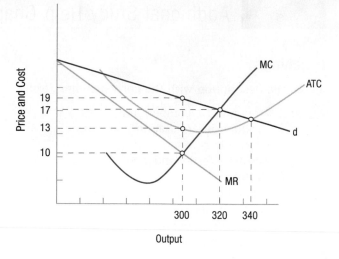

MC-1

4. In the short run, what will be the profit earned by this monopolistically competitive firm?
   a. $2,700
   b. $600
   c. zero
   d. $1,800

5. If demand declines in the long run such that output remains the same in long-run equilibrium as it was in the short run, what will be the price in the long run for the product?
   a. $19
   b. $17
   c. $13
   d. $10

6. In long-run equilibrium for monopolistically competitive firms, which of the following will hold?
   a. P = MC = MR and P = minimum point on LRATC curve
   b. P > MC = MR and P > minimum point on LRATC curve
   c. P > MC = MR and P = minimum point on LRATC curve
   d. P = MC = MR and P > minimum point on LRATC curve

7. In long-run equilibrium for monopolistically competitive firms,
   a. firms sell as much output as they can.
   b. firms differentiate their products by charging more than competitors.
   c. firms sell at the minimum point on the LRATC curve.
   d. firms earn a normal return like competitive firms.

Use Figure MC-2 to answer questions 8 and 9.

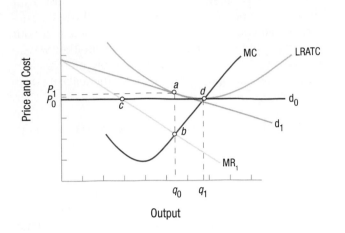

MC-2

8. Long-run equilibrium for the competitive firm is at point
   a. *a.*
   b. *b.*
   c. *c.*
   d. *d.*

9. Long-run equilibrium for the monopolistically competitive firm is at point(s)
   a. *a* and *b.*
   b. *b* and *c.*
   c. *c.*
   d. *d.*

10. Which of the following industries is a monopolistically competitive industry?
    a. automobiles
    b. cigarettes
    c. shoe stores
    d. computer microprocessor chips

11. The most important characteristic of oligopoly is
    a. numerous firms.
    b. insignificant barriers to entry.
    c. mutual interdependence.
    d. sticky or stable price structures.

12. A cartel or joint profit maximization oligopolist will maximize profits by setting
    a. MR = MC = P.
    b. MR > MC = P.
    c. MR = MC < P.
    d. MR = MC > P.

13. The essential characteristic of a cartel is
    a. the industry's demand curve is highly elastic.
    b. collusion between the members is necessary.
    c. the size of the market.
    d. how much profit each cartel member can make.

14. Which of the following industries or organizations operate as a cartel?
    a. steel industry
    b. Organization of Petroleum Exporting Countries (OPEC)
    c. automobile industry
    d. cigarette industry

15. Cartels are inherently unstable because
    a. cartels have too many members to police.
    b. buyers rebel at high prices, forcing demand to drop, causing the cartel to break up.
    c. politicians are able to pass laws prohibiting them.
    d. the incentives to cheat are too great.

16. The kinked demand curve model requires
    a. a lot of firms selling in the market.
    b. high barriers to entry and exit.
    c. different reactions to price changes from rivals.
    d. multiple marginal cost curves.

Use Figure MC-3 to answer questions 17–19.

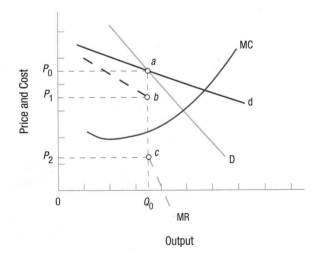

MC-3

17. Equilibrium price for the oligopolist pictured is
    a. P_0.
    b. P_1.
    c. P_2.
    d. somewhere between P_1 and P_2.

18. Demand curve d represents that demand curve where
    a. price is attractive to buyers.
    b. changes in prices are *not* followed by rivals.
    c. changes in prices are followed by rivals.
    d. demand associated with cartel behavior.

19. Demand curve D represents that demand curve where
    a. price is unattractive to buyers.
    b. changes in prices are *not* followed by rivals.
    c. changes in prices are followed by rivals.
    d. demand associated with cartel behavior.

20. Which of the following industries is *not* an oligopoly?
    a. cigarettes
    b. prescription drugs
    c. oil
    d. personal computers

21. Game theory is useful
    a. to keep mathematicians employed.
    b. to help economists understand how monopolistically competitive firms set prices and outputs.
    c. to help economists understand how oligopolists make decisions involving mutual interdependence.
    d. to help economists see the differences between monopolistically competitive firms and oligopolists.

Use the payoff matrix below to answer question 22. Assume that Firms A and B are currently charging $10 for the product and face roughly the same cost and demand curves.

Firm A's Price	Firm B's Price	
	$10	$8
$10	$200,000,$200,000	$100,000,$500,000
$8	$500,000,$100,000	$150,000,$150,000

22. Firm A is considering lowering its price to $8. Under which of the following circumstances would Firm A lower its price?
    a. To beat Firm B to the punch.
    b. It would never lower its price because all other profit opportunities, given its rival's reactions, are lower.
    c. If the pricing decisions shown in the diagram were irreversible and occurred simultaneously (essentially a Prisoner's Dilemma situation).
    d. If it found a way to improve its product.

Essay-Problem

Answer in the space provided.

The questions below call for extended answers. Your answers may not always be the same as those we suggest. While your words will differ, the essence of your answer should be similar. Use these as another way to assess your progress, and how to apply monopolistic competition, oligopoly, game theory, and market structure analysis in general.

1. What is the essence of monopolistically competitive markets?

2. Marketing people have said that "firms sell products, but people buy brands." Consider your local grocery, and explain whether the quotation is true.

3. What is the value of the Coca-Cola brand?

4. If cartels are inherently unstable, why legally ban them at all?

5. Why do auto companies give rebates rather than lower prices?

6. The kinked demand curve helps to explain the stability of prices for some oligopolies. Why is it useful in showing why oligopolists tend not to lower prices?

7. In the Prisoner's Dilemma, why must prisoners be kept apart from each other?

8. Of the four market structures, which is the best for society?

9. Of the four market structures, which one do firms *not* want to be in?

10. Why do monopolies and oligopolies tend to be regulated rather than monopolistically competitive and competitive firms?

What's Next

This and the previous two chapters focused on markets structure. This analysis is a very important tool in the microeconomist's toolkit. This analysis helps us understand why firms act as they do, and all we really need to know are some key market characteristics. In the next chapter, we will put some of the basic market structure analysis to work when we look at resource markets, especially labor markets. Just keep in mind the general idea of market power and how it is derived.

Answers to Chapterwide Practice Questions

Matching

1. f   4. h   7. g
2. d   5. i   8. e
3. b   6. a   9. c

Fill-In

1. differentiated, economic, normal
2. less, higher, MR = MC
3. few, many, interdependent
4. will not, will, stable
5. noncooperative, confess, simultaneously, sequentially

True-False

1. T   5. F   9. F   13. F
2. F   6. F   10. F   14. F
3. F   7. T   11. F   15. F
4. T   8. F   12. F

Multiple Choice

1. d   5. c   12. c   19. c
2. c   6. b   13. b   20. d
3. c   7. d   14. b   21. c
4. d ($19 −   8. d   15. d   22. c
   $13) × 300 =   9. a   16. c
   $6 × 300 =   10. c   17. a
   $1,800.   11. c   18. b

Essay-Problem

1. Differentiated products.
2. It is mainly true because firms try to differentiate their products to gain some pricing power, and people become loyal to brands, but it is not true to the extent that people buy generic products. Do you buy generics for some products? What brand of milk do you buy? What brand of oranges or apples?
3. Because Coca-Cola is considered the most widely recognized brand in the world, its value must be huge. Consider the soft-drink dispensing machine at your school: How much extra would you pay for a Coca-Cola as compared to a grocery store house brand? Now

multiply that by millions of servings a day, and you might get a sense of the value of the brand. Interestingly enough, Coca-Cola values its brand name at $1 on its corporate balance sheet, but you can bet that if it put the brand name up for sale, the asking price would be in the many billions of dollars.

4. Since there is no short-run or long-run benefit to consumers, but only to the cartel members, the existence of cartels is damaging to society. The only question is how damaging. Since this is so one-sided, banning cartels seems like the best solution.

5. The effect to the consumer is the same: Rebates *lead to* lower prices. There seems to be some perception by the auto companies that lowering the price will somehow damage the brand, while rebates are perceived as temporary things. Evidence for this has not been forthcoming. In addition, lowering sticker prices in bad years and increasing them in good ones would lead to the impression that auto companies were exploiting consumers with extremely high price increases. Everyone understands that rebates are temporary incentives to get you to buy now before they expire.

6. The kinked demand curve shows graphically that if one oligopoly firm lowers its price, it will gain market share at the expense of the others, so the others will rush to meet the price decrease—the end result being that everyone is worse off because price will be much less and the increase in quantity sold will be very small. So, no firm wants to undertake that action as long as it thinks others will follow suit.

7. If the prisoners could communicate, they might work out a deal in which none of them confesses because they would see that this is the best strategy for them combined. However, this combined strategy is not the best strategy for each individual when the individual does not know what the others will do.

8. The competitive model is the best for society in that it leads to both production and allocative efficiency.

9. Competitive markets, because firms have no pricing power. The competitive firm is under constant competitive pressure to lower costs. Firms would rather have less pressure on them. What is good for General Motors is not necessarily good for society.

10. The key factor is that barriers to entry exist with monopolies and oligopolies, and these barriers give them considerable market power, while barriers to entry are insignificant for monopolistically competitive firms and are nonexistent for competitive firms. Regulation thus seeks to mitigate the market power of monopolies and oligopolies.

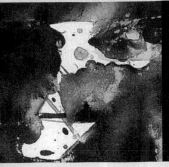

Theory of Input Markets

From Products to Inputs

With this chapter, we turn our attention from product markets to input markets. Behind the production of goods and services lie workers, machinery, and plants. Most firms need employees and capital to operate. You will be able to bring some of your market analysis insights from the previous three chapters to this examination of input markets.

This Is What You Need to Know

STEP 1

After studying this chapter you should be able to

- Define and describe competitive labor markets.

- Derive a supply curve for labor.

- Describe the factors that can change labor supply.

- Describe the factors that can change labor demand.

- Determine the elasticity of demand for labor.

- Derive the market demand for labor.

- Describe monopoly and monopsony power and their impact on imperfect labor markets.

- Determine the present value of an investment.

- Compute the rate of return of an investment.

- Describe the impact of the supply of land on markets.
- Describe the impact of economic profits on entrepreneurs and markets.

Review the Key Terms

Demand for labor (derived demand): Demand for labor is derived from the demand for the firm's product and the productivity of labor.

Supply of labor: The amount of time an individual is willing to work at various wage rates.

Substitution effect: Higher wages mean that the value of work has increased, and the opportunity costs of leisure are higher, so work is substituted for leisure.

Income effect: Higher wages mean you can maintain the same standard of living by working fewer hours. The impact on labor supply is generally negative.

Marginal physical product of labor: The additional output a firm receives from employing an added unit of labor ($MPP_L = \Delta Q \div \Delta L$).

Marginal revenue product: The value of another worker to the firm is equal to the marginal physical product of labor (MPP_L) times marginal revenue (MR).

Value of the marginal product: The value of the marginal product of labor (VMP_L) is equal to price multiplied by the marginal physical product of labor, or $P \times MPP_L$.

Elasticity of demand for labor: Equal to the percentage change in the quantity of labor demanded divided by the percentage change in the wage rate.

Monopsony: A labor market with one employer.

Monopolistic exploitation of labor: When a firm has monopoly power in the product market, marginal revenue is less than price (MR < P) and the firm hires labor up to the point where MRP_L = wage. Because MRP_L is less than the VMP_L, workers are paid less than the value of their marginal product and this difference is called monopolistic exploitation of labor.

Marginal factor cost (MFC): the added cost associated with hiring one more unit of labor. For competitive firms it is equal to the wage rate (W); but for monopsonists, it is higher than the new wage rate because all existing workers must be paid this higher new wage, making MFC > W.

Monopsonistic exploitation of labor: Because monopsonists hire less labor than competitive firms, and workers are paid less than the value of their marginal products, this difference is referred to as monopsonistic exploitation of labor.

Capital: All manufactured products that are used to produce goods and services.

Present value: The value of an investment (future stream of income) today. The higher the discount rate, the lower the present value today, and vice versa.

Rate of return: Uses the present value formula, but subtracts costs, then finds the interest rate (discount rate) at which this investment would break even.

Rent: the return to land as a factor of production. Sometimes called economic rent.

	Work Through the Chapter Tutorials	STEP 3

Competitive Labor Supply

Frequently Asked Questions

Q: **What are the characteristics of competitive labor markets?**

A: Competitive labor markets comprise firms that are price takers. They compete with other firms in the wider market for labor. Labor is assumed to be a homogeneous input: One unit of labor is just as productive as all others. Information about prices and wages is assumed to be widely available, and supply and demand interact to determine the equilibrium wage for the industry. Each firm then decides how much labor to purchase at the going wage rate.

Q: **What is the supply of labor, and why is the supply of labor curve backward bending?**

A: The supply of labor is the time an individual is willing to work (the labor the person is willing to supply) at various wage rates. The supply of labor is positively sloped because at higher wages, workers will substitute work for leisure. However, when wages rise high enough, workers may elect more leisure over greater income, resulting in a backward bending supply of labor curve.

Q: **What causes the supply of labor curve to shift?**

A: Changes in wage rates will change the quantity of labor supplied or cause movements along the supply of labor curve. Demographic changes and changes in the nonmonetary aspects of a job, the wages for alternative jobs, and nonwage income will all shift the supply of labor curve. Such a shift might be precipitated, for instance, by a change in labor force participation rates, a reduction in the risk of a job, or a change in income from other sources.

Keep in Mind

Competitive firms are price takers in both product and labor markets. They get the going wage for homogeneous labor from the market, then determine how many workers to hire. The supply of labor is determined by demographics, nonmonetary wage aspects of the job, wages for alternative jobs, and nonwage income of workers.

Competitive Labor Supply Quick Check

Circle the Correct Answer

1. (T/F) In competitive labor markets, workers are divided into two categories: substitute workers (one worker is similar to another) and income workers (workers who produce more than the average worker).
2. (T/F) The substitution effect for labor is always positive.
3. (T/F) In competitive markets, labor supply is derived from the demand for the firm's product and the productivity of labor.

4. (T/F) A backward-bending supply of labor curve means that the income effect eventually will swamp the substitution effect.

5. At high wage rates, people who begin to choose leisure rather than more work are examples of
   a. the substitution effect.
   b. the income effect.
   c. the competitive labor markets effect.
   d. the consumer surplus effect.

6. The backward-bending supply of labor curve means that at some point
   a. the cost of leisure is too great.
   b. income becomes too high and leisure is more attractive.
   c. the substitution effect will finally win out.
   d. people cannot work any more hours in the day.

7. Which of the following will *not* produce a shift in the supply of labor curve for a book-shelver's job at your school library?
   a. A new staff lounge is opened that includes a microwave.
   b. The admissions department miscalculated last year, and there are now 25% more entering students than projected.
   c. The campus food service just raised starting wages.
   d. The library just raised the wage rate for book-shelvers.

8. If the opportunity cost of leisure is too high,
   a. people will substitute work for leisure.
   b. people will substitute leisure for work.

   c. it will be overcome by the income effect.
   d. it will be overcome by the leisure effect.

9. An increase in the quantity supplied of labor for a particular job results from
   a. more women entering the labor force.
   b. more immigrants entering the country.
   c. an increase in safety regulations for the job.
   d. an increase in the wage rate for the job.

10. Which of the following will *not* produce an increase in the supply of labor curve?
    a. A new policy is instituted making job hours more flexible.
    b. An economic recession leads to a decline in demand for the product.
    c. Wages are increased.
    d. Other firms in the industry raise wages for their workers.

Score: ____

Answers: 1. F; 2. T; 3. F; 4. T; 5. b; 6. b; 7. d; 8. a; 9. d; 10. c

If You Got 9 or 10 Correct

You can handle the concept of labor supply in competitive labor markets. Go on to the next section, "Competitive Labor Demand."

If You Didn't Get at Least 9 Correct

You should have answered most of these questions correctly. They are relatively easy. If not, review this material carefully and concentrate on how the competitive product model applies to input markets. You might review income and substitution effects of labor supply once more.

In any event, keep going, but be prepared to look at this section again. As you focus next on labor demand, you will begin to put the two together. Workers supply labor for one set of reasons, and firms demand labor for another set. Try to keep this perspective. ■

Competitive Labor Demand

Frequently Asked Questions

Q: **Where does the demand for labor come from?**

A: The demand for labor is a derived demand. It is derived from the productive capabilities of labor and the demand for the good or service produced. The demand for labor is equivalent to the marginal revenue product (MRP_L) curve. Marginal revenue product is equal to marginal physical product of labor times the product's marginal revenue.

Q: **How is the competitive firm's demand for labor linked to the value of the marginal product of labor?**

A: Because competitive firms are price takers, marginal revenue is equal to price. So, the competitive firm's demand for labor is equal to what economists call the value of the marginal product (VMP_L). The value of the marginal product is equal to marginal physical product times price ($MPP_L \times P$).

Q: **How do changes in labor demand come about?**

A: Since the demand for labor is a derived demand, changes in labor demand will come about because of changes in labor productivity or changes in product demand. Anything that changes the price of a firm's product will change its labor demand. If new equipment is added and worker productivity increases, labor demand will rise. An increase in the cost of capital increases the demand for labor because labor-intensive production methods become more attractive to firms.

Q: **What is the elasticity of demand for labor?**

A: The elasticity of demand for labor is the percentage change in the quantity of labor demanded divided by the percentage change in the wage rate. An inelastic demand for labor is one where the absolute value of the elasticity is less than one. An elastic demand is greater than 1. Elasticity of demand for labor is determined by the elasticity of demand for the product, the ease of input substitutability, and the size of labor's share in production costs.

Q: **How do competitive firms determine how many workers to employ?**

A: Figure 1 shows that competitive labor markets determine an equilibrium wage of W_e (point e in Panel A). Then individual firms hire employees up to the point where equilibrium wage is equal to marginal revenue product (point e in Panel B). For competitive markets, the marginal revenue product of labor is equal to the value of the marginal product of labor ($MRP_L = VMP_L$) because $MR = P$.

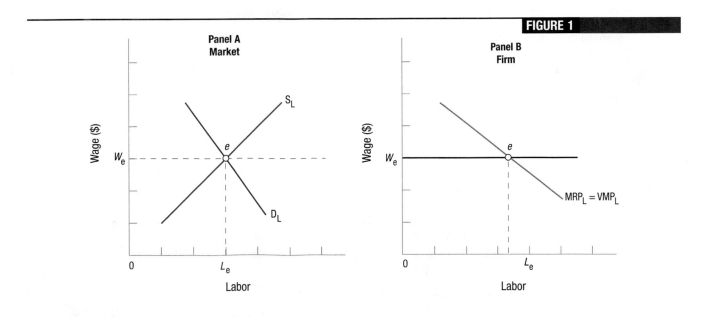

FIGURE 1

Panel A
Market

Panel B
Firm

Key Points to Remember

The demand for labor is a *derived* demand and is based on the demand for the product and the productivity of labor. The demand for labor is equal to the marginal revenue product of labor (MRP_L) and is defined as the marginal physical product of labor times marginal revenue ($MPP_L \times MR$). Remember, competitive firms are price takers so $MR = P$ and, therefore, the competitive firm's demand for labor is also equal to $MPP_L \times P = VMP_L$. Competitive firms hire labor up to the point where VMP_L = wage.

Competitive Labor Demand Quick Check

Circle the Correct Answer

1. (T/F) The competitive firm's demand for labor is derived from demand for the firm's products and the productive capabilities of labor.
2. (T/F) The marginal physical product of labor is equal to the quantity of physical units produced divided by the number of workers.
3. (T/F) For firms in competitive product markets, $VMP_L = MPP_L \times MR$.
4. (T/F) Time is an important factor in the elasticity of demand for labor in competitive markets because in the short run, firms may not be able to adjust to changing wages, but in the long run all production inputs can be adjusted.
5. For a competitive firm, which of the following is *not* true?
   a. $MRP_L = MPP_L \times MR$
   b. $MPP_L = \Delta Q/\Delta L$
   c. $VMP_L = MPP_L \times P$
   d. $MRP_L = VMP_L/\Delta Q$
6. Which of the following will *not* lead to an increase in a particular firm's demand for labor?
   a. an increase in the demand for the firm's product
   b. an increase in the price of capital
   c. an increase in worker productivity
   d. an increase in the firm's wage rate
7. Which of the following does *not* influence the elasticity of demand for labor?
   a. the time firms have to adjust to changing wage rates
   b. ease of input substitutability
   c. nonmoney aspects of the job
   d. labor's share of total production costs
8. If the market supply of labor decreases (shifts to the left) individual firms will
   a. hire more workers to ensure they have enough to produce their products.
   b. outsource some work to India.
   c. see their demand for labor curve decline as well (shift inward to the left).
   d. hire fewer workers.
9. If the interest rate for loans rises in a competitive market, the firm's demand for labor will
   a. not be affected.
   b. decrease because the firm will have to cut back on workers to justify buying more expensive machinery.
   c. increase because the firm will substitute workers for capital.
   d. decrease as machines replace workers.
10. Which of the following influences the elasticity of demand for labor in the computer industry?
    a. wages in the automobile industry
    b. how quickly firms can adjust to changing wage rates
    c. demographic changes in the workforce
    d. the substitution effect of labor

Score: ____

If You Got 9 or 10 Correct

You have successfully made it through some relatively difficult material. You might find it worthwhile to take a quick look at the solved problem below before you move on to the next section, "Imperfect Labor Markets and Other Input Markets."

If You Didn't Get at Least 9 Correct

Be patient in your review of the material. Remember that competitive firms are price takers in both the product and labor market.

Competitive firm labor decisions are the logical extension of the competitive profit maximization of producing output at the point were MR = MC. Since the productivity of labor was an important component of the firm's costs when we analyzed competitive product markets, it is only logical that it will be a prime determinant of just how many workers the firm hires to produce the profit maximizing output.

Overall markets for labor determine wages, and firms look at their production processes and determine the value of workers to them (the MRP_L), then simply hire workers if their $MRP_L \geq W$. This is really a simple concept. Don't make more of it than it is. These decisions are more complex in the next section when we consider monopoly (a single seller in the product market) and monopsony (one buyer of labor). The solved problem below will take you through all of these steps.

Solved Problem: Competitive Labor Market

Consider the following Web site construction firm that is a competitor in both the labor and product markets. Wages are $200 a day, and its output sells for $10 a unit. Answer the following questions:

a. Complete the table below.

Labor	Output	MPP_L	$MRP_L = VMP_L$	Wage
0	0			
1	14	_____	_____	_____
2	30	_____	_____	_____
3	50	_____	_____	_____
4	80	_____	_____	_____
5	108	_____	_____	_____
6	130	_____	_____	_____
7	150	_____	_____	_____
8	168	_____	_____	_____
9	180	_____	_____	_____

b. Graph the supply and demand for labor in the grid provided.

c. How many workers will this firm hire to maximize profits? How large are these profits?

Solution-Discussion

a. See the table on the following page. Marginal physical product of labor (MMP_L) is the change in output from hiring another worker, marginal revenue product (MRP_L) is equal to the value of the marginal product (VMP_L)

because for the competitive price taker, P = MR. Wages (or the supply of labor facing the competitive firm) is assumed to be the wage rate, or $200.

Labor	Output	MPP_L	$MRP_L = VMP_L$	Wage
0	0	—	—	—
1	14	14	140	200
2	30	16	160	200
3	50	20	200	200
4	80	30	300	200
5	108	28	280	200
6	130	22	220	200
7	150	20	200	200
8	168	18	180	200
9	180	12	120	200

b. See Figure 2 below.

FIGURE 2

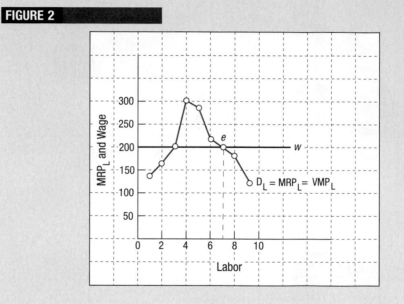

c. This firm will hire workers up to the point were MRP_L = W. In this case, the firm hires 7 workers for total costs of $1,400 ($200 × 7 = $1,400). Total revenue is equal to price times quantity sold or $1,500 (150 × $10 = $1,500). So total profit is equal to $100 ($1,500 − $1,400 = $100).

Working through this solved problem should have clarified any questions you had about competitive labor markets and how firms decide how many workers to hire and at what wage rate. If not, you should review this section on labor demand. The next section starts by analyzing what happens in imperfect labor markets, so you will be using what you have learned about the supply and demand for labor in competitive markets. If you do not understand the material by this point, you will have real trouble in the next section.

Make sure you can write answers to the following questions for competitive markets.

■ What determines the demand for labor?
■ Why do competitive firms hire where MRP_L = W?
■ What are the main determinants of the supply of labor?

- What factors cause the demand for labor to shift?
- What factors influence the elasticity of demand for labor?

Write your answers for these questions, then check them in the text. When you have confidence in your understanding, you will be ready to tackle "Imperfect Labor Markets." ∎

Imperfect Labor Markets and Other Input Markets

Frequently Asked Questions

Q: What is monopolistic exploitation of labor?

A: If wages are determined in a competitive market, a firm will hire labor until $MRP_L = W$. But if the firm enjoys some monopoly power in the product market, marginal revenue product will be less than the value of the marginal product because $MR < P$. The difference between the value of the marginal product and marginal revenue product is known as monopolistic exploitation of labor.

Q: What is monopsonistic exploitation of labor?

A: A monopsony is a market with a single buyer or employer. Marginal factor cost (MFC) is the added cost associated with hiring one more unit of labor. For the monopsonist, the MFC curve lies above the supply of labor curve, because the firm must increase the wages of all workers to attract added labor. If the monopsonist purchases labor from a competitive market, it hires labor up to the point where $MRP_L = MFC > W$. At this point, the value of labor's marginal product exceeds the wage rate; economists refer to this as monopsonistic exploitation of labor.

Q: How are imperfect labor market equilibria diagrammed?

A: Figure 3 puts together a labor market consisting of a monopolist in the product market and a monopsonist in the input market. By bringing in monopoly and monopsony to our labor market analysis, we now have four possible product and labor market equilibria:

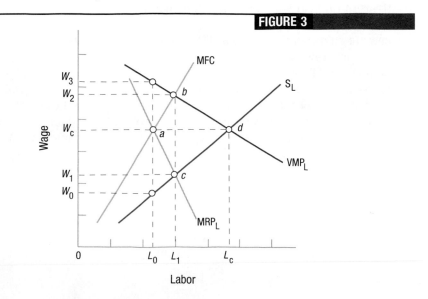

FIGURE 3

■ *Competitive product market and competitive labor market:* Firms hire where $VMP_L = MRP_L = W$ (point d).

■ *Monopoly product market and competitive labor market:* Firms hire where $VMP_L > MRP_L = W$ (point c), resulting in monopolistic exploitation ($VMP_L > W$) or ($W_2 - W_1$).

■ *Competitive product market and monopsony labor market:* Firms hire where $W < MFC = VMP_L = MRP_L$ (point b), but pay the wage W_1 from the supply of labor curve (point c) resulting in monopsonistic exploitation ($VMP_L > W$) or ($W_2 - W_1$).

■ *Monopoly product market and monopsony labor market:* Firms hire where $VMP_L > MRP_L = MFC > W$ (point a). Wages and employment are the lowest in this case (W_0 and L_0), and both monopolistic and monopsonistic exploitation exist ($W_3 - W_0$).

Note that in Figure 3 monopolistic and monopsonistic exploitation just happens to be the same ($W_2 - W_1$), but this will typically not be the case.

Q: What are capital markets, and what role do they play?

A: Capital includes all manufactured goods that are used to produce other goods and services. Capital markets are those markets where financial resources are available for the purchase of capital goods. The loanable funds market determines equilibrium interest rates for these funds. Firms look at their potential investment projects and borrow money to invest when the rate of return on a project is greater than or equal to the market interest rate.

Q: How do firms determine whether potential investments might be profitable?

A: Two approaches are used to determine whether investments are potentially profitable. The present value approach discounts projected future streams of income to determine their present value. This is then compared to the cost of the investment to determine whether it will be profitable. The rate of return approach uses the same present value formula but looks for the rate of return, or discount rate, where the potential income stream and investment costs will be just equal.

Q: What is land to an economist?

A: Land, to the economist, means land and other natural resources that are nearly fixed in supply, or inelastically supplied. Because the supply of land is fixed, the rent on land is determined by demand.

Q: How are entrepreneurship and profits linked?

A: Profits are rewards to entrepreneurs for combining the other inputs of production—land, labor, and capital—in ways that produce goods and services, and for assuming the risks associated with production. Economic profits are profits that exceed normal levels. They act as signals to other entrepreneurs and firms that consumers want more of the profitable product. These signals produce shifts in resources toward those goods that consumers want.

Core Graphs: Imperfect Labor Markets

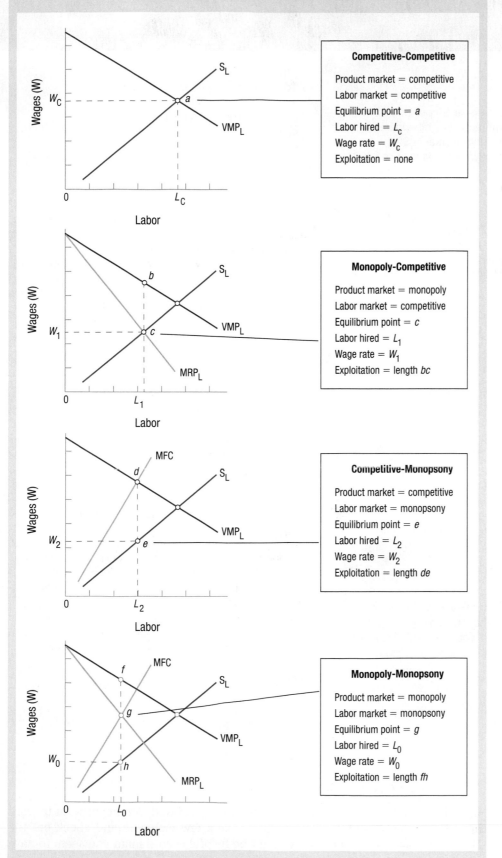

Competitive-Competitive

Product market = competitive
Labor market = competitive
Equilibrium point = a
Labor hired = L_c
Wage rate = W_c
Exploitation = none

Monopoly-Competitive

Product market = monopoly
Labor market = competitive
Equilibrium point = c
Labor hired = L_1
Wage rate = W_1
Exploitation = length bc

Competitive-Monopsony

Product market = competitive
Labor market = monopsony
Equilibrium point = e
Labor hired = L_2
Wage rate = W_2
Exploitation = length de

Monopoly-Monopsony

Product market = monopoly
Labor market = monopsony
Equilibrium point = g
Labor hired = L_0
Wage rate = W_0
Exploitation = length fh

Imperfect Labor Markets and Other Input Markets
Quick Check

Circle the Correct Answer

1. (T/F) If a firm employs 7 workers at $8 per hour, but it must offer $10 per hour to attract an eighth worker, the marginal factor cost of this eighth worker is $24.
2. (T/F) The present value of a payment next year of $750 will be less than $750.
3. (T/F) A market that has a single buyer is called a monopsony.
4. Distance *bc* in Figure 4 is called
   a. monopolistic exploitation of labor.
   b. monopsonistic exploitation of labor.
   c. imperfect exploitation of labor.
   d. optimum exploitation of labor.

FIGURE 4

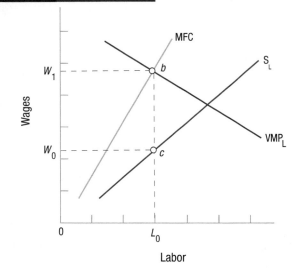

5. You have just retired and want to buy an annuity to make sure you have enough money to pay your annual expenses. You calculate that you need $25,000 per year, and that the market interest rate is 5%. How much will you pay for this annuity?
   a. $5,000
   b. $50,000
   c. $125,000
   d. $500,000

6. To economists, land is a natural resource with
   a. a supply curve that is horizontal.
   b. a relatively elastic supply curve.
   c. lots of trees.
   d. an absolutely inelastic supply curve.
7. Which of the following is *not* correct for a firm that has both monopoly and monopsony power?
   a. It will employ fewer workers than in competitive markets.
   b. It will pay workers less than in competitive markets.
   c. It will exploit workers both monopolistically and monopsonistically.
   d. It will employ fewer workers but at a wage higher than the market wage rate.
8. What is the present value of $1,000 received in 3 years if the interest rate is 6%?
   a. $1,191.02
   b. $ 839.63
   c. $ 869.71
   d. $1,180.00
9. For the rate of return approach, which one is *not* correct?
   a. The rate of return is also called the internal rate of return.
   b. The rate of return considers the cost of capital.
   c. The rate of return approach is superior to the present value approach.
   d. A risk premium adjusts the rate of return for risky projects.
10. For entrepreneurs, which one of the following is *not* correct?
   a. Profits reward entrepreneurs for combining labor, land, and capital to produce goods and services.
   b. Profits reward entrepreneurs for bearing risk.
   c. Economic profits signal entrepreneurs that consumers want more of the good or service.
   d. Economic profits signal entrepreneurs to shift resources to areas of lower demand to shore them up because there is money to be made there.

Score: ____

Answers: 1. T; 2. T; 3. T; 4. b; 5. d; 6. d; 7. d; 8. b; 9. c; 10. d

If You Got 9 or 10 Correct

Nice job on some tough material. Even though you did well, you might want to work through the solved problem below. Also, take a few moments and check out the "Hints, Tips, and Reminders"; they might be helpful even though you seem to have a good grasp of this material.

If You Didn't Get at Least 9 Correct

Don't give up the ship. Monopoly and monopsony in labor markets are difficult topics. It often takes students more than one attempt at this material to really master it. Take a quick look back at the core graphs and make sure you know why each equilibrium point has been selected.

Work through the solved problem below. This numerical example should help you see how market structure in both product and labor markets affects wages and the level of employment.

Solved Problem: Imperfect Labor Markets

Using the data for labor, wage rates, marginal factor cost, value of the marginal product, and marginal revenue product in the table below, answer the questions that follow.

Labor	Wage	MFC	VMP	MRP
0	0	0	0	0
1	50	50	500	500
2	75	100	450	400
3	100	150	400	300
4	125	200	350	200
5	150	250	300	100
6	175	300	250	0
7	200	350	200	-100
8	225	400	150	-200
9	250	450	100	-300

First, graph all four curves in the grid below.

a. Assume that both the product and labor markets are competitive. Label the equilibrium point a. How many employees will be hired? What is the level of labor exploitation in this situation?

b. Now assume that the product market is monopolistic and the labor market continues to be competitive. Label the new equilibrium point b. How many employees will be hired? What is the level of monopolistic exploitation in this situation?

c. Now assume that the product market is competitive and the labor market becomes monopsonistic. Label the new equilibrium point *c*. How many employees will be hired? What is the level of monopsonistic exploitation in this situation?

d. Now assume that the product market is monopolistic and the labor market becomes monopsonistic as well. Label the new equilibrium point *d*. How many employees will be hired? What is the total level of monopolistic and monopsonistic exploitation in this situation?

Solution-Discussion

Figure 5 graphs all four curves.

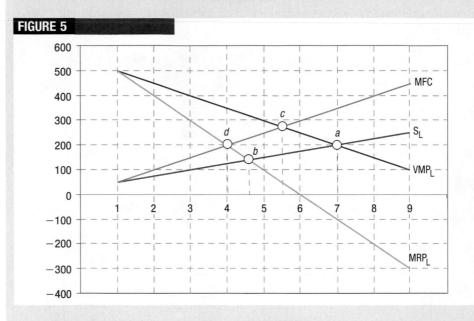

FIGURE 5

a. When both markets are competitive, equilibrium will be found where the supply of labor crosses the value of the marginal product of labor, or point *a* in the figure above. Since both markets are competitive, no exploitation occurs, and labor is paid its VMP.

b. When the product market becomes monopolistic, labor is hired where the supply of labor is equal to the marginal revenue product, point *b* in the figure above. Monopolistic firms are the market and they must lower price to get higher sales, so $MR < P$, and therefore $MRP_L < VMP_L$. Somewhere between 4 and 5 workers are hired and the monopolistic exploitation of labor is equal to $VMP_L - $ wage, or roughly 187.5 (325 − 137.5 = 187.5). The VMP_L between 4 and 5 workers is 325, and the wage from the supply curve for between 4 and 5 workers is 137.5. This is equal to the vertical distance from point *b* to the VMP_L curve in the figure above.

c. When the product market is competitive and the labor market becomes monopsonistic (one buyer of labor), labor is hired where the marginal factor cost (MFC) of labor is equal to the value of the marginal product, point *c* in the figure above. Monopsonistic firms are the only buyers of labor, and their MFC is higher than the supply of labor curve because they must pay everyone a higher wage when they want to hire another worker. Somewhere between 5 and 6 workers are hired and the monopsonistic exploitation of labor is equal to VMP_L − wage, or roughly 112.5 (275 − 162.5 = 112.5). The VMP_L between 5 and 6 workers is 275, and the wage from the supply curve for between 5 and 6 workers is 162.5. This is equal to the vertical distance from point c on the VMP_L curve to the wage rate on the supply of labor curve in the figure above.

d. When the product market is monopolistic and the labor market becomes monopsonistic (one buyer of labor), labor is hired where the marginal factor cost (MFC) of labor is equal to marginal revenue product, point d in the figure above. Four workers are hired, and the sum of both monopsonistic and monopolistic exploitation of labor is equal to VMP_L − wage, or equal to 225 (350 − 125 = 225). The VMP_L for 4 workers is 350, and the wage from the supply curve for 4 workers is 125. This is equal to the vertical distance from the point on the VMP_L curve above point d to the wage rate on the supply of labor curve in the figure above.

Ideally, working through this solved problem with numbers will help you see how imperfect labor markets equilibrate. This is not easy material, but looking at the wages and employment levels for anything other than competitive markets illustrates why economists favor competitive markets both in product markets and in labor markets. Take a moment to look back at the Quick Check and figure out why you missed the question(s) you did, then spend some time with the "Hints, Tips, and Reminders" that follow. ■

Consider These Hints, Tips, and Reminders

STEP 4

1. While not explicitly discussed in the chapter, there is a straightforward relationship among wages, the marginal productivity of labor, and the firm's marginal costs. To see the relationship among these three variables, remember that in competitive markets (we will just look at the competitive labor and product market combination), $VMP_L = P \times MPP_L = W$ is the profit maximization condition. This equation reduces to

$$P = W / MPP_L$$

Also, profit maximization requires that MR = P = MC. Substituting MC for P in the earlier equation yields

$$MC = W / MPP_L$$

Thus, the wage rate divided by the marginal physical product of labor is equal to marginal cost. So, for example, if wages are $200 a day and marginal physical product for the last person hired is 10 units a day, then marginal cost for each unit produced that day is $20. This is just common sense; you produced 10 units that sell for $200, so marginal cost to produce these units is $20 each.

2. Keep in mind that when we are computing marginal physical product for a unit of labor that is producing a particular product, computing MPP_L is relatively easy. However, computing MPP_L for work such as Web site design, research, and artwork is much more difficult and often virtually impossible unless the work is put up for sale via some form of auction market like eBay.

3. The hardest part in this chapter is hiring rules for various markets (competitive, monopoly, and monopsony). Try approaching each through the following way:

First, go to the competition-competition case where supply and demand cross. This will be the *highest* wage and employment combination of all the possibilities.

Second, look at the monopoly-competition case. Ask yourself how monopolies differ from competitive markets. The answer is that marginal revenue is less than price because product demand is downward sloping, so $MRP_L < VMP_L$ and monopolies will hire fewer workers (and sell a smaller output—remember?).

Third, assume that the competitive situation now becomes a competitive-monopsony. Now with a single buyer of labor, each additional unit of labor costs more than the wage rate because all other workers must be paid the new higher wage required to attract more labor. Higher labor costs again mean that fewer workers will be hired, so both wages and employment will be lower than in competitive markets.

Fourth, when you combine monopoly and monopsony, firms will hire the fewest workers at the lowest wages, because employment is determined where $MRP_L = MFC_L$.

4. This chapter focused on labor markets, but the same conclusions would hold for other factor markets under competitive, monopoly, and monopsony conditions.

Do the Homework for Chapter 11
Theory of Input Markets

Instructor _____ Time _____ Student _____

Use the answer key below to record your answers to these homework questions.

1. (a) (b) (c) (d)	6. (a) (b) (c) (d)	11. (a) (b) (c) (d)	16. (a) (b) (c) (d)
2. (a) (b) (c) (d)	7. (a) (b) (c) (d)	12. (a) (b) (c) (d)	17. (a) (b) (c) (d)
3. (a) (b) (c) (d)	8. (a) (b) (c) (d)	13. (a) (b) (c) (d)	18. (a) (b) (c) (d)
4. (a) (b) (c) (d)	9. (a) (b) (c) (d)	14. (a) (b) (c) (d)	19. (a) (b) (c) (d)
5. (a) (b) (c) (d)	10. (a) (b) (c) (d)	15. (a) (b) (c) (d)	20. (a) (b) (c) (d)

1. Which of the following is *not* an assumption describing competitive labor markets?
   a. The firms operating in the market are operating in competitive markets.
   b. Labor is treated as a homogeneous commodity.
   c. Firms in the industry are able to increase their prices to meet the wage demands of their workers and unions.
   d. Information in the industry is accurate and widely available.

2. The backward-bending supply curve of labor means that
   a. workers can always be induced to work more if the wage is high enough.
   b. the substitution effect is always dominant.
   c. worker hours in the day are limited.
   d. when income is sufficiently high, workers desire more leisure.

3. When wages rise and workers increase their hours of work
   a. the income effect is dominant.
   b. leisure time is less expensive, so workers will increase their hours of work.
   c. workers are substituting work for leisure since leisure now has a higher opportunity cost.
   d. because the income effect implies that working more means they will earn higher incomes.

4. Which of the following factors will *not* change labor supply?
   a. An increase in interest rates that increase the interest income a worker receives from large bond holdings.

   b. The wage rates that a competitive firm is paying for the same skills.
   c. A change in immigration rates.
   d. A change in wages offered by employers.

5. The marginal revenue product is
   a. the marginal cost of hiring one more unit of labor.
   b. the revenue the firm receives from adding one more unit of labor.
   c. the additional labor required to produce one more unit of the product.
   d. the revenue the firm receives from selling one more unit of the product.

6. What is the difference between marginal revenue product and the value of the marginal product in competitive labor markets?
   a. The value of the marginal product is higher than marginal revenue product.
   b. The value of the marginal product is lower than marginal revenue product.
   c. Marginal revenue product is based on output, whereas the value of the marginal product is based on sales of the product.
   d. There is no difference because marginal revenue and price are equal.

7. If the demand for the product rises in a competitive market, the demand for labor in a competitive labor market will
   a. not change.
   b. rise until marginal revenue product just equals total variable costs.
   c. rise.
   d. fall.

8. In the table to the right, the marginal product of the second worker is
   a. 20.
   b. 15.
   c. 10.
   d. 5.

Labor	Output
0	0
1	25
2	45
3	60
4	70
5	75

9. In the table to the right, if the competitive price of the product is equal to $20, then the marginal revenue product of the fourth worker is
   a. $200.
   b. $150.
   c. $100.
   d. $50.

10. Which of the following will have the *least* impact on the demand for labor?
    a. a change in the price of the product
    b. a rise in worker productivity due to the introduction of computers in the production process
    c. a change in interest rates
    d. a change in the price of the product with a cross elasticity of demand equal to zero

11. In Figure HW-1, if the firm is a competitor in both the product and input markets, equilibrium wage rates and employment would be which of the following?
    a. $60 and 150 workers
    b. $90 and 150 workers
    c. $60 and 300 worker.
    d. all of the above

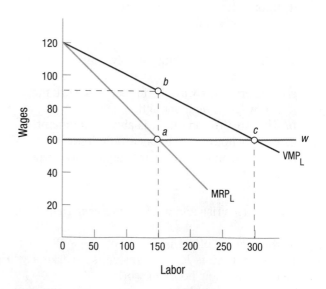

12. In Figure HW-1, if the firm was a competitor in the input market and a monopolist in the product market, equilibrium wage rates and employment would be which of the following?
    a. $60 and 150 workers
    b. $90 and 150 workers
    c. $60 and 300 workers
    d. all of the above

HW-1

13. In Figure HW-1, if the firm was a competitor in the input market and a monopolist in the product market, monopolistic exploitation of labor would equal
    a. zero.
    b. $20.
    c. $30.
    d. all of the above.

14. In Figure HW-2, the firm is a competitor in the product market and a monopsonist in the labor market. Equilibrium wage and employment will be
    a. W_1 and L_0.
    b. W_0 and L_0.
    c. W_2 and L_1.
    d. W_2 and L_0.

15. In Figure HW-2, if the firm is a competitor in both the product and labor markets, equilibrium wage and employment will be
    a. W_1 and L_0.
    b. W_0 and L_0.
    c. W_2 and L_1.
    d. W_2 and L_0.

16. In Figure HW-2, the firm is a competitor in the product market and a monopsonist in the labor market. Monopsonistic exploitation of labor is equal to
    a. $L_1 - L_0$.
    b. length bc.
    c. length ab.
    d. $W_2 - W_1$.

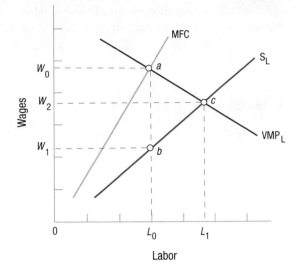

HW-2

17. Which of the following factors does *not* affect the elasticity of demand for labor?
    a. how elastic or inelastic the demand is for the product
    b. how difficult it is to substitute capital for labor
    c. how much the average worker earns weekly
    d. how large labor cost is as a percent of total costs

18. Marginal factor cost is
    a. how much more it costs the firm to produce an additional unit of the product.
    b. the additional cost of replacing a worker with a piece of equipment.
    c. how much more a monopolist must pay to retain good employees.
    d. the added cost of hiring one additional unit of labor.

19. When the supply of land is perfectly inelastic,
    a. rent is determined by how difficult it is to bring more land into productive use.
    b. rent depends entirely on the demand for land.
    c. taxing this land would lead to drastic cuts in the amount of land being used.
    d. rent depends entirely on the degree of regulation of business.

20. If an asset (like land) is expected to produce rent of $2,000.00 a year forever, and interest rates are currently 5%, then a rough approximation of the value of this asset is
    a. $10,000.
    b. $20,000.
    c. $40,000.
    d. $80,000.

Use the ExamPrep to Get Ready for Exams	STEP 6

This sheet (front and back) is designed to help you prepare for your exams. The chapter has been boiled down to its key concepts. You are asked to answer questions, define terms, draw graphs, and, if you wish, add summaries of class notes.

Competitive Labor Supply

Describe the characteristics of competitive labor markets:

Describe the choices an individual makes when determining whether to supply labor to the market:

What is to shape of the individual's labor supply curve?

Describe the substitution effect:

Describe the income effect:

Factors that Change Labor Supply

List of factors that can alter the supply of labor:

Competitive Labor Demand

Define the following:
Marginal revenue product:

The value of the marginal product:

Factors that Change Labor Demand

List the factors that can alter the demand for labor:

Elasticity of Demand for Labor

Define the elasticity of demand for labor:

List of factors that can alter the elasticity of demand for labor:

Competitive Labor Market Equilibrium

In the grid, diagram the competitive firm's labor market equilibrium. (Hint: Assume the overall market has set an equilibrium wage of W_e for labor.)

Imperfect Labor Markets and Other Input Markets

Define monopsony:

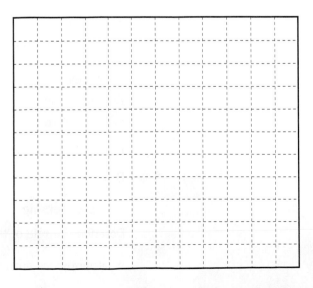

The table below summarizes the four market possibilities for imperfect labor markets (labor and product markets). Use the four grids below to graph and label each of these possibilities.

	Product Market	
Labor Market	Competitive	Monopolist
Competitive	W = VMP	W = MRP < VMP
Monopsony	W < MFC = VMP	W < MFC = MRP < VMP

Capital Markets

Define the following:
Capital:

Capital markets:

Present value:

Rate of return:

Land

Describe the concept of economic rent:

Entrepreneurship

Describe the role of the entrepreneur:

What motivates entrepreneurs?

Additional Study Help Chapterwide Practice Questions

Matching

Match the description with the corresponding term.

____ 1. Supply of labor
____ 2. Income effect
____ 3. Substitution effect
____ 4. Demand for labor (derived demand)
____ 5. Marginal revenue product
____ 6. Value of the marginal product
____ 7. Elasticity of demand for labor
____ 8. Monopsony
____ 9. Exploitation of labor
____ 10. Present value
____ 11. Rate of return
____ 12. Rent
____ 13. Economic profit

a. Derived from consumer demand for a product and the productive capacities of labor.
b. The time a person is willing to spend or the amount of labor a person is willing to supply at various wage rates.
c. The above-normal reward entrepreneurs receive for combining land, labor, and capital to produce goods and services and for assuming the risks that come with producing goods and services.
d. The value of an added worker to a firm.
e. At high enough wage rates, people may conclude that they can earn enough to support their lifestyles by working fewer hours.
f. Defined as marginal physical product times price.
g. The tendency to replace work for leisure as wages rise.
h. A market with a single buyer or employer.
i. Evaluating investment proceeds by asking at what rate of interest the investment will break even.
j. The responsiveness of the quantity of labor demanded to changes in wages.
k. Workers are paid less than the value of their marginal product.
l. Measures how much future returns are worth today.
m. The return or income that flows to land as an input (factor) of production.

Fill-In

Circle the word(s) in parentheses that complete the sentence.

1. The time an individual is willing to work is referred to as the (substitution effect, income effect, supply of labor) _____, while when higher wages lead to fewer hours worked we know that (substitution effect, income effect, supply of labor) _____ is at work, but when higher wages lead to more hours worked, then the (substitution effect, income effect, supply of labor) _____ must dominate.

2. Marginal revenue times the marginal physical product of labor is equal to (value of the marginal, marginal revenue) _____ product of labor. Competitive firms are price takers, meaning that they hire workers up to the point where the wage is equal to the (value of the marginal, marginal revenue) _____ product of labor.

3. Changes in the demand for labor are caused by a change in product demand and (changes in worker productivity, labor's share of production costs, nonwage income) _____. The elasticity of demand for labor is affected by the elasticity of demand for product and (changes in worker productivity, labor's share of production costs, nonwage income) _____.

4. Firms that are monopolies in the product market but face competition in labor markets hire labor where (W = VMP, W = MRP, W = MFC) _____. Firms that are competitive in both markets hire labor where (W = VMP, W = MRP, W = MFC) _____, but monopsonists in the labor market who are competitors in product markets hire labor where (W = VMP, W = MRP, W = MFC) _____.

5. When market interest rates rise, the present value of an annuity will (rise, fall, not change) _____. When a resource like land is fixed in supply, rent is determined by (cost, demand, present value) _____. Entrepreneurs are paid (rent, income, profit) _____ for combining factors to produce a product and for assuming the risk of the business.

True-False

Circle the correct answer.

_T/F_ 1. In a competitive labor market, firms will tightly control or even distort wage information so that workers rarely know what other workers are paid.

_T/F_ 2. In a competitive labor market, labor is regarded as a homogeneous commodity—

one employee is assumed to be just as productive as another.

T/F   3. To the economist, *leisure* implies only those activities that are truly relaxing or enjoyable.

T/F   4. Industry labor supply curves are positively sloped.

T/F   5. When people begin to substitute leisure for the income that comes from work at very high wage rates, this is evidence of the substitution effect.

T/F   6. The more wages rise, the lower the opportunity cost of leisure.

T/F   7. Demographic changes in the workforce, such as an increased labor force participation rate among women, will cause shifts in the supply of labor curve rather than changes in the quantity of labor supplied.

T/F   8. The competitive firm's demand for labor is derived from the demand for the firm's products and the productivity of labor.

T/F   9. For firms in competitive labor markets, $VMP_L = MRP_L$.

T/F   10. A decline in the demand for a product will raise MRP_L for the firm producing it.

T/F   11. The more difficult it is for a firm to substitute capital for labor, the more elastic will be its demand for labor.

T/F   12. The elasticity of demand for labor is more elastic in the short run than it is in the long run.

T/F   13. A monopsony is a market that contains only a single buyer.

T/F   14. A firm that is a monopolist in the product market will offer its workers a wage equal to the value of their marginal product.

T/F   15. The monopsonist will face a positively sloped supply curve for the input of which it is the only buyer.

T/F   16. If a firm employs 5 workers at $10 per hour, but it must offer $12 per hour to attract a sixth worker, the marginal factor cost of this sixth worker is $12.

T/F   17. A firm with both monopoly and monopsony power will hire more workers, but pay them a lower wage than would a competitive firm.

T/F   18. The present value of a payment of $500 next year will be worth something less than $500.

T/F   19. The rate of return approach to evaluating investments proceeds by asking at what rate of interest the investment would just break even.

T/F   20. The single-tax movement initiated by Henry George sought to derive all tax revenues from business profits.

Multiple Choice

Circle the correct answer.

1. Which of the following is *not* true of a competitive labor market?
   a. Wage information is accurate and widely available.
   b. Its firms operate in competitive product markets.
   c. Wage rates reflect the monopsonistic exploitation of labor.
   d. Labor is regarded as a homogeneous commodity.

2. An individual's supply of labor curve will typically be
   a. downward sloping.
   b. upward sloping indefinitely.
   c. upward sloping until daily hours worked equals 24.
   d. upward sloping for some time, then bending backward at very high wage rates.

3. When people begin substituting leisure for the income from work at high wage rates, this is evidence of
   a. the substitution effect.
   b. the income effect.
   c. the monopsony effect.
   d. monopsonistic exploitation of labor.

4. When people choose to work more hours as wage rates rise, this is evidence of
   a. the substitution effect.
   b. the income effect.
   c. the labor-wage effect.
   d. monopsonistic exploitation of labor.

5. The substitution effect for labor is
   a. always positive.
   b. initially positive, but becomes negative at very high wage rates.
   c. always negative.
   d. initially negative, but becomes positive at very high wage rates.

6. Which of the following will *not* produce a shift in the supply of labor curve for a particular job?
   a. demographic changes in the workforce
   b. a change in the nonmonetary aspects of the job, such as its pleasantness or riskiness
   c. a change in the job's wage rate
   d. a change in the wage rates of alternative jobs

7. If workers in the steel industry are given a raise, the supply of labor the iron industry faces can be expected to
   a. grow.
   b. remain about the same.
   c. shrink.
   d. do any of the above—the labor situations in the two industries are completely unrelated.

8. Which of the following would likely cause the supply of labor for a particular job to shrink?
   a. New safety regulations are implemented, making the job less risky.
   b. The wages for several alternative jobs are reduced.
   c. Welfare payments for people who do not work are reduced.
   d. Immigration laws are tightened, reducing population growth.

9. A competitive firm's demand for labor is derived from
   a. demand for the firm's output and workers' income needs.
   b. demand for the firm's output and the productive capabilities of its workers.
   c. political pressures to reduce unemployment rates.
   d. the supply of available labor and its productive capabilities.

10. The number of units of output produced by the last worker hired is labeled
    a. marginal physical product of labor.
    b. marginal revenue.
    c. marginal revenue product of labor.
    d. value of the marginal product.

11. Which of the following is *not* true for a competitive firm?
    a. $VMP_L = MRP_L$
    b. $MPP_L = VMP_L \times MR$
    c. $MRP_L = MPP_L \times MR$
    d. $MPP_L = \Delta Q / \Delta L$

12. Which of the following will *not* change a particular firm's demand for labor?
    a. a change in the price of capital equipment
    b. a change in demand for the firm's product

c. a change in worker productivity brought about by installing a new generation of machinery
d. a change in the wage rates unions will accept

13. If the price of capital drops (interest rates go down), a firm's demand for labor can be expected to
    a. decline.
    b. stay about the same.
    c. increase.
    d. any of the above—there is no relation between the cost of capital and the demand for labor.

14. Which of the following does *not* influence the elasticity of demand for labor?
    a. labor's share of the total production costs
    b. the elasticity of demand for the product
    c. wage rates in alternative jobs
    d. the ease of input substitutability

15. The market demand for labor in a competitive industry is found by
    a. surveying all of the executives in the industry.
    b. summing all wages paid in the industry.
    c. summing the marginal revenue product of labor of all the firms in the industry.
    d. summing the adjusted market demand curves of all of the firms in the industry.

16. If the elasticity of demand for toasters rises, the elasticity of demand for labor in the toaster manufacturing market can be expected to
    a. rise.
    b. remain about the same.
    c. fall.
    d. any of the above—elasticity of product demand and elasticity of demand for labor aren't related to each other.

Fill in the table below for a firm in a competitive labor market, where P = $10 and W = $100, then use it to answer questions 17 and 18.

L	Q	MPP	P	MRP = VMP	W
0	0	0	10	0	100
1	8		10	_____	100
2	18		10	_____	100
3	30		10	_____	100
4	40		10	_____	100
5	48		10	_____	100
6	54		10	_____	100

17. What is the equilibrium level of employment for the firm?
    a. either 2 or 4 workers
    b. 3 workers
    c. 4 workers
    d. 6 workers

18. What is the equilibrium level of employment for the firm if the wage rate falls to $80?
    a. 4 workers
    b. 3 workers
    c. 5 workers
    d. 6 workers

19. Monopsony power is defined as
    a. a market that has only a single seller.
    b. a market that has only a single buyer.
    c. the control a firm has over the price of its product.
    d. the control firms exercise over their workers.

20. A firm with a monopoly in the product market that buys labor in a competitive market can be expected to pay its workers
    a. something less than the prevailing market wage.
    b. the prevailing market wage.
    c. something more than the prevailing market wage.
    d. a wage equal to the value of the marginal product of labor.

21. Which of the following *least* fits the description of a monopsonist?
    a. the U.S. Postal Service
    b. a steel town's lone steel mill
    c. a fast-food restaurant
    d. the U.S. Air Force

22. Marginal factor cost (MFC) of labor is
    a. the amount it costs a firm to hire one more worker.
    b. the wage a firm must pay to the last worker hired.
    c. the difference between the wage of the last worker hired and that of previous workers.
    d. the cost to a firm of replacing a machine with a human worker.

23. Which of the following does *not* occur in cases of monopsonistic exploitation of labor?
    a. Labor is paid less than the value of it marginal product.
    b. The monopsonist offers a wage at the level where $S_L = VMP_L$.
    c. The monopsonist hires at a level where MFC = VMP_L.
    d. The monopsonist's demand for labor equals its VMP_L.

24. If the interest rate is 8%, what is the present value of an investment that promises to yield $500 annually forever?
    a. $62.50
    b. $500

c. $4,000
d. $6,250

25. To economists, land is any natural resource that is
    a. elastically supplied.
    b. essentially unlimited.
    c. inelastically supplied.
    d. used in production.

26. Profits are the rewards to entrepreneurs for all *except* which one of the following?
    a. combining land, labor, and capital to produce goods and services
    b. assuming the risks of producing goods and services
    c. seeing market needs that others have not seen
    d. owning land

Essay-Problem

Answer in the space provided.

The questions below can be challenging. Your answers may not always the same as those we suggest, but they should be close. Use these questions as another learning exercise for the material in this chapter.

1. What are the four inputs?

2. What assumption about competitive labor markets seems the most controversial?

3. Why is the opportunity cost of leisure important in determining the supply of labor?

4. At what point does the labor supply curve become backward bending?

5. Which is likely to have more monopsony power: the New York City school district or a much smaller rural school district in upstate New York?

6. Why would one use the rate of return approach rather than sticking with the present value approach?

7. Does land really have a vertical supply curve?

8. Is entrepreneurship more likely to be found in small companies or large corporations?

9. Why do interest rates affect the demand for labor?

10. Is the substitution effect the same for product markets and input markets?

What's Next

This chapter has covered a lot of material. You now have a good understanding of what input markets are and how they work. In the same way that competitive product markets are the benchmark for market structures, competitive labor markets lead to the best results for workers. In competitive markets, individuals are paid the value of their marginal products. How productive you are determines your wages and your standard of living.

In the next chapter, we look at some specific aspects of labor markets including investment in human capital (education and on-the-job training) that increase productivity and living standards. In addition, we examine economic discrimination and look at the history and impacts of unions and collective bargaining.

Answers to Chapterwide Practice Questions

Matching

1. b	6. f	11. i
2. e	7. j	12. m
3. g	8. h	13. c
4. a	9. k	
5. d	10. l	

Fill-In

1. supply of labor, income effect, substitution effect
2. marginal revenue, value of the marginal
3. changes in worker productivity, labor's share of production costs
4. W = MRP, W = VMP, W = MFC
5. fall, demand, profit

True-False

1. F	6. F	11. F	16. F
2. T	7. T	12. F	17. F
3. F	8. T	13. T	18. T
4. T	9. T	14. F	19. T
5. F	10. F	15. T	20. F

Multiple Choice

1. c	5. a	9. b	13. a
2. d	6. c	10. a	14. c
3. b	7. c	11. b	15. d
4. a	8. d	12. d	

16. a

L	Q	MPP	P	MRP = VMP	W
0	0	0	10	0	100
1	8	8	10	80	100
2	18	10	10	100	100
3	30	12	10	120	100
4	40	10	10	100	100
5	48	8	10	80	100
6	54	6	10	60	100

17. c   20. b   23. b   26. d
18. c   21. c   24. d
19. b   22. a   25. c

Essay-Problem

1. Labor, capital, land, and entrepreneurship.
2. Labor is considered a homogeneous commodity—one unit of labor is a perfect substitute for another.
3. For most people, the cost of leisure rises as the wage rate rises. Having fun costs more when the alternative—working—increases in value. Only those people who are fabulously rich might ignore the call of very high wages.
4. The simple answer is when the income effect swamps the substitution effect. The backward-bending labor supply curve has been observed empirically. In general, it takes high levels of income before the income effect overpowers the substitution effect. But ultimately, it depends on each individual's preferences.
5. Most likely, the smaller rural school district will have more monopsony power because it faces no—or fewer—competitors in the immediate area. The New York City school district, though a large employer of labor, faces competition from suburban school districts.
6. The rate of return approach lets one compare projects of different sizes. A plant expansion might lead to a large income stream, whereas a product expansion might lead to a much smaller income stream. The present value of the first might be much larger than the second. But the second might be much more profitable; the rate of return approach would tell you this.
7. It is useful to think of it in this way. Yet, when housing prices rise spectacularly, this puts pressure on current landholders to improve their land. Landholders drain swampland or remove boulders, so that they can sell this previously unused land to housing developers. However, there is an ultimate physical limit to land—you cannot squeeze 2 acres of land out of 1 acre.
8. Large corporations tend to be bureaucratic, whereas small companies tend to be more flexible. Large corporations can encourage entrepreneurship, but it is tough to do this. Thus, entrepreneurs tend to be driven out of large corporations and form their own companies.
9. Interest rates drive the cost of capital. When capital becomes more expensive, firms seek to substitute less-expensive labor for more-expensive capital. Specifically, if a firm finds that it has to increase production, but the cost of capital has made machinery much more expensive, it will try to hire more workers to meet its production needs.
10. No. In input markets such as labor, when the price (wage rate) rises, people substitute more hours of work. The substitution effect for labor is always positive. In product markets, the substitution effect is negative: When price falls, consumption rises.

Labor Market Issues

12

Everyone Is Affected by Labor Market Issues

In the last chapter, we looked at the theory of input markets. Now we want to look more closely at one particular input: labor markets. We will discuss such topics as the link between education and earnings, economic discrimination, and unions. You undoubtedly will have some personal interest in these topics.

This Is What You Need to Know

STEP 1

After studying this chapter you should be able to

- Describe the relationship between education and earnings.
- Understand how the rate of return on a college degree is computed.
- Know how market equilibrium levels for human capital are determined.
- Understand the different theories of human capital.
- Describe the difference between general and specific training.
- Describe Becker's theory of economic discrimination.
- Describe the concept of segmented labor markets and how they affect wage levels.
- Describe federal laws and policies regarding discrimination.
- Describe the history, costs, and benefits of trade unions.
- Discuss the evolution of labor markets.

Review the Key Terms

Investment in human capital: Investments such as education and on-the-job training that improve the productivity of human labor.

Screening/signaling: The argument that higher education simply lets employers know that the prospective employee is intelligent and trainable and has the discipline potentially to be a good employee.

On-the-job training: Training typically done by employers, ranging from suggestions at work to sophisticated seminars.

General training: Training that improves a worker's productivity in all firms.

Specific training: Training that improves a worker's productivity in a specific firm.

Economic discrimination: When workers of equal ability are paid different wages or in any other way discriminated against because of race, color, religion, gender, age, national origin, or disability.

Segmented labor markets: Labor markets split into separate parts. This leads to different wages paid to different sectors even though both markets are highly competitive.

Comparable worth: An approach to determining wage rates for specific occupations that assumes that every job has essential characteristics that possess an inherent worth independent of market forces.

Secondary boycott: Occurs when unions clash with one firm and put pressure on another firm to enlist the help of the second firm to obtain the union's objectives with the original firm.

Closed shop: Workers must belong to the union before they can be hired.

Union shop: Non-union hires must join the union within a specified period of time.

Agency shop: Employees are not required to join the union, but must pay dues to compensate the union for its services.

Right-to-work laws: Laws created by the Taft-Hartley Act that permitted states to outlaw union shops.

Work Through the Chapter Tutorials

Investment in Human Capital

Frequently Asked Questions

Q: How do workers invest in themselves? How do firms invest in their workers?

A: Workers invest in themselves by going to school or learning a trade. Firms invest in workers through on-the-job training or in-house training for employees.

Q: How can we calculate the return to human capital investment?

A: The value of human capital investment can be determined using investment analysis. Investments in education involve the direct costs of education and foregone earnings. The benefits of such investments are then spread over the individual's working life. Human capital analysis uses present value calculations to determine the return to human capital investment.

Q: What influences the supply and demand for human capital investment?

A: Anything that reduces the availability of funds will reduce investments in human capital. The demand for human capital, meanwhile, is influenced by an individual's abilities and learning capacity. Human capital improves an individual's productivity, thereby resulting in higher lifetime earnings. Productivity thus links education and earnings.

Q: Why can a college degree be considered a signaling device rather than an investment in human capital?

A: Some economists suggest that investments in human capital do little more than serve as screening or signaling devices for employers. With this view, a college degree is merely a proxy for trainability, discipline, good work habits, and intelligence.

Q: What are the two types of on-the-job training, and why do firms tend to offer one and not the other?

A: On-the-job training falls into two categories: general and specific training. General training improves productivity at all firms, while specific training improves productivity only at one specific firm. Firms rarely provide general training; workers must get this training on their own. Firms will, however, provide specific training if the returns are high enough.

Keep in Mind

We saw earlier that over the longer term, productivity determines an individual's standard of living. Investment in human capital typically determines individual productivity, so making investments in ourselves is extremely important. Since you are in college, you probably have a general sense of this.

Investment in Human Capital Quick Check

Circle the Correct Answer

1. (T/F) The major costs of attending college are the direct costs such as tuition and books.
2. (T/F) Firms typically pay for specific training for their workers.
3. (T/F) Learning a trade through an apprenticeship program is a form of human capital.
4. (T/F) Firms are generally reluctant to provide their employees with general training because recouping the investment is difficult given that employees can take the training and apply it elsewhere.
5. To compare the benefits of going to college with the benefits of not going to college, calculate
   a. the present value of expected earnings over one's working lifetime after college.
   b. the present value of expected earnings over one's working lifetime after college, minus the direct costs of going to college.
   c. the present value of expected earnings over one's working lifetime after college, minus the direct costs of going to college and the forgone earnings.

   d. the present value of expected earnings over one's working lifetime after college, minus the direct costs of going to college and the forgone earnings, and compare it to the present value of the earnings over one's lifetime if one did not go to college.

6. Economists who believe that college degrees have little connection to future worker productivity argue for all *except* which one of the following?
   a. All that college degrees do is let employers know which potential employees have a certain level of trainability, discipline, and intelligence. The degree does not guarantee success.
   b. College degrees are solely screening and signaling devices.
   c. College degrees help the degree holder only, not the general public.
   d. Public support for higher education should be minimal.

7. Young people are more likely to seek further education than older people because
   a. they are smarter than their elders.

b. the opportunity costs of seeking further education are higher for older people.

c. their parents push them.

d. it is easier for young people to get loan money.

8. Older people are less likely to go to medical school than younger people because of all except which one of the following?

a. Older people face higher opportunity costs.

b. The time it takes to become a doctor is so long that it leaves much less time for older people to earn income and "pay back" the costs of education.

c. Younger people are better at screening and signaling.

d. Older people are much more likely to have family commitments.

9. Which of the following is *not* an example of specific training?

a. instruction on shipping procedures

b. training on budgeting formulas used by the firm

c. knowledge of the inventory system

d. instruction on using Microsoft Word

10. Which one of the following would you *not* consider in deciding whether to invest in human capital?

a. the interest costs of loans

b. the expected rate of return

c. the cost of earnings forgone, if any

d. clothing costs for the time you are in school

Score: ____

If You Got 9 or 10 Correct

Go on to Economic Discrimination in the next section.

If You Didn't Get at Least 9 Correct

You may be going through this material too quickly. It is not difficult, and it reflects to some degree (no pun intended) why you are taking this course. Be sure you know how to set up the costs and benefits of investment in human capital. This is an important concept. Fortunately, the sections in this chapter cover different issues, and each section stands on its own and does not rely on earlier material. Review the material again and then go on to the next section, "Economic Discrimination." ▪

Economic Discrimination

Frequently Asked Questions

Q: **What is economic discrimination?**

A: Economic discrimination occurs whenever workers of equal ability and productivity are paid different wages or otherwise discriminated against in the workplace because of their race, color, religion, gender, age, national origin, or disability. Lower wages, segregation into different occupations, and restrictions on entry into professions are all examples of economic discrimination.

Q: **What is Gary Becker's analysis of economic discrimination, and why does economic discrimination persist?**

A: Gary Becker offered an account of economic discrimination that assumes some employers have a taste for discrimination. Becker concluded that employers who discriminate lose profit opportunities; therefore, competitive pressures should end this discrimination. Competitive forces, however, may not be enough to end discrimination because of the significant costs associated with hiring and firing and otherwise restructuring a firm's workforce. Some workers, moreover, are less mobile than others. If this is true of a group of workers, such as women, this could lead to wage differences that are not clearly discriminatory.

Q: How can segmented markets cause economic discrimination?

A: Another approach to analyzing economic discrimination in labor markets rests on the existence of segmented markets. Various forces can segment workers from different groups into different, noncompeting sectors of the labor market. The labor market can be split into primary and secondary markets (the dual labor market hypothesis); it can broken into predominately male and female jobs (the job crowding hypothesis); or it can be split into union and non-union or unemployed workers (insider-outsider theory). All these approaches predict separate job markets and different wages for different groups.

Figure 1 shows how segmented markets can lead to wage differentials. Initially, both labor markets pay W_0 (points e in both panels), and no wage differential exists. Assume in one segment (labeled "High-Paying Employment" in Panel A) government restrictions (licenses, discrimination, or union membership) reduce the supply of labor to S_1. This raises wages in that market; excluded workers move to the other market, increasing supply and reducing wages. The result is a wage differential equal to $W_1 - W_2$.

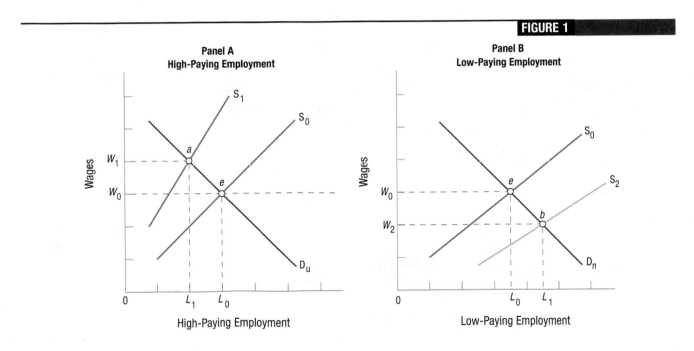

FIGURE 1

Panel A
High-Paying Employment

Panel B
Low-Paying Employment

Q: What public policies prevent economic discrimination?

A: Public policies and laws have been enacted to counter economic discrimination. These include the Equal Pay Act of 1963, the Civil Rights Act of 1964, Executive Order 11246 on affirmative action, Age Discrimination in Employment Act of 1967, and the Americans With Disabilities Act of 1990.

Key Point to Remember

Economic discrimination not only harms the person discriminated against, but also the firm discriminating loses, and society at large loses the higher output that the individual could have produced.

Economic Discrimination Quick Check

Circle the Correct Answer

1. (T/F) The surprising conclusion of Gary Becker's theory of economic discrimination is that discrimination hurts discriminating employers as well as the workers who are discriminated against.
2. (T/F) Male–female wage differentials may persist if females are less mobile than males.
3. (T/F) Gary Becker argued that economic discrimination is economically inefficient, causing discriminating employers to miss profit opportunities.
4. Dual labor markets lead to wage differentials because
   a. women prefer more flexible work.
   b. union workers are more productive than non-union employees.
   c. those excluded from one market retire or leave the labor force.
   d. restrictions in one market reduce the labor supply in that market and increase the supply in the other market.
5. Which segmented labor market theory of economic discrimination divides the workforce into unionized and non-union or unemployed workers?
   a. insider-outsider theory
   b. the job crowding hypothesis
   c. the dual labor market hypothesis
   d. the comparable worth hypothesis
6. Affirmative action for firms doing at least $50,000 in business with the federal government is required by
   a. the Taft-Hartley Act of 1947.
   b. the Equal Pay Act of 1963.
   c. the Civil Rights Act of 1964.
   d. Lyndon Johnson's Executive Order 11246 (1965).
7. Competitive forces may not eliminate economic discrimination because of all *except* which one of the following?
   a. Significant costs may be associated with hiring and firing and otherwise restructuring a firm's workforce.

   b. Women may be less mobile than men.
   c. Women may choose more flexible career paths that do not heavily penalize extended absences from the labor market, and these jobs will tend to pay less.
   d. Women continue to work at different levels of productivity than men in a significant number of jobs in our economy.
8. Which of the following is *not* an example of a segmented labor market theory of economic discrimination?
   a. the job crowding hypothesis
   b. insider-outsider theory
   c. the Becker hypothesis
   d. the dual labor market hypothesis
9. Comparable worth theory maintains that
   a. every job has essential characteristics that possess inherent worth, independent of market forces.
   b. every job is of equal value.
   c. every job in a particular industry is of equal value, though this value may be hidden from view.
   d. market forces eventually will drive out discrimination.
10. What law made it unlawful to "refuse to hire or to discharge any individual . . . because of such individual's race, color, religion, sex, or national origin?"
    a. the Taft-Hartley Act of 1947
    b. the Equal Pay Act of 1963
    c. the Civil Rights Act of 1964
    d. Executive Order 11246 (1965)

Score: ____

Answers: 1. T; 2. T; 3. T; 4. d; 5. a; 6. d; 7. d; 8. c; 9. a; 10. c

If You Got 9 or 10 Correct

Go on to the next section, "Labor Unions and Collective Bargaining."

If You Didn't Get at Least 9 Correct

You didn't read this material very carefully. Economic discrimination is a major public policy issue, and you should understand its various aspects. This is not difficult material; review it again. The next section on unions provides an overview of collective bargaining, its history, and why union memberhip has declined. ■

Labor Unions and Collective Bargaining

Frequently Asked Questions

Q: How are labor unions defined?

A: Labor unions are legal associations of employees formed to bargain collectively with employers over the terms and conditions of employment.

Q: What are the benefits and costs to workers of unionization?

A: Collective bargaining provides workers with increased job security, a more structured work environment, and potentially higher wages. The benefits of unionization, however, do not come free. Monthly dues must be paid to the union, flexibility on the job is often restricted, and infrequently strikes are required, resulting in a loss of wages and possible job loss.

Q: What are the different types of unions in the workplace?

A: A closed shop requires workers to be members of a union before they can be hired. A union shop permits union and non-union hires, but requires new employees to join the union within 30 days. In an agency shop, employees are not required to join the union, but they must pay union dues to reimburse the union for its services. The Taft-Hartley Act of 1947 outlawed the closed shop and permitted states to pass right-to-work statutes that prohibit union shops.

Labor Unions and Collective Bargaining Quick Check

Circle the Correct Answer

1. (T/F) A union's power comes from its willingness to strike to obtain a work agreement with employers.

2. (T/F) In the 1920s, labor unions in the United States were popular with the public and distrusted by government.

3. (T/F) The Taft-Hartley Act of 1947 required unions to bargain in good faith.

4. (T/F) An agency shop is a workplace where workers are required to be members of the union before they can be hired.

5. (T/F) A significant factor in recent labor markets has been the increase in immigration rates.

6. Unions tend to
   a. increase wages for their members but reduce the number of union jobs.
   b. drive up wages for their members and increase the number of union jobs.
   c. go on strike often.
   d. be stronger in the retail service sector than in the automobile manufacturing sector.

7. What is a closed shop?
   a. Workers are required to be a member of the union before they can be hired.

b. Workers are not required to join the union, but they are required to pay union dues to compensate the union for its services.
   c. Workers are not required to join the union or to contribute to it in any way.
   d. Both union and non-union hires are allowed, but non-union hires are required to join the union within 30 days.

8. Why has union membership declined as a percentage of wage and salary workers since World War II?
   a. Strikes have become more frequent, leading to public disapproval.
   b. The service sector has grown substantially, and it is harder to organize.
   c. Unions never recovered from the Taft-Hartley Act of 1947.
   d. Young people are not interested in being union members.

9. Which of the following did the National Labor Relations Act of 1935 *not* do?
   a. require employers to "bargain in good faith" with unions
   b. establish the National Labor Relations Board

c. require unions to "bargain in good faith" with employers
d. prohibit yellow dog contracts
10. Which of the following are *not* among the accomplishments of the 20th-century labor movement?
   a. stronger work safety legislation
   b. Social Security

c. minimum wage laws
d. increases in the number of union jobs

Score: ____

Answers: 1. T; 2. F; 3. T; 4. F; 5. T; 6. a; 7. a; 8. b; 9. c; 10. d.

If You Got 9 or 10 Correct

Move on to the "Hints, Tips, and Reminders," the next step.

If You Didn't Get at Least 9 Correct

You probably went through the material too quickly. It is not difficult. Do a quick review of this section on unions. Although unions today have less than half (as a percent of the labor force) of their peak membership of the 1930s, they are still an important force in our economy, both politically and economically. New strategies are enabling unions to organize the service sector, the fastest growing sector of our economy. As a quick check, list the benefits and costs of unions to workers and make sure you know how unions affect the labor market.

After you have completed this quick review, go on to next section on hints, tips, and reminders. ■

STEP 4   Consider These Hints, Tips, and Reminders

1. This chapter covers three distinct issues that affect labor markets. Investment in human capital and economic discrimination are more analytical than the section on labor unions, so you may need to spend a little more time on these first two sections of the chapter.

2. The analyses of segmented labor market and union–non-union wage differentials are essentially the same. Learn it once, use it twice. Separating labor markets into two different markets and then restricting entry (supply) in one market increases wages in that market but shifts some workers to the unrestricted market, thus increasing supply and reducing wages. This is how a wage differential is created.

3. It is important to keep in mind that labor unions are to some extent victims of their own success. Many of the labor market protections we take for granted are the result of collective bargaining that was later passed into law, and others were supported and lobbied for by unions. But changes from globalization and a shift to a more service-oriented economy have reduced manufacturing employment, a traditional stronghold of unions.

Do the Homework for Chapter 12
Labor Market Issues

Instructor _____ Time _____ Student _____

Use the answer key below to record your answers to these homework questions.

1. (a) (b) (c) (d)
2. (a) (b) (c) (d)
3. (a) (b) (c) (d)
4. (a) (b) (c) (d)
5. (a) (b) (c) (d)

6. (a) (b) (c) (d)
7. (a) (b) (c) (d)
8. (a) (b) (c) (d)
9. (a) (b) (c) (d)
10. (a) (b) (c) (d)

11. (a) (b) (c) (d)
12. (a) (b) (c) (d)
13. (a) (b) (c) (d)
14. (a) (b) (c) (d)
15. (a) (b) (c) (d)

16. (a) (b) (c) (d)
17. (a) (b) (c) (d)
18. (a) (b) (c) (d)
19. (a) (b) (c) (d)
20. (a) (b) (c) (d)

1. Which of the following is *not* a direct cost of a college education?
   a. course textbooks
   b. college tuition
   c. student lab fees
   d. earnings from a full-time job instead of attending college

2. Which of the following does *not* represent general training?
   a. college education
   b. high school education
   c. learning your firm's inventory management system
   d. on-the-job computer software training to use Microsoft PowerPoint

3. Firms will generally not provide general training because
   a. the firm gets no benefit from providing this type of training to employees.
   b. these skills can be used in any firm, not just the firm providing the training.
   c. all employees already have all the general training they can absorb.
   d. management is generally concerned primarily with the bottom line, and the costs of general training will subtract from reported profits.

4. Firms will generally provide specific training because
   a. the firm gets most of the benefit from providing this type of training to employees.
   b. these skills can be used in any firm, including the firm providing the training.

   c. it is a significant fringe benefit to employees.
   d. employees often demand this type of training as a condition of employment.

5. From the view of human capital theory, most people attending college are in their 20s because
   a. college is fun, and people in their 20s want to have fun.
   b. younger people are better at taking tests.
   c. after people have worked for an extended period, their opportunity costs to attending college fall, and so the return from college is too low to be attractive.
   d. younger people have a longer expected work life.

6. Some economists see human capital as just a signaling or screening device. By this, they mean
   a. human capital just builds the resume but adds nothing to the productivity of workers.
   b. human capital enhances productivity of the individual but nothing else.
   c. human capital in the form of higher education adds to productivity, but more importantly, it indicates to prospective employers that the individual has skills that the employer can immediately profit from.
   d. human capital in the form of higher education adds to productivity, but more importantly, it indicates to prospective employers that the individual has discipline, is intelligent, and is trainable.

7. Economic discrimination involves
   a. paying different wages to workers of equal ability and productivity.

b. paying workers different wages based solely on the basis of their race, color, religion, gender, age, national origin, or disability.

c. segregating members of a group into an occupation that is paid a different wage.

d. all of the above.

8. Economic discrimination occurs when
   a. major league baseball pitchers are paid widely different wages.
   b. executive assistants to CEOs are paid higher wages than union organizers.
   c. women are restricted to nursing and teaching, resulting in occupational crowding and low wages.
   d. college professors with advanced degrees earn less than insurance salespeople with high school diplomas.

9. Which of the following is *not* a major act or public policy to combat discrimination?
   a. Equal Pay Act of 1963
   b. Civil Rights Act of 1964
   c. Comparable Worth Act of 1965
   d. Age Discrimination in Employment Act of 1967

10. Economic discrimination in the United States
    a. was never a really serious problem that needed to be solved.
    b. has been gradually rising over the last half century.
    c. changed little in the face of public policy like the Civil Rights Act of 1964.
    d. can cause some people to underinvest in human capital.

11. The segmented market analysis
    a. breaks the labor market into union and non-union workers.
    b. splits occupations into primary and secondary markets.
    c. splits occupations into predominately male and female jobs.
    d. all of the above.

12. Unions often try to increase the demand for their labor by suggesting that we "buy the union label." This is usually done to
    a. help employers increase demand for their products and increase profits.
    b. keep employers from outsourcing computer-programming and high-tech jobs.
    c. increase demand for the product and increase wages for members.

d. increase demand for the product, so volume can grow high enough to reach economies of scale and thus result in lower prices.

13. Union membership as a percent of employment
    a. steadily declined over the last century.
    b. peaked during the depression as individuals needed a union to protect their jobs.
    c. has steadily declined since the end of World War II.
    d. is rising now as more service and technical workers join unions.

14. Work stoppages or strikes
    a. occur frequently.
    b. rarely occur.
    c. inevitably lead to violence.
    d. are outlawed for those in the airline industry.

15. A secondary boycott occurs when
    a. a company is struck for the second time.
    b. a firm's competitors are involved in a strike.
    c. a firm involved in a strike has its suppliers pressured by the striking union.
    d. consumers boycott a firm involved in a strike with its workers.

16. A closed shop is one in which
    a. union members are not allowed to work.
    b. workers must join the union within a month after they are hired.
    c. workers do not have to join the union, but they must pay dues to the union representing the company's workers.
    d. workers must be members of the union to get hired.

17. An agency shop is one in which
    a. union members are not allowed to work.
    b. workers must join the union within 6 months after they are hired.
    c. workers do not have to join the union, but they must pay dues to the union representing the company's workers.
    d. workers must be members of the union to get hired.

18. Featherbedding occurs when
    a. union members are permitted to sleep on the job.
    b. collective bargaining ends in a work stoppage.
    c. redundant workers are employed under a union contract.
    d. workers must be members of the union to get hired.

19. Approximately what percent of workers belong to a union today?
    a. 6%
    b. 15%
    c. 30%
    d. 45%

20. Since World War II, labor union membership as a percent of those employed in the United States has steadily declined because of which of the following?

a. Unions have been shown to be inherently corrupt.
b. Unions have been unable to increase the wages of their members.
c. Unions may have been too successful in the public policy arena by pushing improvements in working conditions, safety, and minimum wages.
d. Government policies have been decidedly anti-union over the last half century.

| | Use the ExamPrep to Get Ready for Exams | STEP 6 |

This sheet (front and back) is designed to help you prepare for your exams. The chapter has been boiled down to its key concepts. You are asked to answer questions, define terms, draw graphs, and, if you wish, add summaries of class notes.

Investment in Human Capital

Education

Describe the relationship between education and earnings:

How do we determine if investment in education is worth it?

Describe the factors that determine the equilibrium levels of investment in human capital:

On-the-Job Training

Describe the following types of on-the-job training:
General training:

Specific training:

Explain why firms will provide specific training, but workers must pay for general training:

Economic Discrimination

Becker's Theory of Economic Discrimination

Describe Gary Becker's theory of discrimination:

What made this analysis unique when it was first proposed?

Segmented Labor Markets

Describe the three segmented labor market theories:

Use the two grids below to illustrate how a wage differential can result from segmented labor markets:

Labor Market 1   **Labor Market 2**

- In both panels, begin with the same labor market supply and demand curves S_0 and D_0 and the same equilibrium wage, W_e. This would be the world without discrimination or market segmentation.
- Now assume that employers and Labor Market 1 discriminate against the group shown in Labor Market 2. Show the new supply curve and equilibrium wage (W_1) for Labor Market 1.
- Those workers discriminated against in Labor Market 1 offer their labor to Labor Market 2. Again, illustrate the new supply curve an equilibrium wage (W_2) for this market.
- Where initially there was no wage differential, what is the wage difference now?

- Describe some market where this type the discrimination still exists today:

Public Policy to Combat Discrimination

Describe the major acts and executive orders designed to eliminate discrimination:

Labor Unions and Collective Bargaining

Describe the two general types of unions:

Describe some of the benefits and costs of the union membership:

Describe the following:
Closed shop:

Union shop:

Agency shop:

Secondary boycott:

Yellow dog contract:

Describe how a union–nonunion wage differential can occur:

Additional Study Help Chapterwide Practice Questions

Matching

Match the description with the corresponding term.

____ 1. Investment in human capital
____ 2. Screening/signaling
____ 3. On-the-job training
____ 4. General training
____ 5. Specific training
____ 6. Economic discrimination
____ 7. Segmented labor markets
____ 8. Union shop
____ 9. Agency shop
____ 10. Closed shop
____ 11. Right-to-work laws

a. A workplace that permits union and non-union hires, but requires that non-union hires join the union within a given period.

b. Improves productivity equally at all firms. It can range from instruction in typing or computers to apprenticeships in plumbing or carpentry. Most employers will not provide this to their workers, who must pursue it at their own expense.

c. Some economists argue that higher education does not raise worker productivity significantly, but it indicates to employers that the graduates possess certain degrees of trainability, discipline, and intelligence.

d. A workplace that requires workers to be union members before they can be hired.

e. Intended to increase worker productivity and raise the wages a worker commands though investing in education, vocational training, or on-the-job training.

f. Improves productivity at one firm only, for example, teaching employees about a company's specific ordering procedures. Employers will often absorb the cost of it if returns from this investment compare favorably to other investment possibilities.

g. Can take many different forms, from instructions by a supervisor on how to help customers or run a cash register to seminars in a more formal setting away from the job.

h. A workplace that does not require union membership, but does require that employees pay union dues to reimburse the union for its services.

i. Theories about this have been developed along several different lines, including the dual labor market hypothesis, job crowding hypothesis, and insider-outsider theory.

j. Workers of equal ability and productivity are paid different wages or are otherwise discriminated against in the workplace because of race, color, religion, gender, age, national origin, or disability.

k. Prohibitions against union shops, thus ensuring that workers need not join unions as a condition of employment.

Fill-In

Circle the word(s) in parentheses that complete the sentence.

1. Individuals and firms invest in human capital to increase (employment opportunities, working conditions, productivity, all of these)_____. Individuals typically must invest in (general, specific) _____ training, but firms will often provide (general, specific) _____ training.

2. Economists have found that there is a (negative, positive) _____ relationship between education and earnings. If higher education is simply a screening/signaling device, it provides employers information that educated workers are (highly productive, expensive, trainable)_____.

3. According to Gary Becker's theory of discrimination, employers (gain, lose)_____ from discrimination, and he felt that (government, competition, the U.S. Chamber of Commerce) _____ would eventually eliminate it.

4. Theories of economic discrimination have been developed using segmented markets. The theory where the market is divided (segmented) by company customs, norms, and policies to inspire employee loyalty is known as (dual labor market hypothesis, job crowding hypothesis, insider-outsider theory)_____, but when labor markets are split into "good jobs" (the primary market) and "not so good jobs" (the secondary market) the theory is (dual labor market hypothesis, job crowding hypothesis, insider-outsider theory) _____.

5. A workplace where any employee can work (union or non-union), but all workers must pay union dues is known as a (closed, union, agency) _____ shop; if only union members are hired, the workplace is a (closed, union, agency) _____ shop. A shop where anyone can be

hired, but all workers must eventually join the union is a (closed, union, agency) _____ shop.

True-False

Circle the correct answer.

__T/F__ 1. The earnings forgone in attending college are typically insignificant as compared to the direct costs of college.

__T/F__ 2. The primary determinants of the decision whether or not to invest in human capital are the interest costs to borrow funds and the rate of return on investments in human capital.

__T/F__ 3. Empirically, the rate of return on college education as an investment in human capital is estimated to be around 40% or 50%.

__T/F__ 4. One reason doctors are highly paid is that, as medical students, they must forgo earning a regular salary for many years.

__T/F__ 5. To finance their education, college students typically turn to private sources of funding first, only turning to government-subsidized loans or family funds as a last resort.

__T/F__ 6. Gary Becker's theory of economic discrimination concludes that discriminatory practices hurt discriminating employers as well as those workers discriminated against.

__T/F__ 7. Any appearance of wage differentials indicates that economic discrimination must be taking place.

__T/F__ 8. One explanation of contemporary male–female wage differentials is that men currently earn far more bachelor's degrees than women.

__T/F__ 9. Affirmative action programs have their origin in Executive Order 11246, issued by President Lyndon Johnson in 1965.

__T/F__ 10. Comparable worth theory maintains that every job is of equal value, and thus all workers should be compensated equally.

__T/F__ 11. The ultimate source of a union's power is its willingness to strike if a satisfactory work agreement is not reached with employers.

__T/F__ 12. The Taft-Hartley Act of 1947 required that employers "bargain in good faith" with unions.

__T/F__ 13. A closed shop is a workplace where workers are required to be members of the union before they can be hired.

__T/F__ 14. Over the past 50 years, union membership as a share of the workforce has generally increased.

__T/F__ 15. Union bargaining tactics often result in higher wages for union members but fewer union jobs.

__T/F__ 16. The increasing influx of immigrants and the growth of the high-tech economy have reduced income inequality in the United States.

Multiple Choice

Circle the correct answer.

1. Which of the following is *not* one of the direct costs of a college education?
   a. books
   b. tuition
   c. forgone wages
   d. student fees

2. In what order will most college students turn to various sources of funds to finance their schooling?
   a. Family funds first, then government-subsidized loans, private loans last.
   b. Private loans first, then family funds, government-subsidized loans last.
   c. Government-subsidized loans first, then private loans, family funds last.
   d. Family funds first, then private loans, government-subsidized loans last.

3. As workers get older and gain more on-the-job experience, the opportunity costs of seeking further education
   a. increase.
   b. remain about the same.
   c. decrease moderately.
   d. fall to zero.

4. Advocates of the screening/signaling view of higher education argue that college degrees give rise to wage differentials primarily by
   a. raising worker productivity.
   b. letting employers know which potential employees have a certain level of trainability, discipline, and intelligence.
   c. improving the communications skills of workers.
   d. putting more money into the pockets of wealthy professors.

5. Which of the following is *not* an example of general training?
   a. a class in public speaking
   b. typing instruction
   c. a carpentry apprenticeship
   d. instruction in a firm's warehousing procedures

6. Which of the following is *not* an example of specific training?
   a. instruction on running a store's cash register
   b. orientation with a company's shipping procedures
   c. weekend classes in spot welding
   d. going over a restaurant's menu with the wait staff

7. Who will generally absorb the costs of specific training?
   a. the people receiving the training
   b. the firm that employs those receiving the training
   c. the parents or family members of those receiving the training
   d. the U.S. Department of Labor

8. Why are firms typically reluctant to provide their employees with general training?
   a. General training does not increase worker productivity.
   b. General training is invariably more expensive than specific training.
   c. Few firms ever provide their employees with any training, general or specific.
   d. Recouping investments in general training is difficult for firms, because employees can take this training and apply it elsewhere.

9. Gary Becker's theory of economic discrimination assumes that
   a. some employers have a taste for discrimination.
   b. men are generally more productive than women.
   c. labor markets frequently divide themselves into noncompeting segments that support different wage rates.
   d. economic discrimination is likely to be around forever.

10. Gary Becker argues that economic discrimination is
    a. highly efficient, helping employers to get the most qualified people on the job.
    b. economically inefficient, causing discriminating employers to miss profit opportunities.
    c. just plain common sense, given that different groups often have different levels of productivity.
    d. likely to be around forever, assuming market forces are allowed to operate freely.

11. Which of the following is *not* an example of a segmented labor market theory of economic discrimination?
    a. the job crowding hypothesis
    b. insider-outsider theory
    c. the Landrum-Griffin hypothesis
    d. the dual labor market hypothesis

12. The job crowding hypothesis
    a. breaks occupations into predominantly male and female jobs.
    b. splits the labor market into primary and secondary sectors.
    c. divides the workforce into unionized and nonunion or unemployed workers.
    d. divides a firm's workforce into newcomers and employees brought up within the firm.

13. Which of the following is *not* among the reasons male–female wage differentials may well be around for some time?
    a. Women may be less mobile than men, often choosing to accept lower wages rather than moving for a job.
    b. The costs to firms of restructuring their workforces in nondiscriminatory ways may be significant, and competitive markets provide little incentive for change.
    c. Many women may continue to choose occupations with more flexible career paths but lower wages.
    d. For most jobs in our economy today, men and women work at different levels of productivity.

14. What law made it unlawful to "refuse to hire or to discharge any individual . . . because of such individual's race, color, religion, sex, or national origin?"
    a. the Taft-Hartley Act of 1947
    b. the Equal Pay Act of 1963
    c. the Civil Rights Act of 1964
    d. Executive Order 11246 (1965)

15. Economic discrimination in the United States
    a. has been gradually increasing over the past 40 years.
    b. remained more or less constant throughout the 20th century.
    c. has been gradually declining over the past 40 years.
    d. was eliminated with the Civil Rights Act of 1964.

16. The Equal Pay Act of 1963 requires that
    a. all jobs be compensated equally.
    b. men and women receive equal pay for equal work.
    c. workers of all ages receive equal pay for equal work.
    d. workers of all races receive equal pay for equal work.

17. Which of the following is *not* true of labor unions?
    a. They are required to bargain in good faith with employers.
    b. Their primary purpose is to engage in collective bargaining with employers.
    c. They are legally barred from charging their members dues.
    d. They sometimes use strikes to achieve their goals.

18. In the 1920s, labor unions in the United States were
    a. small, weak, and distrusted by the public.
    b. disliked by the public, but politically and economically powerful.
    c. both popular with the public and powerful.
    d. protected by numerous prolabor laws and sympathetic courts.

19. Which of the following did the National Labor Relations Act of 1935 *not* do?
    a. require employers to bargain in good faith with unions
    b. establish the National Labor Relations Board
    c. prohibit yellow dog contracts
    d. prohibit unions from coercing or discriminating against workers who chose not to join the union

20. In what type of workplace are both union and non-union hires allowed, though non-union hires are required to join the union within 30 days?
    a. an open shop
    b. a closed shop
    c. a union shop
    d. an agency shop

21. What defines an agency shop?
    a. Workers are required to be members of the union before they can be hired.
    b. Workers are not required to join the union, but they are required to pay union dues to compensate the union for its services.
    c. Workers are not required to join the union or to contribute to it in any way.
    d. Both union and non-union hires are allowed, but non-union hires are required to join the union within 30 days.

22. Since World War II, union membership as a percent of those employed in the United States has
    a. steadily declined.
    b. remained more or less constant.
    c. steadily increased.
    d. grown intermittently but significantly.

23. Which of the following are *not* among the accomplishments of the 20th-century labor movement?
    a. stronger work safety legislation
    b. Social Security
    c. guaranteed employment for those who wish to work
    d. minimum wage laws

24. Approximately what percentage of American workers belonged to unions in the 1990s?
    a. 7%
    b. 15%
    c. 32%
    d. 48%

25. Featherbedding is
    a. union bargaining that ultimately ends in a strike.
    b. union efforts to force non-union personnel to join the union in an agency shop.
    c. added benefits provided to union leaders by management to gain their cooperation.
    d. unnecessary workers hired under union contracts.

26. Which of these trends has *not* been a factor in the recent evolution of the labor market?
    a. There are more two-earner households.
    b. There have been dramatic gains by trade unions.
    c. There is a growing interest in telecommuting.
    d. Immigration rates have increased.

Essay-Problem

Answer in the space provided.

Labor issues affect all of us. The following questions are designed to extend your understanding of these issues. Use our answers as guides to these extensions.

1. What is the essence of the concept of human capital?

2. Stafford Education loans currently have a fixed interest rate of 6.8%. However, for loans disbursed before July 1, 2006, the rate changes every year but is capped at just under 9.825% maximum per year. Explain the cap in light of what you have learned about human capital.

3. Does it make sense for retirees to go back to college?

4. In light of what you learned about general and specific training, what skills would you expect a firm to request in a want ad for an office worker?

5. In competitive markets, how do employers who discriminate shoot themselves in the foot?

6. Why do unions set up picket lines during strikes?

7. Why are there so many last-minute settlements between unions and employees?

8. What is one possible reason for the decline in major strikes?

9. What is the rationale behind an agency shop?

10. What are two key issues in instituting comparable worth?

What's Next

After completing this chapter and the last chapter, you now have a deeper under-standing of labor markets and some of the complex issues facing workers and employers. Since labor income accounts for 70% of our national income, each of us will confront these issues at some point in our working lives. In the next chapter, we look at the environment and apply economic analysis to environmental issues. Given that the population of the United States now exceeds 300 million and warn-ings about global warming approach alarmist proportions, economics provides an analytical framework to apply to these issues.

Answers to Chapterwide Practice Questions

Matching

1. e	4. b	7. i	10. d
2. c	5. f	8. a	11. k
3. g	6. j	9. h	

Fill-In

1. all of these, general, specific
2. positive, trainable
3. lose, competition
4. insider-outsider theory, dual labor market hypothesis
5. agency, closed, union

True-False

1. F	5. F	9. T	13. T
2. T	6. T	10. F	14. F
3. F	7. F	11. T	15. T
4. T	8. F	12. F	16. F

Multiple Choice

1. c	8. d	15. c	22. a
2. a	9. a	16. b	23. c
3. a	10. b	17. c	24. b
4. b	11. c	18. a	25. d
5. d	12. a	19. d	26. b
6. c	13. d	20. c	
7. b	14. c	21. b	

Essay-Problem

1. Investing in people (education, on-the-job training) will lead to increases in productivity. It makes people into better workers and increases their earnings.
2. To invest in human capital, one must weigh the projected benefits against the projected costs. Projected benefits over one's lifetime are very sensitive to the discount rate used in a present value calculation. The higher the cost of capital—in this case, the interest rate on borrowed funds—the lower the benefit of investing in human capital. High inter-

est rates will drive people away from attending college or continuing their education later in life. The government caps the interest rate to encourage people to go on to college.

3. The theory of human capital links investments in human capital with productivity over one's working lifetime. Also, the benefit of college to a retiree might be more psychological, but this is a benefit nevertheless. It is up to the retiree to weigh whatever benefits the education would give against the actual costs.

4. The ad should request skills that just about any firm would want, such as typing, filing, knowledge of word-processing programs, maybe some familiarity with Excel.

5. They pay market wages and yet do not get the best workers because they restrict their worker pool. In effect, they give themselves a higher cost structure.

6. There are two major reasons for picket lines. First, during strikes, employers may try to hire replacement workers, called scabs by the union. The union legally cannot prevent these replacement workers from going to work, but they can organize picket lines to put pressure on replacements who have to cross the picket line to get to work. Second, picket lines are used as information tools for potential buyers of the firm's products, telling the public that a strike is going on. If the picket line leads to public shunning of the firm's products, the firm's decline in sales puts added pressure on it to settle with the union.

7. A union's ultimate power comes from the threat of striking. Its members would prefer not to strike because their income vanishes. On the other hand, a firm would prefer not to suffer from the disruption of a strike. Also, once a strike starts, positions tend to harden and become more radical, adding uncertainty to the possibility of a settlement. It is in the interests of both parties to come to an agreement before a strike occurs. Brinksmanship—waiting until the last minute to settle—is a negotiating tactic that each side uses to get the best possible deal.

8. The federal government has shown a greater willingness to step in and order a cooling-off period, which it can under the law, for potential strikes it considers against the public interest. This willingness has ebbed and flowed, but it is present and must be taken into consideration by major unions contemplating a strike.

9. In an agency shop, one does not have to join the union but has to pay dues to the union to compensate it for its services. The union is the sole negotiator with the firm and negotiates for higher wages and benefits. A non-union worker is the recipient of the higher wages and benefits. If the non-union worker did not pay dues, the worker would be getting these benefits for free, while union members had to pay for them. Out of fairness, the non-union member should contribute toward the union's cost of securing higher wages and benefits for all.

10. First, there is the complexity in any attempt to break down every job into its supposed key components. Second, who decides how to weigh each component?

Public Goods, Common Resources, and Externalities

13

Using Economic Analysis to Understand Environmental Problems Caused by Market Failures

Environmental economics takes economic concepts such as consumer surplus, producer surplus, and market failures, and applies them to environmental problems such as air and water pollution. This will give you a useful framework for analyzing environmental issues. You will get a good understanding of why pollution occurs in markets and what public policy can do to improve the situation.

This Is What You Need to Know

STEP 1

After studying this chapter you should be able to

- Describe the market failures that lead to environmental problems.

- Describe the impact of negative and positive externalities on society.

- Describe the Coase theorem on social costs and the role transaction costs play in the optimal allocation of resources.

- Describe government failures in dealing with market failures.

- Recognize the importance of the discount rate in assessing the intergenerational costs and benefits of environmental policies.

- Use marginal analysis to determine the optimal level of pollution.

- Describe the differences between command and control policies and market-based approaches to environmental regulation.

Review the Key Terms

Consumer surplus: The difference between what consumers (as individuals or the market) would be willing to pay and the market price. It is equal to the area above market price and below the demand curve.

Producer surplus: The difference between market price and the price at which firms would be willing to supply the product. It is equal to the area below market price and above the supply curve.

Social welfare: The sum of consumer and producer surplus.

Market failures: When markets are not competitive or involve public goods, externalities, or common property resources, markets will fail to provide the optimal level of output, and will provide output at too high or low a price.

Public goods: Goods that, once provided, no one person can be excluded from consuming (i.e., nonexclusion), and one person's consumption does not diminish the benefit to others from consuming the good (i.e., nonrivalry).

Nonrivalry: The consumption of a good or service by one person does not reduce the utility of that good or service to others.

Nonexcludability: Once a good or service is provided, it is not feasible to exclude others from enjoying that good or service.

Cost-benefit analysis: A methodology for decision making that looks at the discounted value of the costs and benefits of a given project.

Common property resources: Resources that are owned by the community at large (e.g., parks, ocean fish, and the atmosphere) and therefore tend to be overexploited because individuals have little incentive to use them in a sustainable fashion.

Externalities: The impact on third parties of some transaction between others where the third parties are not involved. An external cost (or negative externality) harms the third parties, whereas external benefits (positive externalities) result in gains to them.

Coase theorem: If transaction costs are minimal (near zero), a bargain struck between beneficiaries and victims of externalities will be efficient from a resource allocation perspective. As a result, the socially optimal level of production will be reached, for example, whether polluters are given the right to pollute, or the victims are given the right to be free of pollution.

Government failure: When the incentives of politicians and government bureaucrats are not in line with the public interest.

Command and control policies: Environmental policies where standards are set and regulations are issued, and these are then enforced by the legal and regulatory system.

Market-based policies: Environmental policies that use charges, taxes, subsidies, deposit-refund systems, or tradable emission permits to achieve environmental ends.

| Work Through the Chapter Tutorials | STEP 3 |

Market Failure

Frequently Asked Questions

Q: What are consumer surplus and producer surplus?

A: Consumer surplus is the difference between what people are willing to pay for a product and what they actually pay for it. Producer surplus is the difference between the revenues firms earn from a product and the costs they would be willing to bear to supply it.

Q: When does market failure occur?

A: Market failure occurs whenever a market does not provide the socially optimal quantity of a product at the socially optimal price. Market failure can occur because of public goods, externalities, or common property resources.

Q: What are public goods?

A: Public goods exhibit both nonrivalry in consumption and nonexcludability. Nonrivalry means that one person's consumption of a good does not reduce the availability of that good to others. Nonexcludability means that once a product has been provided, no consumers can be excluded from consuming the product. Candy bars are a rival and exclusive product; clean air is nonrival and nonexclusive.

Q: What are externalities?

A: Externalities, or spillovers, arise when a transaction benefits or harms parties not involved in the transaction. Pollution and littering are examples of negative externalities, or external costs. Positive externalities, or external benefits, include education and vaccinations.

Q: What is the Coase theorem, and why is it important?

A: The Coase theorem suggests that if transaction costs are near zero, how property rights are allocated (to pollute or to be free from pollution) will not affect the efficiency of the ultimate allocation of resources. The resulting bargain between the parties will lead to an optimal allocation of resources. Benefits, however, will be distributed differently, depending on the original assignment of property rights.

Q: Is competition always the best cure for monopoly?

A: Since monopolies restrict output, if their products involve significant negative externalities, pressing for greater competition could produce socially harmful consequences. Still, to reduce pollution, few people would argue for policies permitting monopolies.

Q: What is the problem with common property resources?

A: Because common property resources are owned by the community, individuals will tend to overuse and overexploit them, as has happened with ocean fishing and some national parks. Solutions to such problems involve either direct government regulation or establishing private property rights.

Key Point to Remember

Market failures are conditions such as externalities, monopoly, public goods, or common property resources that keep markets from providing the socially optimal output. With the exception of public goods, these markets do not collapse, but often require government intervention of some sort to ensure socially optimal outcomes.

Market Failure Quick Check

Circle the Correct Answer

1. (T/F) Total social welfare is equal to consumer surplus minus producer surplus.
2. (T/F) Radio transmissions are a public good because they exhibit both nonrivalry and nonexcludability.
3. (T/F) Consumer surplus is the difference between what people are prepared to pay for a product and what they actually pay for it.
4. (T/F) Downloadable music exhibits nonexcludability because no one is excluded from buying and downloading it.
5. Which of the following is *not* true for externalities?
   a. They can be either negative or positive.
   b. They arise when two parties engage in a transaction, and some third party unrelated to either is harmed or benefited by it.
   c. They are called "the tragedy of the commons."
   d. Negative externalities in an unregulated market will lead to the production of too much of a good at too low a price.
6. The Coase theorem suggests which of the following?
   a. Private negotiations over polluting rights will produce efficient results only if these rights are initially distributed evenly among potential polluters.
   b. Private negotiations over polluting rights will produce efficient results only if these rights are initially distributed to the victims of pollution.
   c. Private negotiations over polluting rights will produce efficient results regardless of the transaction costs.
   d. Private negotiations over polluting rights will produce efficient results if transaction costs are low.
7. What environmental problem arises from common property resources?
   a. negative externality
   b. overexploitation
   c. government failure
   d. high transaction cost
8. Which of the following is an example of a negative externality?
   a. Central Park in New York is too crowded to enjoy.
   b. Residents of a community located near a large factory develop respiratory problems attributable to the factory's smoke.
   c. Lake Ontario sees its fishing population depleted by overfishing.
   d. A community is vaccinated against the flu.
9. When pollution rights are privately negotiated, according to the Coase theorem, what condition must be met for the socially optimal allocation of resources to be brought about?
   a. The initial distribution of pollution rights must be equitable.
   b. The victims must hold the distribution of pollution rights.
   c. Transaction costs must be minimal.
   d. Bargaining must be done in good faith.
10. "The tragedy of the commons" refers to which of the following practices?
    a. a factory releasing sewage into a river
    b. a factory releasing smoke into the air
    c. a city adding to the number of parks, but not as many as the voters want
    d. people walking their dogs in public parks and not cleaning up after them

Score: ____

Answers: 1. F; 2. T; 3. T; 4. F; 5. c; 6. d; 7. b; 8. b; 9. c; 10. d

If You Got 9 or 10 Correct

You have a good grasp of the concepts of market failure including externalities, public goods, and common resource problems. These issues and concepts form the foundation of environmental analysis. You are ready to move on to the more complex material in the next section, "Environmental Policy."

If You Didn't Get at Least 9 Correct

You should have answered most of these questions correctly. If this is not the case, review this section carefully. Make sure you know why you missed a question. Understanding this section is important for understanding the environmental policy material that follows. List the three types of market failure, and describe each one. Do a quick review of the figures in this section; be sure to read the captions under the figures and make sure you understand what is presented.

The remainder of the chapter on environmental policy builds on the analysis of market failure, so you will want to get this material straight before proceeding. Take a moment and work through the two solved problems below on public goods and externalities. Admittedly, they are relatively simple problems, but if you are missing questions in this area, it will be worth your time to make sure you get the concept of public goods and externalities down pat. When you are confident that you can handle public goods and externalities, go on to the next section, "Environmental Policy." ▪

Solved Problem: Public Goods

Using the table below, showing the demand for a public good by three individuals a, b, and c, answer the following questions.

Price	Q_a	Q_b	Q_c	Supply
65	0	0	0	55
60	0	0	0	50
55	0	0	0	45
50	0	0	0	40
45	0	5	0	35
40	0	10	0	30
35	10	15	0	25
30	20	20	0	20
25	30	25	20	15
20	40	30	40	10
15	50	35	60	5
10	60	40	80	0
5	70	45	100	0
0	80	50	120	0

a. In the blank grid below, plot all three demand curves.

b. Plot the total demand for this public good.

c. Given the supply curve, how much at what price will be the public good equilibrium?

Solution-Discussion

a. See Figure 1 below.

FIGURE 1

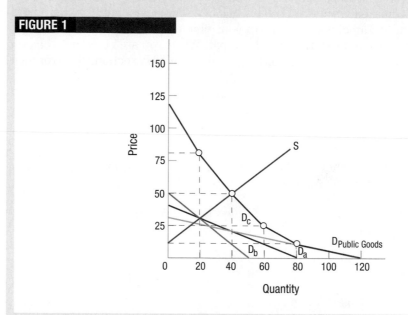

b. Putting together the market demand curve for public goods is a little more challenging than doing the same for normal goods and services. Since all parties get enjoyment from the public good, we essentially need to select a quantity and see how much each person is willing to pay. The three demand curves D_a, D_b, and D_c, correspond to the demands for individuals a, b, and c. Thus, we are adding the prices they are willing to pay for each quantity. So, for a quantity of 40, person a is willing to pay $20, b is willing to pay $10, and c is willing to pay $20, for a total of $50. This corresponds to the price of $50 when quantity is 40 units.

c. Given the supply curve in the table, and the market demand shown in Figure 1, equilibrium is 40 units at $50 total payments.

Solved Problem: Positive and Negative Externalities

Using the table below, showing the private demand (without externalities) for a product, answer the questions that follow.

(1) Private Supply	(2) Private Demand	(3) Price	(4) Social Supply Price	(5) Social Demand Price
120	0	30	___	___
100	20	25	___	___
80	40	20	___	___
60	60	15	___	___
40	80	10	___	___
20	100	5	___	___
0	120	0	___	___

a. In the blank grid below plot the private demand and supply curves. Show equilibrium price and quantity and label the equilibrium point *e*. What is equilibrium price and output without externalities?

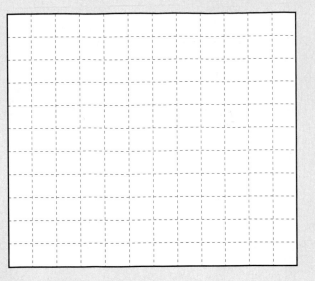

b. Now assume that for each price and output supplied privately, external *costs* are equal to 20% of the per unit price. List the supply price that includes social costs in the fourth column. Graph the social supply curve and label it S_S. Label the new equilibrium point *a*. What is the new price and output where this product sells for its full cost, including external cost?

c. Now, beginning again with the original private supplies and demands, assume this product is education that has external benefits equal to $5 a unit. List the demand price that includes social demand in column 5. Plot the new social demand curve and label it D_S. Label the new equilibrium point *b*. What is the level of education that is socially optimal? What is the level of subsidy that society needs to provide to education to ensure that the socially optimal level of education is provided?

Solution-Discussion

a. See Figure 2. Private equilibrium price is $15, and output is 60 units.

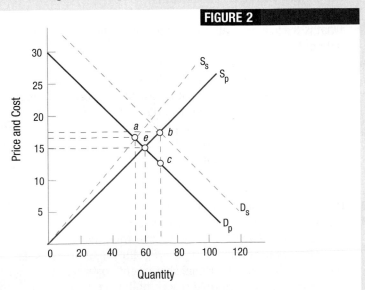

FIGURE 2

b. See the completed table below. Notice that the price in column 4 is 20% greater than the private price shown in column 3. This added price (cost) represents the external costs imposed by the production of this product. The new S_S curve is shown in Figure 2. The new equilibrium price is around $16.50, and the new output level is 53. Making a product pay its full costs, including any negative external costs, will result in a higher price and lower output.

(1) Private Supply	(2) Private Demand	(3) Price	(4) Social Supply Price	(5) Social Demand Price
120	0	30	36	35
100	20	25	30	30
80	40	20	24	25
60	60	15	18	20
40	80	10	12	15
20	100	5	6	10
0	120	0	0	5

c. See the table and Figure 2. The new social demand curve is labeled D_S in the figure. Seventy units of education are now socially optimal, and a $5 per unit subsidy that would shift the private supply curve to the right and pass through point *c* would be sufficient.

Environmental Policy

Frequently Asked Questions

Q: **What is government failure, and when does it occur?**

A: Government failures occur when the incentives of policymakers and bureaucrats do not coincide with the public interest. Government regulators are often captured by the industries they regulate, resulting in regulations that benefit the industry rather than consumers.

Q: **What is the intergenerational aspect of environmental issues, and how do policymakers determine this?**

A: When developing environmental policies, policymakers must consider and evaluate different possible futures. This intergenerational aspect of environmental issues requires a balancing of interests and complicates policymaking. The decisions made will depend on the discount rate chosen. The higher the discount rate, the lower the value we place on events farther into the future, which can result in significant burdens being placed on future generations. Conversely, if we select a low discount rate, the current generation may be overburdened in paying for benefits to be enjoyed by future generations.

Q: **Is the optimal pollution level zero?**

A: Some pollution is acceptable to society. Optimal pollution levels are found where marginal abatement costs equal the marginal benefits. These costs and benefits will vary for different types of pollution, industries, and regions of the country. Figure 3 graphs marginal abatement costs against a marginal damages curve; note that the optimal quantity of pollution is not zero.

Emissions level E_0 represents no abatement at all and at that level marginal damages are high, as shown by the MD curve. As abatement or cleanup occurs (moving left from E_0), marginal damages drop and marginal costs of cleaning up the pollution rise. At emissions level E_1, marginal damages still exceed costs ($b > a$), but once point e is reached, marginal damages and costs are equal. If additional abatement is required, say to E_2, costs greatly exceed the benefits ($d > c$), and we are wasting society's resources. As a result, some pollution (E_e) will typically be socially optimal.

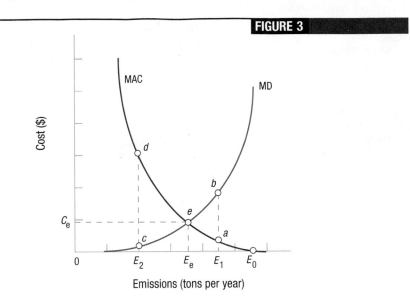

FIGURE 3

Q: **What has been the standard approach to environmental policy in the United States?**

A: Environmental policy in the United States has largely been based on command and control. Command and control policies set standards for polluters—acceptable levels of effluents, for instance—which are systematically enforced through inspections and reports. Another option, though rarely used, is to enact effluent taxes that lead to optimal pollution levels. This is the approach that has been recommended to tackle global climate change; get acceptable levels of carbon dioxide emissions and use marketable permits.

Q: **What are market-based policies, and how do they work?**

A: More recently, market-based policies have been recognized as being more efficient than many command and control policies. First, the government determines a permissible pollution level (ideally, near the optimal level); then, firms are allocated permits to pollute, which they may buy, sell, and trade. Pollution is then limited to this permissible level, and the price of permits adjusts to the costs of abatement.

Key Point to Remember

The optimal level of pollution will not be zero except in extreme cases of highly toxic substances. Some level of pollution, determined where marginal benefits equal marginal costs, will be acceptable to society. In the past, environment protection was based heavily on command and control policies (regulations and prohibitions), but today there is a movement to more market-based solutions that typically lead to better results at lower costs.

Environmental Policy Quick Check

Circle the Correct Answer

1. (T/F) Government failure occurs when the incentives of politicians and government bureaucrats do not coincide with the public interest.
2. (T/F) If policymakers use a low discount rate when setting environmental policies, future generations will bear most of the costs of these policies.
3. (T/F) Government failure occurs when the market does not provide the socially optimal amount of a good at the socially optimal price.
4. (T/F) If marginal abatement costs are higher than the marginal damage caused by pollution, society would be better off with some pollution, not zero pollution.
5. When would a pollution tax be likely to achieve pollution-reduction goals more efficiently than command and control policies?
   a. when the type of pollution is water pollution
   b. when firms have different abatement costs
   c. when abatement costs are low
   d. when abatement costs are high
6. In a marketable permits system for reducing pollution, the government
   a. sets the price of each permit.
   b. forbids anyone except polluters from holding the permits.
   c. calculates marginal abatement costs.
   d. sets a maximum quantity of pollution and issues permits granting the "right" to pollute a certain amount.

7. A regulatory body that requires local factories to limit their discharges into nearby rivers to a specific level is an example of what kind of regulatory policy?
   a. marginal abatement cost
   b. command and control
   c. abatement taxes
   d. marketable permits
8. Which one of the following is *not* true for a command and control environmental policy?
   a. It was favored by policymakers before the 1990s.
   b. It usually sets standards of conduct that are enforced by the legal or regulatory system.
   c. It often uses abatement taxes.
   d. Standards treat all firms in an industry the same.
9. Which of the following is *not* a market-based environmental policy?
   a. plastic-bottle refund systems
   b. rules for usable technologies
   c. tradable permits
   d. user charges for water and wastewater management
10. One benefit of marketable permits is that regulators
    a. do not have to determine marginal abatement costs.
    b. can set any price they want for the permits.
    c. can restrict permit holding to the polluters only.
    d. can restrict the technologies used for pollution control.

Score: ____

Answers: 1. T; 2. F; 3. F; 4. T; 5. b; 6. d; 7. b; 8. c; 9. b; 10. a

If You Got 9 or 10 Correct

You have done well on a difficult area of analysis. Keeping the curves straight in this section is a difficult chore. The reward, of course, is that you have a good grasp of the general types of environmental policies used to combat market failures in the environment. Go on and review the "Hints, Tips, and Reminders."

If You Didn't Get at Least 9 Correct

Review the material slowly. The graphs and concepts in this section are difficult, so spend a little extra time to make sure you understand the following:

- Government failure can happen just like market failure. When bureaucratic goals are not aligned with society's interests, governments can make a mess of the environment.
- The balancing of interests between generations adds significant complexity to environmental policies. Policymakers and politicians must consider the interests of not only their children and grandchildren but also the grandchildren of their great grandchildren. This is especially a factor with an issue like climate change that takes a long time to develop. Economists use discount rates to balance these types of interests. If too high a discount rate is chosen, future generations will

bear an unconscionable burden. If too low a rate is selected, the current generation will sacrifice much, and many in the future will reap the benefits. There is no absolutely correct solution to this problem.

■ Optimal pollution levels are not zero! Policymakers should adjust policies to the point where *marginal* abatement costs are just equal to *marginal* benefits from pollution abatement. Review the discussion surrounding Figure 3 and make sure you understand the reasoning.

■ Policies to reduce pollution fall into two broad categories: command and control and market-based policies. With command and control policies, policymakers set standards (like the 2004 ozone air quality standards set for most metropolitan areas), and local and regional governments must develop plans and policies to meet these requirements over the next decade. Market-based policies use effluent charges, taxes, deposit-refund systems, and tradable permits to reach similar results, typically at lower costs and faster. These approaches often give firms and industries additional incentives to develop and implement the most technically efficient means of reducing pollution.

■ Market-based policies have the advantage of encouraging an industry to meet the goals of pollution reduction at the lowest cost. When taxes are used to encourage pollution reduction, the costs associated with paying taxes on effluents encourage firms and industries to find additional ways to reduce pollution and thus avoid paying the taxes.

■ The idea of tradable permits is not new. It took a long time for policymakers, environmentalists, and the public to accept the idea. Giving corporations the right to pollute went against the grain. Several successful pilot projects, however, changed many minds, and permits are now part of the standard arsenal for policymakers. Market demand and supply adjust to set the price for the allowable pollution permitted. In most instances where permits have been used, the eventual price of permits has been lower than forecasted, suggesting that cleanup costs were less than expected. Marketable permits (based on allowable CO_2 emissions) are the chief mechanisms being used today by Europe to implement the Kyoto accords. In the United States, carbon-trading markets are developing, and California recently introduced mandatory carbon limits (with permit trading) for its power and other industries.

To make sure you have a good handle on these issues, go back to the text and make sure you know the difference between market-based policies and command and control policies. Then take some time to read the "Hints, Tips, and Reminders" below. ■

Consider These Hints, Tips, and Reminders   STEP 4

1. Economists use the terms *externality* and *spillover* synonymously. Negative externalities (e.g., pollution) involve added costs in excess of market prices; hence they are called "spillover costs." Positive externalities (education and vaccinations) involve added benefits to society; hence the name "spillover benefits."

2. When analyzing negative externalities or spillover costs, the focus is on costs, so we use the supply curve; supply involves costs of production. Negative externalities impose higher costs on society, and this is shown by a social supply curve with higher costs. Positive externalities or spillover benefits confer added benefit to society that can be shown by a greater demand for the good or service.

3. Don't let the concept of public goods throw you for a loop. Admittedly, they are a little complex, but keep public goods like national defense and lighthouses in mind when you're faced with a public good problem. My consumption of military protection or the lighthouse's warning does not reduce its value to you (the nonrival characteristic), and once these are provided, no one can be excluded from their protection (the nonexcludability characteristic). Private markets do not provide these products because the public would not be willing to pay (voluntarily) for such services or would pay too little.

4. The fact that the optimal level of pollution is not zero may come as a shock, but it is just a straightforward application of "thinking at the margin" that has been consistently applied throughout this course. No one (neither society nor individuals) wants to spend $100 to get a $5 benefit. That is wasting society's limited resources.

Do the Homework for Chapter 13
Public Goods, Common Resources, and Externalities

Instructor _____ Time _____ Student _____

Use the answer key below to record your answers to these homework questions.

1. (a) (b) (c) (d)   6. (a) (b) (c) (d)   11. (a) (b) (c) (d)   16. (a) (b) (c) (d)
2. (a) (b) (c) (d)   7. (a) (b) (c) (d)   12. (a) (b) (c) (d)   17. (a) (b) (c) (d)
3. (a) (b) (c) (d)   8. (a) (b) (c) (d)   13. (a) (b) (c) (d)   18. (a) (b) (c) (d)
4. (a) (b) (c) (d)   9. (a) (b) (c) (d)   14. (a) (b) (c) (d)   19. (a) (b) (c) (d)
5. (a) (b) (c) (d)   10. (a) (b) (c) (d)   15. (a) (b) (c) (d)   20. (a) (b) (c) (d)

1. Market failure
   a. occurs, for example, when companies fail to provide enough beef to the market, so prices rise.
   b. occurs, for example, when government fails to regulate the market sufficiently such that not enough output is forthcoming.
   c. occurs only in capitalist economies.
   d. can be caused by externalities associated with the production or consumption of some particular good.

2. Public goods are
   a. rival in consumption.
   b. goods where some consumers can be excluded.
   c. goods like public television.
   d. both rival in consumption, and some consumers can be excluded from enjoying the benefits of the goods.

3. Which of the following is *not* a public good?
   a. a lighthouse
   b. National Public Radio
   c. national defense
   d. military aircraft

4. Negative externalities are
   a. the result of a private exchange that imposes costs on others.
   b. the result of product prices being too high for low-income consumers.
   c. the benefits society gets from students in college.
   d. the negative aspects of international trade and outsourcing.

5. Which of the following is *not* a negative externality?
   a. air pollution
   b. high oil prices
   c. clear-cutting in forests
   d. litter

6. Which of the following is a positive externality?
   a. air pollution
   b. honey bees next to an apple orchard
   c. clear-cutting in forests
   d. litter

7. Negative externalities
   a. lead to too little production at market prices that are too high.
   b. are the same as the tragedy of the commons.
   c. lead to too much production at market prices that are too low.
   d. are both nonrival in consumption and nonexclusive once the good is provided.

8. Positive externalities
   a. lead to too little production at market prices that are too high.
   b. are the same as the tragedy of the commons.
   c. lead to too much production at market prices that are too low.
   d. are both nonrival in consumption and nonexclusive once the good is provided.

9. Which of the following goods generates substantial positive externalities?
   a. four-wheeling in the backcountry
   b. eating at McDonald's
   c. getting a college education
   d. traveling to China

10. Common property resources
    a. face a major problem in that they generate negative externalities.
    b. benefit society and therefore are used at optimal levels.
    c. are often overexploited.
    d. cost so much to exploit that Congress has to step in.

11. If a good exhibits both nonrivalry and nonexcludability, it is
    a. a valuable resource that must be conserved.
    b. a common property resource.
    c. a purely private good.
    d. a public good.

12. Which of the following is a public good?
    a. a van that holds 14 people
    b. Yellowstone National Park
    c. cable television
    d. national defense

13. The Coase theorem suggests that
    a. air pollution is not a serious problem if only the government would allow bargaining between the parties involved.
    b. regulating pollution is the only workable solution to reducing pollution.
    c. where bargaining costs are small, the resulting agreements between polluters and victims will be efficient, no matter which party is allocated the rights.
    d. where bargaining costs are small, the resulting agreements between polluters and victims will be efficient, no matter which party is allocated the rights; and more importantly, the distribution of benefits or income will be the same.

14. Government failure often results from
    a. taxing the rich less than the poor.
    b. public policymakers' incentives not always being consistent with the public interest.

    c. too much money chasing too few goods.
    d. politicians discounting future results with too low an interest rate.

15. When policymakers make policy today that affects generations into the future, the use of a very low discount rate means that
    a. policymakers will take the benefits of future generations not yet born into consideration, and will be less likely to use debt today to finance programs that benefit mostly the present generation.
    b. policymakers will be more likely to go into debt today to fund benefits to the present generation.
    c. policies that benefit the present generation will have been paid for by a previous generation.
    d. politicians and policymakers will entirely finance any programs with user fees.

16. The optimal level of pollution
    a. is equal to zero for society.
    b. is that level at which total costs of pollution are minimal.
    c. is that level at which marginal abatement costs equal marginal benefits.
    d. is that level at which total benefits from pollution abatement are maximized.

17. An environmental policy in which the government sets levels, then determines the most efficient policies, sets those rules, and enforces them through regulation
    a. is the best approach to take to solve complex environmental issues.
    b. is a market-based policy.
    c. has historically not been typical of environmental regulation.
    d. is a command and control policy.

18. Setting air quality standards is an example of
    a. market-based policy.
    b. abatement tax.
    c. tradable permit.
    d. command and control policy.

19. One of the arguments against market-based environmental policies is that
    a. they are too efficient.
    b. using market forces to solve a problem created by markets seems inconsistent.
    c. market-based policies can only be used on a tiny fraction of environmental problems.
    d. market-based polices have been shown to not work.

20. The optimal level of pollution is not zero because
    a. policymakers cannot get their act together.
    b. trees need carbon dioxide to survive.
    c. the costs to society would be too high.
    d. government environmental budgets are too low.

Use the ExamPrep to Get Ready for Exams

This sheet (front and back) is designed to help you prepare for your exams. The chapter has been boiled down to its key concepts. You are asked to answer questions, define terms, draw graphs, and, if you wish, add summaries of class notes.

Market Failures

Producer and Consumer Surplus

Define producer and consumer surplus and illustrate both in the grid at right:

Public Goods

Describe the two major aspects of public goods:
Nonrivalry:

Nonexcludability:

Why will the market fail to provide these goods?

Externalities

Describe and provide examples of the following:
Negative externalities:

Positive externalities:

Both producers and consumers produce externalities. Complete the table below by providing examples of these externalities. (*Note:* Examples can be of either positive or negative externalities.)

Origin of Externality	Impact	Victims and Beneficiaries of Externality
	Consumers	Producers
Consumers		
Producers		

Use the grid below to diagram the impact of negative externalities. Begin with the private market supply and demand curves labeled S_P and D_P with equilibrium at point e, equilibrium price at P_e, and equilibrium quantity at Q_e.

- Draw the new supply cure S_1 that includes the full cost to clean the negative externalities. Label the new equilibrium point a; the new price, P_1; and output, Q_1.
- Show why consumer and producer surplus is larger when output is Q_1 rather than Q_e. (*Hint:* Look back at the analysis of Figure 4 in the text.)
- Under what conditions would society want to prohibit the production of some product?
- Why might monopolies mitigate the effects of negative externalities?
- Describe the case for subsidizing the production of those products that have positive externalities. Give some examples of products that are subsidized and some that should be subsidized.

The Coase Theorem

Describe the Coase theorem and its implications for public policy:

Common Property Resources

Describe the "tragedy of the commons":

What are some of the solutions to these types of problems?

Environmental Policy

Describe government failure:

Socially Efficient Levels of Pollution

Why are some levels of pollution efficient?

Environmental Policies

List and describe the two most common types of environmental policies:

Describe how tradable permits work and why they are often highly effective:

Additional Study Help Chapterwide Practice Questions

Matching

Match the description with the corresponding term.

___ 1. Consumer surplus
___ 2. Producer surplus
___ 3. Market failure
___ 4. Public goods
___ 5. Externalities
___ 6. The Coase theorem
___ 7. Common property resources
___ 8. Government failure
___ 9. Command and control policies
___ 10. Marketable permits

a. Environmental policies that set limits on pollution; all firms must comply with these standards.
b. The difference between what people are willing to pay for a product and what they actually pay for it.
c. Occurs when markets do not provide the socially optimal output at the socially optimal price. Either too much or too little of the good is produced, or it is offered at too high or too low a price.
d. The difference between the revenues firms earn from a product and the costs they would be willing to bear to supply it.
e. Goods that exhibit both nonrivalry and nonexcludability.
f. Occurs when government policies fail to bring about optimal resource allocation.
g. Owned by the community rather than subject to individual property rights.
h. Spillovers that arise when two parties engage in a transaction, and some third party uninvolved in the transaction either benefits or is harmed.
i. They grant firms the right to generate pollution and can be bought, sold, or exchanged.
j. Suggests that if externalities are present and transaction costs are small, the market output will be socially optimal no matter whether polluters are given the right to pollute or victims are given the right to be free of pollution.

Fill-In

Circle the word(s) in parentheses that complete the sentence.

1. When producers are able to sell their output for a market price exceeding what they would have been willing to sell the output for, economists refer to this as (consumer surplus, producer surplus, market failure) _____. When markets involve externalities and provide too much output at too low a price, economists call this (consumer surplus, producer surplus, market failure) _____, and when buyers get products for prices that are lower than they would be willing to pay, this is referred to as (consumer surplus, producer surplus, market failure) _____.

2. An oatmeal cookie is a good that is both (rival, nonrival) _____ and (exclusive, nonexclusive) _____ in consumption, whereas Lake Powell in Utah is both (rival, nonrival) _____ and (exclusive, nonexclusive) _____. Public television (PBS) and radio (NPR) are examples of services that are both (rival, nonrival) _____ and (exclusive, nonexclusive) _____.

3. Spillover benefits result in too (little, much) _____ of a good produced at too (high, low) a price; spillover costs lead to too (little, much) _____ production and the resulting output sold at too (high, low) _____ a price.

4. When policymakers are considering policies that have benefits over a long time horizon and their cost-benefit calculations use a low discount rate, they will be (more, less) _____ likely to approve the project.

5. The federal government's approach to reducing pollution from the tail pipes of automobiles has typically been from a (command and control, market-based) _____ perspective, whereas the world's approach to reducing carbon emissions to combat global warming has relied on a (command and control, market-based) _____ perspective.

True-False

Circle the correct answer.

_T/F_ 1. Producer surplus is equal to the price consumers are willing to pay for a product minus the price they actually pay for it.

_T/F_ 2. Total social welfare is equal to consumer surplus plus producer surplus.

_T/F_   3. If firms supply a product to the market at the socially optimal quantity and price, there will be no consumer surplus.

_T/F_   4. Nonrivalry means that once a good has been provided, it is not feasible to exclude some consumers from using it.

_T/F_   5. Spillover costs arise when two parties engage in a transaction, and another party unrelated to the transaction is harmed by it.

_T/F_   6. The Coase theorem suggests that private negotiations over polluting rights will produce efficient results only if these rights are initially distributed evenly among potential polluters.

_T/F_   7. Monopoly production levels may be more socially desirable from an environmental standpoint than competitive levels, though not necessarily.

_T/F_   8. Providing government subsidies for higher education will be both economically efficient and socially equitable if higher education results in positive externalities.

_T/F_   9. If a resource is nonrenewable, this means the current stock of it available for use can never be increased.

_T/F_   10. If policymakers use a high discount rate when setting environmental policies, future generations will bear most of the costs of these policies.

_T/F_   11. For most pollutants, the socially efficient level of pollution is zero.

_T/F_   12. Abatement costs are the costs to society resulting from a certain level of pollution.

_T/F_   13. When various firms have different abatement costs, a pollution tax is likely to achieve pollution reduction goals more efficiently than command and control policies.

_T/F_   14. Marketable permits for pollution have been around in theory since the 1960s, but they were rarely used before the 1990s.

_T/F_   15. One problem with marketable permits is that regulators must be able to determine marginal abatement costs precisely to sell the permits at a price that will achieve the desired results.

Multiple Choice

Circle the correct answer.

1. Consumer surplus is
   a. the difference between the revenues firms earn from a product and the costs they would be willing to bear to supply it.
   b. the number of consumers who want to buy a product but are unable to because supplies have run out.
   c. the difference between what people are prepared to pay for a product and market price.
   d. the excess inventories consumers can purchase at sale prices when supply exceeds demand.

2. Producer surplus is
   a. the difference between market price and the costs firms would be willing to bear to supply it.
   b. the firms in a market that cannot profitably stay in business because the market is overloaded.
   c. the difference between what people are prepared to pay for a product and market price.
   d. the excess inventories producers are left with when supply exceeds demand.

3. Total social welfare is measured as
   a. pollution costs plus abatement costs.
   b. consumer surplus plus producer surplus.
   c. positive externalities minus negative externalities.
   d. abatement costs minus pollution costs.

4. In Figure MC-1, what area represents total social welfare?
   a. $0P_eeQ_e$ c. $0P_0eQ_e$
   b. P_0P_ee d. P_0P_1e

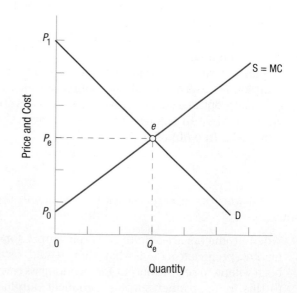

MC-1

5. Which of the following exhibits both nonrivalry and nonexcludability?
   a. positive externalities
   b. public goods
   c. common property resources
   d. negative externalities

6. Which of the following goods exhibits nonrivalry?
   a. candy bars
   b. seats at a ball game
   c. laptop computers
   d. cable or satellite television service

7. Which of the following is *not* a public good?
   a. network television broadcasts
   b. radio transmissions
   c. cable or satellite television transmissions
   d. national defense

8. Which of the following is an example of a spillover cost?
   a. fish being killed by a power plant dumping hot water into a stream
   b. a fishing population being depleted by overfishing
   c. a stream's fish population being revived when farmers living along the stream take erosion control measures
   d. a government-imposed moratorium on fishing in certain waters

9. When pollution rights are privately negotiated, according to the Coase theorem, what condition must be met for the socially optimal allocation of resources to be brought about?
   a. The initial distribution of pollution rights must be equitable.
   b. Transaction costs must be minimal.
   c. Command and control policies must be instituted to ensure that the proper transactions are made.
   d. A large number of parties must be involved in the transactions.

10. When building a dam expands the wetland habitat housing a previously endangered species of bird, this new wetland is an example of a
    a. positive externality.
    b. public good.
    c. common property resource.
    d. negative externality.

11. To what does the "tragedy of the commons" refer?
    a. negative externalities
    b. the failure of a community to provide public goods
    c. the overexploitation of common property resources
    d. positive externalities

12. Which of the following practices, common in the developing world, is an example of the overexploitation of common property resources?
    a. farmers clearing their own lands using slash and burn methods
    b. unfiltered factory emissions polluting the air
    c. untreated sewage being released into rivers
    d. deforestation of public lands by villagers in need of firewood

Figure MC-2 shows negative externalities in a market. Use this figure to answer Question 13.

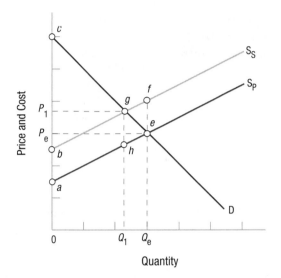

MC-2

13. At output Q_e, social welfare is given by
    a. area *ace* minus area *egf*.
    b. area P_1cg.
    c. area *bcg* minus area *egf*.
    d. area *bcg* minus area *abgh*.

14. Which of the following natural resources is exhaustible, yet capable of renewal?
    a. natural gas
    b. trees
    c. wind energy
    d. gold

15. Government failure results from which of the following?
    a. Government regulators gather large quantities of relevant information on which to base their decisions.
    b. The market does not provide the socially optimal amount of a good at the socially optimal price.
    c. Policymakers are unable to get sufficient information to make good policy.
    d. Economists are allowed to voice an opinion on matters of environmental regulation.

16. A law that requires all power plants to limit their CO_2 emissions to certain specified levels is an example of what sort of environmental policy?
    a. command and control
    b. market-based
    c. tradable permits
    d. charges/taxes

17. In a marketable permits system for reducing pollution, the initial distribution of permits affects
    a. the ability of the system to meet the pollution reduction targets.
    b. the efficiency with which the pollution reduction targets can be met.
    c. the distribution of income among participants in the system.
    d. the market price at which permits eventually come to be bought and sold.

18. In what area of pollution control have marketable permits been most successful to date?
    a. toxic waste
    b. sulfur dioxide emissions that create acid rain
    c. recyclable products
    d. solid wastes

19. Prior to the 1990s, what types of environment policies were most favored by policymakers, both in this country and abroad?
    a. command and control policies
    b. marketable permit systems
    c. taxes and charges on effluents
    d. subsidies for pollution reduction

20. In Figure MC-3 if emissions were at quantity E_1, society would

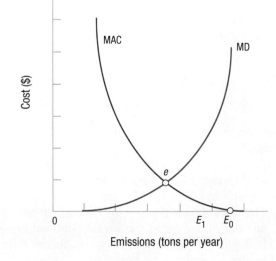

MC-3

a. reduce emissions until they are zero.
b. reduce emissions because the marginal benefit of abatement is greater than its marginal cost.
c. do nothing, because this level is optimal.
d. increase emissions to E_0, because optimal pollution is never zero.

Essay-Problem

Answer in the space provided.

The questions below are designed to extend the concepts from the chapter. Use the suggested answers as a way to assess your progress and extend your ability to use this analysis to better understand environmental economics and policy.

1. What is the essence of market failure?

2. Must government always step in when there is market failure?

3. Pollution from automobiles rises when people are stuck in traffic jams during rush hour. Some local authorities have proposed two bridge toll rates, a higher rate for rush hour and a lower rate for non-rush-hour times (remember our discussion of price discrimination in Chapter 9, "Monopoly"?). Will this two-tier toll structure have any effect on pollution levels?

4. To deal with the "tragedy of the commons" ocean-fishing problem, why doesn't the United States simply restrict the amount of fish each boat can bring into U.S. fish markets at the end of each day?

5. What is a common argument for market-based environmental policies as opposed to command and control policies?

6. National Park rangers at the Grand Canyon have determined that the current level of tourists visiting the park in the summer is causing damage to the canyon because the air quality is being hurt by automobile exhaust. Devise a command and control policy to deal with this. Devise a market policy.

7. What is a common way to deal with "the tragedy of the commons" as concerns local fishing in nearby rivers?

8. The Blue Ridge Mountain Parkway and Skyline Drive in Virginia offer some breathtaking views of the valleys below. The National Park Service charges usage fees that are very low. Why can the 35-mile-per-hour speed limit be seen as a nonmonetary pollution control policy?

9. The federal government uses a command and control policy to deal with pollution caused by automobile emissions. It divides autos into classes, then sets standards for each class. SUVs were placed in the light truck category because they were seen originally as off-the-road vehicles. Light trucks have lower standards than autos—they are allowed to emit more pollution than autos, generally. But with the overwhelming majority of SUVs used as primary vehicles, some critics have said that this categorization has led to unnecessary additional pollution. Construct an argument for leaving SUVs as part of the light truck category. Then construct an argument for placing SUVs in the standard auto category.

10. Are the costs from rent-seeking behavior likely to be higher with command and control environmental policies than with market-based policies such as tradable pollution permits?

What's Next

You now have seen how economic analysis can be used to understand environmental problems. We used the concepts of consumer surplus and market failure, and looked at possible government responses to market failure. In the next chapter, we look at income and wealth distribution and discuss whether it makes sense to think of income disparities in terms of market failure or not.

Answers to Chapterwide Practice Questions

Matching

1. b	4. e	7. g	10. i
2. d	5. h	8. f	
3. c	6. j	9. a	

Fill-In

1. producer surplus, market failure, consumer surplus
2. rival, exclusive, nonrival, exclusive, nonrival, nonexclusive
3. little, high, much, low
4. more
5. command and control, market-based

True-False

1. F	5. T	9. F	13. T
2. T	6. F	10. T	14. T
3. F	7. T	11. F	15. F
4. F	8. T	12. F	

Multiple Choice

1. c	6. d	11. c	16. a
2. a	7. c	12. d	17. c
3. b	8. a	13. c	18. b
4. d	9. b	14. b	19. a
5. b	10. a	15. c	20. b

Essay-Problem

1. There are situations when markets as institutions as they are currently constituted do not provide the socially optimal quantity of a product at a socially optimal price. Three types of market failures were discussed in this chapter: public goods, externalities, and common property resources.

2. No. There are costs to government activity. The benefit from alleviating the damage from the market failure may not surpass the cost of government intervention. This is why local governments usually do not get involved with small companies that have low levels of pollution. And remember, as the analysis by Coase suggests, when transactions costs are low and the number of individuals involved is small, simple bargaining or legal recourse may be sufficient.

3. It should affect pollution levels by giving incentives to drivers to avoid the bridges at rush hour or seek alternative ways, and in this way it will reduce traffic jams and thus reduce pollution, because pollution climbs when cars are stuck in traffic. It is not popular, however, with those who think they are stuck with driving at a certain time and on a certain route. This is equivalent to peak load pricing and price discrimination, where prices at peak time are higher. Theaters charge higher prices for movies at night, and some utilities charge higher prices when power demands are typically higher (early morning and early evening).

4. The fishing problem is international in scope. Restricting local fishing boats will do little to solve the problem because it will have no effect on international fishing boats that prowl international waters. The "tragedy of the commons" results from the fact that no one person or group has any incentive to fish sensibly as long as others do not have to and do not.

5. Cost. Continual regulation can be expensive, and regulators can be captured by the interests they are supposed to control (government failure). Administration costs of market-based policies can be comparatively low compared to command and control policies. Also, market-based policies and the price of permits give those who value a cleaner environment the easy ability to purchase permits to reduce pollution beyond levels originally set by government.

6. A command and control policy would limit the number of tourists who could visit, or limit the number of tourists in automobiles, or restrict automobiles from areas close to the

canyon. Electric-powered buses could be used to transport tourists to the canyon. Similar restrictions on helicopter flights into the canyon have already been proposed to reduce noise pollution and make descending into the canyon a more enjoyable experience. A market-based policy would raise user fees for those tourists with automobiles, or charge higher prices the closer one drove to the canyon itself.

7. Localities deal with the common property rights problem by requiring permits to fish and restricting permit holders to a certain number of fish of a certain size. Localities can still miscalculate, but they are tied in to a state's animal husbandry program.

8. It can be seen as a nonmonetary pollution control policy in two ways. First, if automobiles give off less pollution going 35 miles per hour than at higher speeds, the lower speed limit will have an immediate effect on the pollution level. Second, for those who want to see the vistas but are in a hurry, the 35-mile-per-hour speed limit will tend to push them to leave after a comparatively short period of time, again lowering potential pollution. The parkway is full of curves, so the lower speed limit may be justified for this reason alone, but the lower limit would seem to have positive externalities as well.

9. Leave SUVs as light trucks: Many of the large SUV engines are similar to light truck engines, not standard family autos, so the costs of pollution abatement are higher for SUVs than family autos; it is not fair to put a higher burden on SUV owners than family auto owners.

   Place SUVs in the family auto category: Many of the SUVs use family car engines, not light truck engines. The Toyota Rav4 uses a Camry engine, not some special light truck engine. Therefore, the SUVs should be treated as if they were family autos. Furthermore, if they were so treated, this would be an incentive for auto manufacturers to develop technology to cut back on SUV pollution because SUVs are very profitable for auto makers.

10. The costs of rent-seeking behavior are likely to be higher with command and control policies because regulators, if they are the ones to set and enforce the policies, will need to meet on a continual basis. Government bodies that establish the permits might be lobbied heavily, but once the permits are established, it is much easier for government to resist the call for additional permits and go into regulatory hibernation.

Poverty and Income Distribution

14

Why Do Some People Make More Money Than Others? Is Poverty Inevitable?

Some people are fabulously rich and spend money extravagantly. Other people are poor, sometimes desperately poor. Why are income and wealth distributed the way they are? Should we redistribute them? Or just help those on the bottom of the income ladder? And when we look at those on the bottom, can we determine the causes of poverty? Will poverty ever be eradicated? These are the types of issues covered in this chapter on income distribution and poverty. Economic analysis can help us formulate some answers to these questions.

After studying this chapter you should be able to

- Describe the difference between wealth and income.

- Describe the effects of life cycles on income.

- Analyze functional, personal, and family income distributions.

- Use a Lorenz curve and Gini coefficient to graphically depict the distribution of wealth and income.

- Describe the impact of income redistribution efforts.

- Describe the causes of income inequality.

- Describe the means for determining poverty thresholds.

- Describe the two measures for determining depth of poverty for families.

- Describe the prevailing theories on how to deal with poverty and income inequality.

Review the Key Terms

Income: A flow measure reflecting the funds received by individuals or households over a period of time, usually a week, month, or year.

Wealth: A stock measure of an individual's or family's assets net of liabilities at a given point in time.

Functional distribution of income: The distribution of income for resources or factors of production (land, labor, capital, and entrepreneurial ability).

Personal or family distribution of income: The distribution of income to individuals or family groups (typically quintiles or fifths of the population).

Lorenz curve: A graphical method of showing the income distribution by cumulating families of various income levels on the horizontal axis and relating this to their cumulative share of total income on the vertical axis.

Gini coefficient: A precise method of measuring the position of the Lorenz curve as the area between the Lorenz curve and the equal distribution line divided by the total area below the equal distribution line.

Poverty thresholds: Income levels for various household sizes below which these people are considered living in poverty.

Income deficit: The difference between the poverty threshold and a family's income.

Ratio of income to poverty: The ratio of family income to the poverty threshold. Families with ratios below 0.5 are considered severely poor, families with ratios between 0.5 and 1.0 are considered poor, and those families with ratios between 1.0 and 1.25 are considered near poor.

Work Through the Chapter Tutorials

The Distribution of Income and Wealth

Frequently Asked Questions

Q: **What is the difference between income and wealth?**
A: Income is a flow; it measures the receipts of funds by individuals or households over time. Wealth is a stock; it measures a family's assets net of liabilities at a given point in time.

Q: **Why does income vary over the life cycle?**
A: Family and individual incomes vary significantly over the course of their life cycle. Young people just starting their careers and their families will usually have modest incomes. As people grow older and gain experience, their incomes usually rise, peaking between the ages of 45 and 55. Incomes then normally decline with retirement, as do family responsibilities.

Q: **What is the functional distribution of income?**
A: The functional distribution of income refers to the income distribution among inputs (factors of production). The share of national income going to labor has gradually risen since 1929; it is now fairly stable at around 70%. The remain-

der of the national income is divided among proprietor's income (small business profits), rent, corporate profits, and net interest.

Q: What is the personal distribution of income, and how is it calculated?

A: Personal or family income distribution refers to the percentage of income flowing to families in specific segments of the population. To analyze family income distribution, the U.S. Census Bureau arranges households in quintiles, or fifths, ranging from the 20% of households with the lowest incomes to the 20% with the highest. After totaling and averaging household incomes for each quintile, the Census Bureau computes the percentage of income flowing to each quintile. Since the 1970s, the income distribution in the United States has become more unequal.

Q: What are the primary methods for measuring inequality?

A: Economists have developed two primary methods for measuring inequality: Lorenz curves and Gini coefficients.

Q: What is a Lorenz curve?

A: Lorenz curves cumulate and plot the percent of people below various income levels on the horizontal axis, relating this to their share of income on the vertical axis. Perfectly equal distribution results in a Lorenz curve that bisects the axes, and deviations from this equal distribution curve indicate inequality. Figure 1 is a Lorenz curve for the United States in 2001, showing both income and wealth. Note that income is distributed much more evenly than wealth.

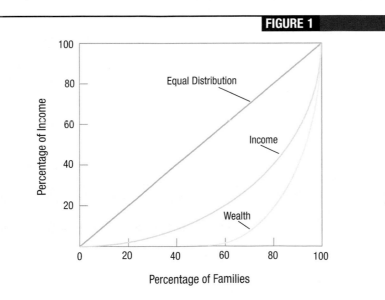

FIGURE 1

Q: What is the Gini coefficient?

A: The Gini coefficient is a precise method of measuring income inequality. The Gini coefficient is defined as the ratio of the area between the Lorenz curve and the equal distribution line in the numerator, and the total area below the equal distribution line in the denominator. When distribution is perfectly equal, the Gini coefficient is zero; when distribution is as unequal as possible, the coefficient rises to 1.0.

Q: How is income distribution affected by redistribution policies?

A: Income distribution is influenced by redistribution policies that include progressive taxes as well as cash and in-kind transfer payments. Redistribution policies are contentious. Those on the political left tend to push for greater redistribution of income and wealth, and those on the right argue that such policies are harmful to economic growth.

Q: **What causes income inequality in the United States?**

A: Income inequality in our society has many causes. Individuals and families invest in human capital to varying degrees, some placing a strong emphasis on education, and others failing to do so. Different education levels are a major factor determining inequalities in income and wealth. Economic discrimination can lead to an income distribution skewed against those suffering discrimination. The growth of two-earner households over the last three decades is a major reason for rising income inequality.

Keep in Mind

Incomes and wealth vary substantially over the life cycle of individuals and families. Lorenz curves and the Gini coefficient are the primary measures of inequality. Income inequality is related to levels of investment in human capital, economic discrimination, and most recently the growth of two-earner households.

The Distribution of Income and Wealth Quick Check

Circle the Correct Answer

1. (T/F) Income is a stock measure whereas wealth is a flow measure.
2. (T/F) Income tends to peak for most people between the ages of 35 and 45.
3. (T/F) American workers currently receive approximately 70% of the national income.
4. (T/F) A Gini coefficient of 1.0 indicates that distribution is perfectly equal.
5. Consider family income distribution from 1970 to 2001, shown in Table 2 in the text (it ignores taxes and transfers). Which group has increased its share of income in this time span?
   a. the lowest quintile
   b. the middle quintile
   c. the highest quintile
   d. the poor
6. The Gini coefficient, used to measure the inequality of income, is
   a. higher in the United States than in most European countries, meaning that income in Europe is more evenly distributed.
   b. lower in the United States than in Canada and Australia.
   c. around 0.111 in the United States, meaning that income is relatively unevenly distributed.
   d. above 2.0 in the United States.
7. Which of the following factors are *not* among the causes of economic inequality in the United States?
   a. living in or near a large city
   b. individuals and families making different investments in human capital

c. rising numbers of two-income households
d. economic discrimination

8. Which one of the following is *not* correct?
   a. A progressive income tax will tax higher incomes at a higher rate than lower incomes.
   b. Food stamps are a transfer payment.
   c. Progressive taxation does not affect income distribution.
   d. Adding transfer payments to the calculation makes income distribution more equal.
9. Which one of the following is *not* correct?
   a. The political left favors greater taxation of income and wealth.
   b. The political right sees income differences as the natural result of a market system.
   c. The political left has been more effective in the United States than in Europe in its redistribution efforts.
   d. The political right is relatively unconcerned about the distribution of income unless it becomes so unequal that it discourages incentives and reduces efficiency.
10. Which of the following factors is *not* among the causes of economic inequality in the United States?
   a. People have different natural abilities.
   b. People have different education levels.
   c. There have been a growing number of two-income households.
   d. Income is taxed at progressive rates.

Score: ____

If You Got 9 or 10 Correct

You have a good working knowledge of the concept of income distribution, how it is measured, and what can be done to change it. Go on to the next section, "Poverty."

If You Didn't Get at Least 9 Correct

Check and make sure you understand why you missed the questions you did. This is relatively easy material, and you probably need to pay a little closer attention. We are near the end of microeconomics, and you have been through much harder material. Pay special attention to the Lorenz curves material; it is the most difficult material in the section. Fortunately, the next section, "Poverty," really stands on its own.

If you had trouble with Lorenz curves, work through the solved problem below; it won't take long, and you will get a quick refresher on how they are constructed and interpreted. ▪

Solved Problem: Lorenz Curves

The table below lists the income distribution (by quintile) for the United States in 1950 and 2000, and for Brazil and Sweden in 2005. Using these data, construct Lorenz curves for each country and plot them in the blank grid provided.

Quintile	United States 1950		United States 2000		Brazil 2005		Sweden 2005	
	Fifth	Sum	Fifth	Sum	Fifth	Sum	Fifth	Sum
Lowest	4.6	_____	3.6	_____	2.5	_____	9.6	_____
Second	11.9	_____	8.9	_____	5.5	_____	14.5	_____
Middle	17.5	_____	14.9	_____	10.0	_____	18.2	_____
Fourth	23.6	_____	23.0	_____	18.2	_____	23.2	_____
Highest	42.4	_____	49.6	_____	63.8	_____	34.5	_____
Total	100.0	_____	100.0	_____	100.0	_____	100.0	_____

Solution-Discussion

Lorenz curves plot the cumulative sum of income on the vertical axis and the cumulative sum of families on the horizontal axis. The first thing you need to do is cumulate each quintile for each income distribution as shown in the table on the next page. Note that the table now has a sum column for each distribution.

The fifths of income are summed from the lowest to the highest. For example, in the U.S. 1950 distribution, the first sum for the lowest is just equal to that fifth's income or 4.6. For the second fifth, we sum the previous fifth (4.6) and the second fifth (11.9) to get 16.5, and so on, until the last fifth's sum equals 100.0.

| Quintile | United States 1950 | | United States 2000 | | Brazil 2005 | | Sweden 2005 | |
	Fifth	Sum	Fifth	Sum	Fifth	Sum	Fifth	Sum
Lowest	4.6	4.6	3.6	3.6	2.5	2.5	9.6	9.6
Second	11.9	16.5	8.9	12.5	5.5	8.0	14.5	24.1
Middle	17.5	34.0	14.9	27.4	10.0	18.0	18.2	42.8
Fourth	23.6	57.6	23.0	50.4	18.2	36.2	23.2	66.0
Highest	42.4	100	49.6	100	63.8	100	34.5	100
Total	100.0	—	100.0	—	100.0	—	100.0	—

Each of the four "Sum" columns are plotted in Figure 2 along with an equal distribution line.

FIGURE 2

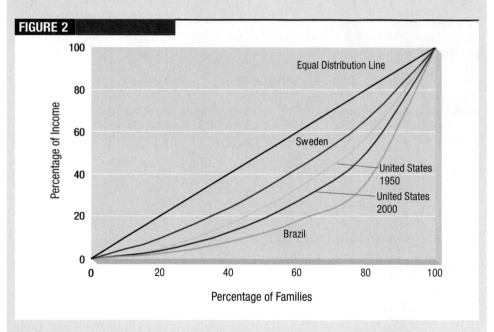

A quick glance at the figure makes it clear that Sweden has the most equal distribution, followed by the United States in the 1950s, then the United States in 2000, and followed by Brazil, the country with the most unequal distribution in income of the four shown. This is the benefit of Lorenz curves. A quick glance and you can tell which distributions are most equal.

Poverty

Frequently Asked Questions

Q: What is the poverty threshold, and how is it calculated?

A: The poverty threshold was first determined by the U.S. Department of Agriculture (USDA). Surveying the food-buying patterns of low-income households, the USDA used these data to estimate the cost of financing a nutritionally balanced diet. It then multiplied the cost of this food plan, adjusting for family size, by 3. The resulting dollar amount is the income threshold beneath which families are officially deemed to be living in poverty. When the Census Bureau calculates the official poverty rate, it counts as income all money income *before taxes,* including cash benefits, but does not include capital gains or noncash benefits such as public housing or food stamps.

Q: **How has the poverty rate changed since 1959?**

A: The poverty rate in the United States fell rapidly between 1959 and 1975, but it has remained roughly stable since then, fluctuating around 12–15%, following the business cycle. Over most of this period, the poverty rate for blacks and Hispanics was roughly twice the rate for whites.

Q: **What are the two major depth-of-poverty measures?**

A: Economists have developed two depth-of-poverty measures that describe the economic well-being of lower-income families: the income deficit and the ratio of income to poverty.

Q: **What is the income deficit?**

A: The income deficit measures how far below the poverty threshold a family's income lies. In 2001, the average income deficit for families living in poverty was just over $7,200.

Q: **What is the ratio of income to poverty, and what does it designate?**

A: The ratio of income to poverty compares family income to the poverty threshold and expresses this comparison as a ratio. The ratio for families with incomes equal to the poverty threshold will equal 1.0; the ratio for those living at half the threshold income will be 0.5. The Census Bureau considers people who live in families with ratios below 0.5 to be "severely or desperately poor," those between 0.5 and 1.0 to be "poor," and those with ratios above 1.0 but less than 1.25 to be "near poor." In 2001, nearly 5% of Americans lived in severely poor families.

Q: **What do experimental measures of poverty consider?**

A: Many researchers have criticized the Census Bureau's official method of determining poverty thresholds. In response, the Census Bureau has developed experimental measures that differ from the old in basing their estimates on after-tax income and counting as income such noncash benefits as food stamps and housing subsidies. Work-related expenses, such as transportation and child care, are deducted from income, as are out-of-pocket medical expenses. When these new measures were applied, poverty rates fell.

Q: **Is poverty a relative or absolute measure, and what are the policy implications of the answer?**

A: Poverty can be a relative or an absolute measure. The official measure of poverty in the United States is based on an absolute number, the poverty threshold. Some researchers, however, think a relative measure would be more useful, for instance, labeling the bottom 20% of American households "poor." Defined this way, poverty can never be eliminated.

Q: **How should we reduce poverty?**

A: The question of how to go about reducing poverty is controversial. The political left sees income and wealth redistribution as the main tool for curing poverty. They suggest expanding welfare-related programs and enhancing the progressivity of the tax system. Those on the right argue that such an approach is too expensive, and that it significantly reduces the incentives to work and produce, thereby reducing the economy's output. These people maintain that the best way to cure poverty is by implementing policies that increase the economic pie shared by all, not just by splitting the current pie more evenly.

Q: **What do current theories say about the possibility of a fair income distribution?**

A: There is no unified theory of income distribution that takes all issues into account, or that tells us what distribution is the fairest. Some contemporary philosophers have weighed in on this issue. John Rawls has argued that low inequality is the fairest, since this is what everyone would choose if they did not know where in the income distribution they would fall. Robert Nozick has replied that it is unfair to use the coercive power of the state to deprive people of their private property to redistribute it to others.

Keep in Mind

The poverty threshold varies by family size and is based on an estimate of a nutritionally balanced low-income food budget, then adjusted for inflation. Controversy surrounds the various methods for curing poverty. Some see income redistribution as the solution, while others argue that economic growth is the answer.

Poverty Quick Check

Circle the Correct Answer

1. (T/F) In general terms, the poverty threshold is defined as the cost of feeding a family a nutritionally balanced diet, multiplied by 3.
2. (T/F) The Census Bureau classifies a family with an income to poverty ratio of 0.70 as severely or desperately poor.
3. (T/F) A poor family's income deficit is the poverty threshold for a family of that size.
4. (T/F) Most of the families classified as poor do not have running water in their homes.
5. The Census Bureau has begun using an experimental measure of poverty that
   a. has virtually eliminated measured poverty.
   b. considers before-tax income.
   c. ignores noncash benefits such as food stamps and housing subsidies.
   d. counts work-related transportation costs.
6. Which one of the following is *not* correct?
   a. The political left sees income and wealth redistribution as the chief means of reducing poverty.
   b. The political right argues that welfare significantly reduces the incentive to work and produce.
   c. The political left believes the possibility of failure is a strong incentive to work and invest.
   d. The political right believes economic growth will alleviate much poverty.
7. Which of the following is correct concerning income distribution?
   a. John Rawls is right and Robert Nozick is wrong: Equity is more important than efficiency.
   b. Robert Nozick is right and John Rawls is wrong: Efficiency is more important than equity.

c. Neither is right nor wrong: There is a tradeoff between equity and efficiency.
   d. John Rawls is closer to the correct political policy because he uses the "maximin" principle.
8. When the Census Bureau began using its new, experimental measure of poverty,
   a. it ignored the effects of taxation.
   b. measured poverty rates generally fell.
   c. it simply took the poverty thresholds from 1963 and updated them for price changes.
   d. it treated cash and noncash benefits differently.
9. Rawls's "maximin" principle focuses on
   a. maximizing welfare for the minimum cost.
   b. maximizing poor people's share of income while minimizing the taxes they pay.
   c. maximizing the welfare of the least-well-off individuals.
   d. maximizing welfare for a minimum number of the poor.
10. Economic analysis
   a. helps us determine the fairest policies for reducing poverty and income inequality.
   b. helps us devise the most effective policies for reducing poverty and inequality.
   c. helps us see that incentives are unimportant in considering policies to reduce poverty and income inequality.
   d. helps us determine whether equity or efficiency is more important.

Score: ____

Answers: 1. T; 2. F; 3. F; 4. F; 5. d; 6. c; 7. c; 8. b; 9. c; 10. b

If you didn't get all of these questions correct, a patient review of the material should be all you need before you move on to the "Hints, Tips, and Reminders" below. It is fairly easy material that is used to explain the nature and extent of poverty. If you missed any questions, review your answers to make sure you know why they were wrong, then move on. ■

	Consider These Hints, Tips, and Reminders	STEP 4

1. This chapter is one of the analytically easiest you will study this semester. The only part that requires some serious work is computing (and graphing) Lorenz curves. That key is to remember to accumulate the income shares from the lowest quintiles to the highest. Lorenz curves provide a quick visual reference for income distributions versus just looking at a table of numbers.

2. The Gini coefficients is not as easy to compute, but it is widely used because it results in a specific number that varies directly from 0 to 1.0, where 0 is an equal distribution and 1.0 is the most unequal. This is very useful for comparisons between countries at a moment in time and over time.

3. Topics like income distribution and poverty involve heavy doses of politics, emotion, and value judgments. Economists do not attempt to suggest what is the "best "or "fairest" distribution of income or wealth (with the exception of extreme distribution levels).

4. Poverty thresholds for the United States are substantially higher than those used by the World Bank and other agencies to measure poverty in the rest of the world. Annual incomes between $350 and $700 are the norm for poverty measurement in developing nations. The material well-being of the poor in the United States vastly exceeds that of the poor in these other nations.

Do the Homework for Chapter 14
Poverty and Income Distribution

Instructor _____ Time _____ Student _____

Use the answer key below to record your answers to these homework questions.

1. (a) (b) (c) (d)   6. (a) (b) (c) (d)   11. (a) (b) (c) (d)   16. (a) (b) (c) (d)
2. (a) (b) (c) (d)   7. (a) (b) (c) (d)   12. (a) (b) (c) (d)   17. (a) (b) (c) (d)
3. (a) (b) (c) (d)   8. (a) (b) (c) (d)   13. (a) (b) (c) (d)   18. (a) (b) (c) (d)
4. (a) (b) (c) (d)   9. (a) (b) (c) (d)   14. (a) (b) (c) (d)   19. (a) (b) (c) (d)
5. (a) (b) (c) (d)   10. (a) (b) (c) (d)   15. (a) (b) (c) (d)   20. (a) (b) (c) (d)

1. Which of the following is true of income?
   a. Most people earn their maximum income when they are 25.
   b. It is a stock.
   c. It is a flow.
   d. Income and wealth are the same.

2. Which of the following is true of wealth?
   a. Wealth is fairly evenly distributed in the United States.
   b. It is a stock.
   c. It is a flow.
   d. Income and wealth are the same.

3. Which of the following is *not* one of the distributions of income studied by economists?
   a. functional distribution of income
   b. personal distribution of income
   c. family distribution of income
   d. annual distribution of income

4. The distribution of income and wealth
   a. are essentially the same thing.
   b. are measured in similar ways, but the distribution of wealth is more unequally distributed.
   c. are measured in similar ways, but the distribution of wealth is more equally distributed.
   d. are measured in similar ways, but the distribution of income is more unequally distributed.

5. In Figure HW-1, the Lorenz curve 0c represents
   a. the most unequal distribution possible.
   b. the Gini coefficient.
   c. the most equal distribution possible.
   d. an unequal distribution that might roughly approximate that of the United States.

6. In Figure HW-1, the Lorenz curve 0dc represents
   a. the most unequal distribution possible.
   b. the Gini coefficient.
   c. the most equal distribution possible.
   d. an unequal distribution that might roughly approximate that of the United States.

7. In Figure HW-1, area A divided by area (A + B) is
   a. the most unequal distribution possible.
   b. the Gini coefficient.
   c. the most equal distribution possible.
   d. an unequal distribution that might roughly approximate that of the United States.

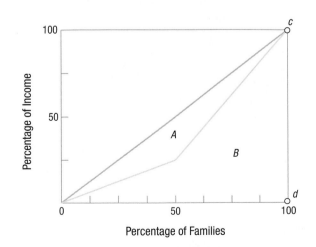

HW-1

8. When income and wealth are redistributed with a progressive income and estate tax,
   a. it has no effect on the Gini coefficient.
   b. the Lorenz curve moves away from the line of equal distribution.
   c. the Lorenz curve doesn't move.
   d. the Lorenz curve shifts inward toward the line of equal distribution.

9. When the Gini coefficient approaches zero,
   a. the income distribution becomes more unequally distributed.
   b. the Lorenz curve moves away from the line of equal distribution.
   c. the people in the society become richer and have a higher gross domestic product.
   d. the distribution of income approaches that of equal distribution.

10. Which of the following factors does *not* seem to be a cause of income inequality in the United States?
    a. different levels of investment in human capital
    b. the progressive income tax
    c. households with two people working
    d. economic discrimination by race, age, or gender

11. When comparing the distribution of income with the distribution of wealth in the United States,
    a. the income distribution is more unequally distributed than wealth.
    b. both have Gini coefficients that are about the same value.
    c. wealth is more unequally distributed than income.
    d. since income is a flow and wealth is a stock, the two cannot be compared.

12. When comparing the characteristics of the lowest income quintile and highest income quintile in the United States
    a. both had the same percentage of householders working full-time.
    b. both included a lot of two-earner households.
    c. the percentage of elderly in the low-income households was higher.
    d. both were equally likely to include individuals who did not work.

13. Poverty in the United States
    a. has steadily risen over the last three decades.
    b. fell dramatically during the 1960s.
    c. tends to fall during recessions and rise in other times.

    d. is unaffected by economic growth because the benefits of economic growth do not "trickle-down" to the poor.

14. Poverty in the United States tends to be the highest
    a. in married-couple families.
    b. in white families.
    c. in female householder families.
    d. in male householder families.

15. Families that the Census Bureau considers to be "severely poor" have a ratio of family income to the poverty threshold of
    a. greater than 1.5.
    b. greater than 1.0 but less than 1.5.
    c. greater than 0.5 but less than 1.0.
    d. less than 0.5.

16. Reducing poverty in the United States
    a. has fallen principally on state and local governments.
    b. has often been accompanied by controversy.
    c. could be eliminated entirely by income redistribution efforts at the local level.
    d. could best be handled by strengthening the laws enabling the poor to join unions.

17. John Rawls proposed the "maximin principle," which suggested that
    a. the maximum economic effort must be extracted from those at the bottom of the income ladder.
    b. maximum incomes must only be permitted for the top 20% of wage earners.
    c. the highest-income people should pay the maximum in taxes.
    d. society should maximize the welfare of the least-well-off individual.

18. Which of the following policies might *not* reduce poverty in the United States?
    a. improving the rate of economic growth
    b. reducing economic discrimination
    c. moving to a flat income tax structure
    d. lowering interest rates on educational loans

19. Today, a family of four has a poverty threshold in the United States
    a. of roughly $12,000.
    b. a little over $30,000.
    c. a little over $20,000.
    d. of just below $8,000.

20. In general terms, poverty thresholds in the United States
    a. are based on the minimum of what families need to live comfortably in a modest rental.
    b. are based on the USDA's least expensive food plan developed in the 1960s, then adjusted for inflation.
    c. are based on extensive surveys of how poor families live and feed family members.
    d. are based on the least expensive food budget adjusted for regional differences in costs.

| Use the ExamPrep to Get Ready for Exams | STEP 6 |

This sheet (front and back) is designed to help you prepare for your exams. The chapter has been boiled down to its key concepts. You are asked to answer questions, define terms, draw graphs, and, if you wish, add summaries of class notes.

The Distribution of Income and Wealth

Describe the following income distribution concepts:
Functional:

Personal:

Use the grid below to diagram the following:

■ Draw a Lorenz curve with equal distribution of income.
■ Draw a Lorenz curve with less than equal distribution.
■ Use the Lorenz curve to define the Gini coefficient.
■ What is the impact of income redistribution on the Lorenz curve?

List some of the programs that lead to income redistribution in the United States:

List some of the causes of income inequality:

Poverty

Describe how poverty is measured:

Describe the two depth-of-poverty measures and their implications for public policy:

Discuss the new measures of poverty and how useful they are to policymakers:

Eliminating Poverty

Discuss how poverty could be eliminated:

Rawls and Nozick

Describe the two philosophical approaches taken to developing theories of a "fair" income distribution by Rawls and Nozick:

Additional Study Help Chapterwide Practice Questions

Matching

Match the description with the corresponding term.

___ 1. Income
___ 2. Wealth
___ 3. Life cycle effects
___ 4. Functional distribution of income
___ 5. Personal or family distribution of income
___ 6. Lorenz curve
___ 7. Gini coefficient
___ 8. Progressive tax
___ 9. Transfer payment
___ 10. Poverty threshold
___ 11. Income deficit
___ 12. Ratio of income to poverty
___ 13. Maximin principle

a. A measure of a household's assets and net liabilities at a given point in time.
b. Compares family income to the poverty threshold and expresses this comparison as a ratio.
c. A means of graphically representing the income distribution by plotting the cumulative percentage of people below various income levels on the horizontal axis and relating this to their cumulative share of total income on the vertical axis.
d. The variation of income for an individual or family during different phases or stages of life.
e. The percentage of income flowing to families in specific segments of the population.
f. The ratio of the area between the Lorenz curve and the equal distribution line and the total area below the equal distribution line.
g. The income level beneath which families are officially deemed to be living in poverty.
h. Income distribution among inputs (factors) of production.
i. Taxes higher incomes at a higher rate than lower incomes.
j. Measures the receipt of funds by individuals or households over some period of time, usually a week, month, or year.
k. A measure of the depth of poverty; that is, it measures how far below the poverty threshold a family's income lies.
l. An idea proposed by philosopher John Rawls that maintains that a society should seek to maximize the welfare of its least-well-off individuals.
m. Cash payments or in-kind benefits, such as housing subsidies or food stamps from government to individuals or families.

Fill-In

Circle the word(s) in parentheses that complete the sentence.

1. Income and wealth vary significantly over families' (portfolios, lifetimes) _____. Income is a (stock, flow) _____, whereas wealth is measured (over time, at a given point in time) _____.

2. Looking at income distribution from the point to view of individuals or families represents the (functional, personal) _____ distribution of income, but when looked at from the viewpoint of factors of production, it is a measure of the (functional, personal) _____ distribution of income.

3. Lorenz curves represent the (cumulative, total, marginal) _____ distribution of income or wealth. Gini coefficients are computed using (factor incomes, Lorenz curves, thresholds) _____ and vary from zero where income is (equally, unequally) _____ distributed to 1.0 where income is (equally, unequally) _____ distributed.

4. The ratio of income the poverty is one way to measure the (incidence, depth, threshold) _____ of poverty.

True-False

Circle the correct answer.

T/F   1. Wealth is a flow of funds measure.

T/F   2. Most individuals and families have very different incomes at different points in their lives.

T/F   3. Since 1929, the share of the national income accruing to corporate profits has hovered somewhere around 10%.

T/F   4. The wealthiest 20% of Americans have about 50% of the national private wealth.

T/F   5. In deriving its official measure of income distribution, the Census Bureau bases its estimates on after-tax income, including cash transfer payments, but not including such noncash benefits as food stamps.

___T/F___ 6. Over the past 30 years, the percentage of income earned by the top quintile of Americans has risen, while the percentages earned by all of the lower quintiles have fallen.

___T/F___ 7. A Lorenz curve plots all of the people below a given income level on the horizontal axis, relating this to their dollar income on the vertical axis.

___T/F___ 8. A Gini coefficient of 0.0 indicates that distribution is perfectly equal.

___T/F___ 9. The United States has one of the lowest Gini coefficients in the world.

___T/F___ 10. The rising technological complexity of the American workplace has been one factor contributing to rising levels of income inequality.

___T/F___ 11. The poverty threshold is determined as the cost of feeding a family a nutritionally balanced diet, multiplied by 4.

___T/F___ 12. The Census Bureau's official measure of poverty treats in-kind benefits such as subsidized housing and food stamps as income.

___T/F___ 13. Although African American and Hispanic poverty rates are still higher than the rate for whites, the poverty rate for both minority groups fell significantly during the 1990s.

___T/F___ 14. A poor family's income deficit is equal to the poverty threshold for a family of that size minus the family's income.

___T/F___ 15. The Census Bureau will classify a family with an income to poverty ratio of 0.45 as "poor."

___T/F___ 16. The official U.S. poverty rate, based on income thresholds, is a relative measure of poverty.

___T/F___ 17. Although politicians frequently disagree on the best approach to reducing poverty, economists virtually all agree that the most effective approach involves favoring redistribution over growth-oriented policies.

___T/F___ 18. Economic analysis can help us to devise the most effective policies for reducing poverty and inequality, but it cannot tell us which of these policies is fair or unfair.

Multiple Choice

Circle the correct answer.

1. After laboring for years in obscurity, a novelist finally publishes a book that shoots to the top of the sales charts. At this moment in her career, she likely has
   a. both a low income and little wealth.
   b. a high income, but little wealth.
   c. a low income, but considerable wealth.
   d. both a high income and considerable wealth.

2. At what point in the life cycle does income peak for most people?
   a. when just entering the workforce, usually in one's early 20s
   b. between ages 25 and 35
   c. between ages 45 and 55
   d. upon retirement, usually around age 65

3. A breakdown of the income flowing to different inputs (factors) of production is referred to as the
   a. functional distribution of income.
   b. operational distribution of income.
   c. personal distribution of income.
   d. family distribution of income.

4. Approximately what share of the national income do American workers currently receive?
   a. 10%
   b. 20%
   c. 50%
   d. 70%

5. Approximately what percentage of the national income does the lowest quintile of Americans earn?
   a. 0–1%
   b. 1–1.5%
   c. 3–4%
   d. 7–8%

6. As measured by the Gini coefficient, the inequality of income distribution in the United States has been _____ since 1970.
   a. steadily falling
   b. steadily rising
   c. holding steady
   d. fluctuating erratically

7. The distribution of income in the United States is _____ than the distribution of wealth.
   a. more equal

b. more unequal

c. about the same as

d. completely unrelated to

8. A Gini coefficient of 0.1 indicates that distribution is
   a. perfectly equal.
   b. relatively equal.
   c. relatively unequal.
   d. as unequal as possible.

9. Which of the following factors is *not* among the causes of rising economic inequality in the United States?
   a. economic discrimination
   b. individuals and families making different investments in human capital
   c. rising number of two-income households
   d. free public education

10. These Lorenz curves for the United States in Figure MC-1 show that
    a. income is less evenly distributed after adjusting for taxes and transfers.
    b. income is more evenly distributed after adjusting for taxes and transfers.
    c. income is relatively evenly distributed before and after adjustment.
    d. wealth is more evenly distributed than income.

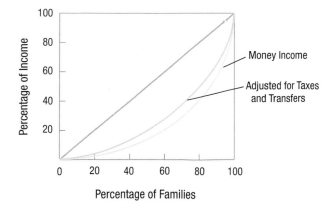

MC-1

11. The Gini coefficient for the distribution shown in Figure MC-1 will likely be
    a. around 0.10 before adjustment and 0.05 after.
    b. around 0.05 before adjustment and 0.10 after.
    c. around 0.40 before adjustment and 0.45 after.
    d. around 0.45 before adjustment and 0.40 after.

12. In very general terms, the poverty threshold is defined as
    a. the cost of renting adequate housing, multiplied by 2.
    b. the cost of buying a family's groceries for a month, multiplied by 2.
    c. the cost of feeding a family a nutritionally balanced diet, multiplied by 3.
    d. median household income, divided by 3.

13. Since 1970, African American and Hispanic poverty rates have been roughly _____ those of non-Hispanic whites.
    a. 4–5 times
    b. 2–3 times
    c. the same as
    d. one third

14. The Census Bureau would classify a family with an income-to-poverty ratio of 0.65 as
    a. severely or desperately poor
    b. poor
    c. near poor
    d. not poor

15. Approximately what percentage of Americans does the Census Bureau classify as "severely poor"?
    a. 2%
    b. 5%
    c. 8%
    d. 11%

16. Which of the following policies has the political left traditionally *not* supported?
    a. a more progressive tax system
    b. greater spending for public education
    c. growth-oriented tax cuts
    d. increases in in-kind transfer payments

17. Rawls's "maximin principle" holds that a society should strive to
    a. maximize its total output.
    b. maximize the percentage of income flowing to the upper quintile of households.
    c. maximize its average income deficit.
    d. maximize the welfare of its poorest individuals.

Essay-Problem

Answer in the space provided.

Use these questions as another way to assess your progress and, more importantly, to dig deeper into income distribution and poverty.

1. Why is it important to consider life cycles when analyzing income distribution?

2. Why is it important to look at the functional distribution of income?

3. We have discussed income distribution as if an equal distribution is to be expected. Is it really?

4. The estate tax is a tax paid by the estate of someone who dies. Its original purpose was to break up wealth holdings passed from generation to generation: Think of the Rockefellers. In the 1990s, estates greater than $600,000 had to pay the estate tax. Congress increased this trigger point, in part because of the bad effect it had on small businesses: On the death of a small business owner, the heirs often had to sell the business to come up with the estate tax, because many small businesses were worth over $600,000. The Democrats argued that the ceiling should be raised to $2,000,000 and left there; if there was need to raise it in the years ahead, this could be done by a future Congress. Republicans argued that the estate tax should be abolished completely because it was a disincentive to people to work hard and establish a dynasty. Which party has the better argument?

5. Consider the way poverty was determined in the 1960s. Construct an argument in favor of this procedure. Now, construct an argument against it.

6. In the late 1800s and early 1900s, there was a large outpouring of private charity. Hull House, education for immigrants, and the Salvation Army all started during this time period. The text talks about public policies to deal with poverty and income distribution problems. Why not rely on private charity?

7. An argument against the use of progressive taxation to redistribute income is that progressive taxation encourages rent-seeking and tax-avoiding behavior, and so encourages inefficiencies. Don't all taxes encourage such behavior?

8. Every now and then, arguments for "workfare" surface in the hope of getting "welfare cheaters" off the welfare rolls. Based on what you have learned in this chapter about the poor, what might go wrong with forcing people on welfare to take various jobs?

9. People who talk about the disincentive effects of welfare point to unemployment insurance. Studies have shown that there is a large amount of job-seeking activity in the weeks before the unemployment insurance runs out, much greater than in the months before. In times of economic slow-down, what can we predict will happen if unemployment insurance is extended from 26 weeks to 52 weeks?

10. What can economics tell us about the efficiency-equity tradeoff?

What's Next

With this chapter completed, you now are near the end of microeconomics. You have used supply and demand analysis to understand how markets work. You have seen how consumers choose to buy goods and services, and why and how firms provide those goods and services. You have seen how market structure affects prices and quantities produced, and how it affects the markets for inputs. You have then gone on to see economic analysis applied to labor issues, environmental issues, and issues of income distribution and poverty.

Answers to Chapterwide Practice Questions

Matching

1. j	5. e	9. m	13. l
2. a	6. c	10. g	
3. d	7. f	11. k	
4. h	8. i	12. b	

Fill-In

1. lifetime, flow, at a given point in time
2. personal, functional
3. cumulative, Lorenz curves, equally, unequally
4. depth

True-False

1. F	6. T	11. F	16. F
2. T	7. F	12. F	17. F
3. T	8. T	13. T	18. T
4. F	9. F	14. T	
5. F	10. T	15. F	

Multiple Choice

1. b	6. b	11. d	16. c
2. c	7. a	12. c	17. d
3. a	8. b	13. b	
4. d	9. d	14. b	
5. c	10. b	15. b	

Essay-Problem

1. We have seen that people earn different amounts of income, depending on their age. Much of this has to do with the gain in experience and skills as people grow older, up to the point where many people start to slow down physically. If one general population group were much younger than another population group, we would expect this younger group to generate less income than the older group. Not recognizing this fact could lead to poor public policy that attempted to deal with a problem that really was not a problem.

2. Looking at the functional distribution helps to dispel myths about workers' share of income versus corporations' share. Respondents to surveys generally believe that corporate prof-

its are a much larger share of income than the 9% or 10% it has been for the past 30 years, and workers' share is less than the 70% it has been in the same time period.

3. The text discussed many factors that would lead one to expect that the income distribution will be unequal: innate abilities, family wealth, schooling, possible discrimination, two-earner households. Luck may be a factor as well. The bothersome thing about income distribution for most is not the likelihood that income will forever be distributed unequally, but the vast differences in income. For many, this is the issue behind income distribution, not the fact that any inequality exists.

4. There is no right answer to this. Republicans are correct in that the estate tax is a disincentive to working hard and accumulate wealth; this is an efficiency argument. But the Democrats speak for many who think the estate tax is a fair (equitable) measure to prevent the accumulation of wealth and the possible privilege it brings with it. This is an example of the efficiency-equity tradeoff, a question to be decided by the voters, not economic analysis.

5. One of the best things about this procedure was its simplicity: Determine a nutritional food budget and multiply by 3. There was no need to determine costs for clothes, housing, medical care, entertainment, and a host of other potential expenditures. On the other hand, over time, living standards change, so it can be argued that food no longer represents one third of a poor family's budget. The procedure should be revised to reflect this.

6. The simple answer is that private charity is not enough. The private charities suggest as much when they request more and greater donations.

7. All taxes encourage rent-seeking and tax-avoidance behavior. The question is whether a progressive tax has rates so high that this behavior swamps the desire to work harder and generate more income. In the 1980s, when the United States' marginal tax rate on the highest incomes was cut by more than half, tax revenues on these income classes grew, suggesting that progressive taxes have high disincentive effects for certain tax rates.

8. Many people on welfare are likely not to have invested in human capital—they may not have the skills to do the job. A better alternative would be to offer training in the skills needed for various jobs, before forcing a job on someone. Build up the human capital first.

9. We can predict that the unemployment rate will rise because people will tend to put off a big job-seeking push until near the end of 52 weeks rather than 26 weeks. However, it should be pointed out that there is no magic number of weeks of unemployment insurance. A society must weigh the efficiency aspects of unemployment insurance with the equity aspects. It is equitable to help people who are out of a job by no fault of their own; but what is a fair number of weeks of help?

10. Economics can tell us about the efficiency aspects of public policies. It cannot tell us what is fair; this is what we as voters have to decide.

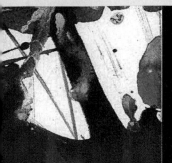

Introduction to Macroeconomics

15

Macroeconomics Looks at the Entire Economy

This chapter introduces you to the basic ideas and goals of macroeconomics. First, you will see how historical events such as the Great Depression shaped the way macroeconomics is studied. Second, you will see how the concept of the business cycle describes our economy's movement from good times to bad times, and back again. Finally, you will see how national income and product accounts (NIPA) were developed by the federal government in the 1930s to measure where our economy is in the business cycle. You will see how to measure gross domestic product (GDP), then will explore whether GDP is an adequate measure of our standard of living. By the end of this chapter, you should have a sense of the basics of macroeconomics.

This Is What You Need to Know

STEP 1

After studying this chapter you should be able to

- Describe the scope of macroeconomics.
- Describe the big events that shaped the study of macroeconomics.
- Describe the goals of macroeconomic policy.
- Describe the business cycle and some of the important macroeconomic variables that affect the level of economic activity.
- Describe the national income and product accounts (NIPA).
- Describe the circular flow of income and discuss why GDP can be computed using either income or expenditure data.
- Describe the four major expenditure components of GDP.
- Describe the major income components of national income.
- Describe the shortcomings of GDP as a measure of our standard of living.

381

Review the Key Terms

Business cycles: Alternating increases and decreases in economic activity that are typically punctuated by periods of downturn, recession, recovery, and boom.

Circular flow diagram: Illustrates how households and firms interact through product and resource markets and shows that economic aggregates can be determined by either examining spending flows or income flows to households.

Gross domestic product (GDP): A measure of the economy's total output; it is the most widely reported value in the national income and product accounts (NIPA) and is equal to the total market value of all final goods and services produced by resources in the United States.

Personal consumption expenditures (PCE): Goods and services purchased by residents of the United States, whether individuals or businesses; they include durable goods, nondurable goods, and services.

Gross private domestic investment (GPDI): Investments in such things as structures (residential and nonresidential), equipment, and software, and changes in private business inventories.

Government spending: Includes the wages and salaries of government employees (federal, state, and local); the purchase of products and services from private businesses and the rest of the world; and government purchases of new structures, equipment, and software.

Net exports: Exports minus imports for the current period. Exports include all the items we sell overseas such as agricultural products, movies, and technology products, while imports are all those items we bring into the country such as vegetables from Mexico, wine from Italy, and cars from Germany.

National income: All income including wages, salaries and benefits, profits (for sole proprietors, partnerships, and corporations), rental income, and interest.

Net domestic product: Gross domestic product minus depreciation or the capital consumption allowance.

Personal income: All income including wages, salaries, and other labor income; proprietors' income; rental income; personal interest and dividend income; and transfer payments (welfare and Social Security payments) received, with personal contributions for social insurance subtracted out.

Disposable personal income: Personal income minus taxes.

Work Through the Chapter Tutorials

The Scope of Macroeconomics

Frequently Asked Questions

Q: What is macroeconomics?

A: Macroeconomics is the study of economic activity from the perspective of the entire economy. It focuses on such issues as economic growth, aggregate output, employment and unemployment, inflation, and interest rates.

Q: **What were the major events in the last century that forced economists to study the macro-economy?**

A: Three major events in the last century propelled the study of macroeconomics. The Great Depression made economists focus on the aggregate economy, away from an earlier emphasis on individual markets. The Depression also focused professional attention on employment and unemployment as macroeconomic issues. Hyperinflation episodes and the damage these caused to other nations led policymakers to put an emphasis on stable prices. Huge budget deficits and the havoc they reap when they are large relative to output have led to a greater sense of fiscal responsibility by policymakers.

Q: **What are the goals of macroeconomics?**

A: The study of macroeconomics has led to several macroeconomic goals. The Employment Act of 1946 mandated that the government pursue policies designed to ensure full employment. This act was amended in 1978, with the government directed to pursue policies designed to stimulate economic growth and maintain stable prices.

Q: **What are business cycles?**

A: Business cycles are the alternating increases and decreases in economic activity typical of market economies. These fluctuations take place around a long-run growth trend.

Q: **How are business cycles defined?**

A: Business cycles contain four phases: the peak or boom, followed by a recession or downturn, leading to the trough or the low point of the cycle, followed by a recovery, leading to another peak. Business cycles vary dramatically in duration and intensity. Figure 1 is a model of a business cycle.

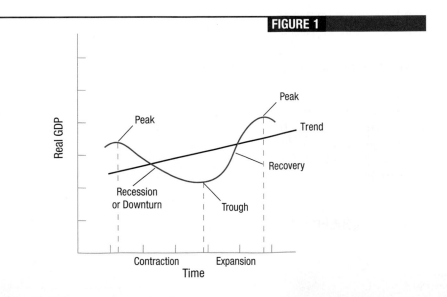

FIGURE 1

The Scope of Macroeconomics Quick Check

Circle the Correct Answer

1. (T/F) Macroeconomics studies economic activity from the perspective of the economy as a whole.
2. (T/F) The Great Depression spurred on economists to spend less time studying the microeconomics of markets and more time studying the macroeconomy.
3. (T/F) Modern macroeconomics looks at aggregate variables such as unemployment, inflation, and interest rates.

4. (T/F) Large government budget deficits typically lead to periods of hyperinflation.

5. Which one of the following is *not* among the macroeconomic policy goals mandated by Congress in 1978?
   a. Maintain price stability.
   b. Avoid budget deficits.
   c. Increase economic growth.
   d. Achieve full employment.

6. Which one of the following is *not* an aspect of business cycles?
   a. They vary in length and intensity.
   b. The National Bureau of Economic Research (NBER) officially dates the "turning points" in the business cycle.
   c. They chart the way aggregate economic activity fluctuates between increases and decreases.
   d. They show how the macroeconomy winds up exactly where it started from, again and again throughout the past century.

7. Which phase of the business cycle typically follows immediately after the trough?
   a. recession
   b. recovery

   c. peak
   d. contraction

8. Congress passed a law in 1946 mandating which one of the following national macroeconomic goals?
   a. no hyperinflation
   b. no budget deficits
   c. full employment
   d. long-term growth

9. Which one of the following is *not* correct regarding business cycles?
   a. They occur periodically.
   b. They are fairly uniform in length.
   c. They have peaks and troughs.
   d. They show that macroeconomic activity alternates between increases and decreases.

10. What is the low point of a business cycle?
   a. recession
   b. depression
   c. contraction
   d. trough

Score: ____

Answers: 1. T; 2. T; 3. T; 4. F; 5. b; 6. d; 7. b; 8. c; 9. b; 10. d

If You Got 9 or 10 Correct

You have a good grasp of the scope of macroeconomics and the concept of business cycles. Go on to the next section, "National Income Accounting."

If You Didn't Get at Least 9 Correct

You should review the material carefully because it contains the basics of macroeconomics. The material is not difficult, though some of it may be unfamiliar to you. Start by skimming the first part of the chapter. Be sure you can list the goals of macroeconomics and the phases of the business cycle. Review the Core Graph below portraying the business cycle. It provides a foundation for your study of macroeconomics.

Core Graph: Business Cycles

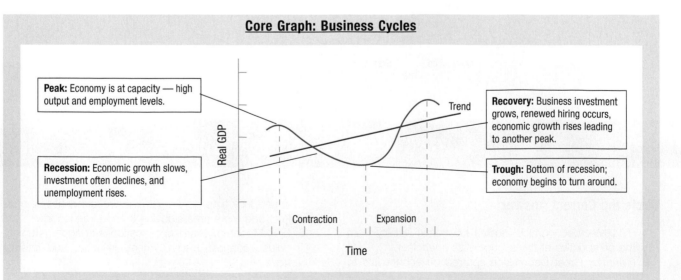

Peak: Economy is at capacity — high output and employment levels.

Recession: Economic growth slows, investment often declines, and unemployment rises.

Recovery: Business investment grows, renewed hiring occurs, economic growth rises leading to another peak.

Trough: Bottom of recession; economy begins to turn around.

Real GDP

Trend

Contraction   Expansion

Time

Most of monetary policy implemented by the Federal Reserve is directed at smoothing out the business cycle and promoting long-term economic growth with stable prices. During deep recessions, government spending and tax policy is focused on reducing the economic impact of the recession and promoting a speedy recovery. As you begin your study of macroeconomics, keep those concepts in mind. ■

National Income Accounting

Frequently Asked Questions

Q: **Why are national income and product accounts valuable?**

A: The national income and product accounts (NIPA) allow economists to judge our nation's economic performance, compare American income and output to that of other nations, and track the economy's condition over the course of the business cycle.

Q: **What are the two major ways of constructing the national income and product accounts?**

A: The major components of NIPA can be constructed in either of two ways: by summing the income of the economy or summing spending. Figure 2, a circular flow diagram of the economy, shows why either approach can be used to determine the country's economic activity. Consumer spending by households is revenue for business, and this revenue is used to produce the products that households purchase. Business spending ultimately represents income to the various inputs (factors) of production. The arrows moving in a clockwise direction represent real goods and services purchased by consumers and real inputs (hours worked) by factors of production. The arrows moving in a counterclockwise direction represent money flows, payments for goods and services (revenues to firms), and money payments to factors of production (wages, profits, etc.). In the end, all spending in the economy represents all income.

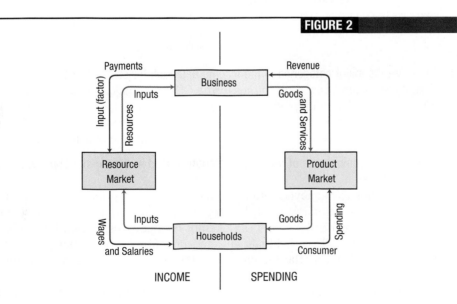

FIGURE 2

Q: **What is gross domestic product (GDP)?**

A: Gross domestic product (GDP) is the standard measure the Commerce Department uses to gauge the economy's output. It is equal to the total market value of all final goods and services produced by resources located in the United States.

Q: **What does gross national product measure, and how does it differ from GDP?**

A: Gross national product (GNP) measures the market value of all goods and services produced by resources supplied by U.S. residents. GNP includes goods produced here and abroad, as long as the production involves resources owned by U.S. residents. The difference between GDP and GNP is small.

Q: **What are the main categories in the expenditures approach for measuring GDP?**

A: Measuring GDP with the expenditures approach means all spending on final goods and services is added together. The four major categories of spending are personal consumer spending, gross private domestic investment, government spending, and net exports (exports minus imports).

Q: **What are personal consumption expenditures?**

A: Personal consumption expenditures (PCE) are goods and services purchased by residents of the United States, whether individuals or businesses. They are divided into three main categories: durable goods, nondurable goods, and services.

Q: **What is gross private domestic investment?**

A: Gross private domestic investment (GPDI) includes investments in residential and nonresidential structures, equipment, and software. GPDI also includes changes in inventories.

Q: **What does the government spending component of GDP measure?**

A: The government spending component of GDP measures the impact government spending has on final demand in the economy. It includes the wages and salaries of government employees and the purchase of products and services from private businesses and the rest of the world.

Q: **What are net exports?**

A: The net export of goods and services is equal to exports minus imports.

Q: **What is the equation for GDP using the expenditures approach?**

A: The four spending categories are commonly abbreviated as C (consumption), I (investment), G (government), and X − M (exports minus imports, or net exports). Together, these four variables constitute GDP:

$$GDP = C + I + G + (X - M).$$

Q: **What are the major categories in the income approach for calculating GDP?**

A: Using the income approach to measuring GDP, the major categories of income are compensation of employees (wages and salaries including benefits), proprietor's income, corporate profits, rental income, and net interest. Several adjustments are required to the national accounts to fully account for GDP.

Q: **What are the components of the major categories used in the income approach for calculating GDP?**

A: Compensation to employees refers to payments for work done, including wages, salaries, and benefits. Proprietor's income is the current income of all sole proprietorships, partnerships, and tax-exempt cooperatives. Rental income is the income that flows to individuals engaged in renting real property. Corporate profits are defined as the income that flows to corporations, as adjusted for inventory valuation and capital consumption allowances. Net interest is the interest paid by businesses less the interest they receive from this country and abroad.

Q: **What are the adjustments needed in the income approach?**

A: National income is the sum of all the income just listed. To get from national income to GDP requires adding in indirect business taxes, an allowance for depreciation of fixed capital, and the payments U.S. residents receive from foreign sources minus the payments they send abroad. These adjustments yield gross domestic income, which is equal to GDP once a small statistical discrepancy is accounted for.

Q: What is net domestic product, and why is it important?

A: Net domestic product (NDP) is defined as GDP minus capital consumption allowance (depreciation). Since some assets are used up in the production process, NDP is a better indicator of sustainable income or output.

Q: How is personal income defined?

A: Personal income includes all income including wages, salaries, and other labor income; proprietors' income; rental income; personal interest and dividend income; and transfer payments, with personal contributions for social insurance being subtracted out.

Q: How is disposable personal income defined?

A: Disposable personal income is defined as personal income minus taxes $(Y - T)$. Disposable income (Y_d) can be either spent (C) or saved (S), yielding the equation: $Y_d = C + S$.

Q: What are the shortcomings of NIPA?

A: The NIPA have some shortcomings. For instance, the national accounts ignore most nonmarket transactions: If you send your clothes to a laundry, GDP rises, but if you wash them yourself, GDP is unaffected. NIPA also fail to account for the environmental impact of economic activity.

National Income Accounting Quick Check

Circle the Correct Answer

1. (T/F) The circular flow diagram shows that an expenditures approach to calculating GDP will equal an income approach.
2. Which of the following equations defines the expenditures approach to calculating GDP?
   a. GDP = C + S
   b. GDP = C + I + G + (X − M)
   c. GDP = C + I + G + S
   d. GDP = C + I + G

Use the following data to answer questions 3 and 4.

Federal government purchases of goods and services	120
Exports	60
Corporate profits	80
Gross private domestic investment	155
Proprietor's income	80
Net interest	40
State and local purchases of goods and services	120
Rental income	20
Personal consumption expenditures	650
Capital consumption allowance	110
Imports	55
Compensation of employees	620

3. Using the expenditures approach, compute GDP.
   _____
4. Using the income approach, compute national income (*Hint*: National income will *not* equal GDP). _____
5. Which one of the following is *not* used to adjust national income to obtain GDP so that the income approach equals the expenditures approach?
   a. depreciation of equipment and buildings
   b. exports *minus* imports
   c. indirect business taxes
   d. payments by residents to foreigners, and vice versa.

Score: _____

If You Got All 5 Correct

You have a good grasp of what the NIPA are and how they are used to calculate gross domestic product. Go to "Hints, Tips, and Reminders."

If You Didn't Get All of Them Correct

You probably went through the material too fast. There are many new terms here. They are worth a little more time spent on getting to know them. Go back and review the material on the NIPA accounts in the text.

Remember that one of the important conclusions from this analysis is that all expenditures in the economy are equal to all income as the Core Graph of the Circular Flow diagram below illustrates.

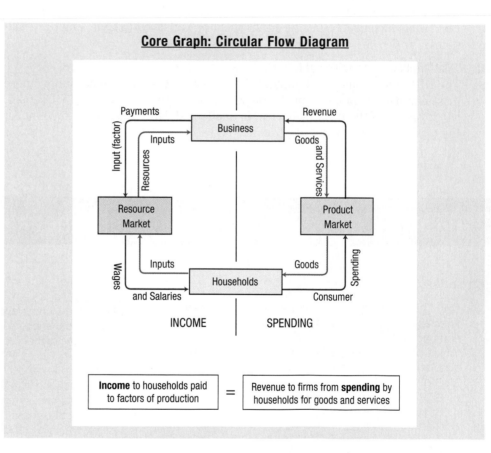

In the blanks below, list the major components of the expenditures approach to calculating GDP; then list the major components of the income approach.

Expenditures Approach

_____

_____

_____

_____

Income Approach

_____

_____

_____

_____

When you have completed this review, answer the questions in the final check below.

National Income Accounting Final Check

1. (T/F) GDP represents the total market value of all final goods and services produced by labor and property by residents of the United States, whether here or abroad.
2. Which one of the following statements about NIPA is *not* correct?
    a. It helps economists compare U.S. income and output to that of other nations.
    b. It tracks the economy's progress over the course of the business cycle.
    c. It is put together by the National Bureau of Economic Research.
    d. It began in the 1930s.
3. Which one of the following statements concerning GDP is *not* correct?
    a. It can be found by adding up all of the spending in the economy.
    b. It can be found by adding up all of the income in the economy.
    c. It incorporates environmental benefits or harm.
    d. It overstates sustainable output because it does not subtract depreciation.

Use the data below to answer questions 4 and 5.

Rental income	20
Personal consumption expenditures	655
Capital consumption allowance	110
Imports	65
Federal government purchases of goods and services	130
Net interest	40
State and local purchases of goods and services	115
Compensation of employees	615
Exports	60
Corporate profits	75
Gross private domestic investment	150
Proprietor's income	90

4. Using the expenditures approach, compute GDP. _____
5. Using the income approach, compute national income. _____

Score: _____

Answers: 1. F; 2. c; 3. c; 4. 1,045; 5. 840

You should have answered 4 or 5 correctly. If you didn't, you can continue to the next step, but you will probably have to review this chapter again. As you read through the "Hints, Tips, and Reminders" next, maybe what you missed will become clearer. ■

Consider These Hints, Tips, and Reminders   STEP 4

1. In macroeconomics, economists use models of the aggregate economy. As you will see, different models give different approaches to solving problems based on the problem and the time period. One important point to remember is that some models give better results in some circumstances, and other models give better results in other circumstances. So spend time to learn the models and consider under what circumstances they work best.

2. Your first macroeconomic model is a circular flow diagram. It is a simple model that shows that any expenditure in the economy represents income to someone else. This is a simple but important conclusion.

3. Get used to thinking about GDP as equal to C + I + G + (X − M). You will see this equation many times throughout the remainder of the course.

4. Don't get bogged down in the calculations of GDP unless your instructor suggests that you must. Knowing the expenditure equation, GDP = C + I + G + (X − M), wil be the most important material from the NIPA section.

5. Maintain a healthy skepticism about GDP and its growth as a valid measure of progress toward a higher standard of living. At a minimum you want to look at GDP per capita. While not perfect, it is the most comparable number between nations we have and keeps us abreast of our rising standard of living. Economists are developing more robust measures, but most have not been widely adopted.

Instructor _____ Time _____ Student _____

Use the answer key below to record your answers to these homework questions.

1. (a) (b) (c) (d)	6. (a) (b) (c) (d)	11. (a) (b) (c) (d)	16. (a) (b) (c) (d)
2. (a) (b) (c) (d)	7. (a) (b) (c) (d)	12. (a) (b) (c) (d)	17. (a) (b) (c) (d)
3. (a) (b) (c) (d)	8. (a) (b) (c) (d)	13. (a) (b) (c) (d)	18. (a) (b) (c) (d)
4. (a) (b) (c) (d)	9. (a) (b) (c) (d)	14. (a) (b) (c) (d)	19. (a) (b) (c) (d)
5. (a) (b) (c) (d)	10. (a) (b) (c) (d)	15. (a) (b) (c) (d)	20. (a) (b) (c) (d)

1. Macroeconomics studies
   a. the most important factors in determining economic growth.
   b. the causes of employment and unemployment.
   c. economic activity from a broad perspective.
   d. all of the above.

2. The Great Depression
   a. is the principal reason we have unemployment today.
   b. caused economists to rethink their approach to analyzing the economy.
   c. was the beginning of the globalization we know today, as countries liberalized their economies and welcomed international trade.
   d. all of the above.

3. The Great Depression
   a. is the principal reason we have unemployment today.
   b. resulted in bank profits swelling, which led to the establishment of the Federal Reserve.
   c. was the beginning of the globalization we know today as countries liberalized their economies and welcomed international trade.
   d. none of the above.

4. Hyperinflation is
   a. low levels of inflation that lead to significant unemployment.
   b. high levels of inflation caused by changes in banking technology.
   c. high levels of inflation brought on by rising oil prices.
   d. none of the above.

5. Which of the following events did *not* do much to shape the macroeconomic analysis we study today?
   a. the Great Depression
   b. globalization and the impact of multinational corporations
   c. episodes of hyperinflation in Germany in the 1920s and many South American countries in the recent past
   d. large swings in budget deficits

6. Which of the following is *not* a major macroeconomic goal?
   a. stable prices
   b. relatively low interest rates
   c. full employment
   d. low economic growth

7. Which of the following is *not* a major macroeconomic goal?
   a. stable prices
   b. relatively low interest rates
   c. full employment
   d. income equality

8. Business cycles are
   a. similar to fashion cycles in the garment industry
   b. recurring periods of cost cutting by business enterprises
   c. recurring episodes of increases and decreases in economic activity
   d. large swings in budget deficits

9. In Figure HW-1, the trough of the business cycle is shown by
   a. point a.
   b. point b.
   c. point c.
   d. point d.

10. In Figure HW-1, the peak of the business cycle is shown by
   a. point a.
   b. point b.
   c. point c.
   d. point d.

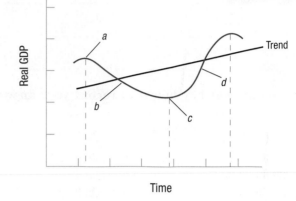

HW-1

11. Actual business cycle dates (peaks and troughs) are determined by
   a. the Department of Commerce.
   b. the Harvard University Economics Department.
   c. the National Bureau of Economic Research.
   d. the President's Council of Economic Advisors.

12. Which phase of the business cycle follows after a recovery?
   a. the peak
   b. the trough
   c. the boom
   d. the recession

13. Which phase of the business cycle follows immediately after a trough?
   a. the peak
   b. the recession
   c. the boom
   d. the recovery

14. Gross domestic product (GDP) is
   a. the final value of all manufactured goods.
   b. the final market value of all manufactured goods by domestic producers both here and abroad.
   c. the total market value of all final goods and services produced by resources in the United States.
   d. the total market value of all goods manufactured by resources in the United States.

15. Which of the following equations best describes the expenditure approach to calculating GDP?
   a. GDP = C + I
   b. GDP = C + I + G + X
   c. GDP = C + I + G + (X − M)
   d. GDP = C + I + G

16. Gross private domestic investment (GPDI) is
    a. a stable component of GDP.
    b. not important for economic growth.
    c. the sum of the total market value of all stocks on the major stock exchanges.
    d. an important determinant of swings in the business cycle.

17. What is the difference between GDP and NDP (net domestic product)?
    a. GDP measures the final value of all goods and services, whereas NDP focuses on the differences between exports and imports.
    b. NDP removes the profits of corporations from GDP.
    c. GDP equals NDP plus a capital consumption allowance.
    d. NDP removes net interest from GDP.

18. Gross domestic product
    a. is a good index of the well-being of people in the United States.
    b. generally ignores nonmarket transactions.
    c. is not used to compare the United States with other countries.
    d. is the market value of all goods manufactured by labor and property in the United States.

19. Gross private domestic investment
    a. essentially represents a change in inventories.
    b. is important for economic growth.
    c. is a key component of government spending.
    d. has little to do with swings in the business cycle.

20. Corporate profits represent what percent of GDP?
    a. over 35%
    b. roughly 25%
    c. roughly 20%
    d. roughly 10%

Use the ExamPrep to Get Ready for Exams

This sheet (front and back) is designed to help you prepare for your exams. The chapter has been boiled down to its key concepts. You are asked to answer questions, define terms, draw graphs, and, if you wish, add summaries of class notes.

Scope of Macroeconomics

Describe three major events that helped define macroeconomics:

List the goals of macroeconomics:

Business Cycles

Define a business cycle:

Draw a business cycle in the grid provided. Show each phase on the business cycle in the grid.

List and define the phases of the business cycle:

National Income Accounting

Draw a circular flow diagram below for consumers and firms. Label spending and income flows.

What does the circular flow tell us about spending and income?

Gross Domestic Product

List the main components of GDP using both the expenditure and income approaches in the table below:

Expenditures	Income
_____	_____
_____	_____
_____	_____
_____	_____
_____	_____

Define net domestic product:

Describe the controversy over GDP as a measure of standard of living:

Additional Study Help Chapterwide Practice Questions

Matching

Match the description with the corresponding term.

___ 1. Business cycle
___ 2. Circular flow diagram
___ 3. Gross domestic product
___ 4. Personal consumption expenditures
___ 5. Gross private domestic investment
___ 6. Government spending
___ 7. Net exports
___ 8. National income
___ 9. Net domestic product
___ 10. Disposable personal income

a. The sum of all earnings by inputs (factors) of production.
b. Includes durable and nondurable goods.
c. Aggregate output adjusted for depreciation.
d. Fluctuations around the long-run growth trend.
e. Consumers can either put this in a savings account or visit their local mall.
f. Shows that aggregate income and aggregate expenditures are equal.
g. Merchandise exports minus imports.
h. The final value of all goods and services produced in the United States.
i. Important item in determining the severity of a recession and the expansiveness of a boom.
j. Wages and salaries of employees are treated as purchases.

Fill-In

Circle the word(s) in parentheses that complete the sentence.

1. Macroeconomics studies the economy from the standpoint of the entire economy and focuses on (wage levels, technical change, economic growth) _____. The three major economic events that shaped macroeconomic thought are the Great Depression, episodes of hyperinflation, and (unemployment, budget deficits, NAFTA) _____.

2. The bottom of the business cycle is called a (recovery, boom, trough, downturn) _____, and is typically followed by a (recovery, boom, trough, downturn) _____, which is then followed by a (recovery, boom, trough, downturn) _____, which eventually results in a (recovery, boom, trough, downturn) _____.

3. The national income and product accounts use the final value of goods and services produced in America to measure GDP and other aggregate values to avoid the problem of (inflation, double counting) _____. The circular flow diagram illustrates that GDP can be computed by measuring expenditures or (prices, incomes) _____.

True-False

Circle the correct answer.

T/F 1. Modern macroeconomic analysis is essentially an extension of the microeconomics of markets.

T/F 2. Hyperinflation is typically associated with a rapid increase in the money supply, typically because a government starts printing huge amounts of new money to finance its deficit spending.

T/F 3. American deficits as a percent of GDP have been relatively low over the past 20 to 30 years.

T/F 4. Prior to the Great Depression, the federal government's most significant domestic responsibility was promoting full employment.

T/F 5. The United States experienced little economic growth over the 20th century due to persistent downturns in the business cycle.

T/F 6. Business cycles are defined as alternating increases and decreases in economic activity.

T/F 7. Over the past century, downturns in the business cycle have been remarkably uniform in their duration and intensity.

T/F 8. The Department of Commerce is responsible for officially dating turning points in the business cycle.

T/F 9. Prior to World War I, the government made many attempts to estimate the output of various sectors of the economy, but without computers, accounting was impossible.

T/F 10. The circular flow diagram makes clear that every dollar spent in our economy is received by someone else as income.

T/F 11. GDP can be estimated by adding up either all of the spending in the economy or all of the taxes paid by individuals and corporations.

T/F 12. GDP represents the total market value of all final goods and services produced by resources located within the United States.

T/F 13. When a U.S.-owned factory in Taiwan earns a profit, this income is counted toward American GDP.

T/F 14. The value of a final good is equal to its costs of production plus its final sales price.

T/F 15. When a U.S.-owned factory in France earns a profit by exporting wine to the United States, this profit is counted toward American GDP.

T/F 16. Cheap foreign cars are a good example of nondurable consumer goods.

T/F 17. Spending on services account for more personal consumption spending than durable goods and nondurable goods combined.

T/F 18. The income approach to GDP adds up compensation to employees, proprietors' income, rental income, corporate profits, and net exports.

Multiple Choice

Circle the correct answer.

1. Macroeconomics studies economic activity from the perspective of
   a. product markets.
   b. the labor market.
   c. the economy as a whole.
   d. the retail industry.

2. Which of the following 20th-century events had the *least* impact on the development of macroeconomics?
   a. episodes of hyperinflation
   b. the Vietnam War
   c. the Great Depression
   d. high budget deficits over the past two to three decades

3. What is the most common cause of hyperinflation?
   a. the discovery of new gold reserves
   b. the government printing too much money to finance deficit spending
   c. increased competition from foreign markets
   d. collapse of a nation's stock market

4. Which of the following were *not* among the macroeconomic goals Congress mandated for government policymakers in 1978?
   a. reduced inflation
   b. expanded economic growth
   c. increased work safety
   d. full employment

5. What are business cycles?
   a. one of the most predictable, uniform phenomena in the economic world
   b. production schedules that manufacturers follow over the course of the year
   c. a sort of scooter popular among young professionals
   d. alternating increases and decreases in aggregate economic activity

6. Which phase of the business cycle typically follows immediately after a downturn or recession?
   a. trough
   b. peak
   c. recovery
   d. boom

7. How long did the longest-lasting expansion of the past half-century last?
   a. 6 months
   b. 11 months
   c. 16 months
   d. 11 years

8. Work on the national income and product accounts (NIPA) began in
   a. the 1930s
   b. the 1940s
   c. the 1970s
   d. the 1990s

9. NIPA are designed to help economists to do all of the following *except*
   a. compare American income and output to that of other nations.
   b. judge the economy's growth and overall performance over time.
   c. track the economy's progress over the course of the business cycle.
   d. predict whether particular industries will grow or decline.

10. GDP can be found by adding up either all of the _____ or all of the _____ in the economy.
    a. spending, taxes
    b. spending, income
    c. investment, income
    d. net interest, taxes

11. If a candy bar that contains $0.25 worth of chocolate and gets packaged in a $0.12 wrapper retails for $0.50, how much does the sale of the candy bar contribute to GDP?
    a. $0.50
    b. $0.37
    c. $0.25
    d. $0.87

12. Gross domestic product (GDP) refers only to output produced by
    a. firms in which U.S. citizens own a majority share.
    b. resources located within the United States.
    c. resources supplied by U.S residents.
    d. corporations that trade on U.S. stock exchanges.

13. Net domestic product (NDP) refers to
    a. $C + I + G + (X - M)$.
    b. GDP minus net exports.
    c. GDP minus capital consumption allowance.
    d. Output produced within the United States minus payments to U.S. entrepreneurs to produce the output.

14. Which of the following is *not* one of the major spending categories that the NIPA use?
    a. gross private domestic investment
    b. personal consumption expenditures
    c. compensation of employees
    d. government expenditures

15. Which of the following is *not* one of the major income categories that the NIPA use?
    a. corporate profits
    b. gross private domestic investment
    c. compensation of employees
    d. rental income

16. Which of the following equations equals disposable income?
    a. $Y = C + S$
    b. $Y = C + I + G + (X - M)$
    c. $Y = I + S$
    d. $Y = C - I$

Essay-Problem

Answer in the space provided.

The questions below are designed to get you to think a little deeper about the issues surrounding macroeconomics. We are just beginning our look at the aggregate economy, but there are issues that you can explore more fully. Use our answers as another way to assess your progress and to discover some of the issues surrounding business cycles and the national income accounts.

1. There were national bank panics and national economic downturns in the United States long before the Great Depression. What was it about the Great Depression that transformed the way people looked at the national economy?

2. Why is it useful to determine peaks and troughs in the business cycle?

3. Innovations happen all of the time in our economy. What is so special about Schumpeter's grouping certain innovations such as railroads and the telegraph into waves?

4. The circular flow diagram teaches us what important point?

5. Of the expenditure categories used in calculating GDP, which one is the least important? Why?

6. Of the major income categories used in calculating GDP, which one is least important?

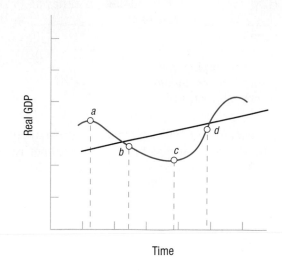

EP-1

7. To calculate sustainable output, why is it important to subtract depreciation from GDP?

8. The national income and product accounts ignore nonmarket transactions. If you pay someone to mow your lawn, this will show up in GDP, but if you mow the lawn yourself, this will not show up. Does this detract from the usefulness of the GDP number?

11. Use Figure EP-1 to answer the following questions.

Label and describe the following points:

     a

     b

     c

     d

12. Use the data below to answer the following questions:

Federal government purchases of goods and services	116
Exports	57
Corporate profits	81
Gross private domestic investment	152
Proprietor's Income	80
Net interest	38
State and local purchases of goods and services	121
Rental income	20
Personal consumption expenditures	649
Capital consumption allowance	109
Imports	55
Compensation of employees	617

9. Periods of hyperinflation typically have started with large government deficits. The United States has generated large deficits over the past 20 years. Why has the United States not suffered from hyperinflation?

10. What are the main macroeconomic concerns?

a. Using the expenditure approach, compute GDP.
b. Using the income approach, compute national income.
c. Why are your answers to parts a and b not equal? Describe generally the adjustments that must be made to national income to get GDP.
d. What is the value of NDP?

What's Next

You now have an introduction to the scope of macroeconomics, the major goals of macroeconomic policymaking, and the use of GDP numbers as a proxy for our national economic well-being. We talked about full employment, price stability, and economic growth as macroeconomic goals. We now want to turn to purely measurement issues. What precisely is inflation? How does the Department of Labor measure employment and unemployment? What is full employment? These are the subjects of the next chapter.

Answers to Chapterwide Practice Questions

Matching

1. d	4. b	7. g	10. e
2. f	5. i	8. a	
3. h	6. j	9. c	

Fill-In

1. economic growth, budget deficits
2. trough, recovery, boom, downturn
3. double counting, incomes

True-False

1. F	6. T	11. F	16. F
2. T	7. F	12. T	17. T
3. T	8. F	13. F	18. F
4. F	9. F	14. F	
5. F	10. T	15. F	

Multiple Choice

1. c	5. d	9. d	13. c
2. b	6. a	10. b	14. c
3. b	7. d	11. a	15. b
4. c	8. a	12. b	16. a

Essay-Problem

1. The difference was in the duration and intensity of the Great Depression, compared to previous national downturns that, though sharp, were of relatively short duration. Unemployment reached 25% during the Great Depression, and some argue that the downturn that started in 1929 really did not disappear until over 10 years later when the United States entered World War II.
2. Policies meant to deal with downturns might hold back recoveries, and policies meant to foster growth might exacerbate downturns. Recognition of troughs and peaks helps policymakers make the correct diagnosis, which helps them select the correct medicine.
3. Schumpeter's point is that innovations have different effects in their own industry and in other industries. Some innovations are more momentous than others. Sometimes inno-

vations have ripple effects throughout the entire economy. Think of the Internet's effect on communications in the past 10 years. The Internet has been a major factor in how people gather information and communicate now. Schumpeter forces us to look at innovations from a macroeconomy perspective.

4. The circular flow diagram, whether simple or complex, teaches us that all spending in the economy has to equal all income.

5. Of the expenditure categories used in calculating GDP, net exports is least important, mainly because of its relative magnitude compared to personal consumption, investment, and government spending.

6. Rental income is by far the smallest category of the major income classes used to calculate GDP.

7. Machinery wears out and needs to be replaced; buildings become dated and need to be replaced. Depreciation takes this wear and tear into consideration. Subtracting depreciation from GDP gives a better sense of what is left for the economy after depreciated capital equipment is replaced.

8. It depends on what you want the GDP number to do. If you want GDP to be an indicator of well-being, then not including nonmarket transactions is a detriment. If you think of GDP as a good proxy for the overall economy, then adding nonmarket transactions will make the number more complex and questionable, and so detract from its usefulness. For example, we can determine what wage you pay to the person who mows your lawn. Would you accept the same wage? If not, an element of uncertainty comes into the calculations.

9. The text noted that large government deficits typically are necessary to start hyperinflation. These deficits must be large relative to the overall economy. They are necessary, but not sufficient. A crucial factor is how governments deal with these deficits. Hyperinflation was caused by governments printing more money to pay for the deficits. So far, the United States has not done that, financing its deficits from increased tax revenues generated during the economic boom of the 1990s, from selling bonds, or from tax increases.

10. According to laws passed by the U.S. Congress, the main concerns are full employment, price stability, and economic growth. Budget deficits and interest rates are important insofar as they affect these three main concerns.

11. a. peak
    b. recession
    c. trough
    d. recovery

12. a. GDP = C + I + G + (X − M)
        C = 649
        I = 152
        G = Federal + State & Local = 116 + 121 = 237
      (X − M) = 57 − 55 = 2
        GDP = 1,040

    b. National income:
       Compensation to employees 617
       Proprietors' income   80
       Corporate profit   81
       Net interest   38
       Rental income   20
       National income   836

    c. Some adjustments are needed to get from national income to GDP. These include such things as depreciation of equipment and buildings (capital consumption allowance), indirect business taxes (sales and property taxes), and payments by residents to foreigners, and vice versa.

    d. NNP = (GDP − capital consumption allowance) = 1,040 − 109 = 931.

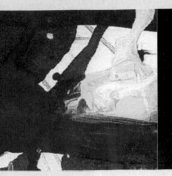

Measuring Inflation and Unemployment

Inflation and Unemployment Are Key Macroeconomic Variables

Macroeconomic policymakers have to deal with the problems of inflation and unemployment. To design effective policies to combat these problems, we first have to be sure that we are talking about the same things. We have a general sense of what is meant by inflation and unemployment; but we need to be precise. How are inflation and unemployment measured? When are they too high? How are inflation measures used? These two concepts are the core of what federal policymakers try to control, so get a good fix on what they are and how they are measured.

| This Is What You Need to Know | STEP 1 |

After studying this chapter you should be able to

■ Define inflation and the various terms associated with inflation.

■ Describe the methods for measuring inflation used by the Bureau of Labor Statistics.

■ Describe the gross domestic product deflator.

■ Use an escalator formula to determine future values.

■ Convert a nominal value to a real or constant dollar value.

■ Describe the economic consequences of the different forms of inflation.

■ Describe the differences between the labor force, employment, unemployment, and underemployment.

■ Describe the different forms of unemployment and their economic consequences.

■ Define the phrase *full employment.*

Review the Key Terms

Price level: The absolute level of a price index, whether the consumer price index (CPI; retail prices), the producer price index (PPI; wholesale prices), or the gross domestic product (GDP) deflator (average price of all items in GDP).

Inflation: A measure of changes in the cost of living. A general rise in prices throughout the economy.

Disinflation: A reduction in the rate of inflation. An economy going through disinflation will typically still be facing inflation, but it will be at a declining rate.

Deflation: A decline in overall prices throughout the economy. This is the opposite of inflation.

Hyperinflation: An extremely high rate of inflation; above 100% a year.

Consumer price index (CPI): A measure of the average change in prices paid by urban consumers for a typical market basket of consumer goods and services.

Personal consumption expenditures index (PCE): A measure of the changes in consumer prices by focusing on consumer expenditures in the GDP accounts.

Producer price index (PPI): A measure of the average changes in the prices received by domestic producers for their output.

GDP deflator: An index of the average prices for all goods and services in the economy, including consumer goods, investment goods, government goods and services, and exports. It is the broadest measure of inflation in the national income and product accounts (NIPA).

Labor force: The total number of those employed and unemployed. The unemployment rate is the unemployed divided by the labor force, expressed as a percent.

Discouraged workers: To continue to be counted as unemployed, those without work must actively seek work (apply for jobs, interview, register with employment services, etc.). Discouraged workers are those who have given up actively looking for work and, as a result, are not counted as unemployed.

Frictional unemployment: Natural unemployment for our economy; includes workers who voluntarily quit their jobs to search for better positions, or are moving to new jobs but may still take several days or weeks before they can report to their new employers.

Structural unemployment: Unemployment caused by changes in the structure of consumer demands or technology. It means that demand for some products declines and the skills of this industry's workers often become obsolete as well. This results in an extended bout of unemployment while new skills are developed.

Cyclical unemployment: Unemployment that results from changes in the business cycle; where public policymakers can have their greatest impact by keeping the economy on a steady, low-inflationary, solid growth path.

Natural rate of unemployment: That level of unemployment where price and wage decisions are consistent; a level at which the actual inflation rate is equal to people's inflationary expectations and where cyclical unemployment is zero.

Work Through the Chapter Tutorials

Inflation

Frequently Asked Questions

Q: **What is inflation?**

A: Inflation, in a general sense, is a measure of changes in the cost of living. It is determined by changes in the price level, as measured by one of the major price indexes. The rate of inflation is the percentage increase in prices over a 12-month period.

Q: **How do economists define inflation, disinflation, deflation, and hyperinflation?**

A: Inflation is defined as a general rise in prices throughout the economy. Disinflation, meanwhile, is a reduction in the rate of inflation, whereas deflation is a decline in prices throughout the economy. Hyperinflation is an extremely high rate of inflation. Most economists refer to inflation above 100% a year as hyperinflation.

Q: **What major price indexes are used to measure inflation?**

A: Four major price indexes are used to measure inflation in the United States: the consumer price index, the personal consumption expenditures index, the producer price index, and the GDP deflator.

Q: **What is the consumer price index (CPI), and how is it calculated?**

A: The CPI is a measure of the average change in prices paid by urban consumers for a market basket of consumer goods and services. Every month, the Department of Labor's Bureau of Labor Statistics surveys thousands of families and retail outlets to track changes in the prices of specific types of consumer goods and services. This market basket of goods contains many product categories, with each category containing many items, and the basket is continually updated for changing consumer preferences. The result of the monthly survey is the cost to purchase the fixed market basket of goods. This cost is then compared to the base period and put into percentage terms using the formula

CPI = (Cost in current period ÷ cost in base period) × 100.

Q: **What is the personal consumption expenditures index (PCE), and how does it differ from the CPI?**

A: The PCE is a little broader index than the CPI. It has a heavier weighting for medical care, apparel, and recreation and a lighter weighting for food and housing. The PCE is based on GDP components and is more reflective of inflation in the wider consumer sector, whereas the CPI is focused on urban consumers.

Q: **What is the producer price index (PPI)?**

A: The producer price index (PPI)—originally known as the wholesale price index (WPI)—measures the average change in prices received by domestic producers for their output. The PPI contains over 10,000 price indexes for specific products and product categories, over 3,200 commodity price indexes, nearly 1,000 indexes for specific outputs of industries in the services sector, and several major aggregate measures of price change.

Q: **What is the GDP deflator?**

A: The GDP deflator is the broadest measure of inflation; it is a measure of the average change in prices of the components in GDP, including consumer goods, investment goods, government goods and services, and exports. The prices of imports are excluded.

Q: How are price indexes used?

A: Price indexes are used for two primary purposes: escalation and deflation. An escalator agreement modifies future payments, usually increasing them, to take the effects of inflation into account. Deflating a series of data with an index involves adjusting some *nominal* (or money) value for the impact of inflation, thereby computing what economists refer to as the *real* (or adjusted for inflation) value.

Q: Who is hurt by inflation? Who is helped?

A: People who live on fixed incomes and creditors are harmed by *unanticipated* inflation, since it decreases the purchasing power of their incoming funds. By the same token, unanticipated inflation helps debtors: It decreases the real value of their debts. These effects are amplified during periods of hyperinflation.

Inflation Quick Check

Circle the Correct Answer

1. (T/F) Inflation is a broad rise in prices throughout the economy.
2. (T/F) Most contemporary economists consider hyperinflation to be a setting in which the rate of inflation climbs to over 100% per month.
3. (T/F) The GDP deflator is the broadest of the four major inflation indexes.
4. What is a decrease in the rate of inflation called?
   a. hyperinflation
   b. hyperdeflation
   c. disinflation
   d. deflation
5. What does the CPI measure?
   a. over 200 goods and services
   b. the average changes in the prices received by domestic producers for their output
   c. the average prices paid by urban consumers for a market basket of consumer goods and services
   d. changes in the cost of living for rural consumers
6. You have just been awarded a cost-of-living increase tied to the CPI. The CPI has gone from 110 to 112. If your salary is $30,000 per year before the increase, what will it be after the CPI increase is factored in?
   a. $29,464
   b. $30,545
   c. $30,600
   d. $33,600
7. Which one of the following is *not* an economic consequence of unanticipated inflation?
   a. Elderly people on fixed incomes are harmed by inflation because the purchasing power of their incomes declines.
   b. Creditors are harmed by inflation because the real value of the payments they receive is reduced if the interest payments are fixed.

   c. There is a redistribution of income from debtors to creditors.
   d. Debtors benefit from inflation because the real value of their payments declines if the interest payments are fixed.
8. The producer price index (PPI) measures
   a. price changes in over 200 categories, each containing more than 200 goods and services.
   b. the average prices paid by urban consumers for a market basket of consumer goods and services.
   c. the average changes in the prices received by domestic producers for their output.
   d. the average change in prices of all of the components of gross domestic product, except for imports.
9. Assume that nominal GDP in 2000 was approximately $10.0 trillion. The GDP deflator, with a value of 100 in base year 1996, was 108 in 2000. What was the value of real GDP for 2000?
   a. $10.80 trillion
   b. $9.26 trillion
   c. $10.00 trillion
   d. $10.40 trillion
10. Which one of the following is *not* correct concerning hyperinflation?
    a. It is an extremely high rate of inflation.
    b. It is usually caused, in part, by extremely high government deficits.
    c. At its worst, the monetary system breaks down and barter takes over.
    d. Hyperinflation devastates everyone in the country.

Score: ____

If You Got 9 or 10 Correct

How inflation is defined and measured is not a problem for you. Be sure you are comfortable with converting nominal values to real values and back again. If you have any doubts, work through the solved problem below, otherwise go on to the next section, "Unemployment."

If You Didn't Get at Least 9 Correct

Slow down and review the material. It is not difficult; you are going through this material too quickly. Take a moment and reread this section in the text. Then spend a little time and write definitions in your own words for the following inflation terms:

- Price level:

- Inflation:

- Rate of inflation:

- Disinflation:

- Deflation:

- Hyperinflation:

Inflation is measured using index numbers. You only really need to be concerned with four measures of inflation: The consumer price index (CPI), the personal consumption expenditures index (PCE), the producer price index (PPI), and the GDP deflator. The first two reflect consumer prices, the PPI measures wholesale business prices, and the GDP deflator represents price changes for the aggregate economy.

All of these indexes are based on a base year where the index is 100. If the CPI for March 2008 was 215, consumer prices are more than double what they were in the base year (1982–84 = 100), or they have gone up by 115% (215 − 100). ▪

Solved Problem: Escalation and Deflation

The only real challenging part of this section is the process of escalation and deflation of series. Escalation is the easy one, so let's begin there.

Escalation: Adjusting Payments for Inflation

If you are earning $10,000 at a part-time job, overall prices rise by 5% (inflation = 5%), and you want your wage to increase by the rate of inflation, how much of a raise would you expect? The answer is easy. A 5% raise will keep you even with inflation, so your new salary needs to be $10,500 or

$$(.05 \times \$10,000) + \$10,000 = \$500 + \$10,000 = \$10,500.$$

When prices rise by x%, you need a raise of x% to keep you even with inflation. This is simple straightforward common sense.

Now when the changes involve index numbers, the calculation gets a little more complicated, but not too much. We have already seen that the CPI for March 2008 was 215 (base years 1982–84 CPI = 100). Now assume the CPI for

March 2003 was 184. Further, let's assume that you rent a commercial property, and you agreed to a 10-year lease in March 2003 with a rental payment of $4,000 a month, with a provision that the rental rate be adjusted by the CPI in 5 years. What is the new monthly rental going to be?

Now we can approach this two different ways. First, we can find the percentage change in the index and then multiply the rental payment by this percentage change; much as we did in the earlier example for a 5% change in earnings of $10,000. Here the index has gone from 184 to 215, for an absolute difference of 31 (215 − 184). Dividing 31 by 184 (the original index value) yields a percentage change of 16.85% (31/184 = .1685 = 16.85%), so prices have risen 16.85% over this 5-year period. Thus, the new rental payment will be 16.85% times $4,000 added to the original $4,000 payment or

$$(0.1685 \times \$4,000) + \$4,000 = \$674 + \$4,000 = \$4,674$$

Second, we can use the general formula for escalation:

$$\text{New} = \text{Original} \times (\text{Current Year Index} \div \text{Original Year Index})$$

Although this looks a little complex, it is not. The current year index (215) divided by the original year index (184) equals 1.1685. When this is multiplied by $4,000 it equals $4,674, the same answer as we computed earlier. This is the simple way to compute escalation. Note, the current year index (215) divided by the original year index (184) is just 1 plus .1685, where .1685 is simply the percentage change in the index.

Deflating Series: Converting Nominal Values to Real Values

Deflating economic series is a little more complicated because you are reducing the nominal value (current dollar value) to a real value (or constant dollar value) that is adjusted for inflation over the period. We use a formula similar to the escalation formula earlier to adjust nominal values to real values:

$$\text{Real} = \text{Nominal} \times (\text{Base Year Index} \div \text{Current Year Index})$$

The mechanics of this formula are the same as the one earlier, but intuitively it is a little more difficult because we are reducing the current value rather than increasing an earlier value for inflation. The question that deflation wishes to answer is how large is current dollar GDP (or any other value affected by inflation) versus an earlier year or quarter, given that the economy has experienced some inflation over this period.

To put this to practical use, let's assume that GDP in the first quarter 2001 was $10,022 billion, and by the first quarter of 2008 is was roughly $14,200 billion. The GDP deflator in the first quarter of 2001 was 101.5 and had grown to roughly 121.5 by the first quarter of 2008. Now, the crucial question is, has real (adjusted for inflation) GDP grown during this period?

We can begin to anticipate the answer by noting that nominal GDP has grown by 41.69% (14,200/10,022 = 1.4169 = 41.69% increase). Prices in the economy as measured by the GDP deflator have increased by 19.8% (121.6/101.5 = 1.198). Thus, if nominal GDP grew faster than inflation, then real GDP must have risen. Now, to see how the two real values compare, we use the formula above and compute real GDP in first quarter 2001 prices:

$$
\begin{aligned}
\text{Real GDP} &= \$14,200 \times (101.5 \div 121,5) \\
&= \$14,200 \times .8353 \\
&= \$11,861
\end{aligned}
$$

Comparing real GDP in first quarter 2001 ($10,022 billion) to first quarter 2008 ($11,861 billion) we see the economy has grown in real terms (adjusted for inflation) by 18.3% ($11,861/$10,022 = 1.183 = 18.3% increase). Notice that the real value of GDP in 2008 (in first quarter 2001 dollars) is less than its nominal value in 2008 ($11,861 versus $14,200), but it exceeds GDP in the base year (first quarter 2001).

Unemployment

Frequently Asked Questions

Q: How does the Census Bureau go about determining the number of people in the labor force?

A: Every month the Census Bureau, in conjunction with the Bureau of Labor Statistics, contacts roughly 60,000 households to determine the economic activity of people. It asks a series of factual questions designed to elicit information that permits the Bureau of Labor Statistics to determine how large the labor force is and whether people are employed or unemployed.

Q: What determines if a person is employed?

A: People are counted as employed if they have done any work at all for pay or profit during the survey week. Regular full-time work, part-time work, and temporary work are all included.

Q: What determines if a person is unemployed?

A: People are counted as unemployed if they do not have a job, but are available for work and have been actively seeking work for the previous 4 weeks. Actively looking for work requires doing things like sending resumes, contacting employers directly, going to job interviews, visiting school placement centers, or contacting private or public employment agencies.

Q: How is the labor force calculated?

A: The labor force is the sum of those people employed and unemployed. It does not include people who may have lost their jobs and are not actively seeking work. The unemployment rate is the number of people unemployed divided by the labor force, expressed as a percent.

Q: What are underemployed and discouraged workers?

A: The Bureau of Labor Statistics also collects data on underemployed and discouraged workers. Underemployed workers are individuals forced by weak economic conditions or changes in the job market to take jobs that do not fully use their education, background, and skills. Discouraged workers are unemployed individuals who have given up hope of finding a job and thus stopped actively seeking work. As a result, they are not classified as unemployed; they are no longer in the labor force.

Unemployment Quick Check

Circle the Correct Answer

1. (T/F) The Bureau of Labor Statistics would classify as employed a person who was laid off from his job 4 weeks ago but is doing 20 hours per week of temporary work as he searches for another job.

2. (T/F) The Bureau of Labor Statistics classifies as unemployed any union workers who are on strike.

3. (T/F) The Bureau of Labor Statistics regards individuals who are working part-time only as underemployed.

4. (T/F) The Bureau of Labor Statistics classifies a person as not in the labor force if he or she was laid off from a

job recently, is currently available for work, but has not actively looked for a job in over 4 weeks.

5. How is the unemployment rate calculated, according to the Bureau of Labor Statistics?
   a. the number of people unemployed plus discouraged workers divided by the labor force
   b. the number of people unemployed plus discouraged workers plus underemployed workers divided by the labor force
   c. the number of people unemployed, whether actively seeking work or not, divided by the labor force
   d. the number of people unemployed divided by the labor force

6. The Bureau of Labor Statistics defines the labor force as
   a. people who are employed, unemployed, underemployed, and discouraged workers.
   b. people who are employed, unemployed, and discouraged workers.
   c. people who are employed and unemployed.
   d. all those willing to work, whether they have a job or not and whether they are actively looking for a job or not.

7. Which of the following activities would the Census Bureau *not* count as an indication that a person is actively looking for work?
   a. checking help-wanted ads
   b. sending resumes off to potential employers
   c. contacting employment agencies
   d. scheduling job interviews

8. What are the primary criteria used by the Census Bureau for classifying people as unemployed?
   a. They must be without a job for 4 weeks and are willing to work.
   b. They must be without a job and are now actively seeking work.
   c. They must be without a job, currently available for work, and have been actively seeking work for the previous 4 weeks.
   d. They must be without a job and not discouraged from seeking work.

9. How would the Bureau of Labor Statistics classify a person who was laid off from her job 4 weeks ago, is currently available for work, has been actively seeking work for the past 4 weeks, and works 20 hours per week without pay in her father's business?
   a. employed
   b. unemployed
   c. underemployed
   d. not in the labor force

10. A person out of work but passively engaged in a job search is considered
    a. part of the labor force in the United States.
    b. part of the labor force in Canada and Europe.
    c. unemployed in the United States.
    d. a discouraged worker in Canada and Europe.

Score: _____

Answers: 1. T; 2. F; 3. F; 4. T; 5. d; 6. c; 7. a; 8. c; 9. a; 10. b

If You Got 9 or 10 Correct

You have a good understanding of the concept of unemployment, employment, and the labor force and how all three are measured. Move on to the next section, "Unemployment and the Economy."

If You Didn't Get at Least 9 Correct

Review the material carefully. This material is not difficult. First, go back to the text and make yourself a little table headed "labor force." List the categories that make up the labor force, and write down a one-sentence definition of each category. Then, write down the categories of people that are not included in the labor force. The next section, "Unemployment and the Economy," brings in further qualifications about the unemployment rate. As you work through more problems in the next section, the way unemployment is measured should make more sense. ∎

Unemployment and the Economy

Frequently Asked Questions

Q: **What causes unemployment?**

A: Our economy will inevitably contain some unemployment. Unemployment is caused by changes in the structure of an industry or the economy, downturns in the business cycle, and people entering the workforce or switching jobs and needing time to find work. Unemployment can result from wage levels that are sometimes kept artificially high (efficiency wages) to reduce turnover or improve morale.

Q: **What are the three major types of unemployment?**

A: Unemployment is split into three types: frictional, structural, and cyclical.

Q: **What is frictional unemployment?**

A: When people are temporarily unemployed because they are switching jobs, they are said to be frictionally unemployed. Frictional unemployment is short term and exists because some workers are always voluntarily or involuntarily changing jobs.

Q: **What is structural unemployment?**

A: Structural unemployment is unemployment brought about by changes in the structure of consumer demands or technology. It is often long term, with workers requiring considerable retraining before they can find work again.

Q: **What is cyclical unemployment?**

A: Cyclical unemployment is unemployment that arises because of downturns in the business cycle. This is unemployment that has the best chance of being affected by changes in government policy. By keeping the economy on a steady, low-inflationary, solid growth path, policymakers can minimize the costs of cyclical unemployment.

Q: **What is the natural rate of unemployment?**

A: The natural rate of unemployment, or full employment, is that rate of unemployment where price and wage changes are consistent, and thus the inflation rate is equal to people's inflationary expectations. It is also where unemployment is only frictional and structural; cyclical unemployment is zero. Economists often refer to the natural rate of unemployment as the nonaccelerating inflation rate of unemployment (NAIRU). This is defined as the unemployment rate most consistent with a low rate of inflation.

Unemployment and the Economy Quick Check

Circle the Correct Answer

1. (T/F) Frictional unemployment is generally short term in character.

2. (T/F) Full employment means zero unemployment.

3. (T/F) Structural unemployment is generally long term in character.

4. (T/F) "Efficiency wages" are wages set above market equilibrium to reduce turnover and boost morale.

5. Which one of the following is *not* true about structural unemployment?
   a. It is usually associated with extended periods of unemployment.
   b. It occurs when a person leaves one job for another job but cannot report to the new employer for several weeks.
   c. It can be caused by changes in technology.
   d. It often necessitates extensive retraining.

6. Which one of the following is *not* correct concerning cyclical unemployment?
   a. Cyclical unemployment comes about because of changes in the business cycle.
   b. Cyclical unemployment is the difference between the current unemployment rate and what it would be at full employment.
   c. Macroeconomic policies have their greatest impact on cyclical unemployment, as compared to frictional and structural unemployment.
   d. Cyclical unemployment is generally short term in duration.

7. The natural rate of unemployment
   a. equals frictional unemployment plus structural unemployment.
   b. does not take inflation into consideration.
   c. includes an average of cyclical unemployment over the life of the business cycle.
   d. is zero.

8. Which type of unemployment is natural for our economy and can be considered beneficial because it allows for searching?
   a. frictional unemployment
   b. structural unemployment
   c. cyclical unemployment
   d. natural unemployment

9. Which type of unemployment is most likely to be affected by macroeconomic policymaking?
   a. frictional unemployment
   b. structural unemployment
   c. cyclical unemployment
   d. natural unemployment

10. Which one of the following is *not* true of the natural rate of unemployment?
    a. It is a level of unemployment consistent with a low rate of inflation.
    b. It is equal to zero.
    c. It is influenced by the demographic makeup of the labor force and the incentives associated with unemployment benefits.
    d. It is the rate of unemployment when cyclical unemployment is zero.

Score: ____

Answers: 1. T; 2. F; 3. T; 4. T; 5. b; 6. d; 7. a; 8. a; 9. c; 10 b

If You Got 9 or 10 Correct

You have a good understanding of the concepts of frictional, structural, and cyclical unemployment and the natural rate of unemployment. As you will see in later chapters, these issues have significant policy implications. You should take a few minutes and look at the "Hints, Tips, and Reminders" below.

If You Didn't Get at Least 9 Correct

This is fairly easy stuff. Review the material and be sure you understand the differences among cyclical, structural, and frictional unemployment. Government can deal with cyclical unemployment much more easily than structural or frictional unemployment. When you have completed this review, glance over the "Hints, Tips, and Reminders" that follow. ■

STEP 4   Consider These Hints, Tips, and Reminders

1. Keep in mind that of our roughly 300 million-plus population, roughly half of those are in the labor force, and the labor force is split between those employed and those unemployed.

2. The key attribute of those considered unemployed is that they must be "actively seeking work."

3. Full employment is not zero. We will always have some unemployment as people pursue new jobs and transition between jobs (frictional unemployment). Further, structural changes, for example, caused by technology, can lead to long-duration unemployment as people need to acquire new skills. As a rough approximation, full employment implies between 4% and 6% unemployment.

4. If the inflation index rose from 100 to 105, prices would have risen 5% over this period. But if the index rose from 120 to 125, the rise in prices would have been only 4.2%, not 5%. Remember that you are looking at *percentage* changes, not just the change in the index.

5. Use your intuition and common sense when deflating nominal values as to real values. If you are deflating today's income to a real (adjusted for inflation) value and there has been inflation over the period, today's real value will be *less* than today's nominal value. If your answer is somehow larger than today's nominal value, you know you're wrong.

Instructor _____ Time _____ Student _____

Use the answer key below to record your answers to these homework questions.

1. (a) (b) (c) (d)   6. (a) (b) (c) (d)   11. (a) (b) (c) (d)   16. (a) (b) (c) (d)
2. (a) (b) (c) (d)   7. (a) (b) (c) (d)   12. (a) (b) (c) (d)   17. (a) (b) (c) (d)
3. (a) (b) (c) (d)   8. (a) (b) (c) (d)   13. (a) (b) (c) (d)   18. (a) (b) (c) (d)
4. (a) (b) (c) (d)   9. (a) (b) (c) (d)   14. (a) (b) (c) (d)   19. (a) (b) (c) (d)
5. (a) (b) (c) (d)   10. (a) (b) (c) (d)   15. (a) (b) (c) (d)   20. (a) (b) (c) (d)

1. A general rise in prices throughout the economy refers to
   a. disinflation.
   b. inflation.
   c. the price level.
   d. deflation.

2. A reduction in the rate of inflation refers to
   a. deflation.
   b. inflation.
   c. the price level.
   d. disinflation.

3. An extremely high rate of inflation refers to
   a. disinflation.
   b. inflation.
   c. the price level.
   d. hyperinflation.

4. The consumer price index (CPI) measures
   a. primarily retail prices of goods manufactured in the United States.
   b. monthly a market basket of 1,000 goods and services purchased in the United States.
   c. the average change in prices paid by urban consumers for a typical market basket of goods and services.
   d. all of the goods and services included in gross domestic product.

5. If the GDP deflator increases from 115.7 to 133.1, the overall increase in prices throughout the economy has been roughly
   a. 5%.
   b. 10%.
   c. 15%.
   d. 20%.

6. Which of the following is *not* a problem in measuring the consumer price index (CPI)?
   a. Public goods and services are excluded.
   b. The number of goods and services surveyed each month is so limited that the index is nearly meaningless.
   c. Environmental impacts are excluded.
   d. Consumer spending surveys are typically 3 to 5 years out of date.

7. In 1976 your mother earned $1,500 a month, and the CPI was 56.9. Today, the CPI stands at 186.6. Approximately what monthly salary would you have to be offered today to earn in real (adjusted for inflation) terms what your mother earned in 1976?
   a. $3,000
   b. $4,000
   c. $5,000
   d. $6,000

8. You will be graduating soon and have been offered a job at an annual wage of $35,000. The current CPI is 186.6, based on a 1984 base year. What is your approximate real wage in 1984 dollars?
   a. $15,000
   b. $18,750
   c. $45,625
   d. $65,000

9. Hyperinflation is *not*
   a. an extremely high rate of inflation.
   b. caused by extremely high deficit spending relative to the size of the economy.
   c. a relatively recent phenomenon.
   d. particularly harmful to individuals and businesses.

10. People who have done any work for pay or profit during the Bureau of Labor Statistics employment survey week are considered
    a. employed.
    b. unemployed.
    c. part of the labor force.
    d. discouraged workers.

11. People who are employed plus those who are unemployed are considered the
    a. employment rate.
    b. unemployment rate.
    c. labor force.
    d. working age population.

12. People who have looked for jobs for an extended period and have finally quit looking during the survey week are considered by the Bureau of Labor to be
    a. homeless.
    b. unemployed.
    c. out of the labor force.
    d. underemployed workers.

13. Businesses fail, people change jobs, and some people are fired. All of this economic activity in the economy naturally leads to
    a. frictional unemployment.
    b. structural unemployment.
    c. cyclical unemployment.
    d. a natural rate of unemployment.

14. Changes in business investment can often lead to ups and downs in the business cycle, and this leads to
    a. frictional unemployment.
    b. structural unemployment.
    c. cyclical unemployment.
    d. a natural rate of unemployment.

15. The unemployment rate that is consistent with a low rate of inflation is
    a. frictional unemployment.
    b. structural unemployment.
    c. cyclical unemployment.
    d. the natural rate of unemployment.

16. Which of the following is true of frictional unemployment?
    a. It is caused by long-run changes in technology.
    b. It is caused when people get discouraged and quit looking for work.
    c. It is caused primarily by the natural consequences of business cycles.
    d. It is a natural by-product of all economic activity.

17. Which of the following is true of structural unemployment?
    a. It is caused by long-run changes in technology.
    b. It is caused when people get discouraged and quit looking for work.
    c. It is caused primarily by the natural consequences of business cycles.
    d. It is a natural by-product of all economic activity.

18. Structurally unemployed individuals
    a. are not considered part of the labor force.
    b. will most likely require some retraining.
    c. are counted as employed if they are on vacation.
    d. are the result of strike breaking by employers.

19. The natural rate of unemployment is
    a. that rate of unemployment consistent with the establishment survey used by the Labor Department.
    b. that rate of unemployment consistent with the household survey used by the Labor Department.
    c. caused primarily by the natural consequences of business cycles.
    d. none of the above.

20. Full employment is
    a. equal to zero unemployment.
    b. defined roughly as the natural rate of unemployment.
    c. the sum of frictional, structural, and cyclical unemployment.
    d. determined primarily by the level of the minimum wage.

Use the ExamPrep to Get Ready for Exams	STEP 6

This sheet (front and back) is designed to help you prepare for your exams. The chapter has been boiled down to its key concepts. You are asked to answer questions, define terms, draw graphs, and, if you wish, add summaries of class notes.

Inflation

Define the following:
Price level:

Inflation:

Inflation rate:

Disinflation:

Deflation:

Hyperinflation:

Consumer price index:

Producer price index:

GDP deflator:

Generally describe how the Bureau of Labor Statistics measures inflation:

Unemployment

Define the following:
Employed:

Unemployed:

Labor force:

Generally describe how these three are measured:

List some of the problems with unemployment statistics:

Unemployment and the Economy

List the three types of unemployment and their descriptions:

Which type of unemployment is most response to government macroeconomic policymaking?

What is generally meant by full employment?

Additional Study Help Chapterwide Practice Questions

Matching

Match the description with the corresponding term.

___ 1. Inflation
___ 2. Disinflation
___ 3. Deflation
___ 4. Hyperinflation
___ 5. Consumer price index
___ 6. Producer price index
___ 7. GDP deflator
___ 8. Labor force
___ 9. Discouraged workers
___ 10. Frictional unemployment
___ 11. Structural unemployment
___ 12. Cyclical unemployment
___ 13. Natural rate of unemployment

a. An extremely high rate of inflation.
b. People who have been unemployed for so long that they have given up actively seeking work.
c. A broad rise in prices throughout the economy, as measured by a price index like the CPI or GDP deflator.
d. Brought about by changes in the structure of consumer demands or technology—long term in nature, with workers often requiring considerable retraining before they can find work again.
e. It measures the average changes in the prices received by domestic producers for their output.
f. A reduction in the rate of inflation.
g. The opposite of inflation; a decline in prices throughout the economy.
h. The rate of unemployment where price and wage decisions are consistent, and the inflation rate is equal to people's inflationary expectations.
i. A measure of the average change in prices of the components of GDP, including consumer goods, investment goods, government goods and services, and exports.
j. A measure of the average change in prices paid by urban consumers for a market basket of consumer goods and services.
k. All people who are either employed or unemployed.
l. When people are temporarily unemployed because they are switching jobs.
m. Unemployment that coincides with downturns in the business cycle. The most likely form of unemployment to be affected by changes in government policy.

Fill-In

Circle the word(s) in parentheses that complete the sentence.

1. When the inflation rate in the economy declines, economists referred to this as (the price level, inflation, disinflation, deflation, hyperinflation) _____, which is different from (the price level, inflation, disinflation, deflation, hyperinflation) _____, which refers to an overall decline in prices throughout the economy. When (the price level, inflation, disinflation, deflation, hyperinflation) _____ rises, an economy suffers inflation; but when prices throughout the economy rise at 100% a year or more, economists referred to this as (the price level, inflation, disinflation, deflation, hyperinflation) _____.

2. Measuring inflation rates by sampling retail establishments each month is done for the (CPI, PCE, PPI, GDP deflator) _____, while keeping track of inflation broadly is done with the (CPI, PCE, PPI, GDP deflator) _____.

3. Converting nominal values to real (adjusted for inflation) values refers to (deflating, disinflating, reinflating) _____ an economic series. When inflation increases unexpectedly, (creditors, debtors) _____ benefit, and (creditors, debtors) _____ lose.

4. Unemployed people are not counted as unemployed if they (lack skills, are not actively seeking work, failed to register for unemployment compensation) _____. The labor force is the sum of those employed and those (unemployed, discouraged) workers _____.

5. If you quit your job and move to Los Angeles to seek a job acting in the movie business, you will be counted as (frictionally, structurally, cyclically) _____ unemployed even though your friends will think you are structurally unemployed (only a small fraction of those who want to act in Hollywood actually make a living doing it). Job losses from a recession would be classified as (frictional, structural, cyclical) _____ unemployment.

True-False

Circle the correct answer.

T/F   1. A price level is the value of a price index as measured, for instance, by the CPI or the GDP deflator.

T/F   2. To say an economy is experiencing disinflation is another way of saying it is experiencing negative inflation, or an overall decline in prices.

T/F   3. When economists mention the inflation rate, they are generally referring to the percentage by which prices increase over a 1-month period.

T/F   4. The consumer price index is the broadest of the four major inflation indexes.

T/F   5. A cost-of-goods index measures the cost of a fixed bundle of goods and services from one period to the next.

T/F   6. The producer price index contains over 10,000 indexes for specific products and product categories, as well as over 3,200 commodity price indexes.

T/F   7. If nominal GDP rises by 2% in a year that inflation (as measured by the GDP deflator) runs at 3%, this means the economy is growing in terms of real GDP.

T/F   8. Most of the problems that may stem from a moderate rate of inflation can be avoided if the inflation is anticipated.

T/F   9. The U.S. unemployment rate peaked during the Great Depression at about 15%.

T/F   10. Those who work without pay for 15 hours per week or more in a family enterprise are "unpaid family workers," according to the Bureau of Labor Statistics.

T/F   11. The Bureau of Labor Statistics counts workers who have recently been laid off but are expecting to be recalled to work soon as employed.

T/F   12. Those people whom the Bureau of Labor Statistics regards as underemployed are individuals who are stuck in jobs that do not fully use their education, background, or skills.

T/F   13. The Bureau of Labor Statistics counts as discouraged workers those individuals who have jobs with which they are unhappy, but who cannot find any other jobs where they would be happier.

T/F   14. Minimum wage laws and collective bargaining both typically raise wages above their equilibrium rate, and this can increase unemployment.

T/F   15. Structural unemployment is typically short term in character.

T/F   16. An economy operating at full employment will have zero unemployment.

T/F   17. As a general rule, government policies can have a strong influence on levels of cyclical unemployment, but little influence over frictional or structural unemployment.

T/F   18. The natural rate of unemployment is a level of unemployment where inflationary pressures are high.

Multiple Choice

Circle the correct answer.

1. What is disinflation?
   a. a general increase in the level of prices
   b. a general decrease in the level of prices
   c. a decrease in the rate of inflation
   d. an extremely high rate of inflation

2. What is deflation?
   a. a general increase in the level of prices
   b. a general decrease in the level of prices
   c. a decrease in the rate of inflation
   d. an extremely high rate of inflation

3. At what rate of inflation would most contemporary economists consider hyperinflation to be setting in?
   a. 1% per month
   b. 100% per month
   c. 10% per year
   d. 100% per year

4. What does the CPI measure?
   a. the average prices paid by urban consumers for a market basket of consumer goods and services
   b. the average changes in the prices received by domestic producers for their output

c. the average change in prices of all of the components of GDP

d. the overall unemployment rate minus cyclical unemployment

5. The market basket the CPI uses to track price changes is composed of
    a. the top 25 consumer goods and services.
    b. 25 different categories, each containing more than 25 goods and services.
    c. over 200 goods and services.
    d. over 200 categories, each containing more than 200 goods and services.

6. What does the PPI measure?
    a. the average prices paid by urban consumers for a market basket of consumer goods and services
    b. the average changes in the prices received by domestic producers for their output
    c. the average change in prices of all of the components of GDP
    d. the overall unemployment rate minus cyclical unemployment

7. If your salary was $50,000 last year, and this year you receive a cost-of-living increase pegged to the CPI, what will your salary be, assuming the CPI has risen from 107 to 109?
    a. $49,083
    b. $50,673
    c. $50,935
    d. $51,243

8. What does real output measure?
    a. an economy's output of physical goods, as opposed to services or intellectual properties
    b. an economy's output, as adjusted for inflation
    c. an economy's output, as measured by total dollar sales
    d. an economy's output as measured by economists rather than television commentators

9. How would the Bureau of Labor Statistics classify a person who was laid off from her job several months ago and is currently available for work, but has not actively looked for a job in over 6 weeks?
    a. employed
    b. unemployed
    c. not in the labor force
    d. unpaid family worker

10. How would the Bureau of Labor Statistics classify a person who was laid off from his job several months ago and is now doing 20 hours of temporary work per week as he actively searches for another job?

a. employed
b. unemployed
c. not in the labor force
d. unpaid family worker

11. The Bureau of Labor Statistics defines the labor force as
    a. all people who are working at full-time, part-time, or temporary jobs.
    b. the sum of those who are employed, those who are unemployed, and discouraged workers.
    c. all people who have held a full-time job some time in the past year.
    d. the sum of those who are employed and those who are unemployed.

12. Which of the following activities would the Census Bureau *not* count as an indication that a person is actively looking for work?
    a. visiting a school job center
    b. attending a regional job fair
    c. asking friends whether they have heard of any job opportunities
    d. scheduling job interviews

13. What are the primary criteria the Census Bureau uses for classifying people as unemployed?
    a. They must have been without a job for at least 3 months and have actively looked for work for at least 2 of those months.
    b. They must have spent at least 5 years in the labor force, but now be unable to find work.
    c. They must not have a job, but they must be at least passively looking.
    d. They must not have a job, but must be currently available for work and have been actively looking.

14. "Efficiency wages" are typically
    a. equal to the minimum wage.
    b. equal to the market equilibrium wage.
    c. somewhat higher than the market equilibrium wage.
    d. designed to keep workers from settling into one job for too long.

15. Frictional unemployment is
    a. the unemployment, usually short term, associated with people who are switching jobs.
    b. the unemployment, typically long term, caused by changes in the structure of consumer demand or technology.
    c. the unemployment that arises due to downturns in the business cycle.
    d. equivalent to the natural rate of unemployment.

16. When a steel plant closes down because the company has moved its production overseas, the resulting unemployment among steelworkers is best described as
    a. frictional unemployment.
    b. structural unemployment.
    c. cyclical unemployment.
    d. natural unemployment.

17. Full employment is generally considered to be a state of the economy where unemployment is
    a. equal to the sum of frictional and structural unemployment.
    b. equal to the sum of frictional, structural, and cyclical unemployment.
    c. equal to structural employment.
    d. at very low levels, between 1% and 2% of the labor force.

18. Which of the following is *not* true of the natural rate of unemployment?
    a. It is equivalent to frictional unemployment plus structural unemployment.
    b. It rises and falls throughout the course of the business cycle.
    c. It is a level of unemployment consistent with a low rate of inflation.
    d. It is a level of unemployment where price and wage decisions are predictable, such that the actual inflation rate closely adheres to people's expectations.

Essay-Problem

Answer in the space provided.

The questions below often approach unemployment and inflation from a new perspective. Don't get upset if your answers are not always the same as those we suggest. Use these questions as another way to improve your understanding of what unemployment and inflation are, how they are measured, and some of the implications for policymaking.

1. To measure inflation, why does the government use a cost-of-goods approach rather than a cost-of-living approach?

2. Why is it important to have an accurate measure of inflation?

3. There was a time when COLAs (cost-of-living adjustments) were important in wage negotiations. Have you ever heard of this term? Why are COLAs not as important now?

4. Why does the government adjust every year the amount of the personal exemption on everyone's income tax form?

5. In the United States, most homeowners have fixed mortgages. In the United Kingdom, it is normal for homeowners to have mortgages with interest rates that fluctuate every year. What accounts for this curious difference?

6. What is an easy way that the government can help the elderly living on fixed incomes in a time of significant inflation?

7. Why would it be bad for you if you received your degree, and at the same time, the government tried to abolish frictional unemployment?

8. We saw that macroeconomic policymaking is more likely to be successful with cyclical unemployment than structural unemployment. Is there nothing the government can do to alleviate structural unemployment?

9. Why might an increase in the inflation rate have no effect on you at all?

10. The federal government now offers savings bonds that are indexed to the inflation rate. The public's response has been underwhelming, to the surprise of government planners. What might account for this lack of interest?

What's Next

With this chapter and the last chapter completed, you now have a good understanding of how the basic macroeconomic concepts of gross domestic product, inflation, and unemployment are measured. We will use these concepts throughout our study of the macroeconomy. In the next chapter, we will put these concepts to work when we look at long-run economic growth.

Answers to Chapterwide Practice Questions

Matching

1. c	5. j	9. b	13. h
2. f	6. e	10. 1	
3. g	7. i	11. d	
4. a	8. k	12. m	

Fill-In

1. disinflation, deflation, the price level, hyperinflation
2. CPI, GDP deflator
3. deflating, debtors, creditors
4. are not actively seeking work, unemployed
5. frictionally, cyclical

True-False

1. T	6. T	11. F	16. F
2. F	7. F	12. T	17. T
3. F	8. T	13. F	18. F
4. F	9. F	14. T	
5. T	10. T	15. F	

Multiple Choice

1. c	6. b	11. d	16. b
2. b	7. c	12. c	17. a
3. d	8. b	13. d	18. b
4. a	9. c	14. c	
5. d	10. a	15. a	

Essay-Problem

1. The main reason is that it is simpler to construct a cost-of-goods index. The measurement of changes to a market basket of goods is involved, though straightforward. To measure changes in the standard of living, the government would have to measure changes in prices of the market basket of goods *plus*, for example, determine how consumers respond to changes in product prices and income, a much more complex undertaking.

2. An accurate measure of inflation lets everyone know what level of inflation is present in the economy, taking away the guesswork that comes from relying on anecdotal and indi-

vidual examples. Policymakers need an accurate measurement to design the right macro-economic policies and to determine whether these policies have been successful. Furthermore, some wage earners have wage increases tied to inflation indices, so accuracy is important.

3. Cost-of-living adjustments were important when the inflation rate was high. They were needed to ensure that real wages did not suffer. For example, if the inflation rate was 10% and your wage increase was 5%, your real wages *decreased* by 5%. COLAs prevented this. With low inflation rates such as now, they are relatively unimportant.

4. The government adjusts the personal exemption amount to take into consideration the effects of inflation. By adjusting the amount, the government keeps the real amount the same.

5. The difference comes from changes in the inflation rate over time. Inflation has fluctuated greatly in the United Kingdom for many years. As we saw in the text, this favors debtors but hurts creditors. Building societies in the United Kingdom (similar to savings and loan companies here) refused to give mortgages with fixed interest rates because they wanted protection from fluctuating inflation rates. This has added a large element of uncertainty into homeowners' budgeting in the United Kingdom.

6. The government can—and now does—index benefits to the elderly such as Social Security, Medicare, and Medicaid. The index incorporates the inflation rate, so there is supposed to be no loss in real benefits.

7. For a start, it would mean that once you received your degree, you would have to take the first job offer you received. Otherwise, you would face frictional unemployment. Search time leads to frictional unemployment, which in reasonable doses may be beneficial for you.

8. A key factor in alleviating structural unemployment is job retraining. The government can offer tax incentives to individuals to encourage them to get this job retraining, and it can offer tax incentives to companies willing to retrain workers.

9. The inflation rate is based on a general rise in prices for goods and services. It affects people differently, depending on the actual goods and services they consume. It is possible, though unlikely, that all of the goods and services you consume will fall in price or remain the same, or that the ones that increase in price are cancelled out by the ones that decrease in price.

10. Three possibilities come to mind immediately. First, inflation is low, so these are not on people's radar screens. Second, since inflation-indexed bonds seem attractive on the face of it, it is likely that people find them less desirable because they offer a fluctuating payment dependent on the inflation rate, not a fixed payment. Third, you must pay taxes each year on the "interest received" even if you do not actually receive it. These bonds are discounted, so you get your interest when the bond matures or when it is sold. Right now, we make a fixed mortgage payment or fixed student loan payment; we want a fixed bond payment, so we can budget and pay our bills, not a real rate plus some undetermined inflation premium. In times of low inflation, certainty in the payment may be more desirable than solid real returns that come in fluctuating payments.

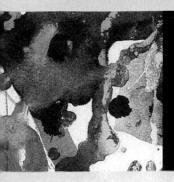

Economic Growth

Economic Growth Is a Key Goal of Macroeconomics

Now that you have examined the main macroeconomic variables of gross domestic product (GDP), inflation, and unemployment and how they are measured, you are ready to consider models of the macroeconomy. In this chapter, you will look at the classical long-run model of the economy and see how it focuses on economic growth. You will be introduced to what generates long-run economic growth, the sources of economic growth, and the role that infrastructure plays in facilitating economic growth. This model underlies long-run macroeconomic analysis.

This Is What You Need to Know

STEP 1

After studying this chapter you should be able to

■ Describe the aggregate production function in terms of classical economic theory.

■ Analyze labor supply and demand and the role of flexible wages.

■ Explain Say's law.

■ Use supply and demand to analyze the relationships among interest rates, savings, and investment.

■ Describe the implications and limitations of classical economic theory.

■ Describe the sources of long-term growth.

■ Describe the sources of productivity growth.

■ Describe modern growth theory.

■ Define infrastructure and explain its importance.

■ Describe the importance of tangible and intangible infrastructure.

Review the Key Terms

Economic growth: Usually measured by the annual percentage change in real GDP, reflecting an annual improvement in our standard of living.

Classical model: A model of the economy that relied on competitive conditions in product, labor, and capital markets, and flexible prices, wages, and interest rates to keep the economy operating around full employment. Anyone unemployed simply was unwilling to work at the prevailing real wage.

Aggregate production function: An equation [Q = Af(K,L)], that relates aggregate output (Q) to technology (A) and to the quantities of inputs (K is capital, and L is labor) it uses in the production process (f).

Say's law: The act of production produces income that leads to an equivalent amount of consumption spending; it is often paraphrased as "supply creates its own demand."

Productivity: How effectively inputs are converted into outputs. Labor productivity is the ratio of the output of goods and services to the labor hours devoted to the production of that output. Higher productivity and higher living standards are closely related.

Capital-to-labor ratio: The capital employed per worker. A higher ratio means higher labor productivity and, as a result, higher wages.

Investment in human capital: Improvements to the labor force from investments in improving skills, knowledge, and in any other way the quality of workers and their productivity.

Infrastructure: The public capital of a nation including transportation networks, power-generating plants and transmission facilities, public education institutions, and other intangible resources such as protection of property rights and a stable monetary environment.

Work Through the Chapter Tutorials

The Classical Model

Frequently Asked Questions

Q: How did classical economists look at the economy, and what did they conclude?

A: Classical economists broke the economy into three markets: the product market, the labor market, and the capital market. All three markets were thought to be highly competitive, allowing prices, wages, and interest rates to adjust to changing conditions. By implication, classical economists predicted a relatively stable economy tending toward equilibrium at full employment.

Q: What is an aggregate production function, and what does it tell us?

A: An aggregate production function describes an economy's production by the formula Q = Af(K,L), where Q is output or income, A is an index of total input (factor) productivity or technology, and f is a function that relates output to inputs of capital (K) and labor (L). This equation tells us aggregate output is directly related to an economy's technological development and to the quantities of labor and capital employed in the production process. Technology, labor, and capital are the three primary factors accounting for long-term economic growth.

Q: How is equilibrium achieved in the labor market?

A: The supply of labor curve reflects the tradeoff workers face between working and leisure. Equilibrium is achieved at the intersection point of the supply of labor and demand for labor curves. At this point, all workers who want to work at the resulting real wage rate are employed. Those who do not work are voluntarily unemployed—they could work, but are unwilling to do so at the going wage. Flexible wages and prices keep the labor market in equilibrium at full employment.

Q: What is Say's law and how does it work?

A: Say's law holds that "supply creates its own demand," or that there can be no deficiency in aggregate demand since the very act of production also generates an income that leads to an equal amount of consumption. Sometimes help is needed from the capital markets, however, to keep the economy at full employment. If consumption falls off, saving will rise. This reduces interest rates, which results in greater investment spending, returning the economy to full employment. This increased investment offsets the decline in consumption.

Q: What is the primary limitation of the classical model?

A: The primary limitation of classical analysis is its exclusive focus on the long run. Policy decisions are often executed with an eye to their short-term political implications, so short-term analytic tools are needed. The classical model assumes, moreover, that labor, product, and capital markets are all highly competitive, which they are if given enough time for adjustment, but in the short run they often do not fit this description.

The Classical Model Quick Check

Circle the Correct Answer

1. (T/F) Classical economists focused on four key competitive markets: labor, capital, product, and land.
2. (T/F) Say's law can be described as "supply creates its own demand."
3. (T/F) In the classical model, those who do not work are voluntarily unemployed; they could work, but are unwilling to do so for the going wage.
4. (T/F) In the classical model, economic growth will be due to good government policies.
5. In the aggregate production function, $Q = A \, f(K,L)$,
   a. aggregate output is totally dependent on the level of technology.
   b. aggregate output is directly related to an economy's technology and to the quantities of inputs it uses in the production process.
   c. aggregate output is directly related to an economy's capital inputs because technology, labor, and land do not vary.
   d. aggregate output is hard to determine because f is unknown.

6. In the classical model, if consumption fell,
   a. the economy would stumble into a recession.
   b. savings would rise, which would lead to a decrease in interest rates, which would spur business investment, which would bring an economy back to full employment.
   c. savings would rise, which would lead to an increase in interest rates, which would hinder business investment, which would lead to a fall in real wages, which would lead to increased hiring, which would bring the economy back to full employment.
   d. savings would rise, which would lead to an increase in interest rates, which would make business investment more profitable, which would spur business investment, which would bring the economy back to full employment.
7. Which one of the following is *not* an element of the classical model?
   a. It concludes that long-run growth can occur due to improvements in labor productivity.
   b. It holds that labor, product, and capital markets are highly competitive.

c. It focuses on the long run.

d. It held that insufficient demand could lead to a general glut.

8. In the aggregate production function, Q = Af(K,L), which one of the following is *not* correct?

a. Increasing labor inputs will lead to rising output if capital and technology are held constant.

b. Increasing capital inputs will lead to rising output if labor and technology are held constant.

c. Increasing technology will lead to rising output if labor and capital are held constant.

d. Increasing technology will lead to rising output only if more capital and labor are added.

9. In the classical model, what guarantees that an economy would quickly follow Says' law (supply creates its own demand)?

a. competitive labor markets

b. competitive capital markets

c. competitive product markets

d. competitive land markets

10. Which one of the following is *not* a part of the classical model?

a. It focuses exclusively on the long run.

b. It assumes that business investment will fall when interest rates fall.

c. It assumes that labor, product, and capital markets are highly competitive.

d. It concludes that high unemployment levels cannot last for long.

Score: _____

Answers: 1. F; 2. T; 3. T; 4. F; 5. b; 6. b; 7. d; 8. d; 9. b; 10. b

If You Got 9 or 10 Correct

The classical model is not an easy model to pick up on the first reading. But you seem to have a good handle on it. Go on to the next section, "Sources of Long-Run Economic Growth."

If You Didn't Get at Least 9 Correct

Slow down when you review the material for this section. This is the key long-run model of the economy, and you need to get this down pat. The classical model uses stylized competitive product, labor, and capital markets to analyze the aggregate economy. Because these markets are competitive, adjustments in these markets keep the economy at full employment.

For our purposes, the classical model is a stylized story summarized as follows:

■ As noted earlier, classical economists split the economy into three *competitive* markets: product, labor, and capital.

■ Competitive product markets determine product prices and output.

■ Labor market demand is based on product demand and labor productivity. Labor supply is based on people's labor–leisure choice. Labor market equilibrium sets wages and employment. All unemployment is "voluntary"; those not working choose not to work for the going wage.

■ The capital market equates business investment with saving and determines equilibrium interest rates that prevent the potential problem of underconsumption.

When you review this stylized story told in this section, ask yourself how flexible wages and product prices keep the economy fully employed. Pay special attention, again, to the role played by competitive markets and flexible wages, interest rates, and product prices.

Keep in Mind

Two key implications result from the classical model:

1. Competition in the major markets and flexible wages, prices, and interest rates work together to keep the economy at full employment.

2. Economic growth results from improvements in technology, additions to capital, and anything that improves the productivity of labor.

With these considerations in mind, we now turn to an examination of the sources of long-run economic growth. ■

Sources of Long-Run Economic Growth

Frequently Asked Questions

Q: Where does economic growth come from?

A: The aggregate production function implies that economic growth can come from three sources: increases in capital, increases in labor, and improvements in technology.

Q: What has been an important driver of economic growth in the United States in the past 100 years?

A: A key factor in U.S. economic growth over the past century has been the expansion of its labor force from population growth and increased labor force participation. These trends have been encouraged by open immigration policies and increased incentives for entering the workforce, such as lower marginal tax rates.

Q: What is productivity growth, and where does it come from?

A: The productivity of labor is the most significant determinant of real wages, and high productivity is the primary reason our standard of living is so high. Sources of productivity growth include increases in the capital-to-labor ratio, increases in the quality of the labor force, and improvements in technology. Technological progress has been the most significant source of the enormous productivity gains the United States and many other countries have enjoyed over the past century.

Q: What is the nature of modern growth theory, and what are its conclusions?

A: Growth theories developed since 1980 focus on the role of technology and knowledge. Innovations have substantial public good aspects as the benefits from new technologies spillover to other firms. Knowledge discovered by one firm quickly becomes public and useful to other firms. With millions of firms engaging in research and development, this public good aspect of knowledge can result in increasing returns and is an important driver of economic growth. Recent developments in microchips, nanotechnology, the sequencing of DNA, and innovative just-in-time production techniques are examples.

Sources of Long-Run Economic Growth Quick Check

Circle the Correct Answer

1. (T/F) The classical model implies that economic growth will come from increases in capital, increases in labor, and improvements in technology.

2. (T/F) Developing countries tend to have shortages of both capital and labor.

3. (T/F) Modern growth theory concentrates on knowledge and technology and especially on the limits of technology to generate growth.

4. (T/F) America's birthrate is rising, suggesting that its labor force will be growing in the years ahead.

5. Which of the following has *not* led to growth in the labor force in the United States?
   a. immigration

b. population growth

c. day care, job sharing, and flexible hours

d. productivity increases

6. Which one of the following has *not* led to labor productivity growth?

a. stable capital-to-labor ratios

b. improvements in computer technology

c. on-the-job training

d. universal public education

7. Which one of the following has *not* helped developing countries improve productivity?

a. global capital movements

b. cheap cell phones

c. low wages

d. inexpensive vaccinations

8. Which one of the following is *not* correct?

a. The higher the value of the goods you produce, the higher will be your earnings and your standard of living.

b. Highly productive nations are places with high standards of living.

c. Nations with high capital-to-labor ratios need more workers in order to improve productivity.

d. Nations with unproductive labor forces have low incomes.

9. Productivity growth is enhanced by all *except* which one of the following?

a. providing universal public education

b. increasing capital-to-labor ratios

c. increasing birthrates

d. improving technology

10. Developing countries have increased economic growth by all *except* which one of the following policies?

a. trade liberalization

b. health education programs that have reduced mortality rates

c. global movement of production facilities

d. commodity price stabilization boards

Score: ____

Answers: 1. T; 2. F; 3. F; 4. T; 5. d; 6. a; 7. c; 8. c; 9. c; 10. d

If You Got 9 or 10 Correct

You can describe the sources of long-run economic growth. Go on to the next section, "Infrastructure and Economic Growth," and discussion of the role infrastructure plays in helping economies grow.

If You Didn't Get at Least 9 Correct

Review the material carefully. The better you understand the sources of economic growth, the better you will be able to weigh the effects of government policies on the economy. Look over this section in the text again. Make up your own list of the sources of economic growth. Keep in mind that nothing in this section is particularly difficult; it is really just common sense.

Continue on, but be prepared to review this section and the first section on the classical model again. The next section, "Infrastructure and Economic Growth," provides further insights on additional elements that jump start and sustain economic growth. ∎

Infrastructure and Economic Growth

Frequently Asked Questions

Q: What is infrastructure, and why is it important?

A: One of the key reasons some nations are rich and others are poor is the different levels of infrastructure in various countries. Infrastructure is defined as a country's public capital. It includes such tangible assets as dams, roads, and bridges, but also such intangible goods as secure property rights, legally enforced contract rights, and a stable financial system.

Q: How is infrastructure measured?

A: Despite the difficulties of measuring infrastructure, the economic freedom index, produced by the Fraser Institute, is a fairly objective means of assessing a country's infrastructure. The index incorporates information from seven categories: size of government, structure of the economy and use of markets, monetary policy and price stability, freedom to use alternative currencies, legal structure and property rights, international exchange, and freedom of exchange in capital and financial markets.

Q: Is there a link between economic freedom and GDP?

A: Those countries with the most economic freedom also have the highest real per capita GDP. It is widely believed that investing in human capital and promoting greater economic freedom will lead to higher growth rates and higher standards of living in the developing world.

Infrastructure and Economic Growth Quick Check

Circle the Correct Answer

1. (T/F) Infrastructure is defined as a country's public capital.
2. (T/F) Dams and roads are tangible infrastructure; public education facilities and telecommunications networks are intangible infrastructure.
3. (T/F) The protection of property rights is an important but intangible part of a country's infrastructure.
4. Economic growth is helped by all of the following *except* which one?
   a. the legal enforcement of contract rights
   b. a stable legal system that protects property rights
   c. informally recognized land ownership
   d. a stable financial system
5. To spur economic growth, underdeveloped countries should
   a. trade with foreigners.
   b. protect property rights.
   c. educate their population.
   d. do all of the above.
6. Which one of the following is *not* correct?
   a. According to the economic freedom index, countries with the most economic freedom have the highest per capita GDP.
   b. Most economists would agree that the best way to help poor nations develop is to encourage economic reforms and the freeing of markets.
   c. Most economists believe that foreign aid is crucial for poor nations.
   d. Governments in poor nations have a crucial role in minimizing inflation and protecting property rights.
7. Which one of the following is *not* part of a country's infrastructure?
   a. a private, paved road running across the estate of the wealthiest person in the country
   b. a bridge over the largest river

c. the national airport
   d. electric lines running from a power plant to the capital
8. Intangible infrastructure includes all *except* which one of the following?
   a. copyright laws
   b. telecommunications networks
   c. legally protected property rights
   d. legally enforceable contracts
9. The Fraser Institute's economic freedom index shows that
   a. economic freedom and per capita GPD are not linked.
   b. economic freedom and per capita GDP are linked in rich countries but not in poor countries.
   c. economic freedom and per capita GDP are linked in poor countries but not in rich countries.
   d. those countries with the most economic freedom have the highest per capita GDP.
10. Which one of the following is *not* correct?
   a. The dominant view after World War II was that poorer countries needed foreign aid in order to generate economic growth.
   b. Peter Bauer argued that opportunities for private profit, not government plans, held the key to economic development.
   c. Most economists now believe that economic freedom and economic development go hand in hand.
   d. Large infrastructure projects such as dams and power plants are needed to stimulate economic growth in developing nations.

Score: ____

Answers: 1. T; 2. F; 3. T; 4. c; 5. d; 6. c; 7. a; 8. b; 9. d; 10. d

If You Got 9 or 10 Correct

You are not having any problems with economic growth, what causes economies to grow, and the infrastructure necessary to achieve growth. Take a quick look at the "Hints, Tips, and Reminders."

If You Didn't Get at Least 9 Correct

Review the material carefully. This material is not difficult, but it often requires some reflection. When you go over this section, try to write down infrastructure items we might take for granted. For example, is there any difference for economic growth between a society where suing your neighbor is a common happening and a society that is more restrained? When you are done, look at the "Hints, Tips, and Reminders" next. ■

STEP 4   Consider These Hints, Tips, and Reminders

1. This is a relatively easy chapter, describing the theory behind economic growth, and is essentially an extension of the analysis in Chapter 2. The only difficult section is on classical theory.

2. Classical analysis is the logical extension of competitive markets applied to the entire economy. Keep in mind it is a good stylized analysis of the *long run*, but as you will see in the next chapter, it does not do a good job of analyzing short-run fluctuations in the economy.

Do the Homework for Chapter 17
Economic Growth

Instructor _____ Time _____ Student _____

Use the answer key below to record your answers to these homework questions.

1. (a) (b) (c) (d)   6. (a) (b) (c) (d)   11. (a) (b) (c) (d)   16. (a) (b) (c) (d)
2. (a) (b) (c) (d)   7. (a) (b) (c) (d)   12. (a) (b) (c) (d)   17. (a) (b) (c) (d)
3. (a) (b) (c) (d)   8. (a) (b) (c) (d)   13. (a) (b) (c) (d)   18. (a) (b) (c) (d)
4. (a) (b) (c) (d)   9. (a) (b) (c) (d)   14. (a) (b) (c) (d)   19. (a) (b) (c) (d)
5. (a) (b) (c) (d)   10. (a) (b) (c) (d)   15. (a) (b) (c) (d)   20. (a) (b) (c) (d)

1. Adam Smith wrote the
   a. Constitution.
   b. *Wall Street Journal.*
   c. Declaration of Independence in 1776.
   d. *Wealth of Nations* in 1776.

2. A production function for the economy suggests that
   a. output in the economy is related to the amount of stock traded on stock exchanges.
   b. employment in the economy is related to government spending on goods and services.
   c. output in the economy is related to the amount of labor employed given the capital stock and technology.
   d. full employment in the economy is the natural state of affairs.

3. According to classical analysis, labor markets will remain in equilibrium at full employment because
   a. people need to work so they can purchase goods and services.
   b. entrepreneurs will open new businesses and hire people to earn higher profits.
   c. technology continually improves living standards.
   d. wages and prices are flexible.

4. Jean Baptiste Say argued that there can be no deficiency in aggregate demand because
   a. demand creates its own supply.
   b. the act of production creates an equivalent amount of income that leads to the same amount of consumption.
   c. capital markets will keep interest rates high to ensure that business will be willing to save what is needed for investment in new plants and equipment.

   d. technology generates new products that consumers want, and their demand keeps the economy at full employment.

5. In the classical model, saving is determined by
   a. the willingness of business to forgo investing in new plant and equipment.
   b. income levels.
   c. the amount of loanable funds available.
   d. interest rates.

6. The major limitations of classical analysis are
   a. its focus on the short run and overly realistic assumptions about the economy and economic actors.
   b. its failure to recognize the role of technology in promoting economic growth.
   c. its focus on the long run and stylistic assumptions.
   d. its failure to recognize the important role of stock markets in channeling funds from sales of stock between investors and speculators to investment in new productive plants and equipment.

7. Classical analysis suggests that economic growth can come from the following three sources:
   a. increases in capital, new products, and a growing labor force.
   b. increases in labor, capital, and technology.
   c. rising stock sales, increases in capital formation, and an increase in the rate of new product development.
   d. improvements in the income distribution, health of the population, and literacy.

8. Classical analysis suggests that in the long run, our standard of living is principally determined by
   a. how the government redistributes income.
   b. capital markets including the stock markets.

c. labor unions and government regulation of business.

d. our productivity.

9. Productivity will generally be higher
   a. the lower the capital-to-labor ratio.
   b. the larger the labor force.
   c. the higher the capital-to-labor ratio.
   d. the smaller the amount of capital available to do the job.

10. Which of the following will *not* increase productivity?
    a. increasing the level of on-the-job training.
    b. increasing the number of hours in the work-week.
    c. a growing capital-to-labor ratio.
    d. spending more money on research and development.

11. The term *infrastructure* refers to
    a. how capital markets are structured.
    b. the general level of government spending in the economy.
    c. a country's public capital like roads and dams.
    d. the internal structure of business and the management techniques used to keep labor highly productive.

12. A stable and secure financial system is important because
    a. it keeps the purchasing power of the currency stable.
    b. it facilitates economic transactions.
    c. it helps credit institutions to develop.
    d. all of the above.

13. Long-run economic growth results from
    a. improvements in technology.
    b. a larger and better-educated labor force.
    c. a higher capital-to-labor ratio.
    d. all of the above.

14. Which of the following elements of a nation's infrastructure is the most difficult to measure?
    a. transportation networks
    b. levels of education
    c. telecommunications networks
    d. contract enforcement and the protection of property rights

15. An economy with a large unskilled labor force would also tend to have
    a. a low capital-to-labor ratio.
    b. high level of investment in human capital.
    c. a high capital-to-labor ratio.
    d. a high standard of living.

16. Productivity in developing countries has *not* been improved by
    a. increased global capital mobility.
    b. trade liberalization.
    c. a growing pool of unskilled low-wage labor.
    d. improved (and cheap) telecommunications equipment.

17. Improvements in technology often arise in developed nations; these improvements help the growth rates of developing economies because
    a. companies in developed nations are quick to gift their new-found technologies to developing nations.
    b. technologies like improved and cheap telecommunications are quickly adapted by developing nations, resulting in improved productivity and growth.
    c. governments in developing nations are quick to adopt the latest technologies to improve the efficiency of government service.
    d. most developed nations have laws that require companies and universities to share their research and development results with their counterparts in developing nations.

18. The extraordinary level of productivity growth we have experienced over the last century can best be explained by
    a. high rate of immigration.
    b. low interest rates that encourage investment by business.
    c. government programs to help the poor.
    d. technology.

19. Classical economic analysis suggests that if the labor force expands,
    a. fewer people will want to work.
    b. stock prices will rise as investors perceive that lower wages will result in higher profits for business.
    c. real wages will adjust to keep the market in equilibrium at full employment.
    d. government will have to institute make-work programs to ensure full employment.

20. Long-run economic growth results from
    a. miracle drugs developed by biotech companies that improve and extend the lives of the population.
    b. technological improvements in online learning that extend a college education to many more people.
    c. improvements in the nation's interstate highway system.
    d. all of the above.

Use the ExamPrep to Get Ready for Exams

This sheet (front and back) is designed to help you prepare for your exams. The chapter has been boiled down to its key concepts. You are asked to answer questions, define terms, draw graphs, and, if you wish, add summaries of class notes.

The Classical Model

List the three markets classical economists used to model the economy and list the variables they thought would be flexible enough to keep the economy at full employment:

Market   **Flexible Variable**

_____

_____

_____

Define Say's law, and explain why it is important:

Explain the role played by the capital markets:

Describe the implications of classical analysis for long-run economic growth:

Sources of Long-Run Economic Growth

What are the sources of long-run economic growth, according to the classical model?

Explain why productivity is important for economic growth and higher standards of living:

List the major sources of productivity growth:

Describe modern growth theory and its implications for economic growth:

Infrastructure and Economic Growth

List some of the important infrastructure elements that aid economic growth:

Additional Study Help Chapterwide Practice Questions

Matching

Match the description with the corresponding term.

___ 1. Aggregate production function
___ 2. Modern growth theory
___ 3. Say's law
___ 4. Long-run classical growth
___ 5. Capital-to-labor ratio
___ 6. Infrastructure

a. The relationship between a country's supply of available capital and its labor supply.

b. It includes such tangible assets as dams, roads, bridges, transportation networks, and educational facilities, and also intangibles such as secure property rights, legally enforced contract rights, and a stable financial system.

c. Suggests that "supply creates its own demand," or that there can be no deficiency in aggregate demand since the act of production also generates income that leads to an equal amount of consumption.

d. Focuses on knowledge spillovers as a major source of economic growth.

e. Describes an economy's production by the formula $Q = Af(K,L)$, where Q is output or income, A is an index of total input (factor) productivity or technology, and f is a function that relates output to inputs of capital (K) and labor (L).

f. Results from growth in labor and capital resources plus improvements in technology.

Fill-In

Circle the word(s) in parentheses that complete the sentence.

1. Long-run economic growth, according to classical economists, came from increases in (labor resources, government, corruption) _____ and improvements in (regulations, technology, data collection) _____.

2. The standards of living that the nation's inhabitants enjoy are a result of their (government, willingness to consume, productivity) _____. Increasing the capital-to-labor ratio results in higher (prices for products, productivity and wages, interest rates) _____. Improvements in technology that spread because the information becomes public and other firms adopt the technology are important elements of (classical, modern growth) _____ theory.

True-False

Circle the correct answer.

_T/F_ 1. Classical economists broke the economy into three competitive markets: the retail market, the wholesale market, and the labor market.

_T/F_ 2. Classical economists argued that workers will supply labor to the market on the basis of what their wages will buy.

_T/F_ 3. Classical analysis tells us that economic growth depends primarily on technological progress and increases in the amounts of labor and capital used in the production process.

_T/F_ 4. Say's law is often paraphrased as "demand creates its own supply."

_T/F_ 5. Classical economists maintained that if demand were temporarily insufficient to absorb the available supply, movements in the labor market would restore the economy to full employment.

_T/F_ 6. Overall, the American economy has greatly benefited from the country's relatively open immigration policies.

_T/F_ 7. Overall, the entrance of large numbers of women into the workforce over the past few decades has hurt the American economy by tightening labor markets.

_T/F_ 8. A developed country will generally have a higher capital-to-labor ratio than a developing country.

_T/F_ 9. The primary reason that U.S. farmers have higher incomes than Nigerian farmers is that they work longer hours.

_T/F_ 10. Technological advances may increase product quality, but they also usually lead to higher prices.

_T/F_ 11. The tangible components of a nation's infrastructure are usually the most difficult to objectively measure.

T/F   12. Even a country with a strong preference for free markets needs some public capital.

T/F   13. The strict enforcement of contracts and property rights tends to stifle innovation and economic growth.

T/F   14. One of the reasons economic growth requires a stable financial system is that price signals function so poorly when they are distorted by inflation or deflation.

T/F   15. Intangible things like enforceable contracts and protected property rights may be counted as part of a nation's infrastructure.

T/F   16. As a rule, those countries with the most economic freedoms enjoy the highest per capita GDP.

T/F   17. A high degree of government planning, as opposed to trusting unpredictable markets, is now thought to be the best strategy for promoting economic growth in developing countries.

T/F   18. Growth is stifled in many developing countries because property rights are recognized only informally rather than being legally defined and protected.

T/F   19. The conventional wisdom on how best to help poorer nations develop has undergone considerable change since the years following World War II.

Multiple Choice

Circle the correct answer.

1. Which of the following is *not* one of the markets into which classical economists broke the economy?
   a. capital market
   b. product market
   c. stock market
   d. labor market

2. What does the production function $Q = Af(K,L)$ tell us?
   a. Aggregate output is a function of input prices and the market demand for goods and services.
   b. Aggregate output is directly related to an economy's level of technology and to the quantities of inputs used in the production process.

   c. Aggregate output is directly related to an economy's level of technology and to the market demand for goods and services.
   d. Aggregate output is a function of wages, interest rates, and rent.

3. Which of the following is an accurate paraphrase of Say's law?
   a. Supply creates its own demand.
   b. Low interest rates drive investment.
   c. In the long run, capital markets promote full employment.
   d. Anything that can go wrong, will go wrong.

4. According to classical economic theory, what is the most significant determinant of saving and investment decisions?
   a. income
   b. interest rates
   c. future expectations
   d. past economic performance

5. What did classical economists believe would restore an economy to full employment if Say's law temporarily failed and output exceeded demand?
   a. the labor market
   b. the product market
   c. the capital market
   d. input markets

6. Which of the following is *not* a true statement about current U.S. demographics?
   a. The U.S. birthrate is rising.
   b. The United States has more immigrants than most other countries.
   c. Americans will soon be growing older as a population.
   d. The U.S. population as a whole has grown faster than its labor force.

7. Which of the following is *not* among the policies the U.S. government has enacted to increase labor force participation.
   a. increased protections for pension funds
   b. an increase in the progressivity of the income tax
   c. support for enhanced retirement benefits
   d. subsidies for day care

8. What has been the most significant factor underlying the tremendous growth of the U.S. economy?
   a. increased productivity
   b. growth of rules governing business behavior
   c. increased use of capital
   d. government coordination of the economy

9. Which of the following would *not* be among the primary sources of rising productivity?
   a. technological advances
   b. improvements in the quality of the labor force
   c. increases in the capital-to-labor ratio
   d. growth of the labor force

10. Developing nations tend to have
    a. considerable capital and labor.
    b. considerable capital, but a shortage of labor.
    c. considerable labor, but a shortage of capital.
    d. shortages of both labor and capital.

11. An economy with a highly skilled labor force will also tend to have
    a. a low capital-to-labor ratio.
    b. a high capital-to-labor ratio.
    c. the same capital-to-labor ratio as a developing country.
    d. a low rate of economic growth.

12. What was the most important factor underlying the tremendous rise in American productivity over the 20th century?
    a. technological progress
    b. increased in the capital-to-labor ratio
    c. improvements in the quality of the labor force
    d. growth of the labor force

13. Which of the following is an intangible component of a nation's infrastructure?
    a. rail lines
    b. power-generating plants
    c. copyright laws
    d. bridges

14. Which of the following would *not* be among the components of a nation's infrastructure?
    a. the financial system
    b. the airline system
    c. roads and bridges
    d. small businesses

15. Which of the following components of a nation's infrastructure are most difficult to measure in objective terms?
    a. the highway system
    b. the enforceability of contracts
    c. the telecommunications network
    d. dams

16. The economic freedom index shows that
    a. those countries with the most economic freedoms have the highest per capita GDP.
    b. those countries with the fewest economic freedoms have the highest per capita GDP.
    c. most of those countries with fewer economic freedoms have per capita GDP's comparable to those of countries with more economic freedoms.
    d. economic freedom and per capita GDP stand in no discernible relation to one another.

17. In the aftermath of World War II, the conventional wisdom held that the best way to help poorer nations develop was by
    a. encouraging economic reforms and the freeing up of markets.
    b. canceling their foreign debts.
    c. sending foreign aid to their governments and assisting in massive construction projects.
    d. promoting political freedom and democracy.

18. Today, most economists would agree that the best way to help poorer nations develop is by
    a. promoting more government control of the economy and the nationalization of heavy industries.
    b. encouraging economic reforms and the freeing up of markets.
    c. sending massive amounts of foreign aid to the government and assisting in large construction projects.
    d. rewarding those dictators who favor our interests with lucrative assistance deals.

Essay-Problem

Answer in the space provided.

The questions below are designed to make you reflect and extend the material on economic growth. Your answers may differ from those we suggest, but use them to assess your progress.

1. What is the simple message about the macroeconomy contained in the classical model that was challenged by the Great Depression?

2. Is productivity growth a benefit to everyone?

3. Why is price stability so important for a developing nation?

4. The classical model assumes that labor markets are highly competitive and therefore that wages will adjust quickly. From your own experience, what might be wrong with this view?

5. Why are the capital markets so important in the classical model?

6. What is the difference between growth in the labor force and growth in labor force productivity?

7. For a time, governments in developing nations were urged to confiscate land from large landholders and redistribute it to the rural poor. Some governments followed this advice and redistributed land in small amounts to the poor, though the government held on to title in the land. Why would this be a problem?

8. Why is it important to consider infrastructure in analyzing economic growth?

9. There is a link between economic freedom and high per capita GDP. Is there a corresponding link between democracy and high per capita GDP?

10. Some studies have shown that business investment tax credits have been important in stimulating economic growth. Why would these credits have this effect?

What's Next

You now have an understanding of how the macroeconomy works in the long run, and what causes long-run economic growth. The classical model assumes a self-correcting macroeconomy that considers short-term problems as purely temporary. In the next chapter, we consider what happens if short-term problems are persistent and severe. We will discuss a macroeconomic model that was initially developed to help explain the Great Depression. This model developed by John Maynard Keynes is the foundation for modern macroeconomic analysis.

Answers to Chapterwide Practice Questions

Matching

1. e	3. c	5. a
2. d	4. f	6. b

Fill-In

1. labor resources, technology
2. productivity, productivity, modern growth

True-False

1. F	6. T	11. F	16. T
2. T	7. F	12. T	17. F
3. T	8. T	13. F	18. T
4. F	9. F	14. T	19. T
5. F	10. F	15. T	

Multiple Choice

1. c	6. d	11. b	16. a
2. b	7. b	12. a	17. c
3. a	8. a	13. c	18. b
4. b	9. d	14. d	
5. c	10. c	15. b	

Essay-Problem

1. The classical model holds that short-term problems in the macroeconomy will correct themselves quickly. Another way of saying this is: Don't worry about short-term problems. The Great Depression resulted in falling incomes, rising bankruptcy, and severe unemployment. These problems lasted a decade and it wasn't until World War II that the economy began to turn around.
2. In the long run, productivity growth helps the macroeconomy. In the short term, it might harm certain individuals and groups. For example, if farmers become more efficient at raising crops, this will help the general populace in the long run, but in the short term it might hurt farmers if productivity gains lead to lower prices. Remember that we are talking about long-run growth in this chapter, not short-term aspects.

3. Prices are signals to producers of potential profitable undertakings. Inflation—a lack of price stability—distorts these signals. Fear of further inflation brings uncertainty into the calculation: People have a harder time judging whether profitable possibilities will be available, so they may not undertake additional economic activities, and thus economic activity drops. This can be more serious in a developing nation than a developed nation because of the relative size of their economies.

4. This is a tough question. Don't worry if you do not get it correct. Wages might adjust upward, but they tend not to adjust downward. It is rare when groups of workers take pay cuts. This sometimes happens, as with airlines facing bankruptcy that seek large wage concessions. But wages are "sticky" and do not adjust downward so easily, as we will see when we look at short-term macroeconomic problems in the next chapters.

5. The capital markets restore macroeconomic equilibrium caused by a drop in consumption (a failure of Say's law). Since people either consume or save, a drop in consumption necessarily leads to an increase in savings. In turn, this increase in savings leads to a decrease in the interest rate because more funds are available, and this encourages businesses to invest more, thus restoring equilibrium at full employment.

6. Growth in the labor force refers to an increase in the number of workers. Growth in labor force productivity refers to the increase in output produced by each worker. Both are desirable for long-term economic growth. Government policy to encourage each one will be different: easing immigration laws would help grow the labor force, while tax benefits to businesses for capital improvements would increase the capital-to-labor ratio and so should translate into higher worker productivity.

7. The problem was that the poor had fewer incentives to consider what was best for the land long term because they did not have title to the land. Without title to the land, they could not sell it, buy land from others (size can be a factor in farming efficiency), or pass it along to heirs. The new landholders were thus at the whim of the government. This proved to be a large disincentive to invest in the land and work it with the long term in mind.

8. The simple answer is that infrastructure is usually taken for granted. Increasing capital or labor or importing technology will have little effect in unstable countries. Economic actors have to believe they will be able to profit from their activities. If this is seriously in question, economic activity will fail to grow.

9. The link between democracy and high per capita GDP is much weaker than the link between economic freedom and high per capita GDP. Some of the recent successes in economic growth from Southeast Asia such as South Korea, Taiwan, Hong Kong, and Singapore have limited democracy. However, economic freedoms often translate eventually into political freedoms.

10. Business tax credits have encouraged business to invest in capital improvement. These improvements have increased the capital-to-labor ratio and have translated into productivity increases. The increases have been modest, but recognizable.

Keynesian Macroeconomics

18

Understanding Short-Term Fluctuations in the Economy Requires a Focus on Aggregate Spending

The classical model we studied in the previous chapter provided insights into the workings of the macroeconomy over the long run, but it isn't particularly helpful in explaining short-run fluctuations. The decade-long Great Depression ushered in a new way of thinking by a British economist, John Maynard Keynes, and the Keynesian model you will learn in this chapter underlies the modern macroeconomics you will study for the remainder of this semester. Learning this model well will make the material in the remaining chapters much easier. This material can be challenging because the emphasis is on the *aggregate* economy and *aggregate* spending. As individuals, we can visualize the working of markets because we interact in them each day, but conceptualizing the workings of the aggregate economy is more abstract. Take your time working through the chapter.

This Is What You Need to Know	STEP 1

After studying this chapter you should be able to

- Name the components of gross domestic product (GDP).

- Analyze consumption using the average propensity to consume (APC) and the marginal propensity to consume (MPC).

- Analyze savings using the average propensity to save (APS) and the marginal propensity to save (MPS).

- Describe the determinants of consumption, saving, and investment.

- Determine aggregate equilibrium in the simple Keynesian model of the private domestic economy.

- Explain why at equilibrium injections equal withdrawals in the economy.

- Explain the multiplier process, how it is computed, and why it operates in both directions.

- Describe macroeconomic equilibrium in the full Keynesian model when government and the foreign sectors are added.

- Explain why the balanced budget multiplier is equal to 1.

- Describe the differences between recessionary and inflationary gaps.

STEP 2   Review the Key Terms

Aggregate expenditures: Consist of consumer spending, business investment spending, government spending, and net foreign spending (exports minus imports): $GDP = C + I + G + (X - M)$.

Consumption: Spending by individuals and households on both durable goods (e.g., autos, appliances, and electronic equipment) and nondurable goods (e.g., food, clothes, and entertainment).

Saving: The difference between income and consumption; the amount of disposable income not spent.

Average propensity to consume: The percentage of income that is consumed (C/Y).

Average propensity to save: The percentage of income that is saved (S/Y).

Marginal propensity to consume: The change in consumption associated with a given change in income ($\Delta C/\Delta Y$).

Marginal propensity to save: The change in saving associated with a given change in income ($\Delta S/\Delta Y$).

Investment: Spending by business that adds to the productive capacity of the economy. Investment depends on factors such as its rate of return, the level of technology, and business expectations about the economy.

Keynesian macroeconomic equilibrium: In the simple model, the economy is at rest; spending injections (investment) are equal to withdrawals (saving), and there are no net inducements for the economy to change the level of output or income. In the full model, all injections of spending must equal all withdrawals at equilibrium; $I + G + X = S + T + M$.

Injections: Increments of spending including investment, government spending, and exports.

Withdrawals: Activities that remove spending from the economy including saving, taxes, and imports.

Multiplier: Spending changes alter equilibrium income by the spending change times the multiplier. One person's spending becomes another's income, and that second person spends some (the MPC), which becomes income for another person, and so on until income has changed by $1/(1 - MPC) = 1/MPS$. The multiplier operates in both directions.

Balanced budget multiplier: Equal changes in government spending and taxation (a balanced budget) lead to an equal change in income (the balanced budget multiplier is equal to 1).

Recessionary gap: The increase in aggregate spending needed to bring a depressed economy back to full employment, equal to the GDP gap divided by the multiplier.

Inflationary gap: The spending reduction necessary (again when expanded by the multiplier) to bring an overheated economy back to full employment.

Work Through the Chapter Tutorials

STEP 3

Aggregate Expenditures

Frequently Asked Questions

Q: How are aggregate expenditures computed?

A: Gross domestic product (GDP) can be computed by adding up all spending or all income in the economy. The spending side consists of consumer spending (C), business investment spending (I), government spending (G), and net foreign spending, or exports minus imports $(X - M)$. Hence, $GDP = AE = C + I + G + (X - M)$. When we only consider the domestic private economy, $GDP = C + I$; and because there is no government to tax incomes or foreign sector, the components of GDP on the income side simply become income, so $GDP = Y$ (income).

Q: How important are personal consumption expenditures?

A: Personal consumption expenditures represent roughly 70% of aggregate spending. What consumers do not spend of their income, they save; thus, disposable income (Y_d) can be divided in consumption (C) and saving (S). Saving equals disposable income minus annual consumption $(S = Y_d - C)$.

Q: What is the relationship between income and consumption?

A: Keynes observed that as disposable income increases, consumption will increase, though not as fast as income. Consequently, as income grows, saving will grow as a percentage of income. This Keynesian approach to analyzing saving differs sharply from the classical approach, which assumed the interest rate to be the principal determinant of saving, and by extension, a principal determinant of consumption.

Q: How is the average propensity to consume and save defined?

A: The percentage of income people consume is known as the average propensity to consume $(APC = C/Y)$. The average propensity to save (APS) is the percentage of income people save (S/Y). Because income (Y) equals consumption plus saving $(Y = C + S)$, if we divide both sides of the equation by Y, $Y/Y = C/Y + S/Y$, so the equation reduces to $1 = APC + APS$.

Q: How is the marginal propensity to consume and save defined?

A: The marginal propensity to consume (MPC) is the change in consumption associated with a given change in income: thus, $MPC = \Delta C/\Delta Y$. The marginal propensity to save (MPS) is the change in saving associated with a given change in income: $MPS = \Delta S/\Delta Y$. Again, because $Y = C + S$, any change in income must be exhausted by the changes in consumption and saving, so $MPC + MPS = 1$.

Q: What factors cause the saving and consumption schedules to shift?

A: Income is the main determinant of consumption and saving, but other factors can shift the entire saving and consumption schedules (they are the determinants of consumption and saving). These include family wealth, expectations about future changes in prices and income, family debt, and taxation.

Q: **What accounts for most of the volatility in GDP?**

A: Gross private domestic investment (the "I" in the GDP equation) accounts for roughly 17–18% of GDP. It is volatile, sometimes increasing by 30% or falling by 10%; these investment swings often account for booms and recessions.

Q: **What determines the level of investment?**

A: Investment levels depend mainly on the rate of return. Investments earning a high rate of return are the investments undertaken first, assuming comparable risk, with projects offering lower returns being undertaken later. Interest rate levels also contribute to determining how much investment occurs, because much business investment is financed through debt. Some other determinants of investment spending include future expectations about returns, technological changes, the quantity of capital goods on hand, and operating costs. The aggregate investment schedule relates investment to income.

Aggregate Expenditures Quick Check

Circle the Correct Answer

1. (T/F) Keynes believed that income is the main determinant of consumption and savings, in contrast to classical economists who thought that the interest rate was crucial.

2. (T/F) If the average propensity to consume is 0.75, and the marginal propensity to consume is 0.70, then if income rises by $4,000, consumption will increase by $3,000.

3. (T/F) According to Keynes, the average propensity to consume and the marginal propensity to consume will normally be equal.

4. (T/F) If a $5,000 increase in income leads to additional savings of $1,250, the marginal propensity to consume is 0.75.

5. Which one of the following statements concerning consumption is *not* correct?
   a. Keynes believed it was a "fundamental psychological law" that as income rises, consumption will rise, but not as fast as income.
   b. Consumption represents 70% of GDP.
   c. Consumption fluctuates between increases of 10% to decreases of 10%.
   d. Expectations about future prices and incomes determine consumption.

6. Which one of the following statements concerning savings is *not* correct?
   a. If income is $30,000 per year and the average propensity to consume is 0.70, annual saving will be $9,000.
   b. A tax decrease generally leads to increases in consumption and savings.
   c. Savings rise as income grows.
   d. Saving is a component of aggregate expenditures.

7. Investment spending is dependent on
   a. the level of consumption in the economy.
   b. the level of personal debt in the economy.
   c. the interest rate.
   d. personal income tax rates.

8. Which one of the following statements concerning consumption is *not* correct?
   a. Wealthy people consume more than other people.
   b. College loans will tend to keep students from consuming even after they graduate and obtain jobs.
   c. Tax increases reduce consumption.
   d. If I think retailers will cut prices because of an economic slowdown, I am more likely to hold off purchasing things now.

9. Which one of the following statements concerning investment demand is *not* correct?
   a. Firms think the economy will enter a recession, so they hold off on purchasing new machines.
   b. Firms have a good deal of inventory on hand, so they hold off on producing more until some of this inventory is sold.
   c. Energy costs rise; firms absorb the costs because there is nothing they can do, and they keep on producing as before.
   d. Businesses think that computers can help them improve customer service and therefore sales, so they purchase more computers.

10. When economists speak of autonomous investment, they mean which of the following?
    a. Business investment varies inversely with interest rates.
    b. Investment is dependent on aggregate wealth.
    c. Aggregate investment grows with income.
    d. Aggregate investment is independent of income.

Score: _____

If You Got 9 or 10 Correct

You have a good feel for the concepts sitting behind aggregate expenditures. You could go on to the next section, "The Simple Keynesian Model." If you missed a question, make sure you know where you went wrong. But because of the importance of the material in this section, it may be useful to work through the solved problem below. It will pay to linger with this section.

If You Didn't Get at Least 9 Correct

Don't panic yet. This material is tough. Go back to the text and review Table 1 and Figure 2; they are the heart of the tough material in this section. Then go on to work the solved problem. ▨

Solved Problem: Aggregate Expenditures

When we focus on the private domestic economy, income equals consumption plus saving $(Y = C + S)$ and aggregate expenditures equal consumption plus investment $(AE = Y = C + I)$.

For this exercise, we will focus on consumption and saving.

1. Complete the table below:

Income	Consumption	Saving	APC	MPC	APS	MPS
–0–						
1,000						
2,000	2,800					
3,000	3,400					
4,000						
5,000						

2. Graph the consumption schedule in the grid below and the saving schedule in the grid on the next page.

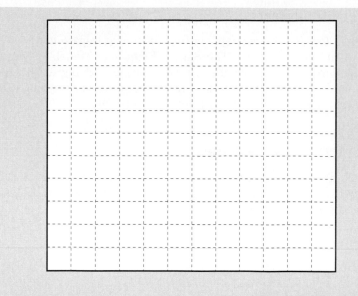

3. If income were to rise to $10,000 in this model, what would APC, APS, MPC, and MPS equal?

Solution-Discussion

1. This was actually kind of a tough problem to begin with; only a few values were available in the original table. By looking at the original, we can see that when income is $2,000, consumption is $2,800; and when income increases to $3,000 (a $1,000 increase) consumption rises to $3,400 (a $600 increase). This tells us that the MPC = $\Delta C/\Delta Y$ = $600/$1,000 = 0.6.

   This is important because we now know that every time income rises by 1 dollar, consumption will rise by 60 cents, and saving will rise by 40 cents, so the MPS will be 0.4. So, we simply ask: When income grows to $4,000 (a $1,000 change), how much will consumption rise? If the MPC is 0.6, then consumption will grow by $600, so when income is $4,000, consumption will also be $4,000 ($3,400 + $600). The MPC works the same way when income falls, so when income drops from $3,000 to $2,000, consumption falls by $600 to $2,200 ($2,800 − $600).

   Once the consumption values are filled in, then computing savings is easy (S = Y − C), and filling in MPC and MPS (0.6 and 0.4, respectively) is straightforward. All that is left is APC and APS, which equal C/Y and S/Y, respectively. See the table below for the completed values.

Income	Consumption	Saving	APC	MPC	APS	MPS
–0–	1,600	−1,600	—	—	—	—
1,000	2,200	−1,200	2.20	0.60	−1.20	0.40
2,000	2,800	−800	1.40	0.60	−0.40	0.40
3,000	3,400	−400	1.13	0.60	−0.13	0.40
4,000	4,000	0	1.00	0.60	0	0.40
5,000	4,600	400	.92	0.60	0.08	0.40

2. See Figure 1.

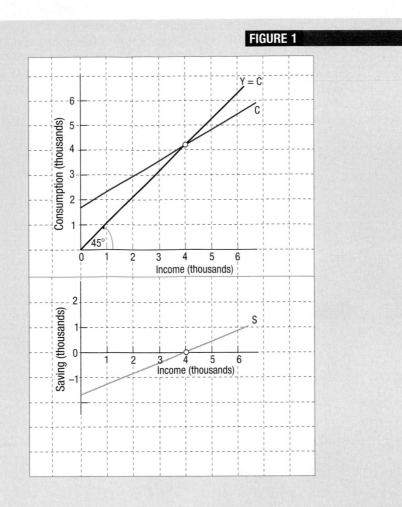

FIGURE 1

3. Again, we use the fact that MPC = 0.6 and MPS = 0.4 to solve this question. Income jumps from $5,000 to $10,000 (a $5,000 change), consumption rises to $7,600 ($4,600 + [.6 × $5,000] = $4,600 + $3,000). Thus saving is equal to $2,400, and,

APC = $7,600 / $10,000 = 0.76
APS = $2,400 / $10,000 = 0.24
MPC = 0.6
MPS = 0.4

Make sure you understand how each of these was computed and you are comfortable with both the consumption graph (the top panel) and the savings graph (the bottom panel). These concepts are fundamental to understanding how the economy achieves equilibrium, discussed in the next section, "The Simple Keynesian Model."

The Simple Keynesian Model

Frequently Asked Questions

Q: How is macroeconomic equilibrium defined in the simple Keynesian model?
A: Ignoring government spending and net exports in the simple Keynesian model, aggregate expenditures (AE) are the sum of consumer and business investment

spending: AE = C + I. When an economy is at equilibrium, aggregate expenditures, income, and output will all be equal; just what is demanded is supplied (AE = Y). And because income can be either spent or saved (Y = C + S), we can determine that, at equilibrium, investment equals saving (I = S). However, if *intended* saving and *intended* investment differ, the economy will have to grow or decline to achieve equilibrium. Note that intended saving or investment is often referred to as "planned" or "desired" saving or investment.

Q: **What role is played by saving and investment in restoring equilibrium in the economy?**

A: In Figure 2, the economy is initially at equilibrium at point a, with saving = 0. Businesses see investment opportunities and want to invest at level I_0 in Panel B. This means that there is an imbalance between desired or intended saving and investment. Aggregate expenditures grow to point e in Panel A as saving climbs to point e in Panel B, where it equals intended investment. The economy is at a new equilibrium at a level of output higher than before. At this new equilibrium *actual* investment equals *actual* saving.

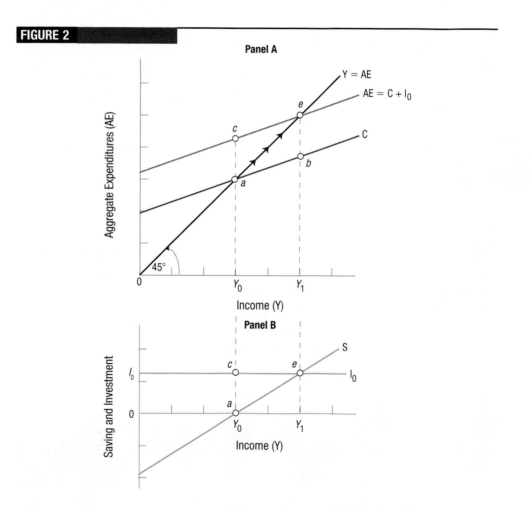

FIGURE 2

Panel A

Panel B

Q: **What is the multiplier effect, and how is it computed?**

A: The multiplier effect describes what happens when new spending occurs in the economy. That *new* spending becomes someone else's *new* income and a portion (the MPC) is spent, creating new income for another person who then spends some (the MPC), and so on. The multiplier is equal to 1/(1 − MPC) = 1/MPS. For example, if the MPC = 0.67, the multiplier will equal 3.

Q: What does it mean that the multiplier works in both directions?

A: We often describe the multiplier as increasing income when new spending is added to the economy. But, it is important to remember that the multiplier works in reverse; remove some spending (let's say people increase their saving because they anticipate a recession), and aggregate income will decline by more than the reduction in spending caused by the increase in saving.

The Simple Keynesian Model Quick Check

Circle the Correct Answer

1. In the simple Keynesian model excluding government and the foreign sector,
   a. at equilibrium actual saving and investment will be equal.
   b. at equilibrium actual income will equal consumption plus investment.
   c. if desired or intended investment is greater than desired or planned saving, income will rise.
   d. all of the above.
2. In this simple Keynesian model shown in Figure 3, if investment I_0 is equal to $100,
   a. equilibrium will be $3,400.
   b. equilibrium will not be at point *a* because intended investment exceeds intended saving.
   c. savings and investment are equal to $100 at point *b*.
   d. all of the above.

c. 3
d. 4

4. When intended saving is greater than intended investment,
   a. actual savings will grow as the economy moves to a new equilibrium at a higher level of income.
   b. the multiplier will push the economy to a higher level of income.
   c. income will fall.
   d. interest rates will fall, pushing investment higher, and thus resulting in a rising level of income and output.

5. In the simple Keynesian model shown in Figure 4, the multiplier is equal to which of the following?
   a. 1
   b. 2
   c. 3
   d. 4

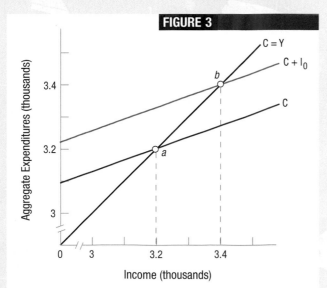

FIGURE 3

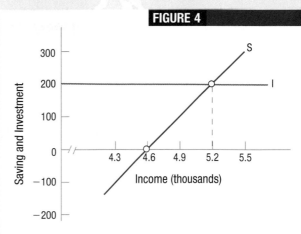

FIGURE 4

3. In this simple Keynesian model shown in Figure 3, if investment I_0 is equal to $100, the multiplier is equal to which of the following?
   a. 1
   b. 2

Score: _____

If You Got All 5 Correct

You did well. The Keynesian model of aggregate spending and income is often difficult to understand, but you handled these reasonably tough questions. If you have any concerns, read through the discussion below. Otherwise, move on to the next section, "The Full Keynesian Model."

If You Didn't Get All of Them Correct

This simple Keynesian model is really not that simple, so don't be discouraged. Look back and make sure you know why you missed the questions you did. Keep in mind the following:

- This simple Keynesian model is a model of the aggregate economy where consumption and saving are based on income, and all income is either spent or saved (no government or foreign sector). So, $Y = C + S$.
- Investment is autonomous (unrelated to income).
- Aggregate spending is equal to consumer spending plus autonomous business investment spending. So, $AE = Y = C + I$.
- Equilibrium occurs where income is equal to aggregate spending, so equilibrium is where $Y = C + I$.
- Now, here's a tricky part. Remember that $Y = C + S$, so equilibrium occurs where $C + S = C + I$, or $S = I$. At *equilibrium* saving and investment are equal.
- But Keynes distinguished between actual saving and investment at equilibrium and intended (or desired) saving by individuals and intended investment by business. Look at Figure 5 (Figure 4 duplicated). At an income of \$4,600 (point *a*), individuals intend to save zero (they are spending all of their income). Business, however, intends to invest \$200, so intended investment exceeds planned saving; the economy will expand to \$5,200, where at point *b*, actual saving and investment will be equal.

FIGURE 5

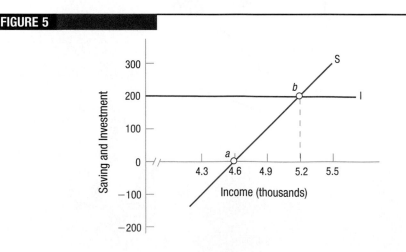

- At equilibrium, we have seen that $S = I$. In this simple model, I (business investment spending) represents an *injection* of spending into the economy, whereas S (savings) represents a *withdrawal* or leakage of funds from the spending stream. This injections-equals-withdrawals framework will be useful when we look at the full Keynesian model in the next section.
- A major contribution of this simple model to our understanding of macroeconomics is the concept of the multiplier. The idea that an increase (or decrease) in

spending of $1 increases (or reduces) income by more than a dollar was an important outcome of Keynesian analysis.
- The round-by-round change in spending and income from an initial change in spending is related directly to the MPC and MPS by the formula $1/(1 - \text{MPC}) = 1/\text{MPS}$.

The Three Key Points You Must Take Away from This Section

1. Equilibrium occurs where spending injections equal spending withdrawals; in this case, where I = S.

2. When planned injections are different from planned withdrawals, the economy will either grow or shrink to reach equilibrium.

3. A change in spending will result in a greater change in income because of the multiplier.

Study the Core Graph below and make sure you understand each of the key points.

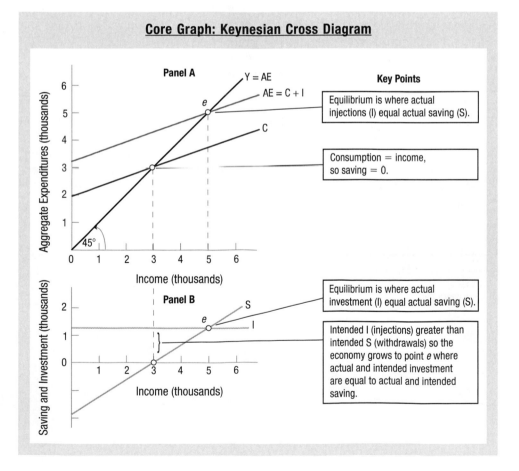

Now go on to the next section, "The Full Keynesian Model," which brings in the government and the foreign sector (net exports). ■

The Full Keynesian Model

Frequently Asked Questions

Q: How does adding government spending affect macroeconomic equilibrium?

A: Government spending is just like any other spending. Equilibrium income grows if government spending increases (or declines if government spending falls) by the change in government spending times the multiplier.

Q: Why do tax changes have different impacts on equilibrium?

A: Tax increases withdraw spending from the economy, but some of the tax increase comes out of saving that was already withdrawn from the spending stream, so only that part drawn from consumption is subject to the multiplier. The result is that the reduction in income from tax increases is smaller than similar reductions in government spending. When taxes are reduced, some of the tax reduction goes into saving, so the impact on the economy is less than a similar increase in government spending.

Q: What is the balanced budget multiplier?

A: The balanced budget refers to the notion that equal changes in government spending and taxes (a balanced budget) result in an equivalent change in income. If both government spending and taxes are increased by $100, equilibrium income rises by $100, and vice versa when both are decreased by $100. Hence, the balanced budget multiplier is equal to 1.

Q: What is a recessionary gap?

A: A recessionary gap is the *increase* in aggregate spending required to propel an economy in recession up to full employment. A recessionary gap is shown in Panel A of Figure 6. The economy is at equilibrium, Y_0, *below* full employment, Y_f. Aggregate expenditures must be increased from AE_0 to AE_1 (the recessionary gap length ab) and, when expanded by the multiplier, will close the GDP gap $Y_f - Y_0$.

FIGURE 6

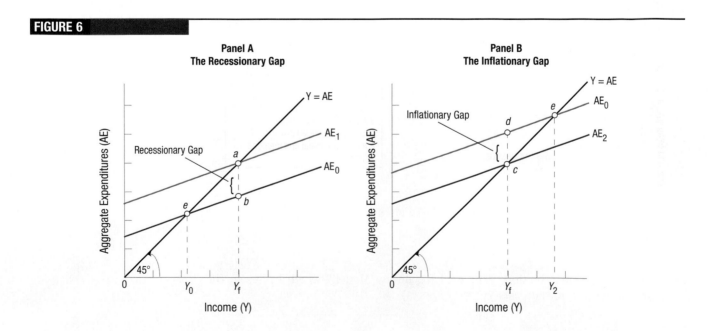

Panel A
The Recessionary Gap

Panel B
The Inflationary Gap

Q: What is an inflationary gap?

A: An inflationary gap is the *reduction* in aggregate spending necessary to bring the economy back to full employment. An inflationary gap is shown in Panel B of Figure 6. The economy is at equilibrium, Y_2, well *above* full employment (Y_f). Aggregate expenditures must be reduced from AE_0 to AE_2 (the inflationary gap length dc) and, when reduced further by the multiplier, will close the GDP gap $Y_2 - Y_f$.

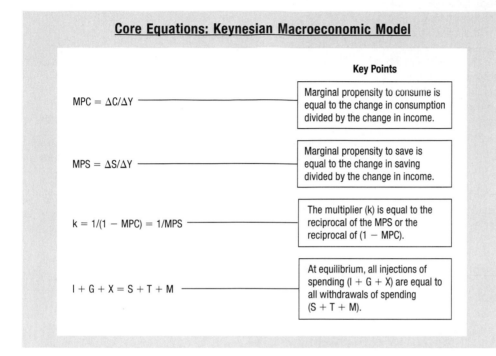

Core Equations: Keynesian Macroeconomic Model

	Key Points
$MPC = \Delta C / \Delta Y$	Marginal propensity to consume is equal to the change in consumption divided by the change in income.
$MPS = \Delta S / \Delta Y$	Marginal propensity to save is equal to the change in saving divided by the change in income.
$k = 1/(1 - MPC) = 1/MPS$	The multiplier (k) is equal to the reciprocal of the MPS or the reciprocal of (1 − MPC).
$I + G + X = S + T + M$	At equilibrium, all injections of spending (I + G + X) are equal to all withdrawals of spending (S + T + M).

The Full Keynesian Model Quick Check

Circle the Correct Answer

1. If the multiplier is equal to 4, government spending rises by $200, and taxes are increased by $200, equilibrium income will
   a. fall by a $200.
   b. fall by less than $200.
   c. rise by $200.
   d. rise by less than $200.
2. If the multiplier is equal to 4, and the government increases taxes by $200, equilibrium income will
   a. fall by $200.
   b. fall by $800.
   c. full by $400.
   d. fall by $600.
3. The reason that government spending has a bigger impact on the economy than a tax reduction of the same magnitude is because
   a. reducing taxes takes too long for a partisan Congress to agree on.

b. regulations keep government spending from being used to buy imported goods.
c. some of the tax reduction goes into saving.
d. tax reductions come with regulations that are too difficult for people to comprehend.

4. When the foreign sector is added to the simple Keynesian model,
   a. imports are *injections,* and exports are *withdrawals.*
   b. net exports have the same impact on the economy as tax increases.
   c. equilibrium income always increases.
   d. exports are *injections* into the economy, and imports are *withdrawals.*

5. At equilibrium in the full Keynesian model,
   a. $I + G + M = S + T + X$.
   b. $S + I + G = M + T + X$.
   c. $I + G + X = S + T + M$.
   d. $I + G + T = S + (X - M)$.

6. If full employment is $5,000, equilibrium income is $4,000, and the multiplier is 4,
   a. the recessionary gap is $1,000.
   b. increase spending of $1,000 will bring the economy to full employment.
   c. the inflationary gap is $250.
   d. a spending increase of $250 will close the GDP gap of $1,000.
7. When equilibrium income exceeds full employment,
   a. the economy is enduring a recessionary gap.
   b. the economy could use a tax reduction to close the GDP gap.
   c. the economy would approach full employment if businesses decided to reduce their investment.
   d. the inflationary gap would be eliminated if government increased spending on health care.
8. In Figure 7, if investment and government spending both equal $20, equilibrium income will be
   a. $250.
   b. $300.
   c. $350.
   d. $400.
9. In Figure 7, the multiplier is equal to
   a. 2.0.
   b. 2.5.
   c. 3.0.
   d. 3.3.

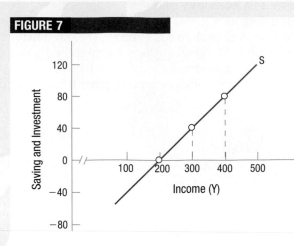

FIGURE 7

10. In Figure 7, if equilibrium income is $400, and the government increases taxes by $100, the new equilibrium will be
    a. $350.
    b. $300.
    c. $250.
    d. $200.

Score: ____

Answers: 1. c; 2. d; 3. c; 4. d; 5. c; 6. d; 7. c; 8. b; 9. b; 10. c

If You Got 9 or 10 Correct

Some of these were tough questions that sought to separate those who really understand the Keynesian model from those whose knowledge is only superficial. Congratulations. Check the "Hints, Tips, and Reminders," then move on.

If You Didn't Get at Least 9 Correct

Admittedly, this was a difficult quiz, but by now you should have the Keynesian model under control. I would recommend that you review the entire chapter again unless it was just the impact of taxes that messed you up.

    If tax changes were a problem, remember that a portion (the MPS) of any tax *increase* comes *from* saving, and that same portion of a tax *decrease* goes *into* savings and does not circulate throughout the economy. The result is that the impact of any tax change is less than the impact of an equivalent change in government spending.

    The rest of this section is a straightforward application of the simple Keynesian model. Review it if you need to, then go on to the "Hints, Tips, and Reminders." ∎

Solved Problem: The Full Keynesian Model

The full Keynesian model brings in both government spending and its power to tax along with foreign sector exports and imports. The table opposite is Table 3 from the text. Use it to answer the following questions. For each question, assume the economy begins in equilibrium with the original table at Y = $4,500.

Keynesian Equilibrium Analysis with Taxes

Income or Output (Y)	Taxes (T)	Disposable Income (Y$_d$)	Consumption (C)	Saving (S)	Investment (I)	Government Spending (G)
4,000	100	3,900	3,925	−25	100	100
4,100	100	4,000	4,000	0	100	100
4,200	100	4,100	4,075	25	100	100
4,300	100	4,200	4,150	50	100	100
4,400	100	4,300	4,225	75	100	100
4,500	100	4,400	4,300	100	100	100
4,600	100	4,500	4,375	125	100	100
4,700	100	4,600	4,450	150	100	100
4,800	100	4,700	4,525	175	100	100
4,900	100	4,800	4,600	200	100	100
5,000	100	4,900	4,675	225	100	100

1. If government spending grows to $150 (the government runs a deficit since taxes are only $100), what will be the new equilibrium level of income? How large is the spending multiplier?

2. If government spending falls to $50 (the government runs a surplus since taxes are $100), what will be the new equilibrium level of income?

3. Assume the economy is running a trade deficit (M > X), so imports equal $200 and exports are only $100. What will be the new equilibrium level of income?

4. Assume the economy is running a trade surplus (X > M), so exports equal $150 and imports are only $100. What will be the new equilibrium level of income?

Solution-Discussion

The key to solving all of these questions is to remember that at equilibrium G + I + X = T + S + M. You simply substitute in the numbers you know and solve for the missing number, then look it up in the table and you have the answer.

1. In this case, government is adding $50 additional spending to this economy, so,

$$G + I + X = T + S + M$$

or,

$$150 + 100 + 0 = 100 + ? + 0$$
$$250 = 100 + ?$$

So, saving = $150, because initially, this table does not include the foreign sector, so M and X are equal to 0. Now S = $150 when Y = $4,700. Thus, the $50 increase in spending led to a $200 increase in income, so the multiplier must equal 4.

2. Since government spending is falling, we can expect that equilibrium income will fall. Following the same procedure again:

$$G + I + X = T + S + M$$

or,

$$50 + 100 + 0 = 100 + ? + 0$$
$$150 = 100 + ?$$

So, saving = $50, because initially, this table does not include the foreign sector, so M and X are still equal to 0. Now S = $50 when Y = $4,300.

3. Now, we bring the foreign sector into the economy. Imports are $200, and exports are $100 (we are running a trade deficit). Again, using the same procedure:

$$G + I + X = T + S + M$$

or,

$$100 + 100 + 100 = 100 + ? + 200$$
$$300 = 300 + ?$$

So, saving must equal zero. Now, S = 0 when Y = $4,100.

4. Now, imports are $100, and exports are $150 (we are running a trade surplus). Again, using the same procedure:

$$G + I + X = T + S + M$$

or,

$$100 + 100 + 150 = 100 + ? + 100$$
$$350 = 200 + ?$$

So, saving must equal $150. Now S = $150 when Y = $4,700.

Notice that in all of these cases, we ended up finding that level of saving that puts the system in equilibrium. That is because in this simple formulation, consumption, savings, and income are the only variables changing. Using this equilibrium equation is the easiest way to solve these types of problems.

STEP 4   Consider These Hints, Tips, and Reminders

1. This and the next chapter are foundation chapters in that the two models discussed form the basic analytical apparatus you will use throughout the remainder of the course. Spend some time and get comfortable with how aggregate spending by consumers, business, government, and the foreign sector determine income and output for our economy.

2. Remember that John Maynard Keynes developed this model during the height of the Great Depression, when unemployment rose to 25% of the labor force. As a result, it is a *fixed price* model. Inflation or a rising price level are not issues the model considers. Changing price levels (inflation) are introduced in the next chapter.

3. Use the 45° reference line in the consumption graph (often called the Keynesian cross diagram) to help you read the graph. Along that line income and aggregate expenditures are equal (a 45° line bisects the axes).

4. Another way to think of the 45° reference line is that any amount of output demanded by consumers and business will be supplied along that line so equilibrium will be where aggregate spending crosses the 45° reference line.

5. Keep in mind that investment includes the amount of inventories of products on hand to be sold. Firms invest in inventories of products to have them available at retail and manufacturers keep inventories because production takes time. Inventories play an important role in how the economy reaches equilibrium. If consumers decide to save more (planned saving rises), consumption falls and inventories rise, ordering for new products falls, signaling to business to adjust output. As output and income decline, consumers readjust their desired saving downward until at equilibrium actual saving and investment are equal.

6. Remember that at equilibrium in the domestic private sector model, *actual* saving equals *actual* investment. Keep in mind that *planned* saving and *planned* investment typically differ. Savers and investors are two different groups, and we would not expect their decisions (plans) to be the same. But at equilibrium, all injections of spending (investment) must equal all withdrawals (savings). More on this below.

7. This is a highly stylized model of our complex economy, but one that provides huge insights into why we can easily slip well below full employment at equilibrium: insufficient aggregate spending. This model forced economists to consider spending as a crucial factor in business cycles.

8. Another major conclusion from this stylized Keynesian model is the existence of a spending *multiplier*. What is important here is that it takes less spending than the full GDP gap to close the gap. If, for example, the multiplier is 2 and the GDP gap is $100, only $50 in spending is needed move the economy to full employment. Note that the *higher* the multiplier, the *less* new spending that is needed to close the GDP gap.

9. The equilibrium in the full Keynesian model with government and the foreign sector really brings home how important it is to remember that at equilibrium all *injections* equal all *withdrawals*. The equation,

$$I + G + X = S + T + M$$

is one you should keep in mind, because it will turn out to be important later on.

10. The recessionary and inflationary gaps are *not* the same as the GDP gap. Both the recessionary and inflationary gaps are the changes in spending necessary, *times* the multiplier, needed to bring the economy to full employment output. Thus, the recessionary or inflationary gaps are equal to the GDP gap *divided* by the multiplier.

Do the Homework for Chapter 18
Keynesian Macroeconomics

Instructor _____ Time _____ Student _____

Use the answer key below to record your answers to these homework questions.

1. (a) (b) (c) (d)	6. (a) (b) (c) (d)	11. (a) (b) (c) (d)	16. (a) (b) (c) (d)
2. (a) (b) (c) (d)	7. (a) (b) (c) (d)	12. (a) (b) (c) (d)	17. (a) (b) (c) (d)
3. (a) (b) (c) (d)	8. (a) (b) (c) (d)	13. (a) (b) (c) (d)	18. (a) (b) (c) (d)
4. (a) (b) (c) (d)	9. (a) (b) (c) (d)	14. (a) (b) (c) (d)	19. (a) (b) (c) (d)
5. (a) (b) (c) (d)	10. (a) (b) (c) (d)	15. (a) (b) (c) (d)	20. (a) (b) (c) (d)

1. Which of the following equations is *not* correct?
   a. GDP = C + I + G + (X − M)
   b. S = Y − C
   c. C = Y − S
   d. Y = C − S

2. Keynes's fundamental psychological law of consumption stated that
   a. people will consume increasing amounts of goods if allowed to.
   b. as income grows, people will increasingly find fewer and fewer things to purchase.
   c. as income grows, people will consume more, but not as much as their income increases.
   d. as interest rate fall, people will buy more durable goods like cars and houses.

3. Which propensity to save or consume measures total consumption divided by income?
   a. average propensity to save

b. average propensity to consume
c. marginal propensity to save
d. marginal propensity to consume

4. Which propensity to save or consume measures change in saving divided by the change in income?
   a. average propensity to save
   b. average propensity to consume
   c. marginal propensity to save
   d. marginal propensity to consume

5. In the simple Keynesian model where Y = C + S and Y = C + I, which of the following is *not* correct?
   a. APS + MPC = 1
   b. MPC = 1 − MPS
   c. APC + APS = 1
   d. MPC = $\Delta C / \Delta Y$

To answer questions 6 to 9, complete the table at right.

6. In the table at right, the average propensity to consume when income is $3,000 is
   a. $2,500.
   b. 0.25.
   c. 0.75.
   d. 0.83.

7. In the table at right, the marginal propensity to consume is
   a. $2,500.
   b. 0.25.
   c. 0.75.
   d. 0.83.

Income or Output (Y)	Consumption (C)	Saving (S)
2,000	_____	_____
2,500	_____	_____
3,000	_____	
3,500	_____	625
4,000	_____	750

8. In the table on the previous page, the average propensity to save when income is $2,000 is
   a. $250.
   b. 0.25.
   c. 0.75.
   d. 0.125.

9. In the table on the previous page, when the average propensity to save and the average propensity to consume are added together the total is equal to
   a. the marginal propensity to consume.
   b. 1.
   c. 0.
   d. the marginal propensity to save.

---

10. While income is the primary determinant of consumption and saving, several other factors are important, including
    a. taxes.
    b. wealth.
    c. household debt.
    d. all of the above.

11. While the rate of return on capital is the primary determinant of investment, several other factors are important, including
    a. expectations about business and the economy.
    b. level of inventories.
    c. the level and speed of technological change.
    d. all of the above.

12. In the simple Keynesian model without government or a foreign sector, and where $Y = C + S$ and $Y = C + I$, equilibrium occurs when
    a. consumers have spent all of their income.
    b. $I = S$.
    c. $APC + APS = 1$.
    d. $MPC = 1$.

---

13. In Figure HW-1, assume that full employment income is $800. If equilibrium is currently $700,
    a. an inflationary gap of $100 exists.
    b. a recessionary gap of $100 exists.
    c. equilibrium saving is 0.
    d. a recessionary gap of $50 exists.

14. In Figure HW-1, assume that full employment income is $800. If equilibrium is currently $900,
    a. a recessionary gap of $50 exists.
    b. an inflationary gap of $100 exists.
    c. equilibrium consumption is $750.
    d. the multiplier is equal to 4.

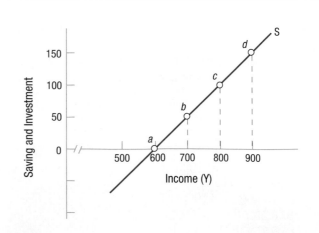

HW-1

15. In Figure HW-1, assume that full employment income is $800. If equilibrium is currently $900,
    a. a reduction that in spending of $100 will bring the economy to full employment.
    b. equilibrium investment is $100.
    c. a reduction in spending of $50 will close the recessionary gap.
    d. the multiplier is equal to 2.

16. In Figure HW-1, if net exports are zero and investment and government spending are each $50, equilibrium income will be at
    a. point *a*.
    b. point *b*.
    c. point *c*.
    d. point *d*.

17. In Figure HW-1, the MPC is equal to which of the following?
    a. 0.25
    b. 0.50
    c. 0.75
    d. 0.83

18. If the marginal propensity to consume is 0.67, and the government increases taxes by $300, equilibrium income will fall by
    a. $200.
    b. $400.
    c. $600.
    d. $900.

19. A balanced budget multiplier of 1 suggests that
    a. increasing income by $1 results in another dollar of government spending.
    b. the MPC = 1.
    c. $1 of government spending has the same impact on the economy as a $1 reduction in taxes.
    d. a $1 increase in both in government spending and taxes leads to a $1 increase in income.

20. Assume the economy is currently at equilibrium at $2,000 and the multiplier is 3. Now assume that exports grow by $400 and imports rise by $200. Equilibrium income will
    a. not change.
    b. decline by $200.
    c. grow by $200.
    d. grow by $600.

This sheet (front and back) is designed to help you prepare for your exams. The chapter has been boiled down to its key concepts. You are asked to answer questions, define terms, draw graphs, and, if you wish, add summaries of class notes.

Aggregate Expenditures

Aggregate expenditures are equal to:

Consumption

Define the following:
APC:

APS:

MPC:

MPS:

List the four major determinants of consumption and saving:

Investment

List the determinants of investment demand:

What is meant by autonomous investment?

The Simple Keynesian Model

Use the grids at right to draw the following:

- Draw a linear consumption schedule in the top panel.
- Draw the corresponding saving schedule in the bottom panel.
- Label the equilibrium point in both panels.
- Now add an investment schedule to both panels.
- Label the new equilibrium point in both panels.

At equilibrium, saving and investment are equal. Explain why this is true.

If intended saving is greater than intended investment, what happens to equilibrium and why?

If intended saving is less than intended investment, what happens to equilibrium and why?

Describe the multiplier process. How is the multiplier defined?

The Full Keynesian Model

Explain why government spending and net exports affect the economy just as any other spending.

Explain why changes in taxes have a smaller impact on the economy than spending changes of the same amount.

Explain why the balanced budget multiplier is equal to 1.

Explain what is meant by a recessionary gap.

Explain what is meant by a inflationary gap.

Explain why GDP gaps can be closed with less of a spending change then that of the entire GDP gap itself.

Additional Study Help Chapterwide Practice Questions

Matching

Match the description with the corresponding term.

___ 1. Aggregate expenditures
___ 2. Consumption
___ 3. Saving
___ 4. Average propensity to consume
___ 5. Average propensity to save
___ 6. Marginal propensity to consume
___ 7. Marginal propensity to save
___ 8. Investment
___ 9. Aggregate equilibrium
___ 10. Recessionary (contractionary) gap
___ 11. Inflationary (expansionary) gap

a. That part of disposable income that consumers do not spend, which can be held in many forms, including savings accounts, bonds, and cash.
b. Equivalent to gross domestic product, consisting of consumer spending, business investment spending, government spending, and net foreign spending.
c. The percentage of income people consume.
d. Includes all personal consumption expenditures. This represents nearly 70% of GDP.
e. The percentage of income people save.
f. The change in saving associated with a given change in income.
g. In the GDP equation, it refers to gross private domestic investment. It is roughly 17–18% of GDP, but is quite volatile. Its primary determinants are the expected rate of return and interest rates.
h. The deficiency in aggregate spending required to bring the economy to full employment assuming no change in prices.
i. Occurs when an economy is at equilibrium above full employment. It is the decrease in aggregate spending necessary to bring the economy back to full employment, assuming no change in prices.
j. Occurs when $I + G + X = S + T + M$.
k. Proportion of additional income that is spent by consumers.

Fill-In

Circle the word(s) in parentheses that complete the sentence.

1. Classical economists focused on (markets, governments, expenditures) _____ in their analysis of the economy, whereas John Maynard Keynes turned his attention to aggregate (markets, governments, expenditures) _____.

2. How much consumers spend of their income is known as the (MPC, MPS, APC, APS) _____, and how much they save is the (MPC, MPS, APC, APS) _____. When income rises, consumers will save a part equal to the (MPC, MPS, APC, APS) _____ times the change in their income.

3. The multiplier is equal to 1 divided by the (MPC, MPS, APC, APS) _____.

4. When (prices, saving, wealth) _____ rise(s), a family will consume more, but a rising level of (household debt, expectations, wealth) _____ can lead to lower levels of consumption.

5. Investment is the most (stable, volatile, costly) _____ of GDP's components, and investment demand by firms is related to their expected rate of return, which is affected by (household wealth, technical change) _____.

6. Investment and exports are (withdrawals, injections) _____ of spending into the economy, whereas imports and saving are (withdrawals, injections) _____. At equilibrium, intended, planned, and actual savings and investment are (equal, different) _____. When intended saving is higher than desired investment, equilibrium output and income will (rise, fall, not change) _____.

7. Tax changes have a (bigger, smaller, the same) _____ impact on the economy as an equivalent amount of government spending. When government spending and taxes are changed by the same amount, equilibrium income will change by (a bigger, a smaller, the same) _____ amount.

8. When (imports, exports) _____ rise, aggregate spending falls, and this leads to a (rise, fall) _____ in equilibrium income. When (imports, exports) _____ rise, this leads to an expansion in income, output, and employment.

9. When the economy is operating below full employment, a(n) (inflationary, multiplier, recessionary)

_____ gap is said to exist, but when the economy is above full employment, a(n) (inflationary, multiplier, recessionary) _____ gap results.

True-False

Circle the correct answer.

T/F   1. If an economy has considerable slack in it, this means businesses can increase their output quickly and without raising costs, thereby holding prices steady.

T/F   2. Classical economists viewed income levels as the primary determinant of consumption levels.

T/F   3. If APC is 0.65, MPS must be 0.35.

T/F   4. If income is $30,000 per year and APC is 0.80, annual saving will be $6,000.

T/F   5. If a $4,000 change in income leads to an additional $1,000 in saving, MPC is 0.25.

T/F   6. The more capital goods a firm currently has on hand, the higher its expected rate of new investment.

T/F   7. In general, the more wealth a family has, the higher its consumption level will be, relative to income.

T/F   8. If consumers anticipate that the price of microwave ovens will rise in the next month, they are more likely to purchase a microwave immediately.

T/F   9. Aggregate consumption is primarily dependent on the rate of return and interest rates.

T/F   10. At equilibrium, aggregate expenditures are equal to income.

T/F   11. If current income is $4,000, the multiplier is 3, and consumers intend to save $100 more than business intends to invest, the new level of equilibrium income will be $3,700.

T/F   12. A multiplier of 4 means that the MPC is equal to 0.25.

T/F   13. One contribution that Keynes made to macroeconomic analysis was his recognition that consumption and investment were related to income and not the interest rate.

T/F   14. Curing an inflationary gap requires policymakers to reduce aggregate spending by the amount current income (output) exceeds full employment income (the GDP gap).

T/F   15. If the economy is in a recession, the MPS = 0.4, and the GDP gap is $1,000, full employment can be achieved if policymakers increase aggregate spending by $400.

Multiple Choice

Circle the correct answer.

1. Which of the following is *not* one of the components of aggregate expenditures (GDP)?
   a. net exports
   b. private saving
   c. government spending
   d. consumer spending

2. Approximately what proportion of GDP does consumption (C) represent?
   a. 35%
   b. 50%
   c. 70%
   d. 85%

3. According to the "fundamental psychological law" Keynes identified, as income rises, consumption will
   a. rise, but not as fast as income.
   b. rise at the same rate as income.
   c. decline as the same rate that income increases.
   d. be unaffected.

4. If income is $60,000 per year and $40,000 of this is spent, what is the average propensity to save (APS)?
   a. 0.33
   b. 0.40
   c. 0.60
   d. 0.66

5. If income is $20,000 per year and APC is 0.65, what is annual saving?
   a. $3,500
   b. $6,500
   c. $7,000
   d. $13,000

6. If MPC is 0.80 and income rises by $5,000, what will the increase in consumption be?
   a. $6,250
   b. $1,000
   c. $5,000
   d. $4,000

7. Which of the following is *not* one of the determinants of consumption and saving?
   a. capital goods on hand
   b. household indebtedness
   c. expectations about future prices and incomes
   d. household wealth

8. Approximately what proportion of GDP does gross private domestic investment (GPDI) represent?
   a. 17–18%
   b. 25–30%
   c. 42–45%
   d. 70%

9. Which of the following is *not* one of the determinants of investment spending?
   a. the quantity of capital goods on hand
   b. business expectations regarding the future state of the economy
   c. household indebtedness
   d. the rate of return

10. Which of the following will necessarily be true of a private domestic economy that is at equilibrium?
    a. S = C
    b. I = S
    c. Y = I
    d. C = Y

Essay-Problem

Answer in the space provided.

The questions below will help you make sure you understand the Keynesian model. Your answers should be close to those we provide. Use these questions as another way to assess your progress with some very abstract material.

1. What is the chief benefit of the Keynesian model over the classical model?

2. How much of your savings activity is influenced by the interest rate you obtain, and how much is influenced by the amount of income you have?

3. If consumption is approximately 70% of spending, why is it almost always less important than business investment?

4. Do ideas of spending over one's life cycle owe more to the classical model or the Keynesian approach?

5. Why were net exports not included in the simple Keynesian aggregate expenditures model discussed in this chapter?

The simple Keynesian model is shown in Figure EP-1. Use the figure to answer questions 6–10. The economy is initially at equilibrium at Y = $3,000.

8. Given the economy described in Figure EP-1, what is the MPC and MPS equal to?

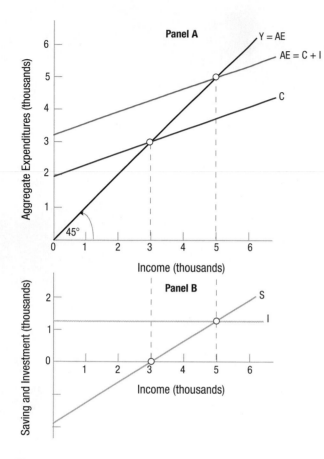

Panel A

Panel B

EP-1

9. The economy starts to pick up steam. Businesses become excited about their economic prospects. They start to invest more in production capacity.
   a. What happens to the investment curve in Panel B? (rises, falls)
   b. What happens to equilibrium savings? (rises, falls)
   c. What effect does this have on the aggregate expenditures curve? (rises, falls)
   d. What happens to national income and output? (rises, falls)

6. How large is aggregate saving at the initial equilibrium level of $3,000?

10. The economy starts to stagger. Businesses are no longer keen about their economic prospects. They start to cut business investment.
    a. What happens to the investment curve in Panel B? (rises, falls) _____
    b. What happens to equilibrium savings? (rises, falls) _____
    c. What effect does this have on the aggregate expenditures curve? (rises, falls) _____
    d. What happens to national income and output? (rises, falls) _____

7. If investment (I) in this economy is equal to $1,200, how large is the multiplier?

What's Next

This chapter provides you with a simple model for understanding how the macro-economy works. In the next chapter, we turn to the modern macroeconomic explanation of the economy, the aggregate demand and supply model. The simple Keynesian model described in this chapter is the basis for the aggregate demand curve in that model. When we add the aggregate supply curve, we have a full and robust model explaining macroeconomic fluctuations.

Answers to Chapterwide Practice Questions

Matching

1. b	4. c	7. f	10. h
2. d	5. e	8. g	11. i
3. a	6. k	9. j	

Fill-In

1. markets, expenditures
2. APC, APS, MPS
3. MPS
4. wealth, household debt
5. volatile, technical change
6. injections, withdrawals, equal, fell
7. smaller, the same
8. imports, fall, exports
9. recessionary, inflationary

True-False

1. T	5. F	9. F	13. F
2. F	6. F	10. T	14. F
3. F	7. T	11. T	15. T
4. T	8. T	12. F	

Multiple Choice

1. b	4. a	7. a	10. b
2. c	5. c	8. a	
3. a	6. d	9. c	

Essay-Problem

1. The Keynesian model gives us more insight than the classical model on how an economy can reach a short-run equilibrium that is less than full employment. Put another way, it shows us why recessions can persist.
2. It was Keynes's great insight that savings is much more a function of income than of the interest rate. If you are like most people, an overwhelming amount of your savings is due to your level of income, not the interest rate you will receive for your savings.

3. Consumption spending tends to be very stable. Business investment fluctuates widely. Consumption would become crucial only in those situations when it dropped precipitously, as it did during the Great Depression.

4. The Keynesian approach emphasizes the importance of income. Life cycle spending is based on the idea of changing income levels over one's life cycle.

5. Unlike other countries, net exports are a relatively small component of gross domestic product for the United States. It was easier to leave them out at the beginning of this chapter, to focus primary attention on consumption, savings, and investment. Net exports still matter, and that is why we added them in constructing the full Keynesian model.

6. Zero

7. When investment rises from 0 to $1,200, income increases by $2,000, so the multiplier is 1.67.

8. When income rises from $3,000 to $5,000 saving rises from 0 to $1,200 so the MPS = $1,200/$2,000 = 0.6. Thus, the MPC = 0.4.

9. (a) rises; (b) rises; (c) rises; (d) rises.

10. (a) falls; (b) falls; (c) falls; (d) falls.

Aggregate Demand and Supply

19

The Aggregate Demand and Aggregate Supply Model Is the Foundation of Modern Macroeconomics

The aggregate demand and aggregate supply (AD-AS) model is the foundation of modern macroeconomics. This is important, but challenging, material. The classical model we studied earlier provided insights into the workings of the macro economy over the long run but is limited in explaining short-run fluctuations and problems. The classical model led to the conclusion that in the long run the three main competitive markets of the economy (product, labor, and capital), along with flexible prices, wages, and interest rates, would keep the economy at or near full employment.

The Great Depression reduced aggregate spending severely, resulting in farm and home foreclosures on a massive scale along with soaring unemployment and bank failures. Output and income were so far below full employment, and stayed that way for a decade, that the classical model was nearly forgotten.

The Keynesian model examined in the previous chapter provided a short-run explanation focused mainly on aggregate expenditures during conditions of serious slack (unemployment) in the economy where inflation pressures were minimal so the price level is assumed to be fixed. That model was the staple for economic explanations of business cycles from the 1940s to the early 1970s, when several supply shocks and serious inflationary episodes showed the flaws in focusing on aggregate expenditures in a fixed price environment. The price level needed to be brought explicitly into a modern framework.

The aggregate demand and aggregate supply model you will learn in this chapter shows both the long run and the short run. This model is not difficult, but learning it well is crucial to your understanding of macroeconomics and the policy material in the remaining chapters. The chapter is divided into three key parts. As you first read through the chapter, stop at the end of each part and try to sum up the key points.

STEP 1

This Is What You Need to Know

After studying this chapter you should be able to

- Describe why the aggregate demand curve has a negative slope.

- Describe the effects of wealth, exports, and interest rates on the aggregate demand curve.

- List the determinants of aggregate demand.

- Analyze the aggregate supply curve and differentiate between the short run and long run.

- Describe the determinants of an aggregate supply curve.

- Define the multiplier and describe why it is important.

- Describe demand-pull and cost-push inflation.

STEP 2

Review the Key Terms

Aggregate expenditures: Consist of consumer spending, business investment spending, government spending, and net foreign spending (exports minus imports), or GDP = C + I + G + (X − M).

Aggregate demand: The output of goods and services (real GDP) demanded at different price levels.

Wealth effect: Families usually hold some of their wealth in financial assets such as savings accounts, bonds, and cash, and a rising aggregate price level means that the purchasing power of this money wealth declines, reducing output demanded.

Aggregate supply: The real GDP that firms will produce at varying price levels. During a depression, the economy has a lot of slack, and the aggregate supply curve will be flat. In the short run, aggregate supply is positively sloped because many input costs are slow to change, but in the long run, the aggregate supply curve is vertical at full employment since the economy has reached its capacity to produce.

Short-run aggregate supply (AS) curve: The short-run aggregate supply curve is positively sloped because many input costs are slow to change in the short run.

Long-run aggregate supply (LRAS) curve: The long-run aggregate supply curve is vertical at full employment because the economy has reached its capacity to produce.

Macroeconomic equilibrium: Occurs at the intersection of the aggregate supply and aggregate demand curves. At this output level, there is no net pressures for the economy to expand or contract.

Multiplier: Spending changes alter equilibrium income by the spending change times the multiplier. One person's spending becomes another's income, and that second person spends some (the MPC), which becomes income for another person, and so on, until income has changed by 1/(1 − MPC) = 1/MPS. The multiplier operates in both directions.

Marginal propensity to consume: The change in consumption associated with a given change in income ($\Delta C/\Delta Y$).

Marginal propensity to save: The change in saving associated with a given change in income ($\Delta S/\Delta Y$).

Demand-pull inflation: Results when aggregate demand expands so much that equilibrium output exceeds full employment output and the price level rises.

Cost-push inflation: Results when a supply shock hits the economy, reducing aggregate supply, and thus reducing output and increasing the price level.

Work Through the Chapter Tutorials	STEP 3

Aggregate Demand

Frequently Asked Questions

Q: What is the aggregate demand curve?

A: The aggregate demand curve shows the quantities of goods and services (real gross domestic product, or GDP) demanded at different price levels.

Q: Why does the aggregate demand curve have a negative slope?

A: The aggregate demand curve is downward sloping for several reasons. For one thing, when price levels rise, household wealth is reduced because the purchasing power of money held in savings accounts, in bonds, and as cash declines. Some purchases are thus put on hold, thereby reducing output demanded. This is known as the *wealth effect*. Second, when the country's aggregate price level rises, U.S. goods become more expensive in the global marketplace, so people in foreign countries purchase fewer of these products, and thus exports decline. Third, as aggregate prices rise, people need more money to carry out transactions. This added demand for money drives up interest rates, which reduces business investment.

Q: What are the determinants of aggregate demand?

A: The determinants of aggregate demand include the components of aggregate spending—consumption, investment, government spending, and net exports. If any of these aggregates change, the aggregate demand curve shown in Figure 1 will shift. If any of the four components of aggregate spending increase, the aggregate demand curve shifts to the right from, say, AD_0 to AD_1. If, for example,

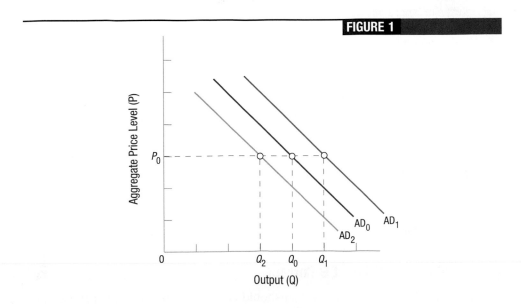

FIGURE 1

imports were to increase or investment to decline, aggregate demand would fall and the aggregate demand curve would shift to the left from AD_0 to AD_2. Also note that the aggregate demand curve slopes down, as noted earlier, and that shifts in the aggregate demand curve affect output for the economy.

Aggregate Demand Quick Check

Circle the Correct Answer

1. (T/F) The aggregate demand curve shows how many goods and services consumers will purchase at varying price levels.
2. (T/F) Because the aggregate demand curve is downward sloping, the price level will have no effect on the economy in the short run.
3. (T/F) The "wealth effect" means that when the aggregate price level rises, people become wealthier.
4. (T/F) The aggregate demand curve slopes downward because of the income effect and the substitution effect.
5. The aggregate demand curve is downward sloping because a rising aggregate price level does all *except* which one of the following?
   a. increases the need for people to use more money to carry out transactions, which raises the cost of borrowing money (interest rates rise), which dampens business investment, which decreases real output
   b. increases the price of goods we would have exported, which lowers exports, which lowers real output
   c. increases the price of goods, which makes imports cheaper, which leads to greater purchase of imports, which increases real output
   d. decreases the purchasing power of family wealth, which reduces consumption, which reduces output demanded
6. Which one of the following is *not* correct?
   a. A surging stock market will shift the aggregate demand curve to the right.
   b. A tax increase will shift the aggregate demand curve to the left.
   c. Excess business capacity will shift the aggregate demand curve to the right.
   d. Growing demand for our goods from other nations shifts the aggregate demand curve to the right.

7. Which one of the following is *not* correct?
   a. When government spending rises, the aggregate demand curve shifts to the right.
   b. New environmental protection regulations shift the aggregate demand curve to the right.
   c. Consumers feel good about the economy, so the aggregate demand curve shifts to the right.
   d. Interest rates fall, so the aggregate demand curve shifts to the right.
8. Which one of the following will *not* occur if the aggregate price level falls?
   a. Interest rates will fall.
   b. Household purchasing power will rise.
   c. The value of bonds will fall.
   d. Exports will rise.
9. Which of the following will *not* shift the aggregate demand curve to the left?
   a. The public's fear of a long, costly war.
   b. Polls show that consumer confidence has fallen.
   c. Our major trading partners all face a deepening recession.
   d. Inflation falls from 9% to 1%.
10. Which of the following will *not* shift the aggregate demand curve to the right?
    a. A president is elected who promises to cut taxes.
    b. The aggregate price level rises.
    c. Congress cuts regulations facing businesses.
    d. Cheap information technology looks like it will increase productivity.

Score: _____

If You Got 9 or 10 Correct

The basics of aggregate demand are not difficult, and you clearly have a good grasp of the basics of aggregate demand. Go on to the next section, "Aggregate Supply."

If You Didn't Get at Least 9 Correct

This is relatively easy material, so you should have been able to answer these questions. Because this is the model you will use for the remainder of the course, go back and review this section now. Make sure you know why you missed the questions you did, and make sure you know why the aggregate demand curve slopes down and what shifts the curve. The next section, "Aggregate Supply," looks at the other side of this stylized model: the real output supplied to the economy by business firms.

Keep in Mind

You should not find this material particularly difficult. It parallels the material from Chapter 3 on supply and demand for individual products. It is clearly different, more abstract, and more stylized than product supply and demand analysis. After all, we all buy products and can visualize the downward-sloping aspect of product demand (we will buy more when the price is lower). Further, it is not difficult to visualize that firms will supply more if prices are higher.

But at the aggregate economy level, these notions are not as concrete visually and take a little more study. Move on to the next section, "Aggregate Supply." You will find it a little more straightforward and easier to grasp. ■

Aggregate Supply

Frequently Asked Questions

Q: **How is the aggregate supply curve defined?**

A: The aggregate supply curve shows the real GDP that firms will produce at varying price levels. The aggregate supply curve has three regions: a horizontal region, where output can be increased without increases in prices; a positively sloped section, where prices rise when GDP grows; and a vertical region, where output cannot grow. These are shown in Figure 2.

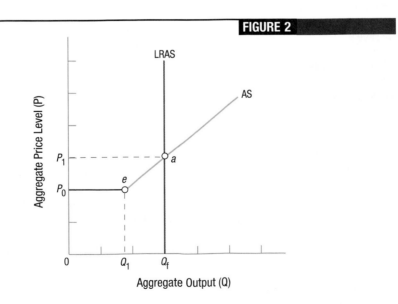

FIGURE 2

Q: **Why is the long-run aggregate supply curve vertical?**

A: The vertical long-run aggregate supply (LRAS) curve reflects the assumptions of classical economic analysis. Over the long run, all variables in the economy, including prices, wages, and interest rates can adjust. This means that an economy in the long run will gravitate to an equilibrium position at full employment.

Q: **What does the short-run aggregate supply curve look like?**

A: The short-run aggregate supply (AS) curve is positively sloped because many input costs are slow to change in the short run. When prices rise, firms do not immediately have to pay higher rents since these are often fixed for a specified term. However, as an industry or the economy as a whole increases its production, firms must start hiring more labor or paying overtime. As each firm seeks more employees, wages are driven up, increasing costs and forcing higher prices.

Q: **What does the flat aggregate supply curve represent?**

A: A flat aggregate supply curve represents the depression period. It applies to an economy with so much excess capacity that businesses can increase their output without having to face rising costs; thus increased output does not lead to inflation.

Q: **What are the determinants of aggregate supply?**

A: The determinants of the aggregate supply curve include changes in input prices, the market power of firms, productivity, taxes, regulation, and business expectations. When one of these determinants changes, the entire aggregate supply curve shifts.

Aggregate Supply Quick Check

Circle the Correct Answer

1. (T/F) If an economy is in a depression, an increase in output will have no effect on the aggregate price level.
2. (T/F) The long-run aggregate supply curve is horizontal.
3. (T/F) The long-run aggregate supply curve has a slight upward slope.
4. (T/F) If an economy faces a horizontal aggregate supply curve, large numbers of machines must be sitting idle or must be underused.
5. The short-run aggregate supply curve is positively sloped because
   a. many input prices such as wages and rents are slow to change in the short run.
   b. the price level does not change in the short run.
   c. as the aggregate price level rises, output falls.
   d. of the income and substitution effects.
6. Which one of the following statements is *not* correct concerning the short-run aggregate supply curve?
   a. The price of steel, aluminum, and iron rises; the aggregate supply curve shifts to the left.
   b. A new tax on corporate profits shifts the aggregate supply curve to the left.
   c. New government regulations requiring extensive data gathering by businesses shifts the aggregate supply curve to the left.
   d. New computer technology promising productivity growth shifts the aggregate supply curve to the left.
7. Which one of the following statements is *not* correct?
   a. Firms think the economy is recovering; the short-run aggregate supply curve shifts to the right.
   b. Wages rise; the short-run aggregate supply curve shifts to the right.

   c. Interest rates fall; the short-run aggregate supply curve shifts to the right.
   d. Huge new oil deposits are discovered in the Louisiana gulf; the short-run aggregate supply curve shifts to the right.
8. If the economy is near full employment, a short-run increase in GDP will
   a. have no effect on the aggregate price level.
   b. will lead to a rise in the aggregate price level.
   c. will lead to a fall in the aggregate price level.
   d. will lead to a fall in wage rates.
9. The short-run aggregate supply curve will shift to the right
   a. when input costs rise.
   b. when taxes rise.
   c. when interest rates rise.
   d. when productivity rises.
10. Which one of the following statements is *not* correct?
   a. Long-run growth is a shifting of the long-run aggregate supply curve to the right.
   b. Increased inflationary expectations will shift the short-run aggregate supply curve to the right.
   c. As businesses become more optimistic, the short-run aggregate supply curve shifts to the right.
   d. Rising interest rates cause the short-run aggregate supply curve to shift to the left.

Score: ____

Answers: 1. T; 2. F; 3. F; 4. T; 5. a; 6. d; 7. b; 8. b; 9. d; 10. b.

If You Got 9 or 10 Correct

This was a relatively easy section, and you have a good understanding of aggregate supply. Go on to the next section, "Macroeconomic Equilibrium," where aggregate demand and supply are combined and used to answer questions about our economy.

If You Didn't Get at Least 9 Correct

Don't panic. This is not difficult material. Reread the section in the text and pay special attention to Figure 4. Be sure you understand the difference between the long-run, short-run, and depression aggregate supply curves.

Then, take a few moments and review Table 2 to make sure you understand what will cause aggregate supply to increase or decline. In general, policymakers want to avoid policies that will reduce aggregate supply. When you have completed this review, go on to the next section, "Macroeconomic Equilibrium," where what you have learned so far in the chapter will be brought together. ■

Macroeconomic Equilibrium

Frequently Asked Questions

Q: How is short-run equilibrium determined?

A: A short-run macroeconomic equilibrium occurs at the intersection of the aggregate supply and aggregate demand curves. When an economy is operating at full employment, this also represents a point of long-run macroeconomic equilibrium. The Great Depression demonstrated, however, that an economy can reach short-run equilibrium at output levels substantially below full employment.

Q: What is the spending multiplier?

A: The spending multiplier, introduced by John Maynard Keynes, described the round-by-round spending that generates income greater than the original amount of new spending. For example, $100 of new spending increases GDP initially by $100. But that $100 becomes income to others, and they will spend a part of that $100 (an amount equal to $100 times their MPC, the marginal propensity to *consume*), and save a part (an amount equal to $100 times their MPS, the marginal propensity to *save*). Again, whatever part is spent becomes new income to others to be partly spent and saved, and so on. The result is that income increases by a multiple of the original change in spending.

Q: How is the spending multiplier computed?

A: The spending multiplier is equal to $1/(1 - \text{MPC}) = 1/\text{MPS}$.

Q: Does the multiplier vary depending on the nature of aggregate supply?

A: Yes. When the economy has a lot of unemployment, as happened during the Great Depression, and the aggregate supply curve is relatively flat, the full impact of the spending multiplier $(1/[1 - \text{MPC}])$ will be felt. This is shown in Figure 3 on the next page between points a and b. In the short run, however, some of the round-by-round spending increases will be absorbed into price increases, as shown between points b and e in Figure 3. The increase in aggregate demand from AD_0 to AD_1 is the same as the increase from AD_1 to AD_2, but the output increase $(Q_1 - Q_0)$ is larger between points a and b than the output increase $(Q_f - Q_1)$ between points b and e. In the long run, once the economy has reached full employment, the LRAS curve is vertical, and increases in aggregate demand do not result in higher output, so the multiplier approaches zero.

FIGURE 3

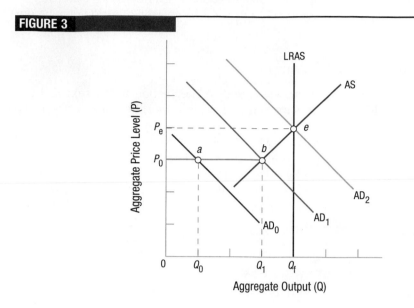

Q: What is demand-pull inflation?

A: Demand-pull inflation occurs when aggregate demand expands so much that equilibrium output exceeds full employment output. This is shown in Figure 4 as a movement from the original equilibrium from point e to point a. On a temporary basis, the economy can expand beyond full employment as workers incur overtime, temporary workers are added, and more shifts are added. All these things increase costs and prices. In the long run, absent an increase in aggregate supply, the economy will move back to full employment and a new equilibrium where prices are permanently higher at point c on the LRAS curve.

FIGURE 4

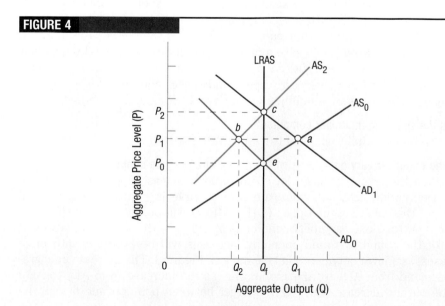

Q: What is cost-push inflation?

A: Cost-push inflation occurs when a supply shock hits the economy, shifting the aggregate supply curve leftward from AS_0 to AS_2 in Figure 4. In the short run, the economy moves from point e to point b, where both prices and unemployment rise and output falls. The oil shock of the 1970s was a good example of cost-push inflation: Because of a sudden decrease in supply, prices rose dramatically, even as output fell. Policymakers will typically increase aggregate demand to something like AD_1 to restore the economy to full employment but at a higher price level. Notice that cost-push inflation is associated with falling real output, whereas demand-pull inflation occurs while output is above full employment.

Core Graph: Macroeconomic Equilibrium in the AD-AS Model

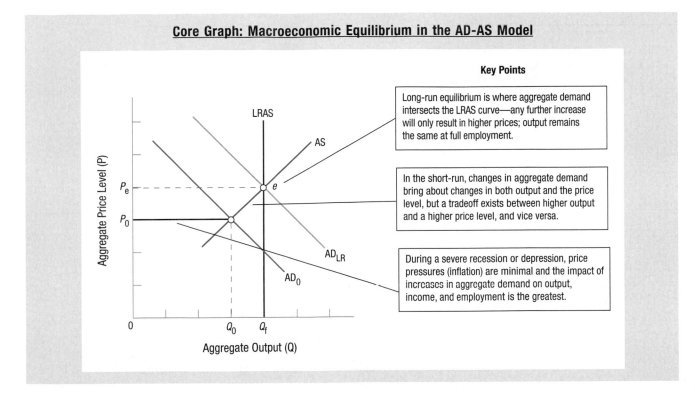

Key Points

Long-run equilibrium is where aggregate demand intersects the LRAS curve—any further increase will only result in higher prices; output remains the same at full employment.

In the short-run, changes in aggregate demand bring about changes in both output and the price level, but a tradeoff exists between higher output and a higher price level, and vice versa.

During a severe recession or depression, price pressures (inflation) are minimal and the impact of increases in aggregate demand on output, income, and employment is the greatest.

Macroeconomic Equilibrium Quick Check

Circle the Correct Answer

1. (T/F) The Great Depression showed that the economy can reach equilibrium with substantial unused resources.
2. (T/F) Policymakers will seek to cure an economy suffering from cost-push inflation by increasing aggregate supply and decreasing aggregate demand.
3. (T/F) Policymakers would rather deal with demand-pull inflation than with cost-push.
4. (T/F) Aggregate demand and aggregate supply are both equally responsive to government policy.

5. (T/F) The spending multiplier is likely to be the largest in the long run.
6. Which one of the following concerning demand-pull inflation is *not* correct?
   a. It occurs when aggregate demand moves equilibrium output beyond the full employment level of output.
   b. Prices and costs will increase.
   c. It is usually caused by aggregate supply shocks to the economy.
   d. Left on its own, the economy eventually will move to a higher price level with lower aggregate supply.

7. Cost-push inflation is caused by
   a. a supply shock that shifts the short-run aggregate supply curve to the left.
   b. a demand shock that shifts the aggregate demand curve to the right.
   c. a supply shock that shifts the long-run aggregate supply curve to the right.
   d. the wealth effect.
8. Which one of the following statements is *not* correct?
   a. The spending multiplier is at its highest level during a deep recession.
   b. The spending multiplier is equal to 1/(1 − MPS).
   c. Cost-push inflation is usually the result of a supply shock.
   d. In the long run, the spending multiplier is extremely small.
9. Demand-pull inflation can occur if
   a. businesses overinvest.

   b. the price of silicon chips rises.
   c. worker productivity rises.
   d. workers become worried about the future and accept wage cuts.
10. Cost-push inflation can occur if
   a. tax rates fall significantly.
   b. the natural gas pipeline linking the Northeast to gas supplies is destroyed by an earthquake and will take 5 years to replace.
   c. workers fear inflation will rise further and negotiate for wage adjustments.
   d. the price of information technology stops dropping.

Score: ____

If You Got 9 or 10 Correct

You have handled the concepts of macroeconomic equilibrium, the spending multiplier, and demand-pull and cost-push inflation well. Go on to the "Hints, Tips, and Reminders."

If You Didn't Get at Least 9 Correct

This is some of the more difficult material in the book, but is fundamental to what you learn in future chapters. Give it another shot. Review this section in the text again before continuing. This material is tough, but it is the foundation for our study of macroeconomics from this point on. Work through the solved problem below and then look through the "Hints, Tips, and Reminders" that follow. ▪

Solved Problem: Aggregate Supply and Demand

Assume the values in the table below represent aggregate demand and supply for the economy. Further assume that full employment is $3,000. Use the table and the grid to answer the questions that follow.

Price Level	AD$_0$	AS$_0$	AD$_1$	AS$_2$
120	1,000	5,000	____	____
110	1,500	4,500	____	____
100	2,000	4,000	____	____
90	2,500	3,500	____	____
80	3,000	3,000	____	____
70	3,500	2,500	____	____
60	4,000	2,000	____	____

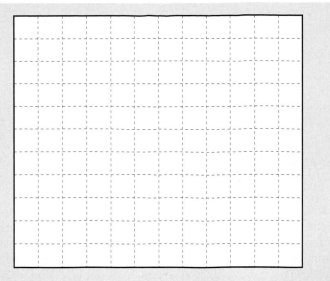

1. Plot the original AD and AS curves in the grid. What is the initial equilibrium and price level? Label the point e.

2. Now assume that aggregate demand doubles. Fill in the table for AD_1 and plot the new AD curve in the grid. What is the new short-run equilibrium output and price level? Label it point a.

3. Given the change in question 2, what will happen in the long run? Approximately what will be the long-run equilibrium output and price level? Label it point b.

4. Return to the original equilibrium at point e. Assume a supply shock hits the economy, reducing short-run aggregate supply but leaving full employment output at $3,000. Assume that AS_0 is reduced by $1,000 at each price level. Fill in the table and plot the new aggregate supply curve (AS_2) in the grid. What is the short-run equilibrium output and price level? Label this equilibrium point c. If policymakers decide to use aggregate demand policy to return the economy to full employment, what will be the long-run equilibrium output and price level? Label this point d.

Solution-Discussion

The completed Figure 5 and table are shown below and on the next page.

FIGURE 5

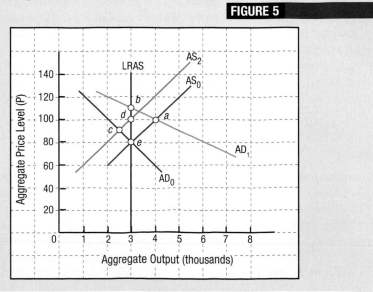

Price Level	AD₀	AS₀	AD₁	AS₂
120	1,000	5,000	2,000	4,000
110	1,500	4,500	3,000	3,500
100	2,000	4,000	4,000	3,000
90	2,500	3,500	5,000	2,500
80	3,000	3,000	6,000	2,000
70	3,500	2,500	7,000	1,500
60	4,000	2,000	8,000	1,000

1. Equilibrium output is $3,000 and the price level is 80 (point *e*).

2. Equilibrium output is $4,000 and the price level is 100 (point *a*).

3. Over time, workers will realize that prices have risen and their real wages have been eroded. They will bargain for higher wages, reducing aggregate supply (not shown in the table or graph), and the economy will move back to full employment at an equilibrium output of $3,000 and the price level of roughly 115 (point *b*). This is an example of demand-pull inflation.

4. The supply shock will move the economy to point *c*, creating a recession with equilibrium output falling to roughly $2,500 and the price level rising to roughly 90. Policymakers can increase aggregate demand to move the economy back to full employment at point *d*, but this means that the price level rises to roughly 100 in the process. This is an example of cost-push inflation.

STEP 4 Consider These Hints, Tips, and Reminders

1. Aggregate demand and supply analysis is more abstract than the market demand and supply analysis you learned in Chapter 3. Our everyday experiences make market analysis more intuitive and easier to grasp. You will need to focus on the reasons for the slope of both aggregate demand and aggregate supply; they differ substantially from market curves.

The components of aggregate spending (consumption, investment, government spending, and net exports) are responsible for shifts in aggregate demand. A growth in any one of these components shifts the aggregate demand curve rightward so that more output is demanded at all price levels, and vice versa.

Aggregate supply is affected by changes in input prices, productivity, taxes, monopoly power, and business expectations. All of these variables affect production and therefore aggregate supply.

2. Keep in mind that aggregate demand is related to spending, whereas aggregate supply is related to production. This will help you keep the determinants of each clearly differentiated.

3. Demand-pull inflation is a relatively straightforward concept, but its adjustment mechanism to long-run equilibrium is more difficult. Spend a little time with this because you will see it in later chapters. When the economy moves along a short-run aggregate supply curve but above full employment, costs and prices rise. Rising prices mean that *real* wages have fallen, and so workers will be looking for the equivalent of a cost-of-living increase to make up for the declines in real purchasing power of their wages. This pushes the short-run aggregate supply curve leftward until equilibrium is reached along the long-run aggregate supply (LRAS) curve at a higher price level.

Do the Homework for Chapter 19
Aggregate Demand and Supply

Instructor _____ Time _____ Student _____

Use the answer key below to record your answers to these homework questions.

1. (a) (b) (c) (d)   6. (a) (b) (c) (d)   11. (a) (b) (c) (d)   16. (a) (b) (c) (d)
2. (a) (b) (c) (d)   7. (a) (b) (c) (d)   12. (a) (b) (c) (d)   17. (a) (b) (c) (d)
3. (a) (b) (c) (d)   8. (a) (b) (c) (d)   13. (a) (b) (c) (d)   18. (a) (b) (c) (d)
4. (a) (b) (c) (d)   9. (a) (b) (c) (d)   14. (a) (b) (c) (d)   19. (a) (b) (c) (d)
5. (a) (b) (c) (d)   10. (a) (b) (c) (d)   15. (a) (b) (c) (d)   20. (a) (b) (c) (d)

1. The aggregate demand curve has a negative slope because
   a. consumers get satiated with too many choices of products and cannot make decisions.
   b. as prices rise, consumers focus their attention on spending on necessities like shelter, causing housing prices to rise rapidly.
   c. as prices rise, household wealth is reduced as the real value of financial assets held in bonds, in savings accounts, and as cash declines, reducing their purchasing power.
   d. as prices rise, Americans are able to get more for their exports.

2. Aggregate demand is determined by
   a. the National Bureau of Economic Research.
   b. changes in consumption, investment, government spending, and net exports.
   c. inflation rates and the marginal propensity to consume.
   d. outsourcing of jobs.

3. The aggregate supply curve is
   a. horizontal during a depression like the Great Depression in the 1930s.
   b. is normally upward sloping in the short run because many input costs are slow to change in the short run.
   c. is vertical over the long run.
   d. all of the above.

4. The aggregate supply curve is
   a. vertical during a depression like the Great Depression in the 1930s.
   b. is normally downward sloping in the short run.
   c. is horizontal over the long run.
   d. none of the above.

5. Using Figure HW-1, assume the economy is initially at equilibrium at point d, and an increase in aggregate demand from AD_1 to AD_0 is equal to $300. In this case, the multiplier is equal to which of the following?
   a. 2.0
   b. 2.5
   c. 3.0
   d. 3.3

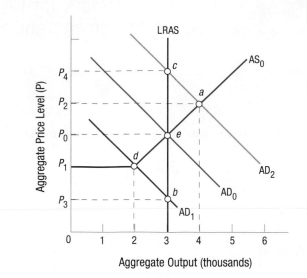

6. Using Figure HW-1, assume the economy is initially at equilibrium at point e. An increase in aggregate demand to AD_2 would result in
   a. cost-push inflation.
   b. prices rising to P_0 over the long run.
   c. prices rising to P_4 over the long run.
   d. policymakers reducing aggregate demand to AD_1 to avoid inflation.

HW-1

7. Using Figure HW-1, assume the economy is initially in equilibrium at point e. Demand-pull inflation would be represented by
   a. a reduction in aggregate demand to AD_1 followed by an increase in government spending to bring the economy back to equilibrium at point e.
   b. point b.
   c. an increase in aggregate demand, followed by adjustments in the product and labor markets resulting in a new equilibrium at point c.
   d. aggregate prices moving immediately from P_0 to P_1.

8. Using Figure HW-1, assume the economy is initially in equilibrium at point b. Cost-push inflation would be represented by
   a. a reduction in aggregate supply to AS_0, typically followed by an increase in unemployment, then an increase in government spending designed to bring the economy back to full employment equilibrium at point e.
   b. point a.
   c. an increase in aggregate demand, followed by adjustments in the product and labor markets, resulting in a new equilibrium at point e.
   d. aggregate prices moving immediately from P_0 to P_1.

9. The wealth effect
   a. prevents consumers from substituting lower-priced goods when prices rise.

b. leads to higher housing prices when the aggregate price level rises.

c. reduces the purchasing power of cash and other monetary holdings such as savings accounts and bonds when the aggregate price level rises.

d. results in higher levels of investment causing the aggregate demand curve to have a negative slope.

10. A rising aggregate price level
    a. results in rising aggregate demand.
    b. results in consumers purchasing more goods and services.
    c. keeps the economy at full employment during a recession.
    d. results in falling exports.

11. Aggregate demand will rise (shift rightward) if
    a. consumer spending rises.
    b. demand for U.S. products by people in foreign countries grows and thus exports rise.
    c. business expectations improve and business doubles its investment in new technology.
    d. all of the above.

12. Increased government spending will
    a. reduce aggregate supply by the amount of the increase in government spending.
    b. increase aggregate supply by the increase in government spending times the multiplier.
    c. increase aggregate demand.
    d. decrease output and employment.

13. Rising imports in the United States
    a. reduce aggregate demand.
    b. could be caused by a rising value of the dollar.
    c. could be caused by rising income in the United States.
    d. all of the above.

14. Rising taxes or increased regulation
    a. gives the aggregate supply curve its positive slope.
    b. would result in a leftward shift in the aggregate supply curve.
    c. would result in a rightward shift in the aggregate supply curve.
    d. has little impact on aggregate supply.

15. Which of the following will *not* a shift the aggregate supply curve?
    a. business expectations about the economy
    b. rising productivity from technical advances
    c. growing exports to Europe
    d. a growing monopolization of important sectors of the economy

16. If the economy is in equilibrium below full employ-
    ment and government spending grows, and as the
    economy expands and output grows, aggregate
    prices rise, then
    a. full employment will never be reached.
    b. the economy is in a depression.
    c. the aggregate supply curve is shifting leftward.
    d. the economy is proceeding along the short-run
       aggregate supply (AS) curve.

17. The Great Depression of the 1930s
    a. was caused by rising imports that reduced
       aggregate demand.
    b. resulted in a huge decline in business invest-
       ment.
    c. had little impact on the modern view of the need
       for macroeconomic policymaking.
    d. was solved by a huge reduction of income tax
       rates on business and the rich.

18. Cost-push inflation
    a. reduces employment along with rising prices.
    b. is caused by excess aggregate spending that
       pushes the economy above full employment.
    c. results from a rise in imports.
    d. is usually conquered by reducing aggregate
       demand and bringing the economy back to full
       employment.

19. If gasoline and diesel fuel prices were to jump
    overnight to from $3 a gallon to $6 a gallon,
    a. the economy would suffer demand-pull inflation
       until policymakers could agree on a plan to
       reduce aggregate demand.
    b. the economy's aggregate demand curve would
       shift rightward.
    c. aggregate supply would expand as business
       invested immediately in fuel-saving hybrid
       delivery vehicles.
    d. the economy's aggregate supply curve would
       shift leftward.

20. When the economy reaches full employment,
    a. increases in aggregate demand will have no
       impact on the economy.
    b. increases in aggregate supply will simply lead
       to higher inflation.
    c. the multiplier will become quite small.
    d. a supply shock will only have a minimal impact
       because the LRAS curve is vertical.

| | Use the ExamPrep to Get Ready for Exams | STEP 6 |

This sheet (front and back) is designed to help you prepare for your exams. The chapter has been boiled down to its key concepts. You are asked to answer questions, define terms, draw graphs, and, if you wish, add summaries of class notes.

Aggregate Demand

Describe three reasons why the aggregate demand curve is negatively sloped:

List the determinants of aggregate demand (*Hint:* Factors that cause the curve to shift):

Aggregate Supply

Describe the aggregate supply curve for the following:

Depression:

Short-run:

Long-run:

Describe the determinants of aggregate supply:

Macroeconomic Equilibrium

- Draw the aggregate supply (AS) and the aggregate demand (AD) curves in the grid below.

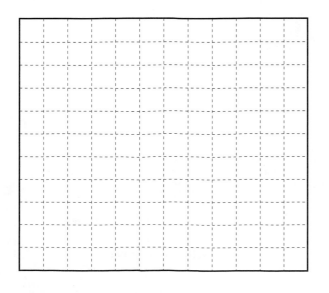

- Label the equilibrium point *e*.
- Draw the long-run aggregate supply (LRAS) curve through point *e*.
- Describe why the spending multiplier is different at different levels of output.

Demand-Pull and Cost-Push Inflation

In the grid below, draw AD and AS curves that represent demand-pull inflation. Describe what causes demand-pull inflation, and describe what happens in the long run if policymakers do nothing.

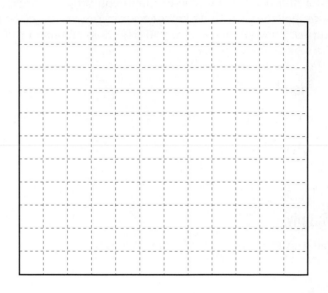

Demand-Pull Inflation

In the grid below, draw AD and AS curves that represent cost-push inflation. Describe what causes cost-push inflation, and describe what happens in the long run if policymakers do nothing.

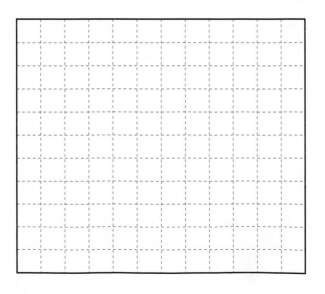

Cost-Push Inflation

Additional Study Help Chapterwide Practice Questions

Matching

Match the description with the corresponding term.

___ 1. Aggregate expenditures
___ 2. Marginal propensity to consume
___ 3. Marginal propensity to save
___ 4. Aggregate demand
___ 5. Aggregate supply
___ 6. Aggregate equilibrium
___ 7. Demand-pull inflation
___ 8. Cost-push inflation

a. Equivalent to gross domestic product, they consist of consumer spending, business investment spending, government spending, and net foreign spending.
b. The change in saving associated with a given change in income.
c. The real GDP that firms will produce at varying price levels.
d. The change in consumption associated with a given change in income.
e. Occurs when aggregate demand expands the economy beyond full employment. Producing above equilibrium drives up the price level and costs, setting in motion forces to move the economy to a new equilibrium where prices are higher.
f. The quantities of goods and services (real GDP) demanded at different price levels.
g. A short-run equilibrium occurs at the intersection of the aggregate supply and aggregate demand curves. When an economy is operating at full employment, this also represents a point of long-run equilibrium.
h. Occurs when a supply shock hits the economy, shifting the aggregate supply curve to the left. At the new equilibrium, prices are higher, unemployment is higher, and output is lower.

Fill-In

Circle the word(s) in parentheses that complete the sentence.

1. One reason the aggregate demand curve has a negative slope is the wealth effect. The wealth effect occurs because households keep some of their wealth in (real estate, gold, cash) _____, and as aggregate prices rise, the purchasing power of this wealth falls. A rising price level also reduces (exports, imports, investment) _____ because higher prices reduce the desirability U.S. goods in foreign markets.

2. The four determinants of the aggregate demand curve include consumption, investment, net exports, and spending by (business, government, foreigners) _____.

3. The aggregate supply curve is flat during (a depression, the short run, the long run) _____, but slopes up during (a depression, the short run, the long run) _____, and is vertical in (a depression, the short run, the long run) _____.

4. The aggregate supply curve will increase (shift rightward) when (input prices, taxes, productivity) _____ increases and will decline (shift leftward) if (expectations, input prices, taxes) _____ decline.

5. The spending multiplier is equal to (1/(1 − MPS), 1/MPS, 1/MPC) _____ and is most powerful (in the short run, in a depression, at full employment) _____, but falls to a small number (in the short run, in a depression, at full employment) _____.

6. When the economy expands beyond full employment, (demand-pull, cost-push) _____ inflation is set in motion. An increase in the price of an economically important commodity could result in (demand-pull, cost-push) _____ inflation.

True-False

Circle the correct answer.

<u>T/F</u> 1. When aggregate price rises, exports tend to rise as well.

<u>T/F</u> 2. When aggregate price rises, interest rates tend to rise as well.

<u>T/F</u> 3. An income tax cut can generally be expected to increase aggregate demand.

<u>T/F</u> 4. The aggregate demand curve shows the quantities of particular goods demanded at different price levels.

<u>T/F</u> 5. The determinants of aggregate demand include input prices, the market power of firms, productivity, and business expectations.

<u>T/F</u> 6. When an economy is at full employment, any further growth in output is extremely difficult.

T/F   7. When an economy is in depression, any increase in output is likely to have inflationary effects.

T/F   8. The determinants of aggregate supply include the market power of firms, taxes, regulation, the price of inputs, productivity, and business expectations.

T/F   9. A rise in productivity will shift the aggregate supply curve to the right.

T/F   10. The aggregate supply curve is negatively sloped.

T/F   11. The Great Depression demonstrated that eventually the economy will always gravitate toward an equilibrium at full employment.

T/F   12. The Great Depression was a turning point in how economists approached macroeconomic analysis.

T/F   13. When cost-push inflation threatens, policymakers are generally quick to take steps to reduce aggregate demand.

T/F   14. Demand-pull inflation occurs when a supply shock hits the economy, shifting the aggregate supply curve leftward.

T/F   15. The oil shock of 1973 produced a dramatic example of demand-pull inflation.

Multiple Choice

Circle the correct answer.

1. Which of the following is *not* among the reasons the aggregate demand curve is negatively sloped?
   a. As price levels rise, interest rates rise.
   b. As aggregate price rises, real household wealth declines.
   c. When domestic prices rise, exports fall.
   d. When the price of a given product rises, consumers will purchase more of its substitutes.

2. Which of the following events would shift the aggregate demand curve to the left?
   a. a rise in interest rates, causing investment to decline
   b. a stock market surge, leading to a rise in consumption
   c. the passage of a spending bill, expanding the federal budget
   d. a revival of the Japanese economy, boosting American exports

3. Cost-push inflation of the 1970s
   a. had only a minor impact on the economy.
   b. resulted from excessive government spending.
   c. was primarily due to oil price increases.
   d. quickly moved the economy to full employment.

4. The aggregate demand curve is
   a. horizontal.
   b. vertical.
   c. upward sloping.
   d. downward sloping.

5. The "wealth effect" refers to the fact that when aggregate price levels rise,
   a. exports decline.
   b. firms cut back on their investments.
   c. the real value of savings accounts, bonds, and cash declines.
   d. interest rates tend to rise.

6. Which region of the aggregate supply curve represents a depression period?
   a. the vertical region
   b. the upward-sloping region
   c. the horizontal region
   d. the downward-sloping region

7. Which region of the aggregate supply curve reflects the classical assumption that an economy will always gravitate toward equilibrium in the long run?
   a. the vertical region
   b. the upward-sloping region
   c. the horizontal region
   d. the downward-sloping region

8. The short-run aggregate supply (AS) curve is
   a. horizontal.
   b. vertical.
   c. upward sloping.
   d. downward sloping.

9. Which of the following are *not* among the determinants of aggregate supply?
   a. productivity
   b. input costs
   c. taxes and regulation
   d. the wealth effect

10. Which of the following will *not* generally be true of an economy in depression?
    a. Inflation rates are consistently high.
    b. Large numbers of machines sit idle.
    c. Many people are willing to work for whatever wage is offered.
    d. Producers can increase their output without raising their costs.

11. A recession occurs when
    a. an economy settles into a short-run equilibrium where aggregate demand is insufficient to keep the economy at full employment.
    b. an economy moves to a short-run equilibrium at a level of output above the full employment level.
    c. aggregate demand expands such that equilibrium output exceeds the full employment level of output.
    d. a supply shock hits the economy, shifting the aggregate supply curve rightward.

12. Cost-push inflation occurs when
    a. an economy settles into a short-run equilibrium where aggregate demand is insufficient to keep the economy at full employment.
    b. an economy moves to a short-run equilibrium at a level of output above the full employment level.
    c. aggregate demand expands such that equilibrium output exceeds the full employment level of output.
    d. a supply shock hits the economy, shifting the aggregate supply curve leftward.

13. Demand-pull inflation occurs when
    a. an economy settles into a short-run equilibrium where aggregate demand is insufficient to keep the economy at full employment.
    b. an economy is in depression.
    c. aggregate demand expands such that equilibrium output exceeds the full employment level of output.
    d. a supply shock hits the economy, shifting the aggregate supply curve leftward.

14. The spending multiplier
    a. gets bigger as the economy approaches full employment.
    b. is equal to $1/(1 - MPS)$.
    c. exists because consumers tend to save any change in income.
    d. is at its maximum during a depression.

15. A rise in exports and a fall in imports
    a. will result in lower output and employment.
    b. will balance each other, so income and output will *not* change.
    c. could be caused by an appreciating dollar.
    d. will shift aggregate demand rightward.

Essay-Problem

Answer in the space provided.

Use these questions to explore some of the extensions of the aggregate demand and aggregate supply model presented in this chapter.

1. What is the chief benefit of the AD-AS model over the classical model?

2. Why are public opinion polls important for aggregate demand and aggregate supply?

3. Why is it easier for policymakers to increase aggregate demand than aggregate supply?

4. Government intervention in the macroeconomy has been criticized as fostering a belief that the macroeconomy is a machine that just needs a little tinkering here and there. Evaluate this criticism based on what you have learned in this chapter.

5. President George W. Bush claimed that his tax cuts brought the economy out of the 2001 recession. How do we know if he is correct?

6. The oil shock of 1973 led to cost-push inflation in the macroeconomy. Are there other things that might lead to economy-wide cost-push inflation?

7. In Figure EP-1, the economy is currently on aggregate demand curve AD_0. Which aggregate demand curve best describes each of the following?
    _____ a. Inflation ravages the economy.
    _____ b. The weak U.S. dollar affects exports.
    _____ c. Interest rates rise.
    _____ d. A rising stock market bolsters consumer wealth and confidence.
    _____ e. Federal tax rates are cut.
    _____ f. Homeowners refinance their mortgages because interest rates have fallen.
    _____ g. The federal government raises corporate income tax rates.

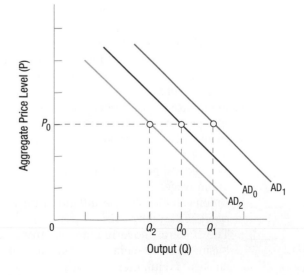

EP-1

_____ h. The federal government institutes a business investment tax credit for purchases of equipment.

_____ i. Government spending increases by 4% per year.

_____ j. People fear that the economy will go into recession.

8. In Figure EP-2, the economy is currently at aggregate supply curve AS_0. Which aggregate supply curve best describes each of the following?

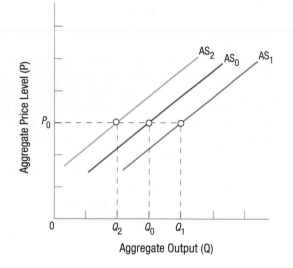

EP-2

_____ a. Oil supplies are disrupted, leading to a rise in the price of gasoline.

_____ b. Improvements in computer technology lead to productivity gains.

_____ c. The corporate tax rate is cut.

_____ d. The federal government creates a 200-page questionnaire that all businesses must fill out every year.

_____ e. An aluminum cartel is formed that doubles the world price of aluminum.

_____ f. Union membership doubles and hard bargaining results in a 25% increase in union wages.

_____ g. Inexpensive solar cells are developed that permit most retail firms to produce their total electrical needs on their rooftops.

_____ h. The federal government raises the minimum wage.

_____ i. Unions think that the inflation rate will rise substantially.

_____ j. The federal government institutes a business investment tax credit for purchases of equipment.

9. In Figure EP-3 the economy is in a recession at point a.

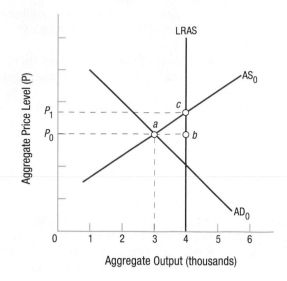

EP-3

a. What is the full employment level of output?

b. If the increase in aggregate spending needed to bring the economy to full employment at point b is $400, how big is the spending multiplier?

c. To move the economy to full employment at point c would require (more than, less than, the same) _____ $400 in aggregate spending.

10. In Figure EP-4, the economy is initially in equilibrium at point a.

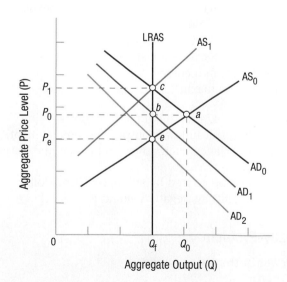

EP-4

a. This is an example of _____.

b. If policymakers want to keep the price level at P_0, what must they do?

c. If policymakers ignore the inflationary pressures, what will happen?

What's Next

This chapter provided you with a model for understanding how the macroeconomy works using aggregate demand and aggregate supply analysis. In the next chapter, we put this model to work when we look at some of the policies government has undertaken to influence the macroeconomy. You will see how useful this model actually is.

Answers to Chapterwide Practice Questions

Matching

1. a	3. b	5. c	7. e
2. d	4. f	6. g	8. h

Fill-In

1. cash, exports
2. government
3. a depression, the short run, the long run
4. productivity, expectations
5. 1/MPS, in a depression, at full employment
6. demand-pull, cost-push

True-False

1. F	5. F	9. T	13. F
2. T	6. T	10. F	14. F
3. T	7. F	11. F	15. F
4. F	8. T	12. T	

Multiple Choice

1. d	5. c	9. d	13. c
2. a	6. c	10. a	14. d
3. c	7. a	11. a	15. d
4. d	8. c	12. d	

Essay-Problem

1. The aggregate demand and aggregate supply model provides a more complete explanation of the causes and results of short-run fluctuations of the business cycle than the classical model.

2. Ideally, public opinion polls tell us what people expect about the economy in the future. Insofar as these polls inform other people, they can become self-fulfilling prophecies. If polls show that people are optimistic, more people may become optimistic and spend.

Unfortunately, it works in reverse as well: Public fears may become magnified if polls show pessimism, leading to decreased economic activity.

3. Government can enact a tax cut, which will have an immediate effect on aggregate demand because withholding tables can be quickly changed, and people will often increase economic activity before they receive the full tax cut. In addition, government spending can be increased rapidly. However, increasing production may necessitate purchasing new plant and equipment, a process that takes time.

4. The criticism has merit in the sense that the macroeconomy is a huge thing, and it is not easy to obtain the result one wants by just a tweak here and a tweak there. Yet, the economy can become stuck in a recession or face inflationary pressures, and general policies may be successful in these instances. Later chapters will explore this issue in greater depth.

5. We have seen that tax cuts in general will increase aggregate demand and increase aggregate supply. Increasing both aggregate demand and aggregate supply should have a beneficial result on moving the macroeconomy out of a recession. The question may be the nature of the Bush tax cuts: Were they across the board, or did they favor small groups? If they favored small groups, did these groups stimulate aggregate demand and aggregate supply in any significant way? Economists have not reached a consensus on this issue.

6. No one expected the cost-push inflation that the oil shock brought. Conceivably, there are strategic resources needed by the United States that are not produced in sufficient quantity here. It is not so easy to identify a resource that would have the same impact as oil; perhaps natural gas supplies would be one.

7. a. AD_1
   b. AD_1
   c. AD_2
   d. AD_1
   e. AD_1
   f. AD_1
   g. AD_2
   h. AD_1
   i. AD_1
   j. AD_2

8. a. AS_2
   b. AS_1
   c. AS_1
   d. AS_2
   e. AS_2
   f. AS_2
   g. AS_1
   h. AS_2
   i. AS_2
   j. AS_1

9. a. $4,000
   b. 2.5 ($1,000/$400)
   c. more than

10. a. demand-pull inflation
    b. Reduce aggregate demand to AD_1.
    c. Economy will adjust to point c at an even higher price level, P_1.

Fiscal Policy

20

Fiscal Policy Is What Government Can Do to Influence the Economy

In the previous chapter, the aggregate demand and supply model was developed to explain how the economy might become stuck in equilibrium with output below the full employment level. In this chapter, we will look at fiscal policy, which concerns how government adjusts spending on goods and services, transfer payments, and taxes to manage the economy and smooth the ups and downs of the business cycle. The government tries to influence both aggregate demand and aggregate supply. Fiscal policy is a key part of what modern governments do.

This Is What You Need to Know

After studying this chapter you should be able to

■ Describe the tools that governments use to influence aggregate demand.

■ Describe mandatory and discretionary government spending.

■ Describe the multiplier effect of increased government spending on the equilibrium output of an economy.

■ Describe expansionary and contractionary fiscal policy.

■ Describe why tax changes have a smaller impact on the economy than changes in government spending.

■ Describe the fiscal policies that governments use to influence aggregate supply.

■ Describe the impact of automatic stabilizers, lag effects, and the crowding out effects in fiscal policymaking.

■ Describe the debate over the size of government and economic policy.

Review the Key Terms

Discretionary spending: The part of the budget that works its way through the appropriations process of Congress each year and includes such programs as national defense, transportation, science, environment, and income security.

Mandatory spending: Authorized by permanent laws and does not go through the same appropriation process as discretionary spending. Mandatory spending includes such programs as Social Security, Medicare, and interest on the national debt.

Discretionary fiscal policy: Involves adjusting government spending and tax policies with the express short-run goal of moving the economy toward full employment, expanding economic growth, or controlling inflation.

Expansionary fiscal policy: Involves increasing government spending, increasing transfer payments, or decreasing taxes to increase aggregate demand to expand output and the economy.

Contractionary fiscal policy: Involves increasing withdrawals from the economy by reducing government spending, transfer payments, or raising taxes to decrease aggregate demand to contract output and the economy.

Supply-side fiscal policies: Focus on shifting the long-run aggregate supply curve to the right, expanding the economy without increasing inflationary pressures. Unlike policies to increase aggregate demand, supply-side policies take longer to have an impact on the economy.

Laffer curve: Plots hypothetical tax revenues at various income tax rates. If tax rates are zero, tax revenues will be zero; if rates are 100%, revenues will also be zero. As tax rates rise from zero, revenues will rise, reach a maximum, and then decline.

Automatic stabilizers: Tax revenues and transfer payments automatically expand or contract in ways that reduce the intensity of business fluctuations without any overt action by Congress or other policymakers.

Data lag: The time policymakers must wait for economic data to be collected, processed, and reported. Most macroeconomic data are not available until at least one quarter (3 months) after the fact.

Recognition lag: The time it takes for policymakers to confirm that the economy is trending in or out of a recession. Short-term variations in key economic indicators are typical and sometimes represent nothing more than randomness in the data.

Implementation lag: The time required to turn fiscal policy into law and eventually have an impact on the economy.

Crowding-out effect: Arises from deficit spending requiring the government to borrow, which drives up interest rates, which in turn reduces consumer spending and business investment.

Fiscal Policy and Aggregate Demand

Frequently Asked Questions

Q: **What are the government's main fiscal policy tools?**

A: Governments try to influence aggregate demand by using fiscal policy. The government's main fiscal policy tools are spending on goods and services, transfer payments, and taxes.

Q: **Why can fiscal policy be so powerful?**

A: Fiscal policy can be powerful because of the multiplier effect. When aggregate spending increases by \$1, the individuals or firms receiving this added dollar will spend part of it, saving the rest. Whatever part of the dollar is spent will be received by some other individual or firm; who will again spend part of the new earnings, saving the rest. This process continues until all the new spending has been exhausted. In this way, the initial \$1 of spending can add considerably more aggregate output and income to the economy than the original \$1. The initial \$1 of spending is multiplied.

Q: **Does the multiplier work only with spending increases?**

A: The multiplier works in both directions: a decrease in spending will reduce equilibrium income and output by the multiplier times the spending decrease.

Q: **Will the multiplier always have the same impact?**

A: The multiplier will have its full effect when an economy is in a depression. Price pressures are nil, and thus the effects of spending increases are multiplied throughout the economy without being absorbed by higher prices. This is shown in Figure 1 as the economy moving from point a to point b when aggregate demand (AD) is increased from AD_0 to AD_1.

When the same economy begins to recover, its short-run aggregate supply curve will be positively sloped, and a similar increase in aggregate demand (from

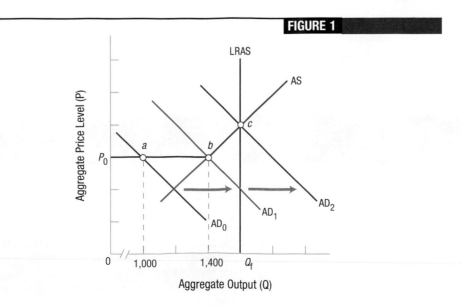

FIGURE 1

AD_1 to AD_2) will have less of an impact on output because higher prices will absorb some of the effects of increased spending (output only moves to point c). When the economy reaches full employment, its long-run aggregate supply (LRAS) curve will be vertical. Spending increases will simply raise the price level without raising equilibrium income or output. When an economy moves beyond full employment, driving up wages and prices, an inflationary spiral sets in.

Q: **What is the short-run goal of fiscal policy?**

A: The exercise of discretionary fiscal policy involves changing government spending, transfer payments, or tax policies with the short-run goal of moving the economy toward full employment, encouraging economic growth, or controlling inflation.

Q: **At equilibrium, what is the relation between injections and withdrawals?**

A: When fiscal policy is added to our model of the economy, equilibrium is achieved when government spending plus business investment plus exports (injections into the economy) equals saving plus taxes + imports (withdrawals or leakages); thus, at equilibrium, $G + I + X = S + T + M$.

Q: **Do changes in government spending and changes in taxes have the same effects?**

A: A change in government spending (G) will cause equilibrium income and output to rise or fall by the spending change times the multiplier. The effect of a change in taxes (T) on the economy is more complex. When taxes are increased, money is withdrawn from the economy's spending stream; when taxes are reduced, consumers and business have more to spend. Yet, a change in taxes will not change equilibrium income and output by the full change times the multiplier. People will put a part of a tax decrease into saving rather than spending it. If there is a tax increase, people will "pay" for some of it by reducing savings. In effect, the multiplier associated with tax changes is smaller than the multiplier associated with government spending.

Q: **What do expansionary fiscal policies do?**

A: Expansionary fiscal policies include increasing government spending; increasing transfer payments such as Social Security, unemployment compensation, and welfare payments; and decreasing taxes. All of these policies focus on aggregate demand. These policies put more money into the hands of consumers and businesses. The opposite policies are contractionary, taking money out of the hands of consumers and businesses.

Q: **Is demand-side fiscal policy a complete blessing?**

A: Exercising demand-side fiscal policy requires tradeoffs between output, unemployment, and price levels. Output can be increased, but only by raising the price level, or prices can be stabilized, but only by reducing output and incurring rising unemployment.

Fiscal Policy and Aggregate Demand Quick Check

Circle the Correct Answer

1. (T/F) The government's chief fiscal policy tools are spending on goods and services, monetary policy, and taxes.
2. (T/F) If an economy has an MPS of 0.2, a $200 increase in government spending raises equilibrium output by $1,000.

3. (T/F) Increases in taxes will not have the same impact on the economy as an equivalent decrease in government spending.
4. (T/F) Mandatory government spending is nearly twice the size of discretionary government spending.
5. Which one of the following is *not* correct?
   a. For an economy at equilibrium, injections will equal withdrawals.

b. An economy will be at equilibrium when I + G + X = S + T + M.

c. Increasing government spending by $1 will lead to an increase in equilibrium output of $1.

d. Increasing taxes will have less of an impact on equilibrium than reducing government spending by the same amount.

6. In Figure 2 which one of the following is *not* correct?
   a. If the economy is stuck at equilibrium at point *e*, the government can increase government spending to shift aggregate demand to the right, thus moving the economy to full employment.
   b. If the economy faces the short-run aggregate supply curve as shown, using fiscal policy to shift the aggregate demand curve should bring the economy to full employment, but at the cost of a higher price level.
   c. In the long run, if the government uses fiscal policy to shift the aggregate demand curve to the right of AD_1, this will merely increase the price level with no effect on output.
   d. The government can shift the aggregate demand curve to the right by decreasing government spending, which will lead to consumers having more money to spend.

7. If the government uses a contractionary fiscal policy in the hope of reducing inflation,
   a. it will have the opposite effect: Contractionary policy will lead to an inflationary spiral.
   b. the price level will fall, but at the expense of lower output.
   c. it should be successful in the short run but not in the long run.
   d. it will have no effect because fiscal policy does not work during times of inflation.

8. In an economy with a marginal propensity to save of 0.4, what effect will a reduction of $100 in government spending have on equilibrium?
   a. reduce it by $250
   b. reduce it by $100
   c. raise it by $100
   d. raise it by $250

9. Which one of the following is *not* correct?
   a. The multiplier has less of an effect on a healthy economy than a depressed economy.
   b. Fiscal policy is used by governments to move an economy to full employment.
   c. Decreasing tax rates should lead to an increase in aggregate demand.
   d. In normal times, expansionary fiscal policy will increase aggregate demand with no effect on the price level.

10. Why do politicians avoid contractionary fiscal policy?
    a. Politicians do not want to be associated with the rise in aggregate prices that always follows contractionary fiscal policies.
    b. Politicians do not want output to fall, which accompanies contractionary fiscal policies, because falling output leads to increasing unemployment.
    c. Contractionary fiscal policy is tougher to bring about than expansionary fiscal policy.
    d. Contractionary fiscal policies often lead to an inflationary spiral.

Score: _____

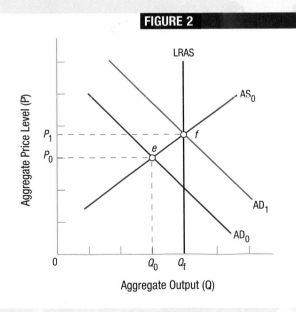

FIGURE 2

If You Got 9 or 10 Correct

You have a good understanding of how governments influence aggregate demand by using fiscal policy, and how multipliers add force to fiscal policy. Go on to the next section, "Fiscal Policy and Aggregate Supply."

If You Didn't Get at Least 9 Correct

Take your time and do the following:

- List the key fiscal policy tools that government uses to influence aggregate demand. Be sure you know how increases and decreases in each tool shift aggregate demand.
- Go back to the text and make sure you see why injections equal withdrawals (I + G + X = S + T + M) at equilibrium. This equation is important, and you will see it again in later chapters.
- Review the concept of the multiplier and make sure you understand why the impact of tax changes is less than changes in government spending.
- Make sure you understand the tradeoffs between expansionary and contraction fiscal policy, and therefore why policymakers typically avoid using contractionary policy.

This is the toughest section in the chapter. The remaining sections will be easier if you have a firm foundation of demand-side fiscal policy. ▪

Fiscal Policy and Aggregate Supply

Frequently Asked Questions

Q: What are some of the advantages and disadvantages of government attempts to use fiscal policy to shift aggregate supply?

A: An advantage is that unlike demand-side policies, supply-side policies do not require tradeoffs between output and price levels; they can expand output without raising prices. Supply-side policies, however, take much longer to work than demand-side policies. The goal of supply-side fiscal policy is to shift the long-run aggregate supply curve to the right, thereby expanding output without raising the price level.

Q: What are some specific fiscal policies used to shift aggregate supply.

A: Fiscal policies to increase aggregate supply include encouraging the acquisition of human capital, facilitating the spread of technology, reducing high marginal tax rates to provide greater incentive to work, encouraging investment in new capital equipment, encouraging investment in research and development, and ending burdensome regulations.

Q: What is the Laffer curve?

A: Economist Arthur Laffer argued that high marginal tax rates discourage working. His point was that there is some tax rate between 0 and 100% that maximizes tax revenue. Beyond that point, higher marginal tax rates lead to lower tax revenues, because high marginal tax rates reduce the incentives to work and take risks. If marginal rates are quite high, he argued, they could be lowered and tax revenues would rise.

Keep in Mind

Supply-side fiscal policy has a political side in addition to the economic aspects we have discussed. Taxes do affect behavior and affect incentives to work, take risk, and invest. For example, high marginal rates can affect investment in human capital (it makes the return from going to college less attractive) and risk taking in business (it reduces profits). But these disincentives can be overstated. They exist, but empirically, they may not be as large as supply-siders might suggest. Further, for some people, supply-side economics has become more political in that they see tax reductions a way to constrain the size of government. Clearly, once tax rates are below the level that maximizes tax revenues, lowering tax rates will not result in higher tax revenues, but less. Supply-side considerations do keep us aware of the fact that if marginal tax rates get too high, or regulations become too burdensome, the economy may benefit from some adjustments.

Fiscal Policy and Aggregate Supply Quick Check

Circle the Correct Answer

1. (T/F) Fiscal policy is more concerned with shifting short-run aggregate supply than long-run aggregate supply.
2. (T/F) Fiscal policy to expand aggregate supply does not require tradeoffs between output and prices, and it works faster.
3. (T/F) Fiscal policies attempt to shift the long-run aggregate supply curve to the left.
4. (T/F) Demand-side fiscal policies do not require tradeoffs between higher output and a higher price level.
5. Which one of the following fiscal policies will *not* increase aggregate supply?
   a. reduced taxes on consumers
   b. reduced taxes on businesses
   c. investment tax credits
   d. a huge expansion of business regulation
6. Arthur Laffer argued for all *except* which statement?
   a. Marginal tax rates are important.
   b. Cutting high marginal tax rates can lead to an *increase* in total tax revenues, not a decrease.
   c. The higher the tax rate, the more that government receives in total tax revenue.
   d. High marginal tax rates act as a disincentive for two-earner families.
7. Which one of the following fiscal policies will *not* increase aggregate supply?
   a. increasing the depreciation period for business equipment from 3 to 5 years
   b. cutting individual marginal tax rates from 35% to 25%
   c. streamlining the drug approval process
   d. providing government grants for basic genome research

8. Which one of the following fiscal policies will *not* expand aggregate supply?
   a. cutting tax rates on income earned
   b. requiring businesses to increase the frequency of their reporting, from quarterly to monthly
   c. a government tax credit for business spending on basic research
   d. government spending on basic research
9. Which of the following is *not* correct?
   a. High marginal income tax rates have minimal effects on aggregate supply.
   b. High marginal income tax rates may so discourage work that cutting them actually could lead to an increase in total tax revenues.
   c. Reductions in marginal income tax rates always leads to increases in tax revenue because economic growth would be so much higher.
   d. Highly burdensome regulations could discourage risk taking and investment, resulting in a lower rate of economic growth for the economy.
10. Which one of the following fiscal policies will *not* shift the aggregate supply curve?
   a. changing individual marginal tax rates
   b. changing investment tax credits for business
   c. changing government funding for basic research
   d. changing the age one can receive prescription drug benefits

Score: ____

Answers: 1. F; 2. F; 3. F; 4. F; 5. d; 6. c; 7. a; 8. b; 9. c; 10. d

If You Got 9 or 10 Correct

You can handle fiscal policy and aggregate supply. Go on to the next section, "Implementing Fiscal Policy."

If You Didn't Get at Least 9 Correct

Slow down. The material in this section is not difficult. Spend a little more time on it. Jot down the key fiscal policies to increase aggregate supply, and be sure you know which way policy increases and decreases shift the aggregate supply curve. Take a moment and reflect on the differences between demand-side fiscal policies and those suggested for the supply-side. Just considering the differences may help you see how each set of policies affects the economy. ■

Implementing Fiscal Policy

Frequently Asked Questions

Q: What are automatic stabilizers?

A: Without overt action by policymakers, tax revenues and transfer payments expand or contract in ways that help counteract the movements of the business cycle. These are called automatic stabilizers.

Q: How do automatic stabilizers work?

A: When the economy is growing briskly, tax receipts from our progressive tax system rise more than just the increase in income as people move into higher tax brackets and transfer payments sink, withdrawing spending from the economy. This acts as a brake to slow the growth of gross domestic product (GDP), keeping the economy from overheating. When the economy goes into recession, the opposite occurs. Tax revenues decline and transfer payments rise. This pumps new funds into the economy, cushioning the impact of the downturn.

Q: Is fiscal policy easy to implement?

A: Using fiscal policy to smooth out the short-term business cycle is difficult because of several lags associated with implementing it. Most of the macroeconomic data needed by policymakers to enact fiscal policy are not available until 1 to 6 months after the fact; this is the *data lag*. And if recent data suggest an economic trend, it can take several quarters to confirm this trend; this is a *recognition lag*. Once lawmakers have recognized a need for action, it may require 18 to 24 months to plan, pass, and implement new economic policies; this is the *implementation lag*. Consequently, by the time fiscal policy is enacted, the economy will have moved to a different point in the business cycle, where the policy enacted could be detrimental.

Q: What is the crowding-out effect, and why is it important in considering fiscal policy?

A: The crowding-out effect arises when the government engages in deficit spending (government spending exceeds tax revenue), increasing the demand for funds, thereby driving up interest rates. This can reduce consumer spending on durable goods and business investment. Deficit spending has an expansionary effect on the economy, but this effect can be diminished when the economy approaches full employment by offsetting reductions in private spending.

Q: What underlying philosophy about the role of government often accompanies the debate over fiscal policy?

A: Often, fiscal policy debates have little to do with the state of the macroeconomy. Underlying the rhetoric of the economic benefits or dangers of tax cuts, budget deficits, and specific spending priorities is a long-standing philosophical debate about the proper size and role of government. The political left favors a larger and more active government, while the political right argues for a more limited role for government.

Implementing Fiscal Policy Quick Check

Circle the Correct Answer

1. (T/F) Automatic stabilizers help smooth the economy without any action on the part of the government.
2. (T/F) When the economy enters a recession, tax revenues tend to fall, and transfer payments rise.
3. (T/F) Tax revenues and government spending are the two principal automatic stabilizers in our economy.
4. (T/F) Recognition lags occur because it often takes several periods of data collection before patterns appear in key macroeconomic indicators.
5. (T/F) Generally, those on the left of the political spectrum favor a larger and more active government, and so they would be more likely than those on the political right to have government engage in fiscal policies.
6. (T/F) Those on the political right often argue against the use of fiscal policy not because they think it will be ineffective, but because they fear the size and power of government, and so they want to limit government's actions.
7. Which one of the following is *not* correct concerning fiscal policy lags?
   a. The data lag arises because it takes time (usually 1–6 months) for governments to collect macroeconomic data.
   b. The recognition lag arises because macroeconomic data can show short-term variation in key indicators.
   c. The implementation lag arises because it often takes time to get fiscal policy changes through the legislative process.
   d. Tax change lags are the worst of the implementation lags.

8. When the government borrows money to engage in deficit spending, it can lead to the crowding-out effect, which
   a. drives up interest rates.
   b. leads to implementation lags.
   c. leads to recognition lags.
   d. can affect the economy for 1 to 6 months.
9. Which one of the following is *not* correct concerning fiscal policy lags?
   a. Because of lags, fiscal policy can compound the effects of the business cycle by overstimulating an economy that is already recovering.
   b. Tax changes are sometimes a preferred fiscal policy tool because the implementation lag is usually shorter than other fiscal policy tools.
   c. The implementation lag can last from 18 to 24 months.
   d. The recognition lag is usually more than 12 months.
10. The crowding-out effect
   a. always occurs when government uses fiscal policy.
   b. may make it tougher for private investors to obtain loans.
   c. only occurs when governments seek to influence aggregate supply, not aggregate demand.
   d. occurs when implementation lags mitigate the effect of fiscal policy.

Score: ____

Answers: 1. T; 2. T; 3. F; 4. T; 5. T; 6. T; 7. d; 8. a; 9. d; 10. b

If You Got 9 or 10 Correct

Go on and review the "Hints, Tips, and Reminders."

If You Didn't Get at Least 9 Correct

A simple review of the material may be all you need because much of the material in this section is definitional. All you may need to do is read through the text again. When you have completed this review, take a look at the "Hints, Tips, and Reminders" that follow.

Consider These Hints, Tips, and Reminders   STEP 4

1. Here are a few concepts—conclusions you should take away from this relatively easy chapter:

■ Mandatory spending is nearly two thirds of federal spending, and this may constrain the ability of fiscal policy to actively alter the business cycle; but with so much of the federal budget in the mandatory category, it may also act to reduce the volatility of the business cycle.

- Changes in government spending have a bigger impact than tax changes because some of the tax goes in or comes from saving, reducing the amount ultimately multiplied.

- Supply-side fiscal policies have a controversial political aspect that often drowns out the straightforward economic incentive aspects. The impact of lowering marginal tax rates as a generator of higher tax revenues and economic growth will decline as marginal tax rates fall. But policymakers should always be aware of the disincentive effects of high marginal rates and excessive regulation.

2. The crowding-out effect briefly mentioned in the chapter becomes more important as the economy approaches full employment. Make a mental note of this issue; you will see it again after you study money and monetary policy, the next two chapters.

Do the Homework for Chapter 20	STEP 5

Do the Homework for Chapter 20
Fiscal Policy

Instructor _____ Time _____ Student _____

Use the answer key below to record your answers to these homework questions.

1. (a) (b) (c) (d)	6. (a) (b) (c) (d)	11. (a) (b) (c) (d)	16. (a) (b) (c) (d)
2. (a) (b) (c) (d)	7. (a) (b) (c) (d)	12. (a) (b) (c) (d)	17. (a) (b) (c) (d)
3. (a) (b) (c) (d)	8. (a) (b) (c) (d)	13. (a) (b) (c) (d)	18. (a) (b) (c) (d)
4. (a) (b) (c) (d)	9. (a) (b) (c) (d)	14. (a) (b) (c) (d)	19. (a) (b) (c) (d)
5. (a) (b) (c) (d)	10. (a) (b) (c) (d)	15. (a) (b) (c) (d)	20. (a) (b) (c) (d)

---

1. Fiscal policy is
   a. the use of government spending to stabilize the business cycle.
   b. the use of higher taxes to slow down a booming economy.
   c. increasing transfer payments during a recession to help those out of work.
   d. all of the above.

2. The simple Keynesian spending multiplier
   a. provides an estimate of how much more consumers will spend when income rises by $100.
   b. is only affected by increases in government spending.
   c. provides an estimate of how much income will grow in response to a change in investment, government spending, or any other new spending in the economy.
   d. is defined as 1 divided by 1 minus the marginal propensity to save $(1/[1 - MPS])$.

3. Discretionary fiscal policy
   a. is of little importance to the economy since it is controlled by politicians.
   b. has little effect on the economy, since anything the government fails to do will be provided by private business and nonprofit corporations.
   c. typically only involves tax cuts for the rich.
   d. is the use of government spending and tax policies to produce full employment in the short run.

4. In Figure HW-1, if the economy was initially in a deep depression and at equilibrium at point e, and aggregate demand expands from AD_0 to AD_1, output will expand to
   a. income and output will not change.
   b. $4,000.
   c. $5,000.
   d. $6,000.

5. In Figure HW-1, if the economy was initially at full employment and at equilibrium at point e, and aggregate demand expands from AD_0 to AD_1, output in the short-run will expand to
   a. income and output will not change.
   b. $4,000.
   c. $5,000.
   d. $6,000.

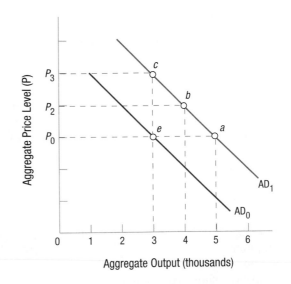

HW-1

6. In Figure HW-1, if the economy was initially at full employment and at equilibrium at point *e*, and aggregate demand expands from AD_0 to AD_1,
    a. the multiplier will be equal to the simple expenditures multiplier suggested by Keynesian analysis.
    b. the new price level will be P_0.
    c. the new price level will be P_2.
    d. the new price level will be P_3.

---

7. In Figure HW-2, if the economy was initially at full employment equilibrium at point *e*, and aggregate demand expands from AD_0 to AD_1,
    a. in the short run, the economy would move to point *b*.
    b. in the long run, the economy would move to point *a*.
    c. nothing would happen, the economy would remain at point *e*.
    d. the economy would experience some inflation and in the short run see reduced levels of unemployment.

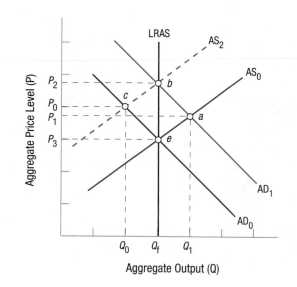

8. In Figure HW-2, if the economy was initially at full employment equilibrium at point *e*, and aggregate demand expands from AD_0 to AD_1,
    a. in the short run, the economy would move to point *a* with long-run adjustments taking the economy to point *b*.
    b. in the long run, the economy would produce output Q_1.
    c. nothing would happen, the economy would remain at point *e*.
    d. the economy would experience some inflation in the short run, but in the long-run return to output level of Q_f with a price level of P_3.

HW-2

9. In Figure HW-2, if the economy was initially at full employment equilibrium at point *b*, and aggregate demand declines from AD_1 to AD_0,
    a. in the short run, the economy would move to point *e*.
    b. in the long run, the economy would move to point *a* with greater output at lower prices.
    c. nothing would happen; the economy would remain at point *b*.
    d. the economy would experience some deflation or disinflation and in the short run see higher levels of unemployment.

10. In Figure HW-2, if the economy was initially at full employment equilibrium at point *e*, and aggregate supply declines from AS_0 to AS_2,
    a. in the short run, the economy would move immediately to point *b*.

b. in the long run, the economy would move to point *a*.

c. the supply shock will initially cause employment to fall and prices to rise, but with expansionary fiscal policy the economy will move back to full employment with a higher price level.

d. the economy would experience some inflation and in the short run see reduced levels of unemployment.

11. In Figure HW-2, assume the economy is initially at full employment equilibrium at point *e*. Which of the following is true?

a. Expansionary fiscal policy would involve increasing tax rates to increase aggregate demand from AD_0 to AD_1.

b. Contractionary fiscal policy would involve reducing government spending to shift the aggregate supply curve from AS_0 to AS_2.

c. Expansionary fiscal policy would involve decreasing tax rates to increase aggregate demand from AD_0 to AD_1.

d. Contractionary fiscal policy would involve decreasing tax rates to decrease aggregate demand from AD_1 to AD_0.

12. Contractionary fiscal policy

a. involves contracting the economy through reducing taxes and government spending.

b. reduces unemployment, but increases the aggregate price level.

c. involves contracting the economy by raising taxes and reducing government spending.

d. none of the above.

13. Expansionary fiscal policy

a. involves expanding the economy through reducing taxes and government spending.

b. reduces unemployment, but increases the aggregate price level if output is close to the full employment level.

c. does not work very well if the economy is in a deep recession because the multiplier is hindered because of rising prices.

d. is mostly used to keep inflation at bay.

14. Supply-side fiscal policy

a. is mainly a short-term fix for mild recessions.

b. is particularly useful for economic conditions like the Great Depression of the 1930s.

c. involves expanding the economy by raising taxes and reducing government spending.

d. is nice in that there is no tradeoff between output and price levels.

15. Supply-side fiscal policy

a. is mainly a short-term fix for deep depressions.

b. takes a long time to have an impact on the economy.

c. involves expanding the economy by increasing government spending.

d. none of the above.

16. Which of the following is *not* an automatic stabilizer?

a. the federal income tax

b. welfare and other transfer payments

c. business investment

d. unemployment compensation payments

17. The crowding-out effect of fiscal policy

a. results from too much money chasing too few goods.

b. is a long-term problem that has little effect on the economy in the short run.

c. results because deficit spending by the government ultimately reduces business investment because interest rates are increased.

d. arises from tax policy that discourages work.

18. Implementing fiscal policy involves several lags. Because information about the economy is only available on a monthly or quarterly basis, this causes a(n)

a. data lag.

b. recognition lag.

c. implementation lag.

d. impact lag.

19. Implementing fiscal policy involves several lags. Even when policymakers have all the information about the economy, it can still take several months before policymakers can detect and confirm the direction of the economy. This lag is called a(n)

a. data lag.

b. recognition lag.

c. implementation lag.

d. impact lag.

20. Implementing fiscal policy involves several lags. Once policymakers have determined that the economy needs some fiscal stimulus or contraction, it still may take several quarters before actual policies are enacted. This is known as the

a. data lag.

b. recognition lag.

c. implementation lag.

d. impact lag.

| | Use the ExamPrep to Get Ready for Exams | STEP 6 |

This sheet (front and back) is designed to help you prepare for your exams. The chapter has been boiled down to its key concepts. You are asked to answer questions, define terms, draw graphs, and, if you wish, add summaries of class notes.

Fiscal Policy and Aggregate Demand

Describe discretionary and mandatory spending:

Describe the simple expenditure multiplier:

Discretionary Fiscal Policy

Describe discretionary fiscal policy:

Describe the impact of government spending on equilibrium income and output:

Describe the impact of tax decreases on equilibrium income and output:

Why are these two different?

Expansionary and Contractionary Fiscal Policy

Describe expansionary fiscal policy:

Describe contractionary fiscal policy:

Fiscal Policy and Aggregate Supply

Describe the goals of fiscal policy and aggregate supply:

Describe the conditions for economic growth suggested by modern growth theory:

List the major fiscal policies designed to increase aggregate supply:

What is the Laffer curve, and what are its implications for fiscal policy?

Compare fiscal policies to expand aggregate supply with fiscal policies to expand aggregate demand. Which one do policymakers prefer? Why?

Implementing Fiscal Policy

Describe the automatic stabilizers, and discuss why they are important:

List and describe the three fiscal policy lags:

Describe the crowding-out effect of fiscal policy:

Additional Study Help Chapterwide Practice Questions

Matching

Match the description with the corresponding term.

___ 1. Multiplier
___ 2. Discretionary fiscal policy
___ 3. Expansionary fiscal policy
___ 4. Contractionary fiscal policy
___ 5. Mandatory spending
___ 6. Automatic stabilizers
___ 7. Crowding-out effect
___ 8. Fiscal policies that expand aggregate supply

a. Involves changing government spending, transfer payments, or tax policies. The short-run goal is moving the economy to full employment, encouraging economic growth, or controlling inflation.

b. When aggregate spending increases, those receiving this new spending will spend some and save the rest. What is spent will be received by others; again, some is spent; some, saved; and so on. In this way, the initial spending adds more output and income to the economy than the original change in spending.

c. Intended to stave off inflation by withdrawing money from the economy; may include reducing government spending and transfer payments, and raising taxes.

d. Intended to raise the economy to full employment by putting more money into the hands of consumers and businesses; may include increasing government spending, increasing transfer payments such as unemployment compensation and welfare payments, and decreasing taxes.

e. Without action by policymakers, taxes and transfer payments will expand or contract in ways that help counter the movements of the business cycle.

f. Spending that is authorized by permanent laws such as Social Security and interest on the national debt.

g. Policies include incentives to expand human capital and facilitate the transfer of technologies, reducing marginal tax rates, encouraging investment in new capital equipment, encouraging investment in research and development, and reducing inefficient business regulations.

h. When the government runs a deficit, this can drive up interest rates, forcing private individuals and firms out of the investable funds market. This can reduce consumer spending on durable goods and business investment.

Fill-In

Circle the word(s) in parentheses that complete the sentence.

1. Government spending that is recommended by the president and approved by Congress each year is referred to as (mandatory, discretionary) _____ spending, while Social Security is an example of (mandatory, discretionary) _____ spending.

2. Discretionary fiscal policy includes adjusting (regulations, civil rights laws, taxes) _____ with the goal of keeping the economy operating near full employment. Added government spending represents (expansionary, contractionary) _____ fiscal policy, while tax increases are (expansionary, contractionary) _____ fiscal policy.

3. The full impact of the multiplier is felt by (government spending, tax changes) _____, but the impact is mitigated for (government spending, tax changes) _____ because part goes into or is taken from savings.

4. If the economy is below full employment, policymakers will want to use (expansionary, contractionary) _____ fiscal policy, and this might include (increasing marginal tax rates on the rich, extending the time unemployed workers can draw unemployment compensation) _____. When the economy is operating above full employment and inflation is a problem, policymakers will make use of (expansionary, contractionary) _____ fiscal policy including (tax cuts, expanded government spending, reduced transfer payments) _____.

5. Fiscal policies directed at aggregate supply can expand output without (economic growth, inflation, tax increases) _____. But one of the problems policymakers face with supply-side fiscal policies is that they take a long time to have an impact.

6. When marginal income tax rates are high, lowering them will likely lead to (lower, higher) _____ tax revenues, but when marginal income tax rates are relatively low, reducing rates further will probably lead to (lower, higher) _____ tax revenues.

7. When the economy is growing rapidly (transfer payments, tax revenues) _____ rise automatically, but when the economy moves into recession we would expect (transfer payments, tax revenues) _____ to rise and (transfer payments, tax revenues) _____ to fall. These automatic stabilizers (do, do not) _____ require congressional action.

8. Collecting information on the economy requires some time, and economists refer to this as the (data, recognition, implementation) _____ lag. The time it takes the government to enact a tax reduction to expand the economy and to change the withholding tables is known as the (data, recognition, implementation) _____ lag.

True-False

Circle the correct answer.

_T/F_   1. When an economy is in equilibrium, total withdrawals from the economy equal total injections into the spending stream.

_T/F_   2. In most situations, an increase in investment spending of $100 will raise equilibrium output by $100.

_T/F_   3. If a $100 rise in investment spending combined with a $50 reduction in government spending results in a $200 increase in equilibrium income, the spending multiplier for this economy must be 2.

_T/F_   4. If an economy has an MPC of 0.6, its spending multiplier will be 2.5.

_T/F_   5. If an economy has a spending multiplier of 4, any change in government spending will raise equilibrium GDP by 4 times the absolute value of the spending change.

_T/F_   6. Discretionary fiscal policy involves adjusting interest rates to promote full employment, encourage economic growth, or control inflation.

_T/F_   7. A change in government spending will have the same effect on equilibrium income as a change in investment of the same amount.

_T/F_   8. An increase in government spending will have the same effect on equilibrium income as a tax reduction of the same amount.

_T/F_   9. When an economy is in equilibrium, $G + S + M = I + T + X$.

_T/F_   10. Fiscal policy is most effective when an economy is in depression.

_T/F_   11. If an economy is at full employment, expansionary fiscal policy will lead to a long-run increase in output without a significant rise in prices.

_T/F_   12. An inflationary spiral is set in motion when an economy expands beyond full employment.

_T/F_   13. Fiscal policies directed at aggregate supply require making tradeoffs between higher output and higher price levels or lower price levels and lower output.

_T/F_   14. Fiscal policies directed at aggregate supply generally take longer to work than demand-side policies.

_T/F_   15. The Laffer curve suggests that raising tax rates will always raise tax revenues; the exception to this rule is when the tax rate is 100%.

_T/F_   16. The high marginal tax rates of the early 1980s strongly encouraged an increase in two-income families.

_T/F_   17. Transfer payments automatically help smooth out the business cycle by falling during boom times and rising when the economy sinks into recession.

_T/F_   18. If the income tax is progressive, incomes will fall faster than tax revenue when the economy experiences a downturn.

_T/F_   19. Though automatic stabilizers such as tax revenues and transfer payments help smooth out the business cycle, they can actually make the implementation of discretionary fiscal policy more difficult.

_T/F_   20. The recognition lag in the fiscal policymaking process is typically 1 to 3 months.

_T/F_   21. An expansionary fiscal policy may actually be counterproductive if it takes so long to implement that the economy is already recovering by the time the policy takes effect.

__T/F__ 22. The crowding-out effect occurs when the government borrows money to engage in deficit spending, thereby driving interest rates up and crowding firms and individuals out of the loanable funds market.

__T/F__ 23. Social Security and the progressive income tax rates tend to slow booms and soften recessions.

Multiple Choice

Circle the correct answer.

1. What is the general formula for the spending multiplier?
   a. $1/(1 - MPS)$
   b. $1/MPC$
   c. $1/(1 - MPC)$
   d. $1/(MPS - MPC)$

2. In a depressed economy with a lot of excess capacity and with a marginal propensity to consume of 0.75, what effect will a $100 increase in government spending have on equilibrium GDP?
   a. reduce it by $250
   b. raise it by $250
   c. raise it by $400
   d. raise it by $750

3. Which of the following is *not* among the standard goals of discretionary fiscal policy?
   a. controlling inflation
   b. promoting economic growth
   c. facilitating immigration
   d. achieving full employment

4. What effect does a tax increase have on the economy's spending stream?
   a. It injects money into the spending stream.
   b. It withdraws money from the spending stream.
   c. It speeds the flow of the spending stream.
   d. It has no effect on the spending stream.

5. What is disposable income (Y_d) defined as?
   a. $Y + T$
   b. $Y - G$
   c. $S + T$
   d. $Y - T$

6. What kind of impact will increasing taxes typically have on equilibrium income, as compared to reducing government spending by a similar amount?
   a. more of an impact
   b. less of an impact
   c. about the same impact
   d. impossible to say without more information

7. If an economy is in the midst of a recovery, how much of an impact will an increase in government spending have on equilibrium output, as compared to if the economy were still depressed?
   a. less of an impact
   b. more of an impact
   c. about the same impact
   d. impossible to say without more information

8. Which of the following is a contractionary fiscal policy?
   a. increasing government spending
   b. expanding transfer payments
   c. subsidizing basic research
   d. raising marginal tax rates

9. If an economy is at full employment, what long-run effect will an expansionary fiscal policy have on it?
   a. increase output and raise the price level
   b. raise the price level without increasing output
   c. reduce the price level without increasing output
   d. increase output and reduce the price level

10. Which of following is *not* true of fiscal policies directed at aggregate supply?
    a. They take longer to work than fiscal policies designed to shift aggregate demand.
    b. They encourage growth in output without triggering inflation.
    c. They require making tradeoffs between greater output and higher price levels.
    d. They were enacted in the United States in the mid-1980s.

11. What is the long-run goal of fiscal policies directed at aggregate supply?
    a. shifting the AD curve upwards
    b. shifting the LRAS curve to the right
    c. shifting the AD curve downwards
    d. shifting the LRAS curve to the left

12. Which of the following fiscal policies would a supply-side economist be *least* likely to favor?
    a. expanding government regulation of business
    b. lowering marginal tax rates
    c. promoting investment in new capital equipment
    d. encouraging investment in research and development

13. Which of the following would *not* be among the likely effects of reducing excessively high marginal tax rates, according to supply-side economists?
    a. increasing the incentive to work
    b. expanding investment spending
    c. increasing the incentive to take entrepreneurial risks
    d. reduced tax revenues

14. What are the two principal automatic stabilizers in the U.S. macroeconomic system?
    a. tax revenues and government spending
    b. investment and government spending
    c. tax revenues and transfer payments
    d. investment and transfer payments

15. As a general rule, when the economy is booming,
    a. tax receipts and transfer payments both rise.
    b. tax receipts rise and transfer payments fall.
    c. transfer payments rise and tax receipts fall.
    d. transfer payments and tax receipts both fall.

16. Which of the following is *not* among the standard lags in the implementation of fiscal policy?
    a. the market lag
    b. the recognition lag
    c. the implementation lag
    d. the data lag

17. What is the typical length of the data lag?
    a. 6 to 12 months
    b. 2 to 4 weeks
    c. 12 to 18 months
    d. 1 to 6 months

18. For which of the following fiscal policies would the implementation lag be shortest?
    a. an increase in government spending by funding the building of new highways
    b. an increase in transfer payments by creating a new federal welfare-to-work jobs program
    c. a decrease in tax payments through a reduction in the federal payroll tax
    d. the promotion of private investment by creating additional tax advantages for individual retirement accounts

19. When the government engages in deficit spending, thereby triggering the crowding-out effect, who gets crowded out of what, and how?
    a. Private contractors get crowded out of projects awarded by government agencies.
    b. Politicians get crowded out of office by unhappy constituents.
    c. Many consumers get crowded out of superior goods markets by rising prices.
    d. Private investors get crowded out of the loanable funds market by higher interest rates.

20. What was the typical level of federal government spending from the 1970s through the late 1990s?
    a. somewhat more than 20% of GDP
    b. just over 15% of GDP
    c. around 35% of GDP
    d. just under 10% of GDP

Essay-Problem

Answer in the space provided.

The questions below take you beyond the material covered in the chapter. Use these questions to assess your progress and to discover some of the added dimensions to fiscal policy.

1. Why is the passage of time not an ally of the multiplier effect?

2. Why do politicians favor demand-side fiscal policies over supply-side fiscal policies?

3. Why are expectations a good antidote to implementation lags?

4. Why is demand-side fiscal policy a sharp instrument in a time of depression but a blunt instrument in other times?

5. Many states have balanced-budget rules. In a time of recession, this rule forces states to consider spending cuts or tax increases. Based on what you have learned in this chapter, could either of these measures be counterproductive?

6. Again, consider state balanced-budget rules. Some state governors have said that they would rather cut state government spending than raise taxes because cutting spending is more beneficial than raising taxes. Based on what you learned in this chapter, why is this reasoning incorrect?

7. Federal budget deficits are projected to be high over the next several years. Why do some people consider these deficits to be the death of demand-side fiscal policy?

8. Supply-side fiscal policies are much more controversial than demand-side policies. Why might the time factor that each policy needs to be effective account for this controversy?

9. Some people have claimed that Keynes saw the economy as an engine that policymakers could finely tune. Why might this criticism of Keynes misinterpret his position?

10. Why is the recognition lag so important in fiscal policy?

What's Next

With the completion of this chapter, you now have a good understanding of fiscal policy, one of the two key approaches that government takes to influence aggregate demand and aggregate supply to smooth out the business cycle. In the next chapter, we begin our examination of the second key approach when we look at money and the economy.

Answers to Chapterwide Practice Questions

Matching

1. b	4. c	7. h
2. a	5. f	8. g
3. d	6. e	

Fill-In

1. discretionary, mandatory
2. taxes, expansionary, contractionary
3. government spending, tax changes
4. expansionary, extending the time unemployed workers can draw unemployment compensation, contractionary, reduced transfer payments
5. inflation
6. higher, lower
7. tax revenues, transfer payments, tax revenues, do not
8. data, implementation

True-False

1. T	7. T	13. F	19. T
2. F	8. F	14. T	20. F
3. F	9. F	15. F	21. T
4. T	10. T	16. F	22. T
5. F	11. F	17. T	23. T
6. F	12. T	18. F	

Multiple Choice

1. c	6. b	11. b	16. a
2. c	7. a	12. a	17. d
3. c	8. d	13. d	18. c
4. b	9. b	14. c	19. d
5. d	10. c	15. b	20. a

Essay-Problem

1. We saw the multiplier effect that comes about when the government spends: The receiver of the spending then spends a portion of this, and the next receiver of this spending goes on to spend a portion, and so on. The more time it takes for a receiver to further spend, the less potent the multiplier effect will be because the spending takes longer to take

effect and affect the economy. Government policymakers want the multiplier process to go quickly; it is not instantaneous.

2. Demand-side fiscal policies are generally more effective in the short-term ones because it takes longer to increase aggregate supply than to increase aggregate demand. Politicians are concerned with reelection: Their relatively shorter time horizon makes them favor fiscal policies that have more immediate results so they can trumpet this in reelection campaigns. Further, politicians are expected to bring in government spending to their state. This leads to a natural tendency to prefer government spending over tax preferences (incentives) for business.

3. We have seen that it often takes many, many months for fiscal policy to make it through the legislative process and take effect. If people expect the legislation to go through, they may act on it before it becomes finalized. Thus, expectation can lead to action before the implementation lag ends, but the expectation needs a high probability of future success before it leads to action. The point is, it is not as if everyone freezes until the policy is finally fully implemented. Activity may start well before this happens.

4. In a time of depression, production capacity is underutilized. Policies that increase aggregate demand are likely to have fairly immediate effects, and they can bring the economy to full employment with few effects on the price level. In other times, the effects are partially eaten up in price increases. For this reason, demand-side fiscal policy is sharper in depression times than otherwise.

5. In a time of recession, reducing government spending or raising taxes would exacerbate the situation, not make it better. Reducing government spending would shift aggregate demand to the left, further reducing aggregate output. Raising taxes would take money out of people's pockets, again reducing aggregate demand and reducing aggregate output. Thus, an unintended consequence of balanced budget rules used to keep government spending in check is to make recessions worse.

6. Budget cuts are more counterproductive than tax increases because the budget cut will have a full effect of depressing spending, while some of the depressed spending from the tax increase would be taken up by reduced savings (a portion of the tax increase would reduce saving rather than reduce consumption).

7. When you hear about massive budget deficits, think of the crowding-out effect. The idea here is that budget deficits will become so large that the federal government will have huge borrowing needs. These huge needs will drive up interest rates unacceptably high. These high rates will make it more difficult for the government to run even more budget deficits in the future. Since running deficits can be a result of demand-side fiscal policy, the government's fiscal policy could be hobbled if it cannot run deficits.

8. The longer it takes for a policy to be effective, the harder it is to claim that a particular policy had a particular effect. With a huge economy, it becomes plausible to say that other factors were at work over a longer time horizon. Supply-side policies typically involve tax cuts to both individuals and companies. For many people who favor an expanded role for the federal government, these tax reductions are viewed as unacceptable.

9. Keynes looked at the economy under extreme conditions: a depression, when the economy was stuck in an equilibrium with output much lower than full employment. Keynes claimed that government must act in extreme situations. This does not necessarily lead to a position that government *should* try to fine-tune the economy all of the time, or that government *could* fine-tune the economy all of the time.

10. Just as no doctor wants to prescribe a remedy for a patient until he or she is sure what the ailment is, so no government official wants to declare that the economy is in a certain state until it is absolutely clear that it is in fact in such a state. Because key indicators normally vary, time is needed for policymakers to make sure that the data are pointing in a certain direction. This tends to lengthen the time of the recognition lag.

The Monetary System

21

Money Makes the World Go 'Round

In the previous chapter, we saw how governments can use fiscal policy to smooth out the business cycle. In this chapter, we start our study of the second tool that governments can use: monetary policy. Money has fascinated people throughout the ages. We will take a quick look at what money is and why it is so useful, then examine the role of banks in an economy. Finally, we will consider the Federal Reserve System (often called *the Fed*), the central banking system in the United States. Throughout this chapter, we will use simple demand and supply concepts to analyze why people want to hold money in their pockets and how money is supplied.

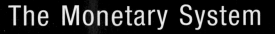

This Is What You Need to Know

STEP 1

After studying this chapter you should be able to

- Describe the functions of money.
- Define the money supply, according to M1 and M2.
- Describe equilibrium in the money market.
- Describe the relationship between the price of bonds and interest rates.
- Describe the functions of financial institutions and the money creation process.
- Describe the history and structure of the Federal Reserve System.
- List the Federal Reserve System's tools for conducting monetary policy.

Review the Key Terms

Money: Anything that is accepted in exchange for other goods and services or for the payment of debt.

Barter: The direct exchange of goods and services for other goods and services.

Medium of exchange: Money is a medium of exchange because goods and services are sold for money, then the money is used to purchase other goods and services.

Unit of account: Money provides a yardstick for measuring and comparing the values of a wide variety of goods and services. It eliminates the problem of double coincidence of wants associated with barter.

Store of value: The function that enables people to save the money they earn today and use it to buy the goods and services they want tomorrow.

Liquidity: How quickly, easily, and reliably an asset can be converted into cash.

M1: The narrowest definition of money; includes currency (coins and paper money), demand deposits (checks), and other accounts that have check-writing or debit capabilities, such as stock market and money market accounts.

M2: A broader definition of money that includes "near monies" that are not as liquid as cash, including deposits in savings accounts, money market accounts, and money market mutual fund accounts.

Transactions demand for money: That part of individual wealth held in money to perform commercial transactions (medium of exchange demand).

Precautionary demand for money: That part of individual wealth held in money to handle unexpected events and expenses.

Speculative demand for money: When inflation is not a problem, holding money for a short period is virtually risk free, whereas holding other assets is more risky. The speculative demand for money varies inversely with interest rates since they are the opportunity costs of holding money in a portfolio.

Fractional reserve banking system: To prevent bank runs (all depositors demanding their deposits in cash at the same time), a portion of bank deposits must be held as vault cash, or else in an account with the regional Federal Reserve Bank.

Money multiplier: Measures the potential or maximum amount the money supply can increase (or decrease) when new deposits enter (exit) the system and is defined as: $1 \div$ reserve requirement. The actual money multiplier will be less since some banks will hold excess reserves.

Federal Reserve System: The central bank of the United States.

Federal Open Market Committee: This 12-member committee is composed of members of the Board of Governors of the Fed and selected presidents of the regional Federal Reserve Banks; it oversees open market operations (the buying and selling of government securities), the main tool of monetary policy.

Reserve requirements: The required ratio of funds that commercial banks and other depository institutions must hold in reserve against deposits.

Discount rate: The interest rate the Federal Reserve charges commercial banks and other depository institutions to borrow reserves from a regional Federal Reserve Bank.

Open market operations: The buying and selling of U.S. government securities, usually treasury bonds, to adjust reserves in the banking system.

What Is Money?

Frequently Asked Questions

Q: What is money?

A: Money is anything that is accepted in exchange for other goods and services or for the payment of debts.

Q: What can be used as money?

A: For a commodity to be used as money, it must be standardizable, so that its value is easy to determine; it must be divisible, so that people can make change; it must be durable; it must be easy to carry; and it must be widely accepted as money by large numbers of people.

Q: What functions does money have?

A: Money has three primary functions in our economic system: as a medium of exchange, a measure of value (unit of account), and a store of value. Using money as a medium of exchange overcomes the problem of double coincidence of wants that plagues barter economies. Similarly, using money as a measure of value drastically reduces the number of prices individuals must determine. Last, because money is a durable store of value, it allows people to save the money they earn today and use it to buy goods and services tomorrow.

Q: What is liquidity, and how docs it relate to money?

A: An asset's liquidity is determined by how quickly, easily, and reliably it can be converted into cash so it can be spent on some good or service. Money is the most liquid asset because it is the medium of exchange and requires no conversion.

Q: How do we measure the money supply?

A: The Federal Reserve System uses two different measures of the money supply. Ranging from the narrowest to a broader measure of money, they are labeled M1 and M2.

Q: What is M1?

A: M1 includes currency (coins and paper money), demand deposits (checks), and other accounts that have check-writing or debit capabilities, such as some brokerage accounts.

Q: What is M2?

A: M2 is composed of M1 plus the "near monies": money that cannot be drawn on instantaneously, but is nonetheless accessible, including savings accounts, small time deposits, and money market mutual fund accounts.

Keep in Mind

Without money, economies could not develop into the sophisticated powerhouses we see today. Money facilitates exchange (as a medium of exchange and a measure of value) and also allows people to save today for purchases tomorrow.

What Is Money? Quick Check

Circle the Correct Answer

1. (T/F) A barter economy suffers from the problem of the necessity of finding someone who has what you want and wants what you have.
2. (T/F) Money is anything that is accepted in exchange for other goods and services or for the payment of debt.
3. (T/F) Money has three primary functions: it is divisible, it is durable, and it is easy to carry.
4. Which one of the following is *not* correct?
   a. Money is a store of value.
   b. Money is highly liquid.
   c. For a commodity to be used as money, it must be widely accepted as money by large numbers of people.
   d. Any commodity can be used as money.
5. Which one of the following is correct concerning the money supply?
   a. M1 does not include checkable deposits.
   b. M1 is not part of M2.
   c. M2 = M1 + "near monies."
   d. M1 = currency and coins only.

Score: ____

Answers: 1. T; 2. T; 3. F; 4. d; 5. c

If You Got All 5 Correct

You have a good sense of what money is. Go on to the next section "Money: Demand and Supply."

If You Didn't Get All of Them Correct

A simple review should do the trick here. Much of this material is definitional.

■ Review this first section and jot down the functions of money.
■ Go back to the text and make sure you know the differences between M1 and M2.

You need to get this terminology down pat before you continue to the next section. Make sure you know the functions of money and the definition of the various measures of the money supply. ■

Money: Demand and Supply

Frequently Asked Questions

Q: **What is the demand for money?**
A: The demand for money refers to the desire of individuals and firms to hold money in their portfolios of assets.

Q: **Why do people hold money?**
A: Money is held for several reasons. As a medium of exchange, it is needed for transactions reasons: to buy and sell goods and services. Some money is held for precautionary reasons, that is, to prepare for unexpected expenses. Third, some part of most portfolios is held as money because other assets are risky. This is called the speculative demand for money.

Q: **How do interest rates affect the speculative demand for money?**

A: The speculative demand for money is inversely related to the interest rate: The higher the interest rate, the higher the opportunity cost of holding money.

Q: **How are the money and bond markets related?**

A: The money and bond markets are closely interrelated. When the demand for money rises, individuals and businesses tend to satisfy this demand first by selling bonds for cash.

Q: **What is a bond?**

A: A bond is a contract between a seller (the company or nation issuing the bond) and a buyer. The seller agrees to pay the buyer a fixed rate of interest (the coupon rate) on the face value of the bond (usually $1,000) until a fixed date (the maturity date of the bond). Once a bond is issued, its yield (interest paid/price of bond) is subject to marketplace forces. As a general rule, as market interest rates rise, the value of bonds (paying fixed dollars of interest) will fall. Conversely, if interest rates drop, the price of bonds will rise.

Q: **What do banks and other financial institutions do?**

A: Banks act as intermediaries, bringing together borrowers and lenders.

Q: **How do banks create money?**

A: Banks operate under a fractional reserve system that allows them to create money. Banks accept deposits, and because bank runs are rare, banks hold only a certain required fraction of these deposits and loan the rest out. Most of the money loaned out will be deposited back into some other bank account. Part of these deposits will be held as new reserves; the rest will again be loaned out. This process continues until the entire initial deposit is held as reserves somewhere in the banking system. By this point, the new money in the economy has expanded to well beyond the size of the original deposit.

Q: **What is the money multiplier, and how is it defined?**

A: The money multiplier measures the potential or maximum amount the money supply can increase (or decrease) when new deposits enter (exit) the system. It is defined by the formula: money multiplier = 1 ÷ reserve requirement. Thus, if the reserve requirement is 20%, the money multiplier is equal to 1/.20 = 5. This means an initial deposit of $1,000 will end up creating $5,000 in new money. The actual money multiplier is lower because of leakages. For instance, some people will hold cash for transactions, reducing the amount put back into the banking system.

Money: Demand and Supply Quick Check

Circle the Correct Answer

1. (T/F) The speculative demand for money refers to the fact that individuals and firms will want to hold some of their assets as money to buy and sell goods and services.

2. (T/F) A bond pays $50 per year in interest. The market interest rate rises. The market price of the bond rises as well.

3. (T/F) The speculative demand for money is inversely related to interest rates.

4. (T/F) If a bond has a face value of $1,000 and pays $80 per year in interest, the bond will be worth less if market interest rates fall.

5. Which one of the following is *not* correct?
   a. An increase in the demand for money will cause interest rates to rise.
   b. Financial institutions bring lenders and borrowers together.
   c. A decrease in the money supply will cause interest rates to fall.
   d. A decrease in the money supply will cause the price of bonds to fall.

6. If the reserve requirement is 25%, what will the money multiplier be?
   a. 0.75
   b. 4.0
   c. 3.0
   d. 0.25
7. The actual money multiplier will be less than the potential money multiplier because of all *except* which reason?
   a. People may want to hold some of their loans as cash for transactions purposes.
   b. Reserve requirements put a brake on bank lending.
   c. Banks may want to keep some excess reserves.
   d. Businesses may hold some of their loans as cash.
8. If the money supply increases, which one of the following will *not* happen?
   a. The price of bonds will rise.
   b. Interest rates will fall.
   c. The speculative demand for money will rise.
   d. The precautionary demand for money will rise.

9. If the reserve requirement is 10%, how much total money will a new deposit of $500 potentially inject into the economy?
   a. $4,000
   b. $5,000
   c. $50
   d. $10,000
10. Which one of the following is *not* correct?
   a. Because of leakages, the actual money multiplier is likely to be less than the potential money multiplier.
   b. Banks may not always want to be "loaned-up."
   c. Reserve requirements make the U.S. banking system a fractional reserve system.
   d. The primary purpose of financial institutions is to create money.

Score: ____

Answers: 1. F; 2. F; 3. T; 4. F; 5. c; 6. b; 7. b; 8. d; 9. b; 10. d

If You Got 9 or 10 Correct

You soaked up a dense section on money demand and how financial institutions create money. Move on to the next section, "The Federal Reserve System."

If You Didn't Get at Least 9 Correct

You will profit from careful review of this section. First, review the relationship between interest rates and bond prices. Then, review the entire section, paying special attention to the example of how banks create money. You need to know how banks create money to understand the role of the Federal Reserve System covered in the next section. Before you go on, work the solved problems below on interest rates and bond prices, and on how banks create money. These are not difficult concepts; a simple run-through should be enough. ∎

Solved Problem: Interest Rates and Bond Prices

The bond in Figure 1 is a railroad and mining bond from Burgos, Spain, issued in February 1920. The total bond issue was for 7,500,000 pesetas, and each bond had a principal value of 500 pesetas. The duration was for 50 years, and the coupon rate was 6%, so each bond paid 30 pesetas per year to bondholders.

Notice the coupons below and around the bond itself. Investors (bondholders) would cut a coupon from the bond and take the coupon to the company (or sometimes banks would handle this transaction), and they would be paid their 30 pesetas for that year. When all the coupons were clipped, it would be time for the company to pay off the bond by giving each bondholder the principal. This is where the term "clipping coupons" came from.

FIGURE 1

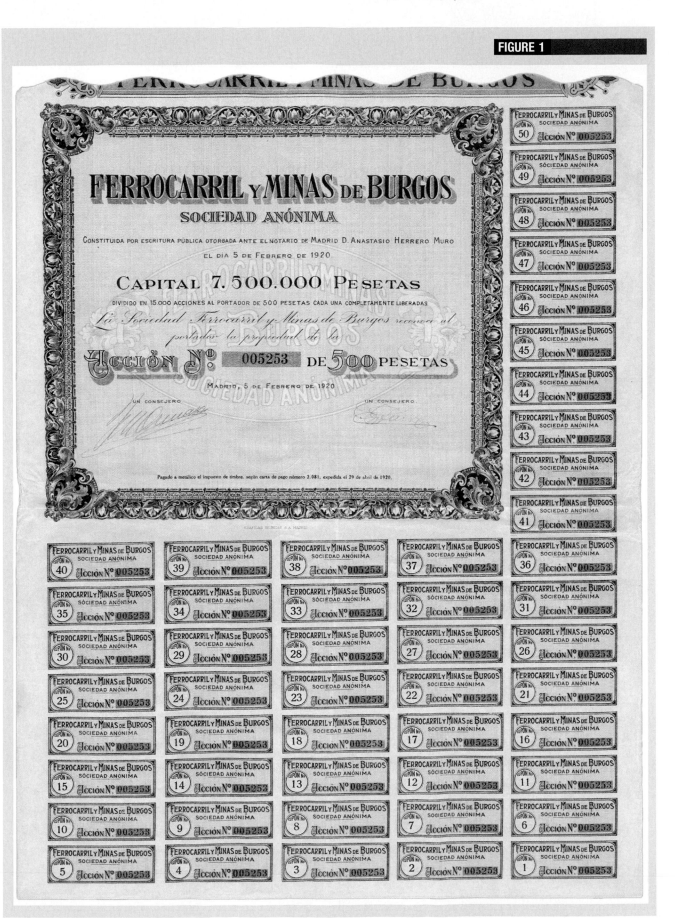

1. If market interest rates rise to 12%, what will happen to the value of this bond?

2. If market interest rates fall to 3%, what will happen to the value of this bond?

3. Using the grids below, show how an increase in the money supply in the money market will affect the bond market.

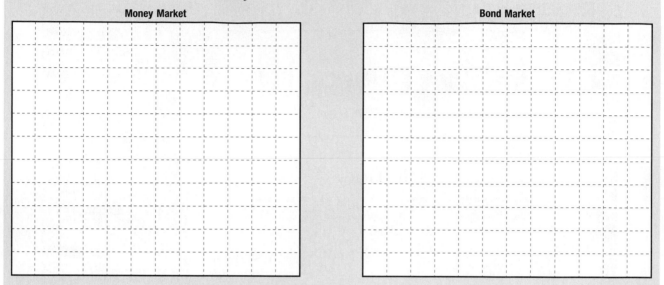

Money Market   **Bond Market**

Solution-Discussion

1. If market interest rates rise to 12% and this bond is still only paying 30 pesetas, then the price of the bond will fall to 250 pesetas because $30/250 = .12 = 12\%$. Thus, a doubling of the market rate of interest cuts our bond price in half.

2. If market interest rates falls to 3% and this bond is still paying 30 pesetas, then the price of the bond will rise to 1,000 pesetas because $30/1,000 = .03 = 3\%$. Thus, when the market rate of interest is cut in half, our bond price doubles.

3. The impact of an increase in the money supply on interest rates and bond prices is shown in Figure 2. An increase in the money supply from M_0 to M_1

FIGURE 2

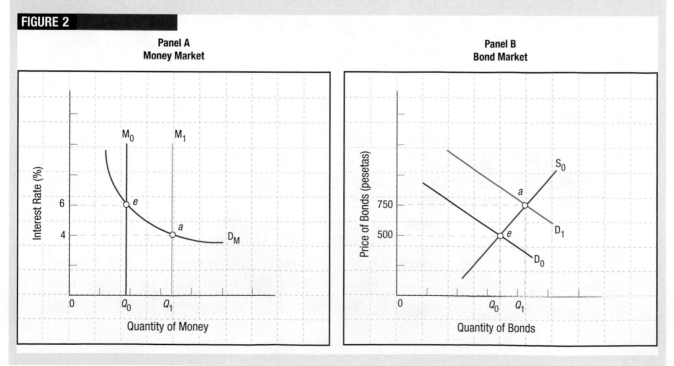

Panel A
Money Market

Panel B
Bond Market

in the money market (Panel A) reduces interest rates from 6% to 4% (point *e* to *a*). More money in the market means that individuals and institutions have more money than they want to hold in their portfolios (this increased money has created an imbalance in portfolios). The result is that people and institutions will now want to purchase more bonds and demand increases for bonds in the bond market (Panel B), shifting the demand curve out to D_1. This raises the price of bonds to 750 pesetas (point *a*), bringing the yield on bonds to 4% ($30/750 = .04 = 4\%$). Make a note of how this explanation differs from that of Figure 1 in the text when the money supply was reduced.

Solved Problem: Bank Creation of Money

One of the unique attributes of a fractional reserve banking system is the ability of banks to create money. This fact means that the Federal Reserve can alter the money supply by injecting a few new reserves into the system, and the banks do the rest, with the end result that the money supply increases by more than just the increase in reserves.

To see how the bank creation process works, assume that the four banks in the following tables are a representative sample from the system, the required reserve ratio is 25%, all banks want to be loaned-up, and any loans from the previous banks are deposited in the next bank in line.

(a) Using the 4-bank T-accounts below, trace the impact of a deposit in First Regional Bank of $1,000.

First Regional Bank

Assets	Liabilities
Reserves	Deposits
Loans	

Second Regional Bank

Assets	Liabilities
Reserves	Deposits
Loans	

Third Regional Bank

Assets	Liabilities
Reserves	Deposits
Loans	

Fourth Regional Bank

Assets	Liabilities
Reserves	Deposits
Loans	

(b) Using the last T-account below, total the changes in deposits, reserves, and loans for the four banks on the previous page.

Totals for First Through Fourth Regional Banks

Assets	Liabilities
Reserves	Deposits
Loans	

(c) When this new deposit has worked its way through the remaining banks in the system, show what the totals for the entire banking system would look like in the T-account below.

Totals for Entire Banking System

Assets	Liabilities
Reserves	Deposits
Loans	

(d) Are the totals for the entire system consistent with the money multiplier?

Solution-Discussion

(a) See the T-accounts below:

First Regional Bank

Assets	Liabilities
Reserves = $250	Deposits = $1,000
Loans = $750	

Second Regional Bank

Assets	Liabilities
Reserves = $187.50	Deposits = $750
Loans = $562.50	

Third Regional Bank

Assets	Liabilities
Reserves = $140.63	Deposits = $562.50
Loans = $421.87	

Fourth Regional Bank

Assets	Liabilities
Reserves = $105.46	Deposits = $421.87
Loans = $316.41	

The reserve requirement is 25%, so $250 of the original $1,000 deposit is kept as reserves for the First Regional Bank on the left side of the T-account, and

$750 in loans are made. These loans ($750) become the deposits for the Second Regional Bank and so on down the line.

(b)

Totals for First Through Fourth Regional Banks

Assets	Liabilities
Reserves = $683.59 Loans = $2,050.78	Deposits = $2,734.37

(c)

Totals for Entire Banking System

Assets	Liabilities
Reserves = $1,000 Loans = $3,000	Deposits = $4,000

(d) Yes, the money multiplier is equal to $1 \div$ reserve requirement $= 1/.25 = 4$; thus $1,000 in new deposits could translate into a $4,000 increase in systemwide deposits.

The Federal Reserve System

Frequently Asked Questions

Q: **What is the Federal Reserve System, and what is its purpose?**

A: The Federal Reserve System (the Fed) is the central bank of the United States. It was established by the Federal Reserve Act of 1913 and has had its mission clarified and expanded by several acts since then. Today, the Fed is required by law to promote economic growth accompanied by high levels of employment, stable prices, and moderate long-term interest rates.

Q: **How independent is the Federal Reserve?**

A: The Federal Reserve is an independent central bank, in that its actions are not subject to executive branch oversight, although the entire Federal Reserve System is subject to oversight by Congress. Experience in this country and abroad suggests that independent central banks are better at fighting inflation than are politically controlled banks. Politicians are reluctant to enact the contractionary policies needed to stave off inflation.

Q: **What is the Fed composed of?**

A: The Fed is composed of a central governing agency—the Board of Governors—and 12 regional Federal Reserve Banks. The Board of Governors consists of seven members appointed by the president and confirmed by the Senate. Board members serve terms of 14 years, after which they cannot be reappointed. The chairman and vice chairman of the Board must already be Board members; they are appointed by the president, subject to Senate confirmation, for terms of 4 years.

Q: **What do the 12 regional Federal Reserve Banks do?**

A: The 12 regional Federal Reserve Banks and their branches provide a nationwide payments system, distribute coins and currency, regulate and supervise member banks, and serve as the banker for the United States Treasury. Each regional bank, moreover, provides the Federal Reserve System with information on economic conditions in its home region. This information is compiled in a report detailing the economic conditions around the country, the *Beige Book*, which the Board of Governors and the Federal Open Market Committee (FOMC) use to determine the course of monetary policy.

Q: What is the Federal Open Market Committee (FOMC)?

A: The FOMC oversees the Fed's open market operations, its primary tool of monetary policy. The FOMC is composed of the seven members of the Board of Governors and five of the 12 regional Federal Reserve Bank presidents. Traditionally, the chairman of the Board of Governors also serves as the chairman of the FOMC.

Q: How many primary tools does the Fed have for conducting monetary policy?

A: The Federal Reserve has three primary tools at its disposal for conducting monetary policy. They are reserve requirements, discount rates, and open market operations.

Q: How does the Federal Reserve use its reserve requirement tool?

A: The Fed can adjust the reserve requirement, the required ratio of funds commercial banks and other depository institutions must hold in reserve against deposits. By raising the reserve requirement, the Fed reduces the potential money multiplier, thus shrinking the supply of money in the economy. The Fed uses this policy tool infrequently, however, given that its impact is so massive and imprecise.

Q: How does the Federal Reserve use the discount rate tool?

A: The Fed can adjust the discount rate, the interest rate it charges commercial banks and other depository institutions to borrow reserves from a regional Federal Reserve Bank. When a bank's reserves fall below the required level, it must borrow money from the Fed or some other source to avoid penalty. Thus, a higher discount rate will encourage banks to hold more reserves. Most of these reserves, however, are borrowed from the Federal Funds Market. The Fed's discount window is a more expensive buffer against day-to-day fluctuations in the demand and supply of reserves.

Q: How does the Federal Reserve use the open market operations tool, the most powerful of its three tools?

A: The Fed's most powerful tool for conducting monetary policy is the open market operations tool. This involves buying and selling United States government securities on the open market to alter reserves in the banking system. When the Fed buys a government security, it pays some private financial institution for the bond, so it adds to aggregate reserves by injecting new money into the financial system. Open market operations are powerful because every dollar the Fed uses to buy up bonds puts a dollar of new reserves into the banking system.

The Federal Reserve System Quick Check

Circle the Correct Answer

1. (T/F) The Federal Reserve is the central bank of the United States and is located in Washington, D.C.
2. (T/F) The Federal Reserve System must seek to establish stable interest rates, while ignoring employment and economic growth issues.
3. (T/F) The Federal Reserve is independent of the executive branch, but subject to oversight by Congress.

4. (T/F) The 12 regional Federal Reserve Banks provide the Board of Governors with information on economic conditions in their home regions.

5. Which one of the following is *not* correct?
   a. There are 12 regional Federal Reserve Banks.
   b. There are 7 members of the Fed's Board of Governors.

c. All members of the Fed's Board of Governors are appointed by the President and confirmed by the Senate.

d. Each Board of Governor member serves for four years.

6. What is the Fed's most effective monetary policy tool?
   a. Reserve requirements.
   b. Open Market Operations.
   c. Discount Rate.
   d. Federal funds rate.

7. Which one of the following statements is *not* correct?
   a. In open market operations, the Fed buys and sells government securities.
   b. If the reserve requirement is 25% and the Fed's Open Market Committee buys $1,000 worth of bonds, this injects $4,000 into the banking system in the form of new reserves.
   c. When the Fed wants to increase the money supply, it buys bonds in the open market.
   d. The Fed's discount rate is now set to be above the federal funds rate.

8. Which of the following is *not* correct concerning the discount rate?
   a. It is the rate the regional Federal Reserve Banks charge depository institutions for short-term loans.
   b. It is set higher than the federal funds rate.
   c. It acts as a buffer in the reserves market against fluctuations in the daily demand and supply for reserves.

d. It accounts for a high fraction of total reserves.

9. Which of the following is not correct concerning open market operations?
   a. Open market operations involve the buying and selling of government securities.
   b. The head of the Federal Open Market Committee reports directly to the Fed Chairman.
   c. The president of the Federal Reserve Bank of New York is a permanent member of the Federal Open Market Committee.
   d. It is the most effective of the Fed's policy tools.

10. What is it about changing reserve requirements that makes it the least used of the Fed's three key policy tools?
    a. Their impact can be large but imprecise.
    b. Their impact is the weakest of the three tools.
    c. Their impact takes the longest to work its way through the financial system.
    d. Their use needs special Congressional approval.

Score: ____

Answers: 1. F; 2. F; 3. T; 4. T; 5. d; 6. b; 7. b; 8. d; 9. b; 10. a

If You Got 9 or 10 Correct

You are ready for the next chapter on how Federal Reserve policy affects the economy. You have a good sense of what the Federal Reserve System is and what policy tools it uses. Take a quick look at the "Hints, Tips, and Reminders," but you probably don't need them.

If You Didn't Get at Least 9 Correct

■ Don't get too concerned. There is a lot of detail here. The key thing to remember is what tools the Fed uses in setting monetary policy. Keep this in mind as you review the material.

■ Go back and reread this section in the text, paying special attention to the Fed's three policy tools.

The next chapter on monetary policy builds on the material in this chapter. You need to have a good sense of how the Fed works to understand how it undertakes monetary policy and how its policies work their way through the economy. ■

Consider These Hints, Tips, and Reminders   STEP 4

1. Money is not just dollars and change. It involves checking accounts and, more broadly, money market and savings accounts.

2. Keep in mind that for banks:

- Deposits are liabilities—the bank must give you your money on demand.
- Loans are assets—people owe the bank money. If you make a loan to a friend by drawing money from your savings account, you have just converted one asset (savings) to another asset (loan).

3. The money multiplier (1 ÷ reserve requirement) is quite different from the spending multiplier described in earlier chapters; don't confuse the two.

4. Keep in mind that the opportunity cost of holding money is the interest you could earn on the funds held in cash. As opportunity costs rise (interest rates rise), people will hold less cash; hence there is a negative slope for the demand for money curve.

5. Spend some time on the relationship between bond prices and interest rates. The components of a bond are the following:

- Principal amount (face value): usually $1,000
- Coupon rate: a fixed percent of the principal paid annually
- Maturity date: principal is paid back to bondholders on this date

For our purposes, the maturity date will typically be far into the future, so you can safely ignore it.

Now, if a $1,000 bond has a coupon rate of 5%, it will pay $50 per year to bondholders. This is the key to the relationship between bond prices and interest rates: Bonds pay a fixed dollar amount to bondholders. Now let's consider yield.

- When the price of the bond is equal to the principal value ($1,000), the bond yield is also 5%. Yield is equal to $50/$1,000 = 5%.
- But what happens to yield if the price of the bond rises to $2,000? Now the yield is 2.5% because $50/$2,000 = 2.5%. Yield falls when bond prices rise!
- If market interest rates rise to 10%, how much will investors be willing to pay for this bond? The bond yields $50 per year, so the question becomes 10% equals $50 divided by what amount? If you are an investor and you will get $50 a year, and you want to earn 10%, you will only be willing to pay $500 for this bond ($50/$500 = 10%).

So, now we see it is the yield (or market interest rate) and bond prices that are inversely related. Thus, when interest rates rise, bond prices fall, and vice versa. Looking at it another way, when bond prices rise, interest rates fall, and vice versa.

Do the Homework for Chapter 21
The Monetary System

STEP 5

Instructor _____ Time _____ Student _____

Use the answer key below to record your answers to these homework questions.

1. (a) (b) (c) (d)   6. (a) (b) (c) (d)   11. (a) (b) (c) (d)   16. (a) (b) (c) (d)
2. (a) (b) (c) (d)   7. (a) (b) (c) (d)   12. (a) (b) (c) (d)   17. (a) (b) (c) (d)
3. (a) (b) (c) (d)   8. (a) (b) (c) (d)   13. (a) (b) (c) (d)   18. (a) (b) (c) (d)
4. (a) (b) (c) (d)   9. (a) (b) (c) (d)   14. (a) (b) (c) (d)   19. (a) (b) (c) (d)
5. (a) (b) (c) (d)   10. (a) (b) (c) (d)   15. (a) (b) (c) (d)   20. (a) (b) (c) (d)

1. When consumers and producers conduct business using money, they are enjoying which of the main functions of money?
   a. unit of account or a measure of value
   b. medium of exchange
   c. debt payment mechanism
   d. store of value

2. Money reduces the number of prices that consumers must know to buy and sell goods and services. This is which of the following main functions of money?
   a. unit of account or a measure of value
   b. medium of exchange
   c. debt payment mechanism
   d. store of value

3. Money is
   a. always backed by gold or some other valuable metal.
   b. not harmed by inflation.
   c. anything accepted in exchange for other goods and services or for the payment of debt.
   d. not that important for growing and expanding economies. (In fact, most of the developed world could get along quite well as barter economies.)

4. M1 includes all of the following *except*
   a. currency.
   b. savings account deposits.
   c. all checkable deposits.
   d. travelers checks.

5. When economists talk about "near money," they are referring to

a. gold or some other valuable metal.
b. shares of stock on the New York Stock Exchange.
c. savings and money market deposits that are readily accessible.
d. anything that can be readily marketed on eBay.

6. Which of the following is the least liquid asset?
   a. gold
   b. shares of stock on the New York Stock Exchange
   c. your car
   d. government bonds

7. If the demand for bonds increases, market interest rates will
   a. fall.
   b. not change since interest rates and bond prices are unrelated.
   c. rise.
   d. do all of the above, because consumers and business investors are fickle.

8. Which of the following is *not* an important element of a bond contract?
   a. the exchange where the bond will be traded
   b. face value of the bond
   c. coupon rate
   d. maturity date

9. How much will a bond be worth if it pays $600 a year and current market interest rates are 6%?
   a. $6,000
   b. $8,000
   c. $10,000
   d. $12,000

10. When someone deposits money into a bank, the bank is required to hold some of that money in their vault or on deposit with the Federal Reserve System. This type of banking system is known as
    a. caveat emptor banking system.
    b. regulated banking system.
    c. demand deposit system.
    d. fractional reserve system.

11. The money multiplier
    a. is equal to 1.
    b. is due to the Federal Reserve loaning money to banks so they can loan it to businesses to invest in new plant and equipment creating more employment and income.
    c. is the reciprocal of the reserve requirement.
    d. is equal to one over the marginal propensity to loan.

12. If the Federal Reserve sets the reserve requirement at 15%, the money multiplier is equal to
    a. 1.0.
    b. 15.
    c. 6.7.
    d. 8.5.

13. The Federal Reserve System was a compromise between competing proposals for a huge central bank and no central bank at all. The current Federal Reserve System has how many regional banks?
    a. 8
    b. 10
    c. 12
    d. 14

14. Which of the following is *not* one of the tools of the Federal Reserve?
    a. the discount rate
    b. open market operations
    c. reserve requirements
    d. demand deposit expansion bonds

15. The Federal Reserve and the 12 regional banks of the Federal Reserve System provide all of the following services *except*
    a. distributing coins and currency.

b. determining tax policy for the nation and regions represented by regional banks.
    c. regulating and supervising member banks.
    d. serving as the banker for the U.S. Treasury.

16. Excess reserves are
    a. the reserves held in excess of that which banks feel they must have to make loans to local businesses.
    b. reserves held with their regional bank.
    c. reserves held that exceed those required by the Federal Reserve System.
    d. used by the Federal Open Market Committee to determine the discount rate.

17. When the Federal Reserve wants to change the money supply in a very measured way and within a short period of time, it uses
    a. the discount rate.
    b. open market operations.
    c. reserve requirements.
    d. restrictions on the use of credit.

18. When the Federal Reserve Open Market Committee conducts monetary policy, it
    a. changes the discount rate.
    b. holds hearings to determine which region of the country needs interest rates reduced to increase investment.
    c. alters reserve requirements.
    d. buys and sells government bonds.

19. The Federal Funds Market
    a. is a market where foreign government securities are bought and sold.
    b. is a market where banks loan each other reserves for short periods.
    c. keeps interest rates for business loans in equilibrium.
    d. buys and sells government bonds.

20. Which tool does the Federal Reserve use most to conduct monetary policy?
    a. the discount rate
    b. open market operations
    c. reserve requirements
    d. the federal funds rate

Use the ExamPrep to Get Ready for Exams	STEP 6

This sheet (front and back) is designed to help you prepare for your exams. The chapter has been boiled down to its key concepts. You are asked to answer questions, define terms, draw graphs, and, if you wish, add summaries of class notes.

What Is Money?

Name and describe the three functions of money:

List the main components of the following measures of the money supply:

M1:

M2:

Money: Demand and Supply

Describe the three motives for holding money:

Bond Prices and Interest Rates

Describe the main components of a bond:

Describe why there is an inverse relationship between bond prices and interest rates:

How Banks Create Money

What is meant by a fractional reserve system?

Describe the general process of how banks create money:

How is the money multiplier defined?

What factors limit the size of this multiplier?

The Federal Reserve System

Describe the three main components of the Federal Reserve System:

Describe the three main tools of the Federal Reserve System:

Describe the difference between the discount rate and the federal funds rate:

What is the most important tool of the Fed? Why?

Additional Study Help Chapterwide Practice Questions

Matching

Match the description with the corresponding term.

___ 1. Money
___ 2. Barter
___ 3. Medium of exchange
___ 4. Unit of account
___ 5. Store of value
___ 6. M1
___ 7. M2
___ 8. Fractional reserve system
___ 9. Money multiplier
___ 10. Federal Reserve System
___ 11. Reserve requirements
___ 12. Discount rate
___ 13. Open market operations

a. An independent central bank charged with promoting economic growth accompanied by full employment, stable prices, and moderate long-term interest rates.

b. Funds that cannot be used instantaneously but are nonetheless highly accessible. These include savings accounts, money market deposit accounts, and money market mutual fund accounts.

c. Anything that is accepted in exchange for other goods and services or for the payment of debts.

d. When money is used as a measure of value, each product on the market can be given one price. This dramatically reduces the number of prices individuals must know.

e. When everyone sells the goods and services they produce for money and uses this money to buy the goods and services they desire.

f. The Fed's narrowest definition of money. It includes currency (coins and paper money), demand deposits (checks), and other accounts that have check-writing capabilities, such as stock market accounts.

g. Because money does not deteriorate (except for inflation), it can serve this important purpose.

h. The Fed's most powerful and most often used tool for conducting monetary policy involves buying and selling United States government securities to adjust reserves in the banking system.

i. Involves the direct exchange of goods and services for one another.

j. Allows banks to create money. When a bank accepts deposits, it retains only a certain required part of this money, loaning the rest back out. A part of these new deposits are again held as reserves; the rest is loaned out again.

k. Measures the potential or maximum amount the money supply can increase (or decrease) when new deposits enter (exit) the system.

l. The required ratio of funds commercial banks and other depository institutions must hold in reserve against deposits.

m. The interest rate regional Federal Reserve Banks charge commercial banks and other depository institutions to borrow reserves.

Fill-In

Circle the word(s) in parentheses that complete the sentence.

1. Money solves the barter problem of (double coincidence of, unlimited) _____ wants. Money serves as a (medium of exchange, unit of account, store of value) _____ when it permits individuals to save today to purchase goods in the future and as a (medium of exchange, unit of account, store of value) _____ by reducing the number of prices consumers need to know.

2. The money definition (M1, M2, currency) _____ includes near monies, while (M1, M2, currency) _____ includes just currency and checkable deposits.

3. People keep some of their portfolio in money for unexpected events. This represents the (transactions, precautionary, speculative) _____ demand for money. That part of money demanded primarily related to the interest rate is the (transactions, precautionary, speculative) _____ demand for money.

4. When the money supply is increased, interest rates (rise, fall, remain the same) _____, and bond prices (rise, fall, remain the same) _____.

5. Banks are able to create money because our banking system is a (full, fractional, multiplied) _____ reserve system. If the reserve requirement is increased, the potential money multiplier will (increase, decrease) _____. With a reserve requirement of 20%, a $200 new deposit in one bank could potentially result in

($400, $800, $1,000) of new money in the economy.

6. The Federal Reserve System is the (political, independent, private) _____ central bank of the United States. It has (8, 10, 12) _____ districts and a Board of Governors consisting of (5, 7, 9) _____ members who serve 14-year terms.

7. The Federal Reserve adjusts the interest rate it charges banks to borrow funds for reserves; this rate is known as the (reserve, discount, open market) _____ rate. When the Fed engages in buying and selling government bonds to alter reserves this is known as (reserve, discount, open market) _____ operations.

8. When the Fed buys bonds, (demand, supply) _____ of bonds (rises, falls) _____ resulting in a(n) (increase, decrease) _____ in market interest rates. When the Fed sells bonds, (demand, supply) _____ of bonds (rises, falls) _____ resulting in a(n) (increase, decrease) _____ in market interest rates.

True-False

Circle the correct answer.

T/F 1. Money consists exclusively of paper currency and coins printed or minted by the government.

T/F 2. The problem of the double coincidence of wants refers to the fact that in a barter economy, exchange requires finding someone who not only has what you want but who also wants what you have.

T/F 3. Money is the commodity with the highest liquidity.

T/F 4. M1 is the Fed's narrowest measure of money.

T/F 5. M2 includes currency, travelers checks, demand deposits, and other checkable accounts, but not savings accounts or small-denomination time deposits.

T/F 6. The transactions demand for money refers to the fact that individuals and firms need to hold some of their assets as money to be able to buy and sell goods and services.

T/F 7. If interest rates go up, the speculative demand for money will also rise.

T/F 8. Bond prices and interest rates are inversely related.

T/F 9. If a bond pays $60 per year in interest and the current market interest rate is 4%, investors will be willing to pay $1,500 for the bond.

T/F 10. A bond now worth $900 that pays $45 per year in interest has a current yield of 2%.

T/F 11. If a bond is initially sold for $1,000, investors may well be willing to pay more or less for this bond as economic circumstances change.

T/F 12. Banks create new money by printing additional currency, as licensed by the Federal Reserve.

T/F 13. "Demand deposits" are so termed because banks are obligated to pay out these accounts on demand.

T/F 14. If the reserve requirement is 20%, this means banks are allowed to loan out only 20% of the deposits they accept.

T/F 15. The Federal Reserve is legally tasked with promoting economic growth accompanied by high levels of employment, stable prices, and moderate long-term interest rates.

T/F 16. Among other duties, the 12 regional Federal Reserve Banks serve as the banker for the United States Treasury.

T/F 17. Open market operations provide the Fed with its most effective tool for conducting monetary policy.

T/F 18. When the Fed raises the reserve requirement, this increases the money multiplier, thus increasing the supply of money in the economy.

T/F 19. When the Fed buys up treasury bonds or other government securities, this reduces the money supply by removing these securities from the open market.

T/F 20. If the reserve requirement is 16%, a new deposit of $100 will potentially inject $625 into the economy.

Multiple Choice

Circle the correct answer.

1. Which of the following is *not* among the primary functions of money?
   a. unit of account
   b. store of value
   c. indicator of supply
   d. medium of exchange

2. In performing which of its primary functions does money solve the problem of the double coincidence of wants?
   a. medium of exchange
   b. unit of account
   c. store of value
   d. none of the above (Money does not solve this problem.)

3. In performing which of its primary functions does money significantly reduce the number of prices the market must determine, as compared to the situation in a barter economy?
   a. medium of exchange
   b. unit of account
   c. store of value
   d. none of the above (Money does not solve this problem.)

4. Which of the following assets is least liquid?
   a. bonds
   b. cash
   c. stocks
   d. real estate

5. Which of the following is *not* a component of M1?
   a. demand deposits
   b. travelers checks
   c. savings deposits
   d. currency

6. Which of the following would economists *not* include among the primary motives people have for holding money?
   a. liquidity demand
   b. status demand
   c. speculative demand
   d. transactions demand

7. The liquidity (or precautionary) demand for money refers to the fact that individuals and firms
   a. generally like to have some money on hand to meet unforeseen expenses.
   b. require some money for buying and selling goods and services.

   c. generally like to hold some of their assets as money since it is safer than other assets.
   d. need some money to purchase beverages for business meetings.

8. The speculative demand for money and interest rates are
   a. identical to one another.
   b. directly related to one another.
   c. inversely related to one another.
   d. unrelated to one another.

9. As a general rule, when interest rates fall, bond prices will
   a. react in any number of unpredictable ways.
   b. fall.
   c. remain constant.
   d. rise.

10. How much will a bond be worth if it pays $40 per year in interest and the current market interest rate is 5%?
    a. $600
    b. $800
    c. $1,000
    d. $1,200

11. What is the yield on a bond sold for $1,000 and paying $37.50 in interest annually?
    a. 37.5%
    b. 26.6%
    c. 3.75%
    d. 0.26%

12. If the money supply increases, the price of bonds can be expected to
    a. fall.
    b. rise.
    c. remain constant.
    d. react in any number of unpredictable ways.

13. What will the asset side of a bank's balance sheet list?
    a. reserves and loans
    b. reserves and deposits
    c. deposits
    d. deposits and loans

14. If the reserve requirement is 18%, approximately how big can the money multiplier be?
    a. 0.55
    b. 1.8
    c. 4.6
    d. 5.6

15. If the reserve requirement is 25%, how much money will a new deposit of $500 potentially inject into the economy?
    a. $2,000
    b. $125
    c. $1,500
    d. $12,500

16. A bank is loaned-up if it has
    a. loaned out all of the deposits it has received.
    b. loaned out all of the deposits it can, retaining only those reserves required by law.
    c. loaned out more money than it has received in deposits.
    d. borrowed the maximum amount allowable from other banks.

17. As an independent central bank, the Federal Reserve is
    a. free from oversight by any elected officials.
    b. free from control by Congress, but subject to oversight by the executive branch.
    c. free from control by the executive branch, but subject to Congressional oversight.
    d. a highly politicized institution.

18. Which of the following is *not* one of the Federal Reserve's legally mandated objectives?
    a. maintaining price stability
    b. promoting economic growth
    c. keeping long-term interest rates moderate
    d. balancing the federal budget

19. How many regional Federal Reserve Banks are there?
    a. 10
    b. 12
    c. 1
    d. 7

20. Which of the following is *not* among the functions of the regional Federal Reserve Banks?
    a. serving as banker for the U.S. Treasury
    b. distributing coins and currency
    c. buying and selling government securities on the open market
    d. providing the Board of Governors with information on economic conditions in their home regions

21. The Fed's most effective tool for conducting monetary policy is
    a. adjusting the reserve requirement.
    b. engaging in open market operations.
    c. printing new money.
    d. adjusting the discount rate.

22. What gets traded on the Federal Funds Market?
    a. government securities
    b. corporate stocks
    c. loans from regional Federal Reserve Banks
    d. bank reserves

23. What is the discount rate?
    a. the rate the regional Federal Reserve Banks charge depository institutions for short-term loans
    b. the rate financial institutions charge one another on the open market for short-term loans
    c. the percentage of deposits banks must legally hold as reserves
    d. the rate at which the regional Federal Reserve Banks compensate depository institutions for maintaining excess reserves

24. When the Fed conducts open market operations, what is it buying and selling?
    a. capital equipment
    b. corporate stocks
    c. previously issued government securities
    d. bank reserves

25. If the reserve requirement is set at 20% and the Federal Open Market Committee buys $10,000 worth of treasury bonds, how much money does this inject into the banking system in the form of new reserves?
    a. $2,000
    b. $10,000
    c. $20,000
    d. $50,000

Essay-Problem

Answer in the space provided.

These questions aim more closely at the role money and the Federal Reserve play in our economy. Some of these questions can be challenging, but don't worry about this. Use these questions as another way to assess your progress and to learn a little bit more about the monetary system and the Federal Reserve.

1. What is the essence of financial markets?

2. Why are checkable deposits considered to be the equivalent of currency in determining M1?

3. Of the currency in your pocket, how much of it is there because of transactions demand? How much for precautionary demand? How much for speculative demand?

4. The chapter talked about banks being *loaned-up.* Considering the possibility of fluctuations in the demand for money, why don't banks hold substantial excess reserves?

5. Why have some people called the Federal Reserve Chairman the second most powerful individual on earth?

6. Why is the president of the New York Federal Reserve Bank a permanent member of the Federal Open Market Committee?

7. What will happen to the demand for money in times of inflation? What will this do to the interest rate?

8. The chapter gave a value of roughly $7 trillion for M2. Assume that reserve requirements are 20%. Now assume that the Federal Reserve lowers this to 10%. How much additional money will this potentially add to bank reserves?

9. The Fed's independence gives it the ability to deal with what economic situation shunned by politicians? (*Hint:* This was discussed in the previous two chapters.)

10. What does newspaper coverage of Federal Reserve Board policymaking tell us about the relative importance of fiscal and monetary policy?

What's Next

In this chapter, we introduced you to the monetary system and the institution of the Federal Reserve. We saw what policy tools the Federal Reserve can wield. In the next chapter, we look at how the Federal Reserve actually uses these tools, how monetary policy works its way through the economy, and other issues concerning monetary policy.

Answers to Chapterwide Practice Questions

Matching

1. c	5. g	9. k	13. h
2. i	6. f	10. a	
3. e	7. b	11. l	
4. d	8. j	12. m	

Fill-In

1. double coincidence of, store of value, unit of account
2. M2, M1
3. precautionary, speculative
4. fall, rise
5. fractional, decrease, $1,000
6. independent, 12, 7
7. discount, open market
8. demand, rises, decrease, supply, rises, increase

True-False

1. F	6. T	11. T	16. T
2. T	7. F	12. F	17. T
3. T	8. T	13. T	18. F
4. T	9. T	14. F	19. F
5. F	10. F	15. T	20. T

Multiple Choice

1. c	8. c	15. a	22. d
2. a	9. d	16. b	23. a
3. b	10. b	17. c	24. c
4. d	11. c	18. d	25. b
5. c	12. b	19. b	
6. b	13. a	20. c	
7. a	14. d	21. b	

Essay-Problem

1. They bring borrowers and lenders together. This facilitates the flow of capital, which encourages economic growth.

2. Checkable deposits are just about as liquid as currency. There are some businesses that do not accept checks (e.g., stores where most goods are priced at around a dollar and some restaurants) but most places accept checks with proper identification.

3. As far as currency in your pocket is concerned, remember that currency is only a part of the definition of money. It is unlikely that any currency is held for speculative demand: You are not likely to buy securities or foreign currencies with this amount of currency, though you could do so with larger checkable deposits. If you expect to make certain purchases soon, the transactions demand is likely to predominate over the precautionary demand for currency held in your pocket. If you do not expect to spend the currency soon, say, on lunch or entertainment, then the precautionary demand probably outweighs the transactions demand. Many people get money before they go on vacation, typically for the unexpected encounter. With today's prevalence of ATMs and credit cards, holding money for precautionary motives has declined.

4. Individual demands for money are fairly stable and predictable, though there is some fluctuation. Think about your need for money over a monthly cycle. If you work, you know that bills will be paid right after you get paid. So there will be a sudden increase in money in your account, then a quick downturn, and then maybe a quiescent period until you get paid again. Banks sum the fluctuations of all of their customers, over periods of time, and can predict fairly accurately what a day-by-day demand for money will be in each month of the year. Thus, there is little need for banks to hold large excess reserves. And as we saw with the federal funds rate and the discount rate, banks can always borrow the difference, though they would prefer not to be in this position.

5. This refers to the fact that the Federal Reserve Chairman is virtually independent (with some Congressional oversight) to pursue policies that affect the U.S. economy. Because the U.S. economy is the largest in the world, it influences other economies. As the saying goes: When the U.S. economy sneezes, the whole world catches cold. The most powerful person, of course, is the president of the United States.

6. Even in this age of computerized security trading, the bulk of these trades still occur in New York. Think *Wall Street*. The actual buying and selling of government securities is done at the New York Fed's trading desk. Hence, the president of the New York Fed is a permanent member of this trading committee.

7. Prices rise in inflationary times. Hence, people will want more money to make their regular transactions. This increased transactions demand for money will drive up interest rates. But interest rates already tend to rise in inflationary times, so increased demand for money will drive interest rates even higher.

8. With a reserve requirement of 20%, the money supply is at $7 trillion. With a lower reserve requirement of 10%, the potential money multiplier climbs to 10. This frees up $700 billion in reserves and will raise potential M2 to $14 trillion, a massive increase of $7 trillion. What will this massive increase do to the economy? This is why the Fed tends to avoid touching the reserve requirement as a tool of monetary policy.

9. Politicians shun inflationary equilibriums because the cure is a contractionary decrease in aggregate demand, which lowers output and raises unemployment. No politician wants to be associated with this. Federal Reserve Board members, because they do not have

to worry about frequent reelections, should be more likely to undertake contractionary policies for the good of the economy. One exception to this was President Reagan, who sided with Fed Chairman Paul Volcker to bring a halt to the high inflation rates and stagflation of the late 1970s and early 1980s.

10. It suggests that the Fed's monetary policy actions are more important than fiscal policy. In the previous chapter, we saw that rising federal deficits could have a crowding-out effect, and so might hamper fiscal policy. This shifts the burden for smoothing out the business cycle to the Federal Reserve. Since financial markets react quickly to changes (or perceived changes) in monetary policy, they represent instant news and get media attention. Fiscal policy is a more extended deliberative process and often doesn't get the same level of attention.

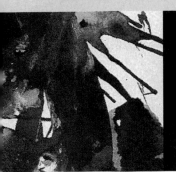

Monetary Policy

22

How Does Government Use Monetary Policy to Influence the Economy?

In an earlier chapter, we saw how governments use fiscal policy to influence the economy. We studied money in the previous chapter to prepare you for fiscal policy's cousin: monetary policy. How does the government use monetary policy to influence the economy? What implementation problems need to be confronted? How does monetary policy balance the goals of price stability, economic growth, and full employment? We cover a lot of material in this chapter.

This Is What You Need to Know

STEP 1

After studying this chapter you should be able to

■ Describe the equation of exchange and its implications for monetary policy.

■ Describe the classical monetary transmission mechanism.

■ Describe Keynesian monetary analysis and the three motives for holding money.

■ Describe the Keynesian monetary transmission mechanism and how it differs from classical theory.

■ Describe the monetarist model of monetary theory.

■ Describe the important differences in the three models of monetary theory and the implications of these differences for monetary policy.

■ Describe the four lags that affect the implementation of monetary policy.

■ Describe why the Fed targets price stability in the long run and inflation rates and output in the short run.

- Determine the effectiveness of monetary policy when demand or supply shocks occur.

- Describe the controversy over whether the Fed should have discretion or be governed by simple monetary rules.

STEP 2   Review The Key Terms

Easy money or expansionary monetary policy: Fed actions designed to increase excess reserves and the money supply to stimulate the economy (expand income and employment).

Tight money, restrictive, or contractionary monetary policy: Fed actions designed to decrease excess reserves and the money supply to shrink income and employment, usually to fight inflation.

Equation of exchange: The heart of classical monetary theory uses the equation, $M \times V = P \times Q$, where M is the supply of money, V is the velocity of money (or the number of times it turns over in a year), P is the price level, and Q is the economy's output level.

Classical monetary transmission mechanism: Because money was assumed to be used only for transactions purposes, that the economy was operating at full employment (Q is fixed), and velocity (V) was dependent on banking technology and thus constant, the equation of exchange suggests the process is quite direct; any change in M will be felt directly in P.

Transactions demand for money: That part of individual wealth held in money to be able to perform commercial transactions (medium of exchange demand).

Precautionary demand for money: Some of individual wealth is held in money to handle unexpected events and expenses.

Speculative demand for money: When inflation is not a problem, holding money for a short period is virtually risk free, whereas other assets are more risky. The speculative demand for money varies inversely with interest rates, since they are the opportunity costs of holding money in a portfolio.

Liquidity trap: When interest rates are so low that people believe they can only rise, they hold onto money rather than investing in bonds and suffer the expected capital loss.

Keynesian monetary transmission mechanism: An increase in the money supply lowers interest rates, thus increasing investment; expanding aggregate demand; and increasing income, output, and employment. The opposite occurs when the money supply is reduced.

Monetarist transmission mechanism: An increase in money will reduce interest rates as portfolios rebalance, leading to a rise in investment or consumption and resulting in an increase in aggregate demand and thus an increase in income, output, or the price level.

Information lag: The time policymakers must wait for economic data to be collected, processed, and reported. Most macroeconomic data are not available until at least one quarter (3 months) after the fact.

Recognition lag: The time it takes for policymakers to confirm that the economy is trending in or out of a recession. Short-term variations in key economic indicators are typical and sometimes represent nothing more than randomness in the data.

Decision lag: After a problem is recognized, it takes some time for the Fed to decide on a policy. Since the Fed meets monthly, the decision lag is relatively short.

Implementation lag: The time required to for monetary policy to have an impact on the economy.

Monetary targeting: Keeps the growth of money stocks such as M1 or M2 on a steady path following the equation of exchange (or quantity theory), to set a long-run path for the economy that keeps inflation in check.

Inflation targeting: Involves setting targets on the inflation rate, usually around 2% a year in recognition that the long-run goal of monetary policy is price stability.

Work Through the Chapter Tutorials

STEP 3

Monetary Theories

Frequently Asked Questions

Q: **What is the classical theory of money?**

A: Classical economics focuses on *long-run* adjustments in economic activity, and concludes that the economy will tend toward equilibrium at full employment in the long run. Classical monetary analysis extends this approach and is grounded in the quantity theory of money. Quantity theory is defined by the equation of exchange:

$$M \times V = P \times Q$$

In this equation, M is the supply of money, V is its velocity, P is the price level, and Q is the economy's output. So, the amount of money in circulation times its velocity (the number of times it turns over) is equal to gross domestic product (GDP, or $P \times Q$).

Q: **In classical theory, changes in the money supply will have what effects, over what time period?**

A: Classical theorists argued that the velocity of money (V) is fixed by the prevailing monetary institutions and technology, and thus is slow to change. Further, aggregate output (Q) is fixed at full employment. The result is that a change in the money supply will translate directly in a change in prices, or

$$\Delta M = \Delta P$$

Thus, quantity theory predicts that in the *long run* changes in the money supply will bring about directly proportionate changes in the aggregate price level.

Q: **Keynesian monetary theory focuses on what time period?**

A: Keynesian monetary analysis was developed during the Great Depression of the 1930s. It examines the *short-run* effects that changes in the money supply have on interest rates and subsequently on investment, consumption, and output.

Q: **In Keynesian theory, what are the three motives for holding money?**

A: Keynes identified three motives that people have for holding money in their portfolios. Individuals and firms need some money to buy and sell goods and services; this is the *transactions* motive for holding money. The *precaution-*

ary motive reflects the desire most individuals and firms have to keep some money on hand to deal with unforeseen circumstances. Finally, Keynes recognized that people sometimes hold money rather than interest-bearing bonds to speculate against changes in interest rates or the price level; this is the *speculative* motive for holding money.

Q: **How does the Keynesian money transmission mechanism work?**
A: According to Keynesian analysis, an increase in the money supply causes the price of bonds to rise and the interest rate to fall. As the Fed buys bonds, this adds to the demand for bonds increasing the price of bonds, reducing interest rates. Falling interest rates boost investment, which raises aggregate demand and thus increases aggregate income, output, and employment. In sequence:

$$\uparrow M \rightarrow \downarrow i \rightarrow \uparrow I \rightarrow \uparrow AD \rightarrow \uparrow Y \rightarrow \uparrow Q$$

Q: **How can the Keynesian money transmission mechanism be shown graphically?**
A: Figure 1 shows the Keynesian monetary transmission mechanism. When the money supply is increased from MS_0 to MS_1 in Panel A, interest rates fall (point a to point b). When interest rates fall, there is an increase in investments, as shown in Panel B (again, from point a to point b). This increased investment raises aggregate demand, income, and output in Panel C. Note that when interest rates are very low, increases in the money supply may have no effect on the interest rate, as shown in a movement from point b to point c in Panel A. Keynes called this a *liquidity trap*. As a result, investment doesn't change in Panel B, nor does income or output change.

FIGURE 1

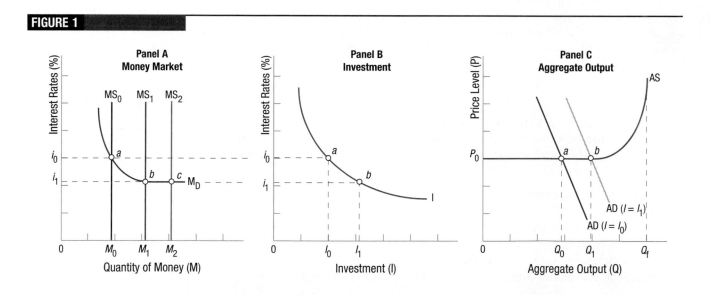

Q: **When did monetarism arise, and what time period does it focus on?**
A: Monetarism, championed by Milton Friedman, first arose in the 1960s as a response to Keynesian monetary analysis. Monetarism assumes the economy will ultimately stabilize itself around full employment, but it supports the use of monetary policy to handle short-run fluctuations.

Q: **What was Milton Friedman's innovation to the theory of money demand?**
A: Friedman pioneered the notion that consumption levels are determined not only by income but also by wealth. He developed the concept of permanent income, the present value of an individual's future stream of labor income as a proxy for wealth. Friedman then altered the demand for money to include wealth (permanent income) and other variables. Friedman's analysis suggests that the

demand for real money balances will be higher if (1) wealth or permanent income is higher, (2) the rate of return on other assets is lower, or (3) the expected rate of inflation is lower.

Q: **What is the monetarist money transmission mechanism?**

A: Friedman argued that individuals will allocate their wealth among various assets until the marginal rates of return are equal. Thus, when the money supply increases, people will discover that they are holding more money than they desire, and the additional supply of money decreases their return on money. Excess money balances will thus be exchanged for other financial and real assets, including bonds, real estate, and consumer durables such as cars and houses. Eventually, portfolios will rebalance and markets will return to equilibrium. Symbolically, the monetarist transmission channel is

$$\uparrow M \rightarrow \downarrow i \rightarrow (\uparrow I \text{ and/or } \uparrow C) \rightarrow \uparrow AD \rightarrow \uparrow Y \text{ and/or } \uparrow P$$

More money means portfolios have too much money, and so rebalancing occurs, resulting in more investment (financial and economic) along with increases in consumption. This leads to greater aggregate demand, resulting in increases in income and aggregate prices.

Monetary Theories Quick Check

Circle the Correct Answer

1. (T/F) In the classical equation of exchange, the velocity of money is assumed to fluctuate rapidly over time.
2. (T/F) Keynes postulated a speculative demand for money, in contrast to the classical focus on the transactions demand.
3. (T/F) In the long run, the classical equation of exchange boils down to $\Delta M = \Delta P$.
4. (T/F) Milton Friedman pioneered the notion that wealth as well as income plays a role in consumption, and therefore that wealth influences the demand for money.
5. Which of the following does *not* describe the Keynesian monetary transmission mechanism?
   a. An increase in the money supply will lower interest rates, which will stimulate investment, which in turn raises aggregate demand, which raises aggregate output and employment.
   b. Monetary policy will have no effect in a depression if an economy is stuck in a liquidity trap.
   c. A liquidity trap can be caused by the speculative demand for money.
   d. The speculative demand for money does not kick in until interest rates hover near zero.
6. Which one of the following does *not* describe the monetarist money transmission mechanism?
   a. An increase in the money supply may affect output or price in the short run.
   b. In the long run, an increase in the money supply will lead to higher prices, with no effect on output.
   c. In a depression, monetary policy will have no effect because people will not be able to rebalance their portfolios.
   d. Money is treated as an asset in a generalized portfolio of assets that might include bonds, stocks, and real estate.
7. Which one of the following statements is *not* correct?
   a. Classical economists believed that an increase in the money supply will increase prices, with no effect on output in the long run.
   b. Keynes believed that fiscal policy was needed to get an economy out of a depression because monetary policy would have no effect.
   c. Monetarists believe that monetary policy will have short-run effects on prices and output, but in the long run an increase in the money supply will affect the price level only.
   d. When interest rates fall, aggregate demand increases in the Keynesian model but decreases in the monetarist model.
8. In the Keynesian monetary transmission mechanism,
   a. when interest rates rise, the speculative demand for money increases.
   b. monetary policy has no effect in the long run.
   c. liquidity traps occur frequently.
   d. an increase in the money supply will increase aggregate demand in normal times.
9. In the monetarist money transmission mechanism,
   a. an increase in the money supply will have no effect on output in the short run.

b. an increase in the money supply will reduce interest rates as individuals rebalance their portfolios, with money one of the assets in that portfolio.

c. velocity fluctuates, just as in the classical model.

d. a decrease in the money supply may cause a liquidity trap.

10. Comparing the classical, Keynesian, and monetarist monetary theories,

a. classical and Keynesian theories both focus on the long run.

b. Keynesian theory postulates that monetary theory may not be effective in a depression, while monetarist theory claims it can be.

c. classical and monetarist theories both claim that monetary policy has no effect in the long run.

d. classical theory focuses on the transactions demand for money, Keynes focuses on the speculative demand for money, and monetarists focus on the precautionary demand for money.

Score: ____

Answers: 1. F; 2. T; 3. T; 4. T; 5. d; 6. c; 7. d; 8. d; 9. b; 10. b

If You Got 9 or 10 Correct

These were tough questions. You have a good grasp of the three monetary theories. You could go on to an analysis of monetary policy lags in the next section. However, because this is difficult material, we suggest you take a few moments and review this material. Review the solved problem below. The extra review will be beneficial when you get to the last section.

If You Didn't Get at Least 9 Correct

■ Don't get too depressed (minor pun). This is some of the more difficult material in the chapter. It often takes several attempts at this material before it really sinks in.

■ Reread this section in the text, and focus on Figures 2, 3, and 4. Make a note of Keynes's reasoning for the liquidity trap during a depression.

■ Work through the solved problem that follows. Be sure to complete the problem yourself before you look at the solution and discussion; this is the heart of the material in this section. ■

Solved Problem: Monetary Transmission Channels

The Fed can alter the money supply by changing bank reserve requirements, altering the discount rate, or buying or selling government bonds. Once one of these actions is undertaken, the changes in the money supply work their way through the economy.

1. In the following grids show the impact of an increase in the money supply in Panel A, followed by the impact on investment in Panel B, and finally the impact on the economy in Panel C. In the space provided below each panel describe the process.

Keynesian Monetary Transmission Channel

Panel A Money Market	Panel B Investment	Panel C Aggregate Output

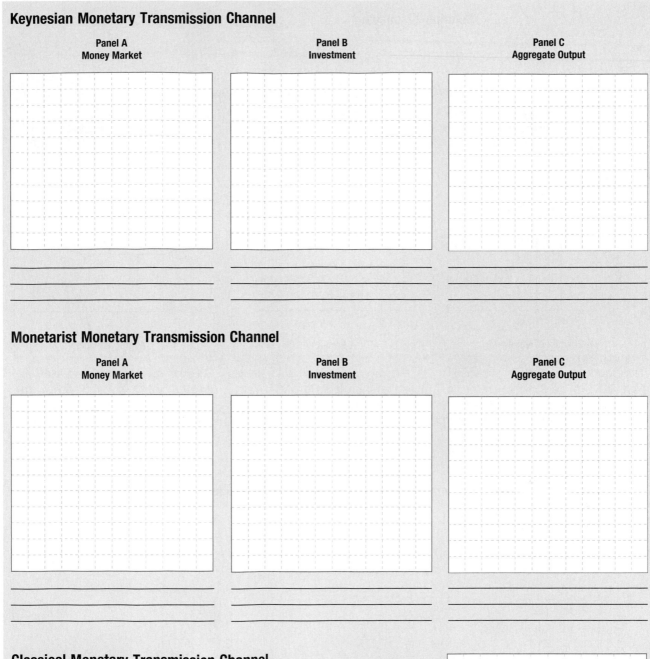

Monetarist Monetary Transmission Channel

Panel A Money Market	Panel B Investment	Panel C Aggregate Output

Classical Monetary Transmission Channel

Using the grid to the right, describe the classical equation of exchange and monetary transmission channel.

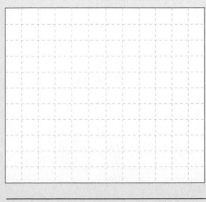

2. Under what the circumstances or economic conditions would each of these monetary transmission channels be expected to operate?

Solution-Discussion

1.

Keynesian Monetary Transmission Channel

Panel A | **Panel B** | **Panel C**
Money Market | Investment | Aggregate Output

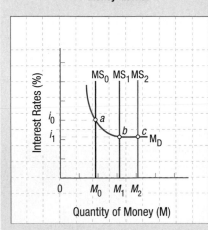 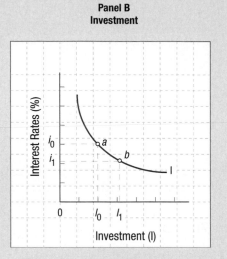 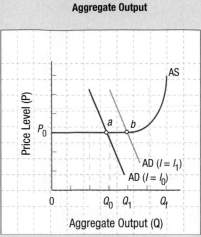

The money supply is increased from MS_0 to MS_1, which reduces interest rates from i_0 to i_1. The Fed buys bonds. This adds to the demand for bonds, increasing the price of bonds and reducing interest rates.

Falling interest rates make more investment projects profitable, increasing investment.

Greater investment increases aggregate demand, and given the excess capacity in the economy, output increases without putting pressure on aggregate prices.

Monetarist Monetary Transmission Channel

Panel A | **Panel B** | **Panel C**
Money Market | Investment | Aggregate Output

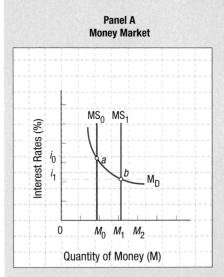 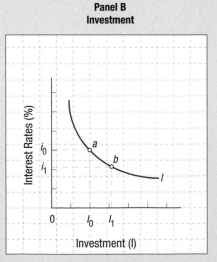 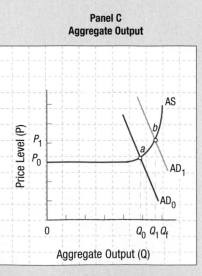

The money supply is increased from MS_0 to MS_1, which reduces interest rates from i_0 to i_1. More money in the market means more people will want to convert to bonds to earn interest, increasing the price of bonds and reducing interest rates.

Increasing money in the economy means people and institutions will rebalance their portfolios, increasing investment in homes, business equipment, and other consumer goods and services.

Greater investment and/or consumer spending increases aggregate demand. In the short run, output will grow and so will consumer prices. In the long run, increases in the money supply will lead to higher prices, and output will remain at full employment.

Classical Monetary Transmission Mechanism

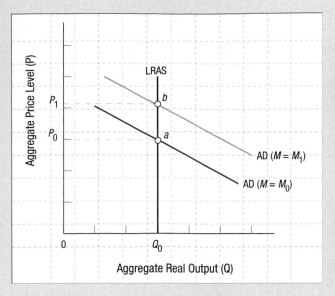

Classical quantity theory states that $M \times V = P \times Q$; and given that velocity is determined by the state of banking technology at the time and output is at full employment, increases in the money supply will translate directly in rising prices ($\Delta M = \Delta P$). More money means aggregate demand will rise, but since the economy is at full employment, output will remain the same and prices will rise.

2.

Keynesian monetary transmission analysis would be most appropriate during severe recessions or depressions. Keynes' analysis was developed during the Great Depression of the 1930s. These depression or severe recession conditions would be most suited to a liquidity trap. When interest rates get low enough, investors and speculators begin to expect interest rates to rise, so holding money is preferred to holding bonds and suffering capital losses (when interest rates finally rise, bond prices will fall).

Monetarist analysis is more appropriate during normal economic conditions (or conditions less extreme than depressions). The changing money supply leads to portfolio adjustments that potentially result in changes to both consumption and investment, as well as changing output and aggregate prices.

Classical monetary transmission is a better explanation for long-run conditions. For example, if monetary authorities continue to increase the money supply at relatively high rates for a long period, the result will be rising prices and little improvement in real output beyond full employment.

Without a clear understanding of the different monetary transmission mechanisms, the debate over rules versus discretion in the last section of this chapter will be difficult to understand. Now move on to the next section on monetary policy lags.

Monetary Policy Lags

Frequently Asked Questions

Q: **Is monetary policy subject to lags, similar to fiscal policy lags?**

A: Monetary policy is subject to four major lags that are similar to the fiscal policy lags studied earlier. They include information, recognition, decision, and implementation lags.

Q: **What is the information (data) lag?**

A: Macroeconomic data are often one to two quarters behind events occurring in the economy. This *information* lag refers to the time it takes for monetary authorities to receive data, bearing in mind that these data are often revised.

Q: **What is the recognition lag?**

A: It takes additional time before certain trends in the data become clear, and often policymakers face an even longer *recognition* lag before they can be certain they are facing a problem in the economy that demands a response.

Q: **What is the decision lag?**

A: There is then a *decision* lag as the Fed weighs the appropriate policy response, although this lag is usually minimal, because the Board of Governors meets monthly.

Q: **What is the implementation lag?**

A: There is an *implementation* lag of months (or even years) before the effects of a change in monetary policy are felt throughout the economy.

Monetary Policy Lags Quick Check

Circle the Correct Answer

1. (T/F) The implementation lag will generally be the longest of the four monetary policy lags.
2. (T/F) The recognition lag is generally from 1 to 3 months as data are collected.
3. Because the Fed meets roughly on a monthly basis, which lag will generally be minimal?
   a. information lag
   b. recognition lag
   c. decision lag
   d. implementation lag
4. "Are you sure these data readings are clear? Seems like fluctuations to me. Maybe we should wait and collect more data." This is an example of
   a. an information lag.

   b. a recognition lag.
   c. a decision lag.
   d. an implementation lag.
5. "The Federal Reserve has just increased the money supply. Is this going to have an effect on my business? I wonder if I should do anything about it now." This is an example of
   a. an information lag.
   b. a recognition lag.
   c. a decision lag.
   d. an implementation lag.

Score: _____

Answers: 1. T; 2. F; 3. c; 4. b; 5. d

If You Got All 5 Correct

This must have seemed like a walk in the park compared to the previous section. You have monetary policy lags down pat. Go on to the next section, "Implementing Monetary Policy."

If You Didn't Get All of Them Correct

A simple review should be sufficient. This is relatively simple material, and it is only a few pages in the text. Do the review, then move on to the next section, "Implementing Monetary Policy." ■

Implementing Monetary Policy

Frequently Asked Questions

Q: In the long run, should the Fed target the price level or output?

A: In conducting monetary policy, the Fed has the broad option of targeting either a stable price level or full employment income and output. Most economists agree that, in the long run, the Fed should target price stability since low rates of inflation have been shown to provide the best environment for long-term economic growth.

Q: Should the Fed have a consistent target in the short run?

A: Probably not. In the short run, demand and supply shocks to the economy may need differing approaches to monetary policy.

Q: With a demand shock, should the Fed target the price level or output?

A: When a demand shock hits the economy, no conflict arises between the twin goals of monetary policy. Not only is the aim of full employment compatible with the objective of stable prices, but also in targeting either one of these objectives, the Fed will take steps that help to bring about the other.

Q: With a supply shock, should the Fed target the price level or output?

A: When a supply shocks hits the economy, in contrast, prices rise and output and employment fall. If the Fed increases the money supply to restore the economy to full employment, this only drives inflation up further. If the Fed enacts a contractionary policy to stabilize prices, this will just lead to a deeper recession. Most economists feel that when a supply shock occurs, expansionary policy is best, since it permits the Fed to spread the shock's impact between income and output losses and price level increases.

Q: Should the Fed use its own discretion or be guided by simple rules?

A: The complexities of implementing monetary policy have led some economists, notably Milton Friedman, to call for simple monetary rules to guide policymakers. Other economists argue that modern economies is too complex to be managed by a few simple rules. Laws and institutions change, the economic behavior of individuals and firms change, and new innovations and technologies mean policymakers should have some discretion over policy.

Q: If simple rules are to be followed, what should the Fed target?

A: Any monetary policymaking rule, whether legally binding or merely advisory, runs the risk of leaving policymakers unable to deal with quickly changing conditions. Economists and Fed policymakers are continually searching for simple rules to guide policy. Most of the proposals that have been offered involve either monetary targeting or inflation targeting.

Q: What is monetary targeting, and how does it work?

A: Monetary targeting aims to secure the steady growth of money stocks such as M1 or M2. With this approach, Fed policymakers use the equation of exchange, or quantity theory, to lay down the long-run path that they would like to see the economy follow. The Fed then keeps a close eye on the economy's various monetary aggregates. If their growth is below the target level, the Fed uses expansionary policy; if money stocks are growing too rapidly, the Fed does the opposite.

Q: **What is the major drawback of monetary targeting rules?**
A: Rules are least likely to be effective when a supply shock hits, given that promoting full employment under these conditions is likely to worsen inflation.

Q: **What is inflation targeting, and how does it work?**
A: Inflation targeting involves setting targets on the inflation rate, usually of around 2% a year. If inflation (or the forecasted rate of inflation) then exceeds this target, the Fed implements a contractionary policy, and vice versa.

Q: **What is the major benefit of inflation targeting rules?**
A: Inflation targeting has the virtue of explicitly acknowledging that the long-run goal of monetary policy is price stability.

Implementing Monetary Policy Quick Check

Circle the Correct Answer

1. (T/F) Most economists think the Fed should target price stability in the long run and output in the short run.
2. (T/F) When a demand shock hits the economy, no conflict arises between the monetary policy goals of price stability and full employment output.
3. (T/F) Most economists think the Fed should target output in the long run and price stability in the short run.
4. (T/F) Monetary policy is less effective countering a supply shock than a demand shock.
5. When a supply shock hits the economy,
   a. a contractionary monetary policy will stabilize prices with little effect on output.
   b. an expansionary monetary policy will restore the economy to full employment with little effect on the price level.
   c. an expansionary monetary policy will spread the shock's impact between income and output losses and price level increases.
   d. the Fed should target output since this is its short-run concern.
6. Which one of the following is *not* correct concerning a monetary targeting rule?
   a. It limits the Fed to expansionary policy, but not contractionary policy.
   b. It aims for steady growth of money stocks such as M1.
   c. It uses the quantity theory to set up a long-run path for money growth.
   d. It is likely to be ineffective under a supply shock.
7. Which one of the following is *not* correct concerning an inflation targeting rule?
   a. It sets an inflation target, usually of around 2% per year.

b. It explicitly acknowledges that the long-run goal of monetary policy is price stability.
c. It prohibits the Fed from pursuing an expansionary monetary policy because this will increase inflation.
d. It requires the Fed to follow a contractionary monetary policy if inflation exceeds the target.
8. Monetary targeting rules
   a. give policymakers enough flexibility to respond adequately to demand and supply shocks.
   b. are primarily concerned with output.
   c. focus on short-run fluctuations of the money stock from a long-run growth path.
   d. focus on the federal funds rate.
9. Inflation targeting rules
   a. focus on the federal funds rate.
   b. require expansionary monetary policy when a negative supply shock hits.
   c. require contractionary monetary policy when a negative demand shock hits.
   d. if followed, would deepen a recession caused by a negative supply shock.
10. Expansionary monetary policy
    a. will *not* be useful to mitigate a supply shock.
    b. is only useful when the economy is hit by a demand shock.
    c. is the essence of Friedman's monetary growth rule.
    d. is useful during both negative demand and supply shocks.

Score: ____

If You Got 9 or 10 Correct

You have a good understanding of when monetary policy is effective and what monetary and inflation targeting rules might be. You could go on to the next section, "Hints, Tips, and Reminders." However, this is a complicated section, and you might find that an extra review is worth the time to make sure you understand all of the concepts.

If You Didn't Get at Least 9 Correct

Relax. This section, along with the first section, contains some of the more difficult material in the book. It is not unusual for students to need several attempts at this material to really master it. Unfortunately, the only easy part of this chapter is the middle section.

Start your review by answering the following questions:

1. Under what conditions will monetary policy be effective? _____

_____

_____

2. When will monetary policy *not* be effective? _____

_____

_____

3. If a demand shock hits the economy, how effective is expansionary monetary policy? _____

_____

_____

4. If a supply shock hits the economy how effective is monetary policy? _____

_____

_____

The answers to these four questions get to the heart of implementing monetary policy. When you finish this review, take some time to review the "Hints, Tips, and Reminders" section, which includes answers to these four questions. ▪

Consider These Hints, Tips, and Reminders   STEP 4

1. The answers to the 4 questions above are the following:
1. Under most normal circumstances.
2. Deep depression, liquidity trap.
3. Expansionary monetary policy will be particularly helpful in this instance because output will rise and the price level will return to its previous level without generating further inflation.
4. Supply shocks are the most difficult for public policy to solve. Contractionary monetary policy aimed at reducing inflation will reduce output and employment making the recession worse. Increasing output with expansionary mon-

etary policy leads to greater inflation. Supply shocks always involve trade-offs between output and inflation when implementing monetary policy.

2. The transactions and precautionary motives for holding money are easy to understand; they represent reasons that we encounter on a regular basis. The speculative motive is not so obvious. For speculative purposes you are holding money (non-interest-earning assets) for two reasons. First, interest rates are low, so bond prices are high. Therefore, you expect that interest rates are going to rise, leading to a fall in bond prices, which means you will be able to buy more bonds for you money. Second, if you expect the price level to fall (defla-tion), money becomes more valuable, so you stand to gain by foregoing the interest and earning more spending power with your money. Keynes was writ-ing during the Depression, when interest rates were low and prices were falling for a short period.

3. The demand for money has a negative slope because of the opportunity costs of holding money when interest rates are lower. Low interest rates mean that it costs you less in interest forgone to hold money in your portfolio.

4. The table below summarizes the three monetary theories discussed in this chapter.

Transmission Channel	Money Supply Impacts	Interest Rate Impacts	Investment and Consumption Impacts	Aggregate Supply Curve
Keynesian	Interest	Investment	Output	Horizontal
Monetarist	Portfolio	Investment and consumption	Output or price	Positively sloped
Classical	Price level	—	Price	Vertical

5. Keep in mind the following four points about implementing monetary policy:
   - In the long run, monetary authorities should target price stability.
   - In the short run, monetary authorities should target the price level and income (output).
   - Demand shocks involve no tradeoffs; targeting either the price level or out-put leads to better outcomes for both.
   - Supply shocks involve tradeoffs: Targeting the price level worsens output, income, and employment; targeting output worsens the price level (infla-tion).

Do the Homework for Chapter 22
Monetary Policy

Instructor _____ Time _____ Student _____

Use the answer key below to record your answers to these homework questions.

1. (a) (b) (c) (d)   6. (a) (b) (c) (d)   11. (a) (b) (c) (d)   16. (a) (b) (c) (d)
2. (a) (b) (c) (d)   7. (a) (b) (c) (d)   12. (a) (b) (c) (d)   17. (a) (b) (c) (d)
3. (a) (b) (c) (d)   8. (a) (b) (c) (d)   13. (a) (b) (c) (d)   18. (a) (b) (c) (d)
4. (a) (b) (c) (d)   9. (a) (b) (c) (d)   14. (a) (b) (c) (d)   19. (a) (b) (c) (d)
5. (a) (b) (c) (d)   10. (a) (b) (c) (d)   15. (a) (b) (c) (d)   20. (a) (b) (c) (d)

---

1. Good monetary policy is designed to promote
   a. economic growth.
   b. stable prices.
   c. full employment.
   d. all of the above.

2. Expansionary monetary policy or easy money policies include
   a. lowering reserve requirements, increasing the discount rate, and buying government securities using open market operations.
   b. raising reserve requirements, increasing the discount rate, and buying government securities using open market operations.
   c. lowering reserve requirements, lowering the discount rate, and buying government securities using open market operations.
   d. raising reserve requirements, increasing the discount rate, and selling government securities using open market operations.

3. Contractionary monetary policy or tight money policies include
   a. lowering reserve requirements, increasing the discount rate, and buying government securities using open market operations.
   b. raising reserve requirements, increasing the discount rate, and buying government securities using open market operations.
   c. lowering reserve requirements, lowering the discount rate, and buying government securities using open market operations.
   d. raising reserve requirements, increasing the discount rate, and selling government securities using open market operations.

4. The quantity theory of money
   a. measures the amount of money in circulation.
   b. explains how an increase in the money supply will increase employment and output in the short run.
   c. suggests that in the long run, a change in the money supply will directly change the aggregate price level.
   d. was a major innovation in economic thinking introduced by John Maynard Keynes during the Great Depression.

5. The equation of exchange is equal to which of the following?
   a. $M + V = P + Q$
   b. $M - V = P - Q$
   c. $M \div V = P \div Q$
   d. $M \times V = P \times Q$

6. Keynesian monetary theory
   a. dominated economic policy during the first part of the 20th century.
   b. was developed during the 1930s and focused more on the short run.
   c. was developed by Keynes and seen as the primary means of bringing an economy out of a deep depression.
   d. stressed the impact of changing interest rates on inflation.

7. Which of the following was *not* one of the three motives Keynes identifies for holding money?
   a. the precautionary motive
   b. the speculative motive
   c. the interest rate motive
   d. the transactions motive

8. The Keynesian speculative motive for holding money
   a. focused primarily on stock brokers and mutual funds.
   b. argued that people might hold money for uncertain or speculative events in their lives.

c. suggested that many individuals speculated in foreign currencies, and this would have a major impact on the U.S. economy.

d. suggested that people held money when they expected interest rates to rise or the price level to fall.

9. The Keynesian monetary transmission channel (or mechanism) suggests that
   a. increases in the money supply will increase interest rates, which will increase investment, resulting in greater employment and income.
   b. increases in the money supply will decrease interest rates, which will result in an increase in investment, resulting in greater employment and income.
   c. increases in the money supply will directly increase the aggregate price level.
   d. increases in the money supply will *not* increase income or output in the short run.

10. When comparing Keynesian and classical monetary theories, which of the following is *not* correct?
    a. Keynes focused on the short run, whereas classical economists focused on the long run.
    b. Keynes focused on the transactions demand for money, whereas classical economists were primarily concerned with the speculative demand for money.

c. For Keynes, the impact of changes in the money supply came through interest rates and their impact on investment, whereas for classical economists, changes in the money supply directly affected the price level.

d. Keynes felt that monetary policy would have little impact during a protracted depression.

11. Permanent income is
    a. the present value of an individual's future stream of income.
    b. a proxy for wealth embedded in human capital.
    c. a weighted average of past incomes.
    d. all of the above.

12. The monetarist monetary transmission channel (or mechanism) suggests that
    a. increases in the money supply will increase interest rates, which will increase investment, resulting in greater employment, income, and a higher price level in the short run.
    b. increases in the money supply will decrease interest rates, which will increase investment or consumption, resulting in greater employment or an increase in the price level in the short run.
    c. increases in the money supply will directly increase the aggregate price level.
    d. increases in the money supply will not increase income, output, or the price level in the short run.

---

13. Assume the economy in Figure HW-1 is initially in equilibrium at point a. Now assume that aggregate demand increases to AD_1. Monetarist analysis would suggest that
    a. the economy would move to point b and remain there over the long run.
    b. as in the classical model, the economy would move immediately to point c.
    c. the economy would move to point b in the short run, then move back to point a over the long run.
    d. the economy would move to point b in the short run, then move back to point c over the long run.

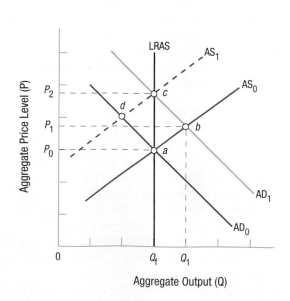

HW-1

---

14. Monetary policy, like fiscal policy, is subject to lags. Economic data are only available periodically, which is what kind of lag?
    a. decision lag

b. implementation lag

c. information lag

d. recognition lag

15. Monetary policy affects bank reserves, interest rates, and decisions by business and households. This introduces

a. a decision lag.

b. an implementation lag.

c. an information lag.

d. a recognition lag.

16. As a general rule, monetary policy should target

a. inflation in the short run and income and output in the long run.

b. only inflation, income, and output in the long run.

c. only inflation in the short run.

d. inflation in the long run and income and output in the short run.

---

17. Assume the economy in Figure HW-2 is initially in equilibrium at point e. Now assume that the economy suffers a supply shock, decreasing aggregate supply to AS_1. If policymakers want to hold the price level constant at P_0,

a. they should increase aggregate demand to AD_1.

b. they should do nothing.

c. they should reduce aggregate demand to AD_2.

d. they should encourage the Federal Open Market Committee (FOMC) to buy bonds.

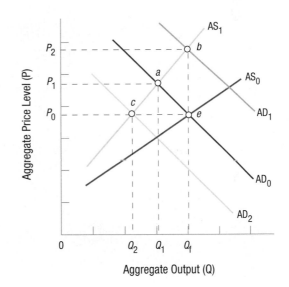

18. Assume the economy in Figure HW-2 is initially in equilibrium at point e. Now assume that the economy suffers a demand shock, decreasing aggregate demand to AD_2. If policymakers want to maintain full employment in the short run,

a. they should increase aggregate demand back to AD_0.

b. they should do nothing.

c. they should implement policies that will increase aggregate supply.

d. they should encourage the FOMC to sell bonds.

HW-2

19. Assume the economy in Figure HW-2 is initially in equilibrium at point e. Now assume that the economy suffers a supply shock decreasing aggregate supply to AS_1. If policymakers want to maintain full employment in the short run,

a. they should implement supply-side policies that will increase aggregate supply like reducing the capital gains tax rate.

b. they should do nothing.

c. they should be willing to accept a much higher aggregate price level.

d. they should encourage the Federal Reserve open market committee to sell bonds.

20. A monetary growth rule
    a. of about 2% would keep the economy at full employment all the time.
    b. would lead to hyperinflation.
    c. may keep policymakers from making things worse.
    d. would not be very helpful if the economy faced modest demand shocks.

Use the ExamPrep to Get Ready for Exams

This sheet (front and back) is designed to help you prepare for your exams. The chapter has been boiled down to its key concepts. You are asked to answer questions, define terms, draw graphs, and, if you wish, add summaries of class notes.

Monetary Theories

The Long Run: Quantity Theory

Define the equation of exchange:

Describe the implications of the equation of exchange for monetary policy in the long run:

Describe the channel (monetary transmission mechanism) through which changes in the money supply influence prices in classical theory:

The Short Run: Interest Rate Channels

Describe why the speculative motive for holding money leads to a negatively sloped demand curve for money:

Describe the conditions under which money would be a better investment than bonds that pay interest:

Describe the Keynesian monetary transmission channel (mechanism):

Monetarist Model

Describe the essential elements of the monetarist model:

Describe the monetarist transmission channel (mechanism):

Monetary Policy Lags

Describe the four monetary policy lags:

1.

2.

3.

4.

Implementing Monetary Policy

Monetary Policy Targets

Describe the appropriate monetary policy targets for the following:
Long run:

Short run:

Describe the appropriate monetary policy for both demand and supply shocks. Be sure to describe the tradeoffs and monetary policy's ability to mitigate the problem.
Demand shocks:

Supply shocks:

Describe the debate about rules versus discretion in monetary policy:

Complete the following table:

Targets	Benefits	Costs
Monetary Targets		
Demand shocks		
Supply shocks		
Inflation Targets		
Demand shocks		
Supply shocks		

Additional Study Help Chapterwide Practice Questions

Matching

Match the description with the corresponding term.

____ 1. Equation of exchange
____ 2. Keynesian monetary transmission mechanism
____ 3. Transactions demand for money
____ 4. Precautionary demand for money
____ 5. Speculative demand for money
____ 6. Monetarist transmission mechanism
____ 7. Information lag
____ 8. Recognition lag
____ 9. Decision lag
____ 10. Implementation lag
____ 11. Monetary rules
____ 12. Monetary targeting
____ 13. Inflation targeting

a. Money balances to help handle unexpected expenses.
b. Simple guides to eliminate or reduce monetary policymaker's discretion.
c. Desired inflation rate of roughly 2% a year.
d. Monetary authorities are looking at preliminary data and cannot determine if additional policy is needed.
e. Money held to benefit from rising interest rates or deflation.
f. A guide to the long-run impact of the rate of growth of the money supply on inflation.
g. Monetary policy takes anywhere from one quarter to 2 years to filter throughout the economy.
h. Changes in individual portfolios of bonds, real estate, consumer durables, and so on, in reaction to monetary policy.
i. Changes in the money supply change the interest rate, and this in turn causes changes in investment, which affects the level of aggregate demand, employment, and output.
j. The time it take policymakers to decide to make changes in policy once they perceive there is a problem in the economy.
k. Money that is needed to make transactions.
l. The Fed maintains a steady growth of monetary aggregates like M1 or M2 by using policy to adjust for differences in growth rates from targeted growth rates.
m. The reporting of macroeconomic data occurs anywhere from 1 month to several quarters after the fact.

Fill-In

Circle the word(s) in parentheses that complete the sentence.

1. The classical equation of exchange states that the quantity of money in circulation times (output, velocity) _____ is equal to the price level times (output, velocity) _____. Because classical economists believed that (velocity, output, inflation) _____ was determined by banking technology and the economy was at full employment, increases in the quantity of money would translate into higher (velocity, output, inflation) _____.

2. Classical economists focused on the (transaction, precautionary, speculative) _____ motive for holding money, whereas Keynes argued that the (transaction, precautionary, speculative) _____ motive was probably most important.

3. Because it takes policymakers time to assess changes in the economy (1 month's reduction in the rate of economic growth does not make a recession), policymakers face a/an (information, recognition, decision, implementation) _____ lag. The Fed meets to make policy on a monthly basis so their (information, recognition, decision, implementation) _____ lag is relatively short, but the (information, recognition, decision, implementation) _____ lag can sometimes take 6 months or longer.

4. For long-run policymaking, the Fed should focus on (full employment, price stability, output) _____, but in the short run, the appropriate policy will depend on the nature of the shocks to the economy. The Fed can use either the price level or output as short-run targets when a (demand, supply) _____ shock hits the economy because improving one benefits the other. But when a (demand, supply) _____ shock occurs, the Fed faces a tradeoff between the price level and output.

5. A monetary growth rule would work well for moderate (demand, supply) _____ shocks, but would not give policymakers the needed flexibility when severe disturbances occur.

True-False

Circle the correct answer.

T/F   1. The quantity theory of money best explains the short-run impact changes in the money supply have on the economy.

T/F   2. The quantity theory of money focuses on the speculative demand for money.

T/F   3. In general, the more broadly defined a money supply is, the lower its velocity will be.

T/F   4. Keynesian monetary theory assumes that an economy will naturally tend toward full employment in the long run.

T/F   5. The speculative motive for holding money will be strongest when interest rates are low and the aggregate price level is expected to rise.

T/F   6. The Keynesian transmission mechanism implies that an increase in the money supply will lower interest rates, thereby increasing investment, aggregate demand, and income.

T/F   7. Monetarist theory assumes that people will hold virtually all of their wealth as either money or bonds.

T/F   8. Monetarist theory concludes that an increase in the money supply may affect output or price levels in the short run, but that the long-run effect will be higher prices.

T/F   9. Monetarists argue that in the long run, increases in the money supply will translate directly into increases in prices.

T/F   10. The information lag in monetary policy-making is typically 1 to 3 months long.

T/F   11. Monetary policymakers like to take counteractive policy measures at the first sign of possible trouble in the economic data they receive.

T/F   12. In monetary policymaking, the decision lag is typically much shorter than the implementation lag.

T/F   13. The effects of changes in monetary policy take time to work their way through the economy because they must first work through individual and firm decision-making processes.

T/F   14. Milton Friedman argued that the difficulty in implementing effective monetary policies in a timely fashion means that we are ill-advised to institute any sort of monetary rules.

T/F   15. The lag that monetary policymakers find to be the most variable is the implementation lag.

T/F   16. Lags do not really pose much of a problem for monetary policymakers because the Fed is tied in directly with the money markets.

T/F   17. Supply shocks are much easier for monetary policymakers to counteract than demand shocks.

T/F   18. In the case of demand shocks, monetary policies aimed at restoring output to its full employment level will also restore prices to their original level, and vice versa.

T/F   19. In the case of supply shocks, monetary policies aimed at restoring output to its full employment will also restore prices to their original level, and vice versa.

T/F   20. The primary disadvantage of monetary rules is that they can be too rigid to allow policymakers to respond adequately to short-term supply or demand shocks.

T/F   21. Monetary targeting involves targeting a particular inflation rate and adjusting monetary policy to keep inflation within certain predetermined limits.

Multiple Choice

Circle the correct answer.

1. Quantity theory is generally adequate for explaining
   a. the short-run impact of monetary growth.
   b. the long-run impact of monetary growth.
   c. the impact of supply shocks to the economy.
   d. the impact of demand shocks to the economy.

2. Keynesian monetary analysis dominated economic thinking
   a. throughout the 1700s and 1800s.
   b. in the early years of the 20th century.
   c. from the Depression of the 1930s through the 1960s.
   d. from the 1970s through the present.

3. In Keynesian analysis, which of the following is *not* among the motives people have for holding money?
   a. speculative motive
   b. transactions motive
   c. inflationary motive
   d. precautionary motive

4. What gives rise to a liquidity trap?
   a. high inflation from excessive government borrowing
   b. disinflation accompanied by economic growth
   c. high interest rates and low investment
   d. low interest rates

5. If classical monetary analysis focused on the transactions demand for money, what does Keynesian analysis emphasize?
   a. the precautionary demand for money
   b. the quantity of currency in the economy
   c. the speculative demand for money
   d. the effects of wealth on consumption

6. In the long-run, which of the following variables do monetarists assume to be fixed?
   a. interest rates
   b. aggregate demand
   c. the velocity of money
   d. the money supply

7. Which of the following is the classical equation of exchange?
   a. $M/V = P \times Q$
   b. $M \times V = P \times Q$
   c. $M \times V = P(100) \times Q$
   d. $M \times V = Q/P$

8. In the classical quantity theory of money, which variables were considered slow to change or were fixed?
   a. M and P
   b. P and Q
   c. V and Q
   d. V and P

9. In Figure MC-1 which one of the following is *not* correct?

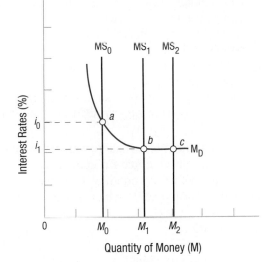

MC-1

a. The figure represents the Keynesian view of the money market.
b. When the money supply increases, interest rates always fall, leading to increased investment.
c. Point *c* represents a liquidity trap.
d. A liquidity trap is caused by the speculative demand for money.

10. In Figure MC-2, which one of the following is *not* correct?
    a. Reducing reserve requirements shifts aggregate demand from AD_0 to AD_1 in the short run.

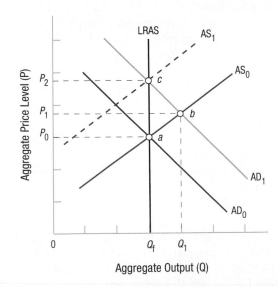

MC-2

b. Increasing the money supply will shift aggregate demand from AD_0 to AD_1, raising output and prices in the short run.

c. Over the long run, an increase in the money supply will move the economy from point a to point b to point c, having no ultimate effect on output but increasing prices.

d. Increasing the money supply will shift aggregate supply from AS_0 to AS_1 in the short run.

11. When monetary policymakers wait several months to confirm that an apparent economic trend is, in fact, real, before responding to it with a policy change, this represents which of the following?
    a. information lag
    b. recognition lag
    c. decision lag
    d. implementation lag

12. Which of the following lags affecting monetary policy will generally be the longest?
    a. information lag
    b. recognition lag
    c. decision lag
    d. implementation lag

13. For monetary policymakers, which of the following lags is of the least consequence?
    a. information lag
    b. recognition lag
    c. decision lag
    d. implementation lag

14. What do most economists believe the Fed should target in the long run?
    a. price stability
    b. high levels of income and output
    c. high inflation rates
    d. low interest rates

15. Which of the following economic events is most difficult to counteract by means of monetary policy?
    a. a short-run decline in aggregate demand
    b. a short-run rise in aggregate demand
    c. a decrease in the demand for electronic equipment
    d. a mild recession

16. If the Fed responds to a negative demand shock with an expansionary monetary policy in an attempt to restore output to its full employment level, what will this do to prices?
    a. drive prices above their original level
    b. leave prices unchanged

c. restore prices to their original level
d. reduce the general price level

17. If the Fed responds to a negative supply shock with expansionary policy in an attempt to restore output to its full employment level, what will this do to prices?
    a. drive prices above their original level
    b. leave prices unchanged
    c. restore prices to their original level
    d. reduce the general price level

18. Which school of economic thought is most associated with calls for monetary rules to guide monetary policymaking?
    a. the classical school
    b. the Keynesian school
    c. the monetarist school
    d. the Austrian school

19. In Figure MC-3, assume the economy is hit with a demand shock, with aggregate supply equal to AS_0 and aggregate demand falling from AD_0 to AD_1.
    a. An expansionary monetary policy will increase the money supply, moving the economy from point a back to point e.
    b. An expansionary monetary policy will increase the money supply, moving the economy from point a to point b.
    c. A contractionary monetary policy is needed to prevent the price level from rising above its original point.
    d. Output and prices move together: Both worsen, or both get better.

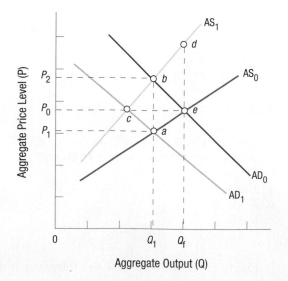

20. In Figure MC-3, assume the economy is hit with a supply shock, with aggregate supply falling from AS_0 to AS_1, while aggregate demand remains at AD_0.
    a. An expansionary monetary policy will increase the money supply, moving the economy back to full employment and at the original price level.
    b. An expansionary monetary policy will increase the money supply, moving the economy back to full employment but at an even higher price level.
    c. A contractionary monetary policy will decrease the money supply, moving the economy back to full employment but at a higher price level.
    d. A contractionary monetary policy will decrease the money supply, moving the economy to a lower output and a higher price level.

Essay-Problem

Answer in the space provided.

The questions below are designed to extend your understanding of monetary policy. Your answers may not always be the same as those we suggest. Gauge whether your answers are close to the recommended ones. Use these questions as another way to assess your progress with monetary policy.

1. Will the recognition lag always be a problem in implementing monetary policy?

2. There are many Federal Reserve watchers who hang on every pronouncement by Fed officials. Could this lead to much shorter implementation lags?

3. In 2002, money market interest rates were hovering around 1%, and bond rates were roughly 4%. Was the U.S. economy facing a liquidity trap?

4. Keynes once likened using monetary policy in a depression as similar to pushing on a string. What did he mean by this?

5. How do monetary policy information and recognition lags compare to fiscal policy information and recognition lags?

6. How do monetary policy decision and implementation lags compare to fiscal policy decision and implementation lags?

7. What is a drawback to monetary policy rules? What is a drawback to discretion?

8. Why might contractionary monetary policy in the short run have more effect on output than prices?

9. Classical economists believed that velocity in the equation of exchange tended to be slow to change. When might velocity change rapidly? (*Hint:* Consider a period of hyperinflation.)

10. Do politicians tend to favor fiscal policy over monetary policy? Why or why not?

What's Next

With this chapter finished, you now have a framework for understanding how the economy works and what tools government can use to smooth out the business cycle and foster economic growth. You know when fiscal policy is appropriate and when monetary policy can be effective. You saw how lags diminish the force of fiscal and monetary policy. We hinted at something else that hinders government policymakers, though we did not explore this in detail. It is now time to face the challenge posed by this shadowy figure: rising federal deficits. How much do deficits tie the government's hands? This is the focus of the next chapter.

Answers to Chapterwide Practice Questions

Matching

1. f	5. e	9. j	13. c
2. i	6. h	10. g	
3. k	7. m	11. b	
4. a	8. d	12. l	

Fill-In

1. velocity, output, velocity, inflation
2. transaction, speculative
3. recognition, decision, implementation
4. price stability, demand, supply
5. demand

True-False

1. F	7. F	13. T	19. F
2. F	8. T	14. F	20. T
3. T	9. T	15. T	21. F
4. F	10. T	16. F	
5. F	11. F	17. F	
6. T	12. T	18. T	

Multiple Choice

1. b	6. c	11. b	16. c
2. c	7. b	12. d	17. a
3. c	8. c	13. c	18. c
4. d	9. b	14. a	19. a
5. c	10. d	15. c	20. b

Essay-Problem

1. It is likely that the recognition lag will always be a problem because there will always be fluctuations in the data. It is unlikely that every indicator will point the same way unless the economy is in a deep recession or obvious inflationary period. Thus, we can expect a recognition lag. The question becomes: How long will the lag be?

2. There have been many Fed watchers for a long time now. Potential Fed actions are debated in the press continually. But the issue with implementation lags is that it often takes people and businesses a while to adapt to Fed policy changes. Even if a policy change is correctly predicted by Fed watchers, people and businesses still may not take action until the policy is actually announced. Therefore, the implementation lag could be slightly shorter than before, in that people and businesses are better prepared, but the length of time it takes them to act would be approximately the same.

3. Not necessarily. A liquidity trap *can* occur when interest rates are very low and when people expect interest rates to climb. Thus, it may be worthwhile to hold money in the hope of soon buying bonds at higher interest rates. In 2002, short-term money market rates were around 1%, but the opportunity cost of holding money was higher because bond interest rates were over 4%. If people did not expect interest rates to rise dramatically in the near future, people would be more likely to wonder what could be done with this money to obtain more interest now, rather than how many weeks (or months) would it be before this money could be used to buy higher-interest bearing assets.

4. If you pull on a taut string, you will make things tighter. But if you push on a stretched string, nothing will happen because the string will just collapse. Recall that Keynes thought an economy in a depression would be facing a liquidity trap. Expansionary monetary policy would have no effect on the liquidity trap. To Keynes, using expansionary monetary policy in that case was just as effective as pushing on a string.

5. They should be the same. In both cases, data have to be gathered, and trends have to be recognized. Fiscal policy is not much different from monetary policy in this regard.

6. Monetary policy decision lags are short compared to fiscal policy. Monetary policymakers meet monthly, while fiscal policy must get through the sausage grinder of Congress and the executive branch. Monetary policy implementation lags, however, can be longer than fiscal policy implementation lags because impacts on the economy must work through the business/consumer investment decision process. For example, the Fed can cut interest rates immediately to stimulate the economy (the decision process); but business and consumer decisions may take quite a while to occur. Even if business expects interest rates to fall, actually bringing an investment online can take years. On the other side, government policymakers have to go through the legislative process to increase spending or cut taxes, but when laws are finally enacted, changing the withholding schedules for tax changes, for example, is fast, resulting in rapidly removing or adding money to the spending stream.

7. Rules can lock in a policy, exacerbating a situation. For example, an inflation target rule for an economy hit by a supply shock would require contractionary policies; this would keep inflation from rising, but at the cost of lowering output. However, discretion makes it difficult for people to plan because they cannot be sure what the Federal Reserve will do under certain situations. When do rules stop being rules if they can be broken? When does discretion stop being discretion if it is bound to certain actions under specific circumstances?

8. Think about price increases and price decreases. Price increases are common. Businesses are reluctant to reduce prices. True, businesses have sales, but they like to broadcast them as temporary, not permanent. Thus, prices tend to be sticky downward. So a contractionary monetary policy is likely to have more of an output effect than a price effect, in the short run.

9. In a time of high inflation or hyperinflation, the value of money diminishes quickly. People want to get rid of money as quickly as possible before prices rise, so they dump money for goods and services and more durable assets. Velocity can become a potent factor at this time. Remember the equation of exchange: $M \times V = P \times Q$. Assume that

output is fixed. Then changes in M and V will equal changes in P. If V is constant, then changes in M equal changes in P. But when velocity climbs, changes in M times changes in V equal changes in P. As velocity climbs, it drives the price level higher.

10. Politicians are in the business of getting reelected. They rush to take credit for spending and taxing policies. Because of the Fed's independence, it is harder for politicians to take credit for Fed policies. For this reason, politicians tend to favor fiscal policy over monetary policy.

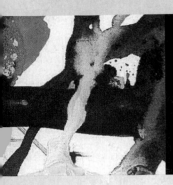

Federal Deficits and Public Debt

23

Is Our Growing Budget Deficit Going to Sink the Economy?

Deficits, deficits, deficits. We hear a constant stream of press reports on the federal government's budget deficit. How important is this issue, really? We try to answer this question in this chapter.

	This Is What You Need to Know	STEP 1

After studying this chapter you should be able to

- Define deficits and the national debt.

- Describe public choice analysis.

- Describe the various approaches to balancing budgets.

- Describe the role of the Federal Reserve in financing debt and deficits.

- Analyze the relationship between budget and trade deficits.

- Explain the difference between internally and externally held debt.

- Describe the crowding-out effect.

- Analyze the sustainability of federal deficits.

Review the Key Terms

Deficit: The amount by which annual government spending exceeds tax revenues.

Surplus: The amount by which annual tax revenues exceed government expenditures.

Public debt: The total accumulation of past deficits and surpluses; it includes treasury bills, notes, and bonds, and U.S. savings bonds.

Public choice theory: The economic analysis of public and political decision making, looking at issues such as voting, the impact of election incentives on politicians, the influence of special interest groups, and rent-seeking behaviors.

Annually balanced budget: Federal expenditures and taxes would have to be equal each year. Annually balanced budgets tend to be procyclical.

Cyclically balanced budget: Balancing the budget over the course of the business cycle by restricting spending or raising taxes when the economy is booming and using these surpluses to offset deficits that occur during recessions.

Functional finance: Essentially ignores the impact of the budget on the business cycle and focuses on fostering economic growth and stable prices, while keeping the economy as close as possible to full employment.

Government budget constraint: The government budget is limited by the fact that $G - T = \Delta M + \Delta B + \Delta A$, where G is government spending and T is tax revenues, thus $(G - T)$ is the federal budget deficit; ΔM is the change in the money supply; ΔB is the change in bonds held by public entities, domestic and foreign; and ΔA represents the sales of government assets.

Budget and trade deficits: These are related by the following equation: $G - T = (S - I) + (M - X)$. So budget deficits must be covered by net domestic saving (private + corporate) or by net foreign saving (in the form of foreigners buying U.S. government bonds).

Internally held debt: Public debt owned by U.S. banks, corporations, mutual funds, pension plans, and individuals.

Externally held debt: Public debt held by foreigners, roughly equal to half of the outstanding U.S. debt held by the public.

Crowding-out effect: Arises from deficit spending requiring the government to borrow, thus driving up interest rates and reducing consumer spending and business investment.

Fiscal sustainability: A fiscal imbalance equal to zero.

Fiscal imbalance: The difference between the present value of future obligations and expected revenues, less government assets, assuming current policies remain unchanged.

Generational imbalance: An estimate of how much of any fiscal imbalance is being shifted to future generations.

Work Through the Chapter Tutorials

Financing the Federal Government

Frequently Asked Questions

Q: How are deficits and national debt defined?

A: A deficit is the amount by which annual government spending exceeds tax revenues. A surplus, when it occurs, is the amount by which the year's tax revenues exceed government spending. The public debt, or national debt, is the total accumulation of past deficits and surpluses.

Q: What securities are held as public debt?

A: Public debt consists of U.S. Treasury securities, including treasury bills, notes, and bonds, and U.S. savings bonds.

Q: What are treasury bills, notes, and bonds?

A: Treasury bills (T-bills) are short-term instruments, with a maturity period of 1 year or less. They do not pay interest; rather, they are sold at a discount, and their yields are then determined by the time to maturity and the discount. Treasury notes are financial instruments issued for periods ranging from 1 to 10 years. Treasury bonds are federal bonds with a maturity period exceeding 10 years. Treasury notes and bonds have stated interest rates and are traded actively, sometimes at discounts but also sometimes at premiums, depending on current interest rates and the coupon rates of the bonds.

Q: What is public choice theory, and what specifically does it look at?

A: Public choice theory involves the economic analysis of public and political decision making. It looks at such issues as voting, the relationship between voting and policy outcomes, the impact of election incentives on politicians, the influence of special interest groups, the analysis of rent-seeking behavior, and the effects of "rational ignorance." Public choice theorists often conclude that collective decision making is often flawed and inefficient.

Q: Who is James Buchanan, and what is his key conclusion?

A: James Buchanan, considered the father of public choice theory, essentially fused the disciplines of economics and political science. Buchanan's analysis assumes that politicians and bureaucrats consider their own self-interest when making public policy. In this sense, they behave no differently than other economic actors. This means our public policies may not always be guided by the public interest.

Q: What is the public choice theory of deficit spending?

A: Public choice economists such as Buchanan argue that deficit spending reduces the perceived cost of current government operations. As a result, taxpayers permit some programs to exist that they would oppose if required to pay the full cost today. Public choice economists charge that this amounts to shifting the cost of government to the next generation.

Q: What are the three general positions concerning a balanced federal budget?

A: Some observers believe the federal government, like state governments, should balance its budget every year. Others argue that balancing the budget over the business cycle is a better approach, while still others have suggested that the federal government should focus on promoting full employment with stable prices, treating the budget deficit or surplus as a secondary concern.

Q: When did the idea of annually balancing the federal budget hold sway, and what is its drawback?

A: The prevailing economic wisdom before the 1930s was that the federal government should balance its budget annually. Today, we know that annually balancing the federal budget would undercut fiscal policies aimed at maintaining full employment. To insist on balancing the budget by reducing spending or increasing taxes when recession looms would require a contractionary policy that would worsen the economic situation and, in the end, increase the deficit.

Q: What is the idea behind balancing the federal budget over the course of the business cycle, and what is its drawback?

A: Some economists have recommended balancing the budget over the course of the business cycle. The basic idea is to restrict spending or raise taxes when the economy is booming to prevent inflationary pressures from taking hold. Surpluses, moreover, should accumulate during boom periods and offset deficits during downturns and recessions. Balancing the budget over the business cycle is good in theory. In practice, however, balancing the budget over the course of the business cycle is extremely difficult and politically risky.

Q: What is the functional finance approach to balancing the federal budget?

A: Economists who favor a functional finance approach to the federal budget believe that the first priority of policymakers should be to keep the economy at full employment with stable prices; whether the budget is in surplus or deficit is only a secondary concern. These economists believe that if the government is successful in providing the appropriate microeconomic mix and successful macroeconomic fiscal policies, deficits and surpluses will be unimportant.

Financing the Federal Government Quick Check

Circle the Correct Answer

1. (T/F) The public debt is the total amount of past government deficits, reduced by the total amount of government surpluses.
2. (T/F) The public debt is held as special Federal Reserve bills, notes, and bonds.
3. (T/F) The deficit is the amount by which annual government spending exceeds tax revenues.
4. (T/F) Gross public debt is over $9 trillion, almost all of it held by the public.
5. Which one of the following is *not* a conclusion of public choice theory?
   a. Politicians and government bureaucrats are motivated by self-interest, just like any other person; they are not always guided by the public interest.
   b. Economic analysis can be used profitably to examine public and political decision making.
   c. Buchanan's law states that government deficits are inevitable.
   d. Deficit spending reduces the perceived cost of current government operations.
6. What is the chief drawback of balancing the federal budget on an annual basis?
   a. It is difficult to do.
   b. Automatic stabilizers make the attempt unlikely to be successful.

   c. Mandating reduced spending or increased taxes when a recession looms would worsen the economic situation, possibly turning a recession into a depression.
   d. The deficit is not that big of a problem.
7. Which one of the following is *not* correct?
   a. Promoters of functional finance are just as concerned with deficits as those who want to cyclically balance the budget.
   b. Cyclically balancing the budget is hard to do because different phases of the business cycle are of different length and severity.
   c. Cyclically balancing the budget is difficult because politicians are loathe to cut spending.
   d. Functional finance focuses on maintaining full employment with stable prices.
8. Public choice theory claims that deficits are caused by
   a. corrupt politicians and bureaucrats.
   b. the ability for the full cost of programs to be pushed off to future generations.
   c. Buchanan's law.
   d. rent-seeking behavior by politicians.
9. Which one of the following is *not* correct concerning cyclically balancing the budget?
   a. It pushes the government to restrict spending or raise taxes when the economy is booming.

b. Theoretically, surpluses from boom times should cancel out deficits from downturns.

c. Automatic stabilizers tend to help in the effort to cyclically balance the budget.

d. It mandates contractionary policies that could deepen a recession into a depression.

10. Functional finance seeks to

a. minimize deficits rather than prevent them.

b. maintain full employment and stable prices, with a balanced budget as a secondary concern.

c. match surpluses with deficits over the course of the business cycle.

d. balance the federal budget on an annual basis.

Score: ____

If You Got 9 or 10 Correct

You have a good grasp of the concepts of public choice theory and the different approaches to balancing the budget. Go on to the next section, "Financing Debt and Deficits."

If You Didn't Get at Least 9 Correct

Jot down the three approaches to balancing the budget. To get a grip on public choice theory, list five things you would do to further your own interest if you were a politician. After each point, indicate whether this is in the public interest as well. This is not difficult material. You should have been able to answer all of the questions correctly. Continue on, but you should probably review this section. Fortunately, the next section, "Financing Debt and Deficits," stands on its own and really does not build significantly on this section. ■

Financing Debt and Deficits

Frequently Asked Questions

Q: How does government finance its debt?

A: Given its power to print money and collect taxes, the federal government cannot go bankrupt. It does, however, face what economists call a budget constraint:

$$G - T = \Delta M + \Delta B + \Delta A$$

where

G = government spending

T = tax revenues, thus $(G - T)$ is the federal budget deficit

ΔM = the change in the money supply

ΔB = the change in bonds held by public entities, domestic and foreign

ΔA = the sales of government assets.

Q: What is meant by "monetizing" the debt?

A: When the Federal Reserve buys bonds, it exchanges cash for bonds. This part of the government's debt is therefore "monetized." The Federal Reserve is increasing the money supply, and therefore the government is financing the deficit by "printing money" ($\Delta M > 0$) or monetizing the debt.

Q: If the Federal Reserve does not buy the government's bonds, who else will?

A: If the Federal Reserve does not purchase the bonds, they must be sold to the public, including corporations, banks, mutual funds, individuals, and foreign entities. This also has the effect of financing the government's deficit ($\Delta B > 0$).

Q: Can the government finance its debt through asset sales?

A: Asset sales ($\Delta A > 0$) represent only a small fraction of government finance in the United States.

Q: What happens when the government borrows to pay for a deficit?

A: When the government runs a deficit, it must borrow funds from somewhere, assuming it does not sell assets. If the government borrows from the public, the quantity of publicly held bonds will rise; if it borrows from the Federal Reserve, the quantity of money in circulation will rise.

Q: If the economy is at equilibrium, how are budget deficits, savings, and trade deficits linked?

A: When an economy is at equilibrium, all injections and withdrawals will be equal; thus: $G + I + X = T + S + M$. By rearranging terms, we find that $G - T = (S - I) + (M - X)$. This equation states that at equilibrium, budget deficits (a positive number on the left side of the equation) must be made up by private savings ($S > I$) or a trade deficit ($M > X$).

Q: What is the link between budget deficits and trade deficits when investment and savings are equal?

A: If investment and saving are equal, $(I - S) = 0$, the link between budget deficits and trade deficits becomes clear. When the budget turns to deficit ($T < G$), a trade deficit will follow ($X < M$), and vice versa.

Q: What is the crowding-out effect of government deficits?

A: If exports and imports are equal ($X = M$), such that the trade balance is zero, budget deficits ($G > T$) must be met by higher private saving ($S > I$). This illustrates the crowding-out effect of government deficits. If G grows while T and S remain constant, investment (I) must fall. Increased deficit spending by the government crowds out private investment.

Financing Debt and Deficits Quick Check

Circle the Correct Answer

1. (T/F) The budget constraint is the total amount the government is allowed to borrow in any given year.

2. (T/F) The crowding-out effect occurs when government borrowing to finance the deficit drives up interest rates, which in turn reduces private investment.

3. (T/F) The government budget constraint shows that the government can either "print money," borrow, or sell assets to finance a budget deficit.

4. (T/F) The Federal Reserve is obligated by law to buy all of the government bonds that the government sells to finance a budget deficit.

5. Which one of the following is *not* correct concerning the government budget constraint?
   a. It can be expressed as $G - T = \Delta M + \Delta B + \Delta A$.
   b. It means that the government can either borrow or engage in asset sales to finance the deficit.
   c. Asset sales are a very small part of financing the deficit.

d. Over 80% of the borrowing is picked up by the public.

6. Which one of the following does *not* occur when the Federal Reserve buys government bonds to finance the deficit?
   a. It pumps new money into the financial system.
   b. It monetizes the debt.
   c. It increases the money supply.
   d. It engages in contractionary monetary policy to mitigate the effects of large deficits.

7. If the economy is in equilibrium, and savings and investment are equal,
   a. a federal budget deficit must be matched by a trade surplus.
   b. a federal budget deficit must be matched by a trade deficit.
   c. a federal budget deficit will have little effect on trade because trade is such a small part of the federal budget.

d. a federal budget deficit encourages savings to grow because people will buy the government's bonds.

8. Which one of the following does *not* describe an aspect of the crowding-out effect?
   a. The government can finance the budget deficit by increasing the quantity of bonds, thereby raising their price and lowering interest rates.
   b. The government can finance the deficit by selling bonds to the Federal Reserve, thereby increasing the money supply.
   c. Government borrowing increases interest rates, which in turn dampens investment.
   d. If government grows, and trade and private saving remain constant, investment must fall.

9. Rising deficits must be paid for by some combination of
   a. rising trade surpluses, rising private savings, and rising investment.
   b. rising trade surpluses, rising private savings, and falling investment.
   c. rising trade deficits, rising private savings, and falling investments.
   d. rising trade deficits, rising private savings, and rising investments.

10. Which one of the following is *not* an asset the government can sell to finance a budget deficit?
    a. offshore oil leases
    b. government land
    c. airwaves (portions of the telecommunications spectrum)
    d. government bonds

Score: ____

If You Got 9 or 10 Correct

You have a good feel for the government budget constraint and the link between budget deficits and trade deficits. Go on to the next section, "The Burden of the Public Debt."

If You Didn't Get at Least 9 Correct

List the three components of the government budget constraint. Then go back to the text and pay special attention to the equation that shows the potential link between budget deficits and trade deficits. This is not an easy equation to work through, because it is a little counterintuitive. You need to get this link down pat. Both of these equations are key equations shown below. After you have reviewed the equations below, continue on to the next section, "The Burden of the Public Debt." ∎

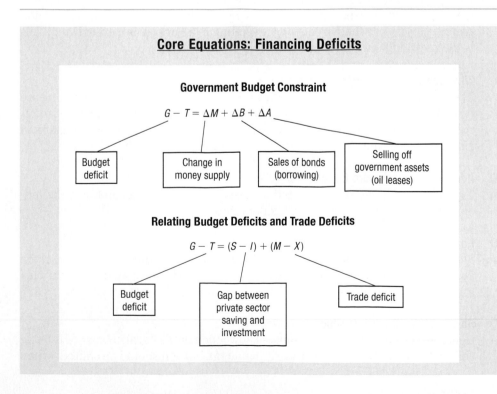

Core Equations: Financing Deficits

Government Budget Constraint

$$G - T = \Delta M + \Delta B + \Delta A$$

| Budget deficit | Change in money supply | Sales of bonds (borrowing) | Selling off government assets (oil leases) |

Relating Budget Deficits and Trade Deficits

$$G - T = (S - I) + (M - X)$$

| Budget deficit | Gap between private sector saving and investment | Trade deficit |

The Burden of the Public Debt

Frequently Asked Questions

Q: What are internally and externally held debt, and why does the difference matter?

A: Much of the national debt held by the public is owned by U.S. banks, corporations, mutual funds, pension plans, and individuals. This is internally held debt. We essentially own this debt. Hence, the taxes collected from a wide array of Americans to pay the interest on this debt is simply paid back out to yet another group of Americans. Foreigners do own part of our national debt. The interest paid on this externally held debt, in other words, the interest paid to foreigners, represents a real claim on our goods and services; it can thus be a real burden on our economy.

Q: Why don't we simply raise taxes and pay off the debt?

A: Many people today "own" some small part of the public debt in their pension plans, but many others do not. If taxes were raised to pay down the debt, those who did not own public debt would be in a worse position than those who did. Servicing the debt requires taxing the general public to pay interest to bondholders. People who own part of the national debt tend to be richer than those who do not. This means money is taken from those at the lower end of the income or wealth distribution and given to those near the top.

Q: What happens to the overall economy when the government sells bonds to the Federal Reserve to finance a budget deficit?

A: When the government runs a deficit, it must sell bonds to either the public or the Federal Reserve. If it sells bonds to the Federal Reserve (which monetizes the debt) when the economy is near full employment, inflation will result.

Q: What happens to the overall economy when the government sells bonds to the public to finance a budget deficit?

A: As the supply of bonds sold on the market rises, prices drop and interest rates rise. The result is that future generations will be bequeathed a smaller and potentially less productive economy, resulting in a lower standard of living. This is the crowding-out effect of deficit spending.

Q: What can lessen the crowding-out effect?

A: The crowding-out effect can be mitigated if the funds from deficit spending are used for public investment. Improvements in the nation's transportation infrastructure, education establishment, and research facilities, for instance, are all aimed at improving the economy's future productive capacity.

Q: How does one measure fiscal sustainability?

A: Two measures have been proposed to assess the fiscal sustainability of the federal budget: fiscal imbalance and generational imbalance.

Q: How is Fiscal Imbalance computed?

A: Ignoring asset sales, fiscal imbalance (FI) computes the difference between the present value of future obligations and expected revenues, assuming that current policies remain unchanged. To be sustainable, FI must equal zero.

Q: How is Generational Imbalance computed?

A: Generational imbalance (GI) estimates how much of the fiscal imbalance is being shifted to future generations. Clearly, some tax burden should be shifted. When current fiscal policy truly invests in the economy, future generations benefit, so some of the present costs may justifiably be shifted to them.

Q: **Does the government have major unfunded liabilities to future generations, and if so, what are they?**

A: The federal government does have huge obligations that extend over long periods. Its two largest programs, Social Security and Medicare, account for one third of all federal spending. Social Security and Medicare are pay-as-you-go programs. The current working generation funds the older generation's benefits; there are no pooled funds waiting to be tapped when needed and as such represent huge unfunded liabilities.

The Burden of the Public Debt Quick Check

Circle the Correct Answer

1. (T/F) Roughly one-quarter of the U.S. total national debt is held by foreign entities.
2. (T/F) An equitable way to pay off the federal debt would be to raise taxes on everyone.
3. (T/F) Roughly half of the U.S. national debt is held by federal agencies.
4. (T/F) One real burden of the public debt is interest paid to foreign bondholders.
5. The crowding-out effect can be mitigated by
   a. the Federal Reserve selling more bonds.
   b. the federal government using deficit spending to give government workers pay increases.
   c. the federal government using deficit spending to fund research spending.
   d. the federal government using deficit spending to encourage current consumption.
6. Which one of the following is *not* correct concerning fiscal sustainability?
   a. For a fiscal policy to be fiscally sustainable, the present value of all projected future revenues must equal the present value of projected future spending.
   b. Generational imbalance is a measure of how much a fiscal imbalance is being shifted to future generations.
   c. It is unfair to shift the present costs of deficit spending on to future generations.
   d. The federal government has large fiscal obligations that extend over long periods.
7. Fiscal policy is *not* currently sustainable because
   a. government accounting is a mess.
   b. Social Security and Medicare are huge pay-as-you-go programs—the current working generation funds the older generation's benefits—with high future liabilities.

c. the government cannot continue to keep running a deficit forever.
   d. politicians will never raise taxes or cut benefits in programs.
8. Fiscal imbalance measures
   a. the difference between current revenues and current spending.
   b. the portion of current deficits being shifted to future generations.
   c. the difference between the present value of future obligations and expected revenues, assuming current policies remain unchanged.
   d. the difference between current revenues and future revenues.
9. The idea of fiscal sustainability arose because
   a. the crowding-out effect has become excessive.
   b. some people have argued that future liabilities of the federal government far exceed projected revenues.
   c. the government cannot run deficits forever.
   d. politicians are always searching for some way to attack the other party.
10. Which one of the following would *not* bring fiscal policy into sustainability in the near future?
    a. Enact massive tax increases to fund future Social Security and Medicare liabilities.
    b. Drastically cut Social Security and Medicare benefits.
    c. Reform government accounting procedures to better estimate future revenues and liabilities.
    d. Abolish automatic stabilizers.

Score: ____

Answers: 1. T; 2. F; 3. T; 4. T; 5. c; 6. c; 7. b; 8. c; 9. b; 10. d

If You Got 9 or 10 Correct

You understand the burden that the public debt will put on this and future generations. Take a quick look at the following "Hints, Tips, and Reminders."

If You Didn't Get at Least 9 Correct

Reviewing the material should be enough. This is not difficult material. Be sure you know the difference between internally and externally held debt, and the real burdens of the national debt. Concentrate for a moment on the issues of fiscal sustainability and generational imbalance when you review this section. Finally, take a look at the following "Hints, Tips, and Reminders." ∎

STEP 4   ## Consider These Hints, Tips, and Reminders

1. The first thing to keep in mind from this chapter is that because of its ability to print money and collect taxes, the federal government cannot go bankrupt, but it is constrained by how deficits must be financed by the following equation:

$$G - T = \Delta M + \Delta B + \Delta A$$

   Each of the following three practices has implications for the economy. Printing too much money (ΔM) can result in inflation. Selling bonds (ΔB) can result in crowding out private investment. Selling assets (ΔA) has limits as well, since the government can eventually run out of assets to sell.

2. The second important conclusion from this chapter is the simple arithmetic of budget and trade deficits as illustrated by

$$G - T = (S - I) + (M - X)$$

   This looks complex, but it is really simple. To see the implications, first assume that $S = I$, so any budget deficit ($G > T$) must be met with a trade deficit ($M > X$).
   Next, assume that imports and exports are balanced ($M = X$), so now any deficit ($G > T$) must be met by ($S > I$), and this means that savings are going into government bonds and not into private investment; thus, the crowding-out effect occurs.

3. The third conclusion to take from this chapter is that the real burden of the debt comes from (1) interest paid to foreign holders of the debt, (2) the impact of crowding out on private investment, and (3) the burden of current public consumption spread to future generations.

Do the Homework for Chapter 23
Federal Deficits and Public Debt

Instructor _____ Time _____ Student _____

Use the answer key below to record your answers to these homework questions.

1. (a) (b) (c) (d)	6. (a) (b) (c) (d)	11. (a) (b) (c) (d)	16. (a) (b) (c) (d)
2. (a) (b) (c) (d)	7. (a) (b) (c) (d)	12. (a) (b) (c) (d)	17. (a) (b) (c) (d)
3. (a) (b) (c) (d)	8. (a) (b) (c) (d)	13. (a) (b) (c) (d)	18. (a) (b) (c) (d)
4. (a) (b) (c) (d)	9. (a) (b) (c) (d)	14. (a) (b) (c) (d)	19. (a) (b) (c) (d)
5. (a) (b) (c) (d)	10. (a) (b) (c) (d)	15. (a) (b) (c) (d)	20. (a) (b) (c) (d)

1. A deficit is defined as
   a. the percent that revenues exceed tax collections.
   b. the dollar amount that federal spending exceed tax collections.
   c. the same thing as the public debt.
   d. all of the above.

2. Public debt consists of
   a. credit card bills of those in the government.
   b. gross domestic product minus personal saving.
   c. the present value of all Social Security payments due in the next 20 years.
   d. treasury securities including treasury bills, notes, bonds, and savings bonds.

3. Public choice analysis
   a. suggests that government is extremely efficient.
   b. suggests that public decision making is inherently flawed and inefficient.
   c. is another form of cost-benefit analysis.
   d. helps government bureaucrats make everyday tough decisions.

4. Public choice economists would argue that
   a. government is efficient and provides many needed services.
   b. deficit spending is necessary when the economy is in a recession.
   c. the size of the public debt is unimportant.
   d. deficit spending is inevitable given the self-interest of politicians.

5. Some economists and politicians have argued that the federal government, like state governments, should be required to balance its budget annually. To do so would
   a. lead to another Great Depression.
   b. lead to procyclical fiscal policy.
   c. result in higher levels of inflation.
   d. make the job of policymakers in Washington easier and more rewarding.

6. Some economists have argued that the federal government's budget should be balanced over the business cycle, running deficits when times are tough and surpluses when times are good. In practice,
   a. raising taxes is a difficult decision for most politicians.
   b. the phases of the business cycle vary in intensity and duration and make balancing the budget over the cycle difficult.
   c. this would happen to some extent automatically if spending and tax rates were stable.
   d. all of the above.

7. The government budget constraint
   a. keeps a lid on federal spending.
   b. means that deficits must be financed by increasing tax rates.
   c. limits the amount of debt a government can finance.
   d. defines how the federal government can finance a deficit.

8. The government budget constraint
   a. says that deficits can be financed by printing money, selling bonds or selling assets.
   b. defines how the federal government can finance a deficit.

c. suggests that government deficits could be financed entirely by printing money.

d. all of the above.

9. Budget and trade deficits

a. are unrelated.

b. are related in that rising deficits must be paid for through rising taxes.

c. tend to move together in the opposite direction.

d. are tied together because rising deficits must be financed by a combination of rising trade deficits, rising private savings, and falling investment.

10. The burden of the national debt is less when

a. it is held by foreigners.

b. interest rates are high.

c. it is held internally.

d. all of the above.

11. When the economy is at full employment and the federal government runs a deficit,

a. selling bonds to the public is a welcomed event for investors who have few alternatives for their money.

b. interest rates will probably fall.

c. rising interest rates will crowd out some private investment.

d. none of the above.

12. Crowding out often occurs

a. when the Federal Reserve buy bonds from the public because the government is running a surplus.

b. when the economy is at full employment and the federal government runs a deficit.

c. when the economy is in a recession and the federal government increases spending for social programs like unemployment compensation and Medicaid.

d. if the Federal Reserve raises reserve requirements and interest rates fall.

13. The crowding-out effect of deficit spending can be mitigated if

a. the federal government focuses its spending on education and research.

b. the Federal Reserve will permit inflation to exceed its targeted levels.

c. the federal government increases spending for social programs like unemployment compensation and Medicaid.

d. consumers will spend more on high-tech products.

14. Generational imbalance in the federal budget

a. is computed and then balanced out by Congress when it passes the budget each year.

b. is roughly $15 trillion at present.

c. is roughly the present value of the difference between future revenues and expenditures assuming current policies remain unchanged.

d. roughly measures how much of the current fiscal imbalance is shifted to future generations.

15. Current national debt and deficit numbers

a. do not accurately portray the extent to which our federal budget is out of balance.

b. are currently measured and reported on a cash basis.

c. do not account for the immense obligations of the federal government that extends over a long period.

d. all of the above.

16. When economists speak of the crowding-out effect of deficit spending, they mean that _____ is crowded out.

a. saving

b. consumption

c. government spending

d. investment

17. If investment and saving are equal ($I = S$) and the federal government is running a deficit, then we would expect

a. our trade balance to be in surplus.

b. that Congress will quickly increase taxes to reduce the deficit.

c. imports to exceed exports.

d. that the Federal Reserve will be rapidly increasing the money supply to accommodate the need of business for more transactions balances.

18. When we speak of the national or public debt, we are referring to

a. U.S. savings bonds.

b. treasury bonds.

c. treasury notes.

d. all of the above.

19. If the federal government were to balance its budget on an annual basis,

a. it would lead to a depression.

b. the business cycle would be dampened.

c. hyperinflation would probably result.

d. swings in the business cycle would probably be more extreme.

20. When the economy enters a recession, we would expect

a. government expenditures to rise.

b. tax revenues to fall.

c. deficits to rise or surpluses to fall.

d. all of the above.

| | Use the ExamPrep to Get Ready for Exams | STEP 6 |

This sheet (front and back) is designed to help you prepare for your exams. The chapter has been boiled down to its key concepts. You are asked to answer questions, define terms, draw graphs, and, if you wish, add summaries of class notes.

Financing the Federal Government

Define the following:

Deficit:

Surplus:

Public debt:

Describe public choice analysis and its implications for public policy:

Describe the following three approaches to federal finance:

Annually balanced budget:

Cyclical balanced budget:

Functional finance:

What is the drawback of each?

Financing Debt and Deficits

Describe the government budget constraint and its implications for public policy:

Describe the relationship between budget and trade deficits:

Describe the implications of this relationship (budget and trade deficits) on financing the deficit:

The Burden of the Public Debt

Describe the following burdens of the public debt:

Externally held debt:

Internally held debt:

Interest payments on the debt:

Discuss the crowding-out effect of private investment in how this effect can be mitigated:

Intergenerational Burdens of Fiscal Policy

Define fiscal sustainability:

Define fiscal imbalance:

Define generational imbalance:

Describe the implications of these measures for public policy:

What are the two government programs that will provide enormous budget pressures in the future? Why?

Additional Study Help Chapterwide Practice Questions

Matching

Match the description with the corresponding term.

___ 1. Deficit
___ 2. Public debt
___ 3. Public choice
___ 4. Annually balanced budget
___ 5. Cyclically balanced budget
___ 6. Functional finance
___ 7. Government budget constraint
___ 8. External debt
___ 9. Internal debt
___ 10. Crowding-out effect
___ 11. Fiscal sustainability

a. Some economists have recommended balancing the budget over the course of the business cycle by restricting spending or raising taxes when the economy is booming to prevent inflationary pressures.

b. Defined by the equation, $G - T = \Delta M + \Delta B + \Delta A$, where G is government spending and T is tax revenues, M is the change in the money supply, ΔB is the change in bonds, and ΔA represents the sales of government assets.

c. Occurs when annual government expenditures exceed tax revenues.

d. The economic analysis of public and political decision making.

e. When the federal government balances its budget every year.

f. The total accumulation of past deficits and surpluses consisting of U.S. Treasury securities including treasury bills, notes, bonds, and U.S. savings bonds.

g. When the government sells bonds to the public to finance deficit spending, prices drop and interest rates rise. As interest rates rise, private investment drops. The result is that future generations will be bequeathed a smaller and potentially less productive economy.

h. That part of our national debt held by foreigners. The interest paid on this represents a real claim on our goods and services, and thus it can be a real burden on our economy.

i. Economists who favor such a policy believe the first priority of policymakers should be to keep the economy at full employment with stable prices; whether the budget is in surplus or deficit is only a secondary concern.

j. That part of national debt owned by U.S. banks, corporations, mutual funds, pension plans, and individuals.

k. The present value of all projected future revenues must be equal to the present value of projected future spending.

Fill-In

Circle the word(s) in parentheses that complete the sentence.

1. When federal tax revenues exceed government spending, the government is running a (deficit, surplus) _____, and when government spending exceeds tax revenues, the federal government is running a (deficit, surplus) _____. The accumulated total of past surpluses and deficits is the national (deficit, debt) _____.

2. Total public debt as a percent of GDP in the United States was roughly (120, 60, 30) _____ % during World War II, but it is approximately (120, 60, 30) _____ % today; currently, public debt held by the public is over (120, 60, 30) _____ % of GDP.

3. Public choice theory integrates economic analysis with (business, household, political) _____ decision making. Public choice analysts typically conclude that public decision making is (efficient, inefficient) _____, because politicians and bureaucrats often focus on (public needs, economic analysis, their self-interest) _____. Public choice theorists typically favor (more, less) _____ government intervention in the market.

4. Balancing the federal budget on an annual basis would lead to the budget having a (pro, counter) _____ cyclical impact on the economy, whereas balancing the budget over the business cycle might reduce the severity of the business cycle, but it is (illegal, not practical) _____.

5. The federal government cannot go bankrupt, but it does face a budget constraint that limits the financing of deficits to printing money, selling assets, and (selling flood insurance along the Gulf

coast, selling bonds, redistributing income) _____.

6. Budget and trade deficits are also linked by the equation $G - T = (S - I) + (M - X)$. When the federal government runs a deficit ($G > T$, $T > G$) _____, and if saving and investment are equal, then ($M > X$, $M < X$) _____. If $M = X$, our trade balance is zero, and the government runs a deficit, then ($I > S$, $S > I$) _____ to pay for the deficit, and this represents (market failure, functional finance, crowding out) _____.

7. Abraham Lincoln noted that (internally, externally) _____ held debt is not a real burden to the country, but the interest on (internally, externally) _____ held debt represents a real claim on our resources. One of the burdens of deficit spending is the crowding out of private investment that occurs when the government sells bonds and increases interest rates, reducing private investment. The impact of crowding out can be reduced if the government directs its spending toward (military purchases, public investment, national health care) _____.

8. When the present value of long-term federal spending exceeds the present value of revenues given current policies, the federal budget is in fiscal (balance, imbalance) _____. Generational imbalance refers to how much of the current fiscal imbalance is shifted to (the elderly, the previous generation, future generations) _____.

True-False

Circle the correct answer.

T/F   1. Treasury notes are financial instruments issued for periods ranging from 1 to 10 years.

T/F   2. Treasury bills (T-bills) are one of the most stable sources of interest in our economy.

T/F   3. James Buchanan, the father of public choice analysis, has argued that politicians and government bureaucrats—unlike private businesspeople—are primarily motivated by the public good in their actions.

T/F   4. Public choice theory suggests that taxpayers would oppose many programs they now support if they were forced to pay the full costs of these programs today as opposed to pushing them off onto future generations.

T/F   5. Prior to the 1930s, most observers agreed that the federal government should try to balance its budget on an annual basis.

T/F   6. Advocates of the functional finance approach to federal financing stress that the government should raise taxes and cut spending during boom times so it can finance deficit spending during recessions, thereby keeping the budget in balance over the long term.

T/F   7. Balancing the federal budget over the course of the business cycle makes good sense in theory, but is difficult to achieve in practice for both technical and political reasons.

T/F   8. Total public debt includes only that debt held by the public, not debt held by government agencies or the Federal Reserve.

T/F   9. Since World War II, the federal government has been in serious danger of going bankrupt on several occasions.

T/F   10. The three primary factors constraining the federal budget are changes in the money supply, changes in the bonds held by the public, and the sales of government assets.

T/F   11. The federal debt is monetized when the government sells bonds to the Federal Reserve.

T/F   12. Asset sales represent a major portion of U.S. government financing.

T/F   13. When the government runs a deficit, it must either borrow funds or sell assets.

T/F   14. When the budget is in deficit ($G > T$), this must be made up either by increased investment ($I > S$) or a trade surplus ($X > M$).

T/F   15. When the government runs significant deficits, this can crowd out private investment.

T/F   16. The crowding-out effect implies that excessive taxation is crowding out consumer spending.

T/F   17. Most of the interest paid on the national debt is lost to the U.S. economy.

T/F   18. When taxes are raised across the board to pay down the national debt, this tends to help lower-income Americans the most.

T/F   19. If the government borrows money to increase its investment in basic research, this may actually spur greater private investment in the future rather than crowding it out.

T/F   20. Using generational accounting, for a fiscal policy to be fiscally sustainable, the present value of all projected future revenues must equal the value of the current federal debt plus the present value of projected future spending.

Multiple Choice

Circle the correct answer.

1. The public debt is
   a. the amount by which annual government expenditures exceed tax revenues.
   b. the amount by which annual tax revenues exceed government expenditure.
   c. the total accumulation of past deficits and surpluses.
   d. the total amount of money private banks, corporations, mutual funds, pension plans, and individuals owe one another.

2. Which of the following is *not* one of the forms the public debt takes?
   a. U.S. savings bonds
   b. mutual funds
   c. treasury notes
   d. treasury bonds

3. Which of the following is *not* one of the conclusions of public choice analysis?
   a. Deficit financing increases the perceived cost of current government operations.
   b. Government action in the economy should be limited.
   c. Politicians and bureaucrats typically pursue self-interest rather than the public good.
   d. Collective decision making is inherently flawed and inefficient.

4. When the economy sinks into recession, the federal budget typically responds automatically with a number of countercyclical measures. Which of the following is one of these automatic, countercyclical responses to a recession?
   a. Government spending drops as overall GDP growth stagnates.
   b. Government spending rises as unemployment claims increase.
   c. Tax revenues increase as incomes rise.
   d. Investment falls as business confidence diminishes.

5. Which approach to federal finances suggests that the government should raise taxes and cut spending during boom times, and cut taxes and increase spending when recession looms?
   a. public choice
   b. annually balanced budget
   c. cyclically balanced budget
   d. functional finance

6. Which of the following equations properly represents the government budget constraint?
   a. $G + T = \Delta M + \Delta B + \Delta A$
   b. $G + T = \Delta I + \Delta S + \Delta A$
   c. $G - T = \Delta S + \Delta A + \Delta T$
   d. $G - T = \Delta M + \Delta B + \Delta A$

7. Which of the following is the *least* significant source of government financing?
   a. tax revenues
   b. the sale of bonds to the public
   c. asset sales
   d. the sale of bonds to the Federal Reserve

8. The federal debt gets monetized when
   a. the Federal Reserve sells bonds.
   b. the Federal Reserve buys bonds.
   c. the government sells treasury bills.
   d. the government buys up treasury bills.

9. If investment and savings are equal ($I = S$) and the federal budget is in surplus ($T > G$), what do we know about the balance of trade?
   a. There is a trade surplus ($X > M$).
   b. There is a trade deficit ($X < M$).
   c. The trade balance is zero ($X = M$).
   d. We cannot know anything about the balance of trade without further information.

10. If the crowding-out effect is in evidence, what is crowding out what?
    a. High tax rates are crowding out business investment.

b. Government deficit spending is crowding out private investment.

c. Consumption is crowding out private savings.

d. Imports are crowding out domestic goods.

11. If budget deficits are rising, which of the following developments will *not* change to meet them?
   a. falling investment
   b. rising private savings
   c. trade deficits
   d. trade surpluses

12. When the government sells bonds to the public, "the public" may include any of the following entities *except*
   a. foreign investors.
   b. mutual funds.
   c. the Federal Reserve.
   d. corporations.

13. Which of the following groups holds the largest portion of the U.S. national debt?
   a. U.S. corporations, mutual funds, pension plans, and individuals
   b. state governments
   c. federal agencies
   d. foreign entities

14. When the government engages in deficit spending, this can crowd out private investment. The crowding-out effect can be mitigated by directing the deficit spending toward any of the following purposes *except*
   a. building more schools.
   b. improving the transportation infrastructure.
   c. subsidizing basic research.
   d. paying the salaries of current government employees.

15. Fiscal imbalance (FI) is a measure of
   a. the difference between the future value of present obligations and current revenues, assuming current policies remain unchanged.
   b. the difference between the present value of future obligations and expected revenues, assuming current policies remain unchanged.
   c. how much current deficits are shifted to future generations.
   d. how much current revenues will be worth in the future.

16. Generational imbalance (GI) is a measure of
   a. the difference between the future value of present obligations and expected revenues, assuming current policies remain unchanged.

b. the difference between the present value of future obligations and expected revenues, assuming current policies remain unchanged.

c. how much of the fiscal imbalance is being shifted to future generations.

d. how much current revenues will be worth in the future.

17. The current national debt held by the public is roughly
   a. $1.2 trillion.
   b. $2.5 trillion.
   c. $3 trillion.
   d. $5 trillion.

18. Assume the government is running a large budget deficit and sells bonds to the Federal Reserve. Which of the following is correct?
   a. The economy feels the effect immediately as an increase in the price level.
   b. The economy will move up the short-run aggregate supply curve to a higher output with a higher price level—and stay there.
   c. The economy will move up the short-run aggregate supply curve in the short run, but eventually price pressures will move the economy back to full employment at a higher price level.
   d. The government would not do this because this is a contractionary monetary policy, pulling reserves from the economy.

19. Assume the government is running a large budget deficit, and so the government sells bonds to the public. What happens?
   a. As the supply of bonds increases, prices drop and interest rates rise. Private investment falls. Private investment is crowded out by this deficit, potentially cutting the size and potential of the future economy.
   b. As the supply of bonds increases, people do not want so many bonds, so interest rates have to fall. This leads to increased investment. This crowds out the government's actions, in the sense that the government will have to offer higher interest rates to sell its bonds.
   c. Government bonds crowd out corporate bonds because people prefer government bonds, so firms cannot raise the investment capital they need to grow.
   d. There is no appreciable change in the economy because the government uses the proceeds from the bond sale for improvements in infrastructure.

Essay-Problem

Answer in the space provided.

The questions below are challenging. Don't get discouraged if your answers are not always the same as those we suggest. Use these as another way to assess your progress, but more importantly, to probe a little more into the issues surrounding deficits and the public debt.

1. Why might the Federal Reserve refuse to buy the government's bonds floated to finance a budget deficit?

2. To change in some degree the Social Security program from pay-as-you-go to a pooled fund, President Bush proposed that each person should be allowed to set up an investment account with a portion of the payroll taxes collected. Give an argument for this proposal. Now, give an argument against this proposal.

3. In March 2004, Alan Greenspan, chairman of the Federal Reserve, stirred up controversy by urging Congress to change the cost-of-living index used to calculate Social Security benefits to be less generous and to raise the age when people can receive retirement benefits. Why did he argue for these changes?

4. Would a public choice proponent be more likely to support budget balancing than functional finance?

5. Consider the September 11, 2001, bombings of the World Trade Center in New York as producing a shock to the U.S. economy. What happened to aggregate demand and aggregate supply? How did this affect the budget of the federal government for 2001 and 2002?

6. If people expect deficits to grow, why would they be reluctant to buy government bonds now?

7. If a private company's debt exceeds its revenue, it can liquidate the business by selling assets and paying off its debts. Is it likely that the federal government will eventually have a "Going Out of Business" asset sale?

8. What is the most likely way for the government to deal with a budget deficit: raise taxes, cut spending, or borrow?

10. Why doesn't the federal government engage in more asset sales to pay off the deficit?

9. If intergenerational burdens are such an issue, why can't this be met by parents increasing their bequests to their children?

What's Next

With this chapter you now have a good understanding of how budget deficits and public debt constrain fiscal and monetary policy. In the next chapter, we look at some key macroeconomic policy challenges facing policymakers. This next chapter takes more of a dynamic perspective on the economy and will further pull together much of what you have learned about fiscal and monetary policy.

Answers to Chapterwide Practice Questions

Matching

1. c	4. e	7. b	10. g
2. f	5. a	8. h	11. k
3. d	6. i	9. j	

Fill-In

1. surplus, deficit, debt
2. 120, 60, 30
3. political, inefficient, their self-interest, less
4. pro, not practical
5. selling bonds
6. $G > T$, $M > X$, $S > I$, crowding out
7. internally, externally, public investment
8. imbalance, future generations

True-False

1. T	6. F	11. T	16. F
2. F	7. T	12. F	17. F
3. F	8. F	13. T	18. F
4. T	9. F	14. F	29. T
5. T	10. T	15. T	20. F

Multiple Choice

1. c	6. d	11. d	16. c
2. b	7. c	12. c	17. d
3. a	8. b	13. c	18. c
4. b	9. a	14. d	19. a
5. c	10. b	15. b	

Essay-Problem

1. When the Federal Reserve buys government bonds, it monetizes the debt, it pumps new money into the financial system in return for purchasing the government's bonds. This new money increases the money supply. The Federal Reserve watches the growth in the money supply, and the Fed may not want to increase it to the extent that it would if it bought all or most of the government's bonds. This is why the money supply acts as a constraint on how much deficit financing the government can do.

2. A major argument for this proposal is that by turning Social Security more into a pooled fund program, it will relieve projected liabilities on future generations. A major argument against this proposal is that it may encourage people to invest recklessly, because they will calculate that the government will not let them starve if they gamble away all of their money.

3. Behind Greenspan's comments on Social Security was a concern about projected future Social Security liabilities and fiscal sustainability. Both of his suggestions—dampening the growth in benefits and raising the age for when people could receive these benefits—would lower future liabilities.

4. Probably yes. Public choice proponents are concerned with voters shifting the cost of programs on to future generations, and thus running deficits. By seeking some type of budget balancing, current programs are paid for by current revenues. Liabilities on future generations will likely be smaller.

5. After the bombings, economic activity dropped. Aggregate demand fell as companies postponed business trips and individuals postponed or canceled trips and vacations. Airlines and hotels were hurt by this drop in demand: They had all of this unused supply, so their profits fell. The general economic downturn held tax revenues in check, while some government spending on relief increased. It is not surprising that by 2002 the federal budget was running a deficit.

6. As budget deficits grow, the government floats more and more bonds. This drives up interest rates. When interest rates rise, current holders of government debt suffer because the price of their bonds falls. This means that current potential bondholders have to deal with the strong possibility that their investment will fall in value in the future. They will seek compensation for this—in higher interest rates.

7. Highly unlikely. The government has much that it can do before it concentrates on asset sales. It can always print money, up to some point, of course, but that point is far away from where the government is now.

8. Politicians avoid raising taxes and cutting spending because neither policy helps them with the electorate. Borrowing is the more likely course for the government to take.

9. Increasing bequests can come about by increasing current savings. As we saw in earlier chapters, the savings rate in the United States is abysmally low. It is overoptimistic to think that this savings rate will change significantly for the better.

10. As long as the federal government can borrow what it needs, it does not need to sell off assets. There is no pressure to do so.

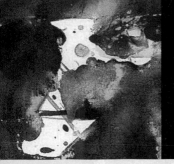

Macroeconomic Policy Challenges

24

How Effective Is Macroeconomic Policymaking?

In earlier chapters, we discussed fiscal and monetary policy, analyzing when they might be effective and when not. In the last chapter, we saw how long-term liabilities from Social Security and Medicare will make fiscal policy unsustainable. We now want to take one final look at the effectiveness of fiscal and monetary policy. In particular, we want to look at recent challenges to macroeconomic policymaking. We start by looking at Phillips curves, which postulate a negative relationship between inflation and unemployment, and consider whether this holds in the long run and the short run. We then go on to consider the rational expectations theory, a recent development that questions whether policies can be effective even in the short run. Finally, we look at jobless recoveries, a situation that occurs when the economy pulls out of a recession but does not produce the jobs it has in previous recoveries. Throughout, the question is: Can macroeconomic policy still be effective?

This Is What You Need to Know

After studying this chapter you should be able to

- Explain what Phillips curves are and what relationship they postulate between inflation and unemployment.

- Describe the natural rate of unemployment.

- Describe stagflation.

- Describe how inflationary expectations can take on a life of their own and stymie policymakers.

- Describe adaptive expectations and its major drawback.

- Describe rational expectations and its implications for policymakers.

- Critique the rational expectations theory.

- Describe what jobless recoveries are.

- Explain why jobless recoveries might arise.

STEP 2 — Review the Key Terms

Phillips curve: The original curve posited a negative relationship between wages and unemployment, but later versions related unemployment to inflation rates.

Natural rate of unemployment: The level of unemployment where price and wage decisions are consistent; a level at which the actual inflation rate is equal to people's inflationary expectations, and cyclical unemployment is zero.

Inflationary expectations: The rate of inflation expected by workers for any given period. Workers do not work for a specific nominal wage but for what those wages will buy (real wages), so their inflationary expectations are an important determinant of what nominal wage they are willing to work for.

Stagflation: Simultaneous occurrence of rising inflation and rising unemployment.

Adaptive expectations: Inflationary expectations are formed from a simple extrapolation from past events.

Rational expectations: Rational economic agents are assumed to make the best possible use of all publicly available information, then make informed, rational judgments on what the future holds. Any errors in their forecasts will be randomly distributed.

Efficiency wage theory: Employers often pay their workers wages above the market-clearing level to improve morale and productivity, reduce turnover, and create a disincentive for employees to shirk their duties.

Jobless recovery: Takes place after a recession, when output begins to rise, but employment growth does not.

STEP 3 — Work Through the Chapter Tutorials

Unemployment and Inflation: Phillips Curves

Frequently Asked Questions

Q: **What was the original discovery made by A. W. Phillips?**
A: In Britain, A. W. Phillips found a negative relationship between unemployment rates and money wages. When unemployment falls, wages rise as firms bid up the price of labor to attract more workers; in contrast, when unemployment rises, wages fall.

Q: What are Phillips curves?

A: Unemployment was later connected to inflation, and the tradeoff between inflation and unemployment has become known as the Phillips curve.

Q: Does a rise in wages always lead to a rise in prices?

A: A rise in wages may lead to a rise in prices, but if worker productivity increases enough to offset the wage increase, product prices can remain stable. The basic relationship among wages, prices, and productivity is $p = w - q$,

where:

p = rate of inflation

w = rate of increase in nominal wages

q = rate of increase in labor productivity

Q: What is the natural rate of unemployment?

A: The natural rate of unemployment is the rate at which inflationary expectations match inflation, and thus inflationary pressures in the economy are nonexistent. This unemployment rate is also known as the nonaccelerating inflation rate of unemployment (NAIRU), and it is often thought to be around 5%. It also is when cyclical unemployment is zero.

Q: What do Phillips curves suggest for policymakers?

A: A negative relationship between unemployment and inflation is represented by the Phillips curve. It suggests that the economy presents policymakers with a menu of choices. By accepting modest inflation, policymakers can keep unemployment low. This is shown in Figure 1. Policymakers can move unemployment lower (a movement from point a to point b) by accepting modest inflation (moving from 0 to p_1 on the vertical axis).

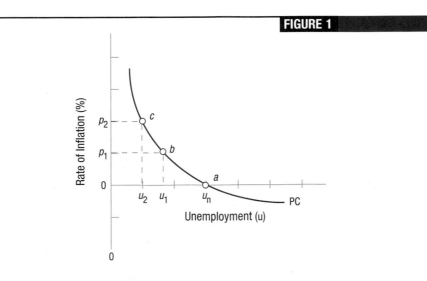

FIGURE 1

Q: What is stagflation, and when did it occur?

A: In the 1970s, policymakers and economists were stymied by the onset of stagflation, when unemployment and inflation rates approached double digits. Unlike the Phillips relationship, which postulated that unemployment would go down when inflation went up, unemployment and inflation both went up.

Q: Do workers incorporate inflationary expectations into their wage negotiations?

A: Workers do not work for the sake of earning a specific nominal wage, but for what this money will buy: a real wage. When bargaining for wage increases, workers will take their past experiences with inflation into account.

Q: What formula links wage increases to unemployment and expected inflation?

A: Wage increases can be related to unemployment and expected inflation by the equation $w = f(u) + p^e$,

where

w = wage increase

$f(u)$ (read "a function of unemployment") = relationship between unemployment and wage increases

p^e = inflationary expectations

Q: What is the wage negotiation process if workers do not expect inflation, but inflation occurs?

A: If workers do not expect inflation, but policymakers trigger inflation to stimulate output and reduce unemployment below its natural rate, then output will rise, and real wages will fall as product prices rise. Workers will then start demanding contract revisions to raise their nominal wages, restoring output to its previous level, but at a higher price level.

Q: What is the wage negotiation process if workers expect inflation, and what does it imply for policymakers?

A: If workers expect a certain rate of inflation when they negotiate their contracts, they will demand a higher nominal wage to account for the expected rise in prices. Thus, if policymakers want to raise output, they must raise inflation to a level even higher than workers expect. This suggests that if policymakers want to keep unemployment consistently below its natural rate, they must be willing to accept a constantly accelerating rate of inflation. This is shown in Figure 2. Note how the economy moves from points a to b to c to d to e, and how inflation ratchets up in Panel B.

FIGURE 2

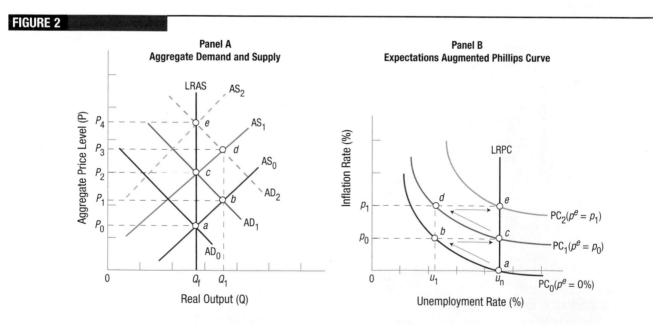

Panel A
Aggregate Demand and Supply

Panel B
Expectations Augmented Phillips Curve

Q: What must policymakers do to get rid of inflationary pressures?

A: If policymakers want to curtail inflationary pressures when they arise, they must be willing to curtail growth in aggregate demand and accept the resulting higher rates of unemployment for a transitional period. As aggregate demand slumps, wage and price pressures will soften, reducing inflationary expectations. As these expectations decline, the Phillips curve will shift leftward, returning the economy to lower inflation and unemployment rates.

Keep in Mind

As workers' inflationary expectations increase, and if policymakers maintain unemployment at a level below the natural rate, then policymakers must be willing to accept a constantly accelerating rate of inflation.

Also, curing inflation pressures requires policymakers to curtail growth in aggregate demand and accept higher unemployment rates during the transition to lower inflation and unemployment rates.

Core Equation: Inflation

$p = w - q$ — Inflation (p) is equal to nominal wages (w) minus the rate of increase in productivity (q). Higher levels of productivity increase permit higher levels of wage increases before inflation becomes an issue.

Unemployment and Inflation: Phillips Curves Quick Check

Circle the Correct Answer

1. (T/F) The original Phillips relationship showed that when unemployment falls, money wages tend to rise.
2. (T/F) Everything else being equal, an increase in worker productivity will lead to a rise in prices.
3. (T/F) The natural rate of unemployment is also called the NAIRU (nonadjusting inflation rate of unemployment).
4. (T/F) The Phillips curve, together with empirical data collected in the 1960s, suggests that keeping the economy at full employment (unemployment = 4%) requires holding the inflation rate at about 3–4%.
5. At the natural rate of unemployment, net inflationary pressures will be
   a. very strong.
   b. nonexistent.
   c. modest, approaching 5%.
   d. negative.
6. Stagflation
   a. is the same as the original relationship between inflation and unemployment shown in the Phillips curve, but the changes occur more slowly.
   b. occurs when inflation becomes stagnant (stable).
   c. is higher inflation met by higher unemployment, not lower unemployment.
   d. is quickly mitigated by increasing aggregate demand.
7. Once workers come to expect inflation, what can policymakers do to lower inflationary expectations?
   a. Increase aggregate demand but make public announcements so workers will know what is going on.
   b. Stop the growth in aggregate demand and accept the higher unemployment that will follow in the transition period.
   c. Announce widespread policy changes but actually do nothing, deceiving workers into lowering their inflationary expectations.
   d. Engage in contractionary monetary policies balanced by expansionary fiscal policies.
8. Which equation properly expresses the relationship among wage increases, unemployment, and expected inflation?
   a. $p = w - q$
   b. $w = f(u) + p^e$
   c. $p = w + q$
   d. $w = p^e + q$
9. If workers expect a certain rate of inflation when they negotiate their contracts,
   a. policymakers must decrease aggregate demand before the contracts are negotiated.
   b. policymakers must be willing to accept a constantly accelerating rate of inflation if they want to keep unemployment consistently below its natural rate.
   c. policymakers must use expansionary policies just to keep unemployment at the natural rate.
   d. policymakers must keep policies secret in order for them to be successful.
10. Phillips curve and natural rate analysis suggest that inflation expectations adjust
    a. only if workers are deceived about policymaking.
    b. immediately.
    c. with a noticeable lag.
    d. only after a period of stagflation has set in.

Score: _____

If You Got 9 or 10 Correct

You seem to have a good grasp of Phillips curves and what policy choices they imply. You could go on to the next section, "Rational Expectations and Policy Formation." However, this is the toughest of the three sections in this chapter, and you might want to review the material below just to make sure that you have a good understanding of Phillips curves.

If You Didn't Get at Least 9 Correct

Don't worry, you are nearing the end of the course, and this is the toughest material in the chapter. It may take some extra effort to master this material. The Phillips curve is really a dynamic representation of the aggregate demand and supply model we have been using all along. We are now modeling inflation: *price changes over time*. This adds another layer of complexity to our analysis. Let's work our way through some of the issues. ■

Wages, Productivity, and Inflation

If wages are rising by 3%, and productivity is growing at a 3% rate, how high will inflation be?

The answer is relatively straightforward, because if you are paying workers more, and they are producing more, then higher costs or prices should not be the result. The 3% increase in productivity offsets the 3% increase in wages, so inflation should be zero.

■ Note, with 3% wage increases and a 3% productivity increase, inflation is zero and workers' real wages (and standards of living) have risen by 3%.

■ This simple relationship, $p = w - q$, ties real economic growth, greater productivity, and rising real standards of living together.

■ Note also that if wage increases are 3%, and productivity is not growing, inflation will be 3%, and workers gain nothing.

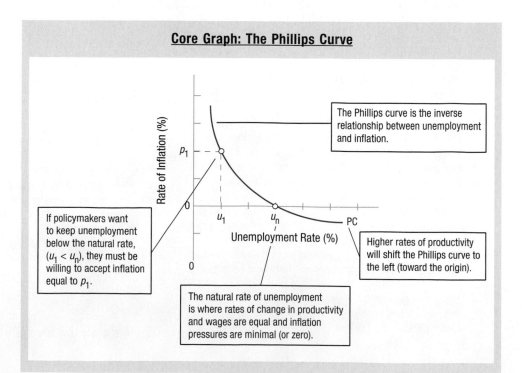

Core Graph: The Phillips Curve

The Phillips curve is the inverse relationship between unemployment and inflation.

If policymakers want to keep unemployment below the natural rate, $(u_1 < u_n)$, they must be willing to accept inflation equal to p_1.

Higher rates of productivity will shift the Phillips curve to the left (toward the origin).

The natural rate of unemployment is where rates of change in productivity and wages are equal and inflation pressures are minimal (or zero).

Adding Inflationary Expectations

We have seen that the Phillips curve is just the negative relationship between inflation and unemployment. Let's write this relationship as $p = f(u)$, so we don't have to write so many words. Remember that p represents inflation. We also know that labor productivity is q, so the relationship becomes

$$p = f(u) - q$$

Graphically, this is shown in Figure 3.

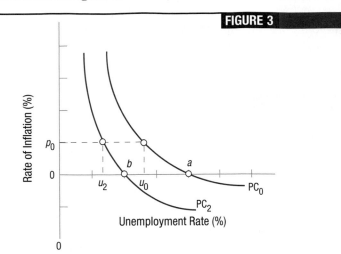

FIGURE 3

In Figure 3, if rates of productivity increase grow from zero (PC_0) to 2% annually, the Phillips curve shifts inward to PC_2, and the natural rate of unemployment is also lower (moving from point a to point b).

Thus, for any Phillips curve, higher rates of productivity will shift the curve toward the origin, and the tradeoff between a given level of unemployment and inflation (p_0) will be better (u_2 versus u_0). Again, higher rates of productivity are good for the economy.

Unfortunately, the same cannot be said for higher inflationary expectations. Inflationary expectations lead to inflationary pressures, so our Philips curve relationship becomes

$$p = f(u) - q + p^e$$

Rising expectations result in the Phillips curve relationship becoming worse for policymakers as the curve shifts rightward, as shown in Figure 4. As inflationary expec-

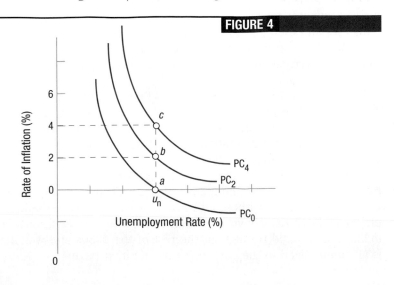

FIGURE 4

tations grow from zero at the natural rate to 2% and then 4% the Phillips curve shifts rightward to PC_2 and PC_4. Note that the inflation rate at point a, b, and c are all equal to inflationary expectations, and unemployment is at the natural rate.

Inflationary expectations raise a difficult dilemma for policymakers: If policymakers try to use aggregate demand policies to hold employment below the natural rate they must be willing to accept accelerating rates of inflation. Let's see why this is true.

Let's begin with unemployment at the natural rate in Figure 5 (assumed to be 6%) and inflation at zero (point a on Phillips curve PC_0). Now assume that policymakers decide to use aggregate demand policies to keep the economy at 4% unemployment. Since 4% unemployment is often suggested as full employment, this may seem like a reasonable fiscal policy. So what happens?

FIGURE 5

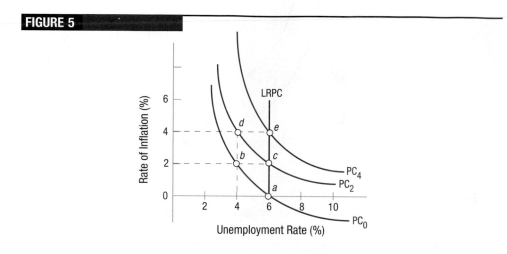

First, the economy moves up to point b, where inflation rises to 2% and unemployment is 4%. An inflation rate of 2% would typically seem like to reasonable tradeoff to get 1 to 2 million more people employed.

But now with inflation at 2%, workers began to expect 2% inflation, so the Phillips tradeoff moves to PC_2, and unemployment gradually moves back to 6% (point c), with inflation now equaling expected inflation of 2%.

Now, to reduce unemployment to 4%, policymakers again increase aggregate demand, and the economy moves up PC_2 to point d in the short run, where the inflation rate is now 4%. Workers begin to expect 4% inflation, and as time marches on, the economy moves back to the natural rate of unemployment, but now at point e on PC_4, and inflation remains equal to expectations.

Thus, to keep unemployment at 4% by increasing aggregate demand and continuing to increase aggregate demand as needed, inflation increases from 2% to 4% to 6%, and so on.

The economy has moved to a point like e with inflation at 4%, and bringing the economy back to point a, with zero inflation at the natural rate of unemployment, is a challenge. Policymakers have to let unemployment rise above the natural rate to cool inflationary expectations. Since this often requires engineering a recession, policymakers do not relish the idea.

At the end of the Carter presidency, for example, both inflation and interest rates were each approaching 20% (yes, 20%). Inflationary expectations were not going to be reduced without a serious recession. The 1981–83 recession saw unemployment rates rise above 10%; thus inflationary expectations dampened, and disinflation continued throughout the rest of the 1980s and well into the 1990s. This is all summarized in the core graph on the next page.

Core Graph: The Phillips Curve and Accelerating Inflation

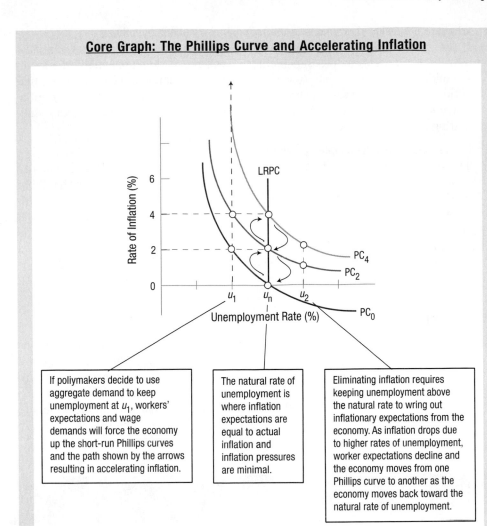

If poliymakers decide to use aggregate demand to keep unemployment at u_1, workers' expectations and wage demands will force the economy up the short-run Phillips curves and the path shown by the arrows resulting in accelerating inflation.

The natural rate of unemployment is where inflation expectations are equal to actual inflation and inflation pressures are minimal.

Eliminating inflation requires keeping unemployment above the natural rate to wring out inflationary expectations from the economy. As inflation drops due to higher rates of unemployment, worker expectations decline and the economy moves from one Phillips curve to another as the economy moves back toward the natural rate of unemployment.

Rational Expectations and Policy Formation

Frequently Asked Questions

Q: **What is the adaptive expectations model, and what is its drawback?**

A: The adaptive expectations model assumes that people form their future expectations by extrapolating from past events. The natural rate of employment model discussed in the previous section is an example of an adaptive expectations model. Workers, for example, are assumed to expect that past rates of inflation, averaged over some time period, will continue into the future. Adaptive expectations theory is therefore a *backward-looking* model of expectations.

Q: **What are the main components of the rational expectations model, and how does it differ from the adaptive expectations model?**

A: The rational expectations model assumes that rational economic agents will use all publicly available information in forming their expectations. This information may include past data, but it will also include current policy announcements and all other relevant information. In this sense, rational expectations theory is a *forward-looking* model of expectations.

Q: **What are the policy implications of the rational expectations hypothesis?**

A: If the rational expectations hypothesis is correct, the implications for policymakers will be enormous. Specifically, it will mean that policymakers cannot stimulate output in the short run by raising inflation unless they keep their actions secret. Otherwise, workers would accurately predict the coming inflation and raise their wage demands immediately, thus raising prices without stimulating an increase in output.

Q: **Has rational expectations been proven to be correct?**

A: The empirical record of rational expectations theory is mixed. New Keynesian economists have critiqued this theory on theoretical grounds, arguing that labor markets are often beset with imperfect information, and that efficiency wages often bring about short-term wage stickiness. (Efficiency wages are wages set above the market-clearing level to improve worker morale and productivity, and decrease turnover.) If wages are sticky, neither workers nor firms can react quickly to changes in monetary or fiscal policy, thus giving such policies a chance of having short-term impacts.

Keep in Mind

The adaptive expectations model assumes people form their future expectations based on an extrapolation of past events (backward looking). The rational expectations model assumes people use all available information to form their future expectations (forward looking).

The rational expectations model suggests that policymakers cannot stimulate output in the short run unless they are able to keep their actions secret.

Rational Expectations and Policy Formation Quick Check

Circle the Correct Answer

1. (T/F) Rational expectations theory is a backward-looking model of expectations: People form expectations based on past experience.
2. (T/F) Rational expectations theory advocates a strong role for the Federal Reserve and the federal government in managing the nation's economy.
3. (T/F) Efficiency wages are wages below market wages that encourage workers to avoid shirking their responsibilities.
4. (T/F) For rational expectations theory to hold, most people have to act rationally most of the time.
5. The rational expectations model assumes that
   a. everyone's expectations will be correct.
   b. mistakes in expectations will tend to clump within the group of workers, not policymakers.
   c. rational economic agents will make the best possible use of all publicly available information.
   d. rational economic agents will focus on illegal inside information.
6. If rational expectations theory is correct, government policymaking
   a. will be effective in the short run but ineffective in the long run.

b. will be effective in the long run but ineffective in the short run.
   c. always will be effective both in the short run and the long run.
   d. will be ineffective in the long run and the short run, unless it is engaged in secretly, in which case it might be effective only in the short run.
7. Which one of the following is *not* a new Keynesian critique of rational explanations?
   a. Efficiency wages often bring about wage stickiness in the short term.
   b. Labor markets are not highly competitive because they are often beset with imperfect information.
   c. People are not rational all of the time.
   d. All labor is not equal.
8. The Federal Reserve announces that it will increase the money supply next month when the Federal Open Market Committee (FOMC) meets. According to rational expectations theory,
   a. the market waits until this policy goes into effect, then adapts to it.
   b. the market immediately undertakes actions as if the policy already was in place.
   c. rational economic agents examine the Federal Reserve's public record to determine if the Fed-

eral Reserve has always followed through on its announcements.

d. rational economic agents ignore the policy announcement if they think the policy is irrational.

9. Which one of the following is *not* correct concerning efficiency wages?

a. They are wages set above market-clearing wages.

b. An employer may use them to improve productivity and morale.

c. They provide a disincentive for shirking.

d. They help get rid of the "sticky wage" problem.

10. Which one of the following is *not* correct?

a. Rational expectations theory suggests that policy-

making will be ineffective in the short run as well as the long run.

b. New Keynesians believe labor markets adjust much more slowly than the rational expectations model predicts.

c. Rational expectations theory is bound to be incorrect because it postulates rational economic agents.

d. Adaptive expectations is a backward-looking model.

Score: ____

Answers: 1. F; 2. F; 3. F; 4. F; 5. c; 6. d; 7. c; 8. b; 9. d; 10. c

If You Got 9 or 10 Correct

You have the concept of rational expectations, its policy implications, and its critique down pat. Go on to the next section on hints, tips, and reminders.

If You Didn't Get at Least 9 Correct

Be sure you know what the theory of rational expectations implies for the effectiveness of policymaking. Go back to the book, paying special attention to the new Keynesian critique of rational expectations. In one sentence, write down a criticism of rational expectations. Then, stop for a moment and mull over the policymaking implications of rational expectations theory and the New Keynesian critique. When you are confident you understand these points, continue on to the next section on jobless recoveries. ■

Consider These Hints, Tips, and Reminders STEP 4

1. In this chapter, spend most of your time on the Phillips curve, what makes it shift, and the role inflationary expectations play. By concentrating on this first section, you will be focusing your time on the most difficult material.

2. Look at this chapter as a summary of how economic theory progresses over time and how different debates work through their way through history.

■ The original work by A. W. Phillips was a historical-empirical look at the changes in money wages related to unemployment.

■ Economists then put a theoretical apparatus behind the curve and related inflation to unemployment.

■ Policymakers began to treat the stable 1960s relationship as a menu from which they could select inflation rates with a given level of unemployment: a simple tradeoff.

■ Stagflation of the 1970s was a shock to policymakers and economists alike as inflation and unemployment both increased and reached double digits.

■ Economists Friedman and Phelps then developed theories to explain stagflation and accelerating inflation by incorporating adaptive inflationary expectations into the model.

■ Then economists wondered why people would wait so long to adjust their expectations about inflation. Rational expectations grew on this inquiry.

■ Today, we see an emphasis in monetary policymaking to keep inflation under control and inflationary expectations at bay. The lessons learned in the 1970s and 1980s were not lost on policymakers, and so policymaking today seems to keep the economy on a steadier course.

3. Remember that the adjustment that occurs from inflationary expectations when the economy grows beyond full employment comes through short-run aggregate supply as workers demand wage adjustments.

4. The fact that the last two recessions (1990–91 and 2001) have shown different patterns of job growth illustrates the inherent difficulty in controlling our economy. This shows why macroeconomic policymaking cannot simply consist of simple rules. Our economy is dynamic, constantly changing, and evolving through technology and our economic relationships with the rest of the world.

Do the Homework for Chapter 24
Macroeconomic Policy Challenges

Instructor _____ Time _____ Student _____

Use the answer key below to record your answers to these homework questions.

1. (a) (b) (c) (d)   6. (a) (b) (c) (d)   11. (a) (b) (c) (d)   16. (a) (b) (c) (d)
2. (a) (b) (c) (d)   7. (a) (b) (c) (d)   12. (a) (b) (c) (d)   17. (a) (b) (c) (d)
3. (a) (b) (c) (d)   8. (a) (b) (c) (d)   13. (a) (b) (c) (d)   18. (a) (b) (c) (d)
4. (a) (b) (c) (d)   9. (a) (b) (c) (d)   14. (a) (b) (c) (d)   19. (a) (b) (c) (d)
5. (a) (b) (c) (d)   10. (a) (b) (c) (d)   15. (a) (b) (c) (d)   20. (a) (b) (c) (d)

1. The Phillips curve
   a. was devised by John Maynard Keynes during the 1930s.
   b. shows why unemployment increases when inflation rises.
   c. shows the negative relationship between unemployment and inflation.
   d. shows how productivity and wages are related.

2. A. W. Phillips, when developing the now-famous Phillips curve,
   a. was interested in how money wages in the United States differed from wages in Britain and South America.
   b. tried to develop a theory of why unemployment increases when inflation rises.
   c. focused on the positive relationship between unemployment and inflation.
   d. empirically compared the rate of change of money wages to unemployment in Britain from 1861 to 1957.

3. The curve in Figure HW-1 is a
   a. rational expectations curve.
   b. demand for inflation curve.
   c. Phillips curve.
   d. curve that shows how productivity and wages are related.

4. A curve like the one in Figure HW-1 suggests that
   a. the tradeoff between unemployment and inflation was quite volatile.
   b. inflation was inevitable in the economy.
   c. there were no real tradeoffs between inflation and unemployment.
   d. policymakers could simply select the level of unemployment and inflation they desired for the economy.

5. Point a in Figure HW-1 represents
   a. the nonaccelerating inflation rate of unemployment.
   b. the natural rate of unemployment.
   c. an unemployment rate where inflation pressures are nonexistent.
   d. all of the above.

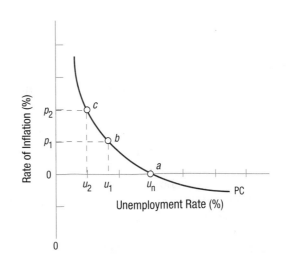

HW-1

6. The basic relationship among wages, prices, and productivity is
   a. that they are unrelated.
   b. inflation is equal to the rate of change in nominal wages plus the rate of change in labor productivity.
   c. if nominal wages rise by 5%, then inflation will also increase by 5%.
   d. inflation is equal to the rate of change in nominal wages minus the rate of change in labor productivity.

7. Stagflation occurs when
   a. unemployment is low and inflation is high.
   b. both unemployment and inflation are high.
   c. both unemployment and inflation are low.
   d. unemployment is high and inflation is low.

8. If policymakers want to increase employment and output above the natural rate,
   a. they must do it gradually.
   b. they are out of luck; it cannot be done.
   c. they must be willing to accept a higher rate of inflation in the short run and accelerating inflation in the longer term.
   d. they must be willing to accept a lower rate of inflation.

9. In Figure HW-2, the natural rate of unemployment is
   a. 8%.
   b. 6%.
   c. 4%.
   d. 0.

10. In Figure HW-2, inflationary expectations are adaptive. If policymakers wish to keep unemployment continually below the natural rate, they will have to
    a. accept an accelerating rate of inflation.
    b. adopt policies that shift the Phillips curve to PC$_2$.
    c. move the economy to point e.
    d. lower federal income taxes on people with incomes below $10,000.

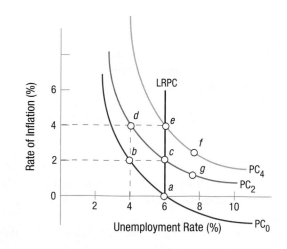

HW-2

11. In Figure HW-2, inflationary expectations are adaptive. Assume that the economy is initially at point e with inflation at 4% and unemployment at 6%. If policymakers wish to reduce inflation to zero by reducing aggregate demand,
    a. they will have to accept an accelerating rate of inflation.
    b. they will have to adopt policies that shift the Phillips curve outward.

    c. the economy will move to point a by following a path through points *efcga*.

    d. the economy will move immediately (or very quickly) to point a.

12. In Figure HW-2, assume that inflationary expectations follow the rational expectations model. Assume the economy is initially at point e with inflation at 4% and unemployment at 6%. If policymakers wish to reduce inflation to zero by reducing aggregate demand,

    a. they will have to accept an accelerating rate of inflation.

    b. the economy will resist the reduction in aggregate demand as consumers attempt to maintain their lifestyles.

    c. the economy will move to point a by following a path through points *efcga*.

    d. the economy will move immediately (or very quickly) to point a.

13. Rational expectations

    a. are backward looking.

    b. rely on people understanding economics and finance and being able to predict the future.

    c. assume that people use all publicly available information to make decisions.

    d. require rational people to adopt the Keynesian macroeconomic model when making a decision affecting the economy

14. Rational expectations

    a. are forward looking.

    b. rely on people understanding economics and finance and being able to predict the future.

    c. assume that rational economic actors base their decisions on inside information.

    d. require rational people to adopt the Keynesian macroeconomic model when making a decision affecting the economy.

15. Assume the economy in Figure HW-3 on the next page is initially in equilibrium at point a, with the aggregate price level at P_0 and output at full employment (Q_f). Now assume policymakers increase aggregate demand to AD_1. If expectations in the economy are rational,

    a. the economy will move to point b.

    b. the economy will move to point b in the short run and gradually move back to point a in the long run.

    c. the economy will move to point b in the short run and gradually move to point c in the long run.

    d. the economy will move to point c very quickly.

16. Assume the economy in Figure HW-3 is initially in equilibrium at point a, with the aggregate price level at P_0 and output at full employment (Q_f). Now assume policymakers increase aggregate demand to AD_1. If expectations in the economy are adaptive,

   a. the economy will move to point b and remain there.

   b. the economy will move to point b in the short run and gradually move back to point a in the long run.

   c. the economy will move to point b in the short run and gradually move to point c in the long run as workers update their expectations to a higher price level.

   d. the economy will move to point c very quickly.

17. Assume the economy in Figure HW-3 is initially in equilibrium at point a, with the aggregate price level at P_0 and output at full employment (Q_f). If policymakers wish to expand output beyond Q_f in the long run, they would need to

   a. expand aggregate demand to AD_1.

   b. increase taxes on capital to expand the Social Security program.

   c. introduce fiscal policies that would shift the long-run aggregate supply (LRAS) curve to the right.

   d. none of the above would expand output beyond Q_f.

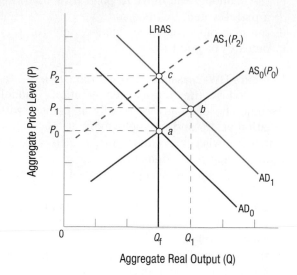

HW-3

18. If the rational expectations critique of policymaking is correct, then

   a. policymakers will be unable to keep unemployment below the natural rate.

   b. when, for example, the Federal Reserve announces a policy change, economic actors will anticipate the long-run results and will move immediately to that equilibrium.

   c. the short-term aspects of public economic policy changes will become mostly ineffective.

   d. all of the above.

19. When output begins to grow at the trough of a recession and employment fails to grow, we call this a

   a. recession.

   b. jobless recovery.

   c. depression.

   d. lagging recovery.

20. Several factors seem to be driving jobless recoveries, including

   a. outsourcing.

   b. rapid increases in productivity.

   c. changes in employment patterns.

   d. all of the above.

Use the ExamPrep to Get Ready for Exams   STEP 6

This sheet (front and back) is designed to help you prepare for your exams. The chapter has been boiled down to its key concepts. You are asked to answer questions, define terms, draw graphs, and, if you wish, add summaries of class notes.

Unemployment and Inflation: Phillips Curves

Describe Phillips curves:

Draw a typical Phillips curve in the grid below.

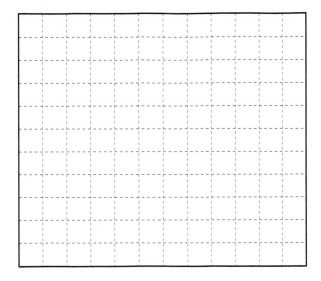

Describe the algebraic relationship among productivity, prices, and wages:

What is stagflation?

Describe the impact of inflationary expectations on Phillips curves:

Describe the natural rate of unemployment:

Explain what policymakers must do to reduce inflationary pressures:

Using the grid below, explain why an economy encounters accelerating inflation if policymakers use fiscal or monetary policy to keep the unemployment rate below the natural rate:

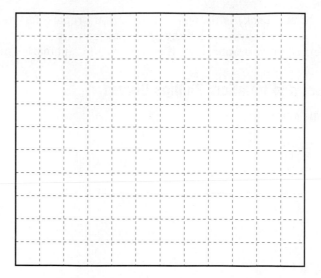

Rational Expectations and Policy Formation

Define rational expectations:

What are the implications for policymakers if the rational expectations hypothesis is correct?

How important has the concept of rational expectations proven to be for policymakers?

Are Job Recoveries Becoming "Jobless Recoveries"?

Define a jobless recovery:

List some of the reasons for jobless recoveries:

Additional Study Help Chapterwide Practice Questions

Matching

Match the description with the corresponding term.

___ 1. Phillips curve
___ 2. Natural rate of unemployment
___ 3. Inflationary expectations
___ 4. Rational expectations
___ 5. Efficiency wage
___ 6. Jobless recovery

a. The rate of unemployment at which expected inflation is equal to actual inflation, such that there are no inflationary pressures on the economy. Also known as the nonaccelerating inflation rate of unemployment (NAIRU).
b. A wage higher than a market-clearing wage, given to improve morale and decrease worker turnover.
c. When economic actors expect a certain amount of inflation, they take any expected price changes into account when negotiating wages or engaging in other economic activities.
d. A stable negative correlation between inflation and unemployment.
e. Once the trough of a business cycle has been passed and output has begun to grow, employment fails to grow.
f. Assumes that economic agents will make the best possible use of all publicly available information in forming their expectations. This information can include past data, but it will also include current policy announcements and any other pieces of information that might give people reason to believe the future will hold certain changes.

Fill-In

Circle the word(s) in parentheses that complete the sentence.

1. Inflation will follow the rate of increase in nominal wages but will be offset by increases in (costs, productivity, regulation) _____.

2. The Phillips curve suggests that increases in (unemployment, the price level) _____ will be associated with reductions in (inflation, exports) _____. This Phillips curve relationship was relatively (volatile, stable) _____ during the 1960s, but began shifting (leftward, rightward) _____ during the 1970s.

3. Inflationary expectations lead to a different Phillips curve for each level of expectations. As the public's inflationary expectations rise, the Phillips curve shifts (rightward, leftward, doesn't change) _____.

4. If policymakers want to keep unemployment below the natural rate, they must be willing to accept (a higher inflation rate, accelerating inflation rates, no change in inflation) _____. Once inflation has reached double digits (at or above 10%), and policymakers want to reduce inflation, they must reduce (aggregate demand, aggregate supply) _____ and expect higher (inflation, wages, unemployment) _____.

5. If the public develops inflationary expectations in a rational manner as described by economists, policymakers will become (highly effective, much less effective) _____ in expanding output and controlling the business cycle.

6. When recoveries do not generate employment as fast as output, they are referred to as jobless recoveries. One important reason for the recent jobless recovery following the 2001 recession was the rapid investment that occurred in the 1990s that increased (inflation, worker productivity, stock prices) _____.

True-False

Circle the correct answer.

_T/F_ 1. The original Phillips curve showed a positive relationship between money wages and unemployment rates.

_T/F_ 2. If wages rise, but worker productivity rises at an even faster rate, prices are likely to remain steady or even fall.

_T/F_ 3. At the natural rate of unemployment, inflationary pressures are typically fairly strong.

_T/F_ 4. In the 1960s, empirical data suggested that a 3–4% inflation rate was necessary to keep unemployment at around 4%.

_T/F_ 5. Stagflation occurs when inflation continues to rise, but unemployment falls.

T/F   6. Real wages tend to fall when actual inflation exceeds expected inflation.

T/F   7. If workers expect inflation of 5%, policymakers can generally expand economic growth by driving the inflation rate up to 5%.

T/F   8. To eliminate inflationary pressures, policymakers must be willing to curtail the growth of aggregate demand and accept the higher rates of unemployment this entails during a transitional period.

T/F   9. Adaptive expectations theory is a forward-looking model of expectations.

T/F   10. Rational expectations theory holds that people form their expectations of the future primarily by extrapolating from past events.

T/F   11. Rational expectations theory suggests that when the Federal Reserve announces a future increase in the money supply, this has virtually the same effect as an actual increase would.

T/F   12. One critique new Keynesian economists offer of rational expectations theory is that the labor market is often beset with imperfect information.

T/F   13. A jobless recovery typically sees no growth in output for several years after the trough in the business cycle has been reached.

T/F   14. Overinvestment in the 1990s probably helped contribute to the jobless recovery following the recession of 2001.

T/F   15. Temporary and part-time workers are less costly for businesses than permanent, full-time workers, and they provide greater flexibility.

Multiple Choice

Circle the correct answer.

1. According to Phillips, when the unemployment rate rises, everything else being equal, money wages will tend to
   a. rise.
   b. fall.
   c. stay about the same.
   d. do any of the above.

2. At the natural rate of unemployment, expected inflation _____ actual inflation.
   a. is less than
   b. exceeds
   c. is equal to
   d. has nothing to do with

3. The Phillips curve suggests that if policymakers want to use expansionary policy to reduce unemployment, they must
   a. reduce inflation to zero, or even to negative levels.
   b. raise interest rates.
   c. take steps to discourage business investment.
   d. accept a higher rate of inflation.

4. When stagflation strikes,
   a. unemployment and inflation are both low.
   b. unemployment is high, but inflation is low.
   c. inflation is high, but unemployment is low.
   d. unemployment and inflation are both high.

5. An expansionary macroeconomic policy is most likely to succeed in increasing output when the inflation it produces is
   a. well anticipated by workers.
   b. negative.
   c. unanticipated by workers.
   d. upwards of 1,000% per year.

6. Given that workers will come to expect certain levels of inflation once they have seen it regularly, what must policymakers do to keep the economy below the natural rate of unemployment for a sustained period?
   a. Continually accelerate the rate of inflation.
   b. Continually reduce the rate of inflation.
   c. Keep the rate of acceleration perfectly constant.
   d. Bring inflation down to zero.

7. In the simple Phillips curve shown in Figure MC-1, the natural rate of unemployment is
   a. 2%.
   b. 4%.
   c. 6%.
   d. 8%.

8. If policymakers wanted to decrease unemployment to roughly 3% in Figure MC-1, they must be prepared to see an inflation rate of
   a. 0.
   b. 2%.
   c. 4%.
   d. 8%.

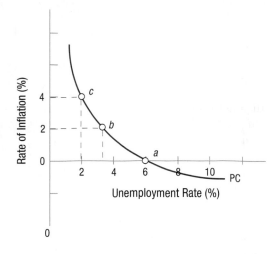

MC-1

Figure MC-2 shows an expectations augmented Phillips curve. Assume the economy is now at point b and is experiencing 2% inflation, and workers are aware of this.

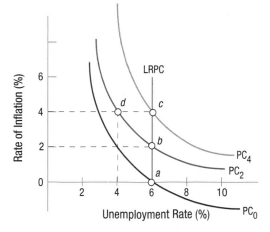

MC-2

9. In Figure MC-2, if policymakers wanted to decrease unemployment to roughly 4% by increasing aggregate demand, they would find that
   a. workers would expect inflation to increase, so the economy would immediately snap from point b to point c.
   b. workers would not expect inflation to increase, so the economy would move to point d and remain there with lower unemployment but an inflation rate of 4%.
   c. workers at first would not expect inflation to increase, so the economy would move to point

d, but when workers recognized the new inflation, they would demand adjustments to their wages, moving the economy back to point c at a 4% inflation rate.
   d. workers would be deceived by the policy, so the economy would move to point d, but workers would demand adjustments once they caught on, moving the economy back to point b.

10. In the rational expectations model, which of the following pieces of information would we *least* expect a rational actor to use when forming expectations of future inflation rates?
    a. a Federal Reserve announcement on monetary policy
    b. economic models studied at college
    c. a government report on current wage levels
    d. a gut feeling that prices are going to go up soon

11. Rational expectations theory suggests that policymakers must do what if their economic policies are to have a short-term impact?
    a. Keep any planned policy changes secret.
    b. Assume that public reaction to any policy changes will be driven largely by emotion.
    c. Implement changes in monetary policy, as opposed to fiscal policy.
    d. Announce any planned policy changes well in advance.

12. To what extent has the policy ineffectiveness proposition of rational expectations theory been borne out by empirical evidence to date?
    a. Empirical evidence fully corroborates the proposition.
    b. Empirical evidence definitively refutes the proposition.
    c. The empirical evidence has been mixed, though it tends not to support the proposition.
    d. No empirical studies have been done in this area.

13. An efficiency wage is a wage set
    a. precisely at the market-clearing level.
    b. somewhat above the market-clearing level.
    c. somewhat below the market-clearing level.
    d. without any consideration of the larger labor market.

14. New Keynesian economists criticize the rational expectations policy ineffectiveness proposition on the grounds that wages are often
    a. kept secret.
    b. set below market-clearing levels.
    c. quick to adjust.
    d. sticky.

15. Under rational expectations theory, if the economy in Figure MC-3 were originally at point a with price level P_0 and output Q_f, an attempt by the Federal Reserve to increase aggregate demand by a well-announced expansionary monetary policy would

   a. lead to an increase in output to Q_1 (point b) in the short run, where it would remain.

   b. lead to an increase in output to Q_1 (point b) in the short run, but the economy would return to output Q_f at point c in the long run.

   c. lead to an immediate movement from point a to point c, meaning that prices would rise immediately with no change in output.

   d. have no effect whatsoever because people would expect the Federal Reserve to act as it had announced and they would have adjusted beforehand.

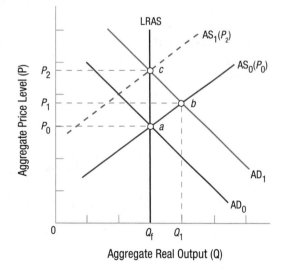

MC-3

16. Which of the following is *not* one of the likely explanations for the jobless recovery that has followed the 2001 recession?

   a. major increases in the government regulation of business

   b. massive overinvestment during the 1990s

   c. increases in worker productivity

   d. a change in business employment patterns, shifting toward more part-time, temporary, and overtime labor

17. How does the recession of 2001 compare to earlier recessions?

   a. more severe than most, but followed by robust job growth

   b. milder than most, and followed by robust job growth

   c. milder than most, but followed by weak job growth

   d. more severe than most, and followed by weak job growth

18. Efficiency wages

   a. are reductions in wages caused by outsourcing.

   b. cause huge increases in productivity.

   c. are used to reduce turnover.

   d. are the result of rational expectations by policymakers.

19. The natural rate analysis developed by Milton Friedman and Edmund Phelps suggests that

   a. inflationary expectations adjust almost immediately to changing economic circumstances.

   b. inflationary expectations adjust with a noticeable lag permitting policymakers a chance to have a short-term impact on the economy.

   c. policymaking is mostly ineffective.

   d. stagflation or jobless recoveries are the natural outcomes of most economic policy.

20. The stable relationship between inflation and unemployment suggested by the Phillips curve was effectively destroyed by the

   a. jobless recoveries in the early 1990s and after the recession of 2001.

   b. stagflation of the 1970s.

   c. new Keynesian critique of rational expectations.

   d. booming stock market bubble in the late 1990s.

Essay-Problem

Answer in the space provided.

The questions below are designed to challenge as well as extend your understanding of macroeconomic policy. Your answers may differ from those we suggest, though they should be fairly close. If they are wide of the mark, you should consider reviewing the chapter.

1. What is the essence of Phillips curves?

2. Why are policymakers so concerned about expected inflation as well as actual inflation?

3. Does the theory of rational expectations expect all of us to be rational?

4. Large, established airlines such as American and United have tried to cut their cost structures to compete more effectively with lower-cost competitors such as Southwest and AirTran. One of the

things they have tried is to obtain wage concessions from pilots, mechanics, and flight attendants. These negotiations have been drawn out and contentious. How does this example support the new Keynesian critique of rational expectations?

5. Over 10 years ago, the U.S. Treasury started to sell inflation-indexed notes and bonds, with the interest rates fluctuating depending on the inflation rate. The response has been underwhelming. Use concepts from this chapter to explain why demand has been low.

6. Now, assume that inflation builds and people notice this. What will happen to the demand for Treasury inflation-indexed securities?

7. The president's economic policy advisors argue that weak business investment is likely one of the key reasons for the jobless recovery. What policy should they put forward to alleviate this situation?

8. Consider your own inflationary expectations, and comment on the effectiveness of the Federal Reserve's monetary policy.

9. If increased worker productivity is a factor behind the jobless recovery, what should policymakers do about this?

10. In presidential election years, the Federal Reserve tries to decrease its policymaking activity so as not to influence the economy in any politically obvious way. Using rational expectations theory, when would we expect the Federal Reserve, in an election year, to act if it fears inflationary pressures are building?

What's Next

You have now seen the challenges to macroeconomic policymaking. Throughout our discussions, we have looked beyond the borders of the United States and brought in other countries when appropriate. We now want to look at the outside world in more depth. How does a global perspective change or modify what we have learned to this point?

Answers to Chapterwide Practice Questions

Matching

1. d	3. c	5. b
2. a	4. f	6. e

Fill-In

1. productivity
2. unemployment, inflation, stable, rightward
3. rightward
4. accelerating inflation rates, aggregate demand, unemployment
5. much less effective
6. worker productivity

True-False

1. F	5. F	9. F	13. F
2. T	6. T	10. F	14. T
3. F	7. F	11. T	15. T
4. T	8. T	12. T	

Multiple Choice

1. b	6. a	11. a	16. a
2. c	7. c	12. c	17. c
3. d	8. b	13. b	18. c
4. d	9. c	14. d	19. b
5. c	10. d	15. c	20. b

Essay-Problem

1. Phillips curves portray a negative relationship between unemployment and inflation. Policymakers can lower unemployment, but at the expense of more inflation. In other words, there is supposed to be a tradeoff between inflation and unemployment.

2. Expected inflation makes people act in ways that may perpetuate the inflation, making the policymaker's job tougher. For example, if workers expect inflation to rise, they will negotiate higher wage increases to take into consideration how inflation affects real wages. These inflationary expectations get built into the system. Strong medicine then may be necessary to wring out these inflationary expectations.

3. No, nor does it need to do this. For rational expectations to be valid, a small group of people have to react rationally to the actions of policymakers. This is often enough to get the rest of us to follow suit. For example, if the Federal Reserve announces a policy change that is likely to increase inflationary pressures in the economy, all it needs is for one large union to negotiate higher wage raises and make inflationary expectations explicit for other unions to follow suit. Additionally, financial markets may only need several large funds to move in the direction contrary to policy to reduce the effectiveness of government policy.

4. The long and contentious negotiations are a good example of wage stickiness: People are very reluctant to negotiate their wages downward. This means that labor markets do not adjust quickly to changes in expectations, however rationally formed.

5. A key concept in the chapter is expectations. When inflation expectations are low or non-existent, we can expect that demand for inflation-backed securities will be low.

6. Demand should grow. As inflationary expectations build, demand should grow in tandem with the expectations. Unexpected inflation takes a big bite out of bond portfolios as interest rates unexpectedly rise and bond prices drop. When inflation begins to rise, the inflation-backed securities take the risk out of having to forecast inflation.

7. To stimulate business investment, the U.S. government traditionally has offered investment tax credits. These credits are both short term and long term in nature. The short-term credits encourage businesses to invest in equipment; often, businesses are allowed to depreciate the cost of machinery over a shorter period of time. The long-term credits encourage research.

8. Most of us have little or no inflationary expectations at this time. Remember from a previous chapter that the Federal Reserve's long-term goal is price stability. This suggests that the Federal Reserve's monetary policy has been very effective.

9. Nothing. Recall that a prime driver of economic growth is increased worker productivity. Since economic growth is a key goal for policymakers, they should do nothing to mitigate this growth. If productivity has some unwanted effects on job growth, these effects should be dealt with individually so as not to destroy the benefits from the productivity growth.

10. If it can hold off, the Federal Reserve will try not to act during the election campaigning, but will act once the election is over. This means that if it becomes fairly clear that inflation is on the horizon, the Federal Reserve might act after Election Day in November. In addition, the Fed will try to begin the inflation mitigation acts with relatively small changes during the run-up to the election.

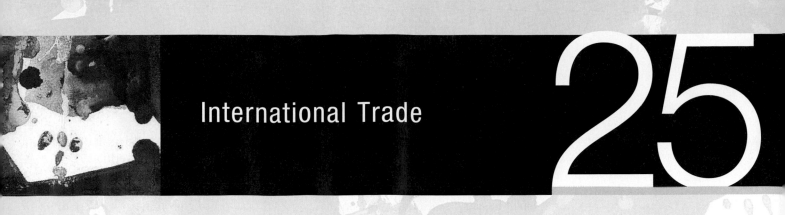

International Trade

25

Free Trade: Blessing or Not?

A key tenet of globalization is that trade is beneficial. Why is this so? Who benefits and who loses from trade? What are the arguments against free trade? We looked at the benefits from trade in Chapter 2. Here we will take a deeper look. We will analyze the benefits that trade brings, show who gains and who loses from trade, describe the common methods used to restrict trade, and then explore some arguments against free trade and globalization.

This Is What You Need to Know	STEP 1

After studying this chapter you should be able to

■ Describe the benefits of free trade.

■ Distinguish between absolute and comparative advantage.

■ Describe the economic impacts of trade.

■ Describe the terms of trade.

■ List the ways in which trade is restricted.

■ Discuss the various arguments against free trade.

■ Describe the issues surrounding increasing global economic integration.

Review the Key Terms

Absolute advantage: One country can produce more of a good than another country.

Comparative advantage: One country has a lower opportunity cost of producing a good than another country.

Terms of trade: The ratio of the price of exported goods to the price of imported goods (P_x/P_m).

Tariff: A tax on imported products. When a country taxes imported products, it drives a wedge between the product's domestic price and its price on the world market.

Quota: A government-set limit on the quantity of imports into a country.

Infant industry: An industry so underdeveloped that protection is needed for it to become competitive on the world stage or to ensure its survival.

Dumping: Selling goods abroad at lower prices than in home markets, and often below cost.

Work Through the Chapter Tutorials

The Gains from Trade

Frequently Asked Questions

Q: What has happened to the volume of foreign trade in the past 25 years, and why?
A: Worldwide foreign trade has quadrupled over the past 25 years. Improved communications and transportation technologies have worked together to promote global economic integration. Most governments around the world have reduced trade barriers in recent years.

Q: Have people always been keen about free trade?
A: Free trade has not always been popular. In 1929–30, as the world economy collapsed, many countries attempted to protect their domestic industries by imposing trade restrictions that discouraged imports.

Q: In the past century, what happened when the United States restricted trade?
A: In 1930, the United States enacted the Smoot-Hawley tariffs, which imposed an average tax of 60% on imported goods. This hurt industries around the world and has been credited with adding to the depth of the global depression.

Q: Is trade a zero-sum game, and if not, why not?
A: In a zero-sum game such as poker, for one party to gain, the other party must lose. Voluntary exchange and trade is a positive-sum game, meaning that both parties to a transaction can gain. These gains arise because of comparative advantage.

Q: What is the difference between absolute advantage and comparative advantage?
A: One country has an absolute advantage over another if it can produce more of some good than the other country. A country has a comparative advantage over another if its opportunity cost to produce some good is lower than the other country's.

Q: **How are trade and comparative advantage linked?**

A: Even when one country has an absolute advantage over another, both stand to benefit from trade if each focuses on the goods or industries with a comparative advantage.

Q: **What are the constraints on trade that every country faces?**

A: There are some practical constraints on trade. First, every transaction involves costs. Second, production is governed by increasing costs and diminishing returns. This makes it difficult for countries to specialize in the production of just one product. Indeed, specializing in one product is risky, since the market for a product can always decline or its production can be disrupted. Third, even though countries that engage in trade benefit, some individuals and groups can be hurt by trade.

Keep in Mind

People generally benefit from trade because trade is a *voluntary* act, and they would avoid it if they did not gain. Although nations as a whole benefit from trade, there are winners and losers within each country, and the losers are far more vocal than the winners. This explains the controversy that sometimes surrounds globalization.

The Gains From Trade Quick Check

Circle the Correct Answer

1. (T/F) International trade is a zero-sum game because both trading countries equally benefit from trade.
2. (T/F) The Smoot-Hawley tariffs imposed by the United States in 1930 worsened the Great Depression.
3. (T/F) If the United States has an absolute advantage over Spain in producing oranges and wine, it will never benefit from trading with Spain for these two products.
4. (T/F) Two countries can gain from trade if one has a comparative advantage over the other in the production of one good, while the other country has a comparative advantage in the production of another good.
5. Comparative advantage is based on
   a. one country being able to outproduce another country in some good.
   b. differences in opportunity costs between two countries.
   c. comparing physical endowments, such as mineral resources, of two countries.
   d. comparing the capital accumulation of two countries.
6. Assume the United States produces two goods: movies and computers. If the United States can produce 100 movies and 20,000 computers each year, what is the opportunity cost of producing one movie?
   a. 1/200 of a computer
   b. 100 computers
   c. 200 computers
   d. 2,000 computers

7. Which one of the following is *not* correct?
   a. Even when one country has an absolute advantage over another, both stand to benefit from trade if each focuses on the goods or industries with a comparative advantage.
   b. Trade is constrained because production faces increasing costs and diminishing returns.
   c. Everyone benefits from trade.
   d. Trade is a positive-sum game.

8. If the United States can produce 100 movies and 20,000 computers in one year, and Canada can produce 5 movies and 2,000 computers, which of the following is true?
   a. The United States will not benefit from trading with Canada, and Canada will not benefit from trading with the United States.
   b. Canada will benefit from trading with the United States, but the United States will not benefit because it has an absolute advantage in producing both items.
   c. Trade will benefit both because Canada has a comparative advantage in producing movies, and the United States has a comparative advantage in producing computers.
   d. Trade will benefit both because Canada has a comparative advantage in producing computers, and the United States has a comparative advantage in producing movies.

9. France has a comparative advantage in the production of perfume, and the United States has a comparative advantage in the production of running shoes.
   a. The United States should try to catch up to France in the production of perfume.
   b. Both countries will benefit if they specialize in the product in which they have comparative advantage and trade with each other.
   c. It is risky for any country to concentrate in producing goods, so France should increase its production of running shoes, and the United States should increase its production of perfume.
   d. Trade will not occur because it will be a zero-sum game in this instance.

10. Which one of the following is *not* a constraint on trade?
    a. Production is limited by increasing costs and diminishing returns.
    b. There are transaction costs with every trade.
    c. Trade can hurt some group or individuals, even if it is beneficial for most people.
    d. Some countries produce few products and have an absolute advantage producing none of them.

Score: ____

Answers: 1. F; 2. T; 3. F; 4. T; 5. b; 6. c; 7. c; 8. d; 9. b; 10. d

If You Got 9 or 10 Correct

You have the basics of the benefits of trade and how these benefits derive from comparative advantage. Go on to the next section, "The Terms of Trade."

If You Didn't Get at Least 9 Correct

■ Give yourself a maximum of 5 minutes and write a one-sentence definition of absolute advantage and comparative advantage.
■ After you do so, check the text and revise or complete your definition of absolute advantage and comparative advantage. You might want to put your revised definitions into the ExamPrep in Step 6.
■ Then, go back to the text and review Figures 2 and 3 and Table 1, making sure you see how both countries can benefit from trade.

The next section, "The Terms of Trade," is more complicated (not just a review of the material in Chapter 2), and it builds on this section. Make sure you understand why people and countries trade so that determining the terms of trade will be easier to pick up. Review the solved problem below, then move on to the next section, "The Terms of Trade." ■

Solved Problem: Mangos and Motorcycles

Amy Yee, in the *Financial Times* (April 28, 2007, p. 2) reported, "After months of negotiations the U.S. has agreed to import Indian mangoes for the first time after clearing concerns about insect importation." She further noted, "In exchange for mangoes India is considering relaxing restrictions to allow the import of Harley-Davidson motorcycles, barred from India because of emissions standards and high taxes." Currently, the United States imports mangoes from Mexico and other Central American countries. This agreement is expected to double trade between India and the United States in the next several years.

Who stands to benefit and lose from this recently negotiated agreement between India and United States?

Solution-Discussion

Clearly, American consumers will benefit because the supply of mangoes will rise and price will undoubtedly fall. The other beneficiaries will be Harley-Davidson (and their workers) because it will enjoy a new market for its products. One suspects that Harley-Davidson was probably lobbying hard for this agreement.

Since there isn't a huge United States mango industry, and most mangos are imported, the losers will be other importers from Mexico and Central America and their American agents.

The Terms of Trade

Frequently Asked Questions

Q: **What are the terms of trade?**

A: The terms of trade determine the prices of imports and exports. If a country exports computers and imports coffee, with two computers trading for a ton of coffee, the price of a computer will be one half the price of a ton of coffee. When countries trade many commodities, the terms of trade are defined as the average price of exports divided by the average price of imports.

Q: **What happens to the price of a good when countries trade?**

A: When two countries begin trading, the price charged for one good may be different in the two countries. In Figure 1, clothing is priced at P_1 in China and P_2 in the United States. As market forces lead each country to focus its production on the goods and industries at which it has a comparative advantage, that good's price will tend to equalize in the two countries, moving to an equilibrium level somewhere between the two original prices. In Figure 1, the equilibrium price after trading, P_e, is between the initial lower price in China and the initial higher price in the United States.

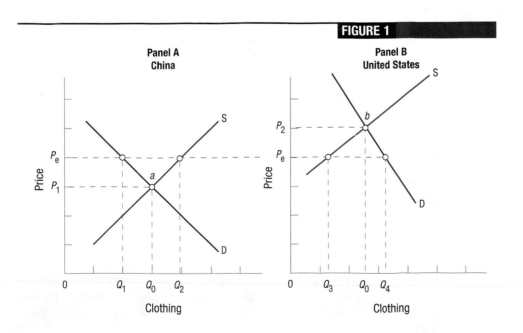

FIGURE 1

Q: **Who gains from trade? Who loses?**

A: Though beneficial to both countries, trade can produce winners and losers. In Figure 1, China has a comparative advantage over the United States in the production of clothing, and so it begins exporting clothing to the United States. Chinese manufacturers and workers will benefit from this increased business, but their domestic consumers will be hurt, however, as the price of clothing rises from P_1 to P_e to meet American demand. In the United States, where clothing had been more expensive, textile manufacturers and workers will be hurt by the competition from the Chinese, but American consumers will benefit as clothing prices fall from P_2 to P_e. Notice that at equilibrium, Chinese exports of $Q_2 - Q_1$ are just equal to American imports of $Q_4 - Q_3$.

Q: **What are the most common forms of trade restrictions?**

A: The most common forms of trade restrictions are tariffs and quotas.

Q: **What is a tariff?**

A: A tariff is a tax on imports. Most tariffs are *ad valorem taxes,* meaning that a product is taxed a certain percentage of its price as it crosses the border. Other tariffs are *unit taxes,* meaning that a fixed tax per unit of the product is assessed.

Q: **Who benefits from a tariff? Who is hurt by a tariff?**

A: Tariffs generate revenues while driving a wedge between a product's domestic price and its price on the world market. When a tariff is imposed on a product, its price will rise. This benefits domestic producers, increasing their sales and the price they can charge, but the resulting price increase hurts domestic consumers. The government collects tariff revenues. In Figure 2, a tariff (T) added to the world price of P_w generates revenue equal to the shaded rectangle.

FIGURE 2

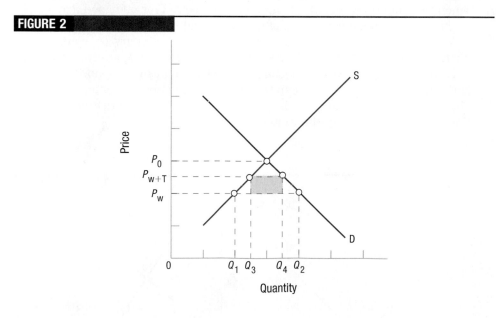

Q: **What are quotas, and how do they differ from tariffs?**

A: Quotas restrict the quantity of imports into a country. Quotas have much the same effect as tariffs, except that they do not generate revenues for the government.

Keep in Mind

Trade tends to equalize prices in both countries after trade. Tariffs and quotas are the two most common forms of trade restrictions, and they lead to roughly the same outcomes except that tariffs produce revenue for governments, so they are the most frequently used.

The Terms of Trade Quick Check

Circle the Correct Answer

1. (T/F) The terms of trade are defined as the average price of exports divided by the average price of imports.
2. (T/F) A quota is similar to a tariff, except that the government collects revenues under a quota but does not under a tariff.
3. (T/F) An ad valorem tax is a tariff calculated as a specific percentage of a product's price.
4. (T/F) A tariff and a quota have the same effect on imports.
5. The United States and Japan both produce cameras. Japan has a comparative advantage over the United States in the production of cameras. After trade, we know that
   a. the price of cameras will rise in both countries.
   b. the price of cameras will fall in both countries.
   c. the price of cameras will rise in Japan and fall in the United States.
   d. the price of cameras will rise in the United States and fall in Japan.
6. The United States becomes convinced that Mexico is dumping its lettuce on the U.S. market and institutes an ad valorem tariff.
   a. This tariff benefits U.S. consumers.
   b. This tariff does not help U.S. lettuce producers because it should be a unit tariff, not an ad valorem tariff.
   c. This tariff benefits U.S. lettuce producers.
   d. This tariff benefits Mexico's lettuce producers.
7. Which one of the following is *not* a reason why governments use tariffs?
   a. Traditionally, governments have used tariffs to generate revenues.

b. Firms that lose from trade seek tariffs as a means of protection from competition.
   c. Unions might seek tariffs as a way to protect jobs.
   d. Consumers seek tariffs to keep out foreign goods.
8. Germany has a comparative advantage over the United States in the production of camera lenses. If Germany and the United States trade,
   a. German consumers will be hurt by a higher price.
   b. U.S. consumers will be hurt by a higher price.
   c. U.S. producers will benefit.
   d. German producers will seek tariff protection.
9. If the United States institutes a tariff on Swiss digital watches,
   a. it will have no effect on the quantity of Swiss watches exported to the United States.
   b. it will have no effect on the price of Swiss watches exported to the United States.
   c. it will benefit U.S. consumers.
   d. it will benefit U.S. digital watch companies.
10. When faced with an influx of cheap foreign goods, consumers will
   a. seek to have an ad valorem tariff instituted.
   b. seek to have quotas instituted.
   c. seek to have a unit tariff instituted.
   d. seek to lower trade barriers.

Score: ____

Answers: 1. T; 2. F; 3. T; 4. T; 5. c; 6. c; 7. d; 8. a; 9. d; 10. d

If You Got 9 or 10 Correct

You have done well on a difficult area. Go on to the next section, "Arguments Against Free Trade."

If You Didn't Get at Least 9 Correct

You should have answered at least nine correctly in this quiz. If this is not the case, review this section and the first section on gains from trade again. Start by making sure that you understand the gains from trade, then jot down the difference between a tariff and a quota. Then, go back to the text, paying special attention to Figure 4. Be sure you know who benefits and who loses from trading in this case. This will help you understand the arguments against free trade covered in the next section.

If you do not understand the benefits from trade and who might lose from trade, separating which arguments are valid and which are not is difficult. Once you finish this review, work through the solved problem below before you go on to the next section, "Arguments Against Free Trade." ■

Solved Problem: Tariffs and Quotas

Using the data for domestic supply and demand for luxury sport utility vehicles (SUVs) in the table below, answer the questions that follow. Note that prices are in thousands of dollars, and quantities demanded and supplied are also expressed in thousands.

Price	Quantity Demanded	Quantity Supplied
140	0	240
120	40	200
100	80	160
80	120	120
60	160	80
40	200	40
20	240	0
0	280	0

a. Plot both curves in the blank grid below.

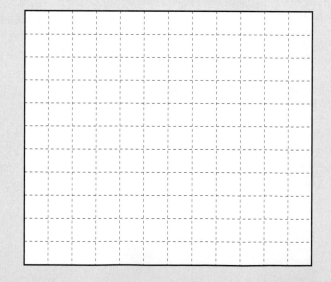

b. Assume the prices for 109 series Land Rovers (sold in Africa, Australia, etc.) and other foreign luxury SUVs are $40,000. How many will be imported into the United States at this price, and how many domestic luxury SUVs will be produced?

c. Now assume that the United States levies a $20,000 per unit tariff to protect domestic Hummers and other luxury SUVs from competition from Land Rovers and other foreign luxury SUVs. What is the reduction in imports of luxury SUVs to this country?

d. How much revenue does the government collect from this tariff? Could the government accomplish the same level of protection by putting an 80,000-unit quota on foreign imports?

Solution-Discussion

a. See Figure 3 below.

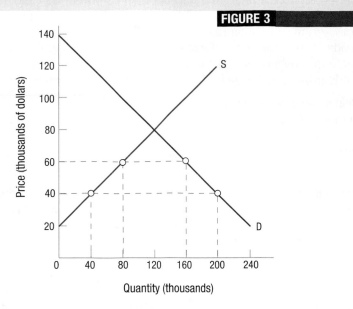

FIGURE 3

b. At a $40,000 price, consumers will buy 200,000 units, of which 40,000 are supplied by the domestic industry and 160,000 are imported.

c. SUV prices rise to $60,000, and 160,000 are purchased, 80,000 are produced domestically, and 80,000 are imported. Thus imports are cut in half.

d. A $20,000 tariff on 80,000 vehicles generates $1,600,000,000 in revenue. Yes, the same level of protection could be accomplished if the government was willing to give up the revenue (not likely).

Arguments Against Free Trade

Frequently Asked Questions

Q: **What is the infant industry argument against free trade?**
A: Despite the many benefits of free trade, some arguments exist for restricting trade. One is that infant industries require some protection. These are industries that are too underdeveloped to achieve a comparative advantage or perhaps even to survive in the global marketplace.

Q: **What is dumping, and why are there laws against it?**
A: Some American trade laws target dumping, which occurs when a foreign firm sells its good cheaper and typically below cost in the United States than in its domestic market. One goal of such dumping may be to drive American firms out of business, thus allowing the foreign firm to come back and impose higher prices on American consumers in the long run. Another may just be to gain a foothold or market share in a foreign market. Or, dumping may simply be a form of subsidized price discrimination. If the federal government determines that a foreign firm is dumping products onto the American market, it can impose antidumping tariffs on the offending products.

Q: **Do we need to restrict trade to be protected from cheap foreign labor?**

A: Some advocates of trade barriers maintain that domestic firms and their workers need to be protected from displacement by cheap foreign labor. Without this protection, it is argued, foreign manufacturers that pay their workers low wages and benefits will flood the market with low-cost products. On balance, however, most economists estimate that the benefits of lower-priced imported goods exceed the costs of lost employment. The federal government has resisted imposing protection measures to protect jobs. Instead, the government funds programs that help displaced workers transition to new lines of work.

Q: **What is the national defense argument against free trade?**

A: In times of national crisis or war, the United States must be able to rely on key domestic industries such as oil, steel, and the defense industry. These industries may require some protection even during peacetime to ensure that they exist when a crisis strikes and importing may be difficult.

Q: **Should trade be restricted if it leads to job losses for domestic workers?**

A: Some critics argue that increased trade and globalization spells job losses for domestic workers. Firms unable to compete with imports will be forced to lay off workers or even close their doors. Increased trade, however, allows firms that are exporters to expand their operations and hire new workers. For workers who lose their jobs, switching industries can be difficult and time consuming and often requires new investments in human capital. American trade policy recognizes this problem. The Trade Adjustment Assistance (TAA) program provides workers with job search assistance, job training, and some relocation allowances.

Q: **What is the environmental argument against free trade?**

A: Concerns about globalization, trade, and the environment usually take one of two forms. Some people are concerned that expanded trade and globalization will lead to increased environmental degradation as companies take advantage of lax environmental laws abroad, particularly in the developing world. Others worry that attempts by the government to strengthen environmental laws will be challenged by trading partners as disguised protectionism. Environmental protection is an income-elastic good: As incomes rise, the demand for environmental protections rises faster. And because trade increases incomes in developed and developing countries, free trade may further the cause of environmental protection.

Q: **Should a country stop trading with another country where wages are low and working conditions poor?**

A: Some antiglobalization activists argue that for the United States to trade with developing countries where wages are low and working conditions are deplorable simply exploits workers in these developing countries. But restricting trade with these countries would probably do more harm than good. Low wages reflect low investments in human capital, low productivity, and low living standards characteristic of developing nations. Blocking trade with these nations may deprive them of their only chance to grow and thus improve in these areas.

Keep in Mind

Most of the arguments against voluntary free trade do not have a solid empirical basis. Trade benefits individuals and nations, or they would not engage in it. Remember, in general the losers from trade are a small segment or industry, and the nation as a whole gains, but the losers are far more vocal than the winners. Infant industries and national defense requirements are situations where nations may wish to restrict trade to protect their industries, but nations must be vigilant to see that these industries continue to be (or become) competitive given their protection from global competition.

Arguments Against Free Trade Quick Check

Circle the Correct Answer

1. (T/F) The national defense argument against free trade claims that key domestic industries such as oil, steel, and manufacturing must be protected even in peacetime to make sure that they are established and ready if called upon during a crisis.

2. (T/F) Concerning jobs lost because of foreign trade, the United States government has tended to focus on job retraining rather than protectionist measures.

3. (T/F) Restricting trade with countries that do not raise their wages to what we consider to be acceptable levels or bring working conditions up to certain standards would probably harm the foreign workers involved because it would block what might be their only chance to escape poverty and misery.

4. Concerning the infant industry argument against free trade, which one of the following is *not* correct?
   a. An infant industry may be too small or undercapitalized to compete in world markets.
   b. Infant industries may be coddled by protection and never mature.
   c. Infant industry protection tends to focus on capital-intensive manufacturing.
   d. Countries with huge labor supplies need to develop capital-intensive industries first to use the labor.

5. Concerning the antidumping argument against free trade, which one of the following is *not* correct?
   a. Firms can use dumping to lower prices so much that foreign companies will be driven out of business; the dumping firm would then raise its prices, offsetting its short-term losses.
   b. If Japan dumps cameras on the U.S. market, U.S. consumers will be hurt.
   c. Firms can use dumping to gain market share.
   d. Dumping violates U.S. trade laws.

6. Concerning the low-foreign-wages argument against free trade, which one of the following is *not* correct?
   a. The argument often arises when workers in advanced economies are displaced by low-wage foreign workers.
   b. The costs of lost employment are usually lower than the benefits of lower-priced goods.
   c. Proponents fail to include the cost of benefits such as health care when calculating the wages for foreign workers.

   d. The United States has tried to help displaced workers transition to new lines of work rather than impose protectionist measures.

7. Concerning the environmental argument against free trade, which one of the following is *not* correct?
   a. One concern is that environmental regulations should not unfairly discriminate against the products of another country.
   b. Freeing trade in agricultural products may lead to less environmental damage (e.g., overuse of land, excessive use of pesticides), not more.
   c. Rising incomes in developing countries, over time, will lead to increased interest in environmental protection.
   d. As incomes rise, the demand for environmental protection rises faster because it is an income-inelastic good.

8. The infant industry argument against free trade might prove detrimental to countries with huge labor supplies if it
   a. encouraged capital-intensive manufacturing rather than labor-intensive industries.
   b. encouraged large industries rather than small ones.
   c. encouraged large countries rather than small countries.
   d. used quotas rather than tariffs.

9. Which one of the following is *not* correct concerning globalization?
   a. Increased globalization has led to some job losses for domestic workers.
   b. Increased globalization usually leads to increased job creation for exporters.
   c. Globalization has pressured firms to increase their comparative advantages.
   d. Globalization has been a mixed bag for consumers.

10. What is the rationale for U.S. antidumping laws?
    a. Dumping hurts American consumers.
    b. Dumping hurts foreign exporters.
    c. Dumping gives foreign firms an unfair advantage over U.S. firms.
    d. Dumping may reflect legitimate instances of lower cost production.

Score: _____

Answers: 1. T; 2. T; 3. T; 4. d; 5. b; 6. c; 7. d 8. a; 9. b; 10. c.

If You Got 9 or 10 Correct

You picked through these tricky little questions quite well. Separating the valid from the invalid arguments in the area of free trade and globalization can be difficult because the rhetoric can sound compelling. Take a few moments are read through the "Hints, Tips, and Reminders" in the next section.

If You Didn't Get at Least 9 Correct

You should have correctly answered at least nine of these questions. If you didn't, you will want to review this chapter one more time. First, review the questions you missed and make sure you understand why you missed the questions you did. The arguments against trade often sound good, and it can be difficult to separate the valid from those that sound reasonable.

Second, review the section on "Arguments Against Free Trade." Many of these arguments have valid points, whereas others are simply nice-sounding rhetoric. It is important that you leave this course with the ability to keep them straight. It is always a good idea to look at each argument with your eye on knowing what group is prone to make the argument, and why. Work through the "Hints, Tips, and Reminders" in the next section; you may find something that helps you get the arguments in this chapter under control. ■

STEP 4   Consider These Hints, Tips, and Reminders

1. The key difference between absolute and comparative advantage is that comparative advantage rests on *opportunity costs*. One nation (firm or individual) can produce a product at a lower opportunity cost than another.

2. Remember that trade is a *voluntary* activity. No nation (or firm or individual) would voluntarily engage in trade unless it expected to benefit. This is why trade is called a positive-sum game.

3. The most difficult material in this chapter is the discussion of the terms of trade; the ratio of the price of exported goods to the price of imported goods. Spend some time with the discussion around Figure 4 in the text. That discussion illustrates why there is often opposition to international trade—some industries (and workers) lose when faced by competition from international firms with a comparative advantage.

4. Don't let tariffs and quotas throw you—they are just two ways to restrict imports and are very similar. Tariffs are taxes, and quotas restrict the amount of imports into a nation. Both result in the same impact (imports are reduced), but tariffs yield revenue to governments. Guess which one governments prefer?

Do the Homework for Chapter 25
International Trade

Instructor _____ Time _____ Student _____

Use the answer key below to record your answers to these homework questions.

1. (a) (b) (c) (d)	6. (a) (b) (c) (d)	11. (a) (b) (c) (d)	16. (a) (b) (c) (d)
2. (a) (b) (c) (d)	7. (a) (b) (c) (d)	12. (a) (b) (c) (d)	17. (a) (b) (c) (d)
3. (a) (b) (c) (d)	8. (a) (b) (c) (d)	13. (a) (b) (c) (d)	18. (a) (b) (c) (d)
4. (a) (b) (c) (d)	9. (a) (b) (c) (d)	14. (a) (b) (c) (d)	19. (a) (b) (c) (d)
5. (a) (b) (c) (d)	10. (a) (b) (c) (d)	15. (a) (b) (c) (d)	20. (a) (b) (c) (d)

1. An absolute advantage exists when
   a. one country exports more to another country than it imports from that country.
   b. one country can produce more of one product than another country.
   c. one country can produce absolutely less of one product than another country.
   d. one country's opportunity cost is less for one product than for another country.

2. A comparative advantage exists when
   a. one country exports more to another country than it imports from that country.
   b. one country can produce more of one product than another country.
   c. one country can produce comparatively less of one product than another country.
   d. one country's opportunity cost is less for one product than for another country.

3. The Smoot-Hawley tariff passed in 1930
   a. helped to moderate the economic consequences of the Depression.
   b. imposed an average tax on imported goods approaching 200%.
   c. had only a modest impact on the world economy.
   d. added to the severity of the global depression.

4. International trade exists because
   a. most countries could not survive without the global flow of goods.
   b. governments force it on its citizens.
   c. nations expect to gain.
   d. treaties negotiated during the 1920s require trade between nations.

5. When one country has an absolute advantage over another country:
   a. trade will never be worthwhile for either country.
   b. that country will push its advantage over the other country and force trade.
   c. both countries may still benefit from trade.
   d. trade will lead to losses for each country.

6. The terms of trade
   a. determine the legal rules for trading between two countries.
   b. are the definitions of comparative and absolute advantage.
   c. set the limits to trading between the two countries and are defined as the maximum exports minus the minimum imports.
   d. are defined as the average price of exports divided by the average price of imports.

7. International trade
   a. is voluntary, so everyone involved must benefit.
   b. is involuntary, so no one really gains.
   c. leads to gains overall to nations, but there will be winners and losers within nations.
   d. reduces product choice for consumers.

8. Which of the following does *not* constrain trade?
   a. There are both winners and losers within nations from trade.
   b. Diminishing returns limit production.
   c. Most countries can only produce one product.
   d. Every trade involves transactions costs.

9. A tariff is
   a. shipping charges associated with international trade.
   b. rules that govern exports.
   c. a limit on the amount of specific goods that can be imported into the country.
   d. a tax on imported goods.

10. A quota is
    a. shipping charges associated with international trade.
    b. rules that govern exports.
    c. a limit on the amount of specific goods that can be imported into the country.
    d. a tax on imported goods.

11. One advantage of a tariff over a quota is
    a. tariffs lead to higher prices, whereas quotas do not.
    b. governments prefer tariffs because they are easier to negotiate and administer.
    c. governments prefer tariffs because they generate revenue.
    d. tariffs lead to less lobbying than quotas because the stakes are lower.

12. Tariffs and quotas
    a. are the backbone of our international economic policies and are designed to help developing countries grow faster.
    b. lead to large-scale lobbying efforts by the companies and industries affected.
    c. have had little effect on the automobile industry, for example.
    d. lead to a better allocation of resources in the United States since these policies protect our smaller and more vulnerable companies and industries.

13. The major beneficiaries from a United States tariff on French wine are
    a. French winemakers and American consumers.
    b. American consumers and the government.
    c. California winemakers and the government.
    d. California and French winemakers.

14. Which of the following is *not* an argument against free trade?
    a. Trade keeps consumer prices too low.
    b. Small industries need protection to achieve comparative advantage in a global environment.
    c. Workers need protection from low-wage foreign workers.
    d. Some industries need protection to ensure that we have them in times of national emergency.

15. When the United States imports products from a country with a wage of less than $2 a day,
    a. that country's workers are harmed.
    b. U. S. workers in the same industry are harmed.
    c. consumers in the United States are harmed.
    d. tariffs must be instituted in the United States to protect the workers in the foreign country from exploitation by multinational corporations.

16. When wages and incomes in developing countries rise,
    a. tariffs on that country's products can be increased without harming workers and incomes in that country.
    b. U.S. workers will have nothing to fear from outsourcing.
    c. consumers in the United States will want to see quotas instituted to keep prices from rising.
    d. the demand for environmental protections will rise.

17. Use the table at right for wine and olive oil production in Greece and Australia. The opportunity cost of one barrel of olive oil in Greece is
    a. two casks of wine.
    b. half a cask of wine.
    c. three casks of wine.
    d. one-third cask of wine.

18. Use the table at right for wine and olive oil production in Greece and Australia. The opportunity cost of one barrel of olive oil in Australia is
    a. two casks of wine.
    b. half a cask of wine.
    c. three casks of wine.
    d. one-third cask of wine.

	Wine (casks)	Olive Oil (barrels)
Greece	10	20
Australia	30	10

19. Use the table on the previous page for wine and olive oil production in Greece and Australia. Assume each country initially produced and consumed half of its possible production of both commodities. Now assume that Greece produces only olive oil and Australia produces only wine, and the two countries agree to split the resulting output. As a result,
   a. Greece will gain an additional 10 casks of wine.
   b. Australia will lose 5 casks of wine.
   c. Australia will gain 10 barrels of olive oil.
   d. Greece will gain 5 barrels of olive oil

20. Use the table on the previous page for wine and olive oil production in Greece and Australia. Assume each country initially produced and consumed half of its possible production of both commodities. Now assume that Greece produces only olive oil and Australia produces only wine, and the two countries agree to split the resulting output. As a result,
   a. Greece will gain an additional 5 casks of wine.
   b. Australia will lose 5 casks of wine.
   c. Australia will gain 5 barrels of olive oil.
   d. Greece will gain 5 barrels of olive oil

| | Use the ExamPrep to Get Ready for Exams | STEP 6 |

This sheet (front and back) is designed to help you prepare for your exams. The chapter has been boiled down to its key concepts. You are asked to answer questions, define terms, draw graphs, and, if you wish, add summaries of class notes.

The Gains From Trade

Define the following:
Absolute advantage:

Comparative advantage:

Describe the gains from trade associated with comparative advantage:

Describe some of the limits to trade and specialization:

Terms of Trade

Describe the process of determining the terms of trade between two industries in two countries.

Describe the impact that trade has on both consumers and workers in the two countries:

Restricting Trade

Use the grid below to illustrate the effects of a tariff. Begin with domestic demand and supply with an equilibrium price of P_0. Then put in the world price of the product P_w below the domestic equilibrium price.

How much of this industry's product is imported?

How much is sold by domestic firms?

Add a tariff (T) to this product.

How much is now imported?

How much is now sold by domestic firms?

Shade in the revenue received by the government from the tariff.

Who benefits from the tariff?

Who are the losers from the tariff?

If the government substituted a quota for the tariff and reduced imports by the same amount, how would this quota differ from the tariff?

Arguments Against Free Trade

Describe the following arguments against free trade:
Protection of infant industries:

Antidumping:

Protection from low foreign wages:

Providing for the national defense:

Concerns about Globalization

Discuss the following concerns about globalization, listing both sides of the argument:

Impact on domestic employment:

Impact of trade on the environment:

Impact on working conditions in developing nations:

Additional Study Help Chapterwide Practice Questions

Matching

Match the description with the corresponding term.

___ 1. Absolute advantage
___ 2. Comparative advantage
___ 3. Terms of trade
___ 4. Tariffs
___ 5. Quotas
___ 6. Infant industry argument
___ 7. Antidumping

a. Determine the prices of imports and exports. When countries trade many commodities, this is defined as the average price of exports divided by the average price of imports.

b. When one country can produce more of some good than can the other country.

c. A tax on imports. It can be an ad valorem tax: a certain percentage of its price. Or it can be a unit tax: a fixed tax per unit of the product.

d. When one country's opportunity cost to produce some good is lower than the other country's.e. When a foreign firm engages in predatory pricing and sells its goods cheaper in the United States than in its domestic market, the U.S. government can impose tariffs on the offending products.

f. An industry that is too underdeveloped to enjoy a comparative advantage or to survive in the global marketplace. Some advocates argue that they require some initial trade protection, usually tariffs or quotas, to allow them to grow and achieve global competitiveness.

g. Restricts the quantity of imports into a country. It has much the same effect as a tariff, except that it does not generate revenues for the government.

Fill-In

Circle the word(s) in parentheses that complete the sentence.

1. When one nation can produce a product at a lower cost than another, it has a(n) (comparative, absolute) _____ advantage over the other country. But just being able to produce more than another country only confers a(n) (comparative, absolute) _____ advantage. Diminishing returns, the market risk associated with specializing in producing one product or commodity, and (transaction costs, terms of trade, low labor costs) _____ place some practical limits on trade.

2. Excise taxes on imported products are (the terms of trade, quotas, tariffs) _____; the price of exports divided by the price of imports is equal to (the terms of trade, quotas, tariffs) _____; and just restricting imports is done with (the terms of trade, quotas, tariffs) _____.

3. Underdeveloped industries that are often protected are (low-wage, infant, capital-intensive) _____ industries, and some antitrade advocates argue that domestic workers need protection from foreign (low-wage, infant, capital-intensive) _____ industries.

4. Selling products at different prices in domestic and foreign markets is referred to as (exploitation, globalization, dumping) _____. Although trade can produce losers among specific industries, overall (workers, consumers, governments) _____ stand to benefit.

True-False

Circle the correct answer.

T/F   1. Roughly one in five American workers owes his or her job to foreign consumers.

T/F   2. Free trade policies have steadily grown more popular around the world since World War II.

T/F   3. In international trade, one country can gain from trade only if another country loses.

T/F   4. If Japan has an absolute advantage over China in the production of automobiles, this means Japan can produce more cars than China.

T/F   5. If France has a comparative advantage over Germany in the production of cheese, this means France is capable of producing more cheese than Germany.

T/F   6. If France has a comparative advantage in the production of wine and Germany has a comparative advantage in the production of beer, both countries can enjoy more wine and beer if each specializes in the area of production where it has a comparative advantage, and the two countries then trade.

T/F   7. If Australia has an absolute advantage over New Zealand in the production of crocodile-skin boots, this means Australia will definitely want to focus some of its resources on producing crocodile-skin boots.

T/F   8. If the United States has been trading baseball caps to Great Britain for years, and they are not subject to significant tariffs, the price of baseball caps in Britain will likely be quite close to their price in the United States.

T/F   9. Calculating the terms of trade between two nations is a relatively simple task for economists.

T/F   10. If the United States is a net exporter to Taiwan, Taiwanese producers will generally be hurt by this trade, but Taiwanese consumers will benefit from it.

T/F   11. As a general rule, tariffs benefit domestic producers but hurt domestic consumers.

T/F   12. A quota is an ad valorem tax assessed on imports as they cross the border.

T/F   13. When consumer groups try to lobby for tariff reductions, they are usually outspent and outlobbied by industry groups supporting the tariffs.

T/F   14. A quota generates more revenues for the government than a tariff.

T/F   15. The infant industry argument for trade barriers suggests that countries with young industries should erect permanent trade barriers to protect these industries.

T/F   16. Developing nations often try to protect their capital industries on the infant industry rationale, even if they would be better served by promoting their more labor-intensive industries.

T/F   17. If China begins selling T-shirts in the United States at a lower price than American producers because China can produce T-shirts less expensively, the federal government is likely to invoke antidumping laws and impose a tariff on Chinese T-shirts.

T/F   18. If the United States were to boycott Burmese textiles because Americans decided wages in Burma were unconscionably low, this move would probably help American textile workers far more than Burmese workers.

T/F   19. Although many industries are vital to securing U.S. national defense, most of them seem capable of thriving even without any special trade protections.

T/F   20. Expanding our trade with other nations typically has the effect of lowering American wages.

T/F   21. Although economic development has clearly caused some environmental degradation, most evidence now suggests that increasing income levels around the world would serve the cause of environmental protection.

T/F   22. The best way to promote higher wages in developing nations is generally to threaten them with a cutoff of trade if they do not start paying their workers more.

Multiple Choice

Circle the correct answer.

1. Approximately what is the combined value of annual U.S. imports and exports?
   a. $500 billion
   b. $800 billion
   c. $1.5 trillion
   d. $3 trillion

2. What was the name of the tariff the United States imposed in 1930 with disastrous results?
   a. Baxter-Taylor
   b. Smoot-Hawley
   c. Jackson-Landreau
   d. Hart-Smalley

3. Which of the following is an example of a positive-sum game?
   a. football
   b. poker
   c. war
   d. international trade

4. If Chile has a comparative advantage over Peru in coffee production, what does this mean?
   a. The opportunity costs of producing coffee are lower in Chile than in Peru.
   b. Chilean coffee is of higher quality than Peruvian coffee.
   c. Chile is capable of producing more coffee than Peru.
   d. The price of Chilean coffee is higher than that of Peruvian coffee.

5. If Chile has an absolute advantage over Peru in coffee production, what does this mean?
   a. The opportunity costs of producing coffee are lower in Chile than in Peru.
   b. Chilean coffee is of higher quality than Peruvian coffee.
   c. Chile is capable of producing more coffee than Peru.
   d. The price of Chilean coffee is higher than that of Peruvian coffee.

6. If Ireland can produce 10,000 additional tons of potatoes every year only by forgoing the production of 100,000 barrels of ale, what is the opportunity cost of 1 ton of potatoes in Ireland?
   a. 0.1 barrel of ale
   b. 10 barrels of ale
   c. 100 barrels of ale
   d. 10,000 barrels of ale

7. Trade between two countries will benefit both
   a. when one country has a comparative advantage over the other in one type of production.
   b. when one country has an absolute advantage over the other in one type of production.
   c. when one country has an absolute advantage over the other in numerous types of production.
   d. in all of the above instances.

8. The United States and South Africa trade cars for diamonds. If 1 car trades for 3 diamonds and each car costs $15,000, what will the price of a diamond be?
   a. $5,000
   b. $15,000
   c. $20,000
   d. $45,000

9. If Chile has a comparative advantage over Peru in the production of coffee and Peru drops its barriers against the importation of Chilean coffee, which two groups will be adversely affected by this new arrangement?
   a. Chilean producers and Peruvian consumers
   b. Chilean producers and consumers

c. Chilean consumers and Peruvian producers
   d. Peruvian producers and consumers

10. If Japan has a comparative advantage in electronics production and China has a comparative advantage in textile production, what will happen to the price of electronics in Japan if the two countries start trading electronics for textiles?
    a. It will drop.
    b. It will rise.
    c. It will hold steady.
    d. Any of the above possibilities is equally likely.

11. If a tariff takes the form of an ad valorem tax, this means:
    a. a fixed tax is assessed for every unit of the product that is imported.
    b. imported goods are taxed every time they are featured in advertisements.
    c. a limit is place on the quantity of a certain product that may be imported.
    d. imported products are assessed a tax equal to a certain percentage of their price.

12. If a tariff takes the form of a per unit tax, this means:
    a. a fixed tax is assessed for every unit of the product that is imported.
    b. imported goods are taxed every time they are featured in advertisements.
    c. a limit is place on the quantity of a certain product that may be imported.
    d. imported products are assessed a tax equal to a certain percentage of their price.

13. Who are the two primary beneficiaries of a tariff?
    a. foreign producers and domestic consumers
    b. domestic consumers and the government
    c. domestic producers and the government
    d. foreign and domestic producers

14. What is the primary difference between tariffs and quotas in terms of their final effects?
    a. tariffs help domestic producers whereas quotas do not
    b. tariffs generate revenues for the government whereas quotas do not
    c. tariffs help domestic consumers whereas quotas hurt them
    d. tariffs are difficult to repeal for political reasons whereas consumer groups can get quotas repealed easily

15. "We should protect the oil industry because we will need to have a secure domestic source of oil

if we ever go to war." This is an example of which of the following arguments for trade barriers?
a. the infant industry argument
b. the antidumping argument
c. the low foreign wage argument
d. the national defense argument

16. "We need to slap a tariff on Japanese televisions because Sony is selling its TVs below cost in the United States." This is an example of which of the following arguments for trade barriers?
a. the infant industry argument
b. the antidumping argument
c. the low foreign wage argument
d. the national defense argument

17. "Mozambique needs to protect its steel industry until it attracts enough capital that it can be competitive in the global marketplace." This is an example of which of the following arguments for trade barriers?
a. the infant industry argument
b. the antidumping argument
c. the low foreign wage argument
d. the national defense argument

18. Which of the following is *not* one the arguments *against* erecting trade barriers on the infant industry rationale?
a. Capital intensive industries are usually the ones protected on this rationale, whereas many developing nations would be better off promoting the development of their labor-intensive industries.
b. Many industries have proven themselves perfectly capable of developing without costly protectionist measures.
c. If a young industry is protected for a short time, this can help it to grow large enough to be competitive in the global market.
d. Many countries coddle their infant industries so much that these industries never really mature and become competitive.

19. If the United States begins importing textiles from Burma, where workers may be paid only $1 per day, which group will this likely hurt the most?
a. Burmese textile workers
b. Burmese textile producers
c. American consumers
d. American textile workers

20. In recent years, when American jobs have been lost due to competition from abroad, the most common response of the federal government has been to:

a. help displaced workers transition to other industries.
b. impose tariffs against foreign products.
c. impose quotas on foreign products.
d. provide domestic producers in the affected industries with subsidies.

21. As incomes rise, especially above the subsistence level, the demand for environmental protections typically:
a. falls.
b. remains constant.
c. rises, though slower than the rise in incomes.
d. rises faster than the rise in incomes.

22. Which of the following policies would probably help workers in developing countries least?
a. expanding political and economic freedoms
b. strengthening the rule of law, especially in the area of property rights
c. instituting rigid trade barriers to protect domestic industries
d. taking measures to promote the influx of foreign capital

Essay-Problem

Answer in the space provided.

Use the questions below as another way to assess your progress. Your answers may differ from ours, but they should not be too far apart. These questions should give you more perspective on issues in international trade.

1. Why is comparative advantage so important for trade?

2. When we hear an argument against free trade, who likely is making the argument?

3. Consider a charge of dumping against two products: cameras and eggs. Why might the charge be mistaken in the case of eggs?

4. We have seen that dumping may put domestic firms at an unfair advantage with a subsidized foreign producer. From the point of view of the domestic consumer, is dumping bad?

5. What did the Smoot-Hawley tariff teach us?

6. What is the difference between buying cheese from a farmer in Wisconsin and from a farmer in Saskatchewan?

7. What groups are hurt if the U.S. puts a tariff on French wine? What groups benefit?

8. Why would an underdeveloped country be apt to have looser environmental regulations than developed countries?

9. When an infant industry is protected, who suffers?

10. Often in this chapter, we have talked about trade without mentioning specific products. Name five products that the United States exports.

11. Use Figure EP-1 to answer the following questions. Points *e* are the initial equilibrium in both markets, and note that camera lenses are measured in thousands.
    a. Initially, how much revenue does U.S. firms make?

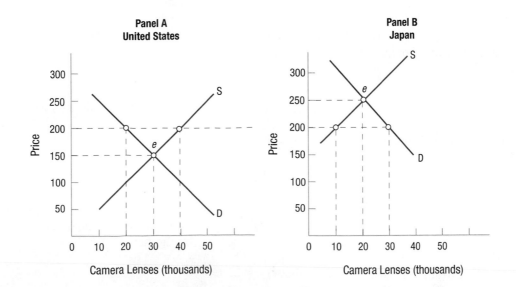

b. After trade with Japan, how much revenue does U.S. firms make?

c. Initially, how much revenue does Japanese firms make?

d. After trade with the United States, how much revenue does Japanese firms make?

e. Which country's firms gain from trade?

f. Initially, how many camera lenses are bought at what price by U.S. consumers?

g. After trade with Japan, how many camera lenses are bought at what price by U.S. consumers?

h. Initially, how many camera lenses are bought at what price by Japanese consumers?

i. After trade with the United States, how many camera lenses are bought at what price by Japanese consumers?

j. Which country's consumers gain the most from trade?

12. Use Figure EP-2 to answer the following questions. The figure illustrates the effects of a tariff of $5 per unit on the world price of $20.

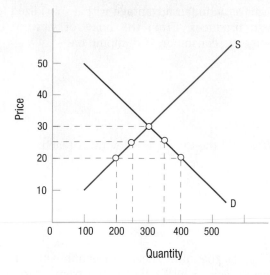

EP-2

a. What is the original equilibrium price and quantity in the home country?

b. If the price in the home country fell to the world price, $20, what quantity would be demanded? What quantity would be supplied by firms in the home country? What quantity would be supplied by foreign firms?

c. If the government imposes a $5 tariff, what quantity is demanded? What quantity would be supplied by firms in the home country? What quantity would be supplied by foreign firms?

d. How much revenue is generated by the $5 tariff?

e. Comparing the world price to the world price plus tariff, who in the home country benefits from the tariff? Who in the home country is hurt by the tariff?

What's Next

International trade deals with products and services. We also want to look at international capital flows to bring in fully an international dimension to macroeconomics and macroeconomic policymaking. We turn to this in the next chapter.

Answers to Chapterwide Practice Questions

Matching

1. b	3. a	5. g	7. e
2. d	4. c	6. f	

Fill-In

1. Comparative, absolute, transactions costs
2. Tariffs, the terms of trade, quota
3. Infant, low wage
4. Dumping, consumers

True-False

1. F	7. F	13. T	19. T
2. T	8. T	14. F	20. F
3. F	9. F	15. F	21. T
4. T	10. T	16. T	22. F
5. F	11. T	17. F	
6. T	12. F	18. T	

Multiple Choice

1. d	7. d	13. c	19. d
2. b	8. a	14. b	20. a
3. d	9. c	15. d	21. d
4. a	10. b	16. b	22. c
5. c	11. d	17. a	
6. b	12. a	18. c	

Essay-Problem

1. Comparative advantage is important because it means that a country does not have to have an absolute advantage over another to trade: trade should take place as long as there is a difference in opportunity costs. This lets poor countries trade even though richer countries are more efficient in all matters of production.
2. Firms and workers who are hurt by free trade. Their concern is legitimate. Their solution, however, may not be in the best interests of everyone.
3. Perishables must be sold in a limited time period. When they start to rot, the value of the product goes down to zero. Lowering the price might be a way to get rid of the product before it goes bad. No such issue of perishability occurs with cameras.
4. No. The domestic consumer obtains a product at a lower price. What is the harm to the consumer in that? For example, why should an American consumer care if Japanese tax-

payers are subsidizing a Japanese producer, and so in effect Japanese taxpayers are subsidizing American consumers?

5. High tariffs can destroy trade, and plummeting trade can lead to immediate drops in national income and output. This can cause or worsen adverse macroeconomic situations, turning a recession into a depression, for example.

6. None, unless the products are vastly different. There is no difference to the consumer in buying a product produced in another state as compared to a product produced in another country. The division between states and countries is arbitrary.

7. French wine producers will sell less wine in the U.S., so they are hurt by the tariff. U.S. consumers will see the price go up. American wine producers, on the other hand, will be helped by the tariff because they will face diminished competitive pressures, and the U.S. government will benefit because it collects the tariff revenues.

8. There is a cost to environmental regulation. For a foreign firm thinking about investing in an underdeveloped country, the higher the cost, the less chance it will invest. This does not mean there will be no environmental regulation at all, nor does it mean that foreign investors will always be less particular about the environment in an underdeveloped country than a developed one. Consider, for example, a firm that wants to build a factory in an underdeveloped country. If it already has an environmentally friendly design, it is probably cheaper to use this design again than to incur the redesign cost. In this sense, foreign investors may improve the environment, not harm it.

9. First, the infant industry may suffer if it is coddled and never learns how to deal with competitive pressures. Second, if the infant industry is subsidized, taxpayers are hurt. Third, consumers are hurt by having the infant industry's product price higher than the market price.

10. There are many American products valued overseas. Here are only a few: Intel computer chips, IBM computers and servers, Coca-Cola, GAP clothes, NIKE athletic shoes, agricultural machinery such as John Deere tractors or Caterpillar heavy machinery.

11. a. $4,500,000
    b. $8,000,000
    c. $5,000,000
    d. $2,000,000
    e. United States
    f. 30,000 @ $150
    g. 20,000 @ $200
    h. 20,000 @ $250
    i. 30,000 @ $200
    j. Japan's

12. a. $30 and 300 sold
    b. 400, 200, 200
    c. 350, 250, 100
    d. $500
    e. Domestic firms and the government; consumers

Open Economy Macroeconomics

26

Macroeconomic Policymaking Is Tempered by Worldwide Responses

So far in this book, we have discussed the macroeconomic policymaking in the context of one country. We now want to broaden our approach and show what happens to the effectiveness of policymaking when worldwide responses come into play. Policymaking becomes more complex as more factors have to be taken into consideration. Nevertheless, the general principles remain the same. Keep this in mind as you read the chapter.

	This Is What You Need to Know	STEP 1

After studying this chapter you should be able to

■ Define the current account and the capital account in the balance of payments between countries.

■ Describe the difference between nominal and real exchange rates.

■ Describe the effects of currency appreciation or depreciation on imports and exports.

■ Describe the effects of changes in inflation rates, disposable income, and interest rates on exchange rates.

■ Describe the differences between fixed and flexible exchange rate systems.

■ Describe the implications for fiscal and monetary policies of fixed and flexible exchange rate systems.

Review the Key Terms

Current account: Includes payments for imports and exports of goods and services, incomes flowing into and out of the country, and net transfers of money.

Capital account: Summarizes the flow of money into and out of domestic and foreign assets, including investments by foreign companies in domestic plants or subsidiaries, and other foreign holdings of U.S. assets, including mutual funds, stock, bonds, and deposits in U.S. banks. Also included are U.S. investors' holdings of foreign financial assets, production facilities, and other assets in foreign countries.

Exchange rate: The rate at which one currency can be exchanged for another, or just the price of one currency for another.

Nominal exchange rate: The rate at which one currency can be exchanged for another.

Real exchange rate: The price of one country's currency for another when the price levels of both countries are taken into account; important when inflation is an issue in one country; it is equal to the nominal exchange rate multiplied by the ratio of the price levels of the two countries.

Purchasing power parity: The rate of exchange that allows a specific amount of currency in one country to purchase the same quantity of goods in another country.

Currency appreciation: When the value of a currency rises relative to other currencies.

Currency depreciation: When the value of a currency falls relative to other currencies.

Fixed exchange rate: Each government determines its exchange rate, then uses macroeconomic policy to maintain the rate.

Flexible or floating exchange rate: A country's currency exchange rate is determined in international currency exchange markets, given the country's macroeconomic policies.

Work Through the Chapter Tutorials

The Balance of Payments

Frequently Asked Questions

Q: What is the balance of payments?
A: The balance of payments includes all payments received from foreign countries and all payments made to them.

Q: How is the balance of payments account divided?
A: The balance of payments account is divided between the current account and the capital account.

Q: **What is the current account?**

A: The current account includes payments for imports and exports of goods and services, incomes flowing into and out of the country, and net transfers of money.

Q: **What is the capital account?**

A: The capital account includes flows of money into and out of domestic and foreign assets. Foreign investment in the United States includes foreign ownership of domestic plants or subsidiaries; investments in mutual funds, stocks, and bonds; and deposits in U.S. banks. U.S. investors in a similar fashion hold foreign financial assets in their portfolios and own interests in foreign facilities and companies.

The Balance of Payments Quick Check

Circle the Correct Answer

1. (T/F) The balance of payments account includes two accounts: the trade account and the financing account.
2. (T/F) If the current account is in deficit, the capital account must be in surplus.
3. (T/F) Money sent back to families in the United States by those working abroad decreases the current account balance.
4. (T/F) The profits from a Toyota truck plant in Tennessee are found in the capital account.
5. Payments for imports and exports of goods and services are shown in
   a. the capital account.
   b. the current account.
   c. the current account for imports and capital account for exports.
   d. the capital account for imports and current account for exports.
6. Which one of the following is *not* a component of the current account?
   a. IBM computers exported to Belgium
   b. wages paid to Americans working abroad minus wages paid to foreigners working in the United States
   c. U.S. foreign aid sent to African countries
   d. a Toyota truck plant in Tennessee
7. Which one of the following is *not* a component of the capital account?
   a. Japanese holdings of U.S. Treasury bonds
   b. American holdings of British common stocks such as Marks & Spencer

   c. Money that people working in the United States send home to their families in foreign countries
   d. A Coca-Cola bottling plant in Asia
8. Which one of the following is *not* a component of the current account?
   a. payments for German binoculars sold in the United States
   b. wages paid to an American working in London
   c. profits from a Coca-Cola plant in Japan
   d. bank of Scotland stock bought by an American working in London
9. Which one of the following is *not* a component of the capital account?
   a. a BMW automobile plant built in North Carolina
   b. the wages sent home to Germany by a German worker at the North Carolina plant
   c. IBM stock purchased by the German worker at the North Carolina plant
   d. BMW stock purchased by American workers at the North Carolina plant
10. If there is an increase in the trade deficit, there must be
    a. an increase in the current account.
    b. an increase in the capital account.
    c. a decrease in the capital account.
    d. an increase in net transfers in the current account.

Score: ____

Answers: 1. F; 2. T; 3. F; 4. F; 5. b; 6. d; 7. c; 8. d; 9. b; 10. b

If You Got 9 or 10 Correct

You have a good grasp of balance of payment accounting. Go on to the next section, "Exchange Rates."

If You Didn't Get at Least 9 Correct

Carefully review this material. It is not hard, but it provides a foundation for the remainder of this chapter. If you do not get this material straight, you might quickly get lost later. Go through the first section, making sure you know where each category fits in the balance of payments accounts. Study Table 1 until you have the categories clear in your mind. Then continue on to the next section. Keep in mind that the material gets substantially more difficult as you move through this chapter. ▪

Exchange Rates

Frequently Asked Questions

Q: **What is an exchange rate?**

A: The exchange rate defines the rate at which one currency can be exchanged for another. A nominal exchange rate is the price of one country's currency for another.

Q: **What is a real exchange rate?**

A: The real exchange rate takes price levels into account. The real exchange rate between two countries is defined as $e_r = e_n \times (P_d/P_f)$,

where

e_r = the real exchange rate
e_n = the nominal exchange rate
P_d = the domestic price level
P_f = the foreign price level

Thus, the real exchange rate is the nominal exchange rate multiplied by the ratio of the price levels of the two countries.

Q: **What is purchasing power parity?**

A: The purchasing power parity (PPP) of a currency is the rate of exchange in which some currency in one country can purchase the same goods in another country. Absolute purchasing power parity would mean that nominal exchange rates equalized the purchasing power in both countries. As a result, the real exchange rate would be equal to 1.

Q: **What happens to exports and imports if there is an excess demand for dollars under a flexible exchange rate system?**

A: If exchange rates are fully flexible, markets determine the prevailing exchange rate. If there is an excess demand for dollars, the dollar will appreciate, or rise in value. As the dollar appreciates, it becomes more expensive for foreigners, reducing the demand for U.S. exports. An appreciating dollar makes foreign imports more attractive for American consumers, increasing imports.

Q: **What happens to exports and imports if there is an excess supply of dollars under a flexible exchange rate system?**

A: If there is an excess supply of dollars, the value of dollars will decline or depreciate. American goods become more attractive to foreigners, increasing American exports and the demand for dollars. When the dollar falls, foreign goods become more expensive for American consumers, driving down American imports.

Q: **Does it matter which currency we look at?**

A: No, but in looking at charts or tables showing exchange rates, it is important to keep in mind which currency is being used to measure the price of others. Does the table show the yen price of the dollar or the dollar price of the yen? Graphs can be viewed as showing either an appreciation or a depreciation, depending on which currency is being considered.

Q: **What happens to the current account when currencies appreciate or depreciate?**

A: Real exchange rates affect the payments for imports and exports, and also affect the current account. If inflation heats up in Britain, production costs will rise. British goods become more expensive, and American goods more attractive to British consumers. American exports will rise, improving the American current account. The opposite occurs in Britain; British imports rise, and the British current accounts suffer.

Q: **What influences the capital account?**

A: Interest rates and exchange rate expectations affect the capital account.

Q: **What happens to the capital account if interest rates change?**

A: If the exchange rate is assumed to be constant, and the assets of two countries are perfectly substitutable, an interest rate rise (fall) in one country will cause capital to flow into (out of) it from the other country.

Q: **What happens to the capital account if the dollar is expected to appreciate in value?**

A: If U.S. currency is expected to appreciate, investors will demand a higher return in, say, Britain to offset the expected depreciation of the U.K. pound relative to the U.S. dollar. Unless interest rates rise in Britain, capital will flow from Britain into the United States until U.S. interest rates fall enough to offset the expected appreciation of the dollar.

Q: **What is a risk premium, and when does it arise?**

A: When capital is not perfectly mobile and substitutable between two countries, a risk premium will be added to interest rates. Expected exchange rate changes and risk premium changes can produce enduring interest rate differentials between two countries.

Exchange Rates Quick Check

Circle the Correct Answer

1. (T/F) A real exchange rate is the price of one currency expressed in terms of another, with no other adjustment.
2. (T/F) If 1 dollar equals 1.5 British pounds, a purchasing power parity rate of 1 means that a Big Mac that costs $3 in the United States will cost 2 pounds in Britain.
3. (T/F) If the nominal exchange rate is $1 = 1.5 British pounds, and the inflation rate is 4% in Britain and 2% in the United States, we know that the real exchange rate will be the same as the nominal exchange rate.
4. (T/F) An appreciation in the dollar should help the U.S. current account (reduce a deficit or increase a surplus).
5. To finance large U.S. federal budget deficits, the Federal Reserve increases the money supply. This leads to a surplus of dollars worldwide. What happens to the U.S. dollar and trade?

   a. The dollar appreciates in value, stimulating imports but curtailing exports.
   b. The dollar appreciates in value, stimulating exports but curtailing imports.
   c. The dollar depreciates in value, stimulating imports but curtailing exports.
   d. The dollar depreciates in value, stimulating exports but curtailing imports.

6. The Federal Reserve raises interest rates. What happens in the foreign exchange market?
   a. Capital flows into the United States from other countries.
   b. Capital flows out of the United States into other countries.
   c. The U.S. dollar depreciates.
   d. There is no change in the foreign exchange market.

7. If the dollar depreciates, this likely will cause
   a. U.S. aggregate supply to rise in the short run and rise in the long run.
   b. U.S. aggregate supply to rise in the short run but fall in the long run.
   c. U.S. aggregate supply to fall in the short run and fall in the long run.
   d. U.S. aggregate supply to fall in the short run but rise in the long run.

8. If the U.S. dollar depreciates against the British pound, what is likely to happen?
   a. British people will buy more American goods.
   b. Americans will buy more British goods.
   c. Americans will take more vacations in Britain.
   d. British people will stop vacationing in Florida.

9. German inflation heats up. Which one of the following is *not* likely to happen?
   a. German production costs rise, making German goods more expensive than American goods.
   b. The German current account will suffer.
   c. German imports of American goods increase.
   d. The Federal Reserve will counter by raising interest rates in the United States.

10. Catherine is going to take a vacation to Scotland. She fears that the dollar will depreciate soon. What is the best thing for her to do?
   a. Buy dollar-denominated traveler's checks now.
   b. Buy pound-denominated traveler's checks now.
   c. Carry U.S. dollars abroad and buy pounds when she arrives.
   d. Use a credit card while on vacation.

Score: ____

Answers: 1. F; 2. F; 3. F; 4. F; 5. d; 6. a; 7. b; 8. a; 9. d; 10. b

If You Got 9 or 10 Correct

You understand well the concept of exchange rates and how they work. Go on to the next section, "Monetary and Fiscal Policy in an Open Economy."

If You Didn't Get at Least 9 Correct

Do a patient review of the material.

- Make a little table with appreciation and depreciation as the rows and imports and exports as the columns. Put up and down arrows in the table to show the movement in imports and exports when currency values change.
- Then, go back to the text and review the material on changes to the current and capital accounts caused by currency appreciation and depreciation.
- Finally, fill in the following table by indicating whether exports and imports *rise* or *fall* in response to an appreciation or depreciation of the dollar.

	Dollar Appreciates	Dollar Depreciates
Exports	_____	_____
Imports	_____	_____

- The next section, "Monetary and Fiscal Policy in an Open Economy," builds on the concepts covered in this section. If you have a shaky grasp on the material now, the next section will be difficult.

Answers to table: Exports-Dollar Appreciates—fall; Exports-Dollar Depreciates—rise; Imports-Dollar Appreciates—rise; Imports-Dollar Depreciates—fall.

Before you go on, use Figure 1 to answer the following questions.

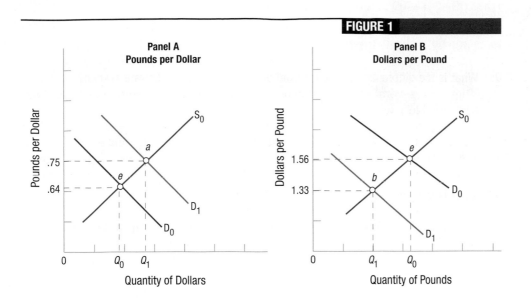

FIGURE 1

1. There is an oversupply of dollars on the worldwide market. What happens to the exchange rate between the United States and Britain? _____

2. Inflation heats up in Britain. What happens to the exchange rate between the United States and Britain? _____

3. Disposable income rises in the United States because of a tax cut. What happens?
   a. The demand for imports in the United States rises, leading to an increased demand for British goods and resulting in appreciation in the British pound.
   b. The demand for imports in the United States rises, leading to an increased demand for British goods and resulting in depreciation of the British pound.
   c. The demand for exports in Britain rises, leading to an increased demand for American goods and resulting in appreciation in the dollar.
   d. The demand for exports in Britain rises, leading to an increased demand for American goods and resulting in depreciation of the dollar.

Answers: 1. The dollar depreciates against the pound, which is a movement from point *a* to point *e* in Panel A and a movement from point *b* to point *e* in Panel B.
2. The dollar appreciates against the pound, which is a movement from point *e* to point *b* in Panel B and a movement from point *e* to point *a* in Panel A.
3. a.

If you got all three correct, go on to the next section, "Monetary and Fiscal Policy in an Open Economy." If you did not get all three correct, go back and review the section on exchange rates. You need to know the relationships found in the figure above. When you are comfortable with this material, proceed to the next section. ■

Monetary and Fiscal Policy in an Open Economy

Frequently Asked Questions

Q: What is the difference between a fixed and a flexible exchange rate system?

A: There are several ways to organize an exchange rate system, including fixed and flexible exchange rate systems. A fixed exchange rate system is one in which governments determine their exchange rates and then use macroeconomic adjustments to maintain these rates. A flexible or floating exchange rate system relies on currency markets to determine the exchange rates, given macroeconomic conditions.

Q: What is the gold standard, and when did it occur?

A: Before the Great Depression, most of the world economies were on the gold standard. Countries had to maintain stocks of gold sufficient to keep the value of their currencies fixed relative to those of others. If a country's imports exceeded its exports, this balance of payments deficit had to come from its gold stocks. Since gold backed the national currency, the country would have to reduce the money circulating in its economy, thereby reducing spending, output, and income.

Q: What happens to monetary policy under a fixed exchange rate system?

A: When exchange rates are fixed, an expansionary monetary policy combined with a neutral fiscal policy will result in a rising money supply and falling interest rates. The rise in the money supply leads to an initial rise in aggregate demand, but the lower interest rates cause capital to flow out of the United States to other countries, which reduces the money supply, reducing the effectiveness of monetary policy.

Q: What happens to fiscal policy under a fixed exchange rate system?

A: Keeping exchange rates fixed and holding the money supply constant, an expansionary fiscal policy will produce an increase in interest rates. As income rises, there will be a greater demand for money, resulting in higher interest rates. Higher interest rates mean that capital will flow into the United States. As more capital flows into these markets, interest rates will be reduced, adding to the expansionary impact of the original fiscal policy.

Q: What happens to monetary policy under a flexible exchange rate system?

A: If exchange rates are flexible, an expansionary monetary policy with no change in fiscal policy will result in a rising money supply and falling interest rates. This leads to a capital outflow and a balance of payments deficit or declining surplus. With flexible exchange rates, consumers and investors will want more foreign currency; thus, there will be depreciation in the exchange rate. As the dollar depreciates, exports increase; U.S. exports look more attractive to foreigners as their currency buys more. The net result is that the international market works to reinforce an expansionary policy undertaken at home.

Q: What happens to fiscal policy under a flexible exchange rate system?

A: Keeping exchange rates flexible and holding the money supply constant, an expansionary fiscal policy with the money supply being held constant will produce a rise in interest rates. Rising income results in a greater demand for money, producing higher interest rates. Higher interest rates mean that capital will flow into the United States, generating a balance of payments surplus or a smaller deficit. This causes the exchange rate to appreciate as foreigners value the dollar more. As the dollar becomes more valuable, exports decline. With flexible exchange rates, an open economy can hamper fiscal policy.

Monetary and Fiscal Policy in an Open Economy Quick Check

Circle the Correct Answer

1. (T/F) Under the gold standard, countries that imported more than they exported had to pay for this with an outflow of gold to other countries.
2. (T/F) Currency markets influence exchange rates under a fixed exchange rate system.
3. (T/F) Under the gold standard, a trade surplus will lead to an inflow of gold, which increases the money supply.
4. (T/F) Though fixed exchange rate systems were the norm for most of the 20th century, most of the world economy now is under flexible exchange rate systems, in which exchange rates are set in international currency markets.
5. Exchange rates are fixed and fiscal policy is held constant. An expansionary monetary policy will be
   a. reinforced by an open economy.
   b. mitigated by an open economy.
   c. unaffected by an open economy because exchange rates are fixed.
   d. multiplied by an open economy.
6. Exchange rates are flexible and fiscal policy is held constant. An expansionary monetary policy will be
   a. reinforced by an open economy.
   b. mitigated by an open economy.
   c. unaffected by an open economy.
   d. multiplied by an outflow of gold.
7. Exchange rates are flexible and monetary policy is held constant. An expansionary fiscal policy will be

   a. reinforced by an open economy.
   b. mitigated by an open economy.
   c. unaffected by an open economy.
   d. multiplied by an outflow of gold.
8. Exchange rates are fixed and monetary policy is held constant. An expansionary fiscal policy will be
   a. reinforced by an open economy.
   b. mitigated by an open economy.
   c. unaffected by an open economy because exchange rates are fixed.
   d. multiplied by an outflow of gold.
9. Exchange rates are flexible and fiscal policy is held constant. A contractionary monetary policy will be
   a. reinforced by an open economy.
   b. mitigated by an open economy.
   c. unaffected by an open economy.
   d. multiplied by an outflow of gold.
10. Exchange rates are flexible and monetary policy is held constant. A contractionary fiscal policy will be
   a. reinforced by an open economy.
   b. mitigated by an open economy.
   c. unaffected by an open economy.
   d. multiplied by an outflow of gold.

Score: ____

Answers: 1. T; 2. F; 3. T; 4. T; 5. b; 6. a; 7. b; 8. a; 9. a; 10. b

If You Got 9 or 10 Correct

You really have a grip on this material. Understanding the effects of monetary and fiscal policy in an open economy is a difficult task. Congratulations! Go on to the "Hints, Tips, and Reminders."

If You Didn't Get at Least 9 Correct

Keep in mind that this is really difficult material. It often takes several attempts to really master it. As you review the material, you will see that there are many steps with each policy change: This leads to that, which leads to this, which leads to that. Jot down the steps in abbreviated form as a learning device. Finally, complete the following table without looking at Table 4 in the text, indicating whether monetary or fiscal policy is reinforced or hampered by the specific exchange rate system. When you are done, take a look at the "Hints, Tips, and Reminders."

	Flexible Exchange Rate	Fixed Exchange Rate
Monetary policy (fiscal policy constant)		
Fiscal policy (monetary policy constant)		

1. Keeping track of what is in the current account and what is in the capital account can be difficult to remember. Here's a hint: Think of capital (as in capital account) as *assets* that people own. Assets owned by foreigners in the United States and assets in foreign countries owned by U.S. citizens are the bulk of the capital account.

2. Make sure you keep the three exchange rates clear in your mind:

   ■ *Nominal exchange rate*: What you can exchange your dollar for in foreign currency.
   ■ *Real exchange rate*: The nominal exchange rate adjusted for the price level in the two countries and a measure of price competitiveness between the two countries.
   ■ *Purchasing power parity (PPP)*: Takes into account what a unit of currency will buy in both countries in terms of goods and services.

   When the price of one currency rises relative to another, the currency is appreciating (getting more valuable). An appreciating dollar would be beneficial to you if you're getting ready to travel to a foreign country, because your dollars would buy more. But exports will fall as U.S. goods are now relatively more expensive.

   A depreciating dollar (becomes less valuable) would harm your travel plans, but your local exporter will benefit because a depreciated dollar would mean that foreign demand for our exports would grow as goods from the United States are now cheaper.

3. Now for the really tough stuff—how monetary and fiscal policy are affected by an open economy. Keep the following points in mind:

   ■ *Fixed exchange rates*: Governments set their exchange rates, then adjust their macroeconomic policies to maintain these rates.
   ■ *Flexible exchange rates*: Countries rely on currency markets to set exchange rates, given each country's macroeconomic policies.

   The following symbolic table summarizes the effects of an open economy on monetary and fiscal policy.

   Notice that the first five columns are the same for each type of exchange rate regime. Expansionary monetary policy lowers the demand for money, which reduces interest rates, so capital flows out of the United States. In contrast, expansionary fiscal policy increases aggregate demand, which increases the demand for money and increases interest rates, so capital flows into the United States. When we look at contractionary policy, the opposite occurs.

Fixed Exchange Rates

(1)	(2)	(3)	(4)	(5)	Interest Rate Changes Because Exchange Rate Is Fixed	
					(6)	(7)
Policy	Instrument	Money demand	Interest rate	Capital flow	Interest rate	Impact
Expansionary monetary policy	↑ MS	↓	↓	↑ outflow	↑	↓ effectiveness
Expansionary fiscal policy	↑ AD	↑	↑	↑ inflow	↓	↑ effectiveness

Flexible Exchange Rates

(1)	(2)	(3)	(4)	(5)	Exchange Rate Changes Because It Is Flexible	
					(6)	(7)
Policy	Instrument	Money Demand	Interest Rate	Capital Flow	Exchange Rate	Impact
Expansionary monetary policy	↑ MS	↓	↓	↑ outflow	depreciates	↑ exports ↑ effectiveness
Expansionary fiscal policy	↑ AD	↑	↑	↑ inflow	appreciates	↓ exports ↓ effectiveness

Keep in Mind

- With *fixed* exchange rates, the impact of capital flows is on *interest rates* because the exchange rate cannot change.
- With *flexible* exchange rates, the impact of capital flows is on the balance of payments and *exchange rates* (the dollar appreciates or depreciates). A changing value of the dollar affects exports that either reinforce or hamper policy.

Thus, with fixed exchange rates, interest rates do the adjusting because exchange rates are fixed, whereas when exchange rates are flexible, they do the adjusting.

Instructor _____ Time _____ Student _____

Use the answer key below to record your answers to these homework questions.

1. (a) (b) (c) (d)	6. (a) (b) (c) (d)	11. (a) (b) (c) (d)	16. (a) (b) (c) (d)
2. (a) (b) (c) (d)	7. (a) (b) (c) (d)	12. (a) (b) (c) (d)	17. (a) (b) (c) (d)
3. (a) (b) (c) (d)	8. (a) (b) (c) (d)	13. (a) (b) (c) (d)	18. (a) (b) (c) (d)
4. (a) (b) (c) (d)	9. (a) (b) (c) (d)	14. (a) (b) (c) (d)	19. (a) (b) (c) (d)
5. (a) (b) (c) (d)	10. (a) (b) (c) (d)	15. (a) (b) (c) (d)	20. (a) (b) (c) (d)

---

1. The balance of payments is split into two main accounts, including,
   a. the international account.
   b. the employment account.
   c. the current account.
   d. the past account.

2. The capital account includes
   a. a new Toyota Land Cruiser plant in Georgia.
   b. a British mutual fund's recent purchase of United Airways bonds.
   c. Ford's new Escort plant in Brazil.
   d. all of the above.

3. The rate at which one currency can be traded for another is called
   a. the real exchange rate.
   b. the nominal exchange rate.
   c. purchasing power parity.
   d. key currency cross rates.

4. The rate at which one currency can be traded for another and is adjusted for the price levels in each country is called
   a. the real exchange rate.
   b. the nominal exchange rate.

   c. purchasing power parity.
   d. key currency cross rates.

5. The rate at which one currency can purchase the same amount of goods and services in another country is called
   a. the real exchange rate.
   b. the nominal exchange rate.
   c. purchasing power parity.
   d. key currency cross rates.

6. If the trade deficit rises
   a. exports exceed imports.
   b. there is an increase in the capital account.
   c. immigrants in this country send more money back home.
   d. a new BMW plant was built in the United States.

7. The real exchange rate between two countries is defined as which of the following?
   a. $e_r = e_n \times (P_d/P_f)$
   b. $e_r = e_n \times (P_d + P_f)$
   c. $e_r = e_n \times (P_d \times P_f)$
   d. $e_r = e_n + (P_d/P_f)$

8. In Figure HW-1, if the exchange rate is fully flexible and the exchange rate initially is e_2, then
   a. the dollar will depreciate.
   b. there is excess supply of dollars.
   c. the British pound will appreciate.
   d. all of the above.

9. In Figure HW-1, if the exchange rate is fully flexible and the exchange rate initially is e_1, then
   a. the dollar will depreciate.
   b. there is excess demand for dollars.
   c. the British pound will appreciate.
   d. all of the above.

10. When a currency appreciates,
    a. its value falls relative to other currencies.
    b. typically supply of that currency is rising faster than the demand for it.
    c. its value rises relative to other currencies.
    d. imports will typically fall.

11. When a currency depreciates,
    a. its value falls relative to other currencies.
    b. typically demand for that currency is rising faster than the supply of it.
    c. its value rises relative to other currencies.
    d. imports will typically rise.

12. When a currency depreciates,
    a. exports will rise.
    b. typically demand for that currency is rising faster than the supply of it.
    c. its value rises relative to other currencies.
    d. imports will typically rise.

13. If a decade long deflation engulfs Japan,
    a. its exports to the United States will fall.
    b. the U.S. current account will move toward a deficit.
    c. U.S. exports to Japan will rise.
    d. the Japanese current account will decline.

14. If disposable income in the United States rises rapidly,
    a. U.S. imports from Britain will fall.
    b. the U.S. current account will move toward a deficit.
    c. interest rates will fall.
    d. the U.S. current account will move to surplus as exports rise.

15. All else equal, if interest rates rise in the United States,
    a. the U.S. current account will move toward a surplus.

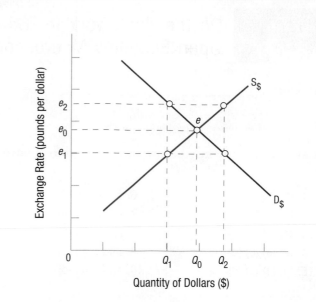

HW-1

  b. interest rate changes do not have an impact on capital flows into and out of the United States.

  c. capital will flow into the United States.

  d. capital will flow out of the United States.

16. All else equal, if the dollar is expected to appreciate relative to the pound,

  a. capital will flow out of the United States.

  b. interest rates will fall in Britain.

  c. capital will flow into the United States.

  d. capital will flow into Britain.

17. If exchange rates are flexible and monetary policy is held constant, fiscal policy will be

  a. unaffected.

  b. reinforced.

  c. multiplied.

  d. hampered.

18. If exchange rates are fixed and fiscal policy is held constant, monetary policy will be

  a. unaffected.

  b. reinforced.

  c. multiplied.

  d. hampered.

19. A continuing interest rate differential between two countries can exist because

  a. capital is not perfectly mobile between the two countries.

  b. capital is not perfectly substitutable between the two countries.

  c. a risk premium is added to one of the interest rates.

  d. all of the above.

20. Assume you are about to travel to Japan, and you expect the dollar to appreciate soon. Which of the following would be your best strategy for currency conversion?

  a. Carry U.S. dollars with you on the trip and buy yen when you arrive.

  b. Buy dollar-denominated traveler's checks now.

  c. Use your credit card while in Japan.

  d. All of the above.

Use the ExamPrep to Get Ready for Exams

This sheet (front and back) is designed to help you prepare for your exams. The chapter has been boiled down to its key concepts. You are asked to answer questions, define terms, draw graphs, and, if you wish, add summaries of class notes.

The Balance of Payments

Describe the current account:

Describe the capital account:

Describe the relationship between the two accounts:

Exchange Rates

Define the nominal exchange rate:

Define the real exchange rate:

Define purchasing power parity:

Describe currency appreciation and depreciation:

Exchange Rates and the Current Account

Describe what happens when inflation rises in one country compared to another:

Describe the impact of changes in disposable income on the current account:

Exchange Rates and the Capital Account

Describe the impact of interest rate changes on the capital account:

Describe the impact of exchange rate changes on the capital account:

Monetary and Fiscal Policy in an Open Economy

Describe the difference between a fixed and flexible exchange rate system:

Complete the table below indicating whether monetary or fiscal policy is reinforced or hampered by the specific exchange rate system, and give a brief explanation why.

	Flexible Exchange Rate	Fixed Exchange Rate
Monetary policy (fiscal policy constant)		
Fiscal policy (monetary policy constant)		

Additional Study Help Chapterwide Practice Questions

Matching

Match the description with the corresponding term.

____ 1. Current account
____ 2. Capital account
____ 3. Exchange rates
____ 4. Nominal exchange rate
____ 5. Real exchange rate
____ 6. Purchasing power parity
____ 7. Flexible exchange rates
____ 8. Fixed exchange rates
____ 9. Currency appreciation
____ 10. Currency depreciation

a. A system in which governments determine their exchange rates and use macroeconomic policy to maintain these rates.
b. When a currency rises in value relative to other currencies.
c. When a currency declines in value relative to other currencies.
d. Includes payments for imports and exports of goods and services, incomes flowing into and out of the country, and net transfers of money.
e. Takes the price levels of both countries into account and is defined as: $e_r = e_n \times (P_d/P_f)$.
f. Includes flows of money into and out of domestic and foreign assets.
g. Defines the rate at which one currency can be exchanged for another.
h. The price of one country's currency for another country's currency.
i. The rate of exchange that allows a specific amount of currency in one country to purchase the same goods in another country.
j. A system that relies on currency markets to determine the exchange rates, given macroeconomic conditions.

Fill-In

Circle the word(s) in parentheses that complete the sentence.

1. Exports and imports are included in the (current, capital) _____ account, income payments into and out of the country are included in the (current, capital) _____ account, and changes in assets owned by foreigners in the United States and U.S.-owned assets abroad are included in the (current, capital) _____ account.

2. When you want to exchange dollars for pesos to go on a Mexican vacation, you will exchange currency based on the (nominal, real, purchasing power parity) _____ exchange rate. Adjusting exchange rates for price levels results in the (nominal, real, purchasing power parity) _____ exchange rate. The (nominal, real, purchasing power parity) _____ exchange rate provides a measure of how the cost of a specific level of goods varies between countries.

3. When a currency (appreciates, depreciates) _____, it now buys less of the other currencies; and when one country's currency (appreciates, depreciates) _____, that country's imports rise. When a country's currency appreciates, other countries import (more, less) _____ of that country's exports.

4. Under a (fixed, flexible) _____ exchange rate system, governments determine their macroeconomic policies and let (currency markets, the World bank) _____ set the exchange rate.

5. Fixed exchange rate systems (hinder, reinforce) _____ fiscal policy, but (hinder, reinforce) _____ monetary policy.

6. In a flexible exchange rate system, expansionary monetary policy will reduce (capital outflows, interest rates, income) _____, leading to an increase in (capital outflows, interest rates, income) _____, which results in the dollar (appreciating, depreciating) _____, which leads to a(n) (increase, decrease) _____ in exports that (hampers, reinforces) _____ monetary policy.

True-False

Circle the correct answer.

_T/F_   1. The balance of payments reflects all payments received from foreign countries and all payments made to them.

_T/F_   2. The capital account includes payments for imports and exports of goods and services, income flows into and out of the country, and net transfers.

T/F   3. If the United States donates $5 million to the International Red Cross for disaster relief in Bangladesh, this will reduce the U.S. capital account balance by $5 million.

T/F   4. When a country runs a current account deficit, it will typically have a capital account surplus, but of a much smaller size.

T/F   5. Credit cards have fundamentally altered the structures governing currency exchange.

T/F   6. If 1 U.S. dollar will buy 1.33 euros, this means 1 euro will buy about 0.75 U.S. dollar.

T/F   7. If 1 U.S. dollar will buy 1.33 euros, and 1.33 euros will buy 0.75 British pound, we know 0.75 British pound will buy 1 U.S. dollar.

T/F   8. Currency arbitrage is a lucrative source of profits for currency speculators.

T/F   9. The real exchange rate between two countries is essentially their nominal exchange rate multiplied by the ratio of the price levels of the two countries.

T/F   10. If the British pound appreciates relative to the euro, British exports to continental Europe will rise.

T/F   11. If you travel from Hungary to Switzerland, and the price of a cup of coffee suddenly goes up, this indicates the purchasing power parity between these two countries is not absolute.

T/F   12. If $2 will buy you a Big Mac in New York, and £2 will buy you a Big Mac in London, this means the purchasing power parity rate between the United States and Britain must be 1.

T/F   13. The two primary reasons firms and individuals demand foreign currency are to purchase foreign goods and services and to invest in foreign assets.

T/F   14. On the foreign exchange market, the demand curve for British pounds will be downward sloping.

T/F   15. If the dollar appreciates relative to the euro, French and German consumers will find U.S. products less attractive.

T/F   16. If the dollar depreciates relative to other currencies around the world, this should help the U.S. current account (i.e., reduce an account deficit or increase a surplus).

T/F   17. If real incomes in Mexico fall, this will likely end up worsening Mexico's current account.

T/F   18. Everything else being equal, capital will tend to flow from countries with lower interest rates to countries with higher interest rates until these interest rates all equalize.

T/F   19. If the dollar depreciates, U.S. aggregate supply will likely rise in the short run as U.S. exports increase, but these gains may well be erased in the long run as domestic production costs rise.

T/F   20. Most world economies are currently on the gold standard.

T/F   21. The Bretton Woods agreement guided the international system of currency exchange from the end of World War II through the 1970s.

T/F   22. If exchange rates are fixed and capital is highly mobile, an expansionary monetary policy will typically have little effect in the long run.

T/F   23. If exchange rates are flexible and fiscal policy is held constant, international currency markets will tend to hamper an expansionary monetary policy.

T/F   24. If exchange rates are flexible and the money supply is held constant, international currency markets will tend to hamper an expansionary fiscal policy.

Multiple Choice

Circle the correct answer.

1. Which of the following is *not* one of the components of the current account?
   a. investments made by foreign companies in domestic plants
   b. income flows into and out of the country
   c. transfers of money into and out of the country
   d. payments for imports and exports of goods and services

2. Which of the following is *not* one of the components of the capital account?
   a. foreign holdings of domestic stocks, bonds, and mutual funds
   b. investments made by foreign companies in domestic plants
   c. payments for imports and exports of goods and services
   d. foreign deposits made into domestic banks

3. A payment made to the United Nations would be classified in the current account as
   a. income flowing out of the country.
   b. a transfer.
   c. an export.
   d. an investment in foreign assets.

4. If a country has a current account balance of −$400 billion, its capital account balance will be
   a. approximately −$400 billion.
   b. approximately $400 billion.
   c. something considerably less than $400 billion.
   d. something considerably more than $400 billion.

5. A nominal exchange rate is
   a. an exchange rate that takes into account the price levels of both countries.
   b. the price of one currency expressed in terms of another.
   c. the rate of exchange that allows a specific amount of currency in one country to purchase the same amount of goods in another country.
   d. the net payments made for the import and export of goods and services.

6. A real exchange rate is
   a. an exchange rate that takes into account the price levels of both countries.
   b. the price of one currency expressed in terms of another.
   c. the rate of exchange that allows a specific amount of currency in one country to purchase the same amount of goods in another country.
   d. the net payments made for the import and export of goods and services.

7. Purchasing power parity is
   a. an exchange rate that takes into account the price levels of both countries.
   b. the price of one currency expressed in terms of another.
   c. the rate of exchange that allows a specific amount of currency in one country to purchase the same amount of goods in another country.
   d. the net payments made for the import and export of goods and services.

8. If 1 U.S. dollar will buy 1.25 Australian dollars, how many U.S. dollars will 1 Australian dollar buy?
   a. 0.25
   b. 1.25
   c. 2.0
   d. 0.8

9. If inflation strikes Mexico, but the price level remains steady in the United States, which of the following sets of effects would we expect to see in the United States?
   a. Both exports to Mexico and imports from Mexico increase.
   b. Exports from Mexico increase, but imports to Mexico decrease.
   c. Both exports to Mexico and imports from Mexico decrease.
   d. Exports from Mexico decrease, but imports to Mexico increase.

10. If the dollar appreciates relative to the Brazilian Real, what will happen to the prices of Brazilian goods for American consumers?
    a. They will fall.
    b. They will rise.
    c. They will remain constant.
    d. We cannot make any predictions without further information.

11. If the dollar depreciates relative to the euro, what will happen to the level of U.S. exports to France and Germany?
    a. It will fall.
    b. It will rise.
    c. It will remain constant.
    d. We cannot make any predictions without further information.

12. If the dollar appreciates relative to the British pound, what will happen to the demand for British pounds?
    a. It will fall.
    b. It will rise.
    c. It will remain constant.
    d. We cannot make any predictions without further information.

13. If disposable income rises in the United States, what will be the effect on the U.S. current account?
    a. It will worsen.
    b. It will improve.
    c. It will remain about the same.
    d. We cannot make any predictions without further information.

14. If a government depreciates (devalues) its nation's currency, what effects does this have?
    a. Exports and imports both become more expensive.
    b. Exports become more expensive, but imports become less expensive.
    c. Imports become more expensive, but exports become less expensive.
    d. Imports and exports both become less expensive.

15. Which of the following statements regarding currency arbitrage is most accurate?
    a. Currency arbitrage is the primary means by which currency speculators make their money.
    b. Currency arbitrage can be very lucrative, but it is also very risky.
    c. Currency arbitrage can be a steady source of smaller profits.
    d. Given the current system of international exchange rates, it is theoretically impossible to make a profit through currency arbitrage.

16. Which of the following is *not* among the likely effects of a currency depreciation?
    a. an improving trade balance
    b. long-run inflation
    c. a short-run increase in imports
    d. an eventual rise in domestic wages

17. Under what system of exchange rates do currency markets determine exchange rates?
    a. a fixed exchange rate system
    b. a flexible exchange rate system
    c. an expanding exchange rate system
    d. the gold standard

18. The Bretton Woods agreement guided the system of international currency exchange
    a. before World War I.
    b. between the two world wars.
    c. from the end of World War II through the 1970s.
    d. from the 1970s until the late 1990s.

19. Under a system of fixed exchange rates, if the money supply is held constant, international currency markets will tend to _____ an expansionary fiscal policy.
    a. hamper
    b. reinforce
    c. have little effect on
    d. have any number of possible effects on

20. Under a system of flexible exchange rates, if the money supply is held constant, international currency markets will tend to _____ an expansionary fiscal policy.
    a. hamper
    b. reinforce
    c. have little effect on
    d. have any number of possible effects on

Essay-Problem

Answer in the space provided.

The questions below are challenging, and this is a challenging chapter. Don't get discouraged if your answers are not always the same as those we suggest. Assess your progress by answering these questions. Also, use these questions to discover more about macroeconomic policymaking in an open economy.

1. You are planning a vacation trip abroad. Do you want the U.S. dollar to appreciate or depreciate?

2. During a presidential election year, the Federal Reserve tends to keep interest rates steady so as not to influence the outcome of the election. It is now April of an election year, and you are planning a vacation abroad in December, after the election is over. You notice that the press runs articles about inflation pressures building in the economy. You begin to believe that the Federal Reserve will raise interest rates as soon as the election is over to dampen inflationary pressures. Should you buy foreign currency now or just before you leave on your trip?

3. Again, it is a Presidential election year and you expect the Federal Reserve to raise interest rates after the November election. You are an exporter of goods. Do you keep production steady or try to concentrate it? If concentrate, do you seek to get more products out the door during summer or after the election?

6. In mid-2003, the United States dollar was strong against the euro. By early 2004, the dollar had depreciated against the euro quite significantly. Many Europeans expected the Federal Reserve to raise interest rates, but it did not. Why should Europeans want the Federal Reserve to raise interest rates?

4. It is a presidential election year, and the Smyth family of Great Britain plans a Florida vacation. They can go in the summer or in December. They expect the Federal Reserve to raise interest rates in the United States just after the election. Should they go on vacation in the summer or in December? Why?

7. An American student studying abroad takes out a bank loan in the United States and receives the loan money in dollars in August. She has to pay tuition in September, December, and March, and has to pay in the foreign currency of the host country. What happens if the dollar depreciates in January?

5. You may read in the newspapers that the United States is running record trade deficits. Using your knowledge of balance of payments accounting, why might we worry about large trade deficits?

8. You may read about central banks entering the foreign exchange market to prop up the value of their country's currency. In basic terms, how do you think this works? Will this be successful over the long term?

9. Why would an American investor want to hold foreign bonds? What is the major risk of holding these bonds?

10. Does the Federal Reserve look over its shoulder at global markets when it sets monetary policy in the United States?

What's Next

After studying this chapter, you now have a better understanding of how monetary and fiscal policymaking in the United States is amplified or mitigated by forces and responses throughout the globe. This chapter's material is complicated. It forces one to go through a detailed step-by-step process in trying to figure out how one action leads to another action. Getting through this chapter is an achievement in itself.

You have now come to the end of this discussion of the principles of macroeconomics. You have used supply and demand analysis to understand how markets work. You have seen how inflation, unemployment, and economic growth are key concerns in macroeconomics. You have seen how the aggregate demand and supply framework can be used to study changes in the macroeconomy, and you have used this framework to analyze the effects of fiscal and monetary policy. You have looked at budget deficits and trade deficits, and you have seen how policymaking is mitigated or amplified on the global stage. What a ride!

I hope you have enjoyed it. Good luck on your exams, and good luck using macroeconomic analysis in the future.

Answers to Chapterwide Practice Questions

Matching

1. d	4. h	7. j	10. c
2. f	5. e	8. a	
3. g	6. i	9. b	

Fill-In

1. current, current, capital
2. nominal, real, purchasing power parity
3. depreciates, appreciates, less
4. flexible, currency markets
5. reinforce, hinder
6. interest rates, capital outflows, depreciating, increase, reinforces

True-False

1. T	7. T	13. T	19. T
2. F	8. F	14. T	20. F
3. F	9. T	15. T	21. T
4. F	10. F	16. T	22. T
5. F	11. T	17. F	23. F
6. T	12. F	18. T	24. T

Multiple Choice

1. a	6. a	11. b	16. c
2. c	7. c	12. b	17. b
3. b	8. d	13. a	18. c
4. b	9. d	14. c	19. b
5. b	10. a	15. d	20. a

Essay-Problem

1. When the dollar appreciates, it buys more foreign currency or foreign goods than before. When you travel abroad, you want your currency to appreciate so your dollars will buy you more.

2. If the Federal Reserve raises interest rates in November, just after the election, this will pull foreign capital into the United States and away from foreign currencies. This should lead to an appreciation in the dollar. As a tourist, you want an appreciated dollar. So your best course of action is to wait until just before your trip to buy foreign currency, not buy it now.

3. If the Federal Reserve raises interest rates in November, the dollar will appreciate. This means that U.S. exports will become more expensive in foreign countries. These higher prices will lead to lower sales. Rather than produce at a steady pace, exporters should concentrate production now and get as much product out the door way before the election, before the dollar appreciates.

4. When interest rates rise in the United States, the dollar should appreciate against the British pound. A depreciated pound buys fewer U.S. goods. Therefore, the British family will find that its money goes further in the summer before the election than in December after the election, assuming that interest rates do in fact rise.

5. Large trade deficits mean we are importing far more than we are exporting. This means that the current account will show a large deficit. This deficit in the current account must be matched by a surplus in the capital account. But a surplus in the capital account means that foreigners are holding more U.S. assets, whether in the form of dollars or U.S. Treasury bonds or other assets. In other words, we are paying for our imports by taking out more and more loans from foreigners. This should cause us worry.

6. The depreciated dollar meant that U.S. goods were cheaper in Europe, so U.S. exports increased. This also means that European goods were more expensive, so Europeans imported more U.S. goods. On the other hand, a depreciated dollar means that European goods are more expensive in the United States, so the United States imported less. From the European perspective, their exports to the United States dropped. An increase in U.S. interest rates would lead to the dollar's appreciation, bringing the trade balance back in the direction of its original equilibrium. Hence, Europeans wanted the Federal Reserve to raise U.S. interest rates. In an open economy, what is good for one country may be bad for another.

7. She will pay her tuition without any problem in September and December. When the dollar depreciates, she will find that she has to come up with more dollars to pay the tuition in March. In other words, the dollar's depreciation hurts this American student studying abroad.

8. In basic terms, a central bank purchases its own currency, using foreign reserves that it holds. This increases the demand for its own currency, so the currency appreciates in value. This is a short-term strategy only, for two major reasons. First, it is limited to the

amount of foreign reserves the central bank holds or can obtain. Second, once foreign currency traders get a whiff of what is going on, they start selling the currency (increase the supply) to force it down in value. Again, this pressure is limited by the amount of currency available, but it can be effective at times.

9. An American investor might want to hold foreign bonds if they pay more than U.S. bonds (they have a higher interest rate). The major risk is that the foreign currency depreciates so much that this wipes out the gain in return. We assume here that the investor seeks out bonds from reputable foreign sources; otherwise, the risk of default may be greater than the risk of depreciated currency.

10. Yes. It has to because foreign markets can amplify the effects of its policies. Just how much the Federal Reserve factors in expected foreign response is the issue.